— — 2014

S

MAUI

KYLE ELLISON

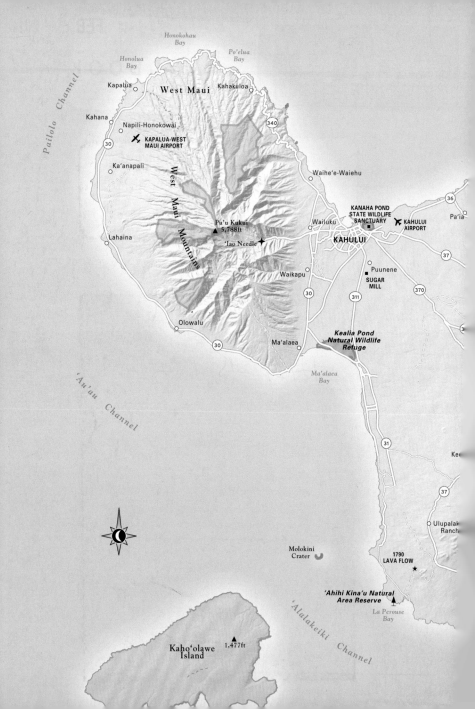

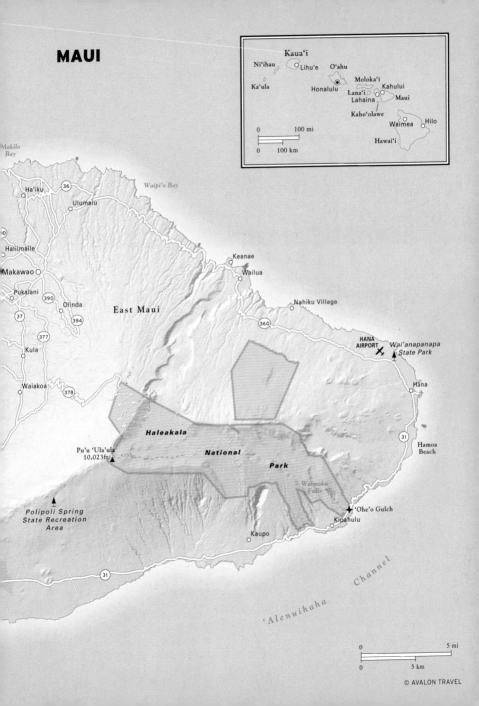

MAUI

Makilo
Bay

Waipi'o Bay

Kaua'i

Ni'ihau Lihu'e O'ahu

Ka'ula Honalulu Moloka'i
Lana'i Kahului
Lahaina Maui
Kaho'olawe Waimea Hilo

Hawai'i

0   100 mi

0   100 km

Ha'iku 36

Ulumalu

Halilmaile

Makawao

Pukalani 390

Olinda 394

37

Kula 377

Waiakoa 378

Keanae
Wailua

East Maui

Nahiku Village

360

HANA
AIRPORT Wai'anapanapa
State Park

Hāna

Haleakala 31 Hamoa
Beach

Pu'u 'Ula'ula
10,023ft National Park

Waimoku
Falls

Polipoli Spring
State Recreation
Area 'Ohe'o Gulch
Kipahulu

Kaupo

31

Channel

'Alenuihaha

0   5 mi

0   5 km

© AVALON TRAVEL

Contents

DISCOVER
Maui

There is a prominent Hawaiian saying about Maui: *Maui no ka oi*. "Maui is the best." Residents and visitors alike can agree that there is something special—even magical—about Hawai'i's second largest island. Yet it's hard to pinpoint exactly one thing that places Maui among the most dreamed-of vacation locations in the world.

The endless stretches of golden sand are an obvious and noteworthy draw, but sand alone doesn't entice millions of visitors to flock to a 727-square-mile dot in the middle of the Pacific. Perhaps it's more than just the image of yourself in a lounge chair on the sand with a mai tai in hand and the soft breeze rustling the palm trees overhead. Maybe it's also the way the trade winds blow across a beach of black sand at Wai'anapanapa State Park, stirring up waves on the sparkling blue waters. Or it's the hope of a close encounter with a giant green sea turtle while snorkeling off the coast of Napili Bay. Or maybe it's the way the setting sun reflects in the waters off Makena, creating an atmosphere that's both fiery and calm in the same fleeting moment.

There's a good chance the secret to Maui's allure lies in the *many* moments that stick with you long after you've left the island behind. Hiking through a bamboo forest so thick it nearly obscures the sun and finding

yourself at the base of a 400-foot waterfall cascading down a rocky cliff. Riding your first wave and feeling the thrill of the surf as you glide across a silky blue break. Waking at 3am to drive up a dark mountainside in the freezing cold to see the first rays of light illuminate the rich colors of Hale-akala Crater.

These are the moments that make a trip to Maui truly *no ka oi*.

Planning Your Trip

Where to Go

West Maui

West Maui pulses with a unique coastal vibe. The historic town of Lahaina was once the capital of the Hawaiian kingdom, and it retains a port town atmosphere. Warm weather and mostly dry conditions make this region a spectacular place for outdoor adventure. Snorkel with sea turtles at Napili Bay, lounge on the beach in Kapalua, ride the zipline above Ka'anapali, or hike to Nakalele Blowhole.

Central Maui

Central Maui is the island's population center and the seat of county government. Most visitors blow through town en route to their beachfront resort, but Central Maui has its own set of sights off the regularly worn trail. The twisting road into 'Iao Valley is the region's most popular attraction. Kepaniwai Heritage Garden exhibits Maui's

multicultural heritage, and down on the shoreline at Kanaha Beach Park, windsurfers and kitesurfers take to the waves along the stretch of Maui's north shore.

South Maui

From the celebrity-laden resorts of Wailea to the condo-dwelling snowbirds of Kihei, South Maui is all about worshipping the sun and enjoying the procession of beaches. Makena remains South Maui's most adventurous venue with snorkeling, scuba diving, hiking trails, kayaking, and some of the island's most photo-worthy beaches. Just offshore, Molokini Crater offers 100-foot visibility and the chance to snorkel with up to 250 species of fish.

Upcountry

Rural, laid-back, and refreshingly cool,

Nakalele Blowhole

Upcountry is Maui's most underrated zone. Agriculture and produce dominate Kula, and everything from vegetables to vineyards, coffee, and goat cheese can be found in this rural and relaxing enclave. Polipoli is the island's little-known adventure zone, where mountain biking, paragliding, and hiking take place in a forest shrouded in mist. Watch the dramatic sunrise from the frosty peak of towering Haleakala, the sacred volcano from which the demigod Maui famously snared the sun.

East Maui: the Road to Hana

The New Age town of Pa'ia is as trendy as it is jovial. Surfers ride waves along undeveloped beaches, patrons shop in locally owned boutiques, and the town is home to some the island's best restaurants. Along the famous, twisting Road to Hana, tumbling waterfalls and rugged hiking trails await. The Pools of 'Ohe'o spill down cliffs to the sea. The hike through a bamboo forest to the base of Waimoku Falls is considered the island's best trek.

Lana'i

Home to 3,300 residents and two large resorts, this island is a playground of outdoor adventure. Whether you are staying here or making a day trip from Maui, everything from hiking to scuba diving, golfing, and surfing can be enjoyed readily without the crowds. Learn about the island's history at the Lana'i Culture and Heritage Center, and make the journey down to Kaunolu to see an ancient village settlement essentially frozen in time.

Moloka'i

Taking time to explore this island offers a chance to experience the roots of native Hawaiian culture. Take a guided tour into historic Halawa Valley, one of the oldest settlements in Hawai'i, or ride on the back of a friendly mule as you visit the former leper colony of Kalaupapa. Watch the sunset from Papohaku Beach, one of the state's longest most deserted stretches of sand, or climb your way high into the mists of the Moloka'i Forest Reserve.

When to Go

Maui isn't postcard-perfect every day of the year. It might not have four distinct seasons, but it definitely has two—summer and winter. During the summer (May-October), areas such as Kapalua, Kahului, North Kihei, and Ka'anapali are prone to trade winds which blow most afternoons. While Hana and Kapalua can see rain during the summer, Lahaina and Kihei can go six straight months without a single drop.

During the winter (November-April), there can be plenty of rain. A winter day on Maui can mean light breezes, sunny skies, and a high of 78°, but it can also mean cloudy skies and rain. Experienced surfers will have the best chance of finding big surf in winter.

The best, most affordable times to travel to Maui are January 15-30, April 15-June 5, and September 15-December 15. Airfare is cheaper, occupancy rates are lower, and many activities are discounted. The two busiest weeks of the year are over Christmas and New Year's, and the two slowest weeks are the first two in December. Whale season runs December 15-May 15, with peak whale-watching January 15-March 30. Visiting Maui during May and September gives you the benefit of summer weather with lower prices and fewer crowds.

Best of Maui in 10 Days

Day 1

Given Hawai'i's time zone, you may wake up before dawn. Take advantage by catching sunrise at Haleakala. Allow two hours of travel from Ka'anapali or Wailea and plan to arrive 30 minutes before sunrise. Spend an hour hiking into the crater. On your way down, have breakfast at Kula Lodge or La Provence. Spend the rest of the day relaxing poolside.

Day 2

Tackle another early-morning activity such as a snorkeling tour. Molokini tours depart from Ma'alaea Harbor, while boats leave Ka'anapali Beach for Olowalu or Honolua Bay. Finish by 2pm and spend the afternoon relaxing on the beach.

Day 3

Enjoy Lahaina, ancient capital of the Hawaiian kingdom. Schedule a surf lesson or explore the town's historic sites. Grab lunch at Aloha Mixed Plate or Cool Cat Café. Then head north to world-famous Ka'anapali Beach, where you can snorkel, cliff jump, play in the surf, or rent a cabana. Explore the shops in Whalers Village, dine at Hula Grill, and catch a showing of 'Ulalena.

Day 4

Catch the 6:45am ferry to the island of Lana'i. Book a Jeep ahead of time and spend the morning exploring. Pick a remote beach such as Polihua, Lopa, or Kaiolohia (Shipwreck Beach). Then head back to Lana'i City for a plate lunch at Blue Ginger.

If you'd rather be hiking, catch the resort shuttle to the Lodge at Koele and spend the morning walking the Koloiki Ridge Trail. Explore Lana'i City before catching a shuttle down to the harbor. Then make the short walk to Hulopo'e Beach. Snorkel along the reef or relax in the shade with a book. Hike around the corner to the Pu'u Pehe Overlook, keeping an eye out for the spinner dolphins. Rinse off at the beach shower, grab a drink at the Four Seasons, and get back to the harbor to catch the 6:45pm ferry back to Maui.

Day 5

Sleep in before grabbing a late breakfast. Those staying in the West Maui should dine at the Gazebo, followed by a stroll along the Kapalua Coastal Trail. Drive to Kahakuloa, stopping en route at the Nakalele Blowhole or Mokulei'a Beach. If the conditions are calm and you can't get enough snorkeling, head to

view of Moloka'i from Ka'anapali Beach

a white spotted toby at Molokini Crater

Keonehe'ehe'e Trail descends 3,000 ft. to the floor of Haleakala Crater

Honolua Bay. End the day with happy hour at the Sea House restaurant.

If you're staying in South Maui, brunch at Kihei Caffe before making the drive to Makena. Spend the day at Maluaka Beach, exploring to the end of the road, and walking the length of Big Beach just before sunset.

Day 6
Drive to Pa'ia. Grab a coffee from Anthony's and stroll down Baldwin Beach, followed by breakfast at Café des Amis. Enjoy the Road to Hana at a leisurely pace, taking time to hike to Twin Falls and explore the Ke'anae Peninsula. Check into your accommodations in Hana and enjoy sunset from Hamoa Beach.

Day 7
Catch the sunrise from Wai'anapanapa State Park. Visit the popular Pools of 'Ohe'o before day-trippers arrive around 11am. Spend a couple of hours exploring the pools and hiking the Pipiwai Trail. If the weather is nice, wrap around the back side of the island on the narrow and rugged "back road." Hike to Alelele Falls, grab a cold drink at the Kaupo Store, and experience a coastline that feels like the end of the earth.

Day 8
Downtime: Sleep in as late as you'd like, lounge by the pool, get a massage. Breathe deeply.

spinner dolphins

Ulupalakua Ranch Store

Day 9

Spend the day in the rural Upcountry. Enjoy brunch on the lanai at Grandma's Coffee House, accompanied by slack key guitar. Stroll down Thompson Road. Drive to Ulupalakua for a midday wine tasting. Double back the way you came to the town of Makawao for some shopping and lunch at Polli's Mexican Restaurant. Spend the afternoon in hippie outpost Pa'ia. Don't linger too long: you need to make it to the Old Lahaina Lu'au by 5pm to celebrate your last night on the island.

Day 10

Gradually make your way toward Kahului Airport. Stop in at the Maui Ocean Center for one last glimpse of marine life. Continuing on to Wailuku, make the short drive into 'Iao Valley to see the famous needle. At Kanaha Beach Park, watch the windsurfers. Think about how you'll miss Maui—and plan your next visit. You'll be back.

'Iao Needle

Best Beaches

D.T. Fleming Beach

Fleming's offers some of the island's best bodysurfing, beachcombing, and coastal hiking. Public restrooms, showers, lifeguards, and parking make this a family-friendly beach. Surfers flock here in winter to tackle the large swells (page 35).

Ka'anapali Beach

Whether you're looking for snorkeling, stand-up paddling, cliff jumping, or scuba diving, you'll find it down at Ka'anapali Beach. This resort district is the see-and-be-seen shoreline for the island's West Side (page 37).

Napili Bay and Kapalua Bay

These two northwestern beaches offer protected snorkeling during summer. Swim with sea turtles at Napili and watch the sun go down from the deck of the Sea House restaurant with a drink in your hand (page 34).

Mokulei'a Bay

During summer, there are few better ways to start the day than by snorkeling at Mokulei'a. Tucked away at the base of the cliffs and hidden from the road, this is also a scenic and sandy spot for watching the large winter surf (page 35).

Keawakapu Beach

Enjoy a sunset stroll down Kihei's nicest beach, or spend your days snorkeling, stand-up paddling, or basking in the sun. Keawakapu has facilities on both ends of the beach, but despite the beach's popularity, there is always room to find your own section of shoreline (page 162).

Maluaka Beach

Maluaka is the most happening beach in Makena, where everything from kayaking to snorkeling and stand-up paddling are readily available. Public restrooms and showers make this a convenient spot for families, and you can walk down the road to historic Keawala'i Church. Or pamper yourself in a beachfront cabana with a relaxing oceanfront massage (page 165).

Makena State Park

Wide, long, and completely undeveloped, aptly-named Big Beach is a local favorite that comes alive at sunset. This legendary shoreline has a lengthy hippie history:

Baldwin Beach

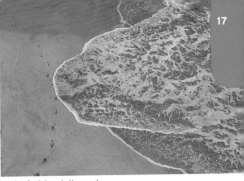

Moloka'i's Papohaku Beach

leaving footsteps in the sand

counterculturists and nudists should visit neighboring Little Beach for Sunday night drum circles (page 166).

Baldwin Beach

This North Shore classic is a local favorite for bodysurfing, bodyboarding, and scenic morning jogs. Undeveloped sand dunes meld into turquoise waters. Families with small children will love the cove at Baby Beach with its protected saltwater lagoon (page 287).

Hamoa Beach

If your vision of paradise involves a book, a palm tree, and the sound of waves at your feet, you'll find it at Hamoa Beach, the nicest beach in Hana. Travelers from Michener to Twain have written of the beauty of its sandy shoreline (page 291).

Hulopo'e Beach Park

This marine reserve has a sandy cove, vibrant reef, and palm-fringed shoreline. Summer months bring good surfing and bodysurfing and easy access to coastal hiking trails. Public restrooms, showers, and picnic tables make this a family-friendly outing on the island of Lana'i (page 323).

Papohaku Beach

On most days your footprints will be the only set in the sand at Papohaku, one of the longest beaches in Hawai'i. This westward-facing shoreline offers Moloka'i's best sunsets. It's perfect for anyone wanting to escape for a little while (page 356).

Big Beach at Makena State Park

Hamoa Beach

Best Snorkeling and Diving

Honolua Bay

A world-renowned surf spot during winter, Honolua Bay has the island's best snorkeling during the calm, warm summer. Hawaiian green sea turtles are a common sight, as are parrotfish, octopus, and the rare spinner dolphin (page 42).

Pu'u Keka'a

The island's most famous snorkeling spot, also known as Black Rock, is one if its best. This rocky promontory on the Ka'anapali strip is a magnet for sea turtles and reef fish. Morning hours offer the calmest conditions. Keep an eye out for the dozens of cliff jumpers who throw themselves off the rock (page 47).

Napili Bay and Kapalua Bay

Within walking distance of each other on the island's northwestern coast, these two bays offer a sandy entry and shallow, protected conditions. Napili has more turtles, while Kapalua has more fish. Summer is the best time of year for calm and flat conditions (page 46).

Olowalu

Often known as "Mile Marker 14," this historic shoreline along the side of the highway is great for beginning snorkelers. The best conditions are during the winter and earlier in the day. The outer reef is covered in turtles and is a playground of healthy coral (page 52).

Makena Landing

The volcanic Makena coastline goes by many names; Turtle Town is perhaps the most relevant to snorkelers. It's pockmarked with caves which form the perfect shelter for sea turtles. Winter months are best along this southern shoreline. Everyone from scuba divers to kayak tours and snorkeling boats frequents the rugged coast (page 177).

Molokini Crater

A crescent-shaped volcanic caldera off the southern coastline of Maui, Molokini Crater offers crystal-clear waters with 100-foot visibility on most days of the year. Over a dozen snorkeling tours make the early morning pilgrimage to the crater, home to over 250 species of fish. For an extreme adventure, scuba divers should tackle the famous Back Wall, which drops straight down for nearly 300 feet (page 169).

a school of *ta'ape* (blueline snapper)

white spotted moray at Hulopo'e Beach Park

a honu (sea turtle) off Makena's coastline

Ulua and Mokapu Beach

These neighboring Wailea beaches are South Maui's most easily accessible, making them ideal for beginning snorkelers. The rocky point between the two beaches teems with tropical reef fish (page 175).

Hulopo'e Beach Park

This Lana'i marine reserve has one of the healthiest reefs in Maui County and fronts a beach ranked as the nation's best. Come face-to-face with multihued parrotfish as they snack on colorful coral, or search the shallows for the *humuhumunukunukuapua'a*, Hawai'i's state fish (page 328).

First and Second Cathedrals

These offshore caverns offer the best scuba diving on Lana'i. Beams of sunlight filter through the water, mimicking church windows of a cathedral—First Cathedral has even been the site of underwater weddings. In addition to the bride and groom, you'll encounter everything from frogfish to lobsters and spinner dolphins (page 329).

Moku Ho'oniki

Advanced scuba divers get their thrills on this Moloka'i deep-water dive. It's home to a large population of scalloped hammerhead sharks (page 361).

First Cathedrals on Lana'i

snorkeling at Molokini Crater

Best Surfing

Honolua Bay

Honolua Bay is a place of local legend, with one of the best right-hand waves in the world during winter. If you're an expert surfer—and show respect to locals by waiting your turn in the lineup—you could end up snagging the wave of a lifetime (page 56).

D.T. Fleming Beach Park

This Kapalua beach is popular with bodyboarders and is best during the winter. It's less crowded than neighboring Honolua, and much more user-friendly, yet should still be reserved for Intermediate to advanced surfers only (page 56).

Pohaku Beach Park

A longboarder's dream wave, S-Turns is the island's most user-friendly winter break and the most accepting of visiting beginning surfers. The long paddle out means a long ride. This rolling, forgiving wave is the perfect spot for honing your skills (page 56).

Ho'okipa Beach Park

The most popular break on the island's North Shore is also the center of the Pa'ia surf scene.

Small days are acceptable for beginners who are still learning, but during the large swells of winter this becomes an experts-only amphitheater of towering 20-foot surf (page 293).

Pa'ia Bay

Walking distance from the center of town, Pa'ia Bay is one of the island's only real beach breaks. It's best for intermediate-advanced shortboarding and bodyboarding (page 293).

The Cove

The Cove is the epicenter of the bustling Kihei surf scene. The shallow, protected cove is home to the south side's numerous surf schools, with gentle waves which are perfect for beginners (page 185).

Lahaina Breakwall

Crowded, shallow, and nearly always sunny, the Lahaina Breakwall is where many visitors stand up and ride their first wave. Surf schools dominate the inside reef, while advanced surfers hang on the outside. While most days are calm with gentle surf, the large south swells of summer are for advanced surfers only (page 58).

Ho'okipa Beach Park

summer surf off Lahaina

Surfboard rentals are available all over Maui.

Launiupoko Beach Park

Keiki learn to ride their first waves here at the most happening beach park on the road to Lahaina. Longboarders can choose from multiple peaks, while the gentle waves and calm conditions make it a perfect spot for beginners (page 60).

Hamoa Beach

More than just a beautiful beach, Hamoa has some of the best surf in East Maui. Intermediate-advanced surfers will find windswell here any time of the year, even during summer when nowhere else on the island has waves (page 296).

Hulopo'e Beach Park

While it might not break often, Hulopo'e Beach has a left-hand wave on par with the best in the state—ideal for intermediate-advanced surfers. Summer is best for this south-facing shore on Lana'i. While spots on Maui can be crowded with 50 people, Hulopo'e will rarely ever have 10 (page 331).

getting barreled at the Bay

The 60-foot waves of Jaws are for experts only—but it's fun to watch.

Best Hikes

Sliding Sands-Switchback Loop

This 12.2-mile sojourn crosses the floor of Haleakala Crater and weaves past cinder cones bursting with color. Keep an eye out for nene and glistening silversword plants. For a real thrill, hike by the light of the full moon (page 226).

Polipoli Spring State Recreation Area

Tucked in one of the least-visited corners of Maui, Polipoli looks more like the Pacific Northwest than a Pacific island. A network of trails weaves through towering redwoods. The silence in the forest is broken only by passing pheasants (page 226).

Na'ili'ili haele

Known as the "bamboo forest," this rugged, slippery trail on the Road to Hana hides a series of waterfalls set deep in the East Maui rainforest. The treacherous trail isn't for everyone, however: Hikers need to be in good physical condition before attempting this trail (page 299).

Makamaka'ole Valley

Hidden along the twisting road between Kahului and Kahakuloa, Makamaka'ole offers some of the most accessible waterfalls in West Maui. This short, steep, and slippery hike should only be attempted by physically fit hikers who are steady on their feet (page 127).

Hoapili Trail

Tucked away in the "deep south," the Hoapili Trail traces the winding footpath of royalty across black fields of lava. This winding, rugged coastal track is an enchanting time portal to ancient Hawai'i. Mornings are best to beat the hot sun (page 193).

Pipiwai Trail

If expansive banyan trees, dark bamboo forests, and numerous waterfalls aren't enough of a thrill, this four-mile trail in Kipahulu reaches a dramatic terminus at the base of 400-foot Waimoku Falls. Often regarded as the island's best hike, this should be on every itinerary for a day spent in Hana (page 302).

Halawa Valley

More than just a hike to a waterfall, a trek in Halawa Valley is a powerful journey to the heart of Hawaiian culture. Halawa Valley is one of the oldest settlements on Moloka'i— and in all of the Hawaiian Islands. This valley

Haleakala Crater

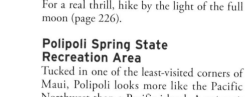

Hike to waterfalls along the Road to Hana.

Munro Trail on Lana'i

is so sacred it can only be explored with a guide (page 367).

Munro Trail

Shaded by the boughs of Cook pines, this weaving dirt track climbs to the summit of 3,370-foot Lana'ihale. Views from this Lana'i trail stretch back toward Maui; on the clearest days, the summit is the only place in Hawai'i where you can get a view of six islands at once (page 333).

Lahaina Pali Trail

Before the coastal road linking Kahului with Lahaina was created, this steep, hot, and dry trail was the preferred way to reach West Maui. Today, the trail offers panoramic views and is perfect for whale-watching, sunsets, and working up a sweat (page 73).

Waihe'e Coastal Dunes and Wetlands Preserve

Hugging the shoreline of sleepy Waihe'e, this coastal track weaves its way past ancient Hawaiian villages along one the island's few remaining sections of undeveloped coastline (page 127).

Na'ili'ili haele, the "bamboo forest"

Hoapili Trail

Best Outdoor Adventures

Paragliding in Polipoli

Paragliding is Maui's most underrated adventure option. The Polipoli flying location has ideal conditions on a cool mountain slope with views gazing out over South Maui. The instructors at Proflyght will have you soaring (page 236).

Kitesurfing at Kite Beach

Kitesurfing was born here on Maui. While experienced kiters can take straight to the water, schools such as Hawaiian Sailboard Techniques give lessons to visitors who are looking to pick up a new sport (page 124).

Snorkeling Molokini Crater

If snorkeling along shore seems too mild, try swimming in the inside of a volcanic caldera. This offshore location offers 100 feet of visibility and 250 species of fish. Companies such as Trilogy Excursions offer daily morning tours (page 169).

Stand-Up Paddling

A great way to get out on the water and work on your balance and core, stand-up paddling has its origins in Maui. While seasoned pros will endure multi-hour "downwinders," even renting a board for an hour is a great introduction to the sport.

Kayaking or Outrigger Canoeing

Many kayak tours combine snorkeling with an upper body workout. Those looking for a cultural connection should snorkel from an outrigger canoe, ancient craft that date back to early Polynesia. Hawaiian Paddle Sports can get you on the water for a private paddling tour.

Surfing in Lahaina

Learn the ancient Hawaiian sport of kings in Lahaina, the one-time royal capital of Hawai'i. Beginners will love the thrill of their first wave, and expert surfers can head to the breaks scattered across the island's west side (page 58).

Ziplining Above the Trees

From kid-friendly short courses to stomach-churning screamers, ziplining has rapidly become one of the island's most popular activities. While all companies provide a thrilling experience, Skyline Eco-Adventures in Ka'anapali offers some of the best views (page 74).

whale-watching

outrigger canoeing

Alelele Falls

Whale-Watching in Ka'anapali

Few things get your heart racing faster than a 50-ton animal leaping out of the water a few feet away. Trilogy Excursions offers whale-watching charters from both Maui and Lana'i. If luck is on your side, you just might end up on a boat that gets "mugged" (page 65).

Scuba Diving Underwater Caves

For as much as is happening above water on Maui, there is nearly as much happening below the surface. Mike Severn's will help divers explore Molokini (page 169), while Trilogy Excursions operates on Lana'i (page 329).

Mountain Biking Makawao or Moloka'i

The slopes of these islands are covered in biking trails. Makawao and Polipoli are the best spots on Maui (page 231), while Moloka'i's forest reserve is an off-road playground (page 367).

Hike Through Bamboo and Waterfalls in Hana

Swimming beneath a waterfall in the rainforest is one of the most singular experiences of a trip to Maui. Luckily, the lush Road to Hana literally drips in cascades, including the Pools of 'Ohe'o (page 284) and Twin Falls (page 298). Hike Maui offers guided trips.

ziplining

scuba diving off Lana'i

Best Historical and Cultural Sites

Bailey House Museum

Step inside this whitewashed missionary home to get a glimpse into 19th-century Maui. This museum also houses ancient Hawaiian artifacts, a surfboard ridden by Duke Kahanamoku, and one of the best bookstores for Hawaiian-themed literature (page 137).

Alexander and Baldwin Sugar Museum

Within sniffing distance of the state's last remaining sugar mill, this small museum takes an informative look at the island's multicultural plantation heritage (page 136).

Hui O Wa'a Kaulua Canoe Hale

The Hui O Wa'a Kaulua is an organization dedicated to the preservation of double-hulled Polynesian voyaging canoes. The group's canoe house is in Lahaina's Kamehameha Iki Park, where volunteers are happy to discuss everything from Polynesian voyaging canoes to native Hawaiian culture (page 89).

Kepaniwai Heritage Gardens

Just a few minutes shy of 'Iao Valley, this small park parallels 'Iao Stream and features traditional housing of the island's immigrant communities (page 140).

Kalaupapa Peninsula

There was once a time when a visit to Kalaupapa meant you'd just been handed a death sentence. Today, go to this remote peninsula on Moloka'i to learn about the struggles of Hawai'i's leprosy patients and Father Damien, the man who gave everything to save them (page 373).

Lana'i Culture and Heritage Center

This small, informative cultural center in the heart of Lana'i City traces the island's history from its original inhabitants through its era as the world's largest pineapple plantation (page 340).

Honokowai Valley

This deep, remote cleft in Mauna Kahalawai was once home to a thriving population of traditional native Hawaiians. When water was diverted, the village had to be

Bailey House Museum

Lana'i Culture and Heritage Center

Alexander and Baldwin Sugar Museum

abandoned. Volunteer efforts are restoring this valley steeped in Hawaiian history (page 83).

Ke'anae Peninsula

Time ticks by as it did centuries ago on this lush peninsula, which offers a refreshing glimpse into "old Hawai'i." This taro-covered promontory is one of the island's last vestiges of native Hawaiian culture (page 275).

Pi'ilanihale *Heiau*

This towering, 50-foot tall *heiau* is the largest remaining in the state, surviving in an area largely unchanged from the times of ancient Hawai'i. The stone platforms encompass an area the size of two professional football fields (page 278).

petroglyphs

Kepaniwai Heritage Gardens

Best for Honeymooners

Pu'u Pehe

Often referred to as "Sweetheart Rock," this iconic promontory five minutes from Hulopo'e is named for two ancient lovers of legend. Today, honeymooning couples can watch the sunset over the water from the panoramic overlook (page 334).

Sunset Cruise

Few Maui activities are more romantic than watching the sunset from the deck of a catamaran with a drink in one hand and your new love in the other (page 64).

Sunday Brunch at Grandma's Coffee House

This Upcountry coffeehouse (page 260) has live slack key music on an intimate outdoor patio. After you've finished your romantic brunch, weave through the pastures along Thompson Road.

Haleakala Sunset

Skip the early morning wakeup call for a sunrise trip and instead visit Haleakala for sunset. The crowds are smaller, the view is spectacular. If you bring some jackets, you can lie on the hood of the car and watch as the stars come out (page 244).

Wai'anapanapa Sunrise

Spend the night in Hana to watch the sunrise from this eastern-facing shoreline, better known as Hana's "black sand beach." You'll have it all to yourself before the daily throngs of visitors arrive (page 278).

Kiss Beneath a Waterfall

The Road to Hana is laden with opportunities for smooching beneath a refreshing cascade (pages 284 and 298).

Dance at the Old Lahaina Luau

Everyone wants to go to a lu'au in Hawai'i, and Old Lahaina is the island's best. In addition to the food and the oceanfront setting, part of the show is devoted to couples who can dance together beneath the stars (page 100).

The Phallic Rock

The Phallic Rock is dedicated to Nanahoa, ancient Hawaiian god of fertility. Women traditionally visited this site in hopes of conceiving a child (page 372).

An Oceanfront Couples Massage

There's nothing more relaxing than a couples massage enjoyed in an oceanfront cabana. Ka'anapali, Wailea, Makena, and Lana'i all offer opportunities to cast your worries away.

a sunset kiss

WEST MAUI

The slopes and shores of West Maui are what many visitors picture when they close their eyes and envision paradise: white sandy beaches, rocky coves, lush valleys, and oceanfront restaurants where the clinking glasses of mai tais and the smooth sounds of a slack key guitar complement the setting sun.

The beaches are some of the best on the island. In winter, Honolua Bay shapes the kind of legendary right-hand point breaks that attract surfers from across the globe. In summer, this same bay offers some of the island's finest snorkeling, where bright parrotfish, shy octopuses, and curious sea turtles occupy an expansive reef.

Hot, busy, and incomparably historic, Lahaina was once the whaling capital of the Pacific as well as the capital of the Hawaiian kingdom. Today, it's Maui's quintessential tourist town. The name "Lahaina" translates as "cruel, merciless sun." Almost every day is sunny in Lahaina. As a result, it buzzes with an energetic fervor that draws pedestrians to the streets, fishers to the harbor, and surfers to the breaks offshore. Some critics say that Lahaina is little more than a tourist trap. While there is some truth in that gripe, when you look past the T-shirt stands, you will notice a town that displays every epoch in the modern history of Hawai'i.

Whether you're scouring the historic relics of Lahaina, swimming with reef fish at Napili Bay, stand-up paddleboarding along the Ka'anapali shoreline, or enjoying the sunset from an oceanfront lu'au, this is the Maui you were dreaming of.

© KYLE ELLISON

HIGHLIGHTS

Whale-Watching

Honolua Bay

Nakalele Blowhole

Kapalua

Napili

Kahana

Kapalua Coastal Trail

Honokowai

Sunset Cruises

Ka'anapali

Surf Spots

Lahaina

Front Street

Ulalena

Lahaina Courthouse

Lahaina Lu'aus

Wailuku

Ma'alaea

PACIFIC OCEAN

0   5 mi

0   5 km

© AVALON TRAVEL

LOOK FOR ◖ TO FIND RECOMMENDED SIGHTS, ACTIVITIES, DINING, AND LODGING.

◖ **Honolua Bay:** In summer, snorkel with sea turtles in this legendary, protected bay. In winter, watch as the island's best surfers drop into waves over 20 feet high (page 42).

◖ **Lahaina Surf Spots:** This ancient capital is one of the island's best places for learning the Hawaiian sport of kings (page 58).

◖ **Sunset Cruises off Ka'anapali Beach:** Feel the trade winds in your hair as you literally sail into the sunset off West Maui's most iconic

beach. Dine on Pacific Rim *pupus* and sip a mai tai during a sunset performance that is different each night (page 64).

◖ **Whale-Watching:** December to April the waters off Maui are home to the highest concentration of humpback whales on the planet. Head out on a whale-watching expedition for an up-close encounter with these leaping, 50-ton creatures (page 65)

◖ **Kapalua Coastal Trail:** Spend an hour scouring the coastline along this luxuriant yet rugged 1.75-mile trail. Along the way you will pass colonies of nesting seabirds, empty Oneloa Bay, hidden Namalu Bay, and some of the country's most beautiful beaches (page 70).

◖ **Nakalele Blowhole:** Take a 15-minute walk down toward this thunderous blowhole where pressure transforms incoming waves into a 100-foot geyser (page 81).

◖ **Lahaina Courthouse:** With an art gallery in the basement, old photos on the ground level, and a museum on the third story, this is one of the town's best spots for educating yourself on the unique history of Lahaina (page 84).

◖ **Front Street:** Get your shopping, people-watching, and dining fixes by walking the length of the island's most famous thoroughfare (page 94).

◖ **'Ulalena:** The history of Hawai'i is told through rhythms, dance, and creative special effects inside the impressive Maui Theatre (page 99).

◖ **Lahaina Lu'aus:** Feast on kalua pig, poi, haupia, and lomi salmon as you take in an authentic cultural performance. **Old Lahaina Luau** is the island's best (page 100).

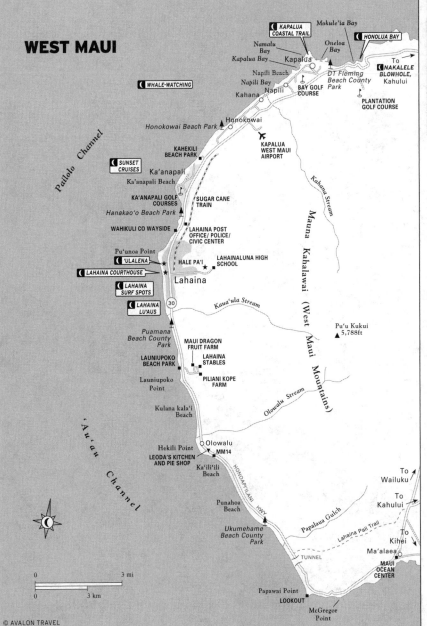

WEST MAUI

Mokule'ia Bay
☾ KAPALUA COASTAL TRAIL
☾ HONOLUA BAY
Namalu Bay
Oneloa Bay
Kapalua Bay   Kapalua
☾ NAKALELE BLOWHOLE, Kahului
Napili Beach   DT Fleming Beach County Park
☾ WHALE-WATCHING
Napili Bay
BAY GOLF COURSE
Kahana   Napili
PLANTATION GOLF COURSE
Honokowai
Honokowai Beach Park
KAPALUA WEST MAUI AIRPORT
KAHEKILI BEACH PARK
☾ SUNSET CRUISES
Ka'anapali
Kahana Stream
Ka'anapali Beach
KA'ANAPALI GOLF COURSES   SUGAR CANE TRAIN
Hanakao'o Beach Park
WAHIKULI CO WAYSIDE   LAHAINA POST OFFICE/ POLICE/ CIVIC CENTER
Pu'unoa Point   LAHAINALUNA HIGH SCHOOL
☾ 'ULALENA   HALE PA'I
☾ LAHAINA COURTHOUSE
Lahaina
☾ LAHAINA SURF SPOTS
Kaua'ula Stream
Mauna Kahalawai (West Maui Mountains)
Pu'u Kukui ▲ 5,788ft
☾ LAHAINA LU'AUS
30
Puamana Beach County Park
MAUI DRAGON FRUIT FARM
LAUNIUPOKO BEACH PARK   LAHAINA STABLES
Launiupoko Point   PILIANI KOPE FARM
Kulana kala'i Beach
Olowalu Stream
Hekili Point   Olowalu
LEODA'S KITCHEN AND PIE SHOP   MM14
Ka'ili'ili Beach
HONOAPI'ILANI HWY
Punahoa Beach
Papalaua Gulch
Ukumehame Beach County Park
Lahaina Pali Trail
To Wailuku
To Kahului
To Kihei
Ma'alaea
TUNNEL
MAUI OCEAN CENTER
Pailolo Channel
'Au'au Channel
Papawai Point
LOOKOUT
McGregor Point
0   3 mi
0   3 km

© AVALON TRAVEL

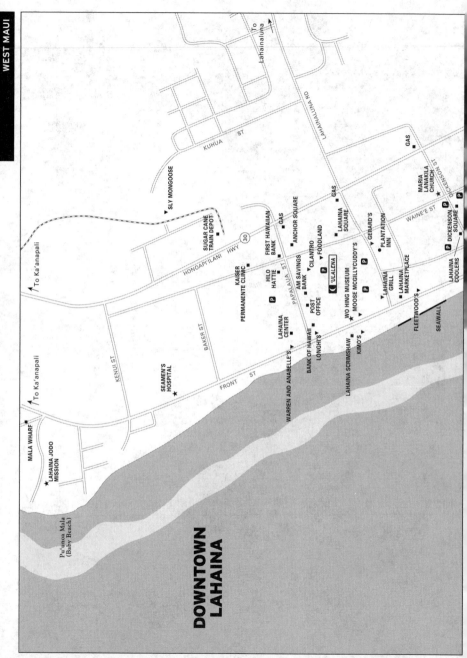

DOWNTOWN LAHAINA

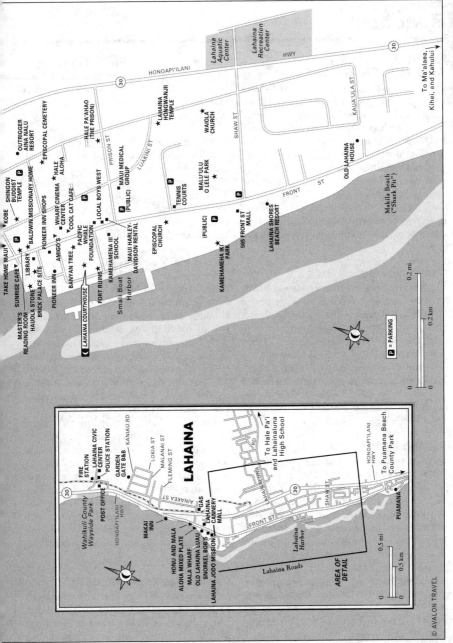

Map labels (upper map — Lahaina detail):

Lahaina Aquatic Center
Lahaina Recreation Center
HWY
HONOAPI'ILANI
To Ma'alaea, Kihei, and Kahului
AHAHINA HONGWANJI TEMPLE
WAIOLA CHURCH
SHAW ST
KAUA'ULA ST
EPISCOPAL CEMETERY
HALE PA'AHAO (THE PRISON)
OUTRIGGER AINA NALU RESORT
SHINGON BUDDIST TEMPLE
KOBE
TAKE HOME MAUI
SUNRISE CAFÉ
MASTER'S READING ROOM
HAUOLA STONE
BRICK PALACE SITE
LIBRARY
BALDWIN MISSIONARY HOME
PIONEER INN SHOPS
AMIGO'S
PIONEER INN
BANYAN TREE
LAHAINA COURTHOUSE
FORT RUINS
Small Boat Harbor
PRISON ST
LUAKINI ST
FRONT ST
PRISON ST
MAUI MEDICAL GROUP
WHARF CINEMA CENTER
COOL CAT CAFE
HALE ALOHA
LOCAL BOYS WEST
PACIFIC WHALE FOUNDATION
KAMEHAMEHA III SCHOOL
MAUI HARLEY DAVIDSON RENTAL
TENNIS COURTS
MALU'ULU O LELE PARK
OLD LAHAINA HOUSE
EPISCOPAL CHURCH
KAMEHAMEHA IKI PARK
(PUBLIC)
505 FRONT ST MALL
LAHAINA SHORES BEACH RESORT
Makila Beach ("Shark Pit")

P = PARKING
0.2 mi
0.2 km

Map labels (inset map — LAHAINA):

LAHAINA
FIRE STATION
LAHAINA CIVIC CENTER
POLICE STATION
GARDEN GATE B&B
KANAU RD
LOKIA ST
MALANAI ST
FLEMING ST
AINAKEA ST
KANIAU RD
To Hale Pa'i and Lahainaluna High School
Wahikuli County Wayside Park
POST OFFICE
HONOAPI'ILANI HWY
MAKAI INN
HONU AND MALA
ALOHA MIXED PLATE
MALA WHARF
OLD LAHAINA LUAU
SNORKEL BOB'S
LAHAINA JODO MISSION
GAS
LAHAINA CANNERY MALL
FRONT ST
SHAW ST
HONOAPI'ILANI HWY
To Puamana Beach County Park
PUAMANA
Lahaina Harbor
Lahaina Roads
AREA OF DETAIL
0.5 mi
0.5 km

© AVALON TRAVEL

Beaches

KAPALUA, NAPILI, AND HONOKOWAI

Known to locals as the Upper West Side (or up north), the beaches along this stretch include tropical, turquoise coves sandwiched between condos and luxurious homes. Napili and Kapalua beaches are the most popular, but past the entrance to Kapalua, the shoreline gets wilder and the crowds start to thin. The wind can howl in the afternoons and massive surf crashes into the coastline October-April. Over the winter the shorebreak often grows up to 10 feet or larger. If the surf is big on the Upper West Side, it's probably flat in Lahaina or Kihei.

Honokowai Beach Park

The farthest point south, **Honokowai Beach Park** is a narrow stretch of sand connected to Kahekili Beach on the northern edge of Ka'anapali. While the beach here is far from being the nicest on the island, there is a large, grassy park with a playground for small children and a couple of shops across the street. This is a nice place to enjoy a picnic or comb the shoreline for shells. Parking for Honokowai Beach Park is in the public lot about a half mile down Lower Honoapi'ilani Road.

Pohaku Beach Park (S-Turns)

More of a surf break than a regular beach, **Pohaku Beach Park** still has some small patches of sand, making it the most accessible beach in the area around Kahana. There is a parking lot at the center of the beach park, and although there aren't any permanent restrooms, there are some showers and picnic tables set in the shade. On both ends of the park are patches of sand passable for laying out a blanket, although the swimming here can be marginal and murky. Nevertheless, this is a popular local hangout which is beautiful on a calm day, and it's the hot spot for longboard surfing on the northwestern shore of the island. To reach Pohaku Beach Park, turn at the junction of Akahele Street and Honoapi'ilani Highway (Highway 30), and make a right on Lower Honoapi'ilani Road, driving until you see the park on your left.

Napili Bay and Kapalua Bay

If you want to see a hot debate, ask which beach is better: **Napili Bay** or **Kapalua Bay.** The camps on each side are staunchly loyal. There are a couple of factors which distinguish one from the other. Although a mere 0.25 mile from each other, the shorebreak at Napili Bay can be larger in the winter whereas Kapalua is more protected. The snorkeling between the two reefs is a tossup, although the general consensus is that Kapalua has a tendency for more fish, whereas Napili has a greater number of sea turtles. Napili Bay is a little larger, although it can also become more crowded. If you are traveling with children, Kapalua Bay is the better bet since the water is calmer and there is easy access to beach showers and restrooms. Kapalua Bay was named the number one beach in America in 1991 and voted as the Best Beach in the World by the readers of *Condé Nast* magazine.

Your best chance for finding parking at Napili Bay is either along the side of Lower Honoapi'ilani Road between Napili Kai and the Kapalua Tennis Club, or, on the south end of the beach, there is some beach parking at the bottom of Hui Drive. The beach parking lot at Kapalua Bay fills up early. If you can't find a parking place, drop all of your beach gear by the stairs leading down to the sand and then circle back to find a parking spot along the road.

Oneloa Bay (Ironwoods)

Hidden from view from the main road through Kapalua, **Oneloa Bay** is virtually always empty. This epic expanse of shoreline sits right along the Kapalua Coastal Trail. Since the swimming

THE BEST BEACH IN AMERICA

If a friend quizzes you on which beach in Maui was voted the number one beach in the United States, and you have to choose between Kapalua Bay, Ka'anapali Beach, D.T. Fleming Beach, Wailea Beach, and Hulopo'e Bay on Lana'i, the correct answer would be...all of them.

Since the rankings began in 1991, each of the five beaches listed above has held the title as the #1 Beach in America, and Hamoa Beach in Hana is consistently ranked in the top five. So how, exactly, is the number one beach determined?

The person behind the rankings is Stephen P. Leatherman, otherwise known as Dr. Beach. He has compiled a sophisticated ranking system of 50 different criteria to measure hundreds of beaches across the nation. Criteria include natural factors such as softness of the sand and width at low tide, as well as human-influenced factors such as availability of lifeguards and ease of public access. Water samples from each beach are collected to determine factors such as turbidity, suspended human material (sewage), and the amount of algae present.

So why is there always a different winner every year? Once a beach has won the title it is subsequently retired from future consideration. With that thought in mind, wouldn't it make sense that the "best of the best" would be the beach which was voted number one when the rankings first started?

If this were the case (and the argument makes a lot of sense), the top beach in the United States when the rankings began in 1991 was Kapalua Bay, so the granddaddy of best beaches in America is here on Maui.

is poor and it's out of sight, it's also out of mind. Mornings on Oneloa can be calm and still, making this a popular spot for sunset wedding shoots. Oneloa is a great beach for communing with nature. To reach Oneloa, either park at the lot for Kapalua Bay and walk for 15 minutes along the Kapalua Coastal Trail or follow Lower Honoapi'ilani Road into the resort complex of Kapalua to a small beach access path and parking lot across from The Ridge condo complex. While there is a small beach shower for rinsing off, the nearest public restrooms are at Kapalua Bay.

D.T. Fleming Beach Park

D.T. Fleming Beach Park was the most recent of Maui's beaches to be named number one beach in the United States, garnering the title in 2006. Unlike any other beach on the island, Fleming's is a hybrid stretch of sand where the southern half is dominated by Ritz-Carlton resort guests and the northern half is popular with locals. This is one of the best beaches on the island for bodysurfing and bodyboarding, although the surf here can get rough and dangerous in the winter. Luckily this is one of the only beaches on the west side with lifeguards. Other amenities include restrooms and showers on the northern section. Out at the point on the southern end of the beach, jagged rocks shape a coastal formation known as **Dragon's Teeth.** Parallel the golf course to reach the end of the point. Once you reach the rocky outcropping, you're greeted with thunderous surf crashing onto the rocks and glimpses of sea turtles poking their heads above the surface. There is a large labyrinth here if you'd like to take a reflective stroll, and this is also a good vantage point for snapping a photo looking back toward the beach. To access D.T. Fleming Beach Park, take Honoapi'ilani Highway (Hwy. 30) 0.9 miles past the main entrance to Kapalua and turn once you've reached the bottom of the hill for the largest parking area. The road will dead-end in the lot.

Mokulei'a Bay (Slaughterhouse)

Mokulei'a Bay is another beach where the crowds are thin since you can't see it from the road. Tucked at the base of dramatic

the empty expanse of Ironwoods at Oneloa Bay

cliffs, Mokulei'a offers some of the best snorkeling on the west side. It's known to locals as Slaughterhouse Beach, but the name is less sinister than it sounds: a slaughterhouse was once located here but is now long gone. The bay is part of the Honolua Bay Marine Life Conservation District, so no fishing or spearfishing—or any other kind of slaughter—is allowed. This is also a popular beach for bodysurfing, although the surf can be treacherous during the large swells of winter. This beach is nearly always deserted in the early morning hours. To reach Mokulei'a, travel 2.5 miles past the entrance to Kapalua and park on the left side of the road, where you will then notice a paved stairway leading down to the beach, as well as a sign that details the rules of the marine reserve.

Punalau Beach (Windmills)

Only a handful of visitors will ever make it to **Punalau Beach** at mile marker 34 of Highway 30 since is hidden from the road. The local name of Windmills derives from an old windmill which once stood here but has long since been destroyed. This is now a popular place for advanced surfers and ambitious beachcombers, who scour the shoreline for flotsam and shells. The road down to the shoreline can often be rough, so unless you have a high clearance vehicle, it's best to leave your car parked by the highway and make the five-minute trek on foot. Bring all of your valuables with you, and also pack a blanket or towel for lying in the sun and soaking up the silence. Rarely are there crowds at Punalau. Since the reef is shallow and can be razor sharp, don't snorkel or swim here. This is also one of Maui's best spots to watch large winter surf, and the left break at the far southern end has been referred to as Maui's version of Pipeline.

Honokohau Beach

Finally, 5.8 miles past the entrance of Kapalua is the rocky beach of **Honokohau Bay.** The best thing about this beach is the scenery, both of the rural valley and the coast. Unfortunately, despite the scenic conditions, car break-ins have

© KYLE ELLISON

the rugged coastline of Windmills

been known to occur, so take your valuables with you. The swimming here is marginal and the waves can be dangerous in the winter.

KA'ANAPALI

Unlike the bays of the Kapalua/Napili section of the island, the beaches in Ka'anapali are long, wide, and lined by resorts. Much like Kapalua, however, the wind can often be a factor here in the afternoon, so it's best to get your water activities in early before the trade winds start blowing.

Ka'anapali Beach

Few stretches of Maui shoreline are more iconic than famous **Ka'anapali Beach**. This long, uninterrupted expanse of sand is lined from end to end with world-class resorts, it was voted as the number one beach in the United States in 2003, and it's the pulsing epicenter of the West Side's see-and-be-seen crowd. It should come as no surprise that the area is a constant hotbed of activity. Pick any island beach activity: surfing, snorkeling, scuba, snuba,

paddleboarding, volleyball, parasailing (summer), or whale-watching (winter), and you'll find it on Ka'anapali Beach. A paved pathway runs the length of the beach and is popular with joggers in the morning.

The best snorkeling is found at Pu'u Keka'a (Black Rock) in front of the Sheraton at the far northern end of the beach. Most of the water sports such as surf lessons take place at KP Point in front of the Ka'anapali Ali'i, and the beach volleyball court is in front of the Sheraton on the north end of the beach. For bodyboarding, the best area is between Whalers Village and Pu'u Keka'a. Since the beach faces directly west, it can pick up waves any time of the year. Be careful on days with big shorebreak, however, and use common sense.

Another favorite activity at Ka'anapali Beach is cliff jumping off Pu'u Keka'a. While this 20-foot jump is popular with visitors and locals, the rock is one of the most sacred places on the island for native Hawaiians who believe it's an entry point for a person's soul passing from this world into the next. To jump off Pu'u Keka'a

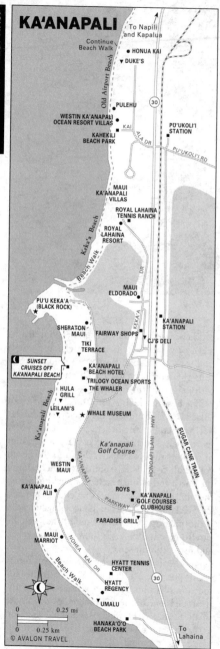

KA'ANAPALI

To Napili and Kapalua

Continue Beach Walk

HONUA KAI
DUKE'S

Old Airport Beach

PULEHU

30

WESTIN KA'ANAPALI
OCEAN RESORT VILLAS

KAI
ALA DR

PU'UKOLI'I
STATION

KAHEKILI
BEACH PARK

PU'UKOLI'I RD

MAUI
KA'ANAPALI
VILLAS

ROYAL LAHAINA
TENNIS RANCH

ROYAL
LAHAINA
RESORT

Keka'a Beach

Beach Walk

MAUI
ELDORADO

DR

KEKA'A

PU'U KEKA'A
(BLACK ROCK)

KA'ANAPALI
STATION

SHERATON
MAUI

FAIRWAY SHOPS

CJ'S DELI

TIKI
TERRACE

SUNSET
CRUISES OFF
KA'ANAPALI BEACH

KA'ANAPALI
BEACH HOTEL

TRILOGY OCEAN SPORTS
THE WHALER

HULA
GRILL

LEILANI'S

WHALE MUSEUM

Ka'anapali Beach

KA'ANAPALI

Ka'anapali
Golf Course

HONOAPI'ILANI HWY

SUGAR CANE TRAIN

WESTIN
MAUI

KA'ANAPALI
ALII

ROYS

KA'ANAPALI
GOLF COURSES
CLUBHOUSE

PARKWAY

PARADISE GRILL

MAUI
MARRIOT

NOHEA KAI DR

HYATT TENNIS
CENTER

Beach Walk

30

HYATT
REGENCY

UMALU

0   0.25 mi

0   0.25 km

HANAKA'O'O
BEACH PARK

To
Lahaina

© AVALON TRAVEL

is to mimic the soul at the moment of death, a legend still told during the evening torch lighting ceremony that takes place before each sunset.

Since Ka'anapali Beach is exposed to the afternoon trade winds, the weather can often be wetter and windier than down the road in Lahaina. The morning hours are best for paddleboarding or snorkeling, and if the wind is blowing too hard by the Sheraton, you can find a pocket of calm at the southern end of the beach by the Hyatt. Also, if you plan on going for a morning swim, realize that there are two areas where large catamarans come ashore to pick up passengers, so keep a keen lookout when in the water in front of Ka'anapali Beach Hotel or Whalers Village.

Unless you're staying at one of the resorts along the Ka'anapali strip, parking is going to be a challenge. Free public parking can be tough to come by, since most public spots are taken by 9am. There is one small public garage between the Sheraton and the Ka'anapali Beach Hotel, a lot between Whalers Village and the Westin, a handful of beach parking stalls in the front lot of the Ka'anapali Beach Hotel, and a small public lot on Nohea Kai Drive that leads down to the Hyatt. While there's always a chance that you'll luck out and snag a spot, more often than not you'll end up having to pay exorbitantly to park in the garage of Whalers Village. Remember, however, that if you end up shopping at a store or eating at a restaurant in Whalers Village, you can validate the parking ticket and not have to pay for parking (each pink sticker is good for three hours).

Kahekili Beach Park

There was a time not too long ago when **Kahekili Beach Park,** named after the great king of Maui, was an undeveloped scrubland of kiawe trees and coastal dunes that existed as an afterthought when compared to Ka'anapali Beach. Over time, there has been so much development at Airport Beach (also known as Ka'anapali North Beach) that it's almost as busy as neighboring Ka'anapali. Yet Kahekili still has a family-friendly atmosphere where locals lounge on the grassy area in front of the beach pavilion or snorkel the offshore reef. The beach here is just as long as Ka'anapali Beach, although the steep grade of the shoreline makes it difficult for jogging. Most visitors use the boardwalk along the shoreline, and if you're up for a stroll you can follow this as it weaves through the Royal Lahaina and Sheraton parking areas to meet up with the Ka'anapali beach path. Unlike Ka'anapali Beach, there are easily accessible public restrooms, and there is a large public parking lot at the Kai Ala entrance from the highway. If the lot is full, there's more parking on the north end of the beach, accessible from Lower Honoapi'ilani Road. The swimming here is much better than at Ka'anapali since there isn't as much catamaran traffic. If Ka'anapali Beach is just a little too busy for you, you'll enjoy how Kahekili offers a world-class beach atmosphere but slinks by at a slower pace.

LAHAINA

The beaches of Lahaina are the most underrated on the island. The swimming is poor due to the offshore reef, but they are sunnier, less crowded, and more protected from the wind than most other beaches on Maui. If it's raining in Kapalua or Napili, or windy on Ka'anapali Beach, 90 percent of the time it's going to be sunny and calm on the beaches of Lahaina.

Makila Beach

Also known as **Breakwall, 505,** or **Shark Pit,** this is the most happening stretch of sand in Lahaina. Most visitors access the beach from Kamehameha Iki Park, and there is beach parking in a small lot or in the back of the Front Street tennis courts. This is the area where most of the surf schools set out from. There is also a beach volleyball court which can get busy during the afternoons. Visitors are encouraged to marvel at the Polynesian voyaging canoes on display as part of the **Hui O Wa'a Kaulua Canoe Club.** This area was once the playground of Hawaiian royalty. You can hear the drums of the Feast of Lele lu'au while watching the sunset from here the north end of the beach, which

can be busy. Visitors rarely wander to the south end of the beach where palm trees hang out over a secluded cove. Locals call this area Shark Pit, referencing the harmless reef sharks which hang around the offshore ledge. The swimming here is poor due to the offshore reef, although it provides calm water for wading with small children. There is one shower but no restroom at this beach.

Pu'unoa and Mala (Baby Beach)

On the northern end of Front Street, the beach which runs along Pu'unoa Point (and known to locals as **Baby Beach**) is an oasis of tranquility where you have to ask yourself if you're still in Lahaina. Shielded from visitors by its residential location—and protected from big surf by the offshore reef—the sand running along this lazy promontory is the perfect spot for a sitting in a beach chair and listening to the waves. Numerous trees provide shade, and the calm waters are ideal for beachgoers with young children or those who want to tan on a raft.

Finding the beach can be a challenge, and parking can be an issue. For the access point with the largest amount of parking, turn off Front Street onto Ala Moana Street by the sign for Mala Ramp. Instead of heading down to the boat launch, proceed straight on Ala Moana until the road ends by the Jodo mission. From here you will see the beach in front of you, and the best section of beach will be a five-minute walk to your left along the sand. Transients sometimes hang out around this parking lot; don't leave any valuables in your car. If you're walking from downtown Lahaina, the quickest access to the nicest part of beach is to turn off Front Street onto Kai Pali Place where you will notice a shoreline access path. If you are coming from downtown Lahaina, this turn will be about three minutes after you pass the Hard Rock Café.

Wahikuli and Hanakao'o Beach Parks (Canoe Beach)

On the northern tip of Lahaina, these two beach parks comprise the strip of land between Front Street and Ka'anapali. **Wahikuli**

© MARK DRIESSEN

a secluded cove at "Shark Pit" (Makila Beach)

is the beach closer to Lahaina, and **Hanakao'o** is the one at the southern edge of the Hyatt. Of the two beaches, Wahikuli offers better swimming, although a secret about Hanakao'o is that on the days when the main stretch of Ka'anapali Beach is windy, Hanakao'o stays tucked in a cove where the wind can barely reach. Hanakao'o is also known as Canoe Beach since this is where many of the outrigger canoe regattas are held on Saturday mornings. As of the time of writing, a new beach path was being constructed so visitors can walk or ride bicycles from the south end of Ka'anapali through Hanakao'o, Wahikuli, and down to Front Street in Lahaina.

SOUTH OF LAHAINA

On the stretch of shoreline between Lahaina and Ma'alaea there are a grand total of zero resorts. Paddleboards and fishing poles rule this section of coast, and even though the swimming is poor, there is one spot which offers good snorkeling. Most visitors choose to pass these beaches by without giving them another thought, but if you do decide to pull over to watch the whales, visit the beach, or photograph the sunset, don't stop in the middle of the road. If you're headed in the Lahaina direction, it's easiest to pull off on the right side of the road and wait for traffic to clear before crossing, or park your car on the right, wait for a break in the traffic, and then cross on foot to the other side.

Olowalu

Known to visitors as Mile Marker 14, the real name of this beach is **Olowalu,** after the village which stretches far back into the valley. The snorkeling here is the best south of Lahaina, although plenty of beachgoers—particularly those with young children—come here simply to wade in the calm waters. While the water may be calm, however, it's also shallow, and the swimming area is nonexistent during low tide, particularly on the days of a full or new moon. Parking is along the side of the highway, although it's easy to get stuck in the sand.

house. There is a large parking lot as well as restrooms and showers, and since most of the parking spots are taken by 8am, there is an overflow lot on the *mauka* (mountain side) of the highway. The water here is too shallow for swimming and the snorkeling is poor, but this is a good place for putting your finger on the local pulse and striking up a good conversation. Who knows? It could end up leading to a free beer and plate lunch!

Puamana Beach Park

There's a decent chance that during your time on the island you'll hear a famous Hawaiian song by the name of "Puamana." This lighthearted, gently flowing melody was written about this section of shoreline that serves as the entry to Lahaina. While there is a private, gated community that goes by the same name, the general public can only visit the small **Puamana Beach Park** one mile north of Launiupoko. As at other beaches in the area, the swimming is poor, although the tables provide a nice setting for a picnic. Longboarders gather along the shore and small groups of beachgoers strum ukulele in the parking lot. If you're looking to take a stroll down the beach, the sandy shoreline fronting the condos is public property, so at low tide you can walk from the beach park to the other end of the private, gated section (although the grassy area is still private and should be treated as such). There aren't any restrooms at the beach park, but there's a refreshing shower in the north end of the parking lot.

© KYLE ELLISON

Puamana Beach Park

Launiupoko Beach Park

Located at the only stoplight between Ma'alaea and Lahaina, **Launiupoko** is the most family-friendly beach park on the west side of Maui. It has a protected wading area for small *keiki,* a decent sandy beach on the south end of the park, a wide, grassy picnic area, and numerous surf breaks that cater to beginner surfers and stand-up paddle surfers. This park is so popular with the weekend barbecue crowd that local families arrive before dawn to stake their claim for a birthday party with a bouncy

WEST MAUI

Snorkeling

Snorkeling is the most popular activity in West Maui. Hundreds of people ply the waters of the island's western shoreline, flipping their fins as they chase after schools of yellow and black *manini* (convict tang). But there is always room to find your own section of reef, and the waters of West Maui teem with everything from graceful green sea turtles to the playfully named *humuhumunukunukuapua'a*—the Hawaiian state fish (the name is translated as "big lips with a nose like a pig").

Mornings are the best time of day for snorkeling on the west side of the island. Different times of year also mean different snorkeling conditions. During the winter, places such as Honolua Bay and Napili can be dangerous due to the huge surf, so summer is the best time for exploring these reefs. Similarly, snorkeling spots on the south shore such as Olowalu can be prone to large surf during summer, although with much less frequency than the northern beaches in winter. Since surf comes in swells only lasting for a few days at a time, there is still the chance you will be able to snorkel at any beach any time of the year—provided you are there between swells. There is a 95 percent chance that Honolua Bay will be good for snorkeling May-September, with only a 20 percent chance December-March. Remaining months of the year will be about 50 percent. If your goal is to snorkel during your time on the West Side, but the surf is too big or the conditions too poor, there is probably another place that is calm and beautiful just a 20-minute drive away.

KAPALUA, NAPILI, AND HONOKOWAI
◖ Honolua Bay
When it comes to snorkeling along Maui's shoreline, **Honolua Bay** is the gold standard.

Some of the island's best snorkeling is in West Maui.

© MARK DRIESSEN

This wide, scenic cleft in the coastline is not only a bio-diverse marine reserve, but it's also protected from the afternoon trade winds. Honolua Bay is one of the most sacred and revered spots on the West Side of the island, and there has been a herculean movement over the last decade to "Save Honolua" and spare the area from development. The valley, bay, and shoreline exude a supernatural beauty. Somewhere between the lush green foliage of the valley and the shimmering, turquoise waters, there is a palpable magic unlike anywhere else. This is also the bay from which the Hokule'a voyaging canoe launched its epic journey to Tahiti in 1976.

Finding the shoreline at Honolua Bay is an adventure in itself. As the highway morphs into a rural county road, the first glimpse you will get of Honolua is from the paved overlook 1.8 miles past the entrance to Kapalua. This is a nice place to pull over for a picture, but there are better lookouts a mile later. Toward the bottom of the hill, parking for the shoreline is in a lush and shaded valley where you might encounter some merchants selling their crafts. To reach the water, find a parking spot wherever you can (all the trails in a 0.5-mile stretch eventually lead to the shoreline), grab all of your snorkeling gear, and make a short, five-minute trek through a dense green understory which chirps with activity and drips with vines.

The "beach" is more a collection of boulders. If you are facing the water, the right side has a much larger snorkeling area and a greater concentration of marine life. The center of the bay has a sandy bottom and is mostly devoid of marine life, so it's best to trace the shoreline and snorkel around to the right. If it's between the hours of 9am and noon and there aren't any charter boats tied up on the right side of the bay, it means that the conditions aren't acceptable enough to bring paying snorkelers here. Also, if you see breaking waves out toward the point and there are over 20 surfers in the water, it means that the visibility is going to be less than stellar and conditions will be dangerous if you venture in too shallow. If it isn't raining on the shoreline but the stream on the left side of

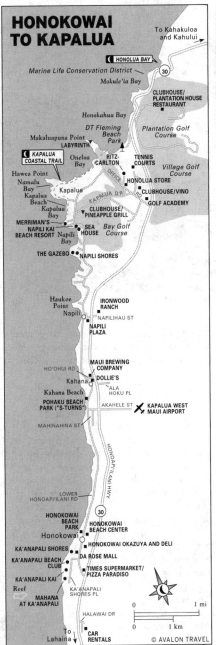

© AVALON TRAVEL

© KYLE ELLISON

Turtles are a common sight when snorkeling in West Maui.

the bay is gushing with brown water, it means that it's raining farther up the mountain and all of the runoff is emptying into the bay. This, of course, will also make for subpar conditions.

If, however, the sun is shining brilliantly, here's your guide to the best snorkeling area: When you enter the water from the rocky shoreline, swim straight out for about 20 yards and then turn right toward the shoreline. You'll want to hug the shoreline in 5-10 feet of water and follow it in a ring around the right side of the bay. If you're on a mission to find Hawaiian green sea turtles, the best spot to check out is the **turtle cleaning station** on the right/center of the bay. It's about 200 yards out from the boat ramp, in line with the bend in the cliff on the right side of the bay, and in about 15-20 feet of water. If you're fortunate enough to snorkel Honolua Bay during winter, dive a few feet underwater to listen for the distant song of humpback whales. Keep a keen eye out for boat traffic, as a number of catamarans make their approach through the middle of the bay.

Mokulei'a Bay

Parking for **Mokulei'a Bay** is along the highway 1.5 miles past the entrance to Kapalua, and the best snorkeling is in the cove on the right side of the bay. Even though Mokulei'a is still a part of the Honolua Marine Life Conservation District, the reef here is completely different than at Honolua Bay, so you're likely to see different species than you would right around the corner. Although there's still the likelihood of seeing a sea turtle, there's also a chance for some spotted eagle rays swimming over the sand by the end of the point or perhaps an octopus clinging to the wall at the far end of the cove. Mokulei'a is a little more exposed to the afternoon trade winds, so morning hours during flat, calm days are the best time for snorkeling.

Namalu Bay (Cliffhouse)

The hidden, craggy shoreline of **Namalu Bay (Cliffhouse)** offers a relaxing setting that could be compared to a Mediterranean coastal village. You can spot green sea turtles, reef fish, and the occasional eagle or manta ray. The

SNORKELING 101

Thousands of island visitors annually strap on a mask for a peek at the underwater world. For those who have never snorkeled, however, the act of breathing through a tube in the middle of the ocean can be harrowing. Follow these basic snorkeling tips for a better first-time experience.

1. Choose the right equipment. Any successful snorkeling mission begins with the proper equipment. Make sure the mask fits by holding it to your face and sucking in with your nose. If the mask stays without you touching it with your hands, it means you have a good seal. For snorkels, no matter what the store clerk says, you don't have to get one with all the bells and whistles. A simple J-shaped snorkel is all that's needed, although some people like the feature where if water gets in the top of the snorkel it won't continue down toward your mouth. For fins, unlike shoes, you want to make sure you have a tight fit around your heel instead of around your toes. If your heel lifts up while the fins are on, it means the fins are too big. If they feel slightly tight when you test them out on land, remember that the water will lubricate the area once you get in the ocean.

2. Learn how to put on the gear. The first thing you want to do before getting in the water is to put a defog solution in your mask to keep it from clouding up. Even though snorkel shops sell fancy gels, the best defog is a home-made solution of baby shampoo and water. For new masks, use toothpaste. Also, to keep your eyes from stinging, don't put sunscreen on your forehead immediately prior to snorkeling since it will end up running into your eyes. When placing your mask on your head, brush all of your hair back so none gets into the mask. If hair gets caught in the mask, it will break the seal and allow water to leak in. The next step is to ensure the mask strap is high on the crown of your head. If the mask strap is touching your ears, it means the mask is too low (young children love to put the mask strap below their ears, which is why their masks always seem to leak). If you're a "nose-breather," remember that your nose is inside a mask, so you need to get used to the sensation of breathing out of your mouth.

When it comes to your fins, the last thing you should ever do on a day when there are waves is to put them on while on the beach and then back your way into the water. Although this works on days when it is calm, this is how you'll end up rolling down the sand with your feet sticking straight in the air when there is shorebreak. Fins are meant for swimming, not walking, so once you fall down with fins on, it's almost impossible to stand back up. The number one rule in Hawaii is never turn your back on the ocean—that's precisely what happens when you back your way into the water. Instead, try holding your fins under your arm (after having put your mask on while onshore), walking out to chest deep water, and putting your fins on once there.

3. Less is more. If you are breathing, and you see fish, then you're doing it correctly. Take long, slow, relaxed breaths in and out of your mouth, and when you swim, use scissor-style kicks with your hands behind your back. Excessive movement will scare away the fish. If you float on the surface (particularly easy with a flotation belt), you'll see more of them.

4. Don't panic. When water ends up in your snorkel, don't panic! To clear the snorkel of water, your two options are to either say the number "TWO" loudly to shoot the water out the top of your snorkel or pop your head out of the water, remove the snorkel from your mouth, and turn the mouthpiece upside down to drain. Similarly, if water gets in your mask, instead of removing the whole mask pull the bottom of the mask away from your face and let the water drain out.

Keep an eye on where you're swimming, don't overexert yourself, and most important, have fun.

center of the bay is about 40 feet deep, whereas the areas ringing the shoreline are a more manageable 5-15 feet. When hanging out on shore, the rocks are the perfect height for cliff jumping, or laying out in the sun and soaking up some rays.

Namalu Bay isn't as crowded as other snorkeling spots because you can't see it from the road. Accessing the bay can be challenging. The more practical way to reach it is via the dirt pathway that traces the coastline from the closest public parking at the Kapalua Bay Villas. To find the eight public spots, turn into the parking area for the Kapalua Spa and make an immediate right toward the Kapalua Bay Villas. You will then make a left, following the sign for beach access parking, and will notice the small public parking area seemingly orphaned among a family of private, residential lots. From here it's a short walk down to the shoreline and the access for the Kapalua Coastal Trail. Alternately, if all the spots here are taken, you can park in the lot by Kapalua Bay and then walk on the paved portion of the Kapalua Coastal Trail before reaching the junction where the pathway turns to dirt. Now that you've found a spot for the car and the trailhead, to get to the actual snorkeling area you will make your way past two brown "Trail" markers and then notice the trail goes in three different directions. The trail to the right is the continuation of the Kapalua Coastal Trail, the gravel trail leading straight heads out to Hawea Point, and the grassy trail that bends off to the left is the one that leads toward Namalu Bay. Follow the trail as it wraps to the left, and when you see the signs that say "proceed at your own risk," understand that that's exactly what you're doing. In 30 seconds you'll find yourself standing atop the cliffs overlooking hidden Namalu Bay.

Kapalua Bay

Kapalua Bay is a sandy cove that is a favorite for those who are snorkeling with small children. The relatively small size means it's easy to scour the entire bay, and you can expect to see colorful parrotfish, lots of goatfish, and

even the occasional green sea turtle. Although depths rarely exceed 20 feet, the best snorkeling is found along the right side of the bay where the rocks extend out to the distant point. If you're a super-snorkeler and the conditions are calm, you can even snorkel around the northern point into neighboring Namalu Bay.

Napili Bay

A short walk from Kapalua Bay is neighboring **Napili Bay,** and you could easily snorkel at both bays without even reparking your car. Whereas Napili Bay doesn't have quite as many fish as Kapalua Bay, there is a higher likelihood of finding a green sea turtle. While many snorkelers hug the wall on the right side of the bay, there is another reef in the center of the bay that's almost exposed during low tide. About 20 yards farther out from here is a second, lesser-visited reef, and although it's deeper at about 15-20 feet, this is the area with the highest concentration of fish. This outer reef is far from shore, so if you're uncomfortable in the water, stay on the inside reefs and enjoy the shallower waters.

Rental Shops

In Kapalua, the most comprehensive shop is **Kapalua Dive Company** (1 Bay Dr., 808/669-3448, www.kapaluadive.com, 8am-5pm daily) on the northern edge of Kapalua Bay. This is a full-service dive and snorkel operation that also offers guided snorkeling tours, just a short stroll down the Kapalua beach path.

In Napili, **Snorkel Bob's** (5425 Lower Honoapiʻilani Rd., 808/669-9603, www.snorkelbob.com, 8am-5pm daily) has a shop in Napili Village next to the Napili General store, with a second location down the street (3350 Lower Honoapiʻilani Rd., 808/667-9999, www.snorkelbob.com, 8am-5pm daily). There is also a **Boss Frog's** (5059 Napilihau St., 808/669-4949, www.bossfrog.com, 8am-6pm daily) in the Napili Plaza shopping center. All offer economical deals on snorkeling equipment. Snorkel Bob's lets you return your gear on a different island if you plan on doing any island hopping.

DON'T STAND ON THE REEF!

At West Side snorkeling spots, signs warn against standing on the reef. While everyone knows to avoid stepping on sea urchins and sharp rocks, the signs are meant to teach about the harm to the reef as opposed to the bottom of your feet.

Unlike beaches which have rocky or sandy bottoms, reefs in Maui are made up of living corals which are as fragile as they are alive. More than just pretty, multicolored rocks, corals are living animals with hard exoskeletons—just as alive as the fish swimming above them or the eels inhabiting their crevices.

As with all things which are alive, however, corals can easily die, and one of the main threats to Maui's corals right now is the number of visitors who stand on the reefs. Granted, it isn't always on purpose, and when many snorkelers go to fix their snorkel mask or readjust their hair tie, they don't realize they're probably killing the ground they're standing on.

Snorkeling areas such as Honolua Bay, Ka-hekili Beach Park, and Olowalu have seen the most damage in recent years. Estimates from recent studies suggest that West Maui has lost as much as 25 percent of live coral growth in the last decade alone. There are other factors involved, such as sedimentation, overfishing, algal blooms, pesticide-laden runoff, and even the petroleum-based sunscreen which washes off visitors' shoulders and ends up settling on the sensitive polyps. Regardless of the exact source, however, the fact remains that Maui's reefs are under attack, and visitors can do their part in protecting this fragile ecosystem by eliminating contact with the reef all together, whether it be while adjusting your snorkel mask in waist-deep water, bracing yourself to take a photo, or swimming along the ocean floor while on an underwater snuba or scuba adventure.

All beachgoers must work toward the health and protection of our island's coral reefs for the sake of our future.

In Kahana, **Maui Dive Shop** (4405 Honoapi'ilani Hwy., 808/669-3800, www.mauidiveshop.com, 8am-9pm daily) is within the Kahana Gateway Center by Maui Brewing Company and offers a full range of rentals as well as information on its dive and snorkeling charters to Molokini and Olowalu.

In Honokowai, locally run **All About Fish** (3600 Lower Honapi'ilani Hwy., 808/669-1710, www.mauifish.net, 9am-5pm Mon.-Sat., noon-4pm Sun.) in the 5A Rent A Space mall offers affordable rentals on a full range of dive equipment. This is a good option if you're staying in a condo in Honokowai and looking for local advice on snorkeling conditions. You can relax knowing you can walk in here to rent some snorkeling gear without somebody trying to sell you a helicopter tour.

KA'ANAPALI
Kahekili Beach Park
In the northern part of Ka'anapali, **Kahekili Beach Park** offers decent snorkeling off the beach park and at the far southern end of the beach. The reef on the northern edge isn't quite as nice as the area in front of the beach park. The reef extends from the shoreline out to about 25 feet of water. Expect to see a healthy amount of herbivorous reef fish here. The moderate depth and easy entry make this a user-friendly snorkeling spot during the early morning hours. At the far southern end of the beach is a rock jetty that also offers good snorkeling, and the rocky promontory here is the "back" of Pu'u Keka'a (Black Rock).

Pu'u Keka'a (Black Rock)
The best snorkeling in Ka'anapali is at **Pu'u Keka'a,** better known as **Black Rock.** At the far northern end of Ka'anapali Beach in front of the Sheraton, this area offers the most consistently beautiful snorkeling conditions and a relatively easy entry. The morning hours are going to be best, and the best chance for seeing

sea turtles here is during high tide, when the water comes up on the side of the rock and all of the *limu* (seaweed) falls into the water. Since this is a favorite delicacy of the green sea turtles, there can occasionally be three or four different turtles all congregating in the shallow cove in only 5-10 feet of water. Since the cliff here is also a favorite place for cliff jumping, steer clear of the immediate landing zone, and if you see the wind whipping up whitecaps out by the point, stay in the cove where it's protected and the current isn't as strong.

Ka'anapali Point

On the other end of Ka'anapali Beach is the reef at **Ka'anapali Point.** While it's not nearly as popular as the reef at Pu'u Keka'a, this reef in front of the Marriott covers a larger area and isn't nearly as crowded. If Pu'u Keka'a is a flotilla of fins, take a 10-minute stroll to the southern end of the beach and try your luck at this lesser-visited spot.

Rental Shops

Every major resort along the strip of Ka'anapali is going to have a rental shack by the sand. Prices vary slightly between all of the operators, although expect to pay the more expensive resort prices rather than what they ask at a snorkeling store off the resort strip. A rental of a couple of hours is commonly $12, although the best deal on Ka'anapali Beach is at the **Maui Dive and Surf** (808/270-9846) kiosk just south of Leilani's at Whalers Village. Snorkeling sets are either $15 for the day or $25 for the week; combine them with a boogie board rental for $35/week.

Snorkeling Charters

A number of catamarans depart directly from Ka'anapali Beach on half-day excursions sailing along the West Maui coastline. For excursions to either Lana'i or Molokini Crater you will still need to go to the Lahaina or Ma'alaea harbors. For all boats departing from Ka'anapali Beach, the preferred snorkeling destination is Honolua Bay. Since the surf at Honolua Bay during the winter can get large, the alternate snorkeling

destination is Olowalu on the south shore. During most days of the year these sleek sailing yachts are able to pull their bows right up on the sand and load passengers directly from the beach, although during days with large surf the shorebreak can be too rough and there's a slight chance the trip might be moved to Lahaina Harbor. If a member of your party has restricted mobility, then trips out of Lahaina Harbor will prove a safer option.

Of the crews departing from Ka'anapali Beach, **Trilogy** (808/874-5649, www.sailtrilogy.com) loads in front of the Ka'anapali Beach Hotel and offers 8am snorkeling charters, thereby making them the first boat to Honolua Bay. Trilogy tours from Ka'anapali are usually aboard *Trilogy IV,* a few feet smaller than other boats along the beach. The maximum capacity on these trips is only about 35 people. All of the food is made fresh on board. Both the Trilogy crew and the level of customer service are widely regarded as the best in the industry. You shouldn't raise a finger; everything is served to you. Due to its slightly smaller size and its lightweight makeup, the *Trilogy IV* is the fastest of the Ka'anapali sailboats. Half-day charters are $119 for adults, include all food and equipment, and usually return to the beach around 1:30pm.

On the stretch of sand in front of Whalers Village, **Teralani** (808/661-7245, www.teralani.net) has two boats that regularly make excursions along the West Maui coastline. The Teralani boats are larger than Trilogy's and cap their trips at 49 people. The primary snorkeling tour departs at 9:30am and returns to the beach around 2:30pm. An abridged trip departs at 11am and returns to the beach at 3pm. All food and equipment are included in the price. There's also an open bar (once you've finished snorkeling, of course), whereas Trilogy charges $5 a drink. With the open bar, however, the price also increases. The adult price of the longer sail is $139 while the four-hour cruise is $112.

Other catamarans departing from Ka'anapali Beach include *Gemini* (808/669-0508, www.geminicharters.com) and *Hula Girl*

(808/665-0344, www.sailingmaui.com), both of which load on the stretch of beach in front of Leilani's restaurant. *Gemini* is just as large as Teralani's boats and offers much the same trip, with a difference being that the primary snorkeling charter departs at 11am and returns to the beach between 3 and 3:30pm. Equipment, food, and open bar are included in the tour, and the adult price is $115. *Hula Girl,* on the other hand, is an ornately painted boat which takes a different approach from the others. At first glance the adult price of only $98 for the five-hour tour (9:30-2:30) appears to be cheap, but that's because it doesn't include the cost of food. Unlike other companies with a set menu, *Hula Girl* has a kitchen on board where chefs make the food to order. There is also free Wi-Fi for anyone who wants to immediately upload the GoPro footage of an encounter with a sea turtle. Scuba diving is offered as an additional upgrade for both certified ($65) and introductory ($75) divers.

LAHAINA
Wahikuli Beach Park
Since the majority of Lahaina is ringed by a barrier reef, there are surprisingly few options for decent snorkeling. The few exceptions should only be snorkeled if they're your only choice. Of the two places to snorkel in Lahaina, the one with the easiest entry is **Wahikuli Beach Park** between Ka'anapali and Lahaina. While much of the bottom here is boring old sand, on the far southern end of the beach is a rocky point that can have a large number of reef fish.

Mala Wharf
In the actual town of Lahaina, the best snorkeling spot is **Mala Wharf,** and since this is a functioning small boat harbor, you need to keep an eye out for boat traffic. The reward, however, is a snorkeling site where legions of sea turtles and numerous reef sharks live under the pilings littering the ocean floor. This is a site most often accessed by boat, but the easiest way to reach it from shore is to park in the public parking area and cross over to where the pier meets the sand. From here, it's a kick out to where the

pier drops into the water. While conditions are nice most times of the year, the only period you wouldn't want to snorkel here is if the river draining into the bay is a rushing torrent of runoff. To find the parking for Mala Wharf, turn off Front Street onto Ala Moana Street, following the signs for Mala Ramp (which is just on the south side of the bridge from the Lahaina Cannery Mall). Once you turn, you will make an immediate right down toward the boat ramp where there are restrooms, showers, and a moderate amount of parking.

Rental Shops
The most comprehensive shop in Lahaina with the largest selection of gear is **Maui Dive and Surf** (315 Keawe St., 808/661-5388, www.mauidiveshop.com, 7am-6pm daily) in the Lahaina Gateway Center. Although when you first walk in it appears to be a massive retail and surf store, the staff here will help you with everything you need from a set of fins to a new dive watch. While short-term rentals are available, this is also a good shop for those looking to purchase their own gear and find something of quality which will last longer than a three-day rental period.

Smaller but just as credible, **Lahaina Divers** (143 Dickenson St., 808/667-7496, www.lahainadivers.com, 8am-8pm daily) will have everything you need for snorkeling, despite the fact it's a full-service dive shop. This is another place you would come if you were looking to own gear for an extended period of time, and since the staff are all divers themselves, they can give you up-to-date information on the current conditions around the West Side.

If, on the other hand, you're just looking for cheap rental gear to get you through your vacation, both **Boss Frog's** (150 Lahainaluna Rd., 808/661-3333, www.bossfrog.com, 8am-5pm daily) and **Snorkel Bob's** (1217 Front St., 808/661-4421, www.snorkelbob.com, 8am-5pm daily) provide economical rentals which can be as low as $2/day. Remember, however, that not only do you get what you pay for, but the main impetus for getting you through the door is to sell activities or upsell you to a fancier mask and snorkel package. If you aren't picky about a mask fitting perfectly or are on a budget, all of the offerings here are completely fine and will get you through a couple of sessions at the beach.

For a similar operation in the center of Lahaina you can also check out **The Snorkel Store** (840 Waineʻe St., 808/669-1077, www.thesnorkelstore.com, 8:30am-5pm daily), a small but friendly shop squirreled away in the Lahaina Square Center a block inland from Front Street. There are often 2 for 1 specials on snorkeling gear. There are also masks with built-in cameras that can potentially take some good videos while you snorkel. The prices here are fair, and the staff won't try to upsell you too hard. This is a good option for renting gear if you're willing to walk a block into a lesser-visited portion of town.

Lahaina Snorkeling Charters

Other than Maʻalaea Harbor, Lahaina Harbor is the island's busiest passenger port with hundreds of visitors daily. Before sunrise, this small, historic harbor teems with activity as fishers fuel their boats and charter captains prepare for the day ahead. All throughout the day the harbor basin is a whirlwind of activity with lines forming and reforming, food coolers being slung across the docks, and fresh fish being laid on ice to the amusement of curious passersby. Behind the famous banyan tree on Front Street, this is where most of Lahaina's snorkeling charters depart from, with a select few opting to set out from Mala Ramp on the northern edge of town. Unlike at Kaʻanapali, however, where all of the snorkeling options are aboard sailing catamarans, snorkeling charters in Lahaina run the gamut from small inflatable rafts to massive two-tiered catamarans which can fit almost 150 people. It's important to match the tour company you go with to the type of experience you're looking for.

SAILBOATS

The company with the largest number of snorkeling charters out of Lahaina Harbor is

Trilogy (808/874-5649, www.sailtrilogy.com), which offers all-day cruises to Lanaʻi as well as a four-hour snorkel along the West Maui coastline. While a couple of other boat companies also travel to Lanaʻi to snorkel for the day, Trilogy is the only one with a commercial permit to have crew and facilities based on the island. The all-day experience is truly in a class of its own.

Departing out of Lahaina Harbor at 10am (during busier times of the year there can also be a 6:30am departure), the 60-foot sailing catamarans travel to Manele Harbor on Lanaʻi where passengers will disembark to snorkel at Hulopoʻe Bay. Since Hulopoʻe faces south, during summer there is the potential for large surf, so the snorkeling can be subpar. While this is only during a handful of days in summer, winter is nearly guaranteed to have pristine conditions. On the beach itself, Trilogy has exclusive access to the left side of Hulopoʻe Bay and it is the only company with lifeguards, beach mats, beach chairs, refreshments, beach volleyball, and all of the snorkeling gear right on the beach. Also included with the price is an optional guided van tour of Lanaʻi City.

The other sailing catamaran departing out of Lahaina Harbor and heading to the island of Lanaʻi is **Paragon** (808/244-2087, www.sailmaui.com), a 47-foot boat which only takes 24 passengers and is the island's fastest catamaran under sail. The seven-hour, $159 trip departs at 8:30am and docks at Manele Harbor on Lanaʻi. You're unsupervised while you snorkel (since the crew doesn't have permission to operate on shore) and you're given a picnic lunch to the enjoy while at the beach. The trip returns to Lahaina around 3:30pm, and on lucky days the crew might even hook up with an *ono* or mahimahi while trolling the fishing lures under sail.

While it mostly focuses on sunset sails and sailing charters, **Scotch Mist II** (808/661-0386, www.scotchmistsailingcharters.com) is a 50-foot Santa Cruz monohull that also operates four-hour sailing and snorkeling charters along the western shoreline of the island for $109.

POWERBOATS

Of the larger diesel boats which operate out of Lahaina Harbor, **Pacific Whale Foundation** (612 Front St., 808/942-5311, www.pacific-whale.org) offers the most options. Its large boats can fit upward of 149 people, and while that's a crowd, there's no arguing with the price. Its five-hour tour to Lana'i departs at 9am. It's only $80 for adults; each paying adult is allotted one child free of charge. Unlike other boats that dock at Manele Harbor, the Pacific Whale Foundation cruises snorkel off the boat, with the two preferred destinations being either Kaunolu (Shark Fin Cove) or the Manele reef outside of the small boat harbor. The level of customer service on a boat this size isn't quite the same as on the more intimate vessels, but for families who are on a budget and want to go snorkeling for the day, it's tough to argue with the affordability.

During summer, a smaller adventure rafting tour departs Lahaina for Lana'i at 7:30am. The price is significantly higher ($119 adult, $75 child), but you get a much more personalized experience than on the larger boat and you're able to hug the shore for a better view of the undeveloped coastline. Another summer rafting excursion ($55) departs at 10:30am to snorkel along the West Maui coastline instead of going all the way to Lana'i. All trips for Pacific Whale Foundation check in at the storefront across the street from the famous banyan tree, and loading is by the main loading dock of the harbor where you will wait for one of the crew to escort you down to the boat.

Also during summer (many of these boats defer to whale watches in the winter), **Lahaina Cruise Company** (877/500-6284, www.lahainacruisecompany.com) has a fleet of aging but functional diesel boats that offer snorkeling charters to Lana'i and along the coastline of West Maui. While much of the focus for these boats is on whale-watching during the winter and cocktail cruises in the evening, there are still snorkeling charters available for those who are on a budget. The cost of the snorkeling tour is an affordable $79 for adults, and trips are offered Monday-Saturday on vessels that can accommodate up to 149 people.

Captain Woody's (808/667-2290, www.captainwoody.net) operates charters of only six people for private excursions. Fishing, snorkeling, and seasonal whale-watching can all be included in these small group tours, and six-hour tours usually depart from Mala Ramp at 7:30am.

RAFTS

For those who don't like crowds, there are a number of rafts that have small group sizes and place you closer to the water than any other type of vessel. Due to their bouncy nature, however, rafts aren't recommended for women who are pregnant or anyone with back problems, and if you're prone to seasickness, they won't be the best option since the waters can often become rough during the afternoon. Some companies will swap their snorkeling charters for whale watches during winter, however, so check ahead of time that snorkeling tours are available for the date of your excursion.

Of all the rafts, **Ultimate Snorkel Adventure** (808/667-5678, www.ultimate-whalewatch.com) is the best option. It operates out of slip 17 of Lahaina Harbor. Group sizes are kept to a minimum at only 16 passengers, and this rigid inflatable is the fastest boat in Lahaina Harbor at speeds in excess of 35 mph. Snorkeling locations are chosen off the island of Lana'i based on the best conditions, and unlike some of the other options which head ashore on Lana'i, this excursion takes place from off the raft. Due to its small size, the raft can navigate close to the shoreline of Lana'i to find blowholes or follow pods of spinner dolphins hanging out by the rocks. Five-hour snorkeling trips are offered at $139, and there is also a two-hour option available along the West Maui shoreline for only $49. Snorkel gear, drinks, and snacks are included in the price of the excursion. This is a great option for those wanting a semiprivate tour with relaxed but professional captain and crew.

Hawaii Ocean Rafting (808/661-7238, www.islandstarexcursions.com) operates out of slip 8 in Lahaina Harbor. Group sizes are kept low on these charters, which are offered as either full-day tours to Lana'i for $115 or half-day tours for $73. Full-day tours depart at 6:30am and return at 2:30pm, whereas the half-day option departs at 7:30am and is back in Lahaina by 12:30pm. Snorkeling gear, snacks, and beverages are included.

For a raft that docks at Manele Harbor and spends time on the island of Lana'i, **Maui Adventure Cruises** (808/661-5550, www.mauiadventurecruises.com) operates two trips out of Lahaina Harbor, one of which allows passengers to spend three hours of beach time at Lana'i's Hulopo'e Bay. This $115 excursion operates on Monday, Wednesday, and Friday, docks in Manele Harbor, and allows its guests to walk Hulopo'e Bay unsupervised. Breakfast, snacks, and a deli lunch are included in the cost of the trip. Excursions depart at both 7am and 9pm from slip #11 in Lahaina Harbor. On Tuesday, Thursday, and Saturday, an abridged 4.5-hour trip is offered for $87 where you will still have the opportunity to snorkel off Lana'i from the boat, rather than docking at Manele Harbor.

Departing from Mala Ramp at 6:30am, **Maui Ocean Riders** (808/661-3586, www.mauioceanriders.com) is the only boat to circumnavigate the island of Lana'i. Covering an astounding 70 miles over the course of the trip, this excursion features multiple snorkeling spots and the opportunity to witness little-seen areas of Lana'i such as the waters off Shipwreck Beach, Polihua Beach, and the snorkeling area known as Three Stone. On calm days this excursion is the best of all the rafting options, although on days when the trade winds are blowing early in the morning, it can be a rough, wet ride that transcends into the "adventure" category.

SOUTH OF LAHAINA
Olowalu

The best snorkeling south of Lahaina is at **Olowalu,** otherwise known as "mile marker 14." The reef here is a wide expanse of coral heads. The outer reef is popular with tour and dive boats, and the inside sections can teem with large parrotfish and Hawaiian green sea turtles. Directly out from the mileage marker is a sand channel that leads through the shallow reef and allows you access to deeper water. If, on the other hand, you venture out from a random spot along the coastline, there is a good chance you will get trapped in a maze of shallow coral heads where the water is often murky and the snorkeling is poor. Morning hours are best at Olowalu. In either situation it's best to snorkel elsewhere because the visibility will be poor and the currents dangerous. **Kayak Olowalu** (808/661-0606, www.kayakolowalu.com) rents gear for only $5 and can be found at the Camp Olowalu location. To reach Camp Olowalu, turn toward the water across from Olowalu General Store and follow the road for a half mile until it ends at the shoreline.

SPEARFISHING

Feeling adventurous? **Spearfish Maui** (808/205-8585, www.spearfishmaui.com, $159/person) will not only take you snorkeling, but teach you the basics of breath holding, free diving tactics, and underwater hunting. After a training with master diver Jeremy, it's off to a dive site along the island's West Side. This isn't for novices; participants should be strong swimmers in good shape. But hundreds of first-time spearfishers have successfully survived the six-hour session (typically 8am-2pm). Many actually catch fish! Don't touch the coral and only aim for fish in the legal size range.

Scuba Diving

Scuba diving from the west side of the island involves one of two options: Departing from a west side harbor for an excursion to Lana'i or diving along the West Maui shoreline. While certified divers should seek out a dive charter, there are also a number of shore operators who offer introductory dives. Or, if you're a certified diver renting gear and planning on diving independently, ask at the rental shop about current conditions and use a dive flag. As with snorkeling, dive spots along the northern section of the island will be largely inaccessible during winter due to large surf. Summer is the best time for diving up north.

KAPALUA, NAPILI, AND HONOKOWAI
Dive Sites

The best shore dive in West Maui is **Honolua Bay,** although slogging all of your gear down to the water can be an exhausting undertaking. If diving from shore, you will want to launch from the center of the beach and hug the right side of the bay where the reef drops off into the sand channel. Maximum depth here can reach about 40 feet, and you can expect to see green sea turtles, a wide variety of reef fish, or even have rare encounters with spinner dolphins. Of the boats offering dive trips to Honolua Bay, *Hula Girl* (808/665-0344, www.sailingmaui.com) offers scuba diving as an add-on to the regular snorkel charter, although most dive charters head elsewhere along the West Side.

For a beginner-friendly introductory dive, **Kapalua Bay** can offer everything from a shallow dive of 25 feet to a more advanced dive of 40 feet rounding the corner toward neighboring Namalu Bay. Unlike at Honolua there are showers and facilities here as well as an easy, sandy beach entry.

Dive Operators

The largest dive operation on the Upper West Side of the island is **Kapalua Dive Company** (1 Bay Dr., 808/669-3448, www.kapaluadive.com, 8am-5pm daily) at the northern end of Kapalua Bay. Introductory beach dives are offered at 10:30am for $85, or you can increase your dive area by taking a scooter dive into neighboring Namalu Bay for $125. To get to areas usually inaccessible from shore, there are also guided kayak dives which depart at 7:30am for turtle-laden areas such as Hawea Point, although inquire at the shop about availability. Those wanting to get certified on vacation can also work with the PADI-certified instructors. Occasional night dives are also offered.

Down in Honokowai, **Tiny Bubbles Scuba** (3350 Lower Honoapi'ilani Rd., 808/870-0878, www.tinybubblesscuba.com, 8am-5pm daily) operates shore dives along the West Maui coast. Under the lead of the vivacious and knowledgeable instructor "Timmerz," all of the instructors for Tiny Bubbles have been diving the Maui shoreline for over a decade and are acquainted with the nuances of Maui diving. Introductory courses are $109, and certified divers can partake in a private, guided beach dive for $89. Night dives and scooter dives are also offered. Depths on these shore dives rarely exceed 35 feet. All gear is included, and as an added convenience, Tiny Bubbles will pick you up from wherever you're staying on the West Side.

Also operating out of Honokowai, **Scorpion Scuba** (3600 Lower Honoapi'ilani Rd., 808/669-1710, www.mauifish.net) is another trusted operator with years of experience on the shorelines of West Maui. The dives here are an exceptional value: Introductory dives are offered for as low as $89 and certified beach dives for as low as $70. All gear is included. Inquire about their certification classes, night dives, and scooter dives. The scuba operation is run out of the All About Fish store in Honokowai where you can pick up any gear you need or ask about conditions and dive sites.

KA'ANAPALI
Dive Sites

The northernmost dive site in Ka'anapali and the one most preferred by independent instructors is **Kahekili Beach Park.** The depth here is shallow and rarely exceeds 35 feet, and the coral begins immediately the moment you get in the water. The reef here parallels the shoreline, with the greatest diversity of life found at 15-25 feet. While the beach itself is long, the healthiest amount of coral is found right off the beach park and is uncrowded compared to neighboring Ka'anapali Beach. There is also easier parking here for lugging all of your gear from the car, and showers and restrooms are conveniently located in the middle of the beach park.

The best dive in Ka'anapali, however, continues to be **Pu'u Keka'a,** otherwise known as Black Rock. Despite the relative ease of the dive and the fairly shallow depths, the rocky promontory has an inexplicable way of drawing in all sorts of marine life. Although not always a guarantee, dives here can frequently involve sightings of sea turtles, reef fish, eels, octopuses, or perhaps something strange such as squid or cowrie. The best way to dive Pu'u Keka'a is either to do a drift dive from the southern end of Kahekili Beach Park and swim around to the front of the rock, or enter the water in front of the Sheraton, swim partway around the rock, and then double back the way you came. Don't swim directly beneath the impact zone of children jumping off the rock; a juvenile habit of island youth is to dive bomb the scuba divers as they send bubbles up from below. This is a great dive for those who have just been certified. For a real treat, consider a night dive.

To dive away from the crowds, head to the large reef at **Ka'anapali Point,** stretching from the Marriott down toward the Hyatt. The depth here ranges 10-30 feet. You'll likely see a large number of turtles, corals, and technicolor parrotfish.

Dive Operators

The Ka'anapali resort diving scene is dominated by **Five Star Scuba** (www.5starscuba. com) which has operations at many of the Ka'anapali resorts. Options include pool sessions and one-tank dives to certification and night dives. A single one-tank dive for certified divers will usually be $89, with the exact dive location determined by what resort you're staying in and where conditions are best.

In front of Ka'anapali Beach Hotel, **Trilogy Ocean Sports** (808/661-7789) also offers one-tank dives, pool classes, and certification courses. Introductory dives are offered at $95, and certified dives are only $69, which is the best deal you'll find along the resort strip.

LAHAINA
Dive Sites

Within walking distance of southern Ka'anapali, **Hanakao'o Beach Park** is the northernmost beach in Lahaina and the site of many introductory classes. This is a good dive if you're practicing your skills over sand. The shallow area is also good for spotting turtles and colorful reef fish.

The best dive in Lahaina is **Mala Wharf,** although it's most often accessed as a boat dive. When Hurricane Iniki came storming through the Hawaiian Islands in 1992, the 30-foot waves it created were strong enough to destroy the outer half of Mala Ramp. Over 20 years later the collapsed pilings are still lying in 25 feet of water, and the result has been two decades of live coral development on what is now one of the island's best artificial reefs. The caverns of the pilings are home to numerous turtles and whitetip reef sharks, some of which can reach up to about six feet. Even though the depth never exceeds 35 feet, this is still a favorite of island dive charters due to its proximity to the harbors and wealth of marine life.

It isn't every day you get to dive the wreck of a 19th-century whaling ship! The *Carthaginian* is an old whaling ship which was scuttled in 100 feet of water by Atlantis Submarines about a half mile offshore from Puamana. A couple of West Side dive charters include this deepwater dive in their weekly schedule, with a maximum depth of about 100 feet. While the *Carthaginian* hasn't yet developed the same amount of live coral as at neighboring Mala Ramp, it's the deepest dive in the area. Winter dives are punctuated by whale song.

Dive Operators

Lahaina Divers (143 Dickenson St., 808/998-3483, www.lahainadivers.com) has the largest number of dive options available. Their two custom-built, 46-foot dive boats departing out of Lahaina Harbor are the largest dive boats on Maui. Two-tank dives range from $139 for dives off Lana'i to $199 for a dive off Moku Ho'oniki (Moloka'i), famous for scalloped hammerhead sharks. There are also trips to the Back Wall of Molokini Crater as well as four-tank dive trips for those who just can't get enough of the water. The full-service dive shop in Lahaina has everything from equipment sales to rentals. Since certain dives are only available on certain days, inquire ahead of time.

On the north end of Lahaina at Mala Ramp, **Extended Horizons** (94 Kupuohi St., 808/667-0611, www.extendedhorizons.com) is another reputable operation that offers tours to Lana'i and the west shore of Maui. Extended Horizons only takes six passengers, and it's the only charter boat on the island to run completely on 100 percent biodiesel. Morning tours check in at 6:30am at the Mala boat ramp for two-tank dives to Lana'i, the cost of which is $149. Other dive options available include trips along the Maui shoreline as well as night dives, beach dives, and certification classes.

A smaller operation offering scuba tours of Lana'i, **Dive Maui** (1223 Front St., 808/661-7333, www.hawaiianrafting.com) departs out of Mala Ramp aboard a rigid aluminum inflatable vessel. The group sizes are small and a deli lunch is included with the two-tank dive. The shop is conveniently located within walking distance from Mala Ramp.

SOUTH OF LAHAINA
Dive Sites

Known to some operators as Turtle Reef or Turtle Point, **Olowalu** is an offshore, turtle-laden area popular with charter boats on the offshore reefs. Maximum depths are about 30 feet and on nice days the visibility is close to 100 feet. This area is also popular with independent dive operators as a "confined water" area for practicing dive skills. If you are shore diving independently, the easiest way to get to deeper water is to enter around the mile marker 14 sign and swim in a straight line until you reach depths of 20-25 feet. When navigating your way through the coral heads, it's imperative to make sure that your gear doesn't drag across the reef, and bring a dive flag with you so that boats know you're below.

Ukumehame is a special spot only accessible by boat charter. Huge manta rays congregate here to be "cleaned" by reef fish who nibble algae off their wings, and the depths here are a moderately deep 30-60 feet. Don't even think about trying to do this dive as a shore dive because the manta ray area is about a 25-minute surface swim from shore and it takes trained dive instructors to determine if the water clarity is good enough for diving. If manta rays have been on your bucket list, inquire with a dive shop about an Ukumehame charter.

SNUBA
Ka'anapali

Shoreline Snuba (808/281-3483, www.shorelinesnuba.com) has six shore-based locations at different resorts. Guided snuba dives are $95 (which is about $20-25 more expensive than on a snorkeling charter), although the experience of breathing underwater for the first time will stick with you for a lifetime.

Surfing

Surfing is more than a hobby in West Maui—it's a way of life. In Lahaina, legions of longboarders begin each morning by watching the sunrise from the water and flotillas of surf schools operate throughout the day. Up north, Honolua is the proving ground of the island's burgeoning surfers, and whenever "The Bay" starts breaking, a palpable buzz goes out through the community. Granted, not all breaks are suitable for beginners. Out of respect for island surfers, only a handful of breaks are included in this guide. Practice common etiquette, and enjoy the serenity that comes with surfing one of the most beautiful spots in the world.

KAPALUA, NAPILI, AND HONOKOWAI

Winter is the best time for surfing "up north," and as a general rule the waves get larger the farther north that you head. With the exception of S-Turns, however, most of the breaks on the Upper West Side are for experienced surfers. Beginners will have better luck at the breaks south of Lahaina.

Surf Spots

Beginning in Honokowai, **Rainbows** is a fickle break that is best for intermediate surfers. The wave is in front of the Ka'anapali Beach Club. Parking can be found by taking the first left on Lower Honoapi'ilani Road across from the Times Supermarket. There can often be some strong currents here, and Rainbows will only break on the largest of northwest swells or any swell which is north or northeasterly.

With a vibe that's similar to San Onofre, **Pohaku Beach Park** in Kahana is the epicenter of the West Side's longboard community and perfect for beginners, commonly known as S-Turns. Travel on Honoapi'ilani Highway until you reach the intersection with Ho'ohui Street with the McDonald's on the corner. Turn toward the ocean, and make a left once

you reach the bottom of the hill. Drive for a quarter mile and you will see the parking lot for S-Turns on your right. When standing in the parking lot, you will notice two distinct breaks: one to the left and one to the right. The break to the left is S-Turns, and the one to the right is Mushrooms. While Mushrooms can be a fun wave, it's shallow on the inside section. Over at S-Turns, you'll notice a couple of A-frame peaks a long paddle offshore. Surfing at S-Turns is as much of a paddle workout as a surfing workout, and you can be forgiven if you need to stop a couple of times to catch your breath on the way out. Beginners stay on the inside section, while more experienced surfers favor the outer peaks. The wave here holds for a long time, so you want to position yourself in the spot just before it's actually breaking. Also, there have been some shark issues at S-Turns in the past, so if the water is murky and no one else is out, there's probably a reason for that. S-Turns starts breaking on a moderate northwest swell, and on the largest of days can reach a few feet overhead.

The surf break at **D.T. Fleming Beach Park** is at the far northern end of the beach. The wave here is a combination of a beach break and a pointbreak, and it can get crowded with bodyboarders during weekends. This is one of the few places on the West Side that picks up windswell, so if it's windy and there aren't waves anywhere else, check Fleming's.

If you're an avid surfer, **Honolua Bay** is a spot that needs no introduction. The wave here is truly one of the best in the world, and holds almost religious significance to the locals who schedule their lives around The Bay. Honolua is reserved for experienced surfers, but even non-surfers should come here during a large swell to watch the island's best pull into the gaping, barreling perfection. Also, Honolua can become crowded, and if you paddle out and nobody recognizes you, your chances of getting a wave decrease by about a half. Granted, on days

WAVES IN HAWAIIAN SCALE

Hawaiians are weird when it comes to their waves.

No, this doesn't have to do with the fact that a high surf advisory is a completely legitimate excuse for missing work, school, or even jury duty, but rather, with the fact that Hawaiians measure the size of waves differently than much of the world.

Unlike places on the mainland that measure the *face* of the waves, Hawaiian surfers instead measure the *back* of the wave. The result is a wave height which is about half what you'd find if it were measured elsewhere. A six-foot wave in California will only be a three-foot wave in Hawai'i.

The history of all this is foggy at best. One leading theory suggests that Hawaiian surfers underestimated the wave size in the 1950s as a humble response to the bravado of California surfers who boasted about the size of the waves they caught. Another theory is that since

Hawaiian lifeguards would be forced to work instead of surf when the waves reached a certain height, they invented a separate scale so that it would require larger waves before they had to go to work.

Whatever the reason, the practical implication is that when you're looking at a surf forecast you need to know if it's being measured on the Hawaiian scale or by face height. On a website such as omaui.com, the forecast is given in face heights, whereas on a website like hawaiiweathertoday.com, the forecast will be in Hawaiian scale.

If you ask a local surfer what the conditions are like, you'll get a reply of either "3 feet Hawaiian," or simply "3 feet," when the head-high waves are obviously larger. Australians have also adopted the Hawaiian scale system of measurement. So while confusion continues to reign, all that matters is assessing your own ability when paddling out to the lineup.

---

when the surf is only about head high and the crowd isn't too thick, there can still be enough waves for everyone—provided you know what you're doing.

Even though **Windmills** is a surf break beyond the ability level of most visitors, it's an epic spot for watching the island's best surfers. The massive left tube barrels with such ferocity it's been called Maui's Pipeline. Many professional surf films have been shot here. The best vantage point is on the side of the road at the edge of a dramatic cliff. If you see cars parked on the side of the road a mile past Honolua Bay, large surf is breaking.

Rental Shops

Experienced surfers will get the best selection at **808 Boards** (808/283-1384, www.808boards. com, $35/day), located by the Napili General Store. They will pick up and drop off the board at no additional charge.

You can also rent a board up north at the **Boss Frog's** locations in Napili (5095 Napilihau St., 808/669-4949, www.bossfrog. com, 8am-6pm daily) and Kahana (4310 Lower Honoapi'ilani Rd., 808/669-6700, www.bossfrog.com, 8am-5pm daily). Rates are around $20/day for soft top longboards or $25/day for fiberglass boards.

For the cheapest boards you'll find on this side of the island, little-known **A&B Ocean Rentals** (3481 Lower Honoapi'ilani Rd., 808/669-0027, 9am-4pm daily) is hidden in Da Rose mall in Honokowai on the ocean side of the highway. Surfboards are only $15/day or $70 for the whole week.

KA'ANAPALI
Surf Spots

The only surf break in Ka'anapali is **Ka'anapali Point,** in front of the Marriott on Ka'anapali Beach. This is where the Ka'anapali surf lessons take place, although the wave here is tricky because it bends at a weird angle. Also, the inside section can get shallow and rocky, so surf school students are given booties. Ka'anapali

Point can pick up both southwesterly and northeasterly swells, which means there can be surf any month of the year.

Rental Shops and Schools

While the waves in Lahaina are more amenable to learning, there are still a number of operators along Ka'anapali Beach for those who would prefer to walk directly from the resort to the lesson. Since Ka'anapali gets windier than Lahaina, it's important to book the first lesson of the day for the best conditions.

For the most affordable lessons, the **Trilogy** beach shack in front of the Ka'anapali Beach Hotel offers two hours for $70. On the other side of Whalers Village, lessons can be booked with **Island Style** (808/244-6858) in front of the Westin or with **Royal Hawaiian** (808/357-8988, www.royalhawaiiansurfacademy.com) at the kiosk at the Marriott. Both places offer two hours for $75. For rentals down by Ka'anapali Point, expect to pay in the $20-40 range depending on the length of rental. Booties are included in the price of all lessons and rentals.

LAHAINA

Lahaina and the areas south of Lahaina have small waves breaking during most of the year, while summer has the most consistent surf. Most days will only have waves in the waist-high range, but on the best swells of summer the surf can reach overhead. If you've rented your own board, there are few better ways to start a day on Maui than with a dawn patrol surf session, as the sun's rays seeping through the valleys of Mauna Kahalawai turn the water a brilliant shade of blue.

C Surf Spots

The most popular surf break in Lahaina is **Lahaina Breakwall,** located between the 505 shopping center and Lahaina Harbor. This is where most of the Lahaina surf schools operate. All of the surf schools hang out in the shallow inside section, whereas the more experienced surfers sit farther outside. The outside section at small levels can be either a left or a right, although when it gets big on a large summer

swell, it can turn into a huge left that can grow to 10 feet or larger. During low tide it can get shallow enough here that you need to paddle with your fingertips and your skeg can scrape the bottom, so high tide is the optimal time for those who are concerned about falling (to tell whether it's high tide or low tide, look at the water in front of 505; if rocks stick out of the water, it's low tide). As the most popular break in Lahaina it shouldn't come as a surprise that this spot can get crowded, a fact of life which has earned it the moniker of Snakewall. If you're a beginning surfer who has rented a board, you're better off going a few miles south to Puamana Beach Park or Guardrails.

Rental Shops and Schools

While rental shops and surf schools are a dime a dozen, these are four trusted schools with sterling reputations.

Inside the 505 shopping center, **Goofy Foot** (505 Front St., 808/244-9283, www.goofy-footsurfschool.com, 7am-9pm daily, no lessons Sun.) has helped over 100,000 students ride their first wave since opening in 1994. Two-hour lessons are $65/person, and the owner, Tim, often enjoys time on the water as the private surf coach for Jimmy Buffett. For board rentals, expect to pay $20 for two hours or $25 for three hours.

One block away on Prison Street are **Royal Hawaiian** (117 Prison St., 808/276-7873, www.royalhawaiiansurfacademy.com, 7am-7pm Mon.-Fri., 7am-3:30pm weekends) and **Maui Wave Riders** (133 Prison St., 808/875-4761, www.mauiwaveriders.com, 7am-9pm daily). Royal Hawaiian has been operating since 1996 and Maui Wave Riders since 1997, and all of the instructors are competent and patient professionals who are guaranteed to get you up and riding. Group rates at Royal Hawaiian are $65/person, whereas Maui Wave Riders is cheaper at $60/person and $50 for kids ages 8-12. For rentals, expect to pay $20 for three hours or $30 for the whole day.

Maui Surfer Girls (808/214-0606, www.mauisurfergirls.com) is the island's premier female-only surf camp operator, although they

SURFING ETIQUETTE

Surfing is a highlight of a visit to Lahaina, but it's important to have a basic grasp of etiquette out in the water.

· **1. Always wear a leash.** Errant boards in the lineup can be dangerous. Nothing ruins a session like having to swim after your board.

· **2. Stay out of the way of any surfer on a wave.** While this can sometimes be difficult when paddling out from shore, the best thing to do is either stop paddling so the surfer can navigate around you, or aim for a line behind the board so it ends up passing in front of you.

· **3. Offer a simple "hello" and a smile to your fellow surfers.** It may or may not be returned, but it's a way of signaling "friend" instead of "foe."

· **4. At more advanced breaks, don't paddle directly to the peak of the wave.** Instead, wait for a while on the shoulder to let the local surfers have a turn. In more advanced lineups such as Honolua Bay, the outer reef at Breakwall, or other spots which aren't named in this guide, waves are earned instead of given, so it's best to keep a low profile for a while. Share the waves. If you just got the last one, don't turn back around and take the next one.

· **5. It's never alright to "drop in" on another surfer.** Although it might seem like a free-for-all out there, surfing etiquette dictates that the surfer closest to the breaking part of the wave has the right-of-way. To initiate a ride in front of this surfer is the worst of surfing offenses and a surefire way to get "stink eye." As a general rule, if you're paddling for a wave, there is already someone riding that wave, and you can see that person's face, then choose a different wave.

· **6. Don't throw your board.** Sometimes in larger surf your board can get ripped away from you, but it's heavily frowned upon to "duck dive" a wave by throwing your board to the side and swimming under the wave. Instead, either duck dive your shortboard under the wave, or, if on a longboard, try to "turn turtle" by flipping upside down with your board and letting the wave crash over you (while holding it with your hands). In the event you are riding a wave and fall, to keep the board from shooting out and hitting someone in the face, reach down and try to grab the part where your leash connects to minimize the distance it can go flying.

· **7. As strange as it seems, don't stare at people.** This is especially true at more advanced breaks such as Honolua Bay. Even if you like someone's tattoo or are trying to read the brand of someone's boardshorts, it comes off as threatening. Strange, but true.

· **8. Assess your own abilities.** "If in doubt, don't go out!" Surfing is meant to be fun and enjoyable. Paddling out into conditions which are outside of your ability level is a good way to get in trouble. Sit and watch the waves for a few minutes before paddling out, assess the vibe once you're out there, and as long as you follow proper surf etiquette, you'll end up having an epic time on the water.

also offer coed group lessons for $75/person. Even though it's a few dollars more than in town, the lessons take place a few miles south of town along a mellow stretch of beach which isn't as crowded as Breakwall. All-inclusive one- and two-week classes are offered during select months of the year to empower teenaged girls through the sport of surfing.

To surf in a secluded location in a private group, try **Hawaiian Paddle Sports** (808/660-4228, www.hawaiianpaddlesports. com), which offers completely private lessons. Share in each other's trials and revel in each other's success. The lessons usually take place along the shoreline south of Lahaina. Since these two-hour lessons are completely private, they are understandably more expensive at $159 for a single person or $109/person for private groups of five or more.

If you're just looking to rent a board in

Summer is the best time for surf in Lahaina.

© MARK DRIESSEN

downtown Lahaina and prefer to teach your-self, you'll get a better deal if you move a few blocks away from the busy surf schools. The **Boss Frog's** (150 Lahainaluna Rd., 808/661-3333, www.bossfrog.com, 8am-5pm daily) in the center of town has soft top boards for either $25/day or $75/week, and fiberglass boards are $35/day. Of course, you can't walk to the surf break from here, so rent or purchase straps for your vehicle.

SOUTH OF LAHAINA

For beginning surfers and longboard riders, the mile-long stretch of coastline between **Puamana Beach Park** and **Launiupoko Beach Park** has numerous breaks with mellow waves for beginners. In between the two parks are peaks which are known as **Guardrails, Woody's,** and **Corner Pockets.** While the beach parks and Guardrails have parking on the ocean side of the road, parking for Woody's is in a dirt lot on the inland side of the highway. There can be small waves here most times of the year, although summer sees the most consistent

surf. If you're a slightly more advanced surfer, park in the lot for Puamana Beach Park and walk the length of shoreline all the way to the right along the Puamana condominium complex. At the far northern end of the beach is another break known as **Beaches** that offers a fun right point welcoming to visiting surfers.

Or, if you're an experienced surfer who prefers to ride a shortboard, the wave at **Olowalu** offers two A-frame peaks that are popular with locals and can get crowded. In a different spot than the snorkeling spot by the same name, the Olowalu surf break is by mile marker 15.5.

At mile marker 12, **Ukumehame Beach Park** is another break which caters to beginners and longboarders but requires a much longer paddle than places such as Guardrails or Puamana. As is the case with long paddles, however, a longer effort means a longer ride. This is a favorite of the island longboarding community. While the beach itself is fairly long, the best waves are found directly in front of the small parking lot.

Tucked right at the base of the cliffs by mile

marker 11, **Grandma's** is the name of the break on the far southern end of Papalaua Beach Park. This is a playful wave that caters to beginners and longboarders.

Stand-Up Paddling

KAPALUA, NAPILI, AND HONOKOWAI

One of the best stretches of coast for paddling is the section between Kapalua Bay and Hawea Point. The sandy entry at Kapalua Bay makes it easy to launch a board into the water. Napili Bay is another popular spot for morning paddles. But never bring a stand-up paddleboard into Honolua Bay.

Rental Shops

In Napili, **Boss Frog's** (5095 Napilihau St., 808/669-4949, www.bossfrog.com, 8am-6pm daily) has paddleboard rentals for $40/day. You can find the same rates down the road at the store in the Kahana Manor (4310 Lower Honoapi'ilani Rd., 808/669-6700, www.bossfrog.com, 8am-5pm daily).

For the cheapest boards on this side of the island, go to **A&B Ocean Rentals** (3481 Lower Honoapi'ilani Rd., 808/669-0027, 9am-4pm daily) in Da Rose mall in Honokowai. It has paddleboards for $35/day or $140 for the whole week.

KA'ANAPALI

Sandy Ka'anapali is the perfect spot for stand-up paddling, but only during the morning hours before the wind picks up. On winter days, the water can be as smooth as glass, with dozens of whales breaching around you. While being out on the water during whale season can be an exciting adventure, the same laws apply to stand-up paddlers as to boats: Paddlers are required to maintain a 100-yard distance from humpback whales—unless, of course, they swim over to you

Rental Shops

Almost every hotel along the main strip has activity huts offering paddleboard rentals. At **Trilogy Ocean Sports** (808/661-7789) in front of the Ka'anapali Beach Hotel, boards are $25 for the first hour and $15/hour after that. In front of the Westin Maui on the south side of Whalers Village, boards are $30 for the first hour and $10 for each additional hour. The cheapest rate is offered by the **Maui Dive and Surf** (808/270-9846, www.mauidiveshop.com) kiosk just south of Leilani's restaurant in Whalers Village, where board rentals are $26 for the first hour or $41 for a four-hour rental.

LAHAINA

Unlike Ka'anapali's large, open stretch of sand, Lahaina is ringed by a barrier reef which can make it shallow and dangerous for paddling. The trained instructors, however, know all of the *pukas* (holes) in the reef, and by allowing them to lead the way, you'll be awarded with sweeping views of the island's West Side. When you are over the Shark Pit, there's a decent chance you'll encounter an endangered Hawaiian monk seal or a harmless whitetip reef shark. While the 505 area can be a little difficult to navigate, it has the added benefit of being protected from the wind and will usually have calm, flat conditions when Ka'anapali is rough and blustery. If you've rented your own board, the best place in the immediate area for stand-up paddling is the stretch of shoreline between Puamana and Launiupoko Beach Parks, where the water isn't nearly as shallow and it's still protected from the afternoon trade winds.

Rental Shops and Schools

Stand-up paddling lessons are offered in the Lahaina Breakwall area by **Royal Hawaiian** (117 Prison St., 808/276-7873, www.royalhawaiiansurfacademy.com, 7am-7pm Mon.-Fri., 7am-3:30pm weekends), **Goofy Foot** (505 Front St., 808/244-9283, www.

TIPS FOR STAND-UP PADDLING

Stand-up paddling has seen an explosion in popularity over the past five years. While taking a lesson is always the best way to ensure success, here are a few tips for those who would rather rent a board and set out on their own.

- Paddle in the morning before the wind comes up.

- When first getting in the water, start on your knees to get the feeling for the board.

- When you stand up, keep your feet shoulder-width apart. You want to be standing in the middle of the board about where the handle is.

- A stand-up paddleboard is like a bicycle; you need momentum for balance, so if you stop paddling, it's like trying to balance on a bicycle without pedaling. When you first stand up from your knees, take a couple of paddles quickly to build up enough momentum so that you won't fall.

- Use the correct side of the paddle. Paddles are like an extension of your hand; you want to use the side of the paddle which would be your palm as opposed to the back of your hand.

- Instead of placing both hands on the shaft of the paddle, put one on the top, and the other on the shaft. To keep a straight line you must alternate paddling on both sides of your body by taking a few strokes on your left and then a few strokes on your right, much like you would in a canoe.

- When paddling, take long, full strokes. Many first-time paddlers have a tendency to poke at the water with short little strokes. Since this doesn't create much momentum, the board becomes wobbly and you're liable to fall. By taking long strokes you create enough momentum for a stable platform and a much more enjoyable paddle.

- Use a leash. A leash is your lifeline if you fall off the board. If you are not sure which ankle to put leash around, act as if you're going to do a cartwheel, and whichever foot you put backwards is the one you should attach the leash to.

- If you are paddling where there are waves, make sure that your board is pointing either into the waves or away from them. When waves hit the side of your board, there is a good chance you'll end up falling.

- When you fall off your board (don't worry, it happens to the best of paddlers), the best thing to do is just let it happen. Most paddleboarding injuries occur when people try to save themselves from falling and end up going down awkwardly. Accept your fate and fall gracefully into the water below.

- Only competent surfers should ever try to surf on their paddleboards. Large, heavy boards can become dangerous in a surf lineup if they go crashing through a crowd, and a spate of injuries related to stand-up paddlers and their large boards have created a rift in the island surfing community. Common surf etiquette is to share the waves with surfers and stay out of the way. In the event you do fall down, make sure that your board doesn't hit someone.

- Most important, enjoy the feeling of the sun on your shoulders, the warm water beneath you, and the views of the island you get from offshore. Bask in the moment of floating across the water, and you'll see why this has become one of the island's hottest activities.

---

goofyfootsurfschool.com, 7am-9pm daily, no lessons Sun.), and **Maui Wave Riders** (133 Prison St., 808/875-4761, www.mauiwaveriders.com, 7am-9pm daily). Rather than mingling with all the surf school students, the stand-up paddling tours go the other direction from the Lahaina Breakwall down to the section of beach known as Shark Pit. Most lessons start with a 20-minute session on the beach where you learn the basics of balancing and paddling. The rates for lessons are highly variable, although at the time of research, Maui Wave Riders offered lessons for $60, Royal Hawaiian for $75, and Goofy Foot for $100. Also in front of the 505 Front Street area, **Maui Paddle Sports** (808/283-9344, www.mauipaddlesports.com, 8am and 10am) offers lessons for $95/person and has personalized ratios of three paddlers per instructor. For rentals, expect to pay in the $35 range for three hours to $45 for all day.

For more personalized service in an area that isn't as crowded, **Maria Souza Stand Up Paddle School** (808/579-9231, www.standuppaddlesurfschool.com) and **Hawaiian Paddle Sports** (808/660-4228, www.hawaiianpaddlesports.com) both offer lessons on beaches south of Lahaina. These operations are run by instructors who have a deep-rooted respect for the island, the environment, and Hawaiian cultural history. While they're more expensive, these tours will leave you with a deeper appreciation

for all things surrounding the ocean. Lessons with Maria Souza's are $159/person and are offered Monday to Friday at 9 and 11am, and lessons with Hawaiian Paddle Sports are $159 for a private lesson or $109/person for private groups of five or more.

SOUTH OF LAHAINA
Rental Shops
For a laid-back rental experience in a unique location, **Kayak Olowalu** (808/661-0606, www.kayakolowalu.com) has stand-up boards available from a campground location for either $20/hr or $30 for a three-hour session. To reach the campground, turn toward the water at Olowalu General Store and follow the signs for Camp Olowalu for half a mile until you reach the shoreline.

Kayaking and Canoeing

West Maui has numerous options for both kayaking and outrigger canoeing. While kayaking isn't as hard on the shoulder muscles and allows you to hug the coastline a little closer, outrigger canoeing comes with a culturally rich experience unique to Polynesia. The morning hours are the best time to paddle, with most operators offering an early morning tour followed by another one during the mid to late morning.

KAPALUA, NAPILI, AND HONOKOWAI
The most popular kayak trip on the Upper West Side of the island is the paddle from D.T. Fleming Beach Park to Honolua Bay. Along this stretch of coastline you will pass rugged rock formations inaccessible from the road, and you'll hug this dramatic coast past Mokuleiʻa Bay and into Honolua. Because of the high surf during winter, these tours are only offered during the summer, and all trips depart D.T. Fleming Beach Park in the early morning hours before the afternoon trade winds pick up. Snorkeling in Honolua Bay is included in the excursions, and you have a high likelihood

of encountering Hawaiian green sea turtles or potentially even Hawaiian spinner dolphins.

Of the companies offering tours up here, **Hawaiian Paddle Sports** (808/660-4228, www.hawaiianpaddlesports.com) operates completely private excursions for $159 for a private tour, $129/person for tours of 2-4 people, and $109/person for tours of five or more. **Maui Kayaks** (808/874-4000, www.mauikayaks.com) offers a three-hour trip for $78/person with a 7am check-in at D.T. Fleming Beach Park.

KAʻANAPALI
Off Kahekili Beach Park in front of the Westin Villas, **Maui Paddle Sports** (808/283-9344, www.mauipaddlesports.com) offers two-hour outrigger canoe rides in a six-man outrigger for $85/person. All canoe tours take place during the morning, but on days with light winds tours can go as late as 1pm.

SOUTH OF LAHAINA
The main areas for kayaking south of Lahaina are either Olowalu (mile marker 14) or Coral

Gardens, off Papalaua Beach Park (mile marker 11). This is a popular area for kayaking in winter since the large surf on the northern shores makes kayaking there impossible. These are fantastic reefs for spotting Hawaiian green sea turtles. While **Maui Kayaks** (808/874-4000, www.mauikayaks.com, $69) and **Hawaiian** **Paddle Sports** (808/660-4228, www.hawaiianpaddlesports.com, private tours from $109-159/person) both offer tours in this area, one tour company which is area-specific is **Kayak Olowalu** (808/661-0606, www.kayakolowalu.com), which either offers tours for $65/adult or unguided rentals for $30-40 for two hours.

Boating

◖ SUNSET CRUISES

Few Maui activities are more iconic than a sunset sail off the West Maui coastline. The feeling of the trade winds in your hair as you glide along the ocean is a sensation of freedom you can't experience on land. Watch as the setting sun paints the sky every shade of orange and pink, while on most days you can also make out a rainbow hovering over the lush valleys of Mauna Kahalawai. Add in some Israel Kamakawiwaʻole tunes, a mai tai, and some Pacific Rim *pupus,* and there's a good chance you'll walk off the boat with a smile on your face and the photo for next year's Christmas card.

Kaʻanapali

While a **sunset sail off Kaʻanapali Beach** can be the most magical moment of your vacation, there are a few things to understand for making the most of the magic. To begin with, make sure to ask when you need to check in, because departure times for sunset sails are 30 minutes different during summer and winter. Secondly, while it's always nice to get a little bit dressed up, remember that you're still going on a moving boat and should be outfitted accordingly. The Kaʻanapali boats are all sailing catamarans which load from the sand, and since some days can have moderate shorebreak, there's a good chance you'll end up wet from the shins down. Also, your shoes will be collected prior to boarding (to keep from tracking sand on the boat), so don't put too much time into matching them with your outfit. There's even a chance that the departure could be moved to Lahaina Harbor due to large surf on the beach. Since this isn't possible to predict until the day before the sail, it's a good idea to double check on the morning of your sail to confirm where the boat will be loading from. The northerly trade winds can often be chilly, so it's a good idea to bring a light jacket. Finally, remember that you'll be sailing. Even though the vessels are wide, stable catamarans, it may be difficult to move around and spray may come over the sides. If your idea of a sunset sail is a stable platform that putts along at three knots, the dinner cruises out of Lahaina are probably a better bet.

Trilogy (808/874-5649, www.sailtrilogy.com) offers sunset sails on Tuesday, Thursday, and Saturday, as well as an Aloha Friday sunset sail that features lives music and Pacific Rim *pupus.* Trilogy's sail isn't marketed as a booze cruise. Three alcoholic beverages (Bikini Blonde beer, premixed mai tais, margaritas, wine, and champagne) are included in the price of the sail, with a three-drink maximum. Unless the surf is high and they need to load out of Lahaina Harbor, all Trilogy tours check-in in front of the Kaʻanapali Beach Hotel. The vessel which Trilogy uses for sunset sails—most often *Trilogy IV*—is the smallest of all the Kaʻanapali catamarans, thereby making them the fastest boat under sail. Regular sunset sails are $69, and the Aloha Friday sail is $79.

In front of Whalers Village, **Teralani** (808/661-7245, www.teralani.net) offers two different sails departing nightly during the busier parts of the year. The original sunset sail is $71/adult and includes a *pupu* menu as well as a full open bar of various beers and mixed drinks. For those who would rather dine on board, the full dinner sail is $94/adult, 30 minutes longer, and includes a filling menu.

Gemini (808/669-0508, www.geminicharters.com) similarly offers sunset sails for $70/adult which feature a *pupu* menu as well as Bikini Blonde beer and mai tais.

The most "yacht-like" experience departing from the beach is on **Hula Girl** (808/665-0344, www.sailingmaui.com), which not only offers the newest boat, but also luxurious upgrades like throw pillows, free Wi-Fi, panoramic viewing from the fly-bridge, and high-tech sailing. Regular sunset sails are offered on Monday, Wednesday, and Friday, and while the $68 price looks in-line with the rest of the options, all food and drink are available for purchase from the kitchen and full-service bar, and such luxury and convenience come at an added price. For a full-service dinner cruise, *Hula Girl* also offers cruises on Tuesday, Thursday, and Saturday for $80/adult featuring upscale Pacific Rim dining options made fresh in the onboard kitchen. It's more of a floating restaurant with an $80 cover charge, with menu items range from $5-23 with a full-service bar slinging top-shelf cocktails at resort bar prices.

Lahaina
DINNER CRUISES

A sailboat is a better venue for a sunset cruise than a powerboat. But for those who would rather be on a large, stable diesel vessel instead of a catamaran, the best dinner cruise out of Lahaina is offered by **Pacific Whale Foundation** (612 Front St., 808/942-5311, www.pacificwhale.org). The power catamaran used for this charter is the nicest of the large diesel boats, and the menu includes locally sourced produce and sustainably harvested seafood. Regular seats are $80, but if you don't want to share a table with another party, upgrade to the premium seating for $100/adult. A maximum of three alcoholic beverages is included in the cruise, as is live performed by a solo musician.

Also out of Lahaina Harbor, **Lahaina Cruise Company** (877/500-6284, www.

mauiprincess.com) offers two different dinner cruises aboard vessels which are a generation older than others. The 2.5-hour dinner cruise aboard *Maui Princess* stays out well past dark (usually until 8pm) and offers rooftop seating aboard a 120-foot vessel. Waiters in gray tuxedos serve meals of prime rib, roasted chicken, or island fish, and the string of white lights illuminating the upper deck aims to create a romantic atmosphere. Dancing is offered in the downstairs portion of the boat. Prices for the cruise are $75/adult, three alcoholic drinks are included, and additional drinks are available for purchase at the bar. A similar cruise is offered aboard *Kaulana,* where dinner consists of a small amount of *pupus* and two drinks are included with the price of the sail. There is a live musician on the aft deck. This is the closest thing to a "booze cruise" that you'll find anywhere on the West Side. Prices for this tour are $47/adult, and the cruise spends two hours motoring along the West Maui shoreline.

SAILBOATS

If you know what it means to "shake a reef," you'll be much happier watching the sunset aboard a small sailboat than on a large, motorized platform.

The only sailing catamaran offering sunset sails out of Lahaina is **Paragon** (808/244-2087, www.sailmaui.com), which provides sailing, *pupus,* beer, wine, and mai tais for only $59/adult. Trips depart on Monday, Wednesday, and Friday. As an added bonus the maximum capacity of the cruise is only 24 people.

Or, if you're a monohull sailor, **Scotch Mist II** (808/661-0386, www.scotchmistsailingcharters.com) offers evening sunset sails for $69 aboard a Santa Cruz 50-foot racing boat which departs from Slip #2.

◀ WHALE-WATCHING

Any single vessel that floats is going to be offering whale-watching between December 15 and April 15. Even though whale season officially lasts until May 15, the whales aren't encountered with enough regularity

© AWAPUHI DANCIL

Whale watching season is December-April.

after mid-April to guarantee sightings. The peak of the season for whale-watching is January through March, and whether you're on a sailboat, powerboat, raft, fishing boat, kayak, or ferry, simply being out on the water turns the experience into whale-watching. Most snorkeling and sailing operators also offer whale-watching during winter, with most boats carrying whale naturalists well-versed in the study of these gentle giants. Since most prices are about the same, the choice ultimately comes down to what sort of vessel best suits your comfort level. Small rafts out of Lahaina Harbor will place you the closest to the water (which is great if you get "mugged"). All sailboats also offer whale-watching trips out of both Lahaina Harbor and Ka'anapali Beach. The large, 149-passenger diesel boats in Lahaina provide the most affordable rates, but you'll be sharing the vessel with over 100 other people and won't get 360° views. Pacific Whale Foundation has the largest presence for whale-watching in Lahaina.

SUBMARINE

If riding a submarine has always been on your bucket list, **Atlantis Submarines** (Slip 18, 808/667-2224, www.atlantisadventures.com/maui, 9am-2pm daily) operates regular charters out of Lahaina Harbor to the *Carthaginian*, a sunken whaling ship sitting in 100 feet of water. If you're wondering how you board a submarine in a harbor, you first board a shuttle boat named *Holokai*, which makes the 10-minute motor to where the submarine descends. Once above the dive site, you will transfer from *Holokai* onto *Atlantis*, and before you know it, the blue of the sky above you has been replaced by the blue of the Pacific around you. Anything from reef fish to sharks or whales could make an appearance. There may even be scuba divers diving at the *Carthaginian*. Rates for the submarine tour are $109/adult and $35/child.

For those who are a little nervous about descending completely underwater and want to see fish without snorkeling, **Reef Dancer** (Slip 6, 808/667-2133, www.mauiglassbottomboat.com) is a yellow "semi-sub" that remains partially submerged for its journey along the coastline. While there is an above deck portion of the sub that never plunges underwater, passengers are seated in an underwater cabin that offers 360° views of the underwater world. All of the boat staff double as scuba divers who can point out anything that might be living along the reef such as eels, octopuses, turtles, or urchins. This is a great way for young children, elderly visitors, or those who aren't comfortable swimming to enjoy Maui's reef system without ever having to get their hair wet. Sixty-minute tours take place three times each morning ($35/adult, $20/child), with a longer 90-minute tour departing Lahaina Harbor at 2:15pm ($45/adult, $25/child).

FISHING

In no place is Lahaina's port town heritage more evident than at dingy yet lovable Lahaina Harbor. The smell of fish carcasses still wafts on the breeze and shirtless, tanned, sweat-covered sailors casually sip beers as they lay the fresh catch on ice. On some days you can buy fresh mahimahi or ono straight from the folks who caught it, or, if you'd rather take your shot at reeling the big one in yourself, there are a slew of sportfishing boats ready to get you on the water. The charters that have the best chance of catching fish are those which leave early and stay out for a full day. These are more expensive, but during a full-day charter you're able to troll around the buoys on the far side of Lana'i or Kaho'olawe, whereas on half-day charters you're confined to shallower water where the fish aren't biting as much (particularly during the winter). On virtually all charters you need to provide your own food and drinks. Although it sounds silly, don't bring bananas on board since it's considered bad luck. Most boats will let you keep what you catch so you can cook it the same night.

Of all the boats in the harbor, one of the companies with the best reputation is **Start Me Up** (808/667-2774, www.sportfishingmaui. com), where prices range from $99/person for a quarter-day charter to $199/person for a full day on the water.

A boat with a sterling reputation is **Die Hard** (808/344-5051, www.diehardsportfishing.com), run by the legendary Captain Fuzzy. Rates for these charters vary, but expect to pay $200/person for six-hour charters and $220/person for full-day, eight-hour charters.

Down at the south end of the harbor away from many of the other boats, **Luckey Strike** (808/661-4606, www.luckeystrike.com) has two different boats and operates on the premise that using live bait for smaller fish is better. Captain Tad Luckey has been fishing these waters for well over 30 years, and as with most captains in the harbor, he has an enviable and well-earned amount of local knowledge to put into every trip.

One of the nicest yachts in the harbor, **Jayhawk** (808/870-6994, www.jayhawkyacht. com), offers private charters for $700/hour on a swanky 48-foot Cabo with all the amenities. It's more than just a fancy ride, however. Captain Steve has been fishing these waters for over two decades and can hook up fish as well as anyone else in the harbor.

PARASAILING

Parasailing isn't available December 15-May 15. Since the waters off West Maui are part of the Hawaiian Islands Humpback Whale National Marine Sanctuary, all "thrillcraft," such as high-speed parasailing boats, are outlawed during the time of year when the whales are nursing their calves. All parasailing operations go dormant during the winter and open up promptly on the morning of May 16. Should you happen to be visiting Maui during the summer or fall, however, parasailing is a peaceful adventure option for gazing at West Maui from hundreds of feet above the turquoise waters. Take a mental picture; it's one of the best views you'll find anywhere on the island.

Ka'anapali

UFO Parasail (800/359-4836, www.ufoparasail.net) departs off Ka'anapali Beach in front of Leilani's restaurant and is one of the two operators departing from the beach. Only eight people are on a boat at a time, which means that your overall time on the water is only a little over an hour. Of that hour, your own personal flight time will last 10-12 minutes depending on the length of your line (you'll end up being 400-500 feet off the water). The staff and captains who run these tours do hundreds of trips over the course of the season, and from a safety and efficiency standpoint, the crew has it down to a science. Taking off and landing on the boat is a dry entry and exit, and you will be blown away by the serenity experienced up in the air. When was the last time you were 1,200 feet away from another human being? Prices range $75-85 depending on the height; you must weigh at least 130 pounds to fly alone.

Down in front of the Hyatt, **West Maui Parasail** (808/661-4060, www.westmauiparasail.com) offers similar tours with the same length of lines at a slightly discounted rate of $70 for 800 feet or $80 for 1,200 feet. If you aren't staying in the Ka'anapali resort area, a perk of going with West Maui Parasail is that free, convenient parking can be had in the Hanakao'o Beach Park area just a three-minute walk from the Hyatt.

WHALE-WATCHING FAQ

The waters off Maui have the highest concentration of humpback whales anywhere on the planet. During peak season (January-March), the main question isn't *if* you're going to see whales, but rather *how many* you will see. Here are answers to commonly asked whale-watching questions:

Q: What kind of whales are in Maui?

A: Although there are rarely seen species such as pilot whales and false-killer whales that inhabit the waters off Maui year-round, 99 percent of the time you will be watching North Pacific humpback whales.

Q: Where are these whales from?

A: These whales were born here in the warm, protected waters of Hawai'i. The humpbacks will then migrate 3,000 miles to their summer feeding grounds in Alaska where they gorge themselves on small fish and krill, and return again in the winter to mate and give birth.

Q: Why don't the whales mate in Alaska?

A: Since baby humpbacks are born with minimal amounts of fat, the water is too cold in Alaska.

Q: Do the whales eat at all in Hawai'i?

A: No. While there's no evidence to suggest that whales wouldn't eat if given the opportunity, the waters off Maui don't contain the same degree of zooplankton and marine organisms that humpback whales feed on. Adults go for months at a time without eating, losing up to one-third of their body weight.

Q: How much do humpback whales weigh?

A: At birth, humpback whales are 10-12 feet long and weigh about a ton. Full-grown adults weigh about one ton per foot, which means that a 45-foot humpback will weigh about 90,000 lbs!

Q: Are males or females bigger?

A: Females are a little bit larger than males, which is known as "reverse sexual dimorphism," a fancy way of saying "I need to give birth to a 2,000 lb. animal, so I need to be bigger than you."

Q: How long do whales live?

A: While an exact life span is undetermined, the general consensus is that whales live about as long as humans do: 50-90 years.

Q: How do you tell the age of a whale?

A: Believe it or not, it's by the earwax. The wax in the ear canal will have a different color and consistency in warm water than cold water. Counting the "rings" in the core of the earwax will show how many annual migrations the whales have undertaken.

Q: How quickly do whales swim?

A: Although they can "sprint" at up to about 20 mph, on average humpback whale travels at a steady rate of 3-5 mph.

Lahaina

The only parasailing operation in Lahaina is **West Maui Parasail** (808/661-4060, www.westmauiparasail.com) out of slip #15. The prices here are the same as at the Ka'anapali operation, but a benefit of parasailing out of Lahaina is that the water is consistently calmer and glassier than in neighboring Ka'anapali. Since the boat ride is only a little over an hour long, you can grab a three-hour public parking spot on the street and not need to pay for an all-day lot.

JET SKIING

Just like parasailing, Jet Skiing is only available May 16-December 14 due to the presence of humpback whales. During summer the island's only Jet Ski operation is **Maui Watersports** (808/667-2001, www.mauiwatersports.com), in Ka'anapali just south of the Hyatt. Even though the area south of the Hyatt is relatively protected from the wind, morning hours are still the best to guarantee the calmest conditions. Also, the Jet Skiing here is fairly regulated and isn't just a free-for-all. Riders are required to ski in a relatively organized pattern, stay inside

Q: How long does it take them to get to Alaska?

A: Whales spend 6-8 weeks migrating between Alaska and the Hawaiian Islands.

Q: I saw humpback whales in Mexico. Are these the same whales?

A: Maybe. While the majority of North Pacific humpbacks spend the winter in Hawai'i, other populations winter off the Baja Peninsula. Occasionally the same whales will be spotted in various breeding grounds in the same season.

Q: How do you identify a whale?

A: In the same way that every snowflake has a different pattern, every humpback whale has a different pattern on the bottom of its fluke. Researchers photograph the bottoms of the flukes and match them up with previous photos to track and monitor a whale's location.

Q: Are whales more active in the morning?

A: No. Since whales only take short "cat naps," there isn't a set time of day when they are asleep. Mornings are often best for whale-watching because the water is calmer and the whales are easier to spot.

Q: How big is a whale's lung?

A: Each lung on a humpback whale is about the size of a small car.

Q: Are humpbacks the world's largest whales?

A: No. Humpbacks are the fifth largest whale, at 45-50 feet. They pale in comparison to blue whales, which can grow upward of 100 feet.

Q: What is "getting mugged?"

A: "Getting mugged" refers to the fact that all boats are required to maintain a 100-yard radius from humpback whales. Should the whales decide to approach the boat it is out of your hands. While the engines are off and the boat is adrift, you need to wait and endure the "mugging" until the whale loses interest. This can be 45 minutes or more.

Q: I would love to see whales up close, but I get seasick. Do you have any suggestions?

A: Seasickness is caused by a disconnect between what your eyes are seeing and what your body is feeling. The best way to avoid it is to stay above deck with your eyes on the horizon. On most boats the bow (front) moves more than the stern (back), so get a seat toward the back. Keep well-hydrated to avoid feeling sick. Caffeine can also cause nausea, so forfeit that morning coffee.

Q: Wow. You know a lot about whales. Any other tips?

A: Unless you're a professional photographer, don't worry so much about fiddling with your camera to get the perfect shot. Just enjoy the live show right in front of you. No two whale-watching trips are equal. The best remedy for a mediocre outing is to go on another one!

the mandated buoys, and maintain a healthy distance from other Jet Skis at any given time. Prices are $70 for a 30-minute ride and $98 for a full hour.

WAKEBOARDING

Captain Ryan at **Wake Maui** (808/269-5645, www.wakemaui.com) now offers wakeboarding trips in the flat water between Lahaina and Ka'anapali. Wake Maui provides the only service of its kind where a six-passenger ski boat is equipped with all the wake toys for a fun day on the water. Since Maui's winds can often be extreme, however, wakeboarding charters usually depart around sunrise to capitalize on glassy conditions. Prices for these dawn patrol wakeboarding sessions are $109/person for trips of three hours, or, if you'd prefer to charter the boat as a private group, two-hour charters can be arranged for $480 or four-hour charters for $739.

Hiking and Biking

HIKING

There aren't nearly as many hiking trails on the West Side of the island as you might expect. Unlike East Maui, which is laden with waterfalls and offers numerous hiking trails, much of the access in West Maui is blocked by private land or lack of proper trails. Also, since much of West Maui sits in the lee of Mauna Kahalawai, there aren't any accessible waterfalls as in East Maui. Nevertheless, the hiking options in West Maui offer their own sort of beauty, from stunning coastal treks to grueling ridgeline hikes.

Kapalua, Napili, and Honokowai
KAPALUA COASTAL TRAIL

Even though it's only 1.75 miles long, the **Kapalua Coastal Trail** might just be the best coastal walk in Hawai'i. The trail is bookended on each side by beaches which have been voted as the #1 beach in the United States—Kapalua Bay and D.T. Fleming Beach Park—and that fact alone should give you a sense of the beauty you're set to encounter. While most walkers, joggers, and hikers begin the trail at Kapalua Bay, you can also access the trail from other junctions at the Kapalua Bay Villas, Oneloa Bay, the Ritz-Carlton, and D.T. Fleming Beach Park.

Aside from the scenery, what makes the Kapalua Coastal Trail legendary are the various environments it passes through. Should you begin at Kapalua Bay, the trail starts as a paved walkway paralleling the beach and weaves its way through ultra-luxurious residences. At the top of a short hill the paved walkway reaches a junction by the Kapalua Bay Villas, where the path suddenly switches to dirt. While signs point to the continuation of the trail, a spur trail leads straight out toward Hawea Point, a protected reserve home to the island's largest

Take a morning walk on the Kapalua Coastal Trail.

© KYLE ELLISON

colony of *u'au kani,* or wedge-tailed shearwaters. The success of the colony can largely be attributed to the work of local volunteer and fisher, Isao Nakagawa, who took it upon himself to place traps for the feral rodents and cats that were preying upon the nests of burrowing shearwaters. Over the course of a decade between 2001 and 2011, Nakagawa was able to increase the number of burrows from a mere handful to over 500, and hikers are asked to stay on the trail during the March-December nesting season. If you follow the grass trail to the left of the three-way junction, it will connect with the trail to Namalu Bay—the rocky, Mediterranean cove hidden in the craggy recesses.

Continuing along the main Kapalua Coastal Trail will take you over a short rocky section before emerging at a smooth boardwalk along Oneloa Bay. The boardwalk here was constructed as a means of protecting the sensitive dunes native to Kapalua, and Oneloa in the mornings is one of the most gloriously empty beaches you'll find on Maui. At the end of the boardwalk the trail will change into stairs and eventually connect with Lower Honoapi'ilani Road. From here you will take a left and follow the sidewalk as it connects with the trail running in front of the Ritz-Carlton before finishing at the water's edge at D.T. Fleming Beach Park. For a side trip, hike out parallel to the golf course to the point on the left side of the beach known as Dragon's Teeth, and there is a massive labyrinth where you can walk in circles and try to make sense of the beauty around you.

VILLAGE WALKING TRAILS

The **village walking trails** are the next most popular hikes in the Kapalua resort area. Weaving their way up the mountainside through the cool and forested uplands, hikers can choose from either the 1.25-mile Cardio Loop or the 3.6-mile Lake Loop, an uphill, butt-burning workout popular with local joggers. More than just a great morning workout, there are also sections of the trail that offer sweeping views looking out toward Moloka'i and the area around Honolua Bay. To find the

access point for the trails, park in the lot for the Kapalua Village Center (between Sansei Restaurant and the Kapalua Golf Academy), and follow a paved cart path winding its way down toward an underpass where you will find the trailhead for both loops. When walking up here, pay attention to the signs and stick to the established trails. If you get lost, just choose a path heading downhill and you will eventually emerge either at the trailhead or the highway.

MAUNALEI ARBORETUM TRAIL

To climb even farther up the mountainside, follow the **Maunalei Arboretum Trail** as it winds its way through a forest planted by the great D.T. Fleming. The manager of Honolua Ranch during the 1920s, Fleming forested the mountainside with numerous plant species from across the globe in an effort to preserve the watershed. Today, over 85 years after the arboretum was established, hikers can still climb the ridges of this historic upland and be immersed in the serenity of a global forest. Trails in the arboretum range from short, 0.5-mile loops, to a moderate, 2.5-mile round-trip which winds its way up Honolua Ridge. Reaching the trails, however, is strange: You need to take a shuttle to the trailhead since access crosses over expensive private property. Shuttles depart from the Kapalua Village building at 9:30am and 11:30am, and there are pickups at the trailhead at 9:50am, 11:50am, and 1:50pm. For more information on the shuttle or to arrange a ride call 808/665-9110. The other—albeit longer—option, is to catch a ride on the shuttle up to the Maunalei Arboretum and then hike your way back down the Mahana Ridge Trail for a grand total of around seven miles.

MAHANA RIDGE TRAIL

The **Mahana Ridge Trail** is the longest continuous trail in the Kapalua resort area and the best option for serious hikers. Although you can access the Mahana Ridge Trail from the village trails, a less confusing and more scenic trailhead may be found in the parking lot of D.T. Fleming Beach Park along the access road from the highway. This trail climbs up the ridge for

PU'U KUKUI: ONE OF THE WETTEST SPOTS ON EARTH

380. That's about how many inches of rain fall annually on the 5,787-foot summit of Mauna Kahalawai.

For those of you doing the math, that's over 31 feet. For those more familiar with snow, going off the general estimate that one inch of rain is equal to a foot of snow, that's about 380 feet of snow–higher than the tallest point in the state of Florida.

The summit of Mauna Kahalawai–known as Pu'u Kukui–is really, *really* wet. There aren't many days when you can see Pu'u Kukui, although if you get a clear morning, take a picture, because it doesn't happen too often.

Even on days when it's sunny along the coastline (Lahaina only gets about 13 inches of rain per year), you can see rain clouds hanging in the valleys of the lushly forested interior. There aren't any roads back here, and there are barely even hiking trails. It's just too wet.

Mt. Wai'ale'ale on Kaua'i is regarded as the wettest place in Hawai'i (average annual rainfall of about 390 inches). Even though a remote area in East Maui known as the Big Bog is alleged to be even wetter (404 inch mean over the last 30 years), Pu'u Kukui still holds a number of rainfall records that no other spot can beat.

In March of 1942, rain gauges at Pu'u Kukui recorded 101 inches of rain in a single month. In 1982, over 704 inches of rain were unleashed on the summit. According to statistics provided by the Weather Channel, both are U.S. records.

---

nearly six miles and offers dramatic ocean and gulch views. Unlike the paved village trails, the Mahana Ridge Trail is a proper hiking trail with narrow areas, moderate uphills, and exposed tree roots. The trail can either be hiked as an out and back trip, or if you are connecting the trail with the Maunalei Arboretum Trail, you can arrange to catch the 1:50pm shuttle for a sticky and sweaty shuttle ride down. A better option is to catch the 9:30am shuttle ride up to the Maunalei Arboretum trailhead in the morning and then hike the Mahana Ridge Trail all the way down to D.T. Fleming Beach Park for a refreshing dip in the ocean. Maps are posted at the Kapalua Adventure Center and are also available online at www.kapalua.com.

OHAI TRAIL

The 1.2-mile Ohai Trail awards hikers with panoramic vistas of the island's North Shore: the cobalt Pacific stretches out uninterrupted until the fjords of Alaska nearly 3,000 miles away. This area is often windy, and the way in which the wind drowns out all other sounds makes it a peaceful respite on the northern coast. The Ohai trailhead is 10 miles past the entrance to Kapalua by mile marker 41 between the Nakalele Blowhole and Olivine Pools. Along the moderate, winding trail there are a few placards with information on the island's native coastal plants. This is also a great perch to watch for tropical seabirds soaring on the afternoon breeze. There isn't any readily available water on this stretch of coastline.

Ka'anapali

KA'ANAPALI BOARDWALK

The **Ka'anapali Boardwalk** is about three miles long from end to end. There are various historical placards scattered along the beach path. The southern terminus of the boardwalk is in front of the Hyatt resort, and the easiest public beach parking is at Hanakao'o Beach Park along the highway between Ka'anapali and Lahaina. From here the boardwalk runs north all the way to the Sheraton about a mile and half later, although if you follow the paved walkway through the lower level of the Sheraton and through the parking lot, you will notice the trail reforms and starts skirting the golf course. The walkway then wraps its way through the Royal Lahaina resort and the parking lot of adjoining hotels. By following the Beach Walk signs you will eventually join with another boardwalk which runs all the way down to the Honua Kai resort.

South of Lahaina
HONOKOHAU DITCH TRAIL

More of a walking and jogging path than a proper hiking trail, the **Honokohau Ditch Trail** runs for two miles through the residential communities of Launiupoko and Puʻunoa. The trail is meant to mimic the irrigation ditches which once provided up to 50 million gallons a day for the surrounding sugarcane fields (which morphed into luxury homes with the closing of Pioneer Mill in 1999), and there are allegedly plans to one day have this trail system run all the way from Olowalu to Kapalua. Until that time comes, hikers will have to enjoy this short stretch weaving its way through dream homes pulled straight from the pages of a magazine. Along the journey, panoramic views can be had over the water toward Lanaʻi. Since this area can become unbearably hot during the middle of the day, it's best hiked during the late afternoon when you can finish it with the sunset. To find the trailhead, the easiest access is to turn uphill at the stoplight for Launiupoko Beach Park and travel up Kai Hele Ku Road, continuing straight at the roundabout. A couple of hundred yards past the roundabout you will see the trailhead on your left, and there is a small amount of parking on the side of the road, although be sure you aren't leaving your car on someone's front lawn.

LAHAINA PALI TRAIL

Hot, dry, and with incomparable views, the **Lahaina Pali Trail** is a literal walk back in time to days when reaching Lahaina wasn't quite so easy. This five-mile, three-hour (one-way) hike is the most strenuous trek in West Maui, as the zigzagging trail climbs for 1,600 feet before reaching a crest by the Kaheawa Wind Farm. While torturous on both your legs and your thirst, the reward for the uphill slog is panoramic views over the central valley and dozens of humpback whales off the coast during the winter.

Tracing its way over a part of the island which receives less than 10 inches of rainfall annually, this trail was originally constructed about 400 years ago during the reign of Piʻilani, who envisioned a footpath wrapping around the island. Once horses were introduced, riders would use this trail to connect Central Maui with the West Side, but when a dirt road was constructed along the coast in 1911, the trail fell into disrepair. Nevertheless, hikers will still encounter evidence of ancient activity such as stone shelters and rock walls. It's surreal to imagine that only 100 years ago this was the preferred route for reaching Lahaina. To get the most out of this hike, pick up the hiking guide the Na Ala Hele trail system has published entitled "Tales from the Trail," which provides an interactive historical tour aligned with markers along the trail. Copies are available at the Department of Land and Natural Resources building in Wailuku (54 High St.), or, if you have a smartphone, download it as a PDF (www.mauiguidebook.com/hikes/lahaina-pali-trail) you can carry with you on the trip.

The downside of this trail is that since it's a one-way hike it can take some logistical planning. The Ukumehame trailhead on the Lahaina-side is at mile marker 10.5 about a half mile after the tunnel in a small dirt parking lot on the inland side of the highway. If you depart from the Ukumehame trailhead, the path ascends moderately and offers pristine views of the coral reefs below. After the trail levels out at 1,600 feet and you reach the crest by the wind farm, it will descend steeply and sharply to the opposite trailhead between Maʻalaea and the junction of Honoapiʻilani Highway (Hwy. 30) and North Kihei Road. Your four options for the return route are to either leave a car at the opposite trailhead, hike back the way you came, hitchhike back to the original trailhead, or turn back the way you came once you reach the wind farm (which is the shortest and most practical option). If you plan on only hiking half the trail, setting out from the

Ma'alaea trailhead offers better views of the valley and Kealia Pond, whereas departing from the Ukumehame trailhead offers better views of the coastline and whale-watching opportunities. For the intrepid and those equipped with headlamps, the Ukumehame side is the best sunset perch on the West Side. Since there is absolutely no shade on this hike and it can get brutally hot, it's imperative to avoid the middle of the day and to pack more water than you would normally need. Also, since this area is so dry, it's a tinderbox ready to ignite at any moment, so don't smoke or use a lighter at any point on your hike. You'll be passing over rocky, rugged terrain, so wear closed-toe shoes.

BIKING

Whether you're going for a 60-mile cycle around the West Maui Mountains or a leisurely ride down Front Street on a beach cruiser, all of the biking on the West Side of the island consists of cycling on island roadways. For serious cyclists looking to rent a proper road bike, **West Maui Cycles** (1087 Limahana Pl., 808/661-9005, www.westmauicycles.com, 9am-5pm Mon.-Sat., 10am-4pm Sun.) in the industrial park of Lahaina is the best bike shop on the West Side. Rentals of mountain bikes and high-performance road bikes range from $50/day to $285/week, or you can also get basic beach cruisers for $15/day. As a fun aside this is also the only shop on the island where you can rent a tandem bicycle if you want to be one of the handful of people per year who choose to cycle the Road to Hana as a tandem duo.

Closer to the center of Lahaina, **Boss Frog's Cycles** (156 Lahainaluna Rd., 808/661-1344, www.mauiroadbikerentals.com, 8am-5pm daily) also offers beach cruisers for $15/day, $50/week, and high-performance road bikes for $50/day. While this location is closer to town and more convenient, die-hard cyclists will appreciate the passion for the sport found at West Maui Cycles.

Adventure Sports

Even though water sports dominate the recreation options on the island's West Side, there are still a number of places where you can get a thrill either on the land or cruising over the water.

ATV RIDES

The best ATV ride on the West Side of the island is with **Kahoma Ranch** (808/667-1978, www.kahomaranch.com), a company with whom you not only have the ability to get dirty and rip across private dirt roads on your own ATV, but at the end when you're all hot and sweaty you can also take a plunge down one of three different waterslides. Aside from the fun of tooling around on ATVs and plunging at high speeds into a swimming reservoir, tour participants are awarded with views looking out at the island of Lana'i and back into Kahoma Valley. The area you tour is closed to the general public, so this is the only way you will see these views. The waterslides themselves aren't at all what you'd expect. When you first see them, you might be skeptical in that they look like little more than tarps stretched over a hole in the ground. When it comes to slides, however, it isn't a beauty contest, and the speeds you can get while careening down one are better than average. The cost for adults riding their own vehicle is $199, whereas a shared ATV is $129. Children are $65, and those as young as five years old can accompany a driver of legal age. Tours take place at 8am, 11am, and 2pm, although the 8am tour doesn't involve the waterslide.

ZIPLINING

Despite the explosion in zipline operators on the island, the only zipline tour in West Maui is **Skyline Eco-Adventures** (2580 Keka'a Dr., 808/878-8400, www.zipline.com, 7am-6pm daily), a company that was

© KYLE ELLISON

zipling above Ka'anapali

the first zipline operator on Maui and continues to be a leader in the industry. When Skyline opened an Upcountry course in 2002, it was in fact the first zipline company in the United States. Seizing upon the initial success, it opened up a second course in the hills above Ka'anapali offering greater views and longer lines than the sister course. Aside from there being eight ziplines crisscrossing the canyons, each one has an historical, environmental, or cultural connection explained to you by the affable guides. Skyline donates 1 percent of profits to environmental preservation and aims to be a carbon-neutral company. The main draw of this trip—nearly more so than the ziplines themselves—is the view looking out toward Lana'i and Moloka'i that incorporates 180° of horizon. Visitors

are also afforded glimpses into the island's valleys as well as of small waterfalls during the wetter months of the year. These tours are so popular they run seven times a day, with the earliest setting out from the Fairway Shops office at 7am. The benefit of an early tour is that the temperature is still cool and the wind hasn't picked up yet, although there can sometimes be some lingering morning rain showers and the dirt roads can be muddy from this moisture. By 11am, the sun can be scorchingly hot. Try to get on the 8am or 9am tour, although there is never a *bad* time to be zipping over a rugged ravine and gazing out at the wide-open Pacific. Children must be 10 years of age for the Ka'anapali course, closed-toe shoes are required, and the maximum weight is 260 pounds.

Horseback Riding

KAPALUA, NAPILI, AND HONOKOWAI

The only horseback riding operator on the island's northwestern side is **Ironwood Ranch** (808/669-4991, www.ironwoodranch.com), a conveniently located option for anyone staying in Kapalua or Napili. Ironwood Ranch is high on the mountainside above Napili. Riders are picked up at a parking lot at the junction of Napilihau Street and Honoapi'ilani Highway (mile marker 29) and shuttled up the mountain by ranch staff. Riders at Ironwood Ranch will be treated to a different section of Napili covered in native plants and hidden trails. The views and sunsets from the ranch are from a higher elevation than you can reach on your own and the guides educate you on this sparsely visited area. Rides range from $90 to $120/person and only involve a maximum of six riders. Private rides can also be arranged for experienced riders.

LAHAINA

In the upper reaches of Launiupoko, trail rides at **Lahaina Stables** (Punakea Lp., 808/667-2222, www.mauihorse.com) head back into the Launiupoko Valley and offer panoramic views looking out over Lahaina. Rides are offered three times daily, at 8:30am, 10:30am, or two hours prior to sunset, the last option offering some of the best sunsets on the island. All of the rides offer glimpses into Hawaiian history and information about the surrounding terrain. It can be a hot, rocky, and dusty ride. Until you reach the upper terminus of the trail at the mouth of the valley, the surrounding foliage won't be nearly as lush as at Ironwood Ranch, although the upside is that this means you won't have to ride in the rain. The weather in this valley is almost always perfect, and although there can occasionally be high winds gusting through the valley, they usually won't have picked up yet for the morning rides and will have subsided by the evening sunset ride. A decent portion of the trail winds its way through the outer reaches of a residential community, although the snack area by the reservoir is tucked back at the mouth of the valley and off in its own little area. Rates for the two-hour rides are $120 for an early morning ride, $130 for a sunset ride, and $145 for the 10:30am ride, which is a bit longer and includes a light lunch.

Golf and Tennis

GOLF

Kapalua, Napili, and Honokowai

For serious golfers, the name Kapalua should be synonymous with the **Kapalua Plantation Course** (2000 Plantation Club Dr., 877/527-2582, www.golfatkapalua.com), a windy, challenging, and scenic course that spreads out across the mountainside above D.T. Fleming Beach Park. This par-73, 7,411-yard course is the most famous course on the island and the site of the Hyundai Tournament of Champions. You're somehow expected to focus on your chip shot when you have the deep blues of the Pailolo Channel opening up before you. You might want to forget the clubs and grab your camera. With the course's fame and prestige, however, come greens fees toward the upper end of the spectrum. Regular golfers will need to shell out $278 for a chance at tackling the Plantation, but those staying in the Kapalua resort receive a discount that knocks the price down to $228. Greens fees decrease as the day wears on, so those opting to play in the late afternoon can squeak in a round for only $128

PROFESSIONAL GOLF AT KAPALUA

Every year, the professional PGA Tour kicks off its season with the Hyundai Tournament of Champions at the Kapalua Golf Course. Formerly known as the Mercedes Championships, this tournament is unique in that only golfers who have won a professional title in the previous year are invited to take part.

The event has been held on the Kapalua Plantation Course every year since 1999. Play usually takes place during the first week in January (so don't expect to get on the Plantation Course at that time). Golf legends including Tiger Woods, Ernie Els, and Vijay Singh have all claimed the title at the Plantation, and in 2013, the winner of the event was set to take home a cool $1.1 million for the effort.

(although expect the wind to be howling). Club rentals are $65 (including two sleeves of balls), and shoe rental is $14. To the find the clubhouse for the Plantation Course, travel along Honoapiʻilani Highway (Hwy. 30) for one mile past the main entrance to Kapalua resort and make a right onto Plantation Club Drive. You will wind your way up the hillside and eventually see the clubhouse on your right.

The **Kapalua Bay Course** (300 Kapalua Dr., 877/527-2582, www.golfatkapalua.com) along the Kapalua shoreline is a touch more forgiving at par 72 and 6,600 yards. While all of the holes offer resort-quality play, the highlight here is hole #5 where the green is sandwiched between Oneloa Bay and D.T. Fleming Beach Park. While putting here you are surrounded by 270 degrees of brilliant blue ocean. Even if your round isn't going quite as you had hoped, this rocky promontory is relaxing enough to bring a temporary moment of peace. Like the Plantation Course, however, the Bay Course is windy in the afternoon, so early morning hours are best for calm conditions. Greens fees here are still expensive at $208 for regular guests and $188 for those staying in Kapalua resort. As with other courses the fees decrease throughout the day, and you can pick up a late afternoon round for as low as $98. (*Tip:* If the weather forecast is calling for *kona* winds, it means that the winds will be light and the conditions in the afternoon will be just as good as the morning. If the weather forecast is for trade winds of anything over 15 knots, then you'll want to schedule an early round). To find the clubhouse for the Bay Course, turn on Kapalua Drive from Lower Honoapiʻilani Road across the street from Oneloa Bay (Ironwoods Beach). Travel up the road by the tennis center and you will see the clubhouse on your right.

The **Kapalua Golf Academy** (1000 Office Rd., 808/662-7740, www.golfatkapalua.com/golf-academy) has been voted as one of the best golf schools in the country, with 23 acres devoted to bettering your game. Everything you could possibly need is available here, from private instruction and video analysis to on-course lessons and custom club fitting. Though the golf instruction is by no means cheap, seasonal packages and specials can sometimes offer surprisingly affordable deals.

Kaʻanapali

There are a number of benefits about playing the courses in Kaʻanapali. They're cheaper than Kapalua and closer to the majority of resorts. Perhaps most important, however, they're less prone to wind and rain, and it takes the trade winds about two hours longer to reach Kaʻanapali than Kapalua. What this means is that an 8am tee time at Kapalua on most days will begin getting blustery around the 6th hole, whereas at Kaʻanapali you could be well into the back nine before the wind becomes a factor. The sacrifice in Kaʻanapali is that the views aren't quite as nice (though they are still spectacular by normal standards), and the greens are just *slightly* less manicured when compared to Kapalua.

Of the two courses in Kaʻanapali, the **Royal**

Ka'anapali (2290 Ka'anapali Pkwy., 808/661-3691, www.kaanapaligolfcourses.com) has the best views and is the nicer course. In addition to paralleling the Pacific Ocean, this par-71, 6,700-yard course is also historic as the island's original course, having opened in 1962. Rates for the Royal course are $249 for non-resort guests, and those staying in Ka'anapali can play for $189. For those willing to tee off after 1pm, the price drops down to $149.

The **Ka'anapali Kai** (2290 Ka'anapali Pkwy., 808/661-3691, www.kaanapaligolfcourses.com) course has most of its holes on the inland side of the highway. The fairways here aren't as nicely maintained as the Royal, although since you're playing at a slight elevation there still are the kind of ocean views you would expect from a resort course in Hawai'i. Rates for the Kai course are $205 for non-resort guests and $149 for those staying in Ka'anapali. Rates drop to $119 after 1pm, club rental is $49, and shoes are available for $10. Both Ka'anapali courses check in at the same clubhouse.

TENNIS
Kapalua, Napili, and Honokowai

For those who are serious about their tennis, the **Kapalua Tennis Club** (300 Kapalua Dr., 808/662-7730, www.golfatkapalua.com/tennis, 8am-6pm daily) is the largest facility on the northwest side of the island and has been ranked as one of the top 50 tennis resorts in the United States. There are "stroke of the day" clinics every day 9am-10am for $25, as well as drop-in doubles sessions on Monday and Wednesday 4pm-6pm for $12/person. If you just want to rent some court time, court fees are $14/person for the day, and racquets are only $6/day if you left your sticks at home.

There are a couple of public courts without any fees at **Napili Park** off Honoapi'ilani Highway between Napilihau Street and the entrance to Kapalua resort. The courts here can be windy in the afternoons and potentially wet in the mornings, but if you're just looking for somewhere to knock a few balls around, then these are the closest.

Ka'anapali

Even though a number of resorts in Ka'anapali have courts available for guests, the facility with the largest number of courts and programs is the **Royal Lahaina Tennis Ranch** (2780 Keka'a Dr., 808/667-5200, www.tennismaui.net, 8am-noon and 2pm-6pm Mon.-Fri., 8am-noon and 2pm-5pm weekends), in the parking lot of the Royal Lahaina Resort. This is the premier tennis facility in Ka'anapali. Morning clinics are $20/person, as are the Saturday morning doubles clinics for intermediate and advanced players. Court fees are only $10/person for those who just want to hit on their own, and racquets can be rented for an affordable $2.50. Private instruction and hitting sessions are available for advanced players. Often when it's raining in Kapalua, the showers haven't made their way down as far as Ka'anapali, and the courts will be nice and dry.

Lahaina

The best courts in Lahaina are at the **Lahaina Civic Center** across from Wahikuli Beach Park. There are nine courts here, and with the slight sea breeze coming off the water, they are a few degrees cooler than the courts on Front Street. Since these are public courts, there is no fee to play, but there also isn't any sort of pro shop or tennis-related facilities. There is a water fountain as well as a public restroom, and a few of the courts are lit at night. To find the courts, turn on Leiali'i Parkway off Honoapi'ilani Highway and make a left on Ka'aahi Street. Parking is available either on the side of the road or in a parking area at the end of the last court.

In the center of Lahaina town, the **Wakida Courts** on Front Street between the banyan tree and Kamehameha Iki Park are named for the legendary Lahaina tennis coach Shigeto "Shigesh" Wakida who trained hundreds—if not thousands—of Lahaina youth over his decades of running the Lahaina tennis program. These courts bearing his name remain as the center of Lahaina's junior tennis scene and are where much of Lahaina chooses to play. Only on the rarest of days will there be any sort of wind or rain at these free courts. A small water fountain offers drinking water, and exceptionally dirty bathrooms are located in the park on the south side of the basketball court. On the far end of the park behind the baseball field, tucked back from the road, are two additional courts. They're nicer than the courts on Front Street, but they are also an unofficial gathering place for Lahaina's homeless community.

Yoga, Fitness, and Spas

YOGA AND FITNESS
Kapalua, Napili, and Honokowai
The best place for workout classes on the northwestern side of the island is the ludicrously luxurious **Kapalua Spa** (100 Bay Dr., 808/665-8282, www.kapaluaspa.com, 5:30am-7pm daily) in Kapalua just north of Kapalua Bay. Despite the fact that this is one of the toniest resort areas in Hawai'i, the fitness specials offered at the spa are some of the most affordable on the island. The best deal is a $200, one-week package that includes three 30-minute private training sessions with a personal trainer, four shadow fitness sessions, and unlimited access to all of the spa facilities such as saunas and steam rooms. What's more, for classes such as yoga, boot camps, and Pilates, a package of five is only $50. Considering that a single-session is $28, this is an unbelievable deal that will leave you refreshed, full of energy, and questioning how you were able to afford hanging out in this luxurious fitness center.

Squeeze in a workout at **Passion of Movement** (5095 Napilihau St., 808/419-6028, www.passionofmovement.com), in the Napili Plaza shopping center. Everything from yoga and Pilates to TRX and P90X is taught in this locally run studio. This is where you'll find Napili locals working on their beach body and perpetuating the healthy island lifestyle. Mat classes range from $18 for a single session to $80 for a block of five classes.

Ka'anapali
With workout equipment and weight lifting options, **Valley Isle Fitness** (2580 Keka'a Dr., 808/667-7474, www.valleyislefitnesscenter.com, 5:30am-10pm Mon.-Thurs., 5:30am-9pm Fri., 7am-7pm Sat., 9am-4pm Sun.) is the largest gym on the West Side. The gym is in the Fairway Shops of Ka'anapali. If you're staying at a place in Ka'anapali that doesn't already have its own workout facilities, you can drop in here for $20/day or get a one-week pass for $75.

If you would rather arrange a private training session or a fast-paced boot camp on the beach, **One Fitness** (925/708-7351, www.facebook.com/onefitnessmaui) is a Ka'anapali-based fitness company run by the legendary Ben Auerbach, who has won gold medals representing the United States in the 400 meters. One Fitness has flexible training options in outdoor venues around the West Side. Whether it's organizing trail runs or sprinting through deep sand, this is a company custom-tailored toward increasing athleticism and fine-tuning the workout goals you've been hoping to attain.

Lahaina
For all-around fitness in a boutique studio, the best place to work out in Lahaina is **Body In Balance** (142 Kupuohi St., 808/661-1116, www.bodyinbalancemaui.com), an intimate, two-story studio where the professional instructors will help you achieve the results you're looking for. The downstairs portion of the studio focuses on weight and strength training, while the upstairs area is where group classes in Pilates, mat work, or spinning take place. The focus here is on long-term visitors looking to sculpt a proper training schedule, although you can also inquire about single classes for as low as $18. To find the gym, drive uphill past the Lahaina Gateway Center and make a right on Kupuohi Street; the gym will be on your right.

For those who can't imagine a vacation that

doesn't involve a WOD, the local CrossFit box is at **Lahaina CrossFit** (219 Kupuohi St., 808/286-9422, www.lahainacrossfit.com, closed Sun.). Those who are already familiar with CrossFit will feel right at home with the short, intense regimens. Single sessions are $20; $55 gets a weekly pass. Classes begin as early as 6am and run through the day until 6pm.

For yoga workouts, even though downtown Lahaina can be hot enough during summer to be an outdoor Bikram studio, locals nevertheless flock to **Island Spirit Yoga** (840 Waine'e St., 808/667-2111, www.islandspirityoga.com) behind the Ace Hardware a block back from Front Street for their daily dose of stretching, breathing, and asana. Single sessions are $17, or you can get a five-class pass for $65. Classes are normally held throughout the morning hours and later in the evenings. A full list of offerings and times can be found on the website.

Bikram Yoga Lahaina (845 Waine'e St., 808/661-6828, www.bikramyogalahaina.net) in the Foodland shopping center offers single-session classes for $20 and an unlimited weekly pass for $50. The studio is on the second floor above Nagasako General Store, has classes as early as 6:30am on Tuesday and Thursday and a variety of class times during the rest of the week.

SPAS

While the following spa and massage services are broken down by their geographic location, if you would rather enjoy an in-room, mobile massage service regardless of where you're staying, **Na Ali'i Massage** (808/250-7170, www.mymauimassage.com) will meet you anywhere on the West Side and offers rates which are much lower than the resorts or local massage parlors. A 60-minute massage is $85, and they also offer a full range of other services such as body scrubs, reflexology, and hand and foot treatments.

Kapalua, Napili, and Honokowai
Just like its workout facility, the **Kapalua Spa** (100 Bay Dr., 808/665-8282, www.kapaluaspa.com, 9am-7pm daily) has the best spa services

on the northwestern side of the island. This spa has been voted as the best luxury destination spa in the United States. This truly is a luxurious wellness retreat unlike any other, incorporating elements of native Hawaiian culture into the treatments for an experience you won't find at smaller, more affordable spas. When your treatment is through, you are welcome to linger and use the spa facilities or sit by the edge of the edgeless pool and listen to the waves lap in the nearby bay. Unlike their fitness packages, however, fees at the spa reflect the higher resort prices, and 50-minute massages—the shortest option—are $160.

For a spa experience outside a resort, **Zensations Spa** (3600 Lower Honoapi'ilani Rd., 808/669-0100, www.zensationsspa.com, 10am-5pm Mon.-Sat., 9am-7pm Sun.) in the 5A mall in Honokowai offers 60-minute massages for $99 as well as a full range of aromatherapy, facial, and body treatment options. The spa is within walking distance of many Honokowai condos.

Maui Massage and Wellness (3636 Lower Honoapi'ilani Rd., 808/669-4500, www.mauimassageandwellness.com, 9am-6pm Mon.-Fri., 10am-5pm weekends) by the Honokowai Farmers Market offers massage and spa services for cheaper than the resort rates. Sixty-minute massages range $105-115, and there are also facials, foot scrubs, and various packages.

Ka'anapali
While nearly every resort in the Ka'anapali complex is going to offer a spa or beauty center, there are a couple which stand out.

At the Westin Maui next to Whalers Village, **Heavenly Spa** (2365 Ka'anapal Pkwy., 808/661-2588, www.westinmaui.com/spa, 8am-7pm daily) has been lauded as one of the top spas in the United States and has 50-minute massages beginning at $145.

For slightly more affordable rates, the **Spa at Black Rock** (2605 Ka'anapali Pkwy., 808/667-9577, www.blackrockspa.com, 8:30am-7pm daily) offers 60-minute massages beginning at $125 in addition to a complete menu of spa packages.

Lahaina

Although there aren't any fancy resort spas in the middle of Lahaina, the upside is that you can get relaxing spa sessions from seasoned professionals at prices that are a fraction of those at the resorts. If you tweaked your neck during a surf lesson at Breakwall or pulled a muscle while jumping off Black Rock, one of the most popular massage centers in town is **Maui Zen Day Spa** (181 Lahainaluna Rd., 808/661-7200, www.mauizen.com, 10am-6pm daily), smack in the middle of Lahaina about one block inland from Cheeseburger in Paradise. Massage sessions range between $99 and $115 depending on the treatment. For an additional $15 the therapists will come and meet you at your resort or condo.

Sights

KAPALUA, NAPILI, AND HONOKOWAI

Despite the prevalence of beaches here, there are still a few sights worth exploring, located along the remote northwestern corner of the island, which is like a miniature Road to Hana without the waterfalls. If you continue all the way around the back of West Maui past the town of Kahakuloa (the road isn't four-wheel drive like your rental car map might say, but it *is* far narrower, curvier, and scarier than the Road to Hana), you can combine the drive with the waterfalls of Makamaka'ole Valley in Central Maui for a full-day experience. This journey is not for the timid; most turn back toward Kapalua once they reach Kahakuloa.

◖ Nakalele Blowhole

Eight miles past the entrance to Kapalua by mile marker 38 is the famous **Nakalele Blowhole.** Outside of Honolua Bay this is the most popular stop along this stretch of coast. It's about a fifteen-minute drive past the entrance to Kapalua if you go straight through without stopping. Blowholes are formed when sea caves grow upward and bore a small opening into the surface of the rock. On the right days, the Nakalele Blowhole can jettison water upward of 100 feet into the air. The best conditions for witnessing Nakalele are when the trade winds are blowing and during the hours around the high tide. To check the current tide tables for the highest time of day, look at www.hawaiitides.com. In the full throes of its performance, Nakalele Blowhole is a natural saltwater geyser erupting on a windswept outcropping, and it's one of the most powerful forces of the sea you can witness on the island. This power, however, needs to be respected, as visitors have been killed by standing too close to the blowhole.

Finding the blowhole can be a challenge for those who don't know where to look. At mile marker 38 there is dirt pullout on the oceanside of the highway, although the trail from here that leads down toward the water will only take you as far as the decrepit old lighthouse and a marginal view of the blowhole. A better access point is a half a mile farther down the road where a second dirt pullout serves as the trailhead for the path leading to the blowhole. Between the two parking areas are dozens of dirtbike tracks which serve as red herrings and don't lead anywhere, so the best thing to do is park by mile marker 38.5 (although there isn't an actual sign) and make your way down from there. The trail to the blowhole is just over a half mile long, and the last half of the trail becomes a scramble down a moderate scree slope which is best left to those who are steady on their feet.

The Olivine Pools

A little over four miles past the Nakalele Blowhole by mile marker 16 (if you've realized that the math doesn't add up, it's because Honoapi'ilani Highway changes into Kahekili Highway) are **the Olivine Pools.** The coastal

Nakalele Blowhole

panoramas from here are breathtaking, and even if you never walk down to the pools, the views alone are reason enough to stop. For most visitors, the whole point of coming here is to swim and bathe in the shallow tidepools perfectly perched on a lava rock outcropping. On calm days when the wind is light and the ocean is mellow and smooth, this can be one of the most serene perches you'll find anywhere on the island. However, the ocean is rarely calm along this stretch of shoreline, and winter can see 20-foot surf cascading over the rocky pinnacle. That makes swimming in the pools exceptionally dangerous. A good rule of thumb is to sit and watch them for a while and wait to see if any waves are crashing into them. If the ocean is calm and isn't reaching the pools, then this is the safest time for swimming or wading. If waves are washing into the pools—even small ones—keep out. Visitors have been swept to their deaths here.

Kapalua Labyrinth

Though not a sight in the traditional sense of the word, the massive white-coral labyrinth which has been constructed on the point between D.T. Fleming Beach Park and Oneloa Bay is a place of palpable power and sweeping ocean views. The rocky point that this labyrinth is set on is a sacred spot to native Hawaiians, who believe it to be one of the places where souls would leap from this world into the next. Though the middle of the day can be marred by high winds, early mornings and the hour just before sunset are great times to walk in your pensive circles. To reach the labyrinth, you can either scramble up the rocks on the southern end of D.T. Fleming Beach Park, or, if approaching from the interior of Kapalua, park in the small parking lot at the juncture of Office Road and Lower Honoapi'ilani Road and follow the small path out toward the point. You will be paralleling the golf course here, so prior to reaching the labyrinth keep an eye out for golfers who might be teeing off into the area.

Honokowai Valley

Inaccessible to the general public, this valley can only be reached by crossing private land as part of a volunteer group which meets on Saturday mornings at 9am at the Puʻukoliʻi train station (junction of Puʻukoliʻi Road and Honoapiʻilani Highway). Easily visible from the highway as a deep cleft in the mountainside, Honokowai Valley was once home to a thriving community of up to 600 different families who farmed, hunted, and built *pili* grass shelters in the deep and protected recesses of the valley during ancient Hawaiian times. When the streams were diverted for sugarcane in the 1800s, however, the water which once irrigated the taro *loʻi* was no longer available for farming. Having been robbed of their vital life source, the valley residents abandoned their homes and left to establish a life elsewhere. For 100 years, this valley sat empty, neglected, and essentially forgotten. Foreign plant species made their in and crowded out the native species which had flourished for decades, and invasive animals such as feral cats and mongooses preyed upon native bird species and drove them to the brink of extinction. This five-mile-long valley running from the shoreline into the heart of Mauna Kahalawai was crumbling beneath the elements it once harnessed to survive.

Enter Ed and Puanani Lindsey, two native Hawaiian land activists who helped establish the group Maui Cultural Lands in 2002. Recognizing the inseparable relationship between the health of the land and the preservation of culture, the duo worked with Kaʻanapali land companies to act as stewards of the land and gradually return the valley to its glory. The invasive species would be removed, endemic species would be planted, and life would once again begin to flourish. Legions of volunteers have donated their efforts to the cause since the founding of the program. Even with the passing of Ed Lindsey in 2009, his vision of a healthy and restored valley continues to live on. Rock walls once completely overgrown have since been uncovered, and for a mile-long stretch of the valley it's not only possible to see what the village would have looked like, but also to make out the irrigation and farming systems which provided life for the community. The valley is a living museum, and all visitors who choose to volunteer are given a short walk around it and are taught the area's cultural significance. All those interested in volunteering can find out more information by contacting the Pacific Whale Foundation's Volunteering on Vacation program at 800/942-5311, ext. 1, or by reading more online at volunteersonvacation.org.

KAʻANAPALI
Puʻu Kekaʻa

Known to most visitors as Black Rock, **Puʻu Kekaʻa** is the correct name for this volcanic outcropping at the northern end of Kaʻanapali Beach. Today the rock is a popular spot for snorkeling, scuba diving, and cliff jumping, although the most popular time of day is about 20 minutes prior to sunset when a torch-wielding, shirtless member of the Sheraton staff scrambles onto the rock and lights a row of carefully placed tiki torches. Once all of the torches are lit, his flaming staff is ceremoniously chucked into the water moments before he performs a swan dive off the rock. More than just a creative marketing plan, the ceremony is a reenactment of the sacred belief that this is one of the spots on the island where a person's soul leaps from this world to the next immediately following death. Ancient Hawaiians dared not venture onto the jagged precipice for fear they wouldn't return. In the 18th century, King Kahekili leapt from the sacred cliff and remained firmly in this world, procing that he possessed incredible *mana,* or spiritual strength. Today, the ceremony held at Puʻu Kekaʻa honors this great king of Maui.

Whalers Village Museum

There's actually more to Whalers Village than high-end luxury shopping and beachfront, barefoot bars. On the third story high above the fancy stores and bustling courtyard, the **Whalers Village Museum** (2435 Kaʻanapali Pkwy., 808/661-5992, www.whalersmuseum.com, 10am-6pm daily, $3 adults, $2 seniors,

$1 children) is the best resource for whale education on the island's West Side. Visitors can wander through the museum to learn everything from *why* whales were hunted in the first place (it wasn't for the meat) to what life was like aboard a 19th-century whaling ship (it was miserable). There is a large display of scrimshaw art (drawings carved on whale's teeth), and there are also movies playing throughout the day that explore the dismal yet fascinating world of 19th-century whaling. During winter, a visit to the museum is the perfect way to fortify the knowledge gained on a whale-watching excursion. Despite the fact the museum discusses whaling, the focus has shifted toward protecting our winter companions today.

LAHAINA

From 1820-1845, this seaside town—which was originally called *Lele*—was the capital of the Hawaiian kingdom. At about the same time that the *ali'i* and royalty were establishing their capital, fleets of New England whaling ships began anchoring in the Lahaina Roads. From 1820-1860, thousands of crusty whalers paddled ashore in wooden rowboats to reprovision their ships, soak their livers, and soothe their rusty loins. Answering the call to save these poor souls, Christian missionaries from New England began to arrive in the early 1820s, bolstered by the support of Queen Ka'ahumanu who had embraced the values of Christianity. Lahaina became a literal and metaphorical battleground between drunken whalers and pious missionaries to win the native Hawaiian populace. Lahaina truly was the Wild West of the Pacific. Today, scores of historic sites pertaining to this era are scattered about town.

Thanks to the tireless work of the Lahaina Restoration Foundation, many of the town's historical sites are well marked and accessible. Pick up a walking tour map from the Lahaina Visitor Center in the Courthouse next to Lahaina Harbor or a *Mo'olelo O Lahaina* historical and cultural walking tour map from the offices of the Lahaina Restoration Foundation on the grounds of the Baldwin Missionary home.

The Banyan Tree

This magnificent tree is the most recognizable landmark in West Maui. You can't miss it at the corner of Hotel and Front Streets, because it spreads its shading boughs over almost an acre. Every night at sunset there is a calming cacophony of hundreds of mynah birds who sing from its upper reaches. This tree is the **largest banyan in the state,** planted in April 1873 by Sheriff Bill Smith in commemoration of the Congregationalist Missions' golden anniversary. Every year during the month of April a birthday party is held for the tree which draws hundreds of people to its shady confines. During most days you can find old-timers sitting here chatting, and artists gather here on weekends to display their artwork under the tree's broad branches. The tree is also a gathering place for the local homeless population.

Fort

On the southwestern edge of the park are the restored coral remnants of the historic Lahaina fort. By 1825 the missionaries had convinced Hawaiian royalty that drunken sailors running amok in town was morally lamentable, so strict laws forbade native women from visiting the ships and whalers from coming ashore after nightfall. These rules, as you can imagine, proved a severe hindrance to any lascivious pursuits, and riots frequently broke out between angry whalers and the missionaries. In 1827, whalers anchored offshore went so far as to lob cannonballs into the lawn of missionary William Richards' house, and it was decided by Hoapili—the governor of Maui—that a fort needed to be built to protect the town from the pent-up whalers. Hence, in 1832, a fort was constructed out of coral blocks with walls 20 feet high and laden with cannons, the restored remnants of which are still visible today. One of the cannons from the fort is across the street at Lahaina Harbor, facing out toward the water to serve as a reminder of the "tensions" which once gripped this town.

◖ Lahaina Courthouse

The old **Lahaina Courthouse** contains the

most informative museum in downtown Lahaina. During its tenure as the town's political center, it also served as governor's office, post office, customs office, and police station, complete with a jail in the underground basement. The jail is now home to the Lahaina Arts Society's **Old Jail Gallery,** and the society has its main **Banyan Tree Gallery** on the first floor. Since renovation in 1998, the **Lahaina Visitor Center** (808/667-9193, 9am-5pm daily) has also occupied a room on the main floor. Here anyone can come for gifts and tourist information and brochures about the town, and there are also numerous coupon books that can help save you a few dollars. In the old courtroom on the second floor, the **Lahaina Heritage Museum** (9am-5pm daily, suggested $3 donation) displays historical objects and old photographs, and there is even the original Hawaiian flag which was lowered from the courthouse on the day it was replaced in 1898 by the American stars and stripes. On the lower level there is also a small theater with informative documentaries about life in the islands, and this is a must-stop venue for anyone with an interest in the history of Lahaina.

Pioneer Inn

Across the street from the courthouse is the historic **Pioneer Inn.** While today it's just a Best Western hotel with restaurants and shops on the bottom, this site is notable as being the island's first hotel. Established in 1901, it continued as the West Side's only accommodations until 1963. If you pop into the lobby, read the hilarious rules which still hang in the rooms and govern the behavior of patrons.

Lighthouse

A tall white lighthouse stands on the northern edge of the main loading dock. During summer months you will also notice local surfers launching themselves into the water by the breakwall here, and it's the perfect spot for soaking up some sun and people-watching. What makes this lighthouse historic, however, is that it's the oldest one in the state of Hawai'i,

constructed in 1840 as an aid to whaling ships navigating offshore.

The Brick Palace Site

In the small park between the harbor and the library is the foundation of an old house. If you didn't know what it was, you'd most likely pass it by. The depressed, flat slab of concrete in the middle of an otherwise grassy park is the foundation of what is believed to have been the first stone building ever constructed in the Hawaiian Islands, dating to 1801 and built for Kamehameha I (who used it as a storeroom). Two ex-cons from Australia supervised the construction from locally made bricks. The building eventually fell into total disrepair.

Hauola Stone

Another site which you would normally walk right by is the **Hauola Stone,** an ancient birthing stone which was reserved for Hawaiian royalty. At the tip of the breakwall on the north side of Lahaina Harbor, this large, smooth stone stands out from the others along the shoreline and is best viewed at low tide. Pregnant *ali'i* would come here to give birth in a natural chair surrounded by the soothing waters, and it's an interesting spot to reflect on what life was like only a short few hundred years ago.

Baldwin Missionary House

On the inland side of Front Street on the corner with Dickenson Street, you will notice the sprawling green lawn and whitewashed front of the historic **Baldwin Missionary House** (10am-4pm daily, $7 adults, $5 seniors). Established in 1834, this restored and peaceful property has stood since the days of the earliest missionaries, and was the home of Doctor/Reverend Dwight Baldwin, his wife Charlotte, and their eight children. Baldwin was the first modern doctor and dentist in Hawai'i (having studied at Harvard), and in the back of the museum are his tools of the trade. This building also served until 1868 as a dispensary, meeting room, and boardinghouse, and Rev. Baldwin was instrumental in not only educating scores of Hawaiian citizens, but also in helping to

PARKING IN LAHAINA

If you're looking for a good way to get into a fight, try finding parking in Lahaina while running late for an activity. A web of narrow streets and overpriced lots, Lahaina for most visitors is an expensive source of angst and confusion when it comes to parking.

But it doesn't have to be that way.

Here are a few tips to help cut through the confusion.

· Most street parking in Lahaina is good for three hours, and there is no such thing as parking meters. If you know that you're only going to be a few hours, there is no need to pay for a parking lot. Free street parking can be found on Dickenson and Waine'e Streets, and there is a large, three-hour parking lot on the corner of Prison and Front Streets. The three-hour lot is heavily patrolled, however, so if you "chance it," you'll most likely end up with a $60 ticket.

· While there is also free street parking on Front Street, attempting to parallel park on Front Street is like singing a solo in front of your school: The whole street is watching you, you are holding up traffic, and the space is most likely too small to begin with. Save yourself the hassle and don't even try.

· If you're eating dinner in Lahaina, there is free parking at Lahaina Harbor between the Courthouse and the harbor 7pm-7am, although you can't park in the back lot by the fishing boats because it's by permit only. On weekends and public holidays, there is free parking all day in the spaces in front of Kamehameha School by the junction of Prison and Front Streets.

· There is also free all-day parking in the lot behind the Front Street tennis courts. The spaces when you first pull in are reserved for the cultural center, but there is a dirt parking lot in the back as well as a paved parking lot by the back tennis courts. There is a sizable homeless population there; don't leave valuables in your car.

· Parking in a paid parking lot doesn't make your car any more secure. Only a few of them are monitored, but car break-ins happen at hiking trailheads and beaches as opposed to downtown Lahaina in broad daylight. The only reason you would ever need to pay for parking in Lahaina is for the convenience of being closer to where you're trying to go. There is enough free parking in Lahaina for everyone, although you might need to walk a few blocks to save a few bucks. Essentially, paying for parking is a convenience, but not a necessity.

· Luakini Street paralleling Front Street is a one-way street, with traffic running north to south on the south end of Dickenson, and south to north on the north end of Dickenson. Confused? Better to just avoid the street entirely.

· Allow yourself enough time. Parking may take 5-10 minutes; factor this in when scheduling your day.

fight the smallpox epidemic which struck the island in 1853. Various rooms contain period furniture and artifacts indicative of missionary life in Lahaina, and coin collectors will appreciate the array of historic coins that were used as legal tender in early Hawai'i, including silver bullion which was minted in Bolivia as early as the 1500s. Entrance to the museum also covers the Wo Hing Museum up the street, and if you purchase a $10 Passport to the Past, admission to the A&B Sugar Museum in Kahului and the Bailey House Museum in Wailuku are also included. While visiting in the daytime is educational enough, for a true experience of missionary life, take part in a candlelit tour 6pm-8:30pm every Friday evening.

Masters' Reading Room

Immediately next door to the Baldwin House is the **Masters' Reading Room,** which was originally a missionaries' storeroom, but was converted to an officers' club for ship's captains in 1834. It was restored to its original condition in 1970, and the downstairs is used for a

MISSIONARIES: "CAME TO DO GOOD AND STAYED TO DO WELL"

All around West Maui, from the Baldwin House in downtown Lahaina to the fallow fields of former sugar plantations, island visitors are surrounded by signs of the missionary influence.

The first Protestant missionaries arrived from New England in 1820 aboard a wooden brig named *Thaddeus* after a tortuous journey around Cape Horn. Led by Hiram Bingham (whose grandson would go on to "discover" Machu Picchu), the original missionaries immediately set to work crafting a moral compass for the wayward Hawaiians, who had abandoned their centuries-old religious system only a year earlier. A written form of the Hawaiian language was created, Bibles were printed, and within a few years a number of the Hawaiian nobility were converted to Christianity.

It didn't take long for the missionaries to start having children. In the same year of their arrival, the first European child was born in the Hawaiian Islands. The introduction of progeny would not only alter the social structure of the mission, but change the political and economic course of the kingdom of Hawai'i. Missionaries were forced to cope with the realities of raising children in faraway Hawai'i. Mission wages were woefully inadequate, a system of education was nonexistent, and sending their children to boarding school on the mainland was expensive and logistically difficult. With the issue of supporting their children weighing heavily on them, nearly half of the missionaries were threatening to abandon their posts by the 1840s.

The American Board of Commissioners for Foreign Missions (which had founded and funded the endeavor) agreed in 1848 to allow missionaries to engage in economic pursuits—including owning property. In an alignment of the economic stars, a momentous event known as the Great Mahele was planned by the Hawaiian monarchy in 1848. According to the terms of the Mahele—or division—a system of land ownership was established in Hawai'i to subdivide lands between the crown, the chiefs, and private citizens. Though native residents had two years to lay claim to their *kuleana*, or homestead lands, many citizens literally "didn't get the memo." By 1850 much of these lands became available for foreign purchase. Suddenly, what was once a religious mission began to take on the outline of a colony.

Though their parents remained dutifully devoted to the faith, the Hawaiian-born children of missionaries instead focused on economic opportunity. Samuel Alexander and Henry Baldwin—children of missionaries who arrived in 1831 and 1832—pooled their money in 1869 to buy 12 acres of Makawao sugar land for the grand total of $110. Today, the Alexander & Baldwin company has over 88,000 acres of land and assets of over $1.4 billion, is traded on the New York Stock Exchange, and has been listed as one of the 1,000 largest companies in America.

Another missionary child—Sanford Dole—became a central figure in the 1893 overthrow of the Hawaiian government and ultimately the president of the short-lived Republic of Hawaii. His cousin, James Dole, turned the island of Lana'i into the world's largest pineapple plantation.

Today, the legacy of Hawai'i's missionaries lives on in the real estate, business, agriculture, and ranching industries of Hawai'i. Names such as Baldwin, Dole, Cooke, Castle, and Rice are plastered on everything from arts center to high schools to public parks.

Think about this while you stand in the Baldwin Missionary House. The people who founded and inhabited these sites would ultimately end up changing the course of Hawai'i's history—for better or for worse.

gift and art gallery associated with the Village Gallery up the road. Uniquely constructed of coral and stone, these two venerable buildings constitute the oldest standing Western structures on Maui.

Plantation Museum

For a look at a period of Lahaina's history that didn't have to do with whalers, missionaries, or Hawaiian royalty, idle on over to the Wharf Cinema Center and climb the stairs to the third story for a glimpse inside the informative **Plantation Museum** (9am-6pm daily, free). Although it isn't much larger than a closet, there are dozens of old photos showing life during plantation times as well as a video detailing harvesting sugarcane. The Pioneer Mill was the social and economic engine of the West Side for the better part of 100 years, and the plantation days are just as much a part of Lahaina's heritage as harpoons, grog, and Bibles. A visit here only takes a couple of minutes, but you'll be glad you stopped in.

Wo Hing Museum

The **Wo Hing Museum** (858 Front St., 10am-4pm daily, $7) is a small Chinese museum sandwiched between the modern commercial ventures of Front Street. Built in 1912 as a social and religious hall for Chinese workers, it's been placed on the National Register of Historic Places. Downstairs are displays, and upstairs is the temple altar. In the cookhouse next door, you can see film clips of Hawai'i taken by Thomas Edison in 1898 and 1906. On the Chinese New Year, the Wo Hing Museum is the center of the activities that play out on Front Street. The entrance fee is also good for entrance to the Baldwin House.

Maria Lanakila Church

If you're wandering central Lahaina around the top of the hour, there's a good chance you'll hear **Maria Lanakila Church** (712 Waine'e St., www.marialanakila.org) before you see it. Stoically occupying the corner of Waine'e and Dickenson Streets, Maria Lanakila is the oldest Catholic church on the island, established

in 1846. The current structure has been around since 1873, and the doors to the church are open to the public.

Hale Pa'ahao

When Luakini crosses Prison Street, turn left and walk a few yards to **Hale Pa'ahao** (10am-4pm daily, free), better known as Lahaina's old prison. This is one of the more historically informative sights in Lahaina. Now the peaceful courtyard inside the prison walls is a place of serenity and calm where benches rest beneath the shade of a mango tree, but there was once a time when this compound housed dozens of sailors and Hawaiians who had violated the laws set forth by the royalty and their missionary advisors. To get an idea of an offense that would land you in the Lahaina slammer, read the list from the 1850s posted on the wall of one of the wooden cells. The top three offenses by island felons were drunkenness, assault, and adultery— just as you would expect of a port town! Though the town's original jail was in the basement of the courthouse by Lahaina Harbor, the need for a larger penitentiary led to the coral blocks of the Lahaina fort being taken apart and moved across town to build the tall walls which surround Hale Pa'ahao today. An old wooden rowboat rests in the corner of the compound, serving as a reminder for how whalers would move between ship and shore en route to getting themselves in trouble.

Waiola Church and Cemetery

Moving south down Waine'e Street, you will soon come to the **Waiola Church and Cemetery** (535 Waine'e St., www.waiola-church.org) on the right side of the road, which is essentially where Christianity on Maui began. The two female members of the royalty, Queen Ka'ahumanu and Queen Keopualani, were among the first to embrace the Christian religion, and when the capital of the kingdom was established in Lahaina, a small church was formally dedicated at Waiola in 1823. Though there have been many ups and downs for the native Hawaiian population

MOKU'ULA: THE ANCIENT CAPITAL OF HAWAI'I

Up until 1845 the town of Lahaina served as the royal capital of Hawai'i. Generations of rulers from King Kamehameha on down ruled the kingdom from this historic, sun-drenched shore, and some of the most notable events in Hawaiian history were witnessed by this very town.

If Lahaina was so important, you ask, then where is the royal palace? Where is the seat of the monarchy? Where, exactly, was the capital?

Unfortunately, when the capital was moved to Honolulu in 1845, the site of the former capital—Moku'ula—was abandoned and left to decay. Where once a large fishpond that was the home of *ali'i* and royalty existed, there now sits an overgrown baseball field frequented by the island's homeless. If ever there were a fall from grace, it is the site of Moku'ula.

All hope is not lost for the former capital, however, as nonprofit group **Friends of Moku'ula** (808/661-3659, www.mokuula. com) is committed to the process of restoring the nearly forgotten site across from the area on Front Street where the 505 shopping center now stands. During the time of ancient Hawai'i when royalty called this place home, there was a 25-acre *loko*, or fishpond named Mokuhinia that was fed by the streams flowing down from Mauna Kahalawai. In the middle of this pond was a small island—Moku'ula—and only the highest chiefs and Hawaiian royalty were allowed to set foot on it. Walking distance from the ocean and framed by the mountainous backdrop, it must have been a sight to behold.

When the capital was moved, the stream was diverted to irrigate the sugar crop, and the Mokuhinia fishpond became a festering swamp of mosquitoes and bugs. Taking matters into their own hands, mill workers filled the pond with dirt in 1914. The ballfield and parking structures that stand in its place were subsequently constructed on top.

Just because Moku'ula isn't visible, however, doesn't mean that it is gone. Archaeologists estimate that the site still exists about three feet below the surface, and digs have yielded artifacts that show evidence of the ancient fishpond. Nevertheless, like many endeavors, raising funds is always an issue, and the Friends of Moku'ula are simultaneously working to raise awareness and funding toward a major restoration of the former royal site. The group envisions the site as more than just a historic landmark, but rather an educational resource about the greater Hawaiian culture.

For a more in-depth look at both the history and future of Moku'ula, take one of the **Maui Nei** (505 Front St., 808/661-9494, www.maui-nei.com) 2.5-hour cultural walking tours which not only cover many of the historic sites of Lahaina, but also spend ample time discussing the case of Moku'ula. Tours are $60/adult, and you can also add a meal at Pacific'O restaurant for an additional $35. If you fancy yourself a historian or have an interest in Hawaiian history, there are few tours that will provide the level of insight offered on this cultural one.

over the last 200 years, one thing which has always remained is the church at Waiola. It's as old and storied as the history of foreigners on Hawaiian land. Queen Keopuolani herself is buried in the Royal Tomb in the small cemetery next door, as is the revered Governor Hoapili and the young Princess Nahi'ena'ena. As you might imagine, this is a spot of immense cultural significance and pride for the Hawaiian people and should be treated with the utmost respect.

Kamehameha Iki Park

Access the beach via **Kamehameha Iki Park** for a stroll along the ocean. In this small, oceanfront park, you will find a thatched roof canoe *hale* as well as signs pertaining to the historical significance of the area. This stretch of shoreline was once a gathering place of Hawaiian royalty. The **Hui O Wa'a Kaulua Canoe Club** continues to maintain their office and workshop on the grounds. There is a beach volleyball court here, and it's is a popular hangout

Lahaina Jodo Mission

© MARK DRIESSEN

with surf schools and visitors. At low tide you can stroll along the shoreline towards Lahaina Harbor and end up back at the center of town.

Lahaina Jodo Mission

On the northern end of Lahaina by Baby Beach and Mala Wharf, you'll find **Lahaina Jodo Mission** (12 Ala Moana St., 808/661-4304, www.lahainajodomission.org) by turning off Front Street where a sign over a building reads "Jesus Coming Soon." Turn left toward the beach and you'll immediately spot the three-tiered wooden pagoda down at the end of the road. The temple bell welcomes you at the entrance gate, and a giant bronze Buddha sits exposed to the elements on a raised stone platform nearby. The largest Buddha found outside of Asia, this seated Amita Buddha image was dedicated in 1968 in commemoration of the centennial of the arrival of Japanese workers in Hawai'i. You may stroll around, and while the buildings are closed to the public, you can climb the steps of the main building to peek into the temple. It's a perfect spot for solitary meditation if you've had enough of frenetic Lahaina. Buddha's birthday is celebrated here every April.

Hale Pa'i Printing Museum

All the way at the top of Lahainaluna Road on the grounds of Lahainaluna High School (which is the oldest American high school west of the Rocky Mountains, having been founded in 1831), **Hale Pa'i Printing Museum** (10am-4pm Mon.-Wed.) provides a phenomenally informative view into the literary past of the Hawaiian Islands. If you're involved in the education field or fancy yourself a historian, this is a must-stop venue for a look at the history of Hawai'i's printed past.

In addition to the old printing press, there are a host of native Hawaiian artifacts. This small, out-of-the-way museum in the parking lot of the island's oldest school is the best learning experience you'll find on the island's West Side about the development of modern Hawai'i.

FROM SUGAR TO COFFEE

The hills above Lahaina, once covered in flowing green sugarcane, have seen the last of their harvest. Though the cane haul roads and irrigation ditches that divided them are still in place, many of the fields themselves either now lay fallow or are overrun with tall grass. Pioneer Mill—the company that had grown sugar in West Maui since 1862 and employed more than 1,600 laborers at its peak—hasn't harvested sugarcane since 1999 when it was forced to close due to mounting debt and rising costs. Nevertheless, many are surprised to find it gone.

As with most things that die, however, something new will grow in its place. Even though some of the land has gone toward development (Launiupoko), other parts are now planted in a different crop that is surging in popularity: coffee.

Although coffee was first commercially grown in West Maui as early as 1988 (on land once used for sugar), the Ka'anapali Estate Coffee enterprise was forced to close in 2002.

MauiGrown Coffee (www.mauigrowncoffee.com) took over the land and now plants over 350 acres of the caffeinated beans. The coffee farms are on the hillside above Ka'anapali just past the Pu'ukoli'i sugar train station. Visitors can take a self-guided drive through rows of the yellow catura, red catuai, typica, and moka beans which are blended into fresh Maui coffee. MauiGrown Coffee's commercial headquarters are—ironically enough—at the base of the old Pioneer Mill Smokestack at the bottom of Lahainaluna Road.

Ka'anapali Coffee Farms isn't the only place you can find coffee in West Maui. High on the slopes above Launiupoko Beach Park, **Piliani Kope Farm** (www.pilianikopefarm.com) is a boutique coffee operation that offers tours and a rustic tasting room.

If you're a coffee aficionado, stop in at either of these farms for more info on the industry and a sip of black elixir. Better yet, buy some beans to take home with you.

Pioneer Mill Smokestack

Set at the bottom of Lahainaluna Road, this lonely site once housed an enormous sugar mill that employed tens of thousands of island workers over the course of a 139-year span. All that remains of the legendary mill now, however, is this 200-foot concrete smokestack which was once the island's tallest structure. During the plantation era, over 40 plantation camps were scattered from Olowalu to Kapalua, and the hills constantly rumbled with the sound of rocks being moved, cane being hauled, or the crackle of cane fires illuminated the sky. With the closure of the mill in 1999, however, the aging structure was torn down and the smokestack was in dire need of repairs. Not wanting to lose an island landmark (for years also a navigational marker for sailors), the Lahaina Restoration Foundation made it its mission to restore the site and protect the historic icon. Information placards are scattered about the site, and those interested in helping protect the

smokestack can participate in the "buy a brick" program to raise funds for additional renovations. Engraved, personalized bricks start at $125. For more information you can contact the Lahaina Restoration Foundation office at 808/661-3262.

While visiting the smokestack, also stop in at the **MauiGrown Coffee** (277 Lahainaluna Rd., 808/661-2728, www.mauigrowncoffee.com, 6:30am-5pm Mon.-Sat.) store for a bag of Ka'anapali coffee and an explanation on how 350 acres of former sugar land have given rise to a new chapter of West Side agriculture.

Sugar Cane Train

The historic **Sugar Cane Train** (975 Limahana Pl., 808/661-0080, www.sugarcanetrain.com, $23 adults, $16 children) continues to be the island's only train ride and as such remains a novelty. It's a misnomer, since there hasn't been any sugarcane since Pioneer Mill shuttered its operations in 1999, and the six-mile route now wraps its way through residential backyards and industrial construction sites. Nevertheless, the old-fashioned trestle is still the highlight of the trip and provides a few views looking out toward the water. The train ride is popular with young children and those with a love for trains, and the narration provides a decent history about the plantation era of Lahaina. Round-trip trains depart Lahaina three times daily at 11:05am, 1pm, and 2pm, and this is also an alternative (albeit expensive) way of transporting yourself to the resort area of Ka'anapali.

SOUTH OF LAHAINA
Olowalu Petroglyphs

For every 1,000 people who snorkel at Olowalu, probably only one makes it back to the *ki'i pohaku*, or petroglyphs behind the Olowalu General Store. Hidden a half mile back in the recesses of Olowalu valley, the 70 rock carvings on the face of Pu'u Kilea date to a time nearly 300 years ago when there was no written language and drawings were one of the only ways of communicating other than storytelling, song, or dance. The Olowalu valley is an area which is heavily steeped in Hawaiian history, and though a century of sugar cultivation and the encroachment of modern development has eroded the traditional village sites, there are still a number of families living back in the valley who aim to perpetuate the lifestyle of their ancestors. To find the petroglyphs, drive on the road behind the Olowalu fruit stand at mile marker 15 and proceed on the paved segment which runs back toward the valley. After half a mile you will see signs for the Olowalu Cultural Reserve, and when the road turns to dirt, the petroglyphs will be on the rock face about 200 yards down. Unfortunately, some of the petroglyphs have been vandalized, so visitors are kindly asked to keep a respectful distance from the rock face. A small table on the other side of the dirt road is a peaceful place for a picnic.

Piliani Kope Coffee Farm

If you've ever been interested in coffee, drink coffee regularly, or are just obsessed with coffee culture, the **Piliani Kope Coffee Farm** (15 Wailau Pl., 808/661-5479, www.pilianikope-farm.com) high on the hill in the Launiupoko subdivision offers tours that will walk you through every step of the coffee process. Hawai'i is the only U.S. state where coffee is commercially harvested. Aside from having a stunning ocean view, this working coffee farm produces some of the island's best coffee and is an educational experience. Ninety-minute tours are held regularly on Tuesday and Thursday during the cooler morning hours at $10/person. The farm just requests that you call a couple of days ahead to confirm the exact timing. During September through December when the farm is processing coffee, there is an in-depth, three-hour, $90/person processing tour covering every single aspect of the growing and roasting process. This tour also includes lunch and offers the island's best insight into what has become the fastest-growing and most successful crop on Maui.

Maui Dragon Fruit Farm

If exotic fruit that you've never heard of is more interesting to you than coffee, then the **Maui Dragon Fruit Farm** (833 Punakea Lp., 808/264-6127, www.mauidragonfruit.com), also in the Launiupoko subdivision, will make for a curious combination of agriculture and adventure. Dragon fruit is a tropical fruit native to Central and South America, although it's most often seen in markets throughout Southeast Asia. With the consistency of an apple but the look of an exotic poppy seed muffin, dragon fruit is one of the most colorfully named as well as colorful produce species on the island. In addition to the dragon fruit, various other crops are grown on this certified organic farm. Daily walking tours take place 1pm-2pm daily for $25/adult. Additional adventure activities are available throughout the farm such as a 450-foot-long zipline and an enormous plastic "Aquaball," which is filled with water and then rolled 450 feet downhill (with you inside, of course). The zipline inclusion is $80/adult or $50/child, and the Aquaball is $100/

adult and $70/child. Zipline tours of the farm take place at 10am, 2pm, and 5pm, and the Aquaball tour is at either 11:30am or 3:30pm.

Combine the farm tour, the zipline, and the Aquaball into a zany package for $140/adult or $100/child.

Shopping

KAPALUA, NAPILI, AND HONOKOWAI

Shopping in the northwestern corner of the island is utilitarian, paling in comparison to the shops of Ka'anapali and Lahaina. Nevertheless, there are still a few stores worthy of a mention of you're staying in the area and need some emergency retail therapy.

In Kapalua, the **Honolua Store** (502 Office Rd., 808/665-9105, 6am-6:30pm daily) has a small apparel and souvenir section to accompany the food market, and if you save your receipt from any purchase, you will receive a free gift on your next time shopping there.

For Polynesian jewelry, **La Perle** (700 Office Rd., 808/669-8466, 10am-7pm Mon.-Sat., 10am-6pm Sun.) is a small shop next to Sansei restaurant which specializes in black pearls and gold jewelry.

Down the road in Kahana, both **HIM** (808/281-1418, www.himmaui.com) as well as **Women Who Run With Wolves** (808/665-0786, www.womenwhorunwithwolves.com, 10am-6pm daily) are in the downstairs portion of the Kahana Manor (4310 Honoapi'ilani Rd.) and offer the best apparel and accessory shopping for men and women that you'll find on the northwest side.

KA'ANAPALI
Whalers Village

Without a doubt, the undisputed epicenter of the Ka'anapali shopping scene is **Whalers Village** (2435 Ka'anapali Pkwy., 808/661-4567, www.whalersvillage.com, 9:30am-10pm daily), smack in the middle of Ka'anapali Beach between the Whaler hotel and the Westin Resort. Three levels of restaurants, clothing boutiques, jewelry galleries, and kiosks, Whalers Village is the see-and-be-seen spot for all of your island

souvenir shopping. While many of the stores are name-brand outlets you're already familiar with (a Prada purse, anyone?), there are still a handful of locally run stores. Get your parking validated since the garage rates are expensive.

If you park in the Whalers Village garage, you can't help but walk directly past **Totally Hawaiian** (808/667-4070, www.totallyhawaiian.com), a clean and brightly illuminated gift gallery featuring the wares of over 100 local artists. Works of craftsmanship from hand-turned wood bowls to hand-painted Hawaiian gourds are all on display, as is an impressive collection of Ni'ihau jewelry featuring shells from the island of Ni'ihau which are some of the smallest and rarest in the world. Stop in for a look. There's a fascinating array of ancient Hawaiian weapons handcrafted from shark's teeth and wood.

"Coastal lifestyle emporium" **Sand People** (808/662-8785, www.sandpeople.com) features a slew of home decor and furnishing which have been inspired by the ocean or shoreline. This is a good place to find that whitewashed driftwood picture frame you've been searching for, or the last-minute wedding gift you've been putting off.

Other popular apparel favorites range from **Blue Ginger** (808/667-5793, www.blueginger.com), a store specializing in women's and children's resort wear, to **Maggie Coulombe** (808/344-6672, www.maggiecoulombe.com), a world-renowned dress fashionista who has clothed some of the world's top celebrities.

Shops at the Hyatt Regency

While nearly all of the Ka'anapali shopping takes place at Whalers Village, there are enough stores in the lobby of the Hyatt at the far southern end of the Ka'anapali strip that it's at least worth a mention. A handful of galleries, souvenir stores, clothing boutiques, and jewelry outlets populate the recesses of the lobby.

LAHAINA

Frenetic and fast-paced, Lahaina is the shopping capital of Maui. The section of Front Street between the Old Lahaina Center and the 505 shopping center is where you'll find the majority of shops.

◖ Front Street

Front Street is a sight unto itself that centers around commerce and a voracious love of shopping. Front Street has been listed as one of the "Great Streets in America" by the American Planning Association. Walking the length of this vivacious thoroughfare is one of the West Side's most popular activities. Along this flat, oceanfront stretch you'll find everything from art galleries to surf shops all compressed together in a nonstop string of merchandise. Most shops are open 9am-10pm.

The **Wyland Gallery** (711 Front St., 808/667-2285, www.wyland.com) offers the artist's trademark array of marine life scenes in a perfect oceanfront location. On the opposite side of the street, acclaimed photographer **Peter Lik** (712 Front St., 808/661-6623, www.peterlik.com) has a popular showroom of his oversize art with the ability to transport you directly into the photograph. Other galleries of note are **Sargent's Fine Art** (802 Front St., 808/667-4030, www.sargentsfineart.com) on the corner of Lahainaluna Road, the **Village Gallery** (120 Dickenson St., 808/661-5199, www.villagegalleriesmaui.com), and **Martin Lawrence** (808/661-1788, www.martinlawrence.com). Those with a passion for art should also remember that every Friday night is **art night** in Lahaina, when many galleries put on their finest show, featuring artist appearances or live jazz, 7pm-10pm.

Bella Lulu (626 Front St., 808/667-5657) and **Serendipity** (752 Front St., 808/667-7070, www.serendipitymaui.com) offer unique female apparel. **Hale Zen** (180 Dickenson St., 808/661-4802, www.halezen.com)—a

shopping for crafts in Lahaina

WHAT'S WITH ALL THE CHEAP ACTIVITY SIGNS?

Walking around Front Street in Lahaina, it only takes about three minutes to notice that every other shop is offering discount activities at rates that are too good to be true. A helicopter ride for $49? Bike down the volcano for $29? A lu'au for $9? There's got to be a catch.

Yes, there is a catch, but it doesn't mean the rates aren't real.

In order to cash in on the advertised rates, you are essentially signing yourself up to endure a timeshare presentation separate from the activity that lasts a couple of hours. While no one plans on going to a meeting while on vacation, it could end up saving you a bundle on many of your island activities in the long run.

A word of caution, however, before you start committing to everything on the whiteboard. Often the activity providers (particularly the Molokini snorkeling tours) are with companies that aren't in the upper echelon of their genre, so comb over the particulars of the agreement (90 percent of afternoon Molokini snorkeling tours don't end up going to Molokini). Before committing to a discounted lu'au, find out which lu'au it is to see if it's one you want to attend.

Even though you might not plan on buying a timeshare, many of these closers could sell ice to an eskimo. You could end up walking out with the most expensive luau you'll ever attend (but you now "own a piece of Maui").

---

two-minute walk up Dickenson Street—is a local favorite for everything from homewares to candles, lotions, and crafts from local artists. For jewelry, stop into **Glass Mango Designs** (858 Front St., 808.662-8500, www.glass-mango.com) for a colorful selection of "wearable art."

A notable stop that has nothing to do with clothing, jewelry, photos, or paintings, is **Lahaina Scrimshaw** (845 Front St., 808/667-9232, www.lahainascrimshawmaui.com), a classic retail outpost featuring the historic seafarers' craft of carving scenes on ivory. Or, just in front of Pioneer Inn, you could always just throw shopping to the wind and get your photo taken with a parrot on your head (Wed.-Sun. evenings).

505 Front Street

Down at the southern end of Front Street, most shops are open 9am-9pm, including several art shops, clothing shops, and a **Whalers General Store** for sundries.

Wharf Cinema Center

Right across from the banyan tree, the **Wharf Cinema Center** (www.thewharfcinemacenter. com) is a three-story beehive of merchandise that constantly buzzes with shoppers. For art,

check out the **Simon-Jon Gallery** (808/667-4088), and for jewelry, the **Jade Tiki** (808/661-2008, www.mauitikigoddess.com) offers Burmese jade in a nice deviation from the ubiquitous black pearl markets. There's also a bookstore on the third story. The most popular souvenirs are from the wooden tiki carvers who sit out on the sidewalk and expertly chisel crafts to the glee of onlookers.

Banyan Tree Market

While the Friday art nights are always a festive event, those who prefer smaller artists are encouraged to visit the fair beneath the banyan tree, held on various weekends throughout the year 9am-5pm. For a full schedule on when the art fair is on, visit www.lahaina-arts/events.

Lahaina Cannery Mall

Although many locals have essentially left it for dead, there are enough visitors who still frequent **Lahaina Cannery Mall** (1221 Honoapi'ilani Hwy., www.lahainacannery. com, 9:30am-9pm Mon.-Sat., 9:30am-7pm Sun.) to keep a few stores open. Stores of note include **Honolua Surf Co.** (808/661-5777, www.honoluasurf.com) which has the same apparel as you would find in Whalers Village or on Front Street for slightly reduced rates, and

Maui Toy Works (808/661-4766), the de facto stop for picking up children's gifts.

Lahaina Gateway Center
On the inland side of the highway across from the Lahaina Cannery Mall is the **Lahaina Gateway Center** (305 Keawe St., www.lahainagateway.com, 9:30am-9pm daily) where you'll find **Local Motion** (808/661-7873, www.localmotionhawaii.com) surf shop, **Mahina** (808/661-0383, www.mahinamaui.com) women's clothing boutique, and **Maui Dive and Surf** (808/661-5388, www.mauidiveshop.com) for ocean-related merchandise. Walking distance along the highway back toward the center of Lahaina, you will also find **West Side Vibes** (1087 Limahana Pl., 808/667-1900, www.westsidevibes.com, 10am-7pm Mon.-Sat., noon-6pm Sun.), the Lahaina head shop for all of your reggae-inspired clothing and smoking-related accessories.

SOUTH OF LAHAINA
Olowalu General Store
The only shopping to be found anywhere south of Lahaina is at **Olowalu General Store** (820 Olowalu Village Rd., 808/667-2883, 5am-7pm daily) where you can pick up refreshingly cheap clothing and Olowalu merchandise. This is a good place for finding a shirt that no one else will have, and also a great place to shop to help support local small businesses.

Entertainment

West Maui is the island's entertainment hot spot. Here you'll find the island's best lu'aus and most happening bars. You can't walk more than 10 yards in Lahaina without tripping over an evening drink special. More than just booze and bad decisions, West Maui is also home to family entertainment options ranging from free hula performances and whale lectures to evening magic performances. Despite the happening surroundings, however, if you're the clubbing type who likes to party into the wee hours of the morning, you'll be out of luck since most bars close by 11pm, and only a handful stay open later than 1am. Also, even though almost all of the nightlife options involve bars and pubs that have lively atmospheres, the options for dancing are woefully inadequate. For the most up-to-date info on the latest evening scene, pick up a free copy of *Maui Time* newspaper, or, check out The Grid section on the website at www.mauitime.com.

KAPALUA, NAPILI, AND HONOKOWAI
Evening Shows
Can't get enough of *ki ho'alu* (slack key guitar)? The **Masters of Slack Key** (5900 Lower Honoapi'ilani Rd., www.slackkeyshow.com, 7:30pm Wed.) performance at the Aloha Pavilion of the Napili Kai Beach Resort is the best show you'll find on the island. Tickets can either be purchased online or at 6:45pm when the doors first open. Prices for the show are normally $38, although you can also book a package dinner combo for $79 which includes a sunset dinner at the Sea House restaurant immediately before the show.

Bars, Live Music, and Nightlife
The late-night karaoke sessions at **Sansei** (600 Office Rd., 808/669-6286, www.sanseihawaii.com, 5:30pm-10pm Mon.-Thurs., 5:30pm-1am Fri.-Sat.) restaurant in the Kapalua resort are the most happening evenings on the northwestern side. This popular sushi and sake bar stays open until 1am on Thursday and Friday during karaoke night, and more so than the drinks and the singing, the main draw is the award-winning late-night menu (10pm-1am) that offers dozens of sushi plates at heavily discounted rates.

A short walk away at the Ritz-Carlton hotel you can find live music in the **Alaloa Lounge** Thursday-Monday evenings. It has the most consistent live music in the Kapalua resort.

In the Kahana Gateway Center, **Maui Brewing Company** (4405 Honoapi'ilani Hwy., 808/669-3474, www.mauibrewingco. com, open until midnight) is the island's only brewery. Sit at the bar so you can keep your beer cold on the slab of ice that's inside the bar. There are over a dozen beers only available on draft at the brewery. My personal favorite brews are the La Perouse White and the Drip Dry Coffee Stout.

Dollie's (4310 Lower Honoapi'ilani Rd., 808/669-0266, www.dolliespizzakahana.com, open until midnight) is the West Side's de facto sports bar where cheap beer and good pizza are served throughout the night. This is where island locals come to catch the Monday Night Football game or Sunday NFL. Fifteen different televisions also show NBA, hockey, college sports, and whichever game you're hoping to catch.

In the strip mall by Times Supermarket in Honokowai **Soup Nutz/Java Jazz** (3350 Lower Honoapi'ilani Rd., 808/667-0787, www. javajazz.net, open until 10pm) has live music seven nights a week 7pm-10pm in an eccentric, artsy, and dimly lit interior. Coffee shop by day and trendy parlor by night, this establishment has a decor that includes a bear rug, a disco ball, and a chandelier made up of dozens of different wine bottles. This is a good place to sit and listen to some underground acoustic artists.

KA'ANAPALI
Whalers Village
Of the few daytime entertainment options which don't involve the beach (or golf), the **free whale talks** in Whalers Village take place with the most regularity. In the Whalers Museum on the third story of the mall, guest speakers from NOAA and the Hawaiian Islands Humpback Whale National Marine Sanctuary regularly give free lectures about the island's winter visitors. Talks are every Thursday, Friday, and Saturday 11am-noon and 2pm-3pm. Mention that you're attending the talk and you'll gain free entry to the museum (usually $3).

Beyond the free whale talks, the center stage area at Whalers Village constantly teems with free events. Stalwarts of the entertainment schedule include lei making classes, hula classes, arts and crafts sessions, and live music on most weekend nights. While the schedule of events is constantly shifting, you can visit www. whalersvillage.com for an up-to-date calendar of the current month's activities.

For live music, at any time of the afternoon you can find a band or ukulele musician strumming live tunes along the Ka'anapali strip. Hula Grill in Whalers Village also has live entertainment every afternoon at the barefoot beach bar, and this is one of the more popular venues for an afternoon drink and soothing island tunes.

Magic Dinner Theater
The only show in Ka'anapali that isn't a lu'au is the **Kupanaha Magic Dinner Theater** (2525 Ka'anapali Pkwy., 808/262-8450, www.kupanaha.com, 4:30pm-7:30pm Mon.-Sat. evenings, $79 adults, $55 teens, $39 kids), which is a great choice if you want to experience a hula performance as well as a magic show but only have a single night to do so. Staged inside the Ka'anapali Beach Hotel, this three-hour show features everything from tableside magic during the dinner service to an illusionist sawing a lady in half. To add some cultural flare, the Kupanaha hula dancers chant and dance their way through ancient Hawaiian lore. You're treated to an authentic cultural performance as well as head-scratching magic without ever having to leave your seat. In addition to the magic and the hula, the food is just as good as you would expect at a nice Ka'anapali restaurant, and this show is a great value for family entertainment considering all that is included.

Lu'aus
There is no shortage of lu'aus to be found along the Ka'anapali strip. While the best lu'au on the island (Old Lahaina Luau) is in nearby Lahaina, there are four lu'aus in Ka'anapali for those who would prefer to simply stroll from

their resort down to the lu'au grounds. Also, if the only reason you want to go to a lu'au is for the fire dancing, you'll want to choose one of the lu'aus here in Ka'anapali for your fire twirling fix. All will feature buffet food mass produced for over 100 people, all will feature local craft artisans, and all will offer some sort of premium seating for an added price. The premium seating doesn't make a difference, so you're better off saving the money and sticking with a regular seat. Also, inquire about exactly what time the show starts, since most schedules vary by about 30 minutes during winter versus summer due to the sun setting at different times. Most, however, begin at either 5 or 5:30pm. Ka'anapali can experience higher winds and a greater likelihood of rain than nearby Lahaina, so the chances of the lu'au needing to be moved inside or cancelled are higher. Most nights are gorgeous, but if you want to guarantee calm conditions, you'll have better luck in Lahaina.

Of the numerous lu'aus in Ka'anapali, the best show is the **Wailele Polynesian Luau** (2365 Ka'anapali Pkwy., 808/667-2525, www. westinmaui.com) at the Westin Maui resort. The fire dancers here are the best, and the food is above average when compared to the other options. Also, the backdrop for the show faces out toward the ocean as opposed to being hunkered in the corner of a resort. The fast-paced performance weaves a storyline of tales from various corners of Polynesia. The one thing you don't get here is the unearthing of the pig experience. Shows take place Tuesday and Thursday evenings (as well as Sunday during busier times of the year), and prices range between $110 and $135 for adults and $65-80 for kids. If you're coming from elsewhere and will be driving to Ka'anapali, the one downside of this show is that parking can be a little challenging. Your best bet is to try and find a free beach parking spot in the lot between Whalers Village and the entrance to the Westin. If you can't find any free spots, your most economical option is going to be parking in the Whalers Village garage and then buying something small (such as an ice cream or a quick beer after the show)

to get your parking validated (one pink sticker is good for three hours of parking).

Ka'anapali Sunset Luau at Black Rock (2605 Ka'anapali Pkwy., 808/877-4852, www. sheratonmauiluau.com) is at the Sheraton resort. The crowds here aren't quite as large as other shows, and the grassy lu'au grounds are more spacious. While the food is fine and the dancers are entertaining, the best part about this show is the atmosphere of looking out at Pu'u Keka'a and experiencing the torch lighting ceremony. While children are welcome to enjoy the show, it mainly caters to couples and adults. The lu'au takes place Monday and Wednesday evenings. Prices range $105-115 for adults and $57-67 for children.

At the far end of the beach at the southern tip of Ka'anapali, the **Drums of the Pacific** (200 Nohea Kai, 808/667-4727) at the Hyatt resort is managed by the same production company (Tihati) as the show at the Sheraton, so you can expect something similar. The lu'au at the Hyatt is larger than the one at the Sheraton. While the fire dancing and the performance are on par with other Ka'anapali shows, the food portion of the evening leaves much to be desired. Prices are $105-115 for adults, $49-61 for kids, and shows take place every evening except Sunday.

On the northern side of Pu'u Keka'a facing out toward the ocean, the **Royal Lahaina Luau** (2780 Keka'a Dr., 808/661-9119, www. royallahaina.com) is a Ka'anapali original and the best option for those traveling with children. This is the island's longest running lu'au (although don't confuse it with *Old* Lahaina Luau, which is better), and while there's no shaking the tourist trap kitsch, there's a palpable charm that goes along with the old-school venue. Everything over on this side of "the rock" is more laid-back than along the main Ka'anapali strip. A nice bonus right away is that parking for the show is ample, easy, and only $5. Although the show doesn't face the beach, it's nevertheless set along a wide stretch of sand, and guests are encouraged to watch the sun go down while sipping a drink from the lu'au grounds. The show features a fire dance finale, and the entertainers will bring children on stage for an impromptu hula lesson. The food is average and what you would expect from a large lu'au. Mai tais and Blue Hawaiians are included in the price of the ticket, but premium drinks will cost extra at the bar. During summer the lu'au takes place daily 6pm-8:30pm, while September through May there aren't any shows on Saturday or Monday and the festivities begin at 5:30pm.

Bars, Live Music, and Nightlife

Most of the bar scene in Ka'anapali plays out at the pool bars within the resorts. My favorite is the **Grotto Bar at the Hyatt,** which is tucked beneath two different waterfalls. While the happy hour and dinner scene can be fun, if you're looking for anything later than 10pm, you're going to have to get a cab down to Lahaina. **Hula Grill** in Whalers Village has live music every afternoon and evening, and neighboring **Leilani's** occasionally has live music during happy hour. There is also live music on the center stage of **Whalers Village** on Friday and Sunday evenings, and most restaurants and lobbies inside the resorts will also provide it during the later afternoons, sunset, and peak dinner hours.

The only place in Ka'anapali with anything that resembles proper nightlife is **Paradise Grill** (2291 Ka'anapali Pkwy., 808/662-3700, www. paradisegrillkb.com, open until 2am) featuring live entertainment every night 10pm-1:30am. Paradise Grill and the associated Mello's Bar are on the corner of Ka'anapali Parkway and Honoapi'ilani Highway. It's the first building you see at the main entrance to the Ka'anapali resort. Most of the late-night entertainment takes place downstairs in Mello's, while the upstairs section of the restaurant usually has live music during the dinner hours 6pm-9pm. Expect to find acoustic music upstairs during dinner, and rock, reggae, and karaoke later hours downstairs.

LAHAINA
Hula Shows
The **free hula shows** at the **Lahaina Cannery**

Mall (1221 Honoapi'ilani Highway by Safeway) take place in the center of the mall at 1pm on weekends, and evening shows begin at 7pm on Tuesday and Thursday.

Theater

At **Warren and Annabelle's** (900 Front St., 808/667-6244, www.warrenandannabelles. com, 5pm Mon.-Sat., $61 show, $101 package), any skepticism you might have had about attending a magic show in Maui will be immediately erased the moment you walk into Annabelle's secret parlor. Much more than a simple sleight of hand show, this enchanting evening revolves around the legend of Annabelle—a ghost—whose swanky parlor you have the pleasure of dining in for the evening. After making your way through a secret entrance, you are welcomed into a plush lounge where the sound of piano keys accompanies the clink of oversize wine glasses. The high level of service starts immediately, as the refined waitstaff zip about with the air of a caffeinated butler. Settling into an overstuffed chair, guests can relax with some beverages from the bar and dine on gourmet *pupus.* Once dinner is through it's on to the intimate 78-seat theater. Be warned that if you sit in the front row you'll end up becoming a part of the show. Two parts magic and three parts comedy, this performance will leave you holding your sides in laughter and shaking your head at the magical mystery taking place on the stage. Do yourself a favor and spend the extra $40 for the package including cocktails and appetizers. Due to Maui County liquor laws, this show is only for those 21 or older. Even though a second show is added at 7:30pm during busier times of the year, reservations are highly recommended.

◖ 'Ulalena

'Ulalena (Maui Theatre, 808/856-7900, www. mauitheatre.com, 6:30pm Mon.-Fri., $40-80) is a captivating show that details the history of the Hawaiian Islands. Told through chant, dance, and visual effects, the show takes place in the 680-seat Maui Theatre which is something you would expect to find in Vegas or

New York—not in the middle of a parking lot in Lahaina. The show is musical, performed without words. Because of the use of creative audience participation, words aren't necessary. (Have you ever experienced 500 people making the sound of a rainstorm with only their hands?). Ticket prices vary depending on seats and packages; the most expensive tickets will allow you to spend 20 minutes with the cast. If you're a fan of shows or have an interest in Hawaiian history, this isn't an evening to be missed.

Art Night

Friday night is **Art Night in Lahaina.** In keeping with its status as the cultural center of Maui, Lahaina opens the doors of its three dozen galleries 7pm-10pm, throws out the welcome mat, sets out food and drink, provides entertainment, and usually hosts a well-known artist or two for this weekly party. Take your time and stroll Front Street from one gallery to the next. Stop and chat with shopkeepers, munch the goodies, sip the wine, look at the pieces on display, corner the featured artist for a comment on his or her work, soak in the music of the strolling musicians, and strike up a conversation with the person next to you who is eyeing that same piece. People dress up, but don't be afraid to come casually.

◖ Lahaina Lu'aus

Lahaina is the best place on the island for taking part in a lu'au. It's drier and calmer than in nearby Ka'anapali. The lu'aus in Lahaina are arguably the two best on the island, and you can't go wrong with either show since they're in oceanfront locations and feature some of the best performers.

Of all the island's lu'aus, **Old Lahaina Luau** (1251 Front St., 808/667-1998, www.oldlahainaluau.com, $99 adults, $69 children) is regarded as the best. The food is the best (you might like poi for once!), the lu'au grounds are immaculate, and everything from the show to the service runs like a well-oiled machine. Despite the fact that the lu'au seats 440 people, it still manages to retain an intimate

atmosphere. You are greeted with a lei made of fragrant fresh flowers. Premium bar selections are included in the price. There is a large *imu* for unearthing the pig (although it gets insanely crowded, so hang by the *imu* early if you want to get a good view), and the private oceanfront setting provides the perfect perch for watching the sun go down. As a logistical bonus, there is ample free parking, or if you plan on having more than a couple of drinks, it's a short cab ride from the resorts in Ka'anapali.

The evening mimics an authentic experience in the surroundings of a Hawaiian fishing village. There is a cultural integrity and commitment to historical accuracy often lost on other shows. However, this means there is no fire dancing, which is a craft that is native to Samoa as opposed to Hawai'i. The show at Old Lahaina Luau traces the history of the original Hawaiians as they migrated across oceans from French Polynesia to establish a unique culture here in Hawai'i. Couples will agree that this lu'au has the most romantic atmosphere.

For seating arrangements, you can either choose between traditional seating on lauhala mats (which are the closest to the stage), or you can sit at tables with chairs which still provide a good view. The only vantage point where it's tough to see the show is from the seats in the far corners. Seating preference is given to those who book the earliest. Check-in for the lu'au is either 5:15pm or 5:45pm depending on the time of year. When you consider all that you're getting—an all you can eat buffet of good food, an open bar of premium drinks, and a professional cultural performance in an oceanfront setting—the tickets are obscenely affordable. Remarkably, shows are offered seven days a week.

The **Feast at Lele** (505 Front St., 808/667-5353, www.feastatlele.com, $115 adults, $85 children) is a lu'au on the oceanfront in the 505 shopping center. "Lele" is the ancient Hawaiian name for the town of Lahaina, and this show begins with a look at the dance which is native to Hawaiian culture. The Feast at Lele then migrates its way through various Polynesian cultures, including those of Aotearoa (New

© KYLE ELLISON

Old Lahaina Luau

Zealand), Tahiti, and Samoa. The combination of cultures makes for a fast-paced, fiery, and heart-pumping performance that is capped off by everyone's favorite, the Samoan fire and knife dancing. Shows take place nightly; check-in begins at 6:30pm and the show begins at 7pm.

Bars and Live Music

Rooted in the grog shop days of its boisterous port town past, Lahaina is Maui's nightlife capital. There are only a handful of places where you can actually dance. Just because places don't stay open late, however, doesn't mean that you can't find live music and a genuinely good time.

For free, family-friendly live music in a historic outdoor setting, the Lahaina Restoration Foundation hosts a **Hawaiian Music Series** 6pm-7:30pm on the last Thursday of every month. Shows take place on the lawn of the Baldwin House, a preserved missionary site on the corner of Dickenson and Front Streets right in the center of town. Musical artists vary from

month to month, but most sessions involve live music and *kanikapila* storytelling. Seating is limited at this popular event, although attendees are encouraged to bring a blanket or beach chair for enjoying the show.

The family-friendly **Friday Town Party** (www.mauifridays.com/lahaina) takes place on the second Friday of every month between the Baldwin House and Wharf Cinema Center. As part of the Maui Fridays series, free event runs 6pm-9pm and features everything from live music and *keiki* competitions to silent auctions and dance performances. Various bars and restaurants feature live music and most restaurants offer specials valid for that night only.

One of the best spots for live entertainment in Lahaina is **Fleetwood's** (744 Front St., 808/669-6425, www.fleetwoodsonfrontst.com), a two-story bar and restaurant that offers the only rooftop perch in Lahaina. As the name suggests this bar was opened by legendary rock musician Mick Fleetwood, and Mick himself has been known to jump in with the band for some impromptu percussion. Live music is offered five nights a week, 6:30pm-9pm, most frequently on the rooftop bar looking out over the Lahaina roadstead.

For the closest thing on Front Street that you'll find to a club atmosphere, **Moose Mcgillicuddy's** (844 Front St., 808/667-7758, www.moosemcgillicuddys.com, open until 2am) is the DJ and dancing hot spot for dollar drinks on Tuesday and Saturday nights. While it's tough to turn down dollar drinks ($5 cover), the place will get insanely crowded with groups of locals looking to start a fight—especially late at night. General sloppiness tends to reign on most evenings. Nevertheless, it's still a good time.

Off Front Street in the Lahaina Cannery Mall, **Lulu's Lahaina Surf Club** (1221 Honoapi'ilani Hwy., 808/661-0808, www.luluslahaina.com, open until 2am) is the town's other dance club. Saturday night is the big night at Lulu's, so there is usually a $5 cover. Live music can sporadically be found on the other nights of the week. While the dance floor is large and there are a couple of pool tables in the back, the mall location detracts from the vintage Lahaina experience. Another problem here seems to have plagued Maui nightlife since the invention of the subwoofer: late nights and loud music can lead to fights.

Also, while the schedule is highly irregular, **Longhi's** (888 Front St., 808/667-2288, www.longhis.com) will occasionally have late-night music until 1am which can feature jazz, rock bands, or visiting DJs. This is the classiest venue in Lahaina, and as of the time of research, Thursday is the best night for late-night dancing.

Both **Cool Cat Café** (658 Front. St., 808/667-0908, www.coolcatcafe.com) and **Kimo's** (845 Front St., 808/661-4811, www.kimosmaui.com) provide live music during the dinner hour seven nights a week. On Friday nights Kimo's can sometimes have music as late as 11pm, although as with most places in Lahaina, there isn't an official dance floor so the atmosphere is relegated to drinks and mingling.

For **karaoke,** the most happening place in Lahaina for late-night sake and singing is **Kobe** (136 Dickenson St., 808/667-5555, www.kobemaui.com, open until 1am) steak house on Friday and Saturday nights from 9:30pm until well after midnight.

A couple of classic watering holes stay open until 2am. On Front Street, **Spanky's Riptide** (505 Front St., 808/667-2337, www.spankys-ripstide.com) in the 505 shopping center on the far southern end is a good place to grab a cheap goblet of PBR, play pool, and engage in conversation with a colorful cast of characters.

Legendary dive bar **Sly Mongoose** (1036 Limahana Pl., 808/661-8097), is in a nondescript location in the Lahaina industrial park, on the inland side of the highway behind Pizza Hut. This is a no-nonsense dive where the beer is cold, the drinks are cheap, the patrons are mostly regulars. This bar isn't walking distance from Front Street, so you'll have to take a cab here.

Food

The number of dining options on the West Side is overwhelming. In most places along the west side, it isn't only the food you're paying for, but also the location. That sunset view doesn't come cheap. It's still possible to get a meal for under $10 per person—just look outside of the main visitor areas.

KAPALUA, NAPILI, KAHANA, AND HONOKOWAI
Continental
There are three facts about Maui you can take home with you: Haleakala is 10,023 feet tall, the island of Maui is 727 square miles, and **C The Gazebo** (5315 Lower Honapi'ilani Rd., 808/669-5621, 7:30am-2pm daily, $9-13) restaurant has the island's best breakfast. This isn't exactly a secret, however, and there is a line out the door by 6:45am. What makes this spot so popular is not only the oceanfront location gazing out toward Moloka'i, but also the famous macadamia nut pancakes and heaping three-egg omelets. Lunch is offered until closing at 2pm. Finding parking can be a little challenging. You can try for a spot along the side of the road along Napili Place, or if everything there is full, you can park by the Napili Bay beach access on Hui Drive and walk to the restaurant across the sand of Napili Bay. If standing on the beach looking out toward the water, the Gazebo is on the point to your left.

Local Style
From the outside, you might wonder what's so special about the hole-in-the-wall **C Honokowai Okazuya and Deli** (3600 Lower Honoapi'ilani Rd., 808/665-0512, 11am-2:30pm and 4:30pm-8:30pm Mon.-Sat., $9-15). You might not notice the restaurant, since the front door is often closed behind a colorfully decorated exterior of bamboo and surfing photos, although once inside you'll find huge portions, great local food, and budget-friendly prices that leave you wondering why you would

ever eat anywhere else. Even though it's inside a strip mall next to the 5A Rent A Space, what this restaurant lacks in atmosphere it makes up for in practicality and taste. Although there are a few seats inside for dining, most visitors use this as a takeaway window for enjoying a meal back at the condo. The food here can rival any on the island, and the prices can be half as much as when the same food is served with an oceanfront view. Try the lemon caper mahimahi if you're looking for fresh fish at an affordable price.

For a budget meal in Kapalua, the deli inside the **Honolua Store** (502 Office Rd., 808/665-9105, 6am-6:30pm, $6) has plate lunches you can enjoy on the plantation-style deck. The loco moco with fried rice will leave you stuffed. While the meals are cheap, the expensive cold drinks are where they make their money back. Service can be slow.

Mexican
In Honokowai, **Ohana Tacos** (3600 Lower Honoapi'ilani Rd., 808/283-7768, 11am-9pm Sun.-Thurs., 11am-8pm Fri.-Sat., $7-11) is a family-run restaurant with a badge of authenticity: It's frequented by the local Spanish-speaking community. This is one of the few places on the island where you can order *sopes* or choose *lengua* as a meat option. Cash only, and only a few outdoor tables.

Italian and Mediterranean
Cornering the casual Italian market, **Pizza Paradiso** (3350 Lower Honoapi'ilani Rd., 808/667-2929, 10am-9pm daily, $19-27) also features cuisine from the greater Mediterranean region. Fresh produce is sourced on the island, the beef is from Maui Cattle Company, and passion goes into the preparation. Try the Big Fat Greek pizza with gyro meat! Organic and gluten-free options are available. Pasta options grace the dinner menu while gyros are the budget-friendly lunch option.

If you would rather enjoy your pizza with a draft beer and sports on the TV, head to **Dollie's Pub and Café** (4310 Lower Honoapi'ilani Rd., 808/669-0266, 11am-midnight daily, $18-25) at the Kahana Manor Shops. Pizzas are available whole or by the slice, with happy hour discounts 3pm-6pm and 10-midnight.

American

On the Kapalua Bay golf course, **Pineapple Grill** (200 Kapalua Dr., 808/669-9600, www. cohnrestaurants.com, 8am-10pm daily, bar $7-12, lunch $12-19, dinner $22-48) is one of the most popular restaurants in Kapalua. Breakfast is a local secret (try the Benedicts or Belgian waffles). The bar menu has affordable island classics such as ahi poke tacos or kalua pork quesadillas topped with Maui onions. Lunch includes burgers and fish tacos and dinner has fine entrées such as Kona kampachi fish plates and shiitake-accented filet mignon.

On the Plantation course, the **Plantation House** (200 Kapalua Dr., 808/669-9600, www. theplantationhouse.com, 8am-9pm daily, $10-22) offers expansive views from the hillside. Considering the luxurious venue, the affordable breakfast and lunch menu makes you feel like you're getting away with something. Enjoy breakfast items like omelets and eggs Benedict while overlooking the Honolua coastline. Lunch offers fresh green salads, teriyaki pineapple burgers, and barbecue pork sandwiches. For dinner, choose fish such as ahi and monchong or meat selections like braised short ribs and chicken stroganoff. The popular bar has an extensive wine list.

For good old-fashioned Southern barbecue, check out the **Iron Imu BBQ** (5315 Lower Honoapi'ilani Rd., 808/298-4575, www.iron-imubbqmaui.com, 5pm-9pm daily, $11-14), a food cart in the parking lot of the Napili Shores. Brisket, rib, sausage, and chicken plates are all there, and you get to choose from a selection of three home-style sides.

Seafood

If you're just trying to find a slab of fish to grill up at the condo, **Fish Market Maui** (3600 Lower Honoapi'ilani Rd., 808/665-9895, www.fishmarketmaui.com, 11am-7pm daily, $6-14) in the 5A strip mall in Honokowai has fresh fish sold by the pound. The prices can be a little high compared to Foodland, but if you're staying at a condo in Honokowai, it's a convenient option within walking distance. There's also a counter inside where you can order a seared ahi steak sandwich served with caramelized onions, tomatoes, and wasabi aioli.

Japanese

If you ask West Side locals where to get sushi, they'll say **⟨ Sansei** (600 Office Rd., 808/669-6286, www.sanseihawaii.com, 5:30pm-10pm Sat.-Wed., 5:30pm-1am Thurs.-Fri., $8-30), a legendary sushi outpost on the main entrance road to Kapalua resort. If you want to maximize your Sansei experience, here's what you do: Call ahead for reservations on Thursday or Friday evening and make them for 5:30pm. This is when the restaurant opens, and they'll usually run an "early bird" special for the first 30 minutes. If you miss the early bird wave and would rather wait a few hours, the same specials are often offered 10pm-1am.

Hawaiian Regional

⟨ Merriman's (1 Bay Club Pl., 808/669-6400, www.merrimanshawaii.com, 3pm-9pm daily, dinner menu begins at 5:30pm, $25-49) is the "nicest" restaurant on the island's northwestern side, and this venue on Kapalua Bay is one of the most scenic dining spots on the island. Arrive early to enjoy a glass of wine while watching the sunset from the oceanfront fire pit. Then enjoy a menu of farm to table fare where over 90 percent of the ingredients are sourced from local farmers, fishers, and ranchers. Acclaimed chef Peter Merriman is one of the founders of the Hawaiian Regional movement, and his genius is evident is everything from the avocado ahi poke salads to citrus ponzu-flavored mahimahi. Five spice roasted Jidori chicken is masterfully paired with Moloka'i sweet potato ravioli, and there are probably nations with constitutions shorter than the wine list (which features over

40 different varietals). Reservations are highly recommended.

The **C Sea House** (5900 Lower Honoapiʻilani Rd., 808/669-1500, www. seahousemaui.com, 7am-9pm daily, dinner $10-24) restaurant at the Napili Kai Beach Resort has an oceanfront patio perfect for watching the sun go down. Happy hour is the best time to visit, but the breakfast rivals island favorite The Gazebo. Try the Molokaʻi sweet potato egg frittata or banana pancakes. Lunch brings kalua pig tacos and dinner specialties include a fisherman's stew of lobster, scallops, shrimp, and vegetables. Get a reservation for Wednesday night, when the places fills up for the slack key guitar concert.

Brewpub

A visit to **C Maui Brewing Company** (4405 Honoapiʻilani Hwy., 808/669-3474, www. mauibrewingco.com, 11am-midnight daily, $12-15) should be at the top of every beer lover's island to-do list. This is the island's only brewery, and while you can find a number of their beers in local supermarkets, at least a dozen more can only be found on tap in the brewhouse. The interior is basic, but this isn't a place you come to for the decor. Even though the beer is the main draw, the Hawaiian beef burger, sliders, and coconut porter beef stew are all hearty accompaniments to a rich pint of stout. There are also filling and affordable pizzas and vegan or gluten-free options.

Coffee Shops

In the Napili Plaza, **The Coffee Store** (5095 Napilihau Rd., 808/669-4170, www.mauicoffee.com, 6am-6pm daily) is the northernmost place on the island completely dedicated to the wonders of the coffee bean. If you're heading out for an early morning stroll on the Kapalua Coastal Trail, this small shop has the usual selection of caffeinated options in addition to selling locally grown beans. Beyond just coffee, food options include health-conscious fare such as acai bowls and zucchini muffins you can enjoy in the comfortable atmosphere.

At the Kahana Gateway Center, **Hawaiian Village Coffee** (4405 Honoapiʻilani Hwy., 808/665-1114, www.hawaiianvillagecoffee. com, 5:30am-6pm daily) is another classic coffee shop with a strong local following and good community vibe. This is the earliest place to open on the northwest side, and the sunrise hours are a collection of late-shift police officers refueling after a long night and sleepy-eyed locals stopping in on their way to work. Although small, the shop has a welcoming atmosphere for reading the morning paper or checking your email on the free Wi-Fi.

KAʻANAPALI

When it comes to dining in Kaʻanapali, there are only three options: restaurants in Whalers Village, restaurants in the resorts, and a handful of restaurants a block off the strip.

Italian

The best Italian in Kaʻanapali is at **Pulehu** (808/667-3200, www.westinkaanapali.com, 5:30pm-9:30pm Thurs.-Mon., $23-39), inside the Westin Kaʻanapali Villas. The antipasti menu features locally-sourced bruschetta and Caprese *insalata*. and Pacific Italian fusion takes over on the main menu where selections of risotto-crusted, pan-seared fish are offered alongside chianti-braised short ribs. Considering the venue and level of cuisine, dishes are surprisingly affordable.

If you just want a slice of pizza, **Nicki's Pizza** (2435 Kaʻanapali Pkwy., 808/667-0333, www. nickispizzamaui.com, 7:30am-9pm daily) in the Whalers Village food court offers filling slices for $4-5.

American

One of the only places for dining in Kaʻanapali that isn't associated with a resort is **CJ's Deli** (2580 Kekaʻa Dr., 808/667-0968, www.cjs-maui.com, 7am-8pm daily, $7-13) in the Fairway Shops. There is a $7 early bird platter at CJ's that includes coffee, and the moderate prices continue throughout the day. CJ's specializes in delicious home-style comfort food, though the counter service can often be a little snippy. Nevertheless, it's a good option if you don't want to pay resort prices. It's BYOB.

Umalu (Hyatt Regency, 808/280-6986, www.maui.hyatt.com, 10am-10pm daily, $13-19) has the best ahi poke nachos on the West Side of the island. Stop reading this sentence right now and go get them. Sure, they're $18, but they're big enough for two people to split. In addition to the nachos there are sandwiches and flatbreads.

On the far other end of the main Ka'anapali Beach strip is the **Tiki Terrace Restaurant** (2525 Ka'anapali Pkwy., 808/667-0124, 6:30am-11am and 6pm-9pm dinner Mon.-Sat., 9am-1pm Sun.) which has the best all-you-can-eat Sunday brunch ($37) on the West Side of the island, with bottomless champagne and a free hula show.

In front of the Honua Kai resort, **Duke's** (130 Kai Malina Pkwy., 808/662-2900, www.dukesmaui.com, 7:30am-9:30pm daily, $10-25) is in the same family of moderately priced restaurants as Kimo's, Leilani's, and Hula Grill. Affordable breakfasts include banana, macadamia nut pancakes, while lunches tend toward sandwiches, burgers, and fish tacos. Dinner entrées are a touch more expensive. Duke's sources ingredients from over 20 different local farms. Afternoon trade winds can make the outdoor dining frustrating, so go for breakfast before 10am, or for dinner after sundown.

Hawaiian Regional

Even though every resort in Ka'anapali has some sort of Hawaiian Regional option, none can hold a candle to world-famous (**Roy's** (2290 Ka'anapali Pkwy., 808/669-6999, www.roysrestaurant.com, 11am-9:30pm daily, $15-45). The location inside the golf clubhouse would be nicer if it had an ocean view, but for what the restaurant lacks in decor, it makes up for in flavor. Chef Roy Yamaguchi was one of the founders of the Hawaiian Regional movement, and his mastery is evident in the misoyaki butterfish and honey mustard-braised short ribs. Even though there are over 30 Roy's locations around the country, every restaurant has a menu and a style unique to the venue.

Dinner entrées are pricey; ordering sandwiches, salads, and appetizers off the lunch menu is more affordable. The chocolate soufflé will change your life; order it half-way through your meal since it takes 20 minutes to prepare.

(**Hula Grill** (2435 Ka'anapali Pkwy., 808/667-6636, www.hulagrillkaanapali.com, 11am-11pm, $13) in Whalers Village is my favorite for oceanfront dining. The barefoot bar has a better atmosphere than the dining room, and it's the only place on the island where you walk through sand to get to your table. There's live music in the afternoons. The Kapulu Joe pork sandwich and the wood-fired goat cheese and roasted pumpkin pizza are two affordable options along an otherwise expensive shoreline.

Across the Whalers Village walkway, **Leilani's On The Beach** (2435 Ka'anapali Pkwy., 808/661-4495, www.leilanis.com, 11am-11pm daily, $15) serves the best fish tacos on the island. The tacos are enormous, served Cajun style, and accompanied by a special sauce that brings it all together. Take advantage of discounts Tuesday 3pm-5pm. Whether you dine on the casual patio or the upstairs in the dining room, save room for a world-famous Hula Pie with macadamia nut ice cream and chocolate cookie crust; it's big enough to share.

At the far southern end of the Ka'anapali strip, **Japengo** (200 Nohea Kai Dr., 808/667-4796, 5pm-10pm daily, $20) has enormous and affordable sushi rolls which rival even Sansei. You'll be amazed that by ordering a big roll and blackened ahi hand rolls, you can dine at a fancy resort and completely stuff two people on fresh sushi. At sushi school (2nd and 4th Sat. each month, 3pm-4:30pm, $35/person), you can learn to make hand rolls from one of the restaurant's master chefs.

Natural Foods

The best gourmet natural foods market on the West Side, **'Aina Gourmet Market** (130 Kai Malina Pkwy., 808/662-2832, www.ainagourmet.com, 7am-9pm daily) is tucked away in the lobby of Honua Kai Beach Resort. 'Aina is in the same restaurant group as Pacifico, I'o, and O'o Farms, and this is a great place for grabbing a cup of 100 percent Maui coffee, organically raised produce, or a healthy panini made from locally sourced ingredients. There are a few tables, or enjoy your meal on the beach.

Coffee Shops

The only local coffee shop in Ka'anapali is **Island Press Coffee** (2580 Keka'a Dr., 808/667-2003, 6am-7pm Mon.-Sat., 7am-4pm Sun.) in the Fairway Shops. The location isn't exactly prime for anyone staying in an oceanfront resort, but if you're up early from jet lag and want to go for an early morning stroll, it's nice that the doors open at 6am most days.

LAHAINA
Continental

Hidden in an oceanfront cove by the Lahaina Library, **Sunrise Café** (693 Front St., 808/661-8558, 7am-3pm daily, $6-9, cash only) is a popular local breakfast spot, although the service can sometimes be a little slow. That aside, this is by far the most affordable, almost-oceanfront breakfast you'll find in Lahaina. Fill up on eggs Benedict or a breakfast platter. Breakfast is served all day. Snag a table on the back patio.

Local Style

There's a place in Lahaina where you can eat good food by the water and the bill won't give you a heart attack. At the northern end of Lahaina next to the Old Lahaina Luau (with which it's affiliated), **Aloha Mixed Plate** (1285 Front St., 808/661-3322, www.alohamixedplate.com, 8am-10pm daily, $8-12) offers affordable plate lunches in a casual oceanfront setting. The plates are paper and the tables are plastic, but who cares? The private setting is up there with some of the most scenic in Lahaina, the food is the best local food you'll find outside of a lu'au, and it's cheap. For lunch and dinner you can sample lu'au items such as lomi lomi salmon or poi. For the main course, get a kalua pig plate lunch (with two scoop rice and macaroni salad) or spring for the Aloha Mixed Plate of shoyu chicken, teriyaki beef, and fresh fish served with rice and mac salad. Breakfast is just as affordable with omelets and loco moco

dishes. There's also a full service bar, although alcohol isn't served at the oceanfront tables.

Mexican

The freshest, healthiest, and best Mexican food in Lahaina is **Cilantro** (170 Papalaua St., 808/667-5444, www.cilantrogrill.com, 11am-9pm Mon.-Sat., 11am-8pm Sun., $9-13), in the Old Lahaina Center next to Jamba Juice and Foodland. The atmosphere here is unassuming, and there is an open-air kitchen where you can watch your food being made. Being set a block off Front Street makes for affordable prices, and the portions are huge. The $10 Mother Clucker Flautas are the tastiest item on the menu (how can you go wrong with chicken drizzled in spicy-sweet roasted jalapeño sauce?). All meals are made from scratch using old-world recipes, and there are even a few gluten-free options. Pair your meal with a creamy horchata drink to round things out.

If you want to pair your Mexican with a margarita, **Amigo's** (658 Front St., 808/661-0210, www.amigosmaui.com, 9am-9pm daily, $9) in the Wharf Cinema Center has a decent bar selection to accompany the largest selection of any Mexican restaurant in town.

Italian

For pasta dishes in a low-key atmosphere, hit **Penne Pasta** (180 Dickenson St., 808/661-6633, www.pennapastacafe.com, 11am-9:30pm daily, $8) in downtown Lahaina just steps from Maria Lanakila Church. Penne Pasta serves quality food quickly and at reasonable rates. The food is cooked southern Italian style, and half of the tomatoes are sourced from outside of Naples. Pastas include linguine pesto, baked penne, and chicken piccata, and pizzas and flatbreads are also available. If you're looking for something lighter for lunch, you can get a Nicoise salad with garlic ahi or an open-face roasted eggplant parmesan.

Opened in 1976, **Longhi's** (888 Front St., 808/667-2288, www.longhis.com, 7:30am-10pm daily, $12-40), has Lahaina's finest Italian. With its black and white tiles and antique chairs, Longhi's is as iconic to Lahaina as a beer at the Pioneer Inn or escaping the heat beneath the shade of the banyan tree. This multilevel establishment has an airy, sophisticated yet casual setting. While pasta dishes form the backbone of the dinner menu, seafood options such as Ahi Torino encrusted in macadamia dance their way across the pages. More affordable breakfast ioptions include eggs Florentine and lobster Benedict. This is the only restaurant in Lahaina that offers a valet service.

Italian Delight (305 Keawe St., 808/662-0077, www.italiandelightmaui.com, 11am-9pm Mon.-Sat., noon-9pm Sun.) in the Lahaina Gateway shops has large New York-style slices ($3-4); two constitute a meal.

French

If you take your fine dining seriously, then you're going to love **Gerard's** (174 Lahainaluna Rd., 808/661-8939, www.gerardsmaui.com, 6pm-8:30pm daily, $50) in the Plantation Inn. Chef Gerard Reversade has been serving French food with an island twist for over 30 years and was one of the pioneers of Hawaiian Regional cuisine. Classics such as foie gras and escargot punctuate the appetizer menu, and favorites include the roasted lamb in lemon/peppermint jelly accompanied by potato au gratin, as well as the fresh fish that changes with the day's selection. Gerard's has received the *Wine Spectator*'s Award of Excellence 19 times for its extensive collection of French and American labels. Ignore the cost and let your taste buds take over. Reservations are imperative.

American

◖ **Lahaina Grill** (127 Lahainaluna Rd., 808/667-5177, www.lahainagrill.com, 6pm-10pm daily, $25-49) is the best restaurant in Lahaina, which is quite an accolade considering the competition. Opened on Valentine's Day of 1990, this restaurant continues to be one of Lahaina's most romantic evenings. Everything from the ambience to the service to the extensive wine list is what you would expect of a fine dining experience. The only thing missing is an ocean view, but for what the restaurant lacks in views it makes up for in a classy bistro setting.

The food is a combination of new American cuisine infused with Pacific Rim favorites, where meat dishes include the coveted Kona coffee-roasted rack of lamb, and seafood selections range from sesame-crusted ahi filets to Maine lobster crab cakes. Much of the produce is sourced locally from independent farmers. Reservations are recommended.

The best burger in Lahaina is at ◖ **Cool Cat Café** (658 Front St., 808/667-0908, www.coolcatcafe.com, 10:30am-10:30pm daily, $10-25). Overlooking the banyan tree, the inside portion of the restaurant is decorated in 1950s decor, while the outdoor patio is livelier. Cool Cats is consistently voted as the island's best burger, and the live music here is better than down the street. All of the meat is massaged with a secret seasoning, and specialty burgers like the Don Ho (teriyaki and pineapple burger), Luna (covered in avocado), and Frisco (served on sourdough bread with grilled onions and jack cheese) are what make it such a legendary choice. There are also fish sandwiches, blackened fish tacos, salads (get the Buddy Holly with chicken strips on top), and a popular bar. It's extra to add fries to your meal (and cheaper to get a basket for the table than to add to each burger separately).

Right next door, sister restaurant **Captain Jack's Island Grill** (672 Front St., 808/667-0988, 8am-midnight daily, $10-25) does for fish what Cool Cat does for burgers. Whether it's fish tacos, fish-and-chips, or fish salad, this casual bar and grill overlooking Front Street has tasty dishes at moderate prices and is always running some sort of special. This is a good family lunch option. Young kids will enjoy the pirate theme that goes hand in hand with the town's nautical history (though whalers weren't exactly pirates).

After Cool Cat, your best bet for a burger on Front Street is **Sure Thing Burger** (790 Front St., 808/214-6982, www.surethingburger.net, 11am-5pm daily, $6-8) inside the Lahaina Marketplace on the corner of Front Street and Lahainaluna Road. The burgers are made from Maui Cattle Company beef and the buns are baked fresh on Maui. While this is only a lunch stand, it's an affordable way to get a burger in Lahaina.

The best burger *off* Front Street is at **Teddy's Bigger Burgers** (335 Keawe St., 808/661-9111, www.teddysbiggerburgers.com, 10am-9pm Sun.-Thurs., 10am-10pm Fri.-Sat., $6-9), inside the Lahaina Gateway Center. These juicy, drip-down-your-arm burgers are made fresh to order. My favorites are the specialty burgers, such as the Kailua Style served with mushrooms and the Hawaiian Style with pineapple.

One of Lahaina's best-kept secrets is **Lahaina Coolers** (180 Dickenson St., 808/661-7082, www.lahainacoolers.com, 8am-midnight daily, $27), a laid-back, local favorite that can rival anywhere in town. All three meals provide reason for visiting (particularly breakfast). The dinner menu is just as good as the fancier names in town. There are also pizzas, pastas, and an affordable bar menu (think kalua pig tacos).

On the far southern end of Front Street, **Betty's Beach Café** (505 Front St., 808/662-0300, www.bettysbeachcafe.com, 8am-10pm daily, $9-14) in the 505 shopping center has affordable breakfast platters, sandwiches, burgers, and plate lunch combos. The best time to visit this hidden beachfront location is brunch on a weekday morning for mimosas.

For quick and easy sandwiches that are filling and affordable, check out **Mr. Sub** (129 Lahainaluna Rd, 808/667-5683, 9am-4pm Mon.-Fri., 9am-3pm Sat., $7-10), on Lahainaluna Road. There are only a couple of tables at this hole in the wall, so you may want to get your turkey, bacon, and avocado sub to go.

Japanese

If there were an award for best cuisine in the most unlikely of locations, **Star Noodle** (285 Kupuohi St., 808/667-5400, www.starnoodle.com, 10:30am-10pm daily, $12) would take the competition by storm. This popular noodle establishment in an obscure corner at the top of the Lahaina Gateway industrial area has been sculpted by Sheldon Simeon, a local chef who made it to the final three contestants on the reality show *Top Chef.* The Asian-infused menu is spectacularly affordable, with bowls of udon, plates of pad thai, and dishes such as miso salmon or chicken in ponzu sauce. If the wait is too long, sit at the bar and order from the main menu.

In downtown Lahaina, **Kobe** (136 Dickenson St., 808/667-5555, www.kobemaui.com, 5:30pm-10pm daily, $22) steak house offers teppanyaki-style dinners where tableside chefs flash their sharp blades through the air, and neatly arranged piles of marinated meat, chicken, and vegetables are expertly flash-fried at your own grill, often culminating in a ball of sake-induced flame. Teppan meals come complete with rice, soup, and tea. You can also order at the separate sushi bar ($6-10 a plate).

Hawaiian Regional

In the 505 shopping area, **Pacific'O** (505 Front St., 808/667-4341, www.pacificomaui.com, 11:30am-10pm daily, $29-46) is one of the best venues in Lahaina for enjoying an oceanfront meal. Many of the ingredients are not only sourced locally, but grown at the organic O'o Farm in Kula, with which the restaurant is associated. The seaside patio is the perfect lunch spot for pairing a sesame fish salad with a crisp glass of white wine, and the fish tacos are affordable at $14 when you consider the oceanfront setting. Reservations are necessary for dinner, where you can feast on entrées such as Pasta 'ele'ele (blackened fresh fish over whole wheat spaghetti in a cilantro pesto) and Hapa/Hapa Tempura (sashimi-grade fish and caviar wrapped in nori). The wine list is one of the most comprehensive on the West Side.

On the far northern end of Lahaina, **Honu** (1295 Front St., 808/667-9390, www.honumaui.com, 11am-9:30pm Mon.-Sat., 4:30pm-9pm Sun., $18-45) offers locally sourced food in an oceanfront setting. *Honu* is the Hawaiian name for sea turtle, and there's a high likelihood that you'll spot a turtle coming up for a breath at some point during your meal. Chef Mark Ellman (one of the original founders of the Hawaiian Regional movement) has

© KYLE ELLISON

Food like this makes Star Noodle a local favorite.

crafted a masterpiece where butternut squash coconut soup complements main courses ranging from lentil quinoa burgers to pork osso bucco. The pizzas are similarly delicious. The extensive craft beer selection features over 50 different microbrews—a rarity among island restaurants. If there's a wait, try sister restaurant **Mala**, next door.

In the heart of Front Street, **Kimo's** (845 Front St., 808/661-4811, www.kimosmaui. com, 11am-10pm daily, $25-32) has a deck looking out over the waters of the Lahaina Roadstead and moderately priced lunch items such as coconut crusted fish sandwiches or koloa pork ribs for $12-16. The dinner entrées in the dining room are pricier, but the signature Molokini Cut, 14-ounce prime rib is served with an au jus that will leave you sopping up the juices however you can. The staff at Kimo's is phenomenal. While dinner is a romantic time to dine, lunch is more moderately priced.

Natural Foods
To the delight of those who care about what

they put in their body, **◖ Choice** (1087 Limahana Pl., 808/661-7711, www.choicemaui.com, 8am-4pm Mon.-Sat., $8) is devoted to the benefits of a healthy, active lifestyle. When you walk in the door (where a sign informs you this is a "bummer free zone"), you can sense the antioxidants and free radicals in the air. The smoothies use all-natural superfood ingredients (spirulina, acai, coconut meat, and almond milk), so your body will thank you. Make your smoothie "epic" by adding superfoods such as kale and blue green algae. A large selection of freshly made kale salads are available after 11:30am each day.

Thai
The best Thai food on the West Side—if not the entire island—is at **Thai Chef** (878 Front St., 808/667-2814, www.thaichefrestaurant-maui.com, 11am-2pm, 5pm-9pm Mon.-Fri., 5pm-9pm Sat., $14), a small, hole-in-the-wall restaurant squirreled away in the parking lot between Longhi's and the Maui Theatre. The family-run restaurant is BYOB if you'd like

to accompany your chicken pad thai with a Singha beer, but beer and wine are available at Foodland across the parking lot. Vegetarians are also well taken care of with plenty of spicy tofu and vegetable dishes. While it's not fancy, you won't be disappointed. Takeout is available; reservations are recommended.

Coffee Shops

For a quick coffee on the run, **Sir Wilfred's** (707 Front St., 808/661-0202, www.sirwilfreds.com, 8:30am-9pm daily) is the island's original coffee shop, having opened its doors in 1976. In 1979 Sir Wilfred's introduced the island's first espresso machine, and the Front Street store is still one of the best spots in Lahaina to stop in and buy some locally grown beans or inquire about fine cigars. Those in need of an early wakeup, however, will unfortunately have to wait until the 8:30am opening time to sip the classic roasts.

If, on the other hand, you're looking for a place you can linger, grab breakfast, get free Internet access, and sip on a proper espresso, try **Café Café** (129 Lahainaluna Rd., 808/661-0006, www.cafecafelahaina.com, 7am-7pm Mon.-Sat.) on Lahainaluna Road next to Mr. Sub sandwich shop. There are a few outdoor tables for sipping your macchiato, and you can also pick up organic, locally sourced, open-faced bagel sandwiches for $5-6.

On the inland side of the highway at the base of the Lahaina Smokestack, **MauiGrown Coffee** (277 Lahainaluna Rd., 808/661-2728, www.mauigrowncoffee.com, 6:30am-5pm Mon.-Sat.) serves 100 percent Maui coffee that's grown in the fields above Ka'anapali. The 6:30am opening time is better than any of the locally run stores in town (Starbucks opens the earliest at 5am; better to spend your money on island-grown coffee). There's seating on the plantation-style porch, and the staff can answer questions on the island coffee industry.

Shave Ice

There are few things better than a cold shave ice on a hot Lahaina day, and the best shave ice in Lahaina is at **Local Boys West** (624 Front St., 808/344-9779, www.localboyshaveice.com, 10am-9pm daily) across the street from the banyan tree. In addition to the copious array of flavors, what makes Local Boys great is the way they offer free Roselani (made on Maui) ice cream, Kauai cream, and azuki beans at the bottom of the shave ice, which any island local knows is the only way to enjoy shave ice.

Market

Believe it or not, the **seafood counter** at the back of the ◖ **Foodland Farms** (345 Keawe St., 808/662-7088, 6am-7pm daily, $7) serves the best *poke* bowl on the island. Get a bowl of ahi tuna and head down to the beach to enjoy it while watching the sunset. The third-pound of yellowfin tuna is prepared in one of a dozen different ways, all served over a bowl of sticky white or brown rice. Try the ahi shoyu, ahi Hawaiian, ahi oyster wasabi, and the Flyin' Hawaiian flavor, where $0.25 of every pound sold goes toward professional baseball player (and Maui local) Shane Victorino's foundation to help disadvantaged youth in Hawai'i.

SOUTH OF LAHAINA
American

The only restaurant between Lahaina and Ma'alaea is ◖ **Leoda's Kitchen and Pie Shop** (820 Olowalu Village Rd., 808/662-3600, www.leodas.com, 10am-8pm daily, $8-12) in the Olowalu store building. Using many sustainable ingredients from local farms, this sandwich and pie shop has quickly become a favorite. The deli sandwiches, potpies, and baked goods are so good, however, that you'll often find a line stretching out the front door. All of the food here is made fresh, so don't expect to get a quick sandwich.

Information and Services

GENERAL INFORMATION
Kapalua, Napili, and Honokowai
For up-to-date information on what's happening in Kapalua, check out the website for the **Kapalua Resort Association** by visiting www.kapaluara.com.

Ka'anapali
The **Ka'anapali Beach Resort Association** website at www.kaanapaliresort.com is a great source of general information on the Ka'anapali area.

Lahaina
For historical inquiries, the **Lahaina Restoration Foundation** (808/661-3262, www.lahainarestoration.org) is a storehouse of information. Pick up its handy brochure, *Lahaina O Mo'olele: A Walking Tour of Historic and Cultural Sites in Lahaina.*

The **Lahaina Town Action Committee** (648 Wharf St., 808/667-9194, www.visitlahaina.com) sponsors cultural events and other activities throughout the year, including Art Night and Halloween, and can provide information about what's happening in the area. It operates the **Lahaina Visitor Center** (808/667-9193) on the first floor of the Old Lahaina Courthouse. For popular events and activities happening in Lahaina, contact the events hotline (808/667-9194), or pick up its *Historic Lahaina Town Walking Map* and the *Maui Historical Walking Guide* brochures, which has information mostly on Lahaina and Ka'anapali.

For art lovers, the nonprofit **Lahaina Arts Society** (808/661-0111, www.lahaina-arts.com) has information about art events in town, and it maintains two galleries at the Old Lahaina Courthouse.

MEDICAL SERVICES
Kapalua, Napili, and Honokowai
Basic medical services are available in Kapalua at **Doctors On Call** (808/667-7676, www.docmaui.com, 8am-9pm daily) at a satellite office by the Ritz-Carlton.

Ka'anapali
The Ka'anapali medical center with the most services is the **West Maui Healthcare Center** (2435 Ka'anapali Pkwy., 808/667-9721, www.westmauidoctors.com, 8am-9pm Mon.-Fri., noon-9pm Sat., 8am-8pm Sun.) on the upper level at the Whalers Village shopping mall in the parking lot behind Leilani's restaurant.

Also in Ka'anapali, **Doctors On Call** (808/667-7676, www.docmaui.com, 8am-9pm daily) has its main office at the Hyatt Regency.

Lahaina
A concentration of specialists is found at the **Maui Medical Group** (130 Prison St., 808/661-0051, 8am-5pm Mon.-Fri., 8am-noon Sat.) in downtown Lahaina. Call for emergency hours.

Professional medical care can also be found at the **Kaiser Permanente clinic** (910 Waine'e St., 808/662-6800) during the same hours.

Pharmacies in Lahaina include the **Lahaina Pharmacy** (808/661-3119) at the Old Lahaina Center, **Longs Drugs** (808/667-4390) at the Lahaina Cannery Mall, and **Walgreen's Pharmacy** (808/667-9515).

BANKING
In Lahaina during normal banking hours, try the **Bank of Hawaii** (808/661-8781) or the **American Savings Bank** (808/667-9561) in the Old Lahaina Center. **First Hawaiian Bank** (808/661-3655) is just a few steps away at 215 Papalaua Street. The only bank north of Lahaina is **Bank of Hawaii** (808/669-3922) at the Kahana Gateway Shopping Center next to McDonald's. There are no banks in Ka'anapali, but there is an ATM is on the lower level of the Whalers Village mall.

GAS
Kapalua, Napili, and Honokowai

There aren't any gas stations in Kapalua or Napili, and only two gas stations in total north of Lahaina. Both, however, will have gas which is a few cents higher per gallon than Lahaina, so if you want to save a small coffee's worth of change then fill up in Lahaina. In Kahana, there's a gas station at the Kahana Gateway Center off Hoʻohui Road, and in Honokowai, there's a gas station between the 5A Rent A Space shopping mall and the Honokowai Marketplace in the parking lot of an ABC store.

Lahaina

There are multiple gas stations on most corners of Honoapiʻilani Highway and its cross streets.

POST OFFICE
Kapalua, Napili, and Honokowai

In the Napili Plaza, **Mail Services Plus** (8am-6pm Mon.-Fri., 10am-2pm Sat.) provides reliable shipping and packaging, sending items via UPS, FedEx, or USPS.

In Honokowai, **Westside Copy & Graphics** (3350 Lower Honoapiʻilani Rd., 808/662-3450, www.wscopyandgraphics.com, 8:30am-5:30pm Mon.-Fri., 10am-1pm Sat.) in the Honokowai Marketplace offers a full range of practical services, from FedEx shipping to mailbox rentals and packaging supplies. The staff here will even package your souvenirs for you so you don't have to worry about schlepping them on the plane.

Lahaina

In Lahaina, the main **U.S. Post Office** (1760 Honoapiʻilani Hwy., 10am-4pm Mon.-Fri.) is by the Lahaina Civic Center on the northern edge of town across from Wahikuli Beach Park; the midtown postal branch (132 Papalaua St., 9am-4pm Mon.-Fri.) is at the Old Lahaina Center next to the Bank of Hawaii and Longhi's restaurant.

In the Wharf Cinema Center across the street from the banyan tree, the **Lahaina Mail Depot** (658 Front St., 808/667-2000, 10am-4:30pm Mon.-Fri., 10am-1pm Sat.) is a post office contract station that, along with the normal stamps and such, specializes in sending packages home.

LIBRARY

The only public library is in Lahaina (680 Wharf St., 808/662-3950, noon-8pm Tues., 9am-5pm Wed.-Thurs., 10:30pm-4:30pm Fri.-Sat.), along Front Street by the Pioneer Inn.

INTERNET SERVICES
Kapalua, Napili, and Honokowai

For free Wi-Fi hotspots you can stop in at **Nachos Grande** Mexican restaurant in the Honokowai Marketplace (Wi-Fi and a margarita!) or, for a more traditional atmosphere, at **Hawaiian Village Coffee** in the Kahana Gateway Center (Wi-Fi and coffee!).

Kaʻanapali

Free access can be a little hard to come by in Kaʻanapali, although there's a free connection at the Starbucks located in the Westin Maui just south of Whalers Village. For a more comfortable perch where you can also snack on a meal, visit **CJ's Deli** (2580 Kekaʻa Dr., 808/667-0968, www.cjsmaui.com, 7am-8pm daily) in the Fairway Shops.

Lahaina

There are a couple of places in Lahaina that offer free Wi-Fi on a consistent basis, and knowing where they are will keep you from joining the three dozen people who are constantly squatting outside of Starbucks in the parking lot next to Foodland.

Along Front Street at the Lahaina Marketplace, the area around **Sure Thing Burger** (790 Front St.), has a Wi-Fi connection for patrons of the burger stand. The downside here is that there aren't any plugs for charging anything in the outdoor courtyard, but it's a nice shaded venue for checking your email.

In the middle of town on Lahainaluna Road, **Café Café** (129 Lahainaluna Rd., 808/661-0006, www.cafecafelahaina.com, 7am-7pm Mon.-Sat.) has free Wi-Fi for patrons.

Toward the southern end of town, **Maui**

Swiss Café (640 Front St., 808/661-6776, www.mauiswisscafe.com, 8am-8pm) offers a service where you pay a predetermined amount and can pick up Wi-Fi 24 hours a day that stretches all the way across the street to the banyan tree. Granted, the fee for this service isn't cheap, and prepaid cards are about $6/hour depending upon the length of time that you purchase. You can also use one of their desktop computers for $0.15 per minute, and this is the closest thing to an "Internet café" you're currently going to find in Lahaina.

There's always the free connection at the various **Starbucks** across town. The Lahaina Cannery Mall location is much larger than the one next to Foodland. There are comfortable outdoor chairs and outlets for you to charge your machine.

Getting There and Around

AIR

Above Kahana is the small **Kapalua-West Maui Airport,** which is a convenient option for those commuting to Honolulu. The interisland fares are often a little higher than at the larger Kahului Airport ($70-80 one way), but when you factor in the hour of driving you save, it's worth the few extra dollars. This small airport is used principally by Island Air and Mokulele Airlines, but it's also used by small commercial tour companies such as Volcano Air Tours. Surrounded by former pineapple fields, the single airstrip is short and used by small propeller aircraft only. The check-in counters, inspection station, boarding gate, and baggage claim are only a few steps from each other.

Island Air operates two flights daily between Kapalua Airport and Honolulu, and Mokulele Airlines has either five or seven flights a day depending on the date. The earliest flight departs for Honolulu at 8:27am, and the last flight of the day is at 6:12pm. It's also possible to connect from here with airports on Moloka'i and Lana'i, although you will need to stop in Honolulu first, so it's easier to take the ferry or a direct flight out of Kahului Airport.

CAR
Rental Car
The largest car rental providers on the West Side are in Honokowai, equidistant between Lahaina Harbor and Kapalua Airport. Here you'll find both **Avis** (11 Halawai Dr., 808/661-4588, 7am-5pm daily) and **Budget** (11 Halawai Dr., 808/661-8721, 7am-5pm daily). Provided you arrive to the harbor or Kapalua Airport during business hours, they have a shuttle that will pick you up.

In the Sheraton resort in Ka'anapali, **Enterprise** (2605 Ka'anapali Pkwy., 808/661-8804, 7am-5pm daily) has a service counter and will pick you up anywhere from Lahaina Harbor to Kapalua.

For car rental in downtown Lahaina, **Hertz** (256 Papalaua St., 808/661-7735, 8am-4pm daily) has a desk in the strip mall on the inland side of the highway by the Subway sandwich shop.

Taxi
In West Maui, taxi options include **West Maui Taxi** (808/661-1122), **AB Taxi** (808/667-7575), and **Paradise Taxi** (808/661-4455). A ride from Lahaina to Ka'anapali is about $15, and from Ka'anapali to Kapalua about $25. Going rates for a cab ride to Kahului Airport from Ka'anapali are about $100, so you might want to think twice about that plan to take a cab to the hotel. For longer trips in the island's most comfortable vans, call **MJ Taxi** (808/283-9309)

Shuttle
Both Kapalua and Ka'anapali offer resort shuttles within the resort and to select areas of West Maui. The free **Kapalua Shuttle** (808/665-9110) runs throughout the resort for guests on an on-demand basis between 6am and 11pm.

WHY DO LOCALS HONK IN THE TUNNEL?

As a general rule, locals don't use their car horns. After all, this isn't Manhattan. Maui drivers are much more apt to wave each other into traffic and throw a big *shaka* out the window than to ever think about touching their horn. For youth who have never left, the only reason cars even have horns is to say hi to your friend as you drive on by.

The one exception to this rule, however, is in the tunnel on the highway between Ma'alaea and Lahaina. When you pass through its dark interior, it isn't uncommon to hear passing vehicles lay on the horn like a cabbie in a traffic jam. The reason has nothing to do with acoustics

or pedestrian safety. It revolves around a local superstition that honking in the tunnel will help ward off spirits. Various iterations exist, with backstories range from mischievous *menehune* (mythical Hawaiian little people) hiding all your stuff from you to the feared "night marchers" coming for your soul.

If soul-seeking night marchers don't sound like guests you want to invite on your vacation, play it safe and do as the locals do. Go ahead and honk as you pass through the tunnel. Once you emerge on the other side, however, don't touch that horn again until the next time.

There's even complimentary transportation to the Kapalua Airport five times daily.

In Ka'anapali, the **resort shuttle** offers free transportation across the resort and runs on a set schedule 9am-9pm.

Motorcycle and Moped

If you want the wind whipping through your hair, there are a number of different motorcycle, Harley, and moped rentals scattered across the West Side. The place with the largest selection of bikes is **Aloha Motorsports** (30 Halawai Dr., 808/667-7000, www.alohamotorsports.com, 8am-5pm daily) in Honokowai across the highway from the Honua Kai resort. It doesn't matter where they're located, however, since the company offers free pickup and drop-off on the West Side. Minimum time for rentals is four hours, although most people opt for 24 hours. Rates for mopeds can be as low as $49 for four hours or $59 for 24 hours, and Harley rentals average around $109 for four hours and $149 for 24 hours. During slower times of the year there can be better specials advertised.

In downtown Lahaina, the best option for hopping on a Harley is at **Cycle City Lahaina** (602 Front St., 667-2800, www.cyclecitymaui.com, 8:30am-6pm daily), which is steps from

the banyan tree. This is a satellite operation of a larger store in Kahului. Rates here are usually around $140 for 24 hours, although lower specials are often advertised.

If you don't need a full-on hog and just want a moped for the day, check out **Motoroshi** (129 Lahainaluna Rd., 808/661-0006, 7am-7pm Mon.-Sat.) moped rentals on Lahainaluna Road. Only a few steps off Front Street in the parking lot of the Café Café coffee shop, its mopeds are available from $40 for three hours to $55 to for the whole day. There are also a number of Vespa scooters which range from $65-95/daily depending on the size of the bike.

BUS

The cheapest way to get about West Maui (albeit much slower), is the **Maui Bus** (808/871-4838, www.co.maui.hi.us/bus). There are four different routes servicing the West Maui area, departures are once per hour, all routes are $2.00/person per boarding, and you can buy a day pass for $4. The bus stations in Lahaina are in the back of the Wharf Cinema Center across the street from the banyan tree, and on the intersection of Front Street and Papalaua Street across the road from the Hard Rock Café. For getting from one side of Lahaina to the other, Bus #23 makes various stops around town from 8am until 11pm. For those traveling from Napili or Kahana to Whalers Village in Ka'anapali (where you can connect with buses to Lahaina and beyond), Bus #30 begins service at 5:30am at the Napili Kai Beach Resort and makes various stops along Lower Honoapi'ilani Road until 9pm. Bus #25 connects Whalers Village in Ka'anapali with the Wharf Cinema Center in Lahaina from 6am until 9pm, and Bus #20 connects the Wharf Cinema Center with Queen Ka'ahumanu Mall in Kahului, making a stop in Ma'alaea for anyone who wants to transfer on a bus down to Kihei.

Since a taxi from Napili to Kahului Airport will cost about $120, if you need to get from Napili to the airport and don't have a car, the cheapest way is to buy a $4 day pass and take Bus #30 to Whalers Village, change to #25 to the Wharf Cinema Center, hop on #20 the Queen Ka'ahumanu Center, and then take #40 to the Kahului Airport. Total transit time for this sojourn is two hours and 10 minutes, but hey, for $4, who's complaining? As a relevant aside, however, you aren't allowed to have more luggage than you can place on your lap or under your seat.

SEA

Though not many visitors access West Maui from the water, those traveling from the islands of Lana'i or Moloka'i will arrive at Lahaina Harbor by interisland ferry. **Expeditions** (808/661-3756, www.go-lanai.com) ferry runs five times daily between Manele and Lahaina Harbors, and the **Moloka'i Princess** (877/500-6284, www.molokaiferry.com) ferry runs daily between Kaunakakai and Lahaina. If coming from Lana'i, the earliest arrival time in Lahaina is 9am, and the latest is 7:45pm. If traveling from Moloka'i, the earliest arrival in Lahaina is 6:45am, and latest is 5:30pm. When arriving in Lahaina by ferry you'll find there are a large number of taxis to get you to your resort, or, if you plan on renting a car, call ahead to the rental car offices listed above and they'll pick you up. If you are traveling from Lana'i, the rental car offices will be closed if you are on the last ferry of the day.

CENTRAL MAUI

The site of Kahului International Airport, Central Maui is the first part of the island most visitors encounter. Kahului is the island's largest town with about 26,000 residents. Neighboring Wailuku is the location of most government offices. More than just the island's business and commercial hub, Central Maui has an underlying charm and a lot of history that stretches beyond the big-box stores and dozens of traffic lights.

Although the backdrop of the verdant mountains and the turquoise water along the shoreline creates a tranquil scene, Central Maui is anything but passive. Kahului's Kanaha Beach Park is home to some of the world's best windsurfing and is one of the beaches where kitesurfing was born. If your idea of a day at the beach involves coconut oil and a gossip magazine, you're better off elsewhere. If you want to put your finger on the pulse of the local water sports scene and are looking to step outside of "resort Maui," this is the place.

Wailuku, just beneath the mist-shrouded cliffs of 'Iao Valley, is in the midst of a renaissance. The culinary scene takes its influence from everything from Filipino to German sources. And even among the residential sprawl, there are still rugged hiking trails, ancient *heiau,* and long, sandy beaches perfect for taking a stroll.

© KYLE ELLISON

HIGHLIGHTS

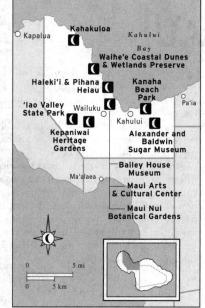

LOOK FOR **(** TO FIND RECOMMENDED SIGHTS, ACTIVITIES, DINING, AND LODGING.

(Kanaha Beach Park: Watch the world's best windsurfers and kitesurfers zip through the air at this grassy, undeveloped, and unheralded beach park (page 120).

(Waihe'e Coastal Dunes and Wetlands Preserve: Hike the trail of this undeveloped preserve as it passes by the ruins of Kapoho fishing village and its associated *heiau* (page 127).

(Maui Arts and Cultural Center: Seeing a movie or live performance in this state-of-the-art facility is one of the best ways to spend an evening on Maui (page 136).

(Maui Nui Botanical Gardens: More than 70 species of taro and dozens of native plants are preserved in this urban garden. A self-guided walking tour discusses traditional irrigation techniques and the role that farming plays in Native Hawaiian culture (page 136).

(Alexander and Baldwin Sugar Museum: Even though the island's sugar industry continues to chug along, there is already a museum dedicated to its legacy. Peer into the daily lives of plantation laborers and read about the herculean undertakings that went into making the industry a reality (page 136).

(Bailey House Museum: Educate yourself on the island's history at this classic Wailuku museum. Displays include authentic Hawaiian artifacts, a surfboard ridden by Duke Kahanamoku, and the best compilation of Hawaiiana literature found anywhere on the island (page 137).

(Kepaniwai Heritage Gardens: This small riverside park highlights the cultures of Maui's immigrant communities. Take an afternoon picnic, dip into the cool waters of 'Iao Stream, and sample the traditional architecture of the island's "mixed plate" community (page 140).

('Iao Valley State Park: The short drive into 'Iao Valley is the easiest way to immerse yourself in the lush interior of the West Maui Mountains. Learn about King Kamehameha's decisive victory at the Battle of Kepaniwai and snap a photo of the iconic 'Iao Needle (page 140).

(Haleki'i and Pihana *Heiau*: These two stone *heiau* were once the religious center of Central Maui. They are notable as the site of the last human sacrifice to take place on Maui (page 142).

(Kahakuloa: Kahakuloa is window into old Hawai'i: one of the last remaining villages where taro is and fish are gathered from the sea. Be sure to buy some banana bread when passing through town (page 143).

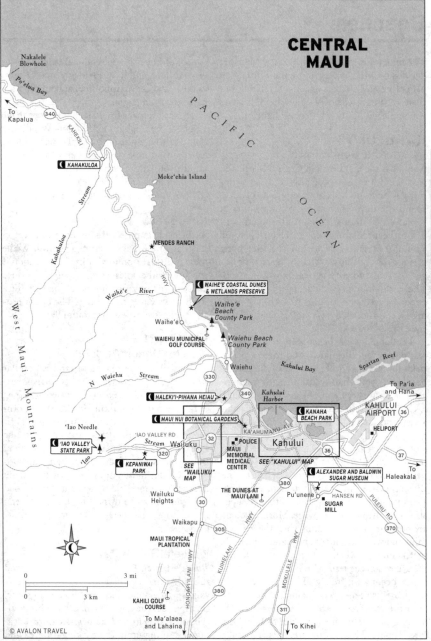

CENTRAL MAUI

Nakalele
Blowhole

Po'elua Bay

To
Kapalua

340

KAHEKILI

Kahakuloa Stream

KAHAKULOA

Moke'ehia Island

West Maui Mountains

MENDES RANCH

Waihe'e River HWY

WAIHE'E COASTAL DUNES & WETLANDS PRESERVE

Waihe'e Beach County Park

Waihe'e

WAIEHU MUNICIPAL GOLF COURSE

Waiehu Beach County Park

N Waiehu Stream

Waiehu

PACIFIC OCEAN

Kahului Bay

Spartan Reef

To Pa'ia and Hana

330

340

HALEKI'I-PIHANA HEIAU

Kahului Harbor

KANAHA BEACH PARK

KAHULUI AIRPORT

36

MAUI NUI BOTANICAL GARDENS

'Iao Needle

'IAO VALLEY RD

'Iao Stream Wailuku

32

KA'AHUMANU AVE

Kahului

HELIPORT

'IAO VALLEY STATE PARK

320

'Iao

KEPANIWAI PARK

POLICE

MAUI MEMORIAL MEDICAL CENTER

SEE "WAILUKU" MAP

SEE "KAHULUI" MAP

36

37

To Haleakala

ALEXANDER AND BALDWIN SUGAR MUSEUM

380

Wailuku Heights

THE DUNES AT MAUI LANI

Pu'unene

HANSEN RD

PUEHU RD

30

Waikapu

305 HWY

SUGAR MILL

370

MAUI TROPICAL PLANTATION

380

KUIHELANI HWY

HONOAPI'ILANI HWY

MOKULELE HWY

0   3 mi

0   3 km

KAHILI GOLF COURSE

To Ma'alaea and Lahaina

311

To Kihei

© AVALON TRAVEL

Beaches

The undeveloped beaches of Central Maui are defined by wind, waves, and water sports. You won't find any tiki bars or activities stands, but there are long stretches of undeveloped beaches where the world's best watermen hang out.

KAHULUI
◖ Kanaha Beach Park

Kanaha is the best beach in Central Maui. You won't find it on any postcards, and the swimming is poor, but this is an enjoyable place to spend the day. The early morning hours at Kanaha offer dramatic views of the mountains before the midmorning clouds roll in. There are a number of sandy beaches interspersed among various rocky points, which, when strung together, make for the perfect morning stroll. Those who want to go for a longer jog can head out on a paved path running from the last parking lot entrance all the way to Stable Road and the town of Spreckelsville.

The large, grassy beach park has showers, restrooms, and lifeguards, and there are also fields for playing Frisbee and one of the island's best beach volleyball courts. There's a campground on western end of the park, although it's been known to attract more unsavory characters and feral cats than actual law-abiding campers.

The beach area itself is broken up into two sections called Uppers and Lowers (Uppers being the farthest to the right when facing the ocean), and there's a protected, roped-off swimming area between the two that is popular with those wanting to wade. Morning hours are popular for spearfishing when the water is calm and with longboard and stand-up paddle surfers on days when there are waves. During the afternoon the trade winds pick up and the beach becomes a frenzy of windsurfers. No windsurfing is allowed before 11am, and by 5pm the wind has usually died down again, making the beach a mellow place to spend the sunset hours. This is also a great place to kill a couple of hours if you've already checked out of your hotel and have a late-afternoon flight, as the rental car return offices are only about a half-mile from the park.

To reach Kanaha from Hana Highway, make a right at the stoplight for Hobron Avenue and then another right onto Amala Place. Drive for about 1.5 miles, and although you'll pass a number of parking lots for other beaches, the best ones for Kanaha Beach Park itself are the last two entrances down at the dead end.

Kite Beach

As the name implies, **Kite Beach** is *the* place on the island for Maui's kitesurfing crowd. While there is little reason to visit in the afternoon if you aren't either kitesurfing or watching others kitesurf, the morning hours can be nice for a stroll or watching the sunrise. The beach usually begins seeing lessons around 9am.

WAILUKU
Waiehu Beach Park

This small strip of grass and sand is popular with locals, who come to surf, spearfish, barbecue, and drink beer on the weekends. The dunes are nice for walking in the early morning, and groups of surfers usually frequent offshore. Since the beach faces almost due east, the sunrises can be particularly rewarding. **Waiehu Beach Park** is a strictly local hangout with little to offer most visitors. To reach Waiehu Beach Park, travel along Waiehu Beach Road until you reach the turnoff for Lower Waiehu Beach Road, and then follow it to the parking lot at the end.

Waihe'e Beach Park

Waihe'e Beach Park is a thin stretch of sand running along a turbulent sea. Due to the prevailing trade winds blowing directly onshore, this spot can be good for beachcombing, although transient and homeless camps occasionally spring up in the parking lot area and

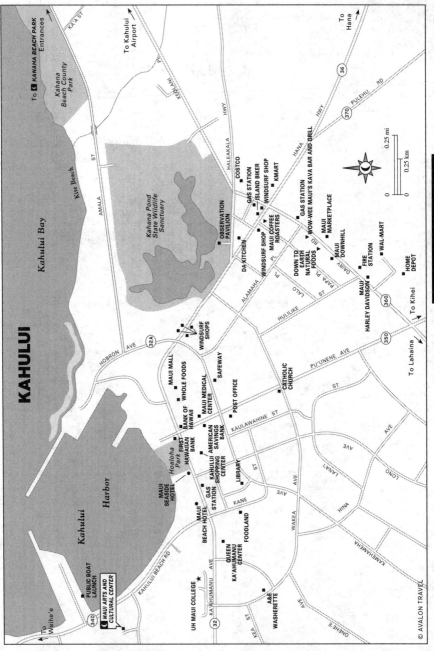

CENTRAL MAUI

© AVALON TRAVEL

CENTRAL MAUI

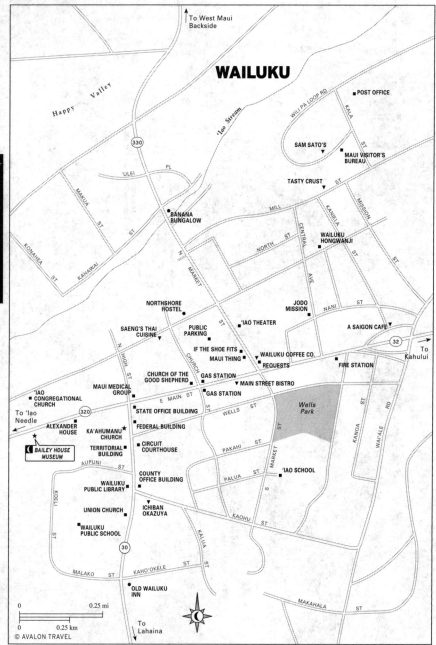

WAILUKU

To West Maui Backside

Happy Valley

'Iao Stream

330

'ULEI PL

MAKUA ST

KONAHEA ST

KAHAWAI ST

WILI PA LOOP RD

■ POST OFFICE

KALA ST

SAM SATO'S ▼

■ MAUI VISITOR'S BUREAU

TASTY CRUST ▼

KANIELA ST

MISSION ST

● BANANA BUNGALOW

N MARKET ST

NORTH ST

MILL ST

CENTRAL AVE

■ WAILUKU HONGWANJI

NORTHSHORE HOSTEL ●

JODO MISSION ■

NANI ST

SAENG'S THAI CUISINE ▼

PUBLIC PARKING ■

'IAO THEATER ■

N HIGH ST

CHURCH ST

IF THE SHOE FITS ■

MAUI THING ■

WAILUKU COFFEE CO. ■

REQUESTS ▼

A SAIGON CAFE ▼

32

To Kahului

FIRE STATION ■

CHURCH OF THE GOOD SHEPHERD ■

GAS STATION ■

MAIN STREET BISTRO ▼

MAUI MEDICAL GROUP ■

GAS STATION ■

'IAO CONGREGATIONAL CHURCH ■

E MAIN ST

320

To 'Iao Needle

■ STATE OFFICE BUILDING

WELLS ST

Wells Park

KANOA ST

WAIALE RD

ALEXANDER HOUSE ●

KA'AHUMANU CHURCH ★

■ FEDERAL BUILDING

☾ BAILEY HOUSE MUSEUM

TERRITORIAL BUILDING ■

■ CIRCUIT COURTHOUSE

PAKAHI ST

KOELI ST

AUPUNI ST

■ COUNTY OFFICE BUILDING

PALUA ST

S MARKET ST

● 'IAO SCHOOL

WAILUKU PUBLIC LIBRARY ■

UNION CHURCH ●

ICHIBAN OKAZUYA ▼

KAOHU ST

KALIA ST

■ WAILUKU PUBLIC SCHOOL

30

MALAKO ST

KAHO'OKELE ST

● OLD WAILUKU INN

MAKAHALA ST

0   0.25 mi
0   0.25 km

© AVALON TRAVEL

To Lahaina

the shoreline can smell of seaweed. To reach Waiheʻe Beach Park, follow Waiehu Beach Road until it turns into Kahekili Highway (Highway 340), and make a right on Halewaiu Road following the signs for the golf course. Before the turnoff into the golf course parking lot, a small road goes to the left, which you can follow all the way to a parking lot. The beach park itself is small, although if you walk on the sand to the left you'll eventually come to a stretch of shoreline that parallels the Waiheʻe Coastal Dunes and Wetlands Preserve.

Surfing

Since the beaches of Central Maui face north and east, the majority of the surfing on this side of the island takes place October-April. Some eastward-facing locations can pick up wind-swell during summer, but often it's choppy, and sloppy. No surf schools operate along this stretch of coast; anyone opting to surf around here needs to be at least an intermediate. Since part of this stretch runs along Maui's fabled North Shore, only the spots which are accessible to the average surfer are mentioned. As for professional watermen who surf the outer reefs when the waves reach 70 feet or more? Thanks, but we'll watch from shore.

KAHULUI

The most popular surf break in Kahului is **Lowers** at **Kanaha Beach Park.** If you're an intermediate to advanced longboarder, then this is the place to come on any sort of northerly swell. To reach the surfing section of the park, travel down Amala Place all the way to the end of the road and park in one of the last two parking lots. Grab your board and wear your slippers as you walk down to the shoreline to avoid kiawe thorns and burrs. Once you're standing on the sand, look for the lifeguard tower you'll paddle out from. The wave at Kanaha breaks on an offshore reef, so reaching the lineup requires a shoulder-burning paddle and at least a couple of rest stops, although a long paddle means a long ride. Given the length of the paddle (usually about 15 minutes), Kanaha is frequented by longboarders and stand-up paddle surfers. When standing in front of the lifeguard tower, you'll notice a defined channel for reaching the lineup, and the surf usually won't close it out until the faces reach 10 feet or higher. Mornings are best before the wind picks up (usually around 11am).

WAILUKU

The most popular surf break in Wailuku is **Big Lefts** in the area known as Paukukalo. This long left-hand wave can get very big on north and northeasterly swells, although it's reserved for advanced surfers only and is heavily localized. Nevertheless, if you're confident in your abilities, are well-acquainted with surf etiquette, and the wind is blowing *kona* (out of the south), "Pakuz" can be one of the best—and most challenging—waves on the island. To access it, turn onto Waiehu Beach Road and then make a right on Ukali Street, following it to the end. The surf break is in front of the parking lot. Don't leave any valuables in your car. The wave here is a rocky beach break that works best at low tide, so be careful paddling out over the shallow rocks.

WINDSURFING

Maui is one of world's top windsurfing destinations. Walking along **Kanaha Beach Park,** you'll hear salty-haired windsurfers conversing in everything from Portuguese to Japanese. The summer trade winds are consistent, arriving like clockwork around 11am to offer 5-6 hours of steady, flat water. During winter, the trade winds aren't nearly as consistent and waves reach 15 feet or higher.

There's strictly no windsurfing before 11am, and Kanaha is split into two main launching areas conveniently named Uppers and Lowers. Many of the windsurfing schools

CENTRAL MAUI

© KYLE ELLISON

dawn-patrol surf session at Paukukalo

operate by Uppers at a cove known as Kook's Beach. Lowers is in the area by the lifeguard tower and is the preferred launching point for most Maui visitors. In between the two areas is a roped-off swimming zone off limits to all windsurfers even if you're swimming your board. If there are waves breaking on the reef, you'll notice a channel off the lifeguard stand where you can get past the break and out beyond the surf.

For more information on Maui windsurfing, go to www.mauiwindsurfing.net for photos, rental operators, and descriptions of the various launching sites. Or, for a live cam of the conditions at Kanaha, check out www.maui-windcam.com.

KITESURFING

The best place for kitesurfing on Maui is at the aptly named **Kite Beach,** a place of hallowed ground where the sport was born. This is the beach where all kitesurfing schools operate, and just as at neighboring Kanaha, it isn't uncommon to watch an Italian guy from Sardinia help a man from Japan launch his kite while a pack of French-speaking onlookers discuss what size kite they're going to use. Even if you aren't a kitesurfer yourself, this is a fantastic spot to sit and watch as hundreds of colorful kites zip through the gusty trade winds. To reach Kite Beach from Hana Highway follow Hobron Avenue toward the Port of Kahului and make a right on Amala Place. Kanaha Kai rental shop will be on your right, then follow the road for a mile until just before a cement bridge. A dirt parking lot on the left side of the road will have a number of vans offering lessons and information. Since Kite Beach is so close to Kanaha, the unwritten rule is that kitesurfers are supposed to stay downwind (closer to Kahului Harbor) of the windsurfers to avoid a high-speed entanglement. Even though this is one of the premier spots on the planet for kitesurfing, the winds can be strong and gusty during the summer (particularly on an east wind), and the waves can be big during winter. Unless you're an advanced kitesurfer,

© KYLE ELLISON

Windsurfers take to the waves.

take a lesson to learn the local conditions and ensure you have the safest, most enjoyable kitesurfing experience possible.

For information relating to Maui kitesurfing, safety, and maps of which areas are prohibited, check out www.kitesurfmaui.org. For a webcam of current wind and weather conditions go to www.kitebeachcam.com.

Stand-Up Paddling

Unlike in South or West Maui, there aren't any stand-up paddleboard lessons offered along the island's central coast. If you have your own board (or have rented one), the best bet for flat-water paddling is **Kanaha Beach Park** on the inside of the reef. Since the reef is a couple of hundred yards offshore, it forms a nice lagoon on the inside, and the water is often calm during the morning before the trade winds pick up. If you're a competent paddle surfer and want to get into the waves, paddle through the channel off the lifeguard stand at Lowers, where you will find waves perfectly suited for stand-up paddle surfing. These are only for advanced paddlers who can handle themselves in large surf.

RENTAL SHOPS

Kahului boasts a large number of rental shops where you can pick up anything from surfboards to stand-up paddleboards and kitesurfing to windsurfing gear. Of all the shops, **HI Tech Surf Sports** (425 Koloa St., 808/877-2111,www.surfmaui.com, 9am-6pm daily) has the largest selection of surf and stand-up paddleboards, which are $25 and $35 per day, respectively. **Hawaiian Island Surf and Sport** (415 Dairy Rd., 808/871-4981, www.hawaiian-island.com, 8:30am-6pm daily) has surfboards start at $20/day or $110/week, and you can save 10 percent by prebooking your board online. There are also stand-up boards for $35/day or $199/week, and the same early booking discounts apply.

If you're a fan of Naish equipment, **Naish** (111 Hana Hwy., 808/871-1503, www.naish-maui.com, 9am-5pm daily) also has a store in Kahului offering a full range of rentals. For windsurfing, **Second Wind** (111 Hana Hwy., 808/877-7467, www.secondwindmaui.com, 9am-6pm daily) offers full packages with all the gear you'll need from $55/day to $575 for a 14-day package.

The shop closest to the beach itself is **Kanaha Kai** (96 Amala Pl., 808/877-7778, www.kanahakai.com, 9am-5pm daily), which offers a 20 percent prebooking special on windsurf bookings of seven days or more. Regular rates without the discount are $50/day for a windsurfing rig to $560 for a 14-day package. You can also get a surfboard for only $90/week, although the selection is smaller than at the stores back in town.

SCHOOLS AND LESSONS

Since Maui can offer some of the most exhilarating, yet challenging, conditions for windsurfing and kitesurfing, those who want to pick up the sports can save themselves hours of frustration by taking lessons from a pro. When it comes to both, one class isn't going to be enough, so ideally you want to book at least a five-hour package to maximize your investment. Then again, every school offers a single-session option for those testing the waters to see if the sport is for them.

One of the largest schools is **Action Sports Maui** (96 Amala Pl., 808/871-5857, www.actionsportsmaui.com), a company that runs its North Shore operation out of Kanaha Kai surf shop on the road toward Kite Beach. Kiting lessons range from $199 for a 2.5-hour intro class

to $2,050 for a 10-day, 30-hour intensive training package. Windsurfing lessons range from $89 for 2.5 hours to $395-575 (group/private) for a five-day course. Action Sports Maui also offers classes which focus on honing individual skills such as jibing, waterstarting, and shortboard basics.

Kitesurfing School of Maui (808/873-0015, www.ksmaui.com) is a school which focuses, as the name suggests, specifically on kitesurfing. The operation is inside the NeilPryde shop in Kahului. A three-hour, one-day class to teach you the basics will cost $270, and a six-hour, two-day class is $495. If you want to delve into the sport, you can spring for the 18-hour, five-day class for $1,295.

Another operation with multisport instruction is **Hawaiian Sailboard Techniques** (425 Koloa St., 808/871-5423, www.hstwindsurfing.com), inside HI Tech Surf Sports. Founder Alan Cadiz has been teaching windsurfing on Maui since 1985, making this the longest-running outfit on the island's North Shore. When kitesurfing came into existence, Cadiz was among some of the first instructors to teach the sport to others, and what's nice about Cadiz's lessons is that an instructor will accompany you on a stand-up paddleboard to talk you through the finer points. Three-hour kitesurfing lessons are $255, and private windsurfing lessons run from $127.50 for 1.5 hours to $459 for a six-hour package.

Aqua Sports (Kite Beach, 808/242-8015, www.mauikiteboardinglessons.com) is right on Kite Beach and offers a $99 two-hour rate for beginners who want to give kiteboarding a try. The classes start at 9am so the beach isn't crowded with other kiters. Even though you don't get in the water, you're able to learn how to control the kite and see if this is a sport you could take up. Additional courses are offered at competitive rates, and online booking specials frequently lower the cost to some of the island's best rates.

Hiking and Biking

HIKING
'Iao Valley

Even though the drive into **'Iao Valley** goes deep into Mauna Kahalawai, the valley itself doesn't have very good public hiking. The only part of 'Iao Valley which could be considered a hike is the 10-minute, paved walking trail leading up to a lookout peering out at 'Iao Needle. If you go out there, you'll notice a railing that keeps visitors from walking into the bush, and on the other side of the railing you'll notice a thin trail which disappears back into the trees. This trail snakes its way through the forest for a couple of miles, although this area is officially off-limits due to the fact that it's easy to get lost—especially if the clouds roll in.

If you want to swim in 'Iao Stream, the best place for accessing the swimming holes is from Kepaniwai Heritage Gardens, where short trails lead down to the refreshing—and cold—water.

◖ Waihe'e Coastal Dunes and Wetlands Preserve

Set on land protected by the Hawaiian Islands Land Trust, this hike passing for two miles along the undeveloped shoreline of Waihe'e has only recently been opened to visitors. Within the 277-acre preserve are the remains of the Kapoho fishing village as well as two different ancient *heiau*. Scholars estimate that the Waihe'e area was populated as early as AD 300-600, which is not surprising, as the freshwater streams, fertile valleys, and lush uplands provide all the natural resources needed for sustaining life. The lonesome shoreline is covered in driftwood and is a great place for beachcombing. This is one of the few places on the island where you can walk down a sandy beach and be the only person around.

The trail itself parallels the shoreline and passes by a couple of abandoned houses before reaching the cultural relics at Kapoho. Expect the round-trip journey to take a little over an hour; add on 30 minutes to explore the coastline or ruins. To reach the trailhead, make a right on Halewaiu Place off Kahekili Highway (Hwy. 340) and follow the signs for Waiehu Golf Course. When the road makes a sharp turn to the right and starts heading toward the golf course, you'll notice an unmarked dirt road going to the left. From this turnoff it's 0.25 mile to the parking area and trailhead, although the unpaved road and small stream crossing are unsuitable for rental cars. You can either park your car here at the turnoff or on the access road which leads down to Waihe'e Beach Park just before the golf course. It's best to park away from the fairway since golfers sometimes drive balls into the parking lot. If you're on your way back from Mendes Ranch or are spending the day driving around the back of the island, this is a fantastic place to not only stretch your legs and explore the shoreline, but to also gain a valuable insight into ancient Hawaiian culture.

Waihe'e Ridge Trail

Driving the Kahekili Highway from Wailuku, the parking area for the **Waihe'e Ridge Trail** is immediately across the road from Mendes Ranch, at the seven-mile marker. This 2.5-mile trail starts innocently enough but does become a switchback farther up. It also crosses some areas that become boggy after a rain. The trail rises to over 2,560 feet with spectacular views into Waihe'e and Makamaka'ole Valleys. The trail continues to Lanilili summit, where on clear days you can see the northern slope of the mountain. This area can get cloudy, blocking the views, although generally if you start hiking before 9am, you'll finish the trail before the clouds start rolling in. This trail takes some energy, so count on three hours for the five-mile trip.

Makamaka'ole Valley

If you're on the hunt for waterfalls, head to the *makai* (ocean-side) section of **Makamaka'ole**

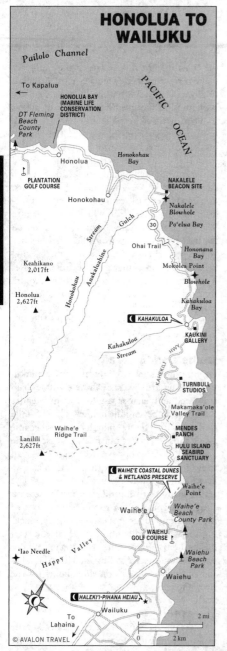

HONOLUA TO WAILUKU

Pailolo Channel

To Kapalua

HONOLUA BAY
(MARINE LIFE
CONSERVATION
DISTRICT)

DT Fleming
Beach
County
Park

Honokohau
Bay

Honolua

PLANTATION
GOLF COURSE

Honokohau

NAKALELE
BEACON SITE

Nakalele
Blowhole

Po'elua Bay

Ohai Trail

Hononana
Bay

Mokolea Point

Blowhole

Kahakuloa
Bay

KAHAKULOA

KAUKINI
GALLERY

Keahikano
2,017ft

Honolua
2,627ft

Kahakuloa
Stream

TURNBULL
STUDIOS

Makamaka'ole
Valley Trail

Waihe'e
Ridge Trail

MENDES
RANCH

Lanilili
2,627ft

HULU ISLAND
SEABIRD
SANCTUARY

WAIHE'E COASTAL DUNES
& WETLANDS PRESERVE

Waihe'e
Point

Waihe'e

Waihe'e
Beach
County
Park

WAIEHU
GOLF COURSE

'Iao Needle

Happy

Valley

Waiehu
Beach
Park

Waiehu

HALEKI'I-PIHANA HEIAU

To
Lahaina

Wailuku

0   2 mi

0   2 km

© AVALON TRAVEL

PACIFIC OCEAN

Honolua Stream

Anakaluahine Gulch

KAHEKILI HWY 30

Valley where a couple of small waterfalls are hidden in the jungle. Although it's a user-friendly, short hike, the trail can be slippery and requires climbing over a couple of boulders. Be respectful of No Trespassing signs and leave the area as you found it.

If approaching from Wailuku, the discreet trailhead is 7.8 miles after making the turn onto Waiehu Beach Road, or 0.8 miles after the Mendes Ranch. At this point the road has climbed in elevation and narrowed at parts to only a single lane. You'll pass a sharp turn in the valley, and when the road starts pointing back toward the ocean, you'll notice a small dirt pullout which can accommodate four or five vehicles. The trailhead is a narrow, well-defined dirt pathway that heads downhill into the brush. There's also a false trailhead that departs from the same parking area but only goes for about five yards. If the trail suddenly ends after 10 seconds, turn around and look for the other one. Once you are on the correct trail, it will wind its way downhill for about 10 minutes before arriving at a small swimming hole where you'll find a rushing waterfall and a rope swing. Along the way you're rewarded with a dramatic view of Makamaka'ole Valley as it wends its way to the ocean below.

The trail continues deeper into the valley toward a waterfall more dramatic than the first. You'll have to climb over a large boulder to keep on the trail, which will then parallel the river over some slippery rocks. The mosquitoes can be vicious in this shaded section, so be sure you've applied repellent or have covered yourself. After tracing the river for 10 minutes, the trail will end at a large banyan tree whose serpentine roots snake down a near-vertical cliff face. In order to reach the pool below, climb down using the roots of the banyan tree as handholds as if it were a natural ladder. As you can imagine, this is a maneuver which requires some athletic ability and skill, so it should only be attempted by those who are agile and accepting of the risks. The reward, however, is a small swimming hole where you can bathe beneath a waterfall in a hidden tropical setting. This spot is popular with many guided hiking tours.

Hike back through time at the Waiheʻe Coastal Dunes and Wetlands Preserve.

HIKING TOURS

Hike Maui (808/879-5270 or 866/324-6284, www.hikemaui.com, 6am-8pm daily) offers knowledgeable guides who will take you to some of the island's most scenic locations. Group sizes are usually fairly small, and again, what makes these hikes worthwhile is not only being taken directly to the trailhead (no arguing about directions in the car!), but also learning about the island's flora, fauna, history, and mythology from local guides who love what they do. Hike Maui meets guests in a large community parking lot in Kahului near the intersection of Kuihelani Highway (Hwy. 380) and Puʻunene Avenue and offers waterfall hikes, trips into Haleakala Crater, and options that combine kayaking with an afternoon hike through the rainforest.

BIKING

Despite the steep grade of the West Maui Mountains there aren't any official mountain biking trails. For road cycling, the most popular ride is heading from Kahului to the fishing village of **Kahakuloa** and back. Distances will vary depending on where you start, but along the way cyclists will be treated to quad-burning ascents, hairpin turns through rainforest surroundings, and sweeping views of the entire North Shore. Sharing the road with cars can be tough considering how narrow it gets, but most cars are traveling so slowly around the tight turns that altercations are rare. If you would prefer to be on a designated bike path that stays on level ground, the **North Shore Greenway** runs from the last parking lot at Kanaha Beach Park all the way to the town of Paʻia, and along the route of the seven-mile bike path only 0.25 mile passes along the shoulder of the main highway. To reach the Kahului terminus of the bike path, follow Amala Place all the way to the end and park in the last parking lot of Kanaha Beach Park. Parts of the bike path go directly behind the airport runway, and this ride is best in the morning due to the strong trade winds which can create momentum-destroying headwinds during the afternoon (the wind normally blows from Paʻia toward Kahului).

Rental Shops

Across the street from K-Mart by the Tesoro Gas Station, **Island Biker Maui** (415 Dairy Rd., 808/877-7744, www.islandbikermaui. com, 9am-5pm weekdays, 9am-3pm Sat.) offers rentals which range from $60/day to $250/week. All bike rentals come with flat repair tools, water bottles, one spare tube, and local insights from staff members who ride

these roads on a regular basis. Both mountain bikes and road bikes are available.

At **Crater Cycles** (358 Papa Pl., 808/893-2020, www.cratercycleshawaii.com, 9am-5pm Mon.-Sat.), rentals range $65-85/day depending on which ride you're going to be doing. The focus here is mainly on mountain biking. If you're looking for information on trail conditions in Polipoli, Skyline Drive, or Makawao Forest Reserve, these are the folks to call.

Horseback Riding and Bird-Watching

HORSEBACK RIDING

The most well-known horseback riding outfit on this side of the island is **Mendes Ranch** (3530 Kahekili Hwy., 808/871-5222, www. mendesranch.com), a family-run operation on the road to Kahakuloa. Just before the seven-mile marker on Kahekili Highway, often you will smell Mendes Ranch before you see it. That's what happens when you have a fully operational ranch with more than 300 head of cattle, but it's all part of the *paniolo* experience. While group sizes can be large and the 1.5-hour rides run $110/person, what separates Mendes from all the other ranches is that you can actually run the horses. That's right: You can gallop at Mendes, so there's no nose-to-tail riding here. The ride itself goes from the family ranch house down the bluffs to the windswept shoreline, and lunch can be included with some of the tours. Expect afternoon rides to be windy and the morning rides to be clearer and calm. The coastal views here aren't accessible by any other means, and Mendes Ranch is a fabulous option to see them.

Much closer to the main resort areas is the central **Makani Olu Ranch** (363 W. Waiko Rd., 808/870-0663, www.makaniuranch. com), another working cattle ranch set back in the Waikapu Valley. Only 25 minutes from Wailea and 35 minutes from Ka'anapali, Makani Olu maintains a herd of 100 long-horn cattle and caps the trail rides at only four riders. The two-hour, $125 ride takes guests

across Waikapu Stream into the forest behind the Maui Tropical Plantation and eventually turns inland and works its way up the valley. The views from this part of the trail look back at Haleakala and the green central isthmus, and this is the only way you can gain access to this remote part of the island. Unlike at Mendes Ranch, all the tours are at walking pace only, which makes them a better option for novice riders. A lunch option is available with the ride, and experienced riders can opt for a $150, private or semiprivate ride that includes 45 minutes in a round pen working on skills. While this is a nice option for families, all riders must be over 10 years old and under 220 pounds.

BIRD-WATCHING

The best bird-watching in Central Maui is at the **Kanaha Pond State Wildlife Sanctuary,** five minutes from the Kahului airport along Hana Highway. This royal fishpond used to provide island *ali'i* with a consistent supply of mullet, although the dredging of Kahului Harbor in 1910 altered the natural flow of water. Today this pond is on the migratory route of various birds and serves as a temporary home to dozens of vagrant bird species. Most important, it's also home to the endangered Hawaiian stilt (*ae'o*), a slender, 16-inch bird with a black back, white belly, and sticklike pink legs. The Hawaiian coot (*'alae ke'oke'o*), a gray-black, duck-like bird that builds large floating nests, may also be seen here. An observation pavilion is maintained on the pond's south edge, accessible through a gate by a short walkway from the parking area. This pavilion is always open and free of charge. Entry to the walking trails within the sanctuary is free, but only by permit on weekdays from the first day of September to the last day of March. Apply 8am-3:30pm Monday-Friday at the **Department of Natural Resources, Division of Forestry and Wildlife** (54 S. High St., Rm. 101, Wailuku, 808/984-8100) and supply the exact dates and times of your intended visit.

The best place for bird-watching in Wailuku is the **Waihe'e Coastal Dunes and Wetlands Preserve,** an expanse of low grassland where various seabirds and native species can be observed.

Adventure Sports

ZIPLINE TOURS

The most beginner-friendly zipline in the central valley is the **Maui Zipline** (1670 Honoapi'ilani Hwy., 808/633-2464, www.mauizipline.com), within the grounds of the Maui Tropical Plantation. This five-line zipline course is affordable at only $90, and children as young as five years old and as light as 50 pounds can take part in the adventure. As you might expect, a course that caters to such young children won't have the same element of extremism as some of the other courses, but the fact that the guides also introduce educational elements into the program (such as the weather patterns of the area and lessons on the surrounding plant species) makes this is a great option for families traveling with children. Cable lengths range 300-900 feet, and there are two cables running parallel to each other so you can go at the same time as a friend or loved one.

While a tame 500-foot zipline might be nice if you're traveling with young children, for those who want to go big or go home, the eight-line **Flyin Hawaiian Zipline** (1670 Honoapi'ilani Hwy., 808/463-4786, www.flyinhawaiianzipline.com, $185) covers 2.5 miles of West Maui mountainside and finishes in a different town. Guests meet at the Maui Tropical Plantation for a 4-by-4 ride back into Waikapu Valley where you will suit up for your midair journey across the mountain. Reservations are highly recommended.

In addition to views toward Haleakala, this zipline ecotour incorporates elements of habitat restoration for Hawai'i's native plants and works to remove nonnative species. The company champions sustainable, educational tourism, and the ecological element of the organization isn't just something done to appear green—it's the real deal.

The most enticing reason to book this tour is the ultra-long, cheek-clenching, three-screamer zipline that runs for more than 3,600 feet—the longest on the island. The lines aren't parallel to each other (so you can't watch your friend's cheeks flap at 50 mph), and the elevation isn't as high as the final, fifth line at Pi'iholo, but you also get a short ATV ride at the end of the tour as they shuttle you from the town of Ma'alaea back to Waikapu. Expect the tour to take 4-5 hours. Small snacks are included. The age limit is 10 years old and weight limit is 75-250 pounds.

ATV TOURS

The only ATV tours in Central Maui are at **Mendes Ranch** (3530 Kahekili Hwy., 808/871-5222, www.mendesranch.com, $79). Trails run from the riding corral down to the shoreline, and the views extend out over the Pacific. Riders must be at least 16 years old to drive one of the ATVs. Over the course of the one-hour ride, guides tell you about the history of Maui, the ranch, and the lineage of the Mendes family. This is one of the only ATV opportunities still available on the island and the only way besides riding a horse that you're going to get to experience the remote stretch of coastline.

HELICOPTER RIDES

Much of Maui is only accessible by helicopter. Helicopter tours are expensive, but if you treat yourself to one splurge, make it a helicopter tour. Eroded valleys, sheer ridgelines, and inaccessible waterfalls are all parts of most Maui helicopter tours, and a one-hour flight spent hovering over the island will be the most memorable hour of your vacation. All pilots flying for the major tour operators have logged thousands of flying hours and put an emphasis on safety. Most pilots also double as geologists, biologists, historians, and naturalists as they narrate tours above the island's interior. Morning hours are best because they offer the clear conditions necessary for visiting spots such as 1,100-foot Honokohau Falls. As an added bonus, during winter, you're able to spot humpback whales as they lounge in the waters below.

All helicopter flights depart from the Kahului Heliport (located 0.5 mile from the junction of Hana Highway and Haleakala Highway), and the two most popular tour options are those combining the West Maui Mountains with Moloka'i and East Maui (Hana) with Haleakala. Regardless of which operator you choose, inquire about getting the two front seats next to the pilot since it's much easier to take photos. Also, if you plan on booking a helicopter tour, remember that you cannot have been scuba diving within a 24-hour period before the flight (snuba, due to the shallow depth, is still permitted). All prices listed below are for online specials given for advance reservations.

Blue Hawaiian Helicopters (1 Kahului Airport Rd., #105, 808/871-8844 or 800/745-2583, www.bluehawaiian.com, 7am-10pm daily) is the largest tour operator and accommodates the largest number of island visitors. With offices on all of the major islands, these guys have been leaders in the Maui helicopter industry since their founding in 1985. They offer tours on two different types of 6-seat helicopters: the A-Star and the Eco-Star. The difference is that the Eco-Star provides individual bucket seats, has larger viewing windows, and can accommodate a greater amount of weight

than the A-Star. As you might expect, flights on the Eco-Star are a little more expensive. Packages run $149/person for a 30-minute tour of the West Maui Mountains to $440/person for a two hour tour of Maui and the Big Island (Hawai'i Volcanoes National Park not included). There's also a tour that touches down at an exclusive landing zone within Ulupalakua Ranch during a stopover of a full-island tour, offering access to a part of the island you would never visit otherwise. As with many other operators, DVDs of your experience can be purchased for an additional $25.

The only other tour operator with Eco-Star (referred to as Whisper-Star) helicopters in their fleet is **Sunshine Helicopters** (1 Kahului Airport Rd., #107, 808/270-3999 or 866/501-7738, www.sunshinehelicopters.com), and the seats in the front will cost you more than those in the back. Prices range from $170/person for a 30-minute West Maui flight to $350/person for a 55-65 minute West Maui and Moloka'i package. If Mendes Ranch horseback riding or the Atlantis Submarine are also on your list of activities, you can book them as a combo package through Sunshine Helicopters and save a little bit on both of the excursions.

A smaller yet reputable operation is **Air Maui** (1 Kahului Airport Rd, Hangar 110, 808/877-7005 or 877/238-4942, www.airmaui.com), a company with prices that are slightly higher but proudly boasting a perfect safety record. Fees range from $175/person for a 30-minute tour to $307/person for a 60-minute tour of West Maui and Moloka'i (which is 15 minutes longer than the same, albeit cheaper Blue Hawaiian Tour).

If you want to be *that* much closer to the scenery, **Alex Air** (108 Kahului Heliport, 808/877-4354, www.helitour.com, 8am-4pm daily) is the only company that offers flights with the doors off. That's right: No doors. No window. Just a waterfall or a mountain zipping past you in real time. Tours with the doors on range from $168/person for a 30-minute West Maui Mountains tour to $229 for a 50-minute tour of West Maui and Moloka'i. Doors-off tours cost a little bit more but are well worth it for the added adventure. If you would rather have a private tour, there are R44 helicopters which can accommodate 1-3 people and range from $450 for a 30-minute tour to $1,200 for a 90-minute East Maui tour combined with a private beach landing.

FLIGHTSEEING TOURS

While helicopters are the best choice for seeing the waterfalls of West Maui and the northern shore of Molokaʻi, the only way that you're going to experience Kilauea Volcano on the Big Island is by taking a flightseeing tour with **Maui Air** (808/877-5500, www.volcanoairtours.com) out of either Kahului or Kapalua Airport. The two-hour flight from Kahului Airport passes by the North Shore of Maui and the waterfalls of Kohala on the Big Island's northwestern tip and circles over Hawaiʻi Volcanoes National Park looking for active lava flows. The plane can accommodate 10 passengers, and you're likely to be sharing the ride with other guests. Those who sit toward the back won't have as much of the wing obstructing the view. At $385/person it isn't a cheap trip, and since weather is a highly variable factor, it can be a gamble. Also, as the eruption at Kilauea is constantly shifting, there's no guarantee of seeing red lava, although on those clear, lava-filled days when everything comes together, this is the best way to experience both islands from the air.

Golf and Tennis

GOLF
Kahului

The only golf course in Kahului is **The Dunes at Maui Lani** (1333 Maui Lani Pkwy., 808/873-0422, www.dunesatmauilani.com, 6:30am-6pm daily), a Scottish-style links course that weaves its way through natural sand dunes. Course designer Robert Nelson utilized the natural topography of the dunes in creating this 6,841-yard course, and as can be expected, it includes a healthy amount of bunkers. On the par-5 18th, two pot bunkers short of the green famously challenge even those with the lowest of handicaps. The afternoon trade winds can make this course difficult, and the greens fees are priced accordingly: $112 for visitors, $99 after 11am, and $79 after 2pm. Rates are substantially cheaper for resident golfers. The central location makes it easy to sneak in a round before heading to the airport.

Wailuku

Set on the hillside in Waikapu, the 6,554-yard **Kahili Golf Course** (2500 Honoapʻilani Hwy., 808/242-4653, www.kahiligolf.com, 6am-6pm daily) is one of the island's best values. Greens fees for visitors are $99, although those teeing off after 2:30pm can squeeze in 18 holes for only $59. The bicoastal views are better than at Maui Lani, although instead of links-style golf you have a course which is set on a gently sloping hillside. Wind can be an issue in the afternoons. It's a 30-minute drive from the resort complexes.

Intermediate golfers who don't want to shell out too much for a round can head to the **Waiehu Golf Course** (200 Halewaiu Rd., 808/243-7400, 6:45am-5pm weekdays, 6am-5pm weekends). This par-72, 6,330-yard municipal course is popular with locals because of the $25 resident's rate, although visitors can expect to pay $55 plus a $20 cart fee. The front nine are fairly straightforward with little elevation gain, and three of the holes go right along the shoreline. The back nine gain a little in elevation and offer views looking out over Waiheʻe Reef, where humpback whales can often be seen jumping during winter. While the views can indeed be spectacular, due to its northeasterly exposure the trade winds can be stiff in the afternoon, so it's best to secure a tee time before 9am to avoid them.

TENNIS
Kahului

The best courts in Kahului are the two at **Kahului**

© KYLE ELLISON

Tee off along the water at the municipal Waiehu Golf Course.

Community Center, located in a shaded area of the large community park. To reach the courts, turn on Onehe'e Avenue behind the Ka'ahumanu Shopping Center and continue for a quarter of the mile. The courts will be on your left.

Wailuku

With six courts, **Wells Park** is the most frequented of any in the central area. This is the headquarters for the Wailuku Jr. Tennis Program, and many of the island's tournaments are held here. The courts are on Wells Street, which runs parallel to Main Street, Wailuku's main thoroughfare.

Four more courts are available at the **War Memorial Sporting Complex,** but while there's a nice backboard to practice on, these courts can be prone to a little more wind. To reach the courts use the parking lot on Kanaloa Avenue off W. Ka'ahumana Avenue. The courts are on the west end of the football stadium and accessible via a small sidewalk.

Yoga, Fitness, and Spas

YOGA
Kahului

The best yoga studio in Kahului is **Kahului Yoga** (283 Lalo St., 808/874-5270, www.kahuluiyoga.com), a small studio in the industrial section of town. There's a full range of classes taught by experienced instructors, and a schedule of classes can be found on the website. Single session rates are $16, and a package of five classes is $75.

Wailuku

The largest yoga studio in Wailuku is **Body Alive** (1995 W. Main St., 808/359-1060, www.bodyaliveyoga.com) in historic downtown close to many shops and restaurants. Single sessions are $15, or a package of five classes can be purchased for $65. A wide range of classes are offered from Flow and Chill yoga to Combat yoga to the cross-fitness fusion of Yogalates (yoga and Pilates). Thai and zen shiatsu massage sessions are also available.

FITNESS
Kahului

The largest fitness center in Kahului is **24 Hour Fitness** (150 Hana Hwy., 808/877-7474, 5am-midnight Mon., 24 hours Tues.-Fri., 6am-10pm weekends), which offers a free three-day pass. It's open longer than anywhere else. Plus it's only five minutes from the airport if you need to squeeze in a workout before a red eye flight.

Anyone with a YMCA membership can head into the **Maui YMCA** (250 Kanaloa Ave., 808/242-9007, www.mauiymca.org. 5:30am-9pm Mon.-Fri., 7am-7pm Sat., 10am-6pm Sun.), which offers a large range of fitness equipment, free weights, a swimming pool, and a locker room.

Wailuku

For those who are addicted to CrossFit, **Maui CrossFit Extreme** (1495 Lower Main St., 808/205-1802, www.mauicrossfitextreme.com) offers five daily classes that mimic the CrossFit philosophy to offer intense workouts in a short period of time.

SPAS
Wailuku

On Main Street by the historic 'Iao Theater, **Green Ti Salon and Massage** (40 N. Market St., 808/242-8788, www.greentimaui.com, 10am-6pm daily) offers massage, acupuncture, facials, waxing, and other spa combination packages. A 50-minute massage costs $65, and you can choose from various options including lomi lomi, Swedish, reflexology, prenatal, and hot stone. Longer sessions are also available. While this small salon might not look like much from the outside, the interior is a calming retreat with an affable staff.

Sights

KAHULUI

◖ Maui Arts and Cultural Center

One of the reasons that Maui is *no ka oi* (the best) is that it truly does have a little of everything: tropical weather, world-class beaches, multicultural cuisine, hidden waterfalls, and live entertainment and cultural exhibitions on par with any metropolitan urban center. Though concerts and events are regularly held at various locations around the island, none offer the big-city professionalism of the $32-million-dollar **Maui Arts and Cultural Center** (1 Cameron Way, 808/242-7469, www. mauiarts.org), a figure that doesn't take into account the massive renovation which was undertaken in 2012.

Although it doesn't look like much from the highway, when you first step inside the Castle Theater or wander through the museum-quality Schaefer Gallery, you quickly realize that this is a place you would expect to find in New York, Chicago, or San Francisco. The 1,200-seat Castle Theater boasts three levels of seating, and the acoustics are designed in such a way that an unamplified guitar can be heard throughout the venue. The 250-seat McCoy Studio is a classic black-box theater which hosts smaller plays and theatrical events. The sprawling, 5,000-person A&B amphitheater has drawn some of the world's biggest musical talents from Elton John to Prince and Jimmy Buffett to The Eagles. The Maui Film Festival is partially held here on a screen inside the Castle Theater, and movies regularly show throughout the year. The constantly changing schedule of performances is listed on the website.

◖ Maui Nui Botanical Gardens

For anyone with an interest in Polynesian flora or sustainable irrigation and farming techniques, the **Maui Nui Botanical Gardens** (150 Kanaloa Ave., 808/249-2798, www.mnbg. org, 8am-4pm Mon.-Sat., free) is an absolute must-stop. From the moment you walk in the entranceway, native trees and their informational placards are displayed in a shaded walkway, and small signs warn you to watch out for falling *ulu,* or breadfruit, which populate the treetops above. As you meander along the self-guided walking tour, various signs discuss the differences between endemic, indigenous, and introduced plant species. A central theme of the garden is the way in which traditional irrigation techniques maximize the ability to farm in a semiarid climate. Freshwater was considered to be among the most precious of resources to Polynesian farmers, and more than 70 species of dryland *kalo,* or taro, are successfully growing in what is otherwise a dry coastal dunes system. Although not as expansive as the botanical gardens in Kula, the way in which the gardens espouse the Polynesian view that humans are but stewards of the land offers reason enough to visit.

◖ Alexander and Baldwin Sugar Museum

There's no place on the island where you can gain a better understanding of Maui's plantation heritage than at the **Alexander and Baldwin Sugar Museum** (3957 Hansen Rd., 808/871-8058, www.sugarmuseum.com, 9:30am-4pm daily, $10), a small, worn-down building in the Central Maui near-ghost town of Pu'unene. This town which was once the beating heart of Maui's sugar industry has been reduced to a faint pulse: A post office, a bookstore, the museum, and the stinky sugar mill are all that remain.

Exhibits discuss everything from how the sugar plant moved across Polynesia in traditional voyaging canoes to historical profiles of the island's first sugar barons. In addition to educating visitors about the growth of the sugar industry, what makes the museum a must-see attraction is the window it provides into the daily lives of the plantation workers who came

DREAM CITY

Not many island visitors spend time in residential Kahului. A sprawl of suburban homes and a maze of intertwined streets, it is a place where even longtime island locals can sometimes get turned around on the back roads. This aging, funky, dated, and low-key venue doesn't end up on many postcards. Rows of cement block homes house multigenerational families. Property values are on the lower end of the island's inflated real estate market.

This hasn't always been the case. Kahului existed for 60 years as a community of plantation camps. With the onset of World War II, many field laborers either joined the military or took jobs in the shipyards or manufacturing. After the war, prosperity swept across the nation. Young soldiers came home and settled down, starting families, and bought homes. It was the height of the American Dream.

But in the 1940s, Kahului didn't have any homes. Everything was owned by the sugar plantation. In 1948, the Alexander and Baldwin sugar plantation realized this opportunity, building 4,000 homes on plantation land. The quarter-acre lots would be sold fee simple giving plantation workers the chance to be homeowners. Seizing upon the national mood, the development was to be called Dream City. In 1950 Kahului became one of the first master planned towns west of the Rocky Mountains. Home prices ranged $6,000-9,000.

Today many of these homes are still owned by the original families, although after 60 years a number are in need of a paint job and a facelift. Even though residential Kahului might not look like much now, it was once a place where dreams came true.

---

from around the globe and endured long days in the fields. The cultural exhibits within the museum include everything from the handsewn Japanese clothing used to protect workers from centipedes to Portuguese bread ovens used by immigrants from the Azores to make their famous staple. There's even an exhibit relating to Filipino cockfighting.

The best thing about visiting this museum, however, is the sense of appreciation you gain for the legions of fieldworkers who continue to toil beneath the midday sun. There aren't too many museums where the culture you read about inside still largely persists just outside the museum walls.

WAILUKU
Ka'ahumanu Church

On South High Street at the turnoff for 'Iao Valley, it's fitting that Maui's oldest existing stone church is named after Queen Ka'ahumanu. This rock-willed woman is the Saint Peter of Hawai'i, upon whom Christianity in the islands was built. She was *the* most important early convert, often attending services in Kahului's humble grass-hut chapel. It's also worth noting that the church was erected on Maui king Kahekili's *heiau*—the squashing of one religion with the growing presence of another. In 1832, when the congregation was founded, an adobe church was built on the same spot and named in her honor. Rain and time washed it away, to be replaced by the island's first stone structure in 1837. Its construction was supervised by the missionary Edward Bailey, whose home stands to the rear, and a three-year renovation project ended in 1976, bringing the church back to form and allowing it placement on the National Register of Historic Places. Services at **Ka'ahumanu Church** (103 S. High St.) are at 9am Sunday, when the Hawaiian congregation sings the Lord's praise in their native language. It's an excellent cultural and religious event to attend.

◖ Bailey House Museum

Regardless of whether or not you're a "museum person," every visitor to Maui should see the **Bailey House Museum** (2375-A Main St., 10am-4pm Mon.-Sat., $7 adults, $2 children

© KYLE ELLISON

Alexander and Baldwin Sugar Museum

7-12) on the road to ʻIao Valley. The Bailey House was built between 1833 and 1850, and from 1837 to 1849 this whitewashed, missionary-style building housed the Wailuku Female Seminary, of which Edward Bailey was principal. With the opening of Lahainaluna High School in 1831 (which is the oldest public high school in the United States west of the Rocky Mountains), it was decided that the young, educated graduates of Lahainaluna would need refined, educated women whom they could eventually take as wives, hence the need for the seminary. After the closing of the institution the Baileys bought the property, began to raise sugarcane, and lived here until 1888. During this time, Edward Bailey became the manager of the Wailuku Sugar Company, and more important for posterity, he became a prolific landscape painter of various areas around the island. Most of his paintings record the period 1866-1896 and are now displayed in the Bailey Gallery, which was once the sitting room of the house. In 1973 it was placed on the National Register of Historic Places.

Inside the museum, the Hawaiian Room houses artifacts of precontact Hawaiʻi such as wooden spears, stone tools, knives made from conch shells, and daggers made from shark's teeth. In the same room there are also stone *kiʻi,* or statues, depicting the Hawaiian war god Ku, expertly crafted wooden calabashes, and an exhibit of artifacts found on the island of Kahoʻolawe from both the pre- and post-bombing eras. Upstairs are two bedrooms which feature detailed information about the lineage of the Hawaiian royalty as well as missionary-era furniture, jewelry boxes, clothing, and handmade quilts. Back downstairs is the room full of Bailey's paintings. Also for those who want to further their knowledge of the islands, the bookstore ranks as the best educational, cultural resource on the island where you can find many of the best titles ever written on Hawaiian history.

There isn't a surfer on the planet who would pass up the chance to see the massive redwood surfboard once surfed by the ambassador of

MAUI SUGAR

© KYLE ELLISON

CENTRAL MAUI

sugar cane fields

Hawaiian Commercial and Sugar Company, a division of Alexander and Baldwin, produces between 170,000 and 185,000 tons of raw sugar annually at its Pu'unene mill—the last sugar mill left in the state of Hawai'i—enough to account for 5 percent of total U.S. production. About 35,000 acres of land on the island are under cultivation, mostly spread across the isthmus. On average, each acre yields about 12 tons of sugar. Aside from the raw sugar, which is sent to Crocket, California, to be refined at the C&H processing plant owned by Hawaiian sugar planters, the Pu'unene mill yields 52,000 tons of molasses annually and gener-

ates 6 percent of Maui's electricity by burning bagasse, the crushed cane left after the juice is extracted.

Maui once had 14 mills spread between Lahaina and Hana. Remnants of the Pa'ia mill (built in 1880, completely rebuilt in 1905, but now mostly dismantled after being shut down in 2000) can still be seen along Baldwin Avenue above the town of Pa'ia. The Pioneer Sugar Mill in Lahaina has also mostly been taken down since its closure in 1999. Concrete remnants of old mill buildings front an old pier in Olowalu, and a mill smokestack still stands along the road in Kipahulu.

aloha himself, Duke Kahanamoku. Placed outside of the museum in an adjacent pavilion, the surfboard was built in 1910. It's accompanied by a 33-foot-long outrigger canoe made from a single koa log.

Tropical Gardens of Maui

As you make your way up the road toward 'Iao Valley, you'll notice the **Tropical Gardens of Maui** (200 'Iao Valley Rd., 808/244-2085, www.tropicalgardensofmaui.com, 9am-4:30pm daily, $5) on the right side of the road.

© KYLE ELLISON

the Bailey House Museum

What separates this garden from the Maui Nui Botanical Gardens in Kahului is that not only is the foliage incredibly lush, but there is also a nursery which is authorized to export plants. What this means is that not only can you spend 30-40 minutes taking a self-guided tour through the tropical surroundings, but if you have a garden at home and would like to import some tropical species, you can speak with the nursery staff about bringing a piece of the surroundings home with you.

(Kepaniwai Heritage Gardens

Tucked away on the banks of 'Iao Stream is **Kepaniwai Heritage Gardens** (870 'Iao Valley Rd., 7am-7pm daily, free), a simple, run-down, but culturally informative park that details Maui's "mixed plate" culture. In addition to numerous pavilions that make great picnic spots (and sometimes double as a great *drinking* spots for locals), the park features a small monument devoted to each of the island's plantation-era immigrant communities. From Japanese to Chinese and Puerto Rican to Portuguese, each monument has an informational placard about the respective culture and a typical dwelling constructed in the traditional style. Along the stream are a few places where you can bathe in the shallow (and cold!) waters, although use some caution scrambling down to it as there aren't any official trails. A visit of 30 minutes will usually suffice.

('Iao Valley State Park

What makes **'Iao Valley State Park** (end of 'Iao Valley Rd., 7am-7pm daily) such a popular attraction is that it's the easiest, most accessible way to delve into the valleys of Mauna Kahalawai. Every other valley in the mountains requires some hiking, some bushwhacking, or some illicit private property crossing, so the park draws its fame from the convenience offered by the three-mile road back into the valley. Don't be alarmed when you arrive and find that it's actually small. Visiting the park doesn't take much time—perhaps an hour at most. 'Iao is not a one-stop destination, but an outing in which the journey is the highlight of the trip.

THE BATTLE OF KEPANIWAI

Given the calming nature of Kepaniwai, it's tough to believe this narrow river canyon was the site of one of Hawai'i's fiercest conflicts. Before King Kamehameha united all the islands under a single crown in 1810, opposing chiefs frequently waged battles in an effort to expand their influence. Having already conquered much of the island of Hawai'i, Kamehameha sailed to Maui in 1790 with 1,200 warriors and landed at the protected waters of Kahului Bay. Though Kahekili—the reigning chief on Maui—was away on O'ahu at the time, Kamehameha met fierce opposition from the Maui warriors who, under the leadership of Kahekili's son Kalanikupule had positioned themselves just a few miles away at the entrance to 'Iao Valley. Using wooden spears and clubs spiked with shark's teeth, Kamehameha's forces chased Kalanikupule's warriors deep into the valley in an evenly matched battle. After two days of fighting neither side could claim victory. It's said that on the third day of battle Kamehameha employed two cannons he had acquired from Western explorers. The spears and stones of the Maui warriors were no match for the explosive cannons, so by the end of the third day Kamehameha's forces had gained a hard-fought victory. Over the course of the battle, not only did the waters of 'Iao Stream run red with the blood of the vanquished, but the bodies of the deceased formed a natural dam which blocked much of its flow. This eerie history lives on today in the name *Kepaniwai*, a word which translates as "the damming of the waters."

The thin ribbon of asphalt which snakes its way up the valley floor is flanked on both sides by towering mountain ridges that get more dramatic as you move your way up the valley.

When you finally reach 'Iao Valley State Park, return visitors will be shocked to find a parking lot attendant collecting fees. Instituted in 2010, parking is now $5/vehicle for nonresidents. Once inside, the "trail" within the park is a paved, semi-crowded walkway which winds its way up 133 steps to a lookout for 2,250-foot Kuka'emoku, better known as the 'Iao Needle. This erosional structure erupts 1,200 feet from the valley floor below and was once used as a lookout point by native Hawaiian settlers. While the Needle itself is worthy of a photo, the towering cliff faces which form the photo's backdrop are even more dramatic. The center of the West Maui Mountains is virtually untouched by modern culture, and it's believed that the bones of Hawaiian royalty are buried in caves back here which are so remote they will never be disturbed.

On the walk back down to the parking lot there are a few short spur trails worthy of a look. One leads down toward the waters of 'Iao Stream, whereas the trail right next to the bridge leads to an ethnobotanical garden highlighting plant species introduced by Polynesian settlers. This loop trail will only take about 10 minutes to explore thoroughly, and there's a nice example of taro irrigation. Overall, 'Iao is a tame adventure, but it's a site that each Maui visitor needs to experience at least once.

Maui Tropical Plantation

The **Maui Tropical Plantation** (1670 Honoapi'ilani Hwy., 808/242-8983, www.mauitropicalplantation.com, 9am-5pm daily, free admission) is a 60-acre working plantation that grows everything from coconuts to star fruit and apple bananas to coffee. Although it mainly caters to the old and the young, the plantation remains an informative stop for anyone interested in Hawai'i's agriculture. Some additions have recently been put in as a way to attract a more active crowd, so the **Maui Zipline** (808/633-2464, www.mauizipline.com) and **Maui Paddler** (808/281-2826, www.mauipaddler.net, 9am-3:30pm daily) outfits both operate on the plantation grounds. While the zipline is a popular tour that caters to small children and beginners, the paddle tour navigates a small lake and teaches you the basics

CENTRAL MAUI

SAY IT RIGHT: "'IAO NEEDLE"

© KYLE ELLISON

The 'Iao Needle is an iconic symbol of Central Maui.

Before learning anything about the 'Iao Needle (or telling anyone that you're going to see it), learn how to pronounce it. Given that not many English words are comprised entirely of vowels, it's understandable that the term can give some people fits.

The most common mispronunciation of this word is "Eye-Ow," as in "Ow, I hurt my eye." The first step toward wrapping your tongue around the proper pronunciation is understanding that vowels are different in Hawaiian than they are in English. Instead of vowels being articulated "a, e, i, o, u" (as they are in English), in Hawaiian they are "ah, eh, ee, oh, oo" (as they are in Spanish). Once you have this vowel structure in mind, it's easy to see that 'Iao Needle is properly pronounced as "Ee-ow."

If all else fails, just remember what *you* would say if you sat on a 1,200-foot tall needle...EE-OWWWW!

---

of outrigger canoe work. Both excursions are tame, although they do offer an educational experience for families who just might want their children to learn something on vacation.

The longtime draw is the **Tropical Express Tram Tour** ($15 adults, $5 children), otherwise known as "the train." This 40-minute train ride makes a large loop through the agricultural fields narrated by a driver who is well versed on the crops. Trams run eight times per day 10am-4pm, and while children will be excited to be on a train, adults will learn something about the crops growing around them.

Kumu Farms (167 Honoapi'ilani Hwy., 808/244-4800, 10am-5pm Tues.-Fri., 10am-3pm weekends), a certified-organic market where you can purchase crops grown right on the property, opened in 2012. There isn't anywhere else in Central Maui where you can buy organic produce that's going to be this fresh. The farm features everything from cilantro to peppers to chard and carrots, as well as the

famous sunrise papayas which are grown at the sister store on Moloka'i. You can also purchase bags of their homemade macadamia nut and basil pesto. If you're staying on the west side of the island and plan on doing some cooking in your condo, there is no better place to pick up your produce on your drive back from Central Maui.

Haleki'i and Pihana *Heiau*

Few island visitors ever stop at the **Haleki'i and Pihana *Heiau*,** which is a shame considering their historical importance. This site is officially classified as a Hawai'i State Park, but the gate to the *heiau* is no longer open for vehicular access and the general condition has fallen into disrepair. It's still easy to park on the residential street in front of the *heiau* and make the five-minute walk to the top of the hill. The 360-degree view stretches from 'Iao Valley to the waters of Kahului Bay. It's one of the best vistas of Central Maui and a

© KYLE ELLISON

the Maui Tropical Plantation

To reach the *heiau,* travel along Waiehu Beach Road until you cross the bridge over 'Iao Stream. On the other side you'll make your first left onto Kuhio Place, and then the first left again onto Hea Place. Since the access gate to the *heiau* will most likely be locked, park your car on the street and walk up the access road.

◖ Kahakuloa

Though technically Kahakuloa is part of Wailuku, this old fishing village is an entity all to itself. Lonely and remote, there are few places left in all of Hawai'i that are quite like Kahakuloa. Many choose to get to Kahakuloa from the west side of the island by following the road past Kapalua, Honolua Bay, and Nakalele Blowhole, but because this road is a loop, Kahakuloa can similarly be accessed from Wailuku. It will take you 30-45 minutes to reach Kahakuloa from Wailuku—and there aren't any gas stations—so be sure you have at least a half a tank of gas before venturing out into the wilderness.

As you leave Wailuku and gain elevation past the town of Waihe'e, the heavy local presence is evident from the "Slow Down! Dis not America" signs. Watch for road bikers as they come zipping around the tight turns, and if it's a sunny day, pull off at one of the various pullouts looking out over the shoreline below. The view here is back at the North Shore of Maui making this a calming place to watch waves crash on the undeveloped shoreline.

Following Kahekili Highway (Hwy. 340) past Mendes Ranch and Makamaka'ole Valley, the road becomes narrow and the foliage dense. The first stop you'll happen upon is **Turnbull Studios** (5030 Kahekili Hwy., 808/244-0101, www.turnbullstudios.org, 10am-5pm Mon.-Fri.), an eclectic sculpture garden that also features paintings and handmade crafts by local Hawaiian artists. The artist has been making sculptures at this mountainside garden for over 25 years. There are only a few parking spaces, and if it's been raining heavily, think twice before going down the short but steep driveway in a low-clearance rental car.

powerful, dramatic, and empty place to watch the sunrise.

In ancient Hawai'i these two *heiau* served as the religious center of the entire Wailuku *ahupua'a,* or land division. Many of Maui's ruling *ali'i* came here to either honor their deceased or commune with religious deities. It's believed that Keopuolani, the woman who would become queen, was born here at Pihana *heiau,* a site which is also believed to have been a *luakini heiau* occasionally used for human sacrifice. Hawaiian scholars believe that one of the last human sacrifices on the island was performed right here at Pihana in 1790 by King Kamehameha after his victory at the Battle of Kepaniwai.

Much of Pihana *heiau* was destroyed during the 19th century when the Hawaiian monarchy converted to Christianity, but numerous walls and terraces from Haleki'i still remain. Treat this place with respect and leave it as you came. This is one of Maui's most accessible sacred sites, and one of the few *heiau* you can visit without a long walk.

© KYLE ELLISON

Haleki'i and Pihana *heiaus* were once the center of Central Maui's religious activity.

Farther down the road you'll reach the **Kaukini Gallery** (808/244-3371, www.kaukinigallery.com, 10am-5pm daily), which is inside a mountaintop home overlooking Kahakuloa Valley. The gallery features more than 120 local artists and their associated paintings, jewelry, ceramics, and handmade crafts, and the views from the parking lot looking up the valley easily make it the most scenic gallery on the island.

Finally, after a few hairpin turns on a narrow one-lane road, you reach the village of Kahakuloa. This place truly is unlike anywhere else on the island, and all sorts of clichés abound: "Old Hawai'i," "turn back time," and "a place that time has forgotten." No matter which one you like, they're all true. Stop just

before you drop into town to pick up banana bread from **Julia's Banana Bread** (www.juliasbananabread.com, 9am-5:30pm) stand in the bright green, wooden building. Across the street is the **St. Francis Xavier Mission church** which was built in 1846, although access is only possible on special occasions.

Driving through this town of 200 residents takes no more than two minutes, and before you know it, you'll be climbing around another hairpin turn and leaving the fishing village behind. At the overlook on the Kapalua side of the village is **Kauikeolani Lunchwagon** (9:30am-4pm daily), a yellow food truck that sells mouthwatering fish-and-chips and where every item on the menu is gloriously deep fried.

THE ROAD TO KAHAKULOA

If driving to Hana was the scariest thing you've ever done, you might want to take a rain check on Road to Kahakuloa. It's one of the most scenic, breathtaking, off-the-map drives you can take. There are sheer drop-offs with no guardrails, completely blind turns, and the occasional rockslide that will send boulders down onto the highway.

There is a lot of confusion about the road that goes around the "back" of the West Maui Mountains. Some rental car maps show the road as four-wheel drive. Others say that it's one lane. Still others say you shouldn't drive it at all. This road can be narrow, frustrating, and downright scary, but if you utilize a few simple tricks, what was once a white-knuckle drive through the wilderness becomes one of the best day trips available on the island.

Despite the dangers, incidents are rare. The road does not require four-wheel drive. It's paved, although some sections can be bumpy. The road is narrow, and at some places is only wide enough for one car, never mind two.

So how do you drive on a one-lane road? The key is to look ahead a mile or so, gauge the oncoming traffic situation, and react accordingly. Go slowly around corners and honk your horn on those you can't see around. Turn the radio off so you can hear if anyone is honking from the other direction. If you need to take a break, use one of the gravel pullouts on the side of the road and let the cars behind you pass. Watch the road that's directly in front of you, but also look across the valley for oncoming traffic which might still be a half-mile away. If you notice that there is an oncoming truck, use the next pullout, wait 20 seconds for the oncoming traffic to pass, and then continue on your way. If you do encounter another car at a narrow junction, you might have to slowly reverse to the nearest pullout and give the other car room to pass. The number one rule is don't sightsee and drive at the same time. If you're the driver, keep your eyes firmly glued to the road. If you want to take photos, pull over.

If you want take this adventurous back road, which direction should you to approach it from? If you're departing from West Maui and moving in a clockwise direction around the mountain, you have the benefit of being on the inside lane and away from the steep cliff faces. Since you are pressed against the mountainside instead of against the ocean, you run the risk of falling rocks coming down after a heavy rain. If you approach from the Wailuku direction and move in a counterclockwise direction around the mountain, be sure the person in the passenger seat isn't afraid of heights.

Buckle up, hold on, and get ready for a ride to remember.

Shopping

KAHULUI

Because of its malls Kahului has the largest amount of shopping on the island. Combine this with the smaller shopping plazas, big-box stores, and individual shops around town, and you can find everything you might need.

The two-story **Queen Ka'ahumanu Shopping Center** (www.queenkaahumanucenter.com, 9:30am-9pm Mon.-Sat., 10am-5pm Sun.) along Ka'ahumanu Avenue is Kahului's largest mall, with the widest selection of stores, many of which are large corporate chains.

The open-air **Maui Mall** (www.mauimall.com, 10am-6pm daily, until 8pm Fri. and 4pm Sun.) is more pedestrian, yet it has a pleasant ambience as its buildings are set around a central T-shaped courtyard. At the intersection of Hana Highway and Ka'ahumanu Avenue, Maui Mall has **Longs Drugs** for everything from aspirin to rubber slippers, a megaplex theater, a handful of clothing and specialty shops, and a couple of places for quick food.

Kahului also has the greatest concentration of water sports shops on the island, many of them at or near the corner of Hana Highway and Dairy Road. Stop here for surf clothing, accessories, boardshorts, or equipment sales. Favorites include **Hawaiian Island Surf and Sport** (415 Dairy Rd., 808/871-4981, www.hawaiianisland.com, 8:30am-6pm daily), **HI Tech Surf Sports** (425 Koloa St., 808/877-2111, www.surfmaui.com, 9am-6pm daily), **Neilpryde Maui** (400 Hana Hwy., 808/877-7443, www.neilprydemaui.com, 9am-6pm daily), and **Maui Tropix** (261 Dairy Rd., 808/871-8726, 9am-8pm Mon.-Sat., 9am-6pm Sun.), which sells the ubiquitous Maui Built wear.

Don't miss a local tradition and one of the most unusual shopping experiences on the island: the **Maui Swap Meet** (310 W. Ka'ahumanu Ave., 808/244-3100, www.mauiexposition.com, 7am-1pm Sat.) on the grounds of the UH Maui College.

WAILUKU

Compared to shopping hot spots such as Lahaina, Pa'ia, or Makawao, Wailuku has woefully little to offer in way of the retail sector. What shopping does occur, however, takes place on Market Street, and between the numerous pawn shops and mom-and-pop stores, it's worth at least poking around when you're in town.

Near the corner of Market Street and Main Street you'll find **If The Shoe Fits** (21 N. Market St., 808/249-9710, www.hotbiskitshoes.com, 10am-5pm Mon.-Fri., 10am-2pm Sat.), which is Maui's only shoe-repair shop and also specializes in specialty footwear. To say that these people love shoes

would be an understatement; they even run the Maui Shoe Academy focused on shoe repair and design.

Also near the corner of Market and Main is **Maui Thing** (7 N. Market St., 808/249-0215, www.mauithing.com, 10am-5pm Mon.-Fri., 10am-4pm Sat.), a clothing store which focuses on Maui-themed clothing and accessories. This is a great store if you're looking for a unique Maui clothing gift you aren't going to find anywhere else on the island.

Across the street is a longtime Wailuku institution, **Requests** (10 N. Market St., 808/244-9315, www.requestshawaii.com, 10am-6pm Mon.-Sat.) music store, which ranks as the last holdout of true island record shops. For music lovers who love walking into a record shop to feel the vinyl, admire the album covers, and talk with people who *really* love music, this shop has been kept alive through the digital music revolution by a loyal customer fan base. Most of the merchandise caters to the reggae and roots lifestyle, but they also have a basement which is chock-full of music that goes back decades.

At the far end of Market Street are two local water sports stores. **TriPaddle Maui** (54 N. Market St., 808/243-7235, www.tripaddle-maui.com, 10am-5pm Mon.-Fri., 10am-3pm Sat.) specializes in everything to do with outrigger paddle sports. **Maui Sporting Goods** (92 N. Market St., 808/244-0011, 9am-6pm Mon.-Fri., 9am-5pm Sat.) is the de facto fishing headquarters for most of Maui's anglers.

Intriguing antiques and pawn shops run the length of Market Street. At **Kama'aina Loan** (98 N. Market St., 808/242-5555, www.kamaainaloan.com, 9am-5pm Mon.-Fri., 10am-4pm Sat.-Sun.), you'll find everything from surfboards to ukuleles to ritual drums used by the shamans of Nepalese tribes.

Entertainment

KAHULUI
Daytime Entertainment
On Saturday (1pm) and Sunday (11am) there are free hula shows and live performances at the **Maui Mall** (70 E. Ka'ahumanu Ave., 808/877-8952, www.mauimall.com), and a monthly calendar of events can be found on the website. Across town, the **Queen Ka'ahumanu Shopping Center** (275 W. Ka'ahumanu Ave., 808/877-3369, www.queenkaahumanucenter.com) offers free hula shows on Monday mornings at 10:30am as well as a rotating schedule of other free performances. As with the Maui Mall, a monthly calendar of events can be found online.

Evening Shows
The best option for evening entertainment in Kahului is the **Maui Arts and Cultural Center** (1 Cameron Way, 808/242-7469, www.mauiarts.org), where a constantly changing schedule of live concerts, movies, exhibits, comedy shows, and family events takes place many nights of the week. Multiple events often happen on the same evening. It's best to check the website for a list of upcoming events.

Bars
The most popular nightlife option in Kahului is the **Kahului Ale House** (355 E. Ka'ahumanu Ave., 808/877-9001, www.alehouse.net, 11am-12:30am Mon.-Thurs., 11am-2am Fri.-Sun.) in the parking lot of the Maui Mall. On Friday and Saturday nights there are either live performances by local artists (mostly reggae) or DJs spinning nightclub tunes.

If you would rather shoulder up to a bar without the fanfare of a full-on nightclub, **Koho's Grill and Bar** (275 W. Ka'ahumanu Ave., 808/877-5588, 7am-10pm Sun.-Thurs., 7am-11:30pm weekends) inside the Queen Ka'ahumanu Shopping Center offers happy hour and evening drink specials.

WAILUKU
Sleepy Wailuku isn't the island's entertainment hub, although there is the monthly **First Friday** event. Market Street in the historic downtown is closed to vehicular traffic 5:30pm-9pm, and the area becomes a festive pedestrian thoroughfare. There's live music in Banyan Tree Park, street performers, food concessions from local restaurants, activities for children, and a beer garden for the adults. This is the original and most popular of the "Maui Friday Town Parties," and more information can be found on the website at www.mauifridays.com/wailuku.

Shows
The only shows which take place in Wailuku are sporadic stage performances at the historic **'Iao Theater** (68 N. Market Street), a Spanish mission-style theater that was opened in 1928 and is listed on the National Register of Historic Places. The 'Iao is the oldest theater building in the Hawaiian Islands and has hosted performers such as Bob Hope and Frank Sinatra over the course of its lengthy history. Massive renovations breathed new life into the venue making the'Iao the heart of the island's live theater community. You can find more information about showtimes at the MauiOnStage website, www.mauionstage.com.

Bars
Every town needs a good dive bar, and the **Steel Horse Saloon** (1234 Lower Main St., 808/243-2200, 10am-2am daily) has got Wailuku covered. This Lower Main Street dive specializes in cheap drinks, rowdy bikers, loud music, and an old-fashioned good time. Set inside a 1930s-era building, the Steel Horse is questionable from the outside and lovable from the moment you walk in the door. On the fringe of the Wailuku Industrial Park, this isn't your typical tourist bar, but live music on

Friday and Saturday nights cranks the atmosphere up another decibel. Free *pupus* (appetizers) are a bonus.

Just down the street, **Tiffany's Bar and Grill** (1424 Lower Main St., 808/249-0052, www.tiffanysmaui.com, 10:30am-12am Mon.-Sat.,

10:30am-11pm Sun.) is another longtime Lower Main Street institution that caters to a heavily local crowd. Karaoke is the name of the game here. Since it's also a full restaurant, you can pick up some more substantial food than at the Steel Horse.

Food

KAHULUI
Local Style
When it comes to plate lunch 🄲 **Da Kitchen** (425 Koloa St., 808/871-7782, www.da-kitchen.com, 11am-9pm Mon.-Sat., $10-17) has the most *ono-kine, broke da mouth grinds* anywhere in town. The restaurant is tucked away in a small strip mall off Ka'ahumanu Avenue; the same mall as HI Tech Surf Sports and Denny's—look for the huge sign that says "Restaurant." Despite the obscure location, it's always packed. Show up hungry; you're sure to leave full. Some of the items on the "Moco Madness" are big enough to split between two people (lunch for under $20). For a tasty, albeit artery-clogging meal, go all-in with fried spam musubi followed by a Polynesian Paralysis Moco of fish tempura, kalua pork, two eggs, onion, mushrooms, and gravy over fried rice.

Mexican
For quick and authentic Mexican food, visit **Las Piñatas** (395 Dairy Rd., 808/877-8707, www.pinatasmaui.com, 8am-8pm Mon.-Sat., 9am-8pm Sun., $7-10), next to Kinko's off Dairy Road. The "Kitchen Sink" burrito is so big that a growing teenager will have trouble cleaning the plate. Bottled beer and *horchata* are available to drink. As the name suggests, over a dozen piñatas dangle from the ceiling. It's a great lunch option if you're heading to or from the airport.

Amigo's (333 Dairy Rd., 808/872-9525, www.amigosmaui.com, 10am-9pm Mon.-Fri., 9am-9pm weekends) is another filling and authentic Mexican option. Don't be fooled by the obscure location behind the gas station and

next to the Minit Stop. Daily specials make this a cheap place to grab a bite. Order a margarita, Mexican beer on draft, or cap off your *carnitas* with a shot of Patrón.

Italian
When you arrive at the Kahului Airport, the first restaurant you see (after the Krispy Kreme) is **Marco's Grill and Deli** (444 Hana Hwy., 808/877-4446, 7:30am-10pm daily, $13-19), on the corner of one of Kahului's major intersections. It's a favorite for grabbing dinner before a red-eye flight. While the sandwiches are filling and tasty, the lunch prices can be high. The dinner menu offers better value, with Italian classics like chicken parmesan and mushroom chicken fettuccini served by a slick and well-groomed waitstaff.

The finest restaurant in Kahului, **Bistro Casanova** (33 Lono Ave., 808/873-3850, www.bistrocasanova.com, 11am-9:30pm Mon.-Sat., $14-38) livens up downtown with a fusion of Mediterranean and Italian cuisine. The tapas menu served after 3pm has affordable crostinis, gnocchi, and grilled calamari. A swanky bar attracts the after-work cocktail crowd. The wine list features over 20 selections from various global wine regions. The dinner menu features meat entrées such as lamb chops and New York steak and pasta dishes like ravioli al tartufo and linguini al funghi.

Pizza in Paradise (60 E. Wakea Ave., 808/871-8188, www.pizza-maui.com, 11am-9pm Mon.-Thurs., 11am-10pm Fri-Sat., $13-26) puts out arguably the best pizza on the island in one of its most unassuming locations. This family-run joint makes its own dough and sauce. Whole pies are available, but the "by the slice" option is nice for lunch on the go. The menu also features subs and pasta, but it's the pizza that keeps locals walking through the door. It's best to not be in a rush; the food can take some time. Parking can be a challenge.

American

It's a chain inside a mall, but the burgers at **Ruby's Diner** (275 W. Ka'ahumanu Ave., 808/248-7829, 8am-9pm Mon.-Thurs., 8am-10pm Fri., 7am-10pm Sat., 7am-9pm Sun., $7-10) are the best in Kahului. Tucked in the lower level of Ka'ahumanu Shopping Center, the 1950s-style diner also serves up massive fountain shakes, sandwiches, salads, and a large breakfast menu.

Also in Ka'ahumanu Shopping Center, **Koho's Grill and Bar** (275 W. Ka'ahumanu Ave., 808/877-5588, 7am-10pm Sun.-Thurs., 7am-11:30pm weekends) offers a daytime menu of sandwiches and omelet plates accompanied by potatoes for breakfast. Surf photography lines the walls, sports plays on the TV, and a wide range of beers, margaritas, and happy hour specials are offered at the bar.

If hunger strikes as you're on your way to or from Lahaina, stop at **Café O'Lei** (1333 Maui Lani Pkwy., 808/877-0073, 8:30am-7:30pm Tues.-Sun., 8:30am-4pm Mon., $8-14), inside the Dunes at Maui Lani golf clubhouse. Sandwiches and burgers are affordable, while entrée items include blackened mahimahi or tiger shrimp linguine. Breakfast is served until 10:30. There's a full bar and an outdoor patio that looks out over the golf course.

Natural Foods

If you're a vegetarian, vegan, or just care about what you put in your body, you will love the salad bar and deli inside the **(Down to Earth** (305 Dairy Rd., 808/877-2661, www.downtoearth.org, 7am-9pm Mon.-Sat., 8am-8pm Sun.) grocery store. There's a wide selection of bottled juices, all-natural snack options, and vitamins and supplements. While the "Fresh Mex" burrito at the deli (which features a wheat tortilla, brown rice, and all vegetarian fillings

for $8) will fill you up, for anyone who isn't a vegetarian the burrito at neighboring Whole Foods is tastier and heartier for the same price.

Japanese

The best Japanese in Kahului is at **Ichiban Restaurant** (65 W. Ka'ahumanu Ave., 808/871-6977, www.ichibanrestaurantandsushimaui.com, 7am-2pm, 5pm-9pm Mon.-Fri., 1:30pm-2pm, 5pm-9pm Sat., $8-12), squirreled away in the Kahului Shopping Center. The building appears to be closed, but once you step inside, the traditional Japanese decor will make you forget you're in an industrial section of Kahului. Rainbow rolls and heaping bowls of udon punctuate the menu. Cap it all off with a Kirin beer or a cup of sake.

At the Ka'ahumanu Shopping Center, **Ramen-Ya** (275 W. Ka'ahumanu Ave., 808/873-9688, 10:30am-9:30pm Mon.-Sat., 10:30am-8:30pm Sun., $7-9) is a hole-in-the-wall that is always packed. It's that good. While the decor isn't quite as authentic as Ichiban, the prices for huge bowls of ramen and udon are tough to beat.

Chinese

The most well-known Chinese restaurant in Kahului is **Dragon Dragon** (70 E. Ka'ahumanu Ave., 808/893-1628, 10:30am-2pm, 5pm-9pm Sun.-Thurs., 10:30am-2pm, 5pm-9:30pm Fri.-Sat., $10-19), inside the Maui Mall. Traditional Chinese options such as moo shu shrimp and vegetables or chow fun Singapore-style dominate the menu. Dim sum options are available during lunch. It isn't the same cuisine you'd find in a Hong Kong back alley, but it's a decent place for Chinese food with moderate prices.

Thai

Thailand Cuisine II (70 E. Ka'ahumanu Ave., 808/873-0225, www.thailandcuisinemaui.net, 10:30am-3:30pm, 5pm-9:30pm daily, $11-16) has been awarded the honor of "Best Ethnic Restaurant on Maui" four separate times. The food is authentic and tasty, but the location at Maui Mall isn't anything special. Menu items feature a classic selection of Thai curries, pad thai noodles, and tom yum soup.

In the same strip mall as Las Piñatas, **Bangkok Cuisine** (395 Dairy Rd., 808/893-0026, bangkokcuisinemaui.com, 11am-2:30pm, 5pm-9:30pm daily) has a similar selection of noodles and curries in a similarly mediocre location. The food is enjoyable and authentic. Although the bill can run a little high, the portions are enormous.

Filipino

Considering the island's sizable Filipino community, you would expect more Filipino restaurants around town, but the only one with any prominence is **Bistro Manila** (230 Hana Hwy., 808/871-6934, 5pm-8:30pm Mon.-Sat.). The local favorite serves dishes so authentic you would think you were in Manila. The restaurant is near some car dealerships in a warehouse off Hana Highway. While there is no liquor license, you are free to pair your pancit, sisig, or pan-fried bangus with beer that you bring in yourself.

German

Industrial Kahului is the last place you would expect to find a Bavarian aprés-ski lodge, but **Brigit and Bernard's Garden Café** (335 Ho'ohana, 808/877-6000, 11am-2:30pm Mon., 11am-2:30pm, 5pm-9:30pm Tues.-Fri., 5pm-9:30pm Sat., $16-32) pumps out stick-to-your-bones German fare that could easily be in the Black Forest. The vaulted A-frame ceiling is hung with colorful steins, cross-country skis, and posters of alpine ski resorts. Order a massive plate of bratwurst or schnitzel served with a huge potato rosti and wash it down with a Bitburger brew. The garden area outside makes for a nice *biergarten*.

Coffee Shops

For local coffee beans head to **(Maui Coffee Roasters** (444 Hana Hwy., 808/877-2877, www.mauicoffeeroasters.com, 7am-6pm Mon.-Fri., 8am-5pm Sat., 8am-2:30pm Sun., $9), the best little coffee shop in all of Kahului. In the same shopping complex as Marco's Grill and Deli, Maui Coffee Roasters has an assortment of brews made from Maui, Kona, Kaua'i, and Moloka'i beans. The full breakfast and lunch menu features bagels, breakfast wraps, sandwiches, and salads. There are a number of tables, free Wi-Fi, and a full range of coffee accessories for sale as well.

Shave Ice

If you're on the way to the airport and crave one last shave ice, stop at **Ululani's** (333 Dairy Rd., 360/606-2745, www.ululanisshaveice.com, 11am-6pm daily), in a small kiosk by the Wow-Wee Maui's Kava Bar and Grill.

If you want to go where the locals go for their shave ice, the **A&E Laundry Center** (125 S. Wakea Ave., 808/877-0353, 5am-9pm daily) by the Queen Ka'ahumanu Shopping Center is the best kept secret on the island. This run-down, industrial haunt (formerly known as the W&F Washerette) has a concession counter which has been known for its shave ice for well over a decade. Only in Hawai'i!

Food Truck

Plate lunch stands occasionally line the harbor. The one with the greatest staying power is the **Geste Shrimp Truck** (Kahului Beach Rd., 808/298-7109, 10:45am-5pm Tues.-Sat., $12, cash only) that parks on Kahului Beach Road, a quarter mile past the turnoff for the Maui Arts and Cultural Center. $12 gets you 12 pieces of shrimp served with crab macaroni salad and two scoops of rice. Based on the aroma of shrimp emanating from the white truck, it's no surprise that it often runs out of food before 5pm.

WAILUKU
Local Style

When—and if—you finally find **(Sam Sato's** (1750 Wili Pa Loop, 808/244-7124, 7am-2pm Mon.-Sat., bakery open until 4pm, $6, cash only), you'll probably say to yourself, *Really? This is the famous restaurant?* Hidden deep with the Wailuku mill yard in a building you can't even see from the road, this family-run institution has been providing

CHEAP EATS: HAWAIIAN PLATE LUNCH

Given Central Maui's large multiethnic population, there is an abundance of plate lunch and budget dining options. Eat like a local by trying at least one of the dishes below.

Plate Lunch

One of the best island standards, these lunches give you a sampling of authentic island food that can include teriyaki chicken, mahimahi, *lau lau*, and *lomi* salmon, among other possibilities. They are usually served on paper plates, packed to go, and often cost less than $8. Standard with a plate lunch are "two-scoop rice" and a generous dollop of macaroni or another salad. Full meals, they're great for keeping down food costs and for instant picnics.

Bento

Bento is the Japanese rendition of the boxed lunch. Aesthetically arranged, these are full meals. They are often sold in supermarkets, gas stations, and in some local eateries with takeout counters.

Saimin

Special saimin shops, as well as restaurants, serve this hearty, Japanese-inspired noodle soup. *Saimin* is a word unique to Hawai'i. In Japan, these soups would be called ramen or soba, and it's as if the two were combined into saimin. A large bowl of noodles in broth, stirred with meat, chicken, fish, shrimp, or vegetables, costs only a few dollars and is big enough for an evening meal. The best place to eat saimin is at a local hole-in-the-wall shop run by a family.

Okazuya

A Hawaiian adaptation of the Japanese restaurant that sells side dishes and inexpensive food, *okazuya* usually have a full menu of savory entrées and side dishes that take their inspiration, like much in the islands, from all the peoples who have made Hawai'i their home. Sometimes they specialize in one type of dish or another. Usually small family-run shops that cater to the local community, they have loyal clients who demand top quality and cheap prices. While not usually on the list of dieters' delights, the food you find at these fine places is filling and will sustain you through the day. Some places are adapting to a leaner menu selection. Some, but not all, have *okazuya* as part of the restaurant name.

Wailuku with dry noodles, plate lunch, and famous *manju* pastries since the 1930s. It's the dry noodles that make Sam Sato's legendary. Served with a side of homemade broth and topped with char siu pork and sprouts, they make an affordable and addictive meal. Despite its fame, Sam Sato's has never lost its local roots. The refreshingly old-school flare is evident in everything from the yellow legal pad that serves as the waiting list to the low prices.

To help you find Sam Sato's: When traveling toward the mountains on Lower Main Street, you will make a right onto Mill Street, and then another right on Imi Kala Street into a baseyard with a number of blue roofs. One final left on to Wili Pa Loop, and you'll see a sign for the restaurant parking lot on your right.

Mexican

Ramshackle little **Fiesta Time** (1132 Lower Main St., 808/249-8463, 10am-8pm Mon.-Sat.) puts out food that is the opposite of its appearance. The plates of food are so affordable and authentic that from the moment you walk in the door, you'll be glad you came. Parking can be an issue.

Italian

Family-owned 🄲 **Giannotto's Pizza** (2050 Main. St., 808/244-5979, www.giannottospizza.com, 11am-9pm Mon.-Sat., 11am-8pm Sun., $7) serves up homemade Italian recipes "just like Mama used to make." Squirreled away into a small corner unit next to the hopelessly mediocre Main Street Food Court, this place is as authentic as the "Joisey" accents emanating from the kitchen, the mafioso photos on the wall, and the cheese pizza sold by the slice. If only the Philly cheesesteak were bigger so it would last longer.

American

The decor is basic and the location is run-down, but the food is the best thing ◖ **Main Street Bistro** (2051 Main St., 808/244-6816, www.msbmaui.com, 11am-7pm Mon.-Fri., $8-12) has going for it. Specializing in "refined comfort food," it offers appetizers such as asparagus milanese and larger items like angel hair pasta with shrimp. The food is also paired with a surprisingly good selection of wines. It's apparent that the owner (who also doubles as the chef) has been doing this for a long time.

You could drive right past local secret **A.K.'s Café** (1237 Lower Main St., 808/244-8774, www.akscafe.com, 11am-1:30pm, 5pm-8:30pm Mon.-Fri., $9-16) and not even know that it's there. The part of town doesn't scream "tropical Hawai'i." Nevertheless, A.K.'s has fish sandwiches, burgers, plate lunches, salads, and local beers on tap that won't empty your wallet.

For good old-fashioned American barbecue, pop into **Bruddah Willy's Sticky Ribs** (1670 Honoapi'ilani Hwy., 808/243-7427, 11am-6pm Thurs.-Sat., $8-12) at the Maui Tropical Plantation. The biggest problem with this finger-lickin' take-out stand is that it's only open three days a week. The meat is soft, juicy, and falls off the bone.

For a hole-in-the-wall hideout that won't break the budget, **Tasty Crust** (1770 Mill St., 808/244-0845, 6am-3pm Mon., 6am-10pm Tues.-Thurs., 6am-11pm Fri.-Sat.) is a diner set in a working-class part of town. This old-school joint (no credit cards or checks, laminate floors, low-slung counter, aging patrons) has been feeding Wailuku for over 50 years. While a full lunch menu offers standard plate lunches, Tasty Crust is known for is its world-famous hotcakes, served all day.

Kahili Restaurant (2500 Honoapi'ilani Hwy., 808/242-6000, www.kahilirestaurant.com, 11am-5pm Mon.-Sat., 9am-5pm Sun., $9-13) at the clubhouse of the Kahili Golf Course

offers views stretching over the central valley and Haleakala. The cuisine ranges from seared beef poke to shrimp linguini. It's a convenient stop on the way to Lahaina.

Japanese

If there were an award for most popular restaurant in the ugliest location, then **Tokyo Tei** (1063 Lower Main St., 808/242-9630, 10:30am-1:30pm, 5pm-8:30pm Mon.-Sat., 5pm-8:30pm Sun., $10-17) would win it. Hidden deep within a dark parking garage in an industrial part of Wailuku, this family-run Japanese restaurant has been serving famous shrimp tempura dishes since 1935. It's consistently voted as the best Japanese cuisine on the island. Dishes include teriyaki steak, yakitori, and teishoku combination platters.

Funky, cheap, and still-ticking **Ichiban Okazuya** (2133 Kaohu St., 808/244-7276, 10am-2pm, 4pm-7pm Mon.-Fri.) is a weathered institution that continues to serve affordable plate lunches in the traditional okazuya style. There isn't anywhere to sit, but if you're low on cash and packing a big appetite, Ichiban Okazuya is the place.

Thai

In Wailuku's funkiest corner, ◖ **Saeng's Thai Cuisine** (2119 W. Vineyard St., 808/244-1567, 11am-2:30pm, 5pm-9:30pm Mon.-Fri., $9-12) offers surprisingly good food in a peaceful garden setting. The pad thai and curries are as authentic as they come. Pair your meal with a Singha beer or wine. The friendly service, peaceful setting, and authentic flavors make it a top pick.

Vietnamese

Sandwiched between a bridge and a low-income housing unit is one of Maui's most popular Vietnamese venues, ◖ **A Saigon Café** (1792 Main St., 808/243-9560, 10am-9:30pm Mon.-Sat., 10am-8pm Sun., $9-15). The affordable clay pot dishes, with heaping mounds of rice, chicken, peas, and vegetables, have made this a Wailuku culinary staple. There are plenty of com dia rice plates, as well as pho, banh hoi, and Vietnamese soup. The portions are enormous, the place is always packed, and there's a full bar. You won't walk away hungry. If locals recommend eating at "Jennifer's," this is the place they mean. Although there's no sign, everyone seems to know it's here. Parking can be a challenge.

Ba-Le (1824 Oihana St., 808/249-8833, www.balemaui.com, 9am-9pm daily) is a casual Vietnamese venue with a French twist. The atmosphere isn't as nice as neighboring A Saigon Café's, but the sandwiches are affordable so it's a nice option for a quick meal on the go.

Coffee Shops

Set in the heart of historic Market Street, **Wailuku Coffee Company** (26 N. Market St., 808/495-0259, 7am-5pm Mon.-Fri., 8am-3pm weekends, $5-8), is where—as the website claims—"the hip come to sip." The lounge atmosphere, free Wi-Fi (for an hour), and funky location contribute to the vibe. Breakfast includes ham, egg, and cheese bagels; lunch features "pitzas" served on pita bread.

Tours

Tour da Food (www.tourdafood.com) takes guests to tucked away mom-and-pop restaurants and introduces them to how "the other side of Maui" eats. Groups are capped at four people. Tsours meet at the Kepaniwai Heritage Gardens up 'Iao Valley Road, where the guide, Bonnie, introduces you to the island's immigrant communities via the architectural monuments dedicated to each group's heritage. This is a fantastic outing if you're a fan of food tours and have a desire to delve deeper into the culture than booking a two-for-one lu'au.

Information and Services

MEDICAL SERVICES

For medical emergencies, try **Maui Memorial Medical Center** (221 Mahalani St., 808/244-9056) or **Kaiser Permanente** (20 Mahalani St., 808/243-6000). Both of these are between downtown Kahului and downtown Wailuku—the medical center up behind the county police station, the clinic across the road from the police station. **Walgreen's** pharmacy (10 E. Kamehameha Ave., 808/872-3301, 8am-10pm Mon.-Fri., 9am-6pm weekends) in Kahului offers a full range of prescription services, as does **Long's Pharmacy** (70 E. Ka'ahumanu Ave., 808/877-0068, 8am-10pm Mon.-Fri., 8am-7pm weekends) in the Maui Mall.

BANKS
Kahului

Kahului has numerous banks with ATMs, and the majority are near the intersection of Ka'ahumanu and Pu'unene Avenues. There are two **Bank of Hawaii** branches (27 S. P'unene Ave., 808/871-8250, 8:30am-4pm Mon.-Thurs., 8:30am-6pm Fri.; Maui Marketplace, 808/871-8260, 8:30am-4pm Mon.-Thurs., 8:30am-6pm Fri., 9am-1pm Sat.); a **First Hawaiian Bank** (20 W. Ka'ahumanu Ave., 808/877-2311, 8:30am-4pm Mon.-Thurs., 8:30am-6pm Fri., 9am-1pm Sat.); an **American Savings Bank** (73 Pu'unene Ave., 808/871-8411, 8am-5pm Mon.-Thurs., 8am-6pm Fri., 9am-1pm Sat.), and a **Central Pacific Bank** (85 W. Ka'ahumanu Ave., 808/877-3387, 8:30am-4pm Mon.-Thurs., 8:30am-6pm Fri.).

Wailuku

For banking in Wailuku there are a **Bank of Hawaii** (2105 Main, 808/243-8268, 8:30am-4pm Mon.-Thurs., 8:30am-6pm Fri.) across the street from Giannotto's Pizza and an **American Savings Bank** (69 N. Market St., 808/244-9148, 8am-4pm Mon.-Thurs., 8am-6pm Fri.) across the street from Wailuku Coffee Company.

GAS

There are gas stations at most major intersections throughout Kahului and Wailuku, although **Costco** (540 Haleakala Hwy., 808/877-5248) will offer gas which is usually $0.20-0.40/gallon cheaper than everywhere else. There are no gas stations once you turn onto Waiehu Beach Road and head toward Kahakuloa.

POST OFFICE
Kahului

The Kahului post office is across the street from Walgreen's Pharmacy (138 S. Pu'unene Ave., 800/275-8777, 8:30am-4pm Mon.-Fri., 9am-noon Sat.).

Wailuku

The Wailuku post office is down in the Millyard area of Wailuku (250 Imi Kala St., 808/244-1653, 9am-4pm Mon.-Fri., 9am-noon Sat.).

LIBRARY
Kahului

The **Kahului Public Library** (90 School St., 808/873-3097, noon-8pm Tues., 9am-5pm Wed.-Sat.) is tucked quietly under tall shade trees not far from Queen Ka'ahumanu Shopping Center.

Wailuku

The historic **Wailuku Public Library** (251 High St., 808/243-5766, 9am-5pm Mon.-Wed. and Fri., 1pm-8pm Thurs.) is just down the street from Ka'ahumanu Church and is smaller than the library in nearby Kahului.

INTERNET SERVICES

While both public libraries in the area have computer terminals you can reserve for a limited amount of time, free wireless connections can be found in Kahului at the **Maui Marketplace Starbucks** (270 Dairy Rd., 808/871-7884, 4:30am-9:30pm Mon.-Sat., 5:30am-9:30pm Sun.), the **Queen Ka'ahumanu Shopping Center Starbucks** (275 W. Ka'ahumanu Ave., 808/871-6290, 5am-9pm Mon.-Thurs., 5am-10pm Fri.-Sat., 5am-8pm Sun.), **Whole Foods supermarket** (70 Ka'ahumanu Ave., 808/872-3310, www.wholefoodsmarket/stores/maui, 7am-9pm daily), **Maui Coffee Roasters** (444 Hana Hwy., 808/877-2877, www.mauicoffeeroasters.com, 7am-6pm Mon.-Fri., 8am-5pm Sat., 8am-2:30pm Sun.), and **Wow-Wee Maui's Kava Bar and Grill** (333 Dairy Rd., 808/871-1414, 10am-9pm Mon.-Fri., 10am-10pm weekends).

In Wailuku, the best place to find free Internet access is at the **Wailuku Coffee Company** on Main Street (26 N. Market St., 808/495-0259, www.wailukucoffeeco.com, 7am-5pm Mon.-Fri., 8am-3pm weekends).

Getting There and Around

CAR
Rental Cars

At the Kahului Airport, **Hertz** (808/893-5200), **Avis** (808/871-7575), **Budget** (808/871-8811), **Enterprise** (808/871-6982), **Alamo** (888/826-6893), and **Thrifty** (808/847-4389) all offer the standard corporate options for island rental cars. Other options in Kahului (which are usually cheaper) include **Maui Car Rentals** (181 Dairy Rd., 808/877-3300 or 800/567-4659, www.mauicarrentals.net), **Aloha Rent A Car** (190 Papa Pl., 808/877-2436 or 800/533-5929, www.mauirentacar.com), **Kimo's Rent A Car** (440 Alamaha St., 808/280-6327, www.kimosrentacar.com), and the budget service **Discount Hawaii Car Rental** (800/292-1930, www.discounthawaiicarrental.com).

While it's always nice to get reward points with the corporate options, there are benefits to renting from a local place. Rental cars are targets for break-ins. If you have a car that looks like a local's car instead of a standard tourist car, it's less likely thieves will scout it for valuables.

The only reason you need a 4WD vehicle on Maui is if you decide to go hunting in Polipoli, fishing at some remote location, or venture onto soft sand. Many visitors spend a lot of money on 4WD (often double the price of a 2WD) and never end up using it. Rent a 4WD vehicle just for the day you need it.

MOTORCYCLE

If the idea of zipping oceanside on a massive Harley is your preferred method of getting from A to B, **Maui Harley Davidson** (150 Dairy Rd., 808/831-2614, www.hawaiiharleyrental. com, 9am-5pm daily) offers rentals from the Kahului shop only five minutes from Kahului Airport.

BUS

The Queen Ka'ahumanu Shopping Center is the central hub of the **Maui Bus,** and if you are connecting from one bus to another, there is a good chance that you'll end up making a stop at the mall. All segments on the bus cost $2/person (or $4/person for a day pass), and this is the terminus and starting point for routes heading up-country as well as to Kihei and Lahaina.

If you're just trying to get across town, buses on the Wailuku Loop (Route #1) make various stops around Wailuku and run hourly 6:30am-9:30pm. Similarly, buses on the Kahului Loop (Route #5) make various stops around Kahului and run hourly 6:30am-9pm. If you're trying to get to the Kahului Airport from Queen Ka'ahumanu, you have to get on the Upcountry Islander bus (Route #40) which runs every 90 minutes 6:10am-9:10pm. For more information, a full schedule, or to see routes to other parts of the island, you can visit www.mauicounty.gov and navigate to "For Residents" and then "Maui Bus."

SOUTH MAUI

If one word defines South Maui, it's "beaches." South Maui is graced with dozens of sandy stretches waiting for your footprints, including the island's longest beach, Sugar Beach, and one of its smallest, Pa'ako Cove. You could visit a different beach every day of a weeks-long vacation and still leave some areas untouched. Best of all, because much of South Maui faces west, the end of each day comes with a sunset that somehow surpasses the day before. It's the picture of paradise.

It's also one of the driest and hottest areas in the state. Mornings in South Maui are perfect for snorkeling or stand-up paddling, while the Maui Ocean Center in Ma'alaea provides the opportunity to explore Maui's underwater world regardless of the conditions outside.

Here the mega-resorts of West Maui give way to rows of condos, making South Maui one of the fastest growing zip codes in the United States. The beaches of Kihei and Wailea are full of amenities. In the luxurious enclave of Wailea in particular, names such as Fairmont and The Four Seasons are paired with high-end shopping and dining.

But South Maui still has a wild side waiting to be explored. The far southern coastline is still rugged, with semi-nudist drum circles at Little Beach and walking trails that were once the footpaths of kings.

© KYLE ELLISON

HIGHLIGHTS

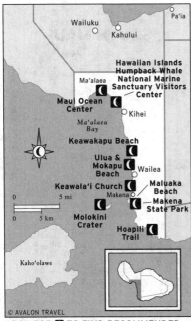

© AVALON TRAVEL

LOOK FOR ◖ TO FIND RECOMMENDED SIGHTS, ACTIVITIES, DINING, AND LODGING.

◖ **Keawakapu Beach:** While the northern end of Keawakapu Beach teems with activity, the southern expanse is one of South Maui's most peaceful getaways (page 162).

◖ **Maluaka Beach:** Peacefully ensconced in front of the Makena Beach and Golf Resort, Maluaka Beach is the perfect place for a morning stand-up paddle along a historic coastline (page 165).

◖ **Makena State Park:** Better known to locals as "Big Beach," this state park actually includes three beaches—one of them nude. It's one of the last stretches of sand free of development. The sunsets are legendary (page 166).

◖ **Molokini Crater:** The water inside this offshore caldera is some of the clearest in the world. Imagine standing on the deck of a boat looking at fish swimming 60 feet beneath you. The snorkeling is the best in the state and the scuba diving is world-class (page 169).

◖ **Ulua Beach and Mokapu Beach:** When it comes to snorkeling from the shoreline, these protected, sandy beaches offer friendly conditions and an abundance of marine life (page 175).

◖ **Hoapili Trail:** This ancient footpath of kings meanders through the island's most recent lava flows. Sunbathe on an empty white-sand beach and wander deserted Hawaiian fishing villages whose stone foundations stand frozen in time (page 193).

◖ **Maui Ocean Center:** Want see sharks, eagle rays, and dozens of fish, all without getting your hair wet? The Maui Ocean Center aquarium is the perfect place for learning about Maui's unique marine ecosystem. It's also one of the island's best attractions for families (page 201).

◖ **Hawaiian Islands Humpback Whale National Marine Sanctuary:** Learn about Maui's most exciting winter visitors with free educational displays in an oceanfront setting. When you're done learning about the whales, walk next door to view the remnants of an ancient Hawaiian fishpond (page 203).

◖ **Keawala'i Church:** Walk the grounds of this historic, oceanfront house of worship, where sermons are still given in the native Hawaiian language (page 204).

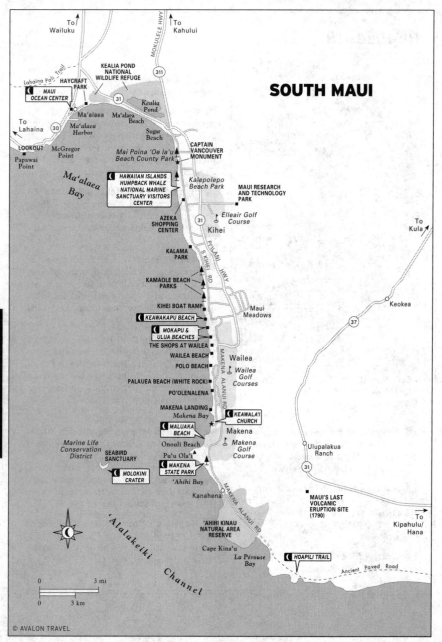

SOUTH MAUI

To Wailuku

To Kahului

MOKULELE HWY

311

KEALIA POND NATIONAL WILDLIFE REFUGE

Lahaina Pali Trail

HAYCRAFT PARK

31

🌙 MAUI OCEAN CENTER

Kealia Pond

Maʻalaea

Maʻalaea Beach

Maʻalaea Harbor

To Lahaina

30

Sugar Beach

LOOKOUT

Papawai Point

McGregor Point

Maʻalaea Bay

Mai Poina ʻOe laʻu Beach County Park

CAPTAIN VANCOUVER MONUMENT

🏛 HAWAIIAN ISLANDS HUMPBACK WHALE NATIONAL MARINE SANCTUARY VISITORS CENTER

Kalepolepo Beach Park

MAUI RESEARCH AND TECHNOLOGY PARK

AZEKA SHOPPING CENTER

31

Elleair Golf Course

Kihei

To Kula

KALAMA PARK

S KIHEI RD

PIILANI HWY

KAMAOLE BEACH PARKS

Keokea

37

KIHEI BOAT RAMP

Maui Meadows

🌙 KEAWAKAPU BEACH

🌙 MOKAPU & ULUA BEACHES

THE SHOPS AT WAILEA

MAKENA ALANUI RD

WAILEA BEACH

Wailea

POLO BEACH

Wailea Golf Courses

PALAUEA BEACH (WHITE ROCK)

POʻOLENALENA

MAKENA LANDING

Makena Bay

🌙 KEAWALAʻI CHURCH

🌙 MALUAKA BEACH

Makena

Marine Life Conservation District

Onouli Beach

SEABIRD SANCTUARY

Puʻu Olaʻi

Makena Golf Course

Ulupalakua Ranch

🌙 MOLOKINI CRATER

🌙 MAKENA STATE PARK

ʻAhihi Bay

31

Kanahena

MAUI'S LAST VOLCANIC ERUPTION SITE (1790)

ʻAhihi Kinau Natural Area Reserve

MAKENA ALANUI RD

To Kipahulu/ Hana

Cape Kinaʻu

La Pérouse Bay

🌙 HOAPILI TRAIL

Ancient Paved Road

ʻAlalakeiki Channel

0   3 mi

0   3 km

© AVALON TRAVEL

SOUTH MAUI

MAUI SNOW

Although on the rarest of winter mornings it's possible to snorkel in Kihei beneath a snow-capped Haleakala Crater, it's more often the case that you'll wake up in Ma'alaea or North Kihei to find your car blanketed in a thin dusting of "Maui snow." The difference: Maui snow is black, dirty, and can fall during any sort of temperature.

Maui snow is the black ash that can blanket the ground after a sugarcane field has been burned. When sugarcane is ready to be harvested, mass fires are lit in the middle of the night, and if there is any breeze, all of the communities downwind of the blaze will wake up to find black ash has covered their cars, patios, and anything left outdoors. Such cane blizzards are more of a nuisance than anything dangerous (although anyone with asthma might be affected by the cane smoke in the air).

Beaches

When it comes to beach weather, even though South Maui is dry, other elements such as the wind and clouds can greatly affect the comfort level. As a general rule, the closer you are to Ma'alaea, the earlier in the day it gets windy—particularly in the summer. Since the afternoon trade winds begin their march in Ma'alaea, they progressively move from north to south through Kihei, Wailea, and ultimately Makena. During trade wind weather patterns, a thick cloud known locally as "the Makena cloud" forms over Haleakala and extends out toward the island of Kaho'olawe; although this doesn't normally happen until the early afternoon. So the morning hours are the best time to hit the beach. In the afternoon, the pocket of beaches in south Kihei and Wailea have the best chance of being sunny and calm. Winter months aren't as windy; this is also when humpback whales can be seen leaping offshore. Is it any wonder so many snowbirds choose to spend the winter here?

MA'ALAEA

Sugar Beach

If your picture-perfect vision of Hawai'i is enjoying a long, lonely stroll down an isolated beach, then **Sugar Beach** is going to be your favorite spot on the island. Bordered on one side by Kealia Pond National Wildlife Refuge and the waters of Ma'alaea Bay on the other, this undeveloped strip runs for five miles all the way to the condos of North Kihei. Nesting green sea turtles often haul out on the sand here to lay their eggs, and the Turtle X-ing signs which once graced the highway were the target of memorabilia thieves for years.

There isn't any snorkeling. Although there can sometimes be waves for boogie boarding during summer, the main attraction here is taking a long, quiet stroll. Most afternoons are marked by fierce trade winds, so the early morning hours are the best time to visit. To access Sugar Beach you can begin at the northern terminus at Haycraft Beach Park, the southern terminus in North Kihei, or at numerous entry points along North Kihei Road.

KIHEI
Mai Poina 'Oe Ia'u Beach Park

For locals this beach is essentially known as the "Kanaha of Kihei" due to the windsurfers who gather along the shoreline. In the morning this is a nice beach for a stroll, as it's much more tranquil than the fast pace of South Kihei. There isn't any swimming or snorkeling, though there are picnic tables and pavilions

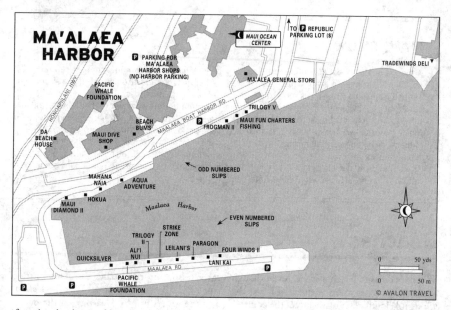

if you're thinking of having a picnic. This is also a nice place for stand-up paddling in the morning.

Kalepolepo Beach Park

Set on the northern edge of the headquarters for the Hawaiian Islands Humpback Whale National Marine Sanctuary (say that 10 times fast), **Kalepolepo Beach Park** is—from a historical perspective—Kihei's most underrated beach. What makes this little-visited enclave so special are the ancient Hawaiian fishponds. Masterfully restored in recent years by local volunteers, the fishponds were once reserved for royalty and the site of a native Hawaiian settlement. Historical placards within the park detail the area's rich cultural history. The fishponds also create a protected swimming area nice for small children. The snorkeling is murky and it isn't a great beach for swimming, but it's worth a stop while driving down South Kihei Road to look at the fishponds and get a feel for this unheralded part of town.

Waiohuli Beach

Even in ultra-crowded Kihei it's nice to know

there are still some places you can stop and hear yourself think. Small, hidden, and essentially forgotten, **Waiohuli Beach** is one of those spots. Not only is this beach rarely frequented by visitors, but locals hardly make it here either. There isn't any snorkeling and the water is too shallow for swimming, so what makes this beach great is the ability to sit on a sandy shoreline and hear nothing but the lapping of waves and intermittent gusts of wind. At the end of Waiohuli Road—a residential street next to the Kihei Veterinary Clinic—there is room to park next to the public beach access sign labeled number "117." *Limu* (seaweed) will often wash onto the beach at high tide. If you walk to the north end of the beach at low tide you can follow the sand all the way to Waipuilani Beach Park. Afternoons are characterized by stiff winds and there aren't any facilities. But if solitude and serenity are exactly what you're searching for, then Waiohuli is where to find it.

"The Cove"

This popular surf spot at the far south end of Kalama Beach Park has a small horseshoe of sand where you can lay out in the sun. While taking a walk down the beach would take no more than 15 seconds, it's still an entertaining spot to sit and watch the surf school students navigate through the learning process. This is a great people-watching spot full of volleyball players, canoers, stand-up paddlers, and surfers. While it isn't the nicest beach in Kihei, if you're in the Kalama Village area and want to kill time at the beach while a family member shops, this small stretch of sand will do the trick.

Kamaole I, II, and III

The **Kamaole Beach Parks** form the core of Kihei's beach scene. Grassy areas run parallel to the roadway, and all of the parks have showers, restrooms, picnic tables, and barbecue grills for putting together a relaxing sunset meal. Kam I has a beach volleyball court on the north side of the park.

The best way to experience these beaches is to take a stroll along the coastline and link all three parks together. The lava rock headlands can be rough on your feet and kiawe trees drop thorns; wear footwear if you plan on walking all three beaches. The tidepools between Kam II and Kam III are a particularly nice place to explore. When you reach the southern end of Kam III, there's a walking trail that runs for 0.75 mile to the Kihei Boat Ramp.

Mornings are usually calm on these beaches and the best time for stand-up paddling and snorkeling, since by noon the wind can pick up and turn the surface to whitecaps. Summers often have some shorebreak. On the biggest of days the surf can turn dangerous. Parking for Kam I and Kam II is at free spots curbside, although parking can be limited during the busier months of the year. Larger Kam III has its own parking lot dedicated to beachgoers. There is also overflow parking between Kam III and the boat ramp.

Sometimes you will hear locals say they enjoy spending time at **Charley Young Beach**; this is just another name for the northern end of Kam I. What's nice about this beach is that it's protected from the wind when the southern section of the beach is choppy. It's the perfect place to lay a blanket down, relax for a while,

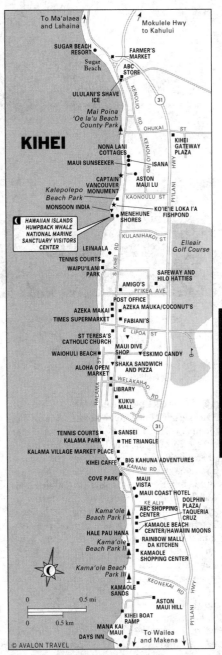

KIHEI

SOUTH MAUI

© AVALON TRAVEL

© KYLE ELLISON

Kamaole I Beach

and soak up the sun with a good book. Parking for Charley Young is along Kaiau Place, which is a small offshoot of South Kihei Road not far from the Cove Park.

Keawakapu Beach

Outside of Kam III, **Keawakapu** is Kihei's most popular beach. This long, sandy stretch is more protected from the wind than the beaches farther north, and water sports are the name of the game. A small rental shop on the north end of the beach rents out stand-up paddleboards, kayaks, and snorkeling gear, and during the calm morning hours this beach is a bustle of activity. Snorkeling is best around the north and south headlands, while the sandy, gentle entry in the middle section of the beach is an enjoyable place to go for a quick swim. There is ample parking on the north end of the beach, and there is a lot off South Kihei Road on the north side of the Days Inn.

For as much activity as the north end of the beach sees, however, the south end of the beach can be an oasis of calm by comparison. To reach the south end of Keawakapu you can either take a stroll down the length of the beach, or if you would rather drive, when South Kihei Road begins to head uphill toward the resorts of Wailea, continue driving straight until the road dead-ends in a small parking lot. There aren't many spaces here, but there is a small shower for hosing off. As if two entrances weren't enough, there's also a central entrance to Keawakapu that's known as Sidewalks with public parking on the corner of Kilohana Drive and South Kihei Road.

Afternoons during the summer can be windy, although by sunset the winds have backed off and it's one of the best beaches in Kihei for a sunset stroll. An interesting fact about Keawakapu is there is a 52-acre artificial reef a half mile offshore comprised of 150 cars, 2,250 tire modules, 35 concrete slabs, 1,500 concrete "Z" modules, and one sunken fishing boat. Even though the reef is much too far to reach from shore, it's strange to think when you gaze out toward Kaho'olawe it's all still down there nevertheless.

© KYLE ELLISON

sunset from Keawakapu Beach

WAILEA
Ulua Beach and Mokapu Beach

Ulua and Mokapu are the northernmost of Wailea's beaches, separated by a small, grassy headland. Mokapu is on the north side of the hill, Ulua is on the south, and the point that separates the two is one of the best spots for snorkeling in Wailea. Ulua is slightly larger than Mokapu and more protected from the surf. Mokapu Beach is also the northern terminus of the Wailea Coastal Walk, although the trail technically crosses the sand dune on Mokapu and continues down the beach to the southern end of Keawakapu. Restrooms and showers are available. A large public parking lot is at the bottom of Ulua Beach Road, just north of the Shops at Wailea.

Wailea Beach

Home to Maui's "see and be seen" crowd, **Wailea Beach** epitomizes Wailea. Fronted by the Grand Wailea and the Four Seasons Maui, this is a beach where corporate CEOs and professional athletes mingle with regular travelers.

Out on the sand everyone is working on the same tan. Beyond luxury, however, this beach is also characterized by fun. Wailea Beach buzzes with activity, and there's a trampoline for the kids, snorkeling around Wailea Point, stand-up paddleboard rentals, outrigger canoe tours, and dozens of visitors playing in the surf who are happy to just be spending a day on Maui. Despite the private nature of the resorts, public access to the beach is quite easy, as there is a large public parking lot just past the entrance for the Four Seasons. In the parking lot there are public restrooms and showers.

Polo Beach

Polo Beach is the southernmost of Wailea's resort beaches, and is the southern terminus of the Wailea Coastal Walk. The cloud-white Fairmont Kea Lani dominates the shoreline, its Arabian spires providing a unique backdrop to the shimmering blue waters. Of all of Wailea's beaches, Polo Beach is the most popular with locals due to the large public parking area being a convenient place for launching stand-up

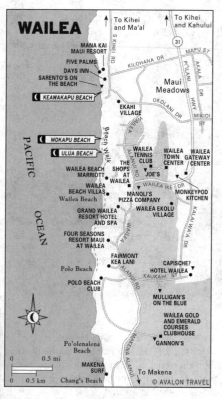

although unfortunately, the mega-mansion sprawl has finally found its way to the shoreline. Compared to a spot like Wailea Beach, however, Palauea is still mellow and empty. Similar in appearance to Keawakapu Beach in Kihei, this long stretch of sand is lined with private luxury homes. For the time being, parking for Palauea is along the side of Makena Road. Public access paths scattered along the roadway lead through the kiawe trees and down to the beach. There's good snorkeling along both the north and south ends of the beach. Boogie boarding can be good here in the summer, although on large south swells the waves can get treacherous. If the nearby beaches of Wailea are too crowded and you want to find your own corner to relax in, Palauea is off the radar of most South Maui visitors. Since there aren't any facilities or showers, expect to track a lot of sand into your car on the drive home. Or drive your salty body down to Polo Beach next to the Fairmont Kea Lani and use the public showers by the parking lot.

Po'olenalena Beach

Once frequented only by locals, **Po'olenalena Beach** can now get so busy it's tough to find a space in the potholed parking lot. Despite the lack of parking, however, the beach itself is big enough that it never feels too crowded. Volleyball enthusiasts will enjoy the pickup games on Sunday afternoons. Po'olenalena is also a local favorite for watching the sunset. Stop in for the evening show. Boogie boarding can be good here on most days of the year, although in summer the waves can get strong. The south end of the beach has more rocks than the north. There are public restrooms on the north side by the gravel parking lot.

If you show up and the beach is too crowded, there's a small trail that departs from the parking lot and passes through some trees on the north end of the beach. The trail continues around a rocky point and brings you to a cove not visible from the road with much fewer people. The hidden location can lead to some beachgoers opting to tan their nether regions,

paddleboards and kayaks. There are public restrooms, showers, and one small barbecue grill. Polo Beach can also be good for boogie boarding in summer, and there is a small activity booth on the north side of the beach if you want to rent a paddleboard or kayak. To reach Polo Beach, travel south along Wailea Alanui Road before making a right on Kaukahi Street and following it to the end.

MAKENA AND BEYOND
Palauea Beach (White Rock)

If there were an official border between Wailea and Makena, then **Palauea Beach** would probably straddle it. Known to locals as White Rock, for decades this was a lesser-visited stretch of shoreline in an otherwise heavily developed area. Bonfires and guitars once outnumbered private lawns and security cameras,

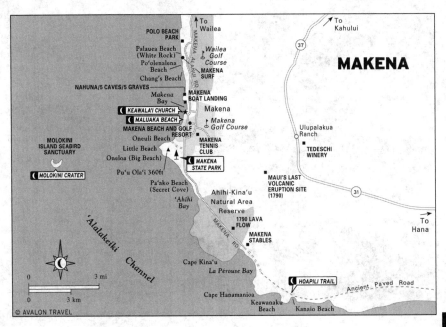

so don't be surprised if you round the corner and get a bit of a show.

To find Po'olenalena, travel on Wailea Alanui Road until you see Wailea Golf Club Drive on your left. Continue straight for one more minute and you will see the parking area for the beach on your right. To access the small public parking lot on the south side of the beach, look for the lot just before the Makena Surf on the right side of the road. Barely visible and only 10 spots large, it's next to the yellow fire hydrant numbered 614.

Chang's Beach

If you're looking for a tiny pocket of sand with exceptional snorkeling and not many people, then **Chang's Beach** will be your favorite spot in Makena. Not many make it to this beach because it's hidden from the road. Chang's Beach is about a mile and half past the Fairmont Kea Lani on Makena Alanui Road. Just look for the small parking lot immediately past the Makena Surf. If you find a spot in the parking lot *before* the Makena Surf building (the one by the fire hydrant 614), walk south for 100 yards past the gated entrance, and another small parking lot will be on your right. From here there is a small trail that leads down to the shore and the fingernail of sand. If you're wondering who "Chang" is, it's the name of a local Chinese family who inhabited the area long before tourism was ever on Maui's radar.

◖ Maluaka Beach

Directly in front of the Makena Beach and Golf Resort, **Maluaka Beach** is everything you've ever wanted in a beach. Locals refer to it as Prince Beach, since the hotel used to be called the Maui Prince. There's good snorkeling around the north end of the beach, fun waves for boogie boarding during the summer, ample parking, restrooms and showers, a grassy area for relaxing, and a beach activity stand right on the shoreline for renting a stand-up paddleboard or snorkeling equipment. This beach is perfect. Mornings are best at this beach for a couple of reasons, but mainly because during summer the wind can turn the sea to whitecaps.

© JENNA STRUBHAR

Maluaka Beach is a favorite of island locals.

The afternoons can also be overcast when you get this far south, as Makena sits directly beneath a cloud that forms every afternoon across the slope of Haleakala.

To reach Maluaka Beach there are two different entrances. On the north side, coming in on Makena Alanui, you make a right on Honoiki Street, then a left onto Makena Road, and a public parking lot is across from Keawala'i Church. For the south entrance, continue on Makena Alanui until you pass the entrance for the Makena Beach and Golf Resort, continue past the turnoff for the golf and tennis club. As the road bends around to the right, you'll see another sign for Makena Road on your right. Make a right, and follow it all the way to the parking area.

◀ Makena State Park

Makena isn't short on shore. Despite the number of sandy getaways, however, one beach in particular will forever define the rugged beauty carefree spirit of Makena: **Big Beach,** also known by its Hawaiian name, Oneloa.

If locals tells their friends they're going to "Makena," they mean this largest of the two beaches within Makena State Park.

In the early 1970s, Makena State Park was an internationally famous hippie commune where hundreds of draft-dodgers, nudists, and societal dropouts gathered in a grove tucked back in the kiawe trees. Drugs were rampant, nudity was the norm, and a growing community of sun-seeking hippies lived out an existence that defined free love. The more conservative South Maui community didn't take kindly to the "freeloaders" squatting in the bushes, and Big Beach was the site of some heated social tensions.

Although Big Beach visitors have since put their pants on, the same can't be said for neighboring **Little Beach** (www.littlebeachmaui. com). A short 30-foot walk over the bluff from the north end of Big Beach will bring you to a stretch of sand where there isn't a tan line in sight. An anachronistic aura permeates Little Beach. The bluff that separates the two beaches seems made not from stone, but from 40 years of compressed time; moving from one side to the other transports you back to an era when it was hip to be free.

In addition to the undeveloped beauty, one of the biggest reasons locals visit Big Beach is for a shorebreak unlike anywhere else on the island. This is the most popular beach on the island for local bodyboarders. This is not the place for casual boogie boarding unless you are a professional. During times of big surf the rip currents can be strong, so unless it's completely flat, think twice before entering the water.

To reach Big Beach and Makena State Park, travel on Makena Alanui road for a mile past the entrance to the Makena Beach and Golf Resort. There are three different access points to the beach, conveniently known as First Entrance, Second Entrance, and Third Entrance. The first two have large parking areas, but Third Entrance (0.5 mile south of First Entrance) is just a dirt area on the side of the road. If you plan on going to Little Beach, the closest parking spot will be at First Entrance. Don't leave any valuables in your vehicle, as car break-ins have been known to be a problem. There are no showers at Big Beach. The nearest place to wash off the sand is at Maluaka Beach a half a mile to the north.

Oneuli Beach

Sparsely visited **Oneuli Beach** is also part of Makena State Park, although it's nowhere near as scenic as neighboring Big or Little Beach. Although it is often referred to as the "black sand beach," the sand is more of a dark brown and nowhere near the deep black of the sand at Wai'anapanapa Beach on the outskirts of Hana. This beach sits at the base of Pu'u Olai, the volcanic red hill towering over Makena, and there is good snorkeling off the left side of the beach on the calmest of days. This spot is popular with locals and a good place to get away from it all. Despite the novelty factor of visiting the "black sand beach," there are better beaches in the area. To reach Oneuli Beach, make a right turn off Makena Alanui Road 0.2 mile past the turnoff for Maluaka Beach and 0.2 mile before the first entrance to Big Beach. The

entrance road is dirt and poorly paved. Cars with a low clearance might have a tough time.

Pa'ako Beach (Secret Cove)

If you want to go back home and tell your friends you found the "secret beach" on Maui, then take the time to sniff out this gem. The problem, however, is that even though this is called **Secret Cove,** the tiny inlet of sand is anything but a secret. Weddings take place here on a daily basis, and the chances of having it all to yourself are slim. To access this beach, you need to walk through a hole in a lava rock wall just south of the Third Entrance for Big Beach. You need to pay attention to find the tiny opening. As you climb up and over a little hill where Big Beach ends, you will notice a lava rock wall running along the right side of the road. You will also notice raised speed tables on the road itself. Next to the second speed table you will see a blue Beach Access sign and a shoulder-width opening in the lava rock wall. If you're not sure if you're at the right spot, a telephone pole on the other side of the street has the code "E2 3" written on it. Parking is only along the ocean side of the road, but on many occasions (due to the popularity of the "secret" beach), it's easier to just park at the Third Entrance for Big Beach and walk the rest of the way.

Keawanaku Beach

Break out your hiking boots and set off for **Keawanaku Beach.** Even most locals have never heard of this beach, and on most days you're guaranteed to be the only person there. Reaching Keawanaku isn't easy; you're going to have to hike over some rugged terrain. Follow the road 3.1 miles past the First Entrance to Big Beach. The road dead-ends in the parking lot of La Perouse Bay. For most visitors this marks the end of the line, and despite the remote location, it can get crowded. For you, however, La Perouse is just the start, because reaching Keawanaku requires an hour-long hike on the Hoapili Trail. You need to be in good shape to make the trek out to the beach. Pack *lots* of water and wear closed-toed shoes since the

SOUTH MAUI

© KYLE ELLISON

Keawanaku Beach on Maui's remote southern coastline

jagged *a'a* lava will rip slippers to shreds. Since there's no shade on this hike, it's best to start early to beat the wind and heat. It's also imperative that you stick to the trail and leave cultural artifacts undisturbed. The trail is outside of cell phone range, so be sure you're prepared and take extra precautions.

The trail starts simply enough and hugs the shoreline past a couple of coves. After 10 minutes you'll pass a small cross on the ocean side of the trail that denotes the La Perouse surf break, and after five more minutes the path will take a turn to the left toward a sign for the Hoapili Trail. At this point the trail departs from the coast and snakes across the center of the lava field. In the distance to your right you will see the lighthouse for Cape Hanamanioa.

Keawanaku will be 20 minutes after making the left onto the Hoapili Trail. As an indicator of where the beach is, you will see a short, lone palm tree surrounded by a grove of kiawe trees springing from the black lava field. Once you've located where the beach might be, keep a keen eye out for the short spur trail which winds its way down to the sand. Although rocky, the trail itself is still noticeable, and if you find yourself asking *"Am I still on the trail?,"* then chances are, no, you're no longer on the trail.

What makes this beach special is its rugged remoteness and the way you can listen to nothing but the wind. On the far left side of the beach there's a small trail which heads around the point and passes the remnants of an old stone fishing village.

Snorkeling

MA'ALAEA

Although you will often see little red dive flags fluttering in the wind off the harbor at **Ma'alaea Bay,** these are local spearfishers who are diving for *tako* (octopus). Don't mistake this for a nice snorkeling spot. Although Ma'alaea Bay once had a teeming reef prior to the 1990s, nearly 100 percent of it has died due to invasive algae species overcrowding the reef. It has been a case study for what will happen to all the island's reefs if environmental dangers go unmitigated.

◖ Molokini Crater

When it comes to snorkeling, what Ma'alaea is known for is the harbor that serves as the starting point for boats to **Molokini Crater,** a half-submerged volcanic caldera that rises from 300 feet of water. The reason Molokini is such a world-renowned dive destination is the fact that the visibility can stretch more than 100 feet on any day of the year. There isn't anywhere else in Hawai'i where you can find water this clear. The deep crater isn't affected by breaking surf in the same way that the beaches along the coastline can be. Since only a tiny bit of Molokini rises out of the water, the amount of runoff after a period of rain isn't enough to affect water quality. Whereas the back of Molokini Crater drops off to almost 300 feet, the inside bowl where snorkel boats tie up is only about 40 feet deep, and the best snorkeling is along the rim of the crater in 15 feet of water. At Molokini you have a great chance of finding colorful parrotfish, endemic reef species, octopuses, eels, and—if you're lucky—maybe a harmless whitetip reef shark. One species notably absent from Molokini, however, are Hawaiian green sea turtles, although most tour operators combine a trip to Molokini with a second snorkeling spot along the coast of Maui so that you can check turtles off the list.

Snorkeling at Molokini is such a popular activity that one of the biggest critiques is it seems there are more humans in the water than fish. One of the best ways to avoid the mass of humanity is to get on the earliest boat you can. Since this often necessitates a 5am wakeup, schedule it early in your trip when you're still jet-lagged and waking up early anyway. If you visited Molokini 20 years ago and are returning for another trip, you might notice there are fewer fish than the last time you were at the crater. The fish feeding that was a popular activity during the 1980s completely disrupted the area's natural food chain. The larger fish drove out the smaller fish, and a handful of species began to take over the entire reef. In an effort to return the crater to its former health, Molokini is now a tightly controlled marine preserve, and you will be required to fill out a form which outlines the rules for visiting. Boat trips from Ma'alaea take about an hour to reach the crater.

Boats to Molokini fall into three categories: small, medium, and large. As you might expect, the cheaper the ticket to Molokini, the more people there are going to be on the boat, which also means the more people there are going to be in the water snorkeling with you. The larger boats can have upward of 100 people on board during the busier months of the year. All of these large boats are diesel catamarans, but if you would prefer to sail on your excursion to Molokini, there are three sailboat companies that travel with 20-50 people on board.

Tree raft companies offer group sizes of no more than 24, which get you to Molokini quickly and easily. These trips can be economical, and the small groups ensure personalized service. However, the food won't be as good as on larger boats, and the bathroom situation can often be tight.

There are three departure points for reaching Molokini: Ma'alaea Harbor, Kihei Boat Ramp, and Maluaka Beach in Makena. Notice that Lahaina Harbor is *not* a departure point for Molokini Crater. Of the three departure points,

SOUTH MAUI

TIPS FOR VISITING MOLOKINI

- **Time of day is important.** Molokini Crater is rarely accessible in the afternoon due to the trade winds blowing out of the north or the east. During about 80 percent of the year the trade winds are so strong that Molokini Crater is filled with four-foot wind waves by noon. This is why all of the boats leave early in the morning. So when you are presented with a discount tour to Molokini and you see it departs at 2pm (conditions permitting), understand that the conditions will only rarely be permitting. You might get lucky, but chances are you'll end up snorkeling at a spot named Coral Gardens along the Maui shoreline.

- **The ride back to Ma'alaea is going to be rough.** For 80 percent of the year (and almost 100 percent of summer), the ride back to Ma'alaea Harbor is *very* rough. It's not dangerous; it's just that it's blowing 30 knots and sheets of sea spray coming over the bow. Some people love the ride; others are terrified. It's best to grab a protected seat toward the back of the boat and brace yourself.

- **Do you *really* need that wet suit?** The water temperature in Maui fluctuates between 73 degrees in the winter to 79 degrees in the summer—colder than the Gulf of Mexico, but still warmer than most oceans around the world. If you go on one of the large diesel boats, you will be asked if you want to rent a wet suit. The crew receives a commission on wet suit rentals, so expect a sales pitch. Only spend extra money on a wet suit if you think you will actually need it.

- **There aren't any turtles at Molokini.** Molokini Crater offers dozens of species of fish, impossibly clear water, and healthy, vibrant corals, but the one thing missing is green sea turtles. All of the turtles are found along the southern shoreline, so if you want to see some turtles, book a charter that stops along the shoreline.

- **Large surf means green turtles.** Wait. Aren't turtles always green? This means that if there is large surf along the southern shoreline (more frequent in summer than winter), then the water color at Turtle Town will be closer to green than blue. If the visibility along the shoreline isn't what you expected, it's due to increased surf.

- **Molokini isn't always accessible.** Molokini is inaccessible most afternoons due to the trade winds; if the wind is blowing out of the north, then the crater isn't accessible in the morning either. Often this wind switch can occur within a matter of minutes, so there is a slight chance you might end up snorkeling at a Plan B spot, which usually still ends up being a good trip.

nearly all boats leave out of Ma'alaea Harbor. The only boats starting from Kihei Boat Ramp are the three rafts—Blue Water Rafting, Seafire, and Redline Rafting—as well as most scuba diving boats. In Makena, the sailing catamaran *Kai Kanani* departs directly in front of the Makena Beach and Golf Resort, and its early trip is one of the first boats to arrive at Molokini. Matching the correct harbor with the correct time of day with the correct boat for your experience comprises the first three steps in ensuring an enjoyable outing.

Rental Shops

The best place for renting snorkel gear in Ma'alaea is at **Maui Dive Shop** (300 Ma'alaea Harbor Rd., 808/244-5514 www.mauidiveshop.com, 6am-6pm daily) in the Ma'alaea Harbor Shops. There is a wide range of snorkeling equipment for rent or purchase, and you can pick up an optical mask if you normally wear prescription glasses. Maui Dive Shop is affiliated with the *Ali'i Nui* sailing catamaran in the harbor just across the street, so you can often secure discounts on your rental gear if you end up combining it with a snorkeling charter (although snorkeling gear is provided on the boat free of charge).

DON'T FEED THE FISH!

There was a time when bread crumbs, frozen peas, and fish food were as integral to a snorkeling outing as a mask and fins. Though other places in the world still allow fish feeding for the enjoyment of snorkelers, here in Hawai'i, feeding fish has had a devastating effect on the marine ecosystem—particularly on coral reefs.

You shouldn't feed fish in the ocean for the same reason you don't feed bears in the woods: It isn't their normal diet. When fish learn to subsist on a foreign food source, they neglect their natural one, which in this case is the algae that grows on the reef and needs thinning out.

The next time you go snorkeling in Hawai'i, in addition to looking at all of the bright, colorful aquatic species, listen to what you hear underwater. The sound is similar to the "snap, crackle, and pop" of milk being poured over breakfast cereal, which is actually the sound of dozens of reef fish all feeding on algae. When herbivorous reef fish gorge themselves on the foreign food you introduce into the water, they become so full that they neglect to clean the reef of algae. Consequently, the coral polyps which form the reef become so overgrown that they struggle to breathe and ultimately die.

Aside from the adverse effect on the coral, larger fish species have been known to drive out the smaller fish species in areas where people feed fish. Many visitors to Molokini notice there are fewer fish than when they visited in the 1980s. It's also the reason for the stringent requirements currently in place.

Remember that some fish have sharp teeth. Many visitors have oval-shaped scars on their fingers from introducing food into the water. For your own safety as well as the health of the reef, don't feed the fish!

Snorkeling Charters

When it comes to charter boats in Maui, **Trilogy Excursions** (Slip 62 and Slip 99, 808/874-5649, www.sailtrilogy.com) has been setting the gold standard for 40 years. At $120/ adult their Molokini trip is pricier than the budget options, but you always get what you pay for. Trilogy boats only have 40-50 passengers, snuba is available as an upgrade, and since Trilogy has two catamarans in Ma'alaea Harbor, if you show up for your trip and the boat is empty, there's a good chance you just need to get to the other side of the harbor. Trips depart at 8am, make stops at two snorkeling spots, and return to the harbor six hours later.

Another family-run sailboat that visits Molokini is **Paragon** (Slip 72, 808/244-2087, www.sailmaui.com). This is a great trip for anyone whose priority is sailing instead of snorkeling. *Paragon* only makes one stop for snorkeling (which is almost always Molokini), and the emphasis on the trip back toward Ma'alaea is racing at top speeds on their high-performance 47-foot catamaran. The boat can reach upward of 20 knots. There are only 20 people on the boat. Trips depart at 7:30am, are five hours long, and cost $100/adult.

Along with *Trilogy II* and *Kai Kanani* down in Makena, *Ali'i Nui* (Slip 56, 808/875-0333, www.aliinuimaui.com) is a sailing catamaran that edges closer to yacht than regular charter boat. With sleek black and white trim, this 65-foot catamaran is also one of the island's widest at 36 feet, thereby ensuring a stable platform. *Ali'i Nui* is affiliated with Maui Dive Shop. While their snorkeling excursion is more expensive than the other excursions ($147/adult), they also include complimentary transportation to and from your hotel if you're staying on the west or south side of Maui. *Ali'i Nui* still offers scuba diving whereas many other companies have switched to snuba. *Ali'i Nui* visits Molokini three times per week (Tues., Thurs., and Sat.), opting on the other days to sail to Olowalu (or as they call it, "Turtle Point").

The company with the largest presence in Ma'alaea Harbor is **Pacific Whale Foundation** (300 Ma'alaea Boat Harbor Rd., 808/249-8811, www.pacificwhale.org), a nonprofit organization which has its headquarters in the Ma'alaea

Harbor Shops. Instead of checking in down at the harbor, check in at their shop. These cruises are more economical than some of the higher-priced excursions, although on busier days you could potentially be sharing the boat with more than 100 fellow passengers.

For snorkeling trips to Molokini with Pacific Whale Foundation there are four different options. The "standard" itinerary departs at 7am, features two snorkeling spots, and is currently listed at $85/adult. If you would rather sleep in a little bit and only want to see Molokini, the 9am Molokini Eco Express only lasts 3.5 hours at $55/adult. An 8:30am trip makes stops at both Molokini *and* at a bay off Lana'i ($95/adult), although this means spending *a lot* of time crossing the channel, which can often be rough on the way home. If you would prefer to be on a smaller vessel, the 7:30am Molokini Wild Side excursion costs $110/adult and spends a greater amount of time focusing on the marine and bird species found in the waters of South Maui.

The **Pride of Maui** (101 Ma'alaea Boat Harbor Rd., 808/242-0955, www.prideofmaui.com) offers a five-hour excursion aboard a large power catamaran for $96/adult. Trips depart at 8am from an area next to the U.S. Coast Guard station, although this is another popular boat which can frequently load over 100 passengers. During the summer and fall months (when it isn't whale season), there's also an afternoon snorkel trip to a location along the West Maui shoreline which runs for 3.5 hours and is only $48/adult. Turtle sightings are guaranteed on these trips, although the winds can often be howling in the afternoon, so don't expect calm conditions.

The **Four Winds II** (Slip 80, 808/879-8188, www.fourwindsmaui.com) catamaran offers both morning and afternoon excursions. Despite the fact that *Four Winds II* has a mast, often it's so windy in Ma'alaea Bay that the boat isn't able to sail. Small children will love the glass bottom part of the boat when stopped at Molokini, and unlike other boats which also make a stop along the shoreline, *Four Winds* makes Molokini its only stop so you have

plenty of time to relax and explore the crater at your own pace. The downside of this, however, is that you won't get the chance to snorkel with turtles. The trip departs at 7am and costs $98/adult. There's also an afternoon charter at a much reduced price of $45 which goes to a spot named Coral Gardens tucked out of the wind.

One of the cheapest trips to Molokini is on **Frogman II** (Slip 87, 888/700-3764, www.frogman-maui.com). *Frogman* offers excursions often tied in with a promotion at Boss Frog's charters, and as long as your expectations aren't too high, you can still have an enjoyable day on the water. The price for the morning trip is only $60/adult. *Frogman* also offers an afternoon trip at the cheap rate of only $30/adult, although it can only make it to Molokini on the rarest and calmest of afternoons. On most occasions *Frogman* ends up tying up next to *Four Winds II* at Coral Gardens, and while it might not be the same as Molokini, for that price you can't complain. If you want to upgrade to the next level of quality (but also upgrade the number of people on the boat), the sister boat is **Quicksilver** (Slip 44, 888/700-3764, www.frogman-maui.com), whose Molokini snorkeling trip visits two spots for $85/adult. While this trip is similar to those offered by the other large powerboats, what *Quicksilver* is known for is the semi-formal dinner cruise, which features live music. Rates for the dinner cruise are $70/adult, and the boat often tucks around the corner of West Maui to get a good angle on the sunset and hide from the wind.

If you want to visit Molokini from Ma'alaea but don't want to spend a lot of time getting there, **Aqua Adventure** (Slip 51, 808/573-2104, www.mauisnorkelsnuba.com) leaves at 7:30am and cruises at speeds much faster than the larger boats, so you can sleep in a little longer but still get to the crater at the same time. The small passenger numbers are also a plus on this boat (they cap the number at 40), and snuba is the name of the game when it comes to getting people in the water. You can of course just choose to snorkel, but if your main priority is getting to Molokini quickly and snuba diving once you're there, this trip costs $105/adult for two snorkeling spots and is an additional upgrade for snuba.

A similar operation that features snuba and small crowds is **Lani Kai** (Slip 76, 808/244-1879, www.mauisnorkeling.com), a trip which departs at 7am and visits two snorkeling locations for $98. Like other operations Lani Kai also has an afternoon charter, and for $44 you can cruise the cliffs over to Coral Gardens and tie up next to *Four Winds* and *Frogman,* with the difference being there are far fewer people on your boat than theirs.

The 58-foot *Mahana Nai'a* (Slip 47, 808/871-8636, www.maui-snorkeling-adventures.com) looks a little funny now that the mast from its sleek sailing days has been removed, but the family-run boat still chugs along, offering $90/adult snorkeling cruises to Molokini and the South Maui coastline.

KIHEI

Mornings are the best time of day for snorkeling in Kihei, and summer can have consistent winds and periods of surf which affect visibility. Although the snorkeling in summer can still be enjoyable, winter mornings are the best bet for light winds and clear visibility, and as an added bonus, if you dive down a few feet while snorkeling, you're guaranteed to hear whale song reverberating in the distance.

Snorkeling Spots

North Kihei doesn't offer anything in the way of snorkeling because the water is too shallow and murky. The northernmost beach in Kihei where you would want to snorkel is **Charley Young** beach, which is also known as the north end of Kamaole I. There's a rocky point here on the right side of the beach that offers good snorkeling, although during periods of high surf it can become popular with boogie boarders. Down at the other end of the beach, the rocky point between **Kamaole I** and **Kamaole II** is another area where you can find reef fish, a few eels, and maybe even a Hawaiian green sea turtle. Similarly, the rocky point that separates Kamaole II from **Kamaole III** is another nice place for a morning snorkel.

A half-mile to the south of Kamaole III is **Keawakapu** beach where there is good snorkeling on both the north and south side of the bay. The north end can get crowded due to the large public parking lot and bustling activity stand, and during busier periods of the year you have a better chance of being kicked in the face than finding a turtle. Not many people follow the outer edge of this reef in front of the hotel, however, so if you want to escape the crowd, either get here early before everyone arrives or just snorkel to the far side where the crowds thin out. To combine a morning snorkel with a leisurely morning stroll, park at the northern end of Keawakapu Beach and walk to the southern point. There are fewer crowds, it's a larger area for snorkeling, and the walk back to your car is one of the best beach walks on the island.

Rental Shops

The streets of Kihei are covered in snorkel shops. Since choosing a shop can be overwhelming, it's important to understand the nature of the snorkel rental business on Maui. Most snorkel shops and activity stands in Kihei are fronts for activity sales and timeshare presentations, so you may hear a sales pitch for a helicopter ride or vacation rental when your intention is just to go snorkeling.

Top picks for rental shops in the South Maui area are the **Maui Dive Shop** locations sprinkled from Ma'alaea to Wailea. There are two different venues in Kihei (2463 S. Kihei Rd., 808/879-1533, www.mauidiveshop.com, 7am-9pm daily; 1455 S. Kihei Rd., 808/879-3388, 6am-9pm daily), and the corporate store in central Kihei opens at 6am. Maui Dive Shop also operates the *Ali'i Nui* catamaran, so there will be a sell on that particular activity, but *Ali'i Nui* is a beautiful boat that puts on a good trip, and you can frequently get discounts with a snorkel gear and snorkeling trip combo.

The other snorkel shop you'll see with just as much frequency is **Boss Frog's** (main office 1770 S. Kihei Rd., 808/874-5225, www.bossfrog.com, 8am-5pm daily), which has three locations scattered across Kihei. Boss Frog's offers

WHAT IS SNUBA?

On many of the boats that visit Molokini Crater you will be presented with the opportunity to upgrade to a snuba dive, but what exactly does that mean?

In short, snuba (SNOO-Bah) is the safest, easiest, and fastest way to experience what it's like to breathe underwater. It is similar to scuba diving in that you are breathing off a regulator. The difference is that instead of having to wear pounds of gear, take an in-depth class, and swim with a tank on your back, during a snuba dive the air tank rests on a raft above the surface, and the only pieces of equipment you wear are a weight belt and a lightweight shoulder harness. A 10-foot-long hose descends from the inflatable raft above you and connects to your regulator, so it's almost like a 10-foot-long snorkel which, instead of going up to the surface, goes up to an air tank. Since snuba is so much more user-friendly than scuba diving, it's the perfect activity for those who have snorkeled a time or two, but have always been a little hesitant about actually making the transition from snorkeling into scuba diving.

Here are some commonly asked questions when it comes to snuba diving:

Q: What is the minimum age for snuba?
A: Eight.

Q: How deep will I go?
A: Ten feet if diving at Molokini Crater, and up to 20 feet if diving elsewhere.

Q: How long can I stay underwater?
A: In most cases you will be sharing an air tank with another diver. Most dives last between 20 and 25 minutes.

Q: Do I need to know how to swim?

A: Yes. Because the whole point behind snuba is to experience what it's like to breath *underwater*, flotation for nonswimmers defeats the point of the activity.

Q: I've never snorkeled before. Can I still snuba?
A: It's helpful to have snorkeled a few times before, but there are people who have never snorkeled who try snuba and do great. As a quick self-test, pinch your nose and breathe out of your mouth for 30 seconds. If this feels awkward, you might want to pass on snuba diving.

Q: Can I fly or travel to Haleakala after a snuba dive?
A: Yes, since you don't descend as deep in snuba diving as you would scuba diving, your body doesn't accumulate enough nitrogen for flying to be a problem.

Q: Do I need to be in good health to snuba?
A: Although the range of physical limitations is more lenient in snuba than it is in scuba diving, you still need to complete a standard medical form.

Q: If I'm congested, can I snuba dive?
A: Not unless you want to have unbearable sinus pain.

Q: My ears hurt when I dive underwater, can I still snuba?
A: Yes. Your instructor will teach you how to equalize the air spaces in your ears so that you won't feel any pressure.

Q: How much does snuba diving cost?
A: While every operation is different, most boats offer snuba as a $59-69 upgrade.

the cheapest deals on snorkel rentals on the island, but the company is heavily embedded in the activities sales market, often timeshare-related. If you rent snorkeling gear for a week (which can be as low as $9), you will also get a discounted snorkeling trip on their boat out of Maʻalaea, the *Frogman II.*

Snorkel Bob's has multiple stores across Kihei, with one in the Kamaole Beach Center (2411 S. Kihei Rd., 808/878-7449, www.

snorkelbob.com, 8am-5pm daily), and another in the Azeka II shopping area in Central Kihei (1279 S. Kihei Rd., 808/875-6188, 8am-5pm daily). Snorkel Bob's is a statewide chain that also incorporates activity sales, and you're sure to see their quirky ads if you flip through any island visitor magazines. Snorkel Bob's is known for selling gear that they design themselves, and a nice feature of the operation is that you can rent gear on one island and return it on another island completely free of charge. Packages range from $2/day for a basic mask and snorkel rental to $44/week for a package that includes prescription lenses and fins.

There are a host of other operations throughout Kihei that offer snorkel rentals, and it can come down to which place is closest and most convenient.

Snorkeling Boats

While most of the boats leaving from Kihei Boat Ramp are scuba diving charters, there are still a few rafting boats that focus on sightseeing and snorkeling. The back of the raft is always the most stable area, whereas the front is where most of the bouncing occurs. They only carry about 24 people, so if you don't like crowds and just want a mellow, informative day on the water, these are going to be the trips for you.

Of all the rafting options, the top pick is **Blue Water Rafting** (808/879-7238, www.bluewaterrafting.com) which meets at the boat ramp at 6:30am. If you've already been to Molokini once before and are looking for an adventure snorkel, Blue Water Rafting has a trip to the Kanaio Coast where you can snorkel along a rugged volcanic coastline most visitors will never get to see. This forgotten southwestern coastline is pockmarked with thundering sea caves and jagged lava formations, and there are multiple places where you can see the remnants of ancient fishing villages. The captains are geologists, historians, and marine naturalists all rolled into one. They're skilled enough to hug the coast so closely you could almost reach out and touch it. The waters in this area can often be rough, however, so this isn't the best trip if you're prone to motion sickness. You can either book the four-hour Kanaio Coastline tour from $100/adult and $79/child, or you can combine it with an 11am excursion to Molokini for $125/adult and $100/child. If you only want to book a two-hour tour to Molokini, the cost is $50/adult and $39/child and it departs at 11:30am, which can sometimes be too late to beat the afternoon trade winds. For anyone doing the math, however, this is one of the most affordable options for visiting the crater if all you're looking for is a ride there and back. There is no breakfast, coffee, or bathroom on board.

The other primary snorkeling option out of Kihei Boat Ramp is **Redline Rafting** (808/757-9211, www.redlinerafting.com), which also offers tours to Molokini and the Kanaio Coast. Tours meet at 6:30am, and at $140/adult and $100/child the cost is a little higher than Blue Water Rafting, but they also include breakfast and coffee and have a (small) bathroom on board. Although they are still one of the only boats that traverses the Kanaio Coast, they don't go as far down the coast as Blue Water, spending more time in Makena and Molokini.

If you've always wanted to look like you're in the U.S. Coast Guard, **Seafire** (808/879-2201, www.molokinisnorkeling.com) offers a trip at 7:30am on its orange and silver jet-drive raft that not only looks like a Coast Guard boat, but is driven by a member of the Coast Guard Reserve. Trips last for three hours. At $55 it's one of the best budget options for reaching Molokini Crater.

WAILEA
◀ Ulua Beach and Mokapu Beach

The best two locations for snorkeling in Wailea are **Ulua Beach** and **Mokapu Beach,** which are listed together because the rocky point that separates them is where you'll find the most marine life and coral. Ulua (the southernmost of the two) is more protected and offers a gentle, sandy entry. This is the perfect spot for beginning snorkelers. Morning hours are calm and the best time for finding turtles. As at neighboring Kihei, winter is guaranteed to offer the best visibility. If you're staying at one of the Wailea resorts, you can reach the beaches by strolling along the Wailea Coastal Walk. If you are driving, there are two small public parking lots which can fill up early; arrive before 9am. To reach the parking area, turn on Ulua Beach Road off Wailea Alanui Drive just north of the Shops at Wailea, and follow the road down until the parking lots at the end.

Mokapu Beach offers some of South Maui's best snorkeling.

© KYLE ELLISON

Wailea Point

The second most popular spot for snorkeling in Wailea is **Wailea Point,** a rocky promontory rife with green sea turtles which separates the Four Seasons and Fairmont Kea Lani. The easiest point of entry is from the south side of Wailea Beach in front of the Four Seasons. The only downside of entering from the beach is that it can be a long swim to the good part of the reef. You'll notice some people trying to enter and exit the water by launching off the point itself, and while this can be efficient, it's also a great way to slip on the rocks or have a wave wash you into some sea urchins. Entering from the beach is the safest bet, although be prepared for a five-minute swim over sand.

Rental Shops

Inside the Shops at Wailea there's a **Maui Dive Shop** (3750 Wailea Alanui Rd., 808/875-9904, www.mauidiveshop.com, 8am-9pm daily) which is similar to the other stores throughout South Maui. The staff can offer good advice on snorkeling locations, it's within walking distance of many of the hotels, and the rental prices will be cheaper than what the activity booth stands will charge inside the resorts.

MAKENA AND BEYOND

As you move south from Wailea to Makena, you'll notice that the terrain becomes just a little rawer. While Makena offers some of the south side's best snorkeling, the entry and exit points can be a little more challenging than at Kihei or Wailea beaches. Makena is a little more exposed to southerly swell than the beaches to the north are, so not only is visibility affected, but the waves can sometimes crash into the lava rocks with such a fury it's the last place you would want to find yourself. High surf is most typical in summer. Just watch the shoreline for five minutes before going in the water so you can get an idea of how large the waves are. During winter, nearly every day will be flat and calm.

Snorkeling Locations

The best place for beginner-level snorkeling

in Makena is **Maluaka Beach** in front of the Makena Beach and Golf Resort. There's a rocky point that wraps around the north end of the beach, and the entry from the sand into the water is gentle and forgiving. The sailing catamaran *Kai Kanani* loads all their passengers from shore here, so if you see the boat motoring toward you, give it a clear path to the sand.

While Maluaka might be the *easiest* place to snorkel in Makena, the best snorkeling overall can be found at **Makena Landing.** Getting in the water can be a little challenging here, but once you make it out past the shallow areas, you'll be glad you made the effort. There are multiple entry and exit points for Makena Landing, the most common of which is the public parking area off Makena Road. To reach the parking area, drive along Makena Alanui until you reach Honoiki Street and the turn for Keawala'i Church. When you reach the bottom of Honoiki, turn right, and follow the road for a quarter of a mile until you see a parking area on your left. The entry from here can be shallow, but be careful to not step on any *wana,* or black sea urchins, a common sight between the rocks. Once in the water, hug the coastline as it wends its way around the rocky point to the north, and when you have rounded the tip, you'll notice there is a long finger of lava underwater that extends out toward Molokini. This is what's known as the South Finger, and there's a sea cave here that houses green sea turtles. This area is often referred to as Turtle Town by many of the snorkel boat operators, and unless you want to share the water with 200 other snorkelers, try to be out here before 10am, when all of the Molokini charter boats begin mooring offshore. If you swim north from the South Finger, you will pass over lime green coral heads. Keep an eye out for moray eels or the strange-looking flying gurnard. Eventually, you'll come to the North Finger, another underwater lava formation that houses many turtles. This finger is often covered in bright red slate-pencil urchins that the ancient Hawaiians would use for red dye, and eagle rays and manta rays are sometimes seen off the deeper end of the finger.

An alternate entry point for Makena Landing is via the north side at a spot known as **Five Graves.** Parking is scarce here, and the entry can be challenging, but it's a much shorter swim to reach the fingers. The beach access is tough to find, however, so you need to pay close attention. Instead of turning into the parking lot on Makena Road, continue driving up and over the hill. When the road drops back down to the shoreline, you'll notice a dirt area on the right that can fit about five cars. Park here. On the other side of the street you'll notice a small trail. You'll know this is the right path if you see five graves in a small graveyard on the left. Follow this trail to the shoreline. The easiest place to get in and out of the water is a protected nook in the rocks on your right. Although the beach area to the left of the trail looks like it would be the easiest, it's shallow for a long way out, and you don't want to contend with the breaking waves. On calm days this is the quickest means of reaching the fingers.

Moving south, there are a few places which offer decent snorkeling inside **Makena State Park,** the best of which is the point that separates Big Beach from Little Beach. The best thing to do is to park in the first entrance to Big Beach and turn right when you hit the sand. This will bring you to the far northern end of the beach where you can enter the water to snorkel around the point. The surf can get big here in the summer, so this is only possible on a flat day. For more direct access to the best part of the reef, clamber up and over the hill to Little Beach and snorkel in the cove off the left side of the bay. If there are waves in the bay, however, it's best to go elsewhere because this will put you right in the path of oncoming boogie boarders.

Some say that the best snorkeling in South Maui is at **Ahihi Kinau.** But once popular spots such as the Fishbowl and the Aquarium are closed to the general public until 2014—and potentially longer. The only place where you can still snorkel in the Ahihi Kinau Natural Area Reserve is a small cove a mile past Pa'ako Beach (Secret Cove). Even though the parking situation here can be abysmal, the snorkeling

SOUTH MAUI

SOUTH MAUI

THE AQUARIUM IS CLOSED

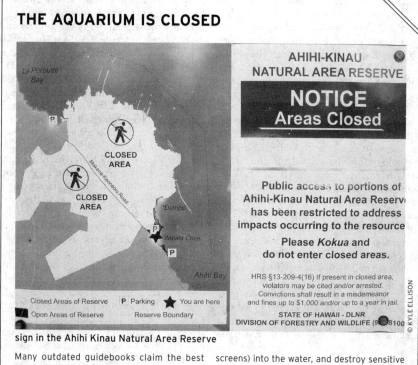

sign in the Ahihi Kinau Natural Area Reserve

Many outdated guidebooks claim the best snorkeling in South Maui are at two areas in the Ahihi Kinau Natural Area Reserve known as the Aquarium and the Fishbowl, hidden near the end of the paved road and accessible via a trail through the island's most recent lava flow.

The problem is that these areas became *too* popular. What was once a sensitive and protected part of the island was overrun with visitors who would leave trash, introduce foreign matter (such as petroleum-based spray-on sun- screens) into the water, and destroy sensitive ponds. It seemed the only solution for keeping troublemakers out was to keep *all* visitors out, so the area was closed in 2008.

The area still hasn't recovered from over- use. A site originally planned to re-open in 2010 remains closed until mid-2014, and potentially longer. These areas are off-limits to the public. There are many other spots for good snorkel- ing along the island's south side. Be part of the solution, not part of the problem.

warrants the effort. If you're not sure if you're at the right place, the house number of the large estate just past the cove is 7750 and it has a large lava rock wall in front of it. While this cove is not within the dramatic lava flow like the other Ahihi spots, it is still a scenic area for finding reef fish and green sea turtles. Entry into the water can be difficult since you need to go over lava rocks, so on days when there are waves breaking all the way into the cove, find somewhere else to snorkel.

On the other side of the hill from the Ahihi Kinau snorkeling area is a cove that's referred to simply as **Dumps.** There's a small gravel park- ing lot here just before the road begins its trek across the lava flow, and a short five-minute trail leads down to a rocky beach. While the snorkeling here can be good at times, there isn't that much more to find here that you can't see at any other South Maui snorkeling spot. The waves can get *very* large in summer, and you only want to snorkel here if the conditions are completely calm. To reach Dumps, travel 1.6 miles past the first entrance for Big Beach. Don't leave valuables in your car; break-ins are an ongoing problem.

Finally, just when you think that the road will never end, the asphalt gives way to a gravel parking lot in a spot known as **La Perouse Bay.** The lava field that you drive over en route to La Perouse is the remnants of Haleakala's last eruption, and if you look up the side of the mountain while traversing the lava field, it's obvious where the lava escaped from the mountain. The ribbon of black rock that weaves toward the sea is so well-defined it looks as if a child chose the wrong crayon to draw an erupting volcano, opting for black instead of orange. Most literature will tell you that the lava flow dates to 1790, although recent evidence suggests it might have been earlier. The bay is named for the French explorer Jean Francois de Galaup Compte de La Pérouse, who in 1786 was the first European to set foot on the island of Maui in this very spot. As you enter the parking area there's a stone structure memorializing this event, and it's fascinating to think that at a time when the United States had already fought a revolution, the island of Maui was still unknown to the Western world.

The snorkeling in La Perouse Bay can be phenomenal, although there are also times when it can be a total bust. Early mornings are best before the trade winds fill the bay with whitecaps, and summer can bring large surf which turns the shoreline into a cauldron of white water. On calm days, however, the best snorkeling is found to the right of the parking lot where you must scramble across a lava rock point to reach the protected inlet. The water here is an enchanting color of turquoise against the young black lava rock. There's a definite "wilderness" factor when snorkeling in a place like La Perouse as opposed to just in front of

your hotel, and although it's possible to follow the rocky shoreline out and around the distant point, it isn't a good idea because it can be tough to make it back to shore. Stay within the bay. A pod of Hawaiian spinner dolphins which has been known to frequent the area. Be careful when clambering over the slippery rocks.

Rental Shops

If you make it all the way down to Makena and realize that you left your mask back in your hotel, you can still rent equipment for the day at the beach activities center in front of the Makena Beach and Golf Resort.

Snorkeling Boats

Kai Kanani (808/879-7218, www.kaikanani. com) is the only option for snorkeling boats leaving out of Makena. Only a few years old and still sparkling, it has all the added amenities you would expect from a luxury yacht with top-notch captains. *Kai Kanani* departs directly from Maluaka Beach in front of the Makena Beach and Golf Resort, which, if you're staying in Makena, makes it a far more convenient option for sailing to Molokini than driving all the way to Ma'alaea Harbor. If Molokini was too crowded the last time you visited, *Kai Kanani's* early-morning Molokini express charter ($63/adult) departs the beach at 6:30am and guarantees you're the first boat at the crater. This trip is just over two hours long, and while its second trip of the day ($138/adult) visits the crater when it's far more crowded, the fact that it's four hours long as opposed to two allows for twice the amount of snorkeling time. Another added benefit of *Kai Kanani* is if you're concerned about getting seasick, the journey time from Maluaka Beach to Molokini is much shorter than the journey between Molokini and Ma'alaea. Summer can occasionally have big surf crashing onto Maluaka Beach, so if you have someone in your party with mobility issues, it can be tough to wade through the water to board the boat. In this case a trip out of Ma'alaea Harbor might be a better choice.

Scuba Diving

South Maui has some of the island's best shore diving. With so many locations and so many different operators, planning your dives can be overwhelming. The following information should help you match your ability level with the operations and locations which suit you the best. Remember that to avoid decompression sickness, you will not be able fly, go on a helicopter tour, or go to the top of Haleakala Crater for 24 hours after finishing your last scuba trip. This is a basic scheduling oversight that many divers forget, so when booking a dive excursion, check your schedule to see if you have any of these activities planned for the following day. Due to the shallow depth of only 10-20 feet, these same restrictions don't apply to snuba diving.

MA'ALAEA
Dive Sites

While **Molokini Crater** can be a great place to snorkel, to truly tap into the magic of the crater you need to put a tank on your back and go and see what's down there. For experienced divers, Molokini ranks in the upper echelon of dive locations around the world. For novice divers who have just been certified, it's a window into a new aquatic universe. Only certified divers are allowed to dive at Molokini Crater. If you aren't certified but still want to experience Molokini from below, sign up for a 20-minute snuba dive to depths of up to 10 feet.

What makes the crater such an exceptional dive spot is the combination of two different factors: Its pelagic location means there is the possibility of seeing anything, and there are multiple dive spots within the crater that cater to a wide range of ability levels. Novice divers will want to inquire about trips that go to either Middle Reef or Reef's End, as depths on these dives don't usually exceed 70 feet. Middle Reef is home to large schools of pelagic species such as jacks and reef sharks, and the sand channel houses curious-looking garden eels. There's also a huge drop-off at the Middle Reef section where it can be easy to exceed your dive profile, so keep an eye on your depth gauge when swimming over the ledge. Similarly, at Reef's End, the dive traces the wall of the underwater caldera to the point where it drops off into the abyss. Since this underwater promontory sits on the fringe of the crater, this is the area with the best chance of sightings of bottlenose dolphins, manta rays, humpback whales, and even the occasional whale shark. There was even a great white shark sighting out here captured on video by Ed Robinson's dive charters, although encounters like this are so rare they aren't even worth worrying about. While Middle Reef and Reef's End are both fantastic dives, the best and most advanced dive in Molokini Crater is a drift dive of the legendary Back Wall. Beginning at Reef's End, divers will follow the current along the back of Molokini where a vertical wall drops over 250 feet to the ocean floor below. If you're the type of diver who dabbles in nitrox or mixed gases, this is the deepest dive available anywhere in Maui County, although you should still stay within the recreational dive limit of 145 feet.

Even though diving at Molokini offers a chance of seeing sharks, if you want a 100 percent guarantee of diving with sharks, the most unique dive on the island is offered at the **Maui Ocean Center** where you can go diving *inside the shark tank*. As part of its Shark Dive Maui program, certified divers are able to spend 30-40 minutes surrounded by various species of sharks, some of which can include hammerhead and tiger sharks. The dive has a maximum limit of four divers, costs $199, and is only offered on Monday, Wednesday, and Friday mornings. The cost includes the tank and the weight, although divers will need to provide the rest of their gear. Although diving at an aquarium might seem like cheating, even some of Maui's most seasoned divers claim it's a great dive. More than just a novelty, this is your best opportunity to be completely surrounded by the ocean's most feared and misrepresented creatures.

One of the island's newest wreck dives is a **Helldiver** WWII airplane which was abandoned by a pilot on a training run off Sugar Beach. When the pilot ejected, his plane sank in 50 feet of water, and for the better part of 60 years this plane sat forgotten in the mudflats off Ma'alaea. When a local fisher tipped off a Kihei dive instructor that there was probably something down there, the exploratory dive mission yielded a historical discovery which is now property of the U.S. military; divers aren't allowed to touch or enter the aircraft. While there isn't an overwhelming amount of marine life here, this is a unique dive you won't find in many people's logbooks. There aren't any regularly scheduled trips to the Helldiver, but many South Maui operators periodically plan excursions to the site, so inquire about when the next outing might be.

Rental Operators

The only retail operator in Ma'alaea that rents out dive gear is **Maui Dive Shop** (300 Ma'alaea Harbor Rd., 808/244-5514, www.mauidiveshop.com, 6am-6pm daily) in the Ma'alaea Harbor Shops. Although most dive operations will furnish their own gear, this is a good place to pick up equipment if you're diving at the Maui Ocean Center, are planning a dive off a nearby shoreline, or need some accessories such as a flashlight or a knife.

Dive Boats

Although most Molokini dive boats depart from the Kihei Boat Ramp, two that depart from Ma'alaea Harbor are the 48-foot **Maka Koa** which is operated by Maui Dive Shop (808/875-1775, www.mauidiveshop.com) as well as the 40-foot *Maui Diamond II* (Slip 23, 808/879-9119, www.mauidiamond.com). Maui Dive Shop offers two-tank trips to Molokini Crater three times per week, and the second dive is either along the shoreline of Maui or at the St. Anthony wreck off Kihei. Rates for a two-tank dive are $139, and BC and regulator

rental is an additional $20. Snorkelers are allowed to accompany divers for a reduced rate of only $80, and this is a good option for the novice to intermediate diver who wants to explore in the 65-70 feet range. In addition to providing a good trip, an added perk of booking with Maui Dive Shop is that they provide complimentary transportation from your hotel to Ma'alaea Harbor. If you're driving yourself to the harbor, check-in is at 6:30am at the store in the Ma'alaea Harbor Shops.

For a few dollars less, *Maui Diamond II* offers 2-tank trips to Molokini and the South Maui shoreline for $129, and BC and regulator rental is an additional $15. If you aren't a certified diver, you have the option of partaking in a Discover Scuba Diving introductory class in which you will snorkel at Molokini and then dive with an instructor at the second spot along the shoreline. The rate for the snorkel and introductory dive combo is $145, although the price is inclusive of all your equipment. This boat is a little older and a little slower, but they feed you well, so the added transport time can be devoted to digestion.

KIHEI
Dive Sites

The only real dive site in Kihei is the **St. Anthony Wreck** off the south end of Keawakapu Beach. Maui Dive Shop offers dives to this part of a massive artificial reef system twice-weekly as part of a two-tank excursion combined with Molokini.

Rental and Shore Dive Operators

If you're a certified diver who needs to rent some gear, get some gear serviced, pick up some tanks for a shore dive, or book a guided shore dive with an instructor, there are a number of different retail operators throughout Kihei. My top pick in Kihei is **Maui Dreams** (1993 S. Kihei Rd., 808/874-5332, www.mauidreamsdiveco.com, 7am-6pm daily) in the shop is across from the southern end of Kalama Park. These guys *love* to dive, and they offer a full range of excursions from scooter dives ($99) to night dives ($79) to regular introductory dives if it's your first time trying the sport ($89). Guided shore dives for certified divers are $69. Maui Dreams is also the only PADI 5-Star Instructor Development Center in South Maui, which means they train instructors. At $399 the certification courses are more expensive than others, and it's $499 if you haven't already completed the academic portion online (PADI E-learning).

Inside the Azeka Makai shopping center on the ocean side of the highway, **B&B Scuba** (1280 S. Kihei Rd., 808/875-2861, www.bbscuba.com, 8am-6pm Mon.-Fri., 8am-5pm weekends) offers guided shore dives for only $59, and they can also arrange a guided kayak dive to some of the spots which would normally only be accessible by boat. Like other operators, they also offer night dives ($65) as well as scooter dives ($119) along the South Maui shoreline. Whereas some other operators in town focus strictly on recreational diving, these guys are a little more hardcore. In addition to offering PADI certification classes ($349), they also offer IANTD tech diving classes such as trimix, nitrox, and rebreather training. They provide basic gear rental and tank pumping.

Check out **Scuba Shack** (2349 S. Kihei Rd., 808/891-0500, www.scubashack.com), which is tucked behind the gas station across from Kamaole I Beach. Guided dives are pricier here. Certified divers can book a guided shore dive for $85, whereas introductory divers will need to shell out $105. Certification classes last three days and are $350, and the shop also offers a full range of gear and equipment rentals.

Dive Boats

All dive boats in Kihei leave from Kihei Boat Ramp, which is just south of Kamaole III Beach. Parking is tight in the main lot, so it's best to head to the overflow lot on the right. The scene at the boat ramp in the morning can be kind of hectic—especially in the dark. If you can't find your boat, ask any staff member; each charter has its own corner of the parking lot. Most boats offer coffee aboard their trips if you still need a wakeup, and most boats also offer private bathrooms if the coffee just goes

right through you. Since a number of boats that leave out of Kihei Boat Ramp don't have offices, bring a credit card or cash so you can process payment on board. If you plan on diving during your time in Maui, bring your certification card.

Of all the choices in Kihei, the unanimous top pick among island locals is always **Mike Severn's** (808/879-6596, www.mikeseverns-diving.com), Kihei's original dive boat operation. Although a number of the other operators in Kihei all provide exceptional service, it's impossible to beat the instructors at Mike Severn's. Not only do the instructors take the time to show you the species outlined in books—but they also wrote them. Since Mike Severn's caters to seasoned divers, the instructors don't mandate an underwater game of "follow the leader." They give you the freedom to enjoy the dive at your own pace. Two-tank dives are $130 (plus $15 BC, regulator, and computer rental), and dives meet at 6am at the Kihei Boat Ramp aboard the 38-foot *Pilikai*.

Pro Diver (808/875-4004, www.prodiver-maui.com) is one of the last dive boats to cap its trips at only six divers (whereas other boats will usually max at 12 divers with two instructors). The small group size guarantees a personal experience, and their 34-foot boat meets at 6am at Kihei Boat Ramp. Two-tank dives are offered at $139, and it's an additional $15 for gear rental in the event you don't have your own.

Also ranking among the South Maui elite, **Ed Robinson's** (808/879-3584, www.mauiscuba.com) caters to advanced divers and underwater photographers. If you're afraid you're going to get stuck with a group of greenhorns, you can confidently sign on with Ed Robinson's and know that everyone aboard is relatively skilled. Meet at 6:30am at the Kihei Boat Ramp. Regular two-tank dives are offered Monday, Thursday, and Saturday for $129, and more advanced two-tank drift dives are offered Sunday and Friday for the same price. If you just can't get enough bottom time, there's also a three-tank dive on Tuesday which departs on a different boat, and if you're an experienced, extreme diver who wants to go off the regular commercial radar, there is an Adventure X dive on Wednesday for $149. Unlike other dive operations out of Kihei Boat Ramp, Ed Robinson's now has a shop in central Kihei in an industrial yard at 165 Halekuai Street across from Eskimo Candy seafood restaurant that also serves as a dive museum.

In addition to offering shore dives and rental options, **B&B Scuba** (1280 S. Kihei Rd., 808/875-2861, www.bbscuba.com) also has a dive boat which does two-tank dives out of Kihei Boat Ramp aboard the 40-foot *Kilikina II*. When it comes to diving, these guys don't screw around; they're out on the water by 5:45am, and since the goal is to beat all of the crowds and get an early start, it's frowned upon to show up late. The payoff for the early wakeup, however, is that you reach your first dive site before any other boats are around, and if that first dive site is Molokini, there is a certain magic to having the solitude most visitors will never get to experience. As an added scheduling bonus, you're usually back to the dock by 10am, and the wallet-friendly price of $119 is also a strong selling point.

Two outfits focusing primarily on recreational divers are **Makena Coast Dive Charters** (808/874-1273, www.mauiunderwater.com) and **Scuba Shack** (808/891-0500, www.scubashack.com). Both have boats leaving from Kihei Boat Ramp, offering one dive at Molokini and one dive along the South Maui shoreline.

WAILEA
Dive Sites

Unlike Ma'alaea or Kihei, which only serve as departure points for diving elsewhere, Wailea offers shore dives with shallow depths perfect for novices. Unlike the shore dives in Makena which require scrambling over jagged lava rocks, the entry points in Wailea are sandy and easy. Of all the beaches in Wailea, the best for a morning shore dive is the point at **Ulua Beach.** This is where most dive operators bring students during their certification courses, as the maximum depth is about 35 feet. There is ample parking at the bottom of Ulua Beach

Road, and the concrete walkway down to the shoreline is convenient for hauling tanks and gear. Although the dive wraps around the point toward Mokapu Beach, it's best to enter and exit the water from the Ulua side since it's more protected from wind and waves. Expect to see a number of Hawaiian green sea turtles along with healthy coral formations, endemic reef fish, and perhaps a rare spotted eagle ray or spiny lobster.

Although most dive operations operate off Ulua Beach, if you're renting your own gear you can dive at **Wailea Point.** Entry for the dive is off the south side of Wailea Beach, and while you might trip over a cabana en route to the shoreline this is a great place for seeing turtles on days with clear visibility (which are more common in winter than summer). The nearest public access and parking lot are on the south end of the Four Seasons resort. Since this area can sometimes be visited by snorkeling charters, it's good to get out early before the crowds (and wind) arrive.

Rental Operators
The only dive shop in Wailea is **Maui Dive Shop** (3750 Wailea Alanui Rd., 808/875-9904, www.mauidiveshop.com, 8am-9pm daily) within the Shops at Wailea. You can pick up dive-related accessories and inquire about current conditions, although since this is a satellite store, if you're in need of gear and tank rental, you're better off with one of the larger outlets in Kihei.

MAKENA AND BEYOND
Dive Sites

In addition to being one of the best shore dives in Makena, **Makena Landing** also takes the cake as the spot with the greatest number of names (others include **Nahuna, 5 Caves,** and **5 Graves**). As if four names weren't enough already, this general area is also referred to as **Turtle Town** by many charter boat operators, which was concocted to sell snorkeling tours. Each of the many monikers is accurate for different reasons: Geographically, the dive lies within the Makena Landing area and is close to Makena Landing park. There are multiple caves here where sea turtles and whitetip reef sharks often hang out, all accessible to divers. You walk right past five tombstones if you choose to use the northern beach access. Nahuna is the Hawaiian name for this area.

What makes this dive so fantastic is not only the chance to see turtles, but also pelagic species such as manta rays, spotted eagle rays, bottlenose dolphins, and large ʻawa. Throughout the winter, divers are surrounded by whale song. For those more interested in macro photography, there can also be nudibranchs, harlequin shrimp, flying gurnards, slate pencil urchins, and a wide range of eels. On calm days the visibility can often reach 100 feet, although on days where there is a south swell (usually in the summer), visibility can be reduced to 20 feet at best.

While many dive boats frequent this area, the easiest place to enter from shore is the parking lot by Makena Landing park. Once in the water, turn to the right and follow the coastline until you reach a long finger of lava. This is what's known as the South Finger, and the depth here is only about 15 feet. Follow the South Finger away from the shoreline, and halfway to the end you will notice a large cave which you can swim through from below. There are numerous turtles that hang out in here, and there is almost always a whitetip reef shark under a ledge. Emerging on the other side of the cave, you can kick your way parallel to the shoreline across a field of peculiar coral formations, whereby you will eventually reach the North Finger after three minutes of swimming. If you somehow haven't seen a turtle yet, there is another large cave on the north side of this finger where turtles are known to hang out.

Since this area is popular with charter boats, arrive early before the crowds, and always dive with a dive flag. For an alternate entry on calm days, park at the small beach access on Makena Road on the north side of the hill past Makena Landing park. There will be a few dirt parking spaces on the right, and the small beach access trail that leads past the five graves.

Another nice shore dive is the **Ahihi Kinau** cove 1.5 miles past the first entrance for Big Beach. The depth here goes to about 40 feet. Since this cove is protected from the wind, it offers pristine diving conditions as long as the surf isn't up. Expect to find green sea turtles and the rare spinner dolphin if you're on the outer edge of the reef. The entry into the water can be tricky since you have to navigate your way over slippery rocks, but you don't need to worry about boats in this cove, although it can often be packed with snorkelers as the morning wears on, making parking an issue.

Surfing

If you look at a map of South Maui, you'll notice that much of it actually faces west. This means that South Maui can get waves at any time of year. It's the southwest swells of summer that bring the best waves, but large northwest winter swells can also wrap into select areas to provide the occasional out of season surf. If you're a complete beginner, the only spot in South Maui you should attempt to surf is The Cove in South Kihei, but if you're an intermediate or advanced surfer, there are other spots to check out.

MAʻALAEA

Realistically, the chances of you surfing in Maʻalaea during your time on Maui are slim, because most of the breaks are either way too fickle or way too advanced. Maʻalaea is one of the few spots on Maui that actually faces almost due south, which means that summer is the only time there will be waves.

Surf Spots

Those familiar with Maui surfing have probably heard of the Maʻalaea Pipeline, also known as **Freight Trains.** This wave needs a huge south swell to start working, but when it does, it's one of the fastest right-hand waves in the world. Don't start frothing with excitement thinking you're going to surf it anytime soon, however, as Freight Trains can turn off for up to a decade. On medium-size south swells it's still possible to surf here, but the coral reef makes it exceptionally shallow and you need to be an advanced surfer. To reach Freight Trains, park along Hauoli Road across the street from Ma'alaea General Store, and either cut through the condominium grounds or follow the shoreline as it departs from the harbor.

The most consistent wave in Ma'alaea is a spot known as **Off the Wall.** This is an A-frame, shifty peak that breaks directly in front of the harbor wall, and you can usually only surf here in the morning hours before the afternoon trade winds start howling. To access Off the Wall, park in the dirt parking area between Buzz's Wharf restaurant and the beginning of the harbor breakwall. From this little corner of harbor the paddle out to the peak is easy, and it beats jumping off the breakwall and clambering over the slippery rocks. Expect short but fun rides, and while it isn't the best break in all of South Maui, it's at least a nice place to get wet.

Half a mile up the highway when you're headed toward Lahaina is **McGregor Point,** a right-hand pointbreak that's a poor man's Honolua Bay. Although McGregor's rarely gets bigger than head-high, the spot can offer a long wave and is best surfed in the morning before the wind comes up. Parking for McGregor's is in a dirt lot on the road heading toward the lighthouse. Be careful when pulling off the highway because it can be a sketchy turn. To get down to the shoreline you have to clamber down a thin, steep trail, which can be tough if you're surfing with a longboard. Only surf here if surfing is a regular hobby.

Rental Shops

The only rental shop for surfboards in Ma'alaea is **Da Beach House** (300 Ma'alaea Rd., 808/986-8279, www.dabeachhousemaui. com, 10am-5:30pm daily) inside the Ma'alaea Harbor Shops. Surfboards rent for $25/day or $75/week, and there are stand-up paddleboards for $40/day or $125/week. There are also boogie boards and beach chairs, and this is a good place to pick up a board if you're planning on surfing some of the beginner breaks on the road toward Lahaina. Since most of the boards are of the "soft top" variety which cater to beginner surfers, however, there isn't anywhere within Ma'alaea itself that you could ever hope to use one. There are usually DVDs playing inside which feature footage from the legendary swell of 2005 when Freight Trains was the best it's ever been.

KIHEI
Surf Spots

The surf epicenter for all of Kihei is **The Cove** park, at the southern end of Kalama Park. This is where all of the surf schools give lessons, and while the waves are gentle, the downside is that it can get ultra-crowded. On some days you'll swear you could walk on water across all of the longboards crammed into the small area, but in the early morning hours before all the surf schools show up, this is still a fun (albeit small) wave. If your goal in Hawai'i is to try surfing for the first time, then this is where you'd come.

If the Cove gets too crowded and you've progressed past the beginner stage, just to the north is a peak known as **Kalama Bowls** that you could almost reach by paddling from the Cove. Some people just paddle out from the rocks in front of Kalama Park, and while the wave is better here (and less crowded), the water can get murky and it's more exposed to the wind.

For intermediate or advanced level surfers, the best wave in Kihei is an A-frame that breaks next to the **Kihei Boat Ramp.** This is a fickle wave that needs a big southwest or west swell to start working, and you need to be careful of the boat traffic coming in and out of the harbor area. Access can be a little tricky since you're asked to not walk in the sand dune area that runs along the shoreline. If you're on a longboard and are up for a paddle, you could always paddle from the far southern tip of Kamaole III Beach. It can get crowded and have a local vibe, so if you're surfing on a "soft top" board, then don't paddle out.

Shortboarding in Kihei can be found at **Sidewalks** on the south-central end of Keawakapu Beach. This is a beach break that offers a fast wave, and the vibe here isn't nearly as strong as at the boat ramp or farther south. Nevertheless, it's still an intermediate wave that isn't suitable for longboards or beginners. Parking for Sidewalks is at the public lot on the corner of Kilohana Drive and South Kihei Road, or all the way at the southern end of South Kihei Road where it comes to a dead end in the parking lot.

Rental Shops and Schools

When it comes to surf lessons in Kihei, there's only one place to go, and that's The Cove. This is the best place on the island for lessons because the water is just the right depth, it's a gentle wave, and rarely is it completely flat. Although heading here for a lesson is the obvious choice, finding out exactly *who* to go with is more of an undertaking. In the area surrounding The Cove there are no fewer than five or six operators all crammed into the same city block. Even with the wide selection, it's best to make a reservation as many operations fill up. Nearly all lessons take place in the morning hours between 8am and noon before the trade winds have filled in, and all operations offer a standard length of two hours for every lesson. If you've moved past the phase of learning how to pop up and ride straight, most operations also offer "surf safaris" where they will act as your personal surf guides for the day and take you out to different breaks where the current conditions suit your ability level. As you can imagine the rates for something like this are higher than taking a two-hour lesson.

One of the few places in The Cove area that has an actual shop (as opposed to just a van stacked with boards) is **Big Kahuna Adventures** (1913 S. Kihei Rd., 808/875-6395, www.bigkahunaadventures.com, 7:30am-7pm Mon.-Sat., 7:30am-5pm Sun.) inside Kihei

© KYLE ELLISON

There is no shortage of boards at the surf schools.

Kalama Village. Lessons are the standard $60/person for a two-hour lesson and take place at two different times in the morning, and those participating in a lesson meet at the surf truck parked across the street from the shop.

Another place that has actual walls is the **Surf Shack** (1993 S. Kihei Rd., 808/875-0006, www.surfshackmaui.com, 7:30am-3pm daily) across the street from The Cove park inside the Island Surf building. Lessons are $59 to be in a group of up to six people, or private lessons begin at $125 for a single student and go all the way up to $350 for a private group of 4 ($87.50/person).

When it comes to the "van shops," one of the largest operations in the area is **Maui Wave Riders** (1975 S. Kihei Rd., 808/875-4761, www.mauiwaveriders.com), a company that also has a Lahaina location and has helped thousands of visitors stand up on their first wave. Lesson rates are $60/person to be included in a group of up to six people, $85/person for a semiprivate lesson, and $140 if you're looking for some one-on-one instruction.

Although they function on a smaller scale, another operation providing lessons in both Kihei as well as on the west side is **Maui Beach Boys** (808/283-7114, www.mauibeachboys.com), a company that offers the same prices of $60/person for a group lesson and $85 for a semiprivate lesson, although private instruction is a few dollars cheaper at only $129 for a two-hour session.

Surf Yoga Maui (808/264-9136, www.surfyoga.com) combines surf lessons with a yoga workout. Lessons are offered on an individualized scale ($90/person semiprivate, $140 private instruction). If you're worried about integrating downward dog while you're sitting out in the lineup, instructors can also provide surfing lessons separate from yoga classes.

If you're just looking to rent a surfboard for the day and only need a basic longboard, head to any of the **Boss Frog's** (www.bossfrog.com) locations around town. Not only are they cheaper than renting from the surf schools ($20/day as opposed to $25), but the surf school rentals often cap your time limit

at four hours whereas Boss Frog's is open until 5pm. There are three locations in Kihei, including the stores in Dolphin Plaza (2395 S. Kihei Rd., 808/875-4477), across from Kukui Mall (1770 S. Kihei Rd., 808/874-5225), and in the Long's Shopping Center (1215 S. Kihei Rd., 808/891-0077). All Boss Frog's are open 8am-5pm.

On the other hand, while the Boss Frog's stores and similar rental agencies are great if you only need a beginner board for the day, the best service for intermediate surfers who want to rent a board for the duration of their trip is **808 Boards** (808/283-1384, www.808boards.com, 7am-5:30pm), who will not only match you up with a board that will suit your ability, but will also drop off and pick up the board where you're staying for no extra charge. Rates are competitive with any other rental shop in town: you can get a beginner board from $25/day to $100/week, or a premium fiberglass board from $35/day to $140/week.

Island Surfboard Rentals (808/281-9835, www.islandsurfboardrentals.com) rents longboards from $56 for two days to $180 for the week. Shortboards will only cost $40 for two days and $130 for the week. The selection of funboards, fishes, and shortboards is superior to that at other rental agencies. They'll even include a leash, some wax, and some inside knowledge of the current swell conditions at no extra cost.

WAILEA
Surf Spots
On the north side of **Mokapu Beach,** Stouffer's is a local spot for shortboarding. If you're an intermediate surfer this is an A-frame peak that can pick up southwest swells in the summer and large west swells in the winter. Parking is either at the south lot of Keawakapu Beach or in the public parking at the bottom of Ulua Beach Road.

MAKENA AND BEYOND
Surf Spots
Not many visitors surf in Makena, although it isn't because there isn't any surf in Makena.

SOUTH MAUI

There simply aren't any surf breaks which are suitable for visitors. If you're an intermediate to advanced surfer, your best bet is on the north end of the park at **Little Beach**. To reach the wave you need to carry your board up and over the hill that separates Little Beach from Big Beach. Since this beach is clothing optional, there may be naked people sharing the lineup with you. If surfing naked is on your bucket list, this is your chance. There are some other breaks farther south, but they are advanced and localized. You can watch the powerful surf, but don't plan on bringing a board with you.

Stand-Up Paddling

KIHEI

Kihei is one of the best spots on the island for stand-up paddling, and all of the major surf schools will also offer paddleboard services. Getting out on the water in the morning is imperative with stand-up paddling because once the trade winds pick up it can become impossible to paddle upwind. For a truly meditative experience, rent a board the evening before and get up early the next morning for a sunrise paddle. The rays of sunlight emerging from behind Haleakala best seen from the water. One of the best runs in Kihei is to go from Sugar Beach to the Menehune Shores condominium and back, or you can always just putt around the coastline by Kamaole and stop at whichever beach is calling your name.

Rental Shops and Schools

Learning to stand-up paddle can often consist of a single lesson. Professional instructors can give you all the pointers you need—such as where to stand on the board, how far apart to keep your feet, and the correct side of the paddle to use—and after the one lesson you should be solid enough to rent a board on your own.

Of all the schools in Kihei, **Maui Wave Riders** (1975 S. Kihei Rd., 808/875-4761, www.mauiwaveriders.com) offers 90-minute lessons which run $60 if you're part of a group, and $85 if it's a semiprivate lesson. For $140, you can get a one-on-one session with an instructor guaranteed to get you up and paddling.

Maui Beach Boys (808/283-7114, www.mauibeachboys.com) offers slightly longer classes (two hours) at a slightly higher price ($79).

You can also try out a multisport operator such as **South Pacific Kayaks and Outfitters** (808/875-4848, www.southpacifickayaks.com), which offers two-hour lessons for $75 as part of a group, $99 semiprivate, or $139 for the private experience.

If you don't feel like being packed in with the rest of the students around The Cove, you can opt for a multisport operator such as **Blue Soul** (3414 Akala Dr., 808/269-1038, www.bluesoul.com) that will arrange for a custom experience suited to your location and ability level. Rates with Blue Soul are $80 for a semiprivate lesson, $120 for a private, and lessons usually last 1.5 hours.

If you want to rent a board and paddle on your own, one of the cheapest options is **Auntie Snorkel** (2439 S. Kihei Rd., 808/879-6263, www.auntiesnorkel.com, 8:30am-8pm daily) in the Rainbow Mall in South Kihei. Boards will only cost you $35 (versus $40/hr at some high-end resort stands), and since stand-up boards can be a pain to strap to your car, this location is best if you are staying by Kamaole Beach I or II so that your condo, the store, and the beach are all within walking distance of each other.

WAILEA

If you're staying in Wailea, there are stand-up operators along Wailea Beach. Situated in the thick of the action is the **Maui Beach Club** in front of the Grand Wailea, which is an activities company that provides stand-up paddleboard rentals and guided tours. As you might

© KYLE ELLISON

Stand-up paddling is the perfect start to a day in Maui.

expect, however, the rates for a single hour can be steep, and the best deal if you plan on putting in a lot of beach time is to buy a four-day membership to the beach club which gets you unlimited paddleboard, kayak, and boogie board rental for $103/person.

If you would prefer to take part in a guided tour, **Paddle On** (888/663-0808, www.paddleonmaui.com) offers early morning tours out of Polo Beach in front of the Fairmont Kea Lani. These tours have a flexible itinerary. The main focus is simply on being out on the water and communing with the tranquil calm of morning. Inquire about meditative sunrise tours.

MAKENA AND BEYOND

The only place in Makena for stand-up paddleboard rentals and lessons is at the beach activities stand in front of the **Makena Beach and Golf Resort** (5400 Makena Alanui, 808/874-1111, www.makenaresortmaui.com) steps from the sand of Maluaka Beach. Lessons are available from $60/hr, or you can rent a board and go on your own for $40/hr. Advance

reservations are required for a lesson. During summer it takes the wind longer to reach here than at areas such as Kihei, which means that your window for paddling lasts an hour or two longer.

For a lengthier, guided stand-up paddling tour, the crew at **Hawaiian Paddle Sports** (808/660-4228, www.hawaiianpaddlesports.com) can meet you at Makena Landing where you can take part in a two-hour lesson and tour of the historic Makena coastline. Unlike with other operators, these are private tours, and rates vary between $159 for a solo person to $109/person for private groups over five.

WINDSURFING

While the north shore of the island is the windsurfing center of Maui, occasionally there are days when the wind direction makes Kihei a better option. This usually happens when the wind is out of the due north or there is a strong *kona* wind blowing out of the south. If it happens to be one of the days when Kihei is better than Kanaha, the most popular area for launching is **Mai Poina 'Oe Ia'u Beach Park** in North Kihei toward the intersection of Ohukai and South Kihei Road. There's a large grassy area here for rigging your equipment. Don't go too far from shore because the wind can drop off in an instant. Despite the fact that this is the second most popular part of the island for windsurfing after the north shore, all of the rental shops for windsurfing gear are in Kahului.

Kayaking and Canoe Paddling

When all factors are considered, Makena is the best area for kayaking and paddling. Not only is the area far more culturally rich, but it takes the wind about an hour longer to reach down here than in neighboring Kihei or Wailea.

If you are trying to choose between an outrigger canoe and a regular kayak, the main difference is that the canoes have a cultural component that doesn't exist with a plastic kayak. The original Polynesians didn't navigate here on a Hobie craft, and when you take part in an outrigger canoe tour, you get the chance to learn about a mode of transportation which is central to Polynesian culture.

When it comes to a paddling tour, don't let the food be a deciding factor. Most tours are only a few hours long, and you can only do so much when it comes to paddling with food. Since many companies will charge substantially more for a tour with food, you're better off having a hearty breakfast or bringing a few snacks for a tour which is only 2-3 hours long.

My top pick for paddling activities is **Hawaiian Paddle Sports** (808/600-4228, www.hawaiianpaddlesports.net), a private tour operator that offers excursions on both the west side as well as the south side of the island. Every single tour is geared to the individual's specific ability level, and owner and head guide Tim Lara perfectly fuses adventure and sustainability with a deep-rooted respect for Hawaiian culture and surroundings. The guides are all accomplished watermen and women who are active in volunteering in the local community. The company was awarded the silver level of certification by the Hawai'i Ecotourism Association. While the private component can be pricier than a group tour, it's guaranteed to be a cultural, historical, environmental, and thoroughly enjoyable tour which will exceed your expectations. For South Maui, Hawaiian Paddle Sports offers three-hour excursions in both outrigger canoes and kayaks, which depart from Makena and incorporate snorkeling, paddling, and storytelling. Trips cost $149 per person for the outrigger canoes and $109-159 per person for kayaking depending on the size of your group. If you're an Ironman triathlete on vacation, tackle the Molokini Challenge where you leave at the break of dawn and make the 3.5-mile channel crossing to Molokini Crater (conditions permitting).

KIHEI

Though the actual location of your kayak tour is variable, **Big Kahuna Adventures** (1913 S. Kihei Rd., 808/875-6395, www.bigkahunaadventures.com, 7:30am-7pm Mon.-Sat., 7:30am-5pm Sun.) in Kihei Kalama Village can arrange a half-day kayaking excursion if you enquire at the office.

Down the street in the Island Surf building, ask **Surf Shack** (1993 S. Kihei Rd., 808/875-0006, www.surfshackmaui.com, 7:30pm-3pm daily) about its combination packages of surf lessons and kayak excursions if you want to spend a full day out on the water. There is a second location at the north end of Keawakapu Beach (2960 S. Kihei Rd.) open 8am-5pm daily.

WAILEA

While there are a number of options for paddling tours in Wailea, the one that focuses the most on Hawaiian culture is **Hawaiian Outrigger Experience** (808/633-3547, www.

© KYLE ELLISON

Makena's historic shoreline is one of the best places for kayaking.

hoemaui.com) operating from Wailea Beach. A play on words, the acronym, *HOE,* translates as "paddle!" in the Hawaiian language. From the moment you begin this tour, you will realize this is as much a cultural experience as it is about spending a morning on the water. In addition to the time you'll spend snorkeling with *honu* (Hawaiian green sea turtles), you'll gain authentic cultural insight from instructors who are not only richly ingrained in the Hawaiian community, but also exude the genuine spirit of aloha.

If a full-on paddling tour is too much exertion for you, another activity with cultural roots is the family-operated **Maui Sailing Canoe** (808/281-9301, www.mauisailingcanoe.com) which departs off Polo Beach. The distinctly red sail of the sailing canoe *Hina* is visible off the shoreline of Wailea on most mornings, and this is the only tour where you can harness the light breeze to slowly sail along the coastline similar to the Polynesians who voyaged here centuries ago. Snorkeling time is also included in the tour, and this is a nice

combination of snorkeling, paddling, sailing, learning, and relaxing in the sun. Rates for the tour are $99/adult and $79 for children. With a maximum of only six people, this is perfect adventure for families wanting to do something different.

Wailea Watersports (808/875-2011, www.waileawatersports.com) also meets at Polo Beach for traditional kayak tours along the Wailea coastline. Tours depart at 8am and cruise the rocky shore between Wailea and Makena. One of the unique features of this tour is the opportunity to go bottom fishing directly off your kayak. Regular tours cost $75/person or $120 if going by yourself, and if you want to try catch your own dinner, you'll have to get up a little bit earlier (6am tour) and fork out a little more cash ($150/person).

MAKENA

Only two places in Makena feature canoe paddling or kayaking: **Maluaka Beach** in front of the Makena Beach and Golf Resort and **Makena Landing** beach park on Makena Road.

Unless you book with the operators through the Makena Beach and Golf Resort, more likely than not you're going to be departing out of Makena Landing.

The only options with land-based facilities are the tours which depart from the **Makena Beach and Golf Resort** (5400 Makena Alanui, 808/874-1111, www.makenaresortmaui.com). Rent your own kayak for $25-30/hour or take part in a two-hour guided snorkeling tour for $75 with one of the knowledgeable guides. You're paying for instructors who know the history of the area—and are highly entertaining. If you want to take part in a paddling experience that's far more culturally oriented (and will give you a better workout), there are also **outrigger canoe tours** which depart from in front of the hotel and cost the same as the kayaks at $75 for a two-hour trip. Snorkeling time is included with both tours. The beach parking area is half a mile past the main entrance to the resort.

The rocky shoreline of Makena Landing is the preferred spot of all other kayak operators, most of whom also have operations elsewhere on the island. My top pick out of Makena Landing is **Hawaiian Paddle Sports** (808/600-4228, www.hawaiianpaddlesports.net), but other operators you can choose from include **Kelii's Kayaks** (808/874-7652, www.keliis-kayaks.com), **Aloha Kayaks Maui** (808/270-3318, www.alohakayaksmaui.com), as well as **Makena Kayak and Tours** (808/879-8426, www.makenakayaks.net), whose prices are usually the cheapest among many of the competitors. Most tours are about $55-70 for a 2.5-hour tour and $85 for a four-hour tour. There are usually two tours offered per day. If you plan on kayaking out of Makena Landing, do yourself a favor and book the early tour, because not only will you beat the wind, but you'll beat the crowds of snorkel boats that converge on the area later on in the morning.

Fishing

MA'ALAEA

For the recreational angler who only wants to spend four hours on the water, the most personalized service you'll find in Ma'alaea Harbor is **Maui Fun Charters** (Slip 97, 808/572-2345, www.mauifuncharters.com). This boat only takes a maximum of six passengers and is perfect for a private charter or a day out with the kids. An important difference between this boat and other fishing boats is that these guys focus on bottom fishing instead of sportfishing, so instead of spending hours trolling in circles in hopes of snaring "the big one," these guys will drift closer to shore and most likely catch a greater number of varied—albeit smaller—fish. If your goal for your fishing trip is to take something home with you that you can fry up back at your place, then this is your best bet. Trips cost $139/person, or if you have six people in your party, save $40 by paying the private rate of $799 for the boat.

If, on the other hand, you want to try your luck at reeling in a trophy fish, **Strike Zone** (Slip 64, 808/879-4485, www.strike-zonemaui.com) offers bottom fishing as well as sportfishing excursions. You know these guys are successful from the dozens of dried fish tails adorning the gate to their slip. The morning charters which leave at 6:30am ($168/adult) last six hours and are a combination of bottom fishing and sportfishing. If your goal is to bring in a mahimahi, ono, or tuna, there are trips which run three days a week focusing exclusively on sportfishing for these larger species. This boat can accommodate up to 15 passengers and is a good option for larger groups (such as a bachelor party or wedding party). With captains and crew who have spent decades in the Maui sportfishing business, you know you're in good hands.

Hiking and Biking

HIKING
Kihei

Kihei isn't exactly a place for hiking. The closest thing to hiking in Kihei is taking long walks down the beach, the best of which is the stroll down five-mile-long **Sugar Beach** which runs between North Kihei and Ma'alaea. You can access the beach from Haycraft Park on the Ma'alaea side, from Kenolio Park on the Kihei side, or at any of the access points along North Kihei Road. Mornings are best before the wind comes up, and when it comes to unobstructed coastal strolls, this is the longest and grandest on the island.

Another popular **coastal walk** in Kihei connects the trio of Kamaole Beaches by following the trails around their respective headlands. Starting at Charley Young Beach on the north end of Kamaole I (parking is in a public lot on Kaiau Place), you can walk to the south end of Kamaole III by going along the shoreline and around the rocky points. Although it's always nice to feel the sand between your toes, the rocks around the headlands can be sharp, so if you have sensitive feet, it might be best to bring footwear.

If you want to extend the coastal walk just a little bit farther, there is a short, 0.5-mile **walking path** that parallels the coastline from the southern end of Kamaole III Beach and finishes at the Kihei Boat Ramp. Along the way you will pass signs educating you about the coastal dune system and the *u'au kani* seabirds that come to shore to nest in the dunes. There are a few benches sprinkled along the walking path that make either a good resting point or, in winter, a place to sit down and watch for whales.

Wailea
WAILEA COASTAL WALK

If your idea of a hike means throwing on some Lululemon, talking on your iPhone, and stopping to pick up some Starbucks, then the **Wailea Coastal Walk** is going to be your favorite hike on the island. Although you have a better chance of seeing a celebrity along the trail than any form of wildlife (although an axis deer was recently rescued from the water by an outrigger canoe tour), this paved pathway that runs from Ulua Beach to Polo Beach is undeniably gorgeous. The round-trip walk covers a distance of 3.5 miles, and along the way you'll pass a host of native coastal plants which have been put in in an effort to revitalize the area's natural foliage. You'll also pass the Grand Wailea, Four Seasons, Kea Lani, Marriott, and Wailea Beach Villas. To reach the "trailhead" for the walkway, you can either park in the public lot at Ulua Beach (at the bottom of Ulua Beach Road) or in the public lot on the southern end of the trail at Polo Beach (at the bottom of Kaukahi Street).

Makena and Beyond
◖ HOAPILI TRAIL

Anyone who heads out on the **Hoapili Trail** will realize right away that this isn't your average hike. Hot and barren and set in the middle of nowhere, the Hoapili Trail isn't as much about hiking as it is about taking a literal step back in time. Although walking the full length of the 5.5-mile trail (round-trip) takes most visitors about four hours, even spending an hour on the coastal section introduces you to a side of the island most visitors never see.

During the reign of respected King Pi'ilani in the 1600s, a walking path was constructed to encircle the entire island. It was reserved for the use of royalty. In the two centuries following his death, however, much of the trail fell into disrepair. In 1824, Governor Hoapili, trusted advisor of King Kamehameha, ordered sections of the trail reconstructed. Using laborers who had been found guilty of adultery under newly adopted Christian laws, rocks were assembled, a path was made, and the road took on a structure that remains untouched to this day.

© KYLE ELLISON

SOUTH MAUI

Hike the footpath of kings on the Hoapili Trail.

The trailhead for Hoapili (also known as the "King's Highway") is located in the parking lot of the La Perouse Bay snorkeling area at the end of Makena Alanui Road, 3.1 miles past the first entrance to Big Beach. If you're still confused on how to get here, just drive south on Makena Alanui Road until the road dead-ends in a lava field and you can't drive any farther.

From the La Perouse Bay parking lot you'll notice a trail that parallels the shoreline and weaves its way along the coast toward the south. Before you set out on the trail, however, understand that this place is hot, barren, mostly devoid of shade, and traverses jagged *a'a* lava that's so sharp you'll want some proper hiking boots. Finally—and most importantly—however much water you would normally take on a four-hour hike, double it, and then you should have enough. Two liters per person might seem like too much, but remember that when you get back from the hike the nearest drinking water is a food truck all the way back at Big Beach. Since much of this hike is outside of cell phone range, it's important to be prepared. One way to reduce the chance of overheating is to start this hike early in the morning so that you don't get trapped in the heat of the day. Don't leave any valuables in your car.

After you've followed the shoreline for 15 minutes, you'll notice a small cross on the ocean side of the trail that denotes a popular surfing spot known as Laps (short for La Perouse). It's an experts-only spot that sees 15-foot surf in the summer. After the surf spot the trail will climb in elevation for 10 minutes before arriving at a junction and veering off to the left. There will be a sign informing you that you're entering the King's Highway and to respect the historic sites. The sign will also indicate that Kanaio Beach is two miles ahead, and if you see a sign asking you to leave the artifacts untouched—but not the sign that mentions Kanaio Beach—don't worry, you just turned left a little soon and you will see the sign after walking for five more minutes.

When on the inland section of trail where the path deviates from the coastline, there's a short spur trail that leads down to the lighthouse at Cape Hanamanioa, although there isn't much to see down here except for the old weathered light. A better side trip is to take the short spur trail found 20 minutes later that leads down to Keawanaku Beach, where you're almost guaranteed to have the beach to yourself. After the turnoff for Keawanaku, the trail continues for another 20 minutes until you finally reach the coast again at Kanaio Beach, a salt and pepper-colored shoreline that's composed of equal parts black lava rock and sunbleached coral. You'll notice the remnants of multiple structures which were once a part of an ancient fishing village, and although the thatched roofs no longer remain, the lava rock walls conjure images of what this coast must have been like in the days before contact with Europeans.

Although Kanaio Beach is the turnaround point for the majority of hikers, the King's Highway continues all the way until it joins with Highway 31 on the "back road to Hana." To reach the highway, however, would require an overnight stay along the trail; camping is permitted along the shoreline from points east of Kanaio Beach. For the average hiker who wants to travel just a *little* farther, however, a sandy road continues from Kanaio Beach and winds its way along the coast. Another 20 minutes of walking from Kanaio will bring you to a shoreline that's completely bathed in bleached white coral, and on the southern end of the "white beach" is an ancient Hawaiian *heiau* set out on the point that looks much the same now as it must have when it was built.

BIKING

Despite the flat terrain and sunny weather, South Maui doesn't have the same number of biking options that you might find upcountry or on the road to Hana. The most scenic ride in all of South Maui is the one between Wailea and the end of the road at La Perouse Bay. Early mornings are the best time for cycling, as the road can get narrow and congested with visitor traffic. On the far northern end of Kihei, a bike path parallels Mokulele Highway, running almost all the way toward Kahului. The wind can be brutal in the afternoons and the scenery is nothing but cane fields and the highway. South Maui is best for a leisurely ride on a beach cruiser, swapping spandex for a bikini or boardshorts and pedaling the flat shoreline with the sun on your face.

Kihei

If you're looking for proper cycling during your stay in South Maui, your best bet is going to be at **South Maui Cycles** (1992 S. Kihei Rd., 808/874-0068, www.southmauibicycles.com, 10am-6pm Mon.-Sat.) across the street from the south end of Kalama Park. Rental prices on road bikes range $22-60/day depending on the caliber of bike, and there are also weekly rates which range $99-250/week. This is a full-service bicycle shop that also offers sales and repairs. If you have any questions about Maui cycling, the informative staff will be able to answer them.

Or, for those who just want a rental for beach-hopping throughout the day, basic beach cruisers are available from **Boss Frog's Bike Shop** (1770 S. Kihei Rd., 808/661-3333, www.bossfrog.com, 8am-5pm daily) for $15/day or $50 week. There are also mountain bikes, hybrid bikes, and proper road bikes to accompany the cruisers, and you can also pick up a cruiser at another location in the Dolphin Plaza across from the southern end of Kamaole II Beach Park.

Makena and Beyond

Although it isn't an actual shop, if you are staying at the **Makena Beach and Golf Resort** (5400 Makena Alanui Rd., 808/874-1111, www.makenaresortmaui.com), the hotel offers free bicycles for guests to use anywhere in the Makena and Wailea area. Don't expect a high-performance road bike, but otherwise, it's a great way to wake up in the morning and explore Makena on two wheels completely free of charge.

Golf and Tennis

GOLF
Kihei

If you just want to go out and play a relaxing round without shelling out resort prices, **Elleair Golf Course** (1345 Pi'ilani Hwy., 808/874-0777, www.elleairmauigolfclub.com) is one of the island's best golf values. It offers views looking out toward Molokini Crater and the West Maui Mountains. This par-71 course isn't as challenging as the Wailea Gold course, but it still provides an enjoyable round for the everyday golfer. Club and equipment rentals are available from the pro shop, and there's a driving range for working on your stroke before your round. The afternoon trade winds can have a major effect on the play here. Rounds can usually be found in the $85-115 range. To save a few dollars, check the website for online specials. They also offer an affordable nine-hole twilight special if you want to sneak in a few holes after a morning excursion to Molokini.

Wailea

The **Wailea Gold** (100 Wailea Golf Club Dr., 808/875-7450, www.waileagolf.com) course is the best course in all of South Maui. This is where the pros play when they come to town, and the 7,000+-yard course (don't worry—there are six different tee boxes) and 93 bunkers will challenge even those with the lowest of handicaps. Guests staying in the Wailea resort complex can play a morning round for $190, whereas guests from other resorts will have to shell out $209. May 1-December 20, the rates are only $179 for all visitors regardless of where they're staying. As at other courses across the island, afternoon rounds are heavily discounted. Club rental and practice facilities are located at the main Wailea clubhouse.

If the length and level of difficulty of the Gold course are intimidating, the **Wailea Emerald** (100 Wailea Golf Club Dr., 808/875-7450, www.waileagolf.com) course has been called the "pretty sister" of the Gold course and is reputed to be easier for shorter hitters. Although the course isn't quite as long, this is still a proper resort course with all of the technical challenges and amenities, so you still need to bring your A-game to get any birdies. Greens fees will run the same as at the Gold course.

If you're a fan of the movie *Old School*, or want to play an "oldie but goodie," the **Wailea "Old Blue"** (100 Wailea Golf Club Dr., 808/875-7450, www.waileagolf.com) course constructed in 1972 is the South Maui original and the second course to be built on Maui (behind Ka'anapali). More forgiving than the other two courses, rates for "Old Blue" are more affordable and usually hover around the $90-170 range depending on what time of day you play and what time of year it is. After you card your best round of your vacation, head down to Manoli's to celebrate at the bar.

Makena and Beyond

When everything is factored in—design, price, views, and location—my favorite South Maui golf course is the **Makena Golf Course** (5415 Makena Alanui Rd., 808/879-3344, www. makenaresortmaui.com/golf), also known as the Makena North course. The course is a 10-minute drive south from Wailea, and the wind down here isn't as much of a factor. The natural design of the course forces you to weave your way around kiawe trees and drive over ravines which are laden with jagged lava rocks, so you can forget about playing from out of bounds. In addition to being challenging, the views afforded from the back nine look out over four different islands. The prices are more affordable than at neighboring Wailea. Unfortunately, the course is closed through the first quarter of 2014 for a major renovation, although look for it to be nicer than ever when it eventually does reopen. Although a regular morning round will run $185, guests of certain resorts can play for $169, it's only $119 after 12pm, and only $90 if you tee off after 3pm (so you can still squeeze in a round during the longer days of summer).

TENNIS
Kihei

The nicest public courts in Kihei are at **Waipuilani Beach Park** in front of the Maui Sunset condo complex. There are three different sets of courts clustered into groups of two, and the parklike surroundings and ocean view are a definite asset. The only downside is that the wind can be so strong during the afternoon hours it's almost impossible to play, so mornings are best. There is no pro shop here, and public parking for the tennis courts is in the parking lot along Waipuilani Road.

While the Waipuilani courts are more popular with visitors, the four courts at **Kalama Park** are where most of Kihei locals play. The surroundings aren't quite as nice as at Waipuilani, but the courts are lit at night and more protected from the wind. Local junior tennis programs frequently operate here in the afternoons, so morning hours or evenings are

© KYLE ELLISON

the challenging natural design of the Makena Golf Course

808/879-1958, www.waileatennis.com, 7am-6pm daily) is the largest tennis facility in South Maui. This is where the bulk of the island's professional events and tennis clinics are held, and the likes of the Bryan brothers and Andre Agassi have swung through here in recent years. There are three lit courts, multiple teaching pros, a large backboard, and a grandstand-style stadium court with a multi-terraced rock wall. At Wailea you can do everything from get your racquet restrung to join a morning clinic, and it's the longest-running tennis community on the south side of the island.

Makena and Beyond

For those staying in Makena (or willing to drive 10 minutes farther), the **Makena Tennis Club** (5400 Makena Alanui Rd., 808/874-1111, www.makenaresortmaui.com/tennis, 7am-7pm daily) offers six recently resurfaced courts and two lit courts which stay open until 9pm (with advance notice). The overall numbers here are smaller than at Wailea, but the stronger sense of community in Makena is evidenced by the small fire pit used for casual gatherings. The small pro shop offers tennis merchandise and racquet restringing, although it's closed daily noon-3pm. As at Wailea there are private lessons, rentals, and clinics available, but one difference between Wailea and Makena is that Makena can see just a little less rain and wind if the elements are inclement up the road.

best for finding an open court. The Kalama courts are on the far north end of Kalama Park behind the public basketball court and across the street from the Kukui Mall.

Wailea

With 11 courts and a medium-size pro shop the **Wailea Tennis Club** (131 Wailea Ike Pl.,

Yoga, Fitness, and Spas

YOGA AND FITNESS
Kihei

When it comes to finding a yoga class in Kihei, the challenge is choosing which of the many operators you'll join for some sun salutations. One of the most complete class schedules is at the **Kihei Community Yoga Center** (1847 S. Kihei Rd., 808/269-2794, www.kiheiyoga.com), an operation that provides mats free of charge and holds multiple classes daily. Drop-in

rates are $16, and a package of five sessions is $75. Those who buy a package can sometimes get discounted rates with local massage operators, so inquire about any specials they might currently be running. The studio location isn't anything amazing (it's across the street from Kalama Park), but this is a great place to mingle with the local yoga community if you plan on spending any length of time on the island.

Farther north in the center of Kihei is the

Maui Yoga and Kickboxing (115 East Lipoa St., 808/463-8811, www.mauihotyoga.com, multiple classes daily) studio for anyone who wants to combine a yoga session with some sparring or self-defense classes. The medium-size studio is curiously covered in dolphin paintings. Drop-in rates are $17, and if you're a fan of doing yoga in a hot room, then these guys have you covered.

If you aren't a full-fledged yogi and just want to enjoy a cheap, casual session overlooking the water, **Yoga Supernova** (2480 S. Kihei Rd., 808/250-7599, www.yogasupernova.com, 8am-9:15am Mon.-Wed., 5pm-6:15pm Thurs., 8am-9:15am Fri.-Sat.) offers one class per day that meets on the grass in front of the Hale Pau Hana resort. The cost is only $10, and although mats are provided free of charge, you can always just use a beach towel if you choose to bring one with you. The class schedule has been known to vary, so check out the website or call to find out about the current situation.

You can also check out **Maui Massage and Yoga** (2450 S. Kihei Rd., 808/214-0129, www.johannawaters.com, 8am-9:15am Thurs. and Sun.) which meets two days/week in front of the Kamaole Nalu Resort. The cost is only $10 for a 75-minute session, you need to bring your own mat or towel, and you need to find street parking somewhere near the resort. It can get a little busy, but it's tough to beat the price and oceanfront setting.

To hear the waves crash from inside an actual studio, head to **Maui Yoga Path** (2960 S. Kihei Rd., 808/874-5545, www.mauiyogapath.maui.net, 8am-9:15am daily), located beneath the Five Palms restaurant in the Mana Kai Resort and facing out toward Keawakapu Beach. In addition to the morning session, there are also varying classes which run on certain afternoons. Although the cost is more expensive at $20/session, you can walk right outside the front door and cool off in the Keawakapu waters.

If yoga isn't your thing and you're looking to move some real weight around, **Maui Powerhouse Gym** (1279 S. Kihei Rd., 808/214-6737, www.mauipowerhousegym.com, 5:30am-10pm Mon.-Fri., 7am-7pm Sat., 8am-5pm Sun.) within the Azeka Shopping Center offers short-term memberships and free 1-day trials.

In North Kihei on the inland side of the highway, **The Gym Maui** (300 Ohukai Rd., 808/891-8108, www.thegymmaui.com, 5:30am-8pm Mon.-Fri., 8am-noon weekends) offers $10/day drop-in rates for visitors, and is located right across the street from the Kihei **CrossFit** (808/874-1155) center that offers $20 workout sessions at multiple points during the day.

Wailea

While all of the major resorts in Wailea offer yoga classes as part of their fitness center offerings, periodic yoga classes are also taught at **REPS Fitness Center** (161 Wailea Ike Pl., 808/875-1066, www.repsfitness.com) to accompany the $18 spin classes, $15 Pilates classes, and range of personal training and workout options. Yoga class schedules vary, so contact the gym beforehand to find out the current times.

Makena and Beyond

If you're a guest of the **Makena Beach and Golf Resort** there are twice-weekly complimentary yoga sessions which take place on the oceanfront lawn.

SPAS
Kihei

Despite the fact that **Valley Isle Day Spa** (1847 S. Kihei Rd., 808/298-9246, www.valleyisledayspa.homestead.com, 8am-8pm daily) is in a Central Kihei strip mall, the services inside could still be exactly what you're looking for. The rates here are far more affordable than the fancy resorts ($95 for 60-minute massage), and like other spas, they also offer aromatherapy, reflexology, facials, body treatments, couples packages, and a decent range of beauty products.

If you're staying in Ma'alaea or North Kihei and don't want to travel all the way down to South Kihei or Wailea, **Massage Maui** (145

N. Kihei Rd., 808/357-7317, www.massage-maui.com) is another low-key massage option where you can either meet the masseuse in the Sugar Beach location or arrange for an outcall massage where the therapist visits you in your condo. A 60-minute massage will cost $95, and outcall services will usually run about $20 higher than the in-spa price.

Wailea

When it comes to choosing the best spa in South Maui, it is tough to argue with a 50,000-square-foot luxury arena that has been voted not only as the best spa in the Hawaiian Islands, but also among the top 10 spas in all of the United States. Such is the case with **Spa Grande** (3850 Wailea Alanui Dr., 800/772-1933, www.spagrande.com), the palatial spa inside the Grand Wailea which completely redefines the concept of pampering. All guests are advised to arrive an hour early so as to enjoy a casual—and complimentary—soak in the termé hydrotherapy baths before moving on to your scheduled treatment. Can't decide between the Roman hot tub, Japanese Furo baths, or honey-mango loofah exfoliation? Do them all. They're included with your package! Of course, you're ultimately paying for all of the extravagance (a 50-minute massage treatment will be $155-175 on average). Along with an enormous selection of facials and treatment options, there's also a beauty salon and fitness center.

The Spa at Four Seasons (808/874-8000, www.fourseasons.com/maui/spa, 8am-9pm daily) is just as lavish and over the top, and a nice perk here is the option of getting a massage in an oceanfront cabana. The prices are often a touch higher than at Spa Grande, but the offerings of wellness options, facials, body treatments, and massage are no less impressive.

Other Wailea resort spas include those at the **Fairmont Kea Lani** (4100 Wailea Alanui Dr., 808/875-2229, www.fairmont.com) and the **Mandara Spa** (3700 Wailea Alanui Dr., 808/891-8774, www.mandaraspa.com, 8am-8pm daily) at the Wailea Marriott.

If the high prices of the resorts are too much to stomach, but you don't want to travel far, then the **Maui Zen Day Spa** (Wailea Gateway Center, 808/874-6000, www.mauizen.com, 10am-6pm daily) is just up the road at the Wailea Gateway Center and offers much of the same services at a moderately discounted rate. It's in the upstairs section of an upscale strip mall, but if the only thing that matters is relieving that stress in your neck, you can come up here to work it out and still have some money left over for dinner. A 60-minute massage will cost $99, and they also offer facials, acupuncture, aromatherapy, and in classically Wailea style—botox injections.

Aroma Stone Wailea Healing Center (161 Wailea Ike Pl., 808/264-9999, www.aromastonewailea.com) is another "out of resort" option that only requires a five-minute drive, yet saves you enough money you could almost come back for a second round. Close to the Wailea Tennis Center in between the Shops at Wailea and the Wailea Gateway Center, this healing zone offers 60-minute massage treatments for $90 that focus on the use of hot stones and aromatherapy.

Makena

The best option for a spa treatment this far south is at the oceanfront **Makena Kai Day Spa** (5400 Makena Alanui Rd., 808/875-5858, 9am-6pm daily) on the beautiful shores of Maluaka Beach. Value is the name of the game: the $115, 50-minute massage treatment beats the resort prices just 10 minutes up the road. If you're looking for an oceanfront massage at a comparatively affordable price, then your best bet is going to be found at the end of the road.

Horseback Riding and Bird-Watching

HORSEBACK RIDING
Makena and Beyond
The only horseback riding in South Maui is found *way* down south at the end of the road at **Makena Stables** (8299 South Makena Rd., 808/879-0244, www.makenastables.com), a family-run outfit that has been leading horseback riding tours since 1983. The trails here meander over Ulupalakua Ranch land only accessible via a private tour. Along the way there's a good chance of spotting axis deer or wild goats that clamber across the jagged *a'a* lava. This is one of the few horseback riding operations on the island with the possibility of riding your horse directly along the shoreline. The only other way you can access this stretch of coastline on horseback is if you take a tour from Triple L Ranch beginning in Upper Kanaio. Since Triple L is 40 miles from Wailea, however, and Makena Stables is only seven, this is the obvious choice if your vacation is based in South Maui. Not only do the views stretch out over the waters of La Perouse Bay to the island of Kaho'olawe in the distance, but you ride directly through the island's most recent lava flow, taking time to stop at Kalua O Lapa, the volcanic vent from which Madame Pele leaked her fiery liquid only a few centuries ago. Group sizes are capped at six and riders must be under 205 pounds. To escape the brutal South Maui sun, take a sunset ride during the coastline's most artistic and romantic hour.

BIRD-WATCHING
Kihei
If there were a bird to be associated with South Maui it would be the Pacific golden plover, or *kolea*. Like many of the condo dwellers that occupy the beaches of Kihei during the winter, the *kolea* leaves its summer home in the Arctic in favor of warm, tropical Maui winters. The term *kolea* is a tongue-in-cheek nickname for visitors who regularly spend winters in Maui.

One of the best places to see *real* birds in South Maui is at the **Kealia Pond National Wildlife Refuge** (www.fws.gov/kealiapond) between Ma'alaea and North Kihei. This 700-acre reserve is home to over 30 species of birds, the most notable of which are the *a'eo* (Hawaiian stilt), *'alae ke'oke'o* (Hawaiian coot), and *koloa maoli* (Hawaiian duck). The greatest number of species can be found here during winter. There are short walking trails which leave from the visitor center (mile marker 6 on Mokulele Hwy.) into the Kealia Pond area. For those traveling from Ma'alaea to North Kihei, there's also a short boardwalk that parallels the shoreline and offers a number of informative placards about the island's native wildlife. The boardwalk takes about 30 minutes to walk to the end and back, and if you plan on visiting it's best to approach from the Ma'alaea side of the road because there's no left turn allowed into the parking lot off North Kihei Road.

Although there's a good chance you won't see any birds at all, another place to try your luck is on the beachwalk running between the Kihei Boat Ramp and the south end of Kamaole III Beach. The coastal dune system here is home to *'u'au kani* (wedge-tailed shearwaters), and the fledgling season is usually October-December. Those with an interest in Maui County's seabirds should check out the **Maui Nui Seabird Recovery Project** (www.mauinuiseabirds.org).

Although **Molokini Crater** is best known as a marine reserve and world-class snorkel and dive destination, few people know that the 161-foot tall islet is also a seabird sanctuary above water. Molokini Crater is home to a healthy population of *'u'au kani*. If you're an avid birder and are planning a trip to Molokini, bring a pair of binoculars to check out what's happening *above* water.

Makena and Beyond
The best place for bird-watching in Makena

is at **Oneuli Beach** by Makena State Park. Although the chances of seeing many species of birds are slim, this coastal wetland area is home to avians such as the *'auku'u* (black-crowned night heron), *'alae ke'oke'o* (Hawaiian coot), and *ulili* (wandering tattler).

Sights

MA'ALAEA
◖ Maui Ocean Center

There isn't a snorkeling spot on the island where you're going to see as wide a range of marine life as at the **Maui Ocean Center** (192 Ma'alaea Rd., 808/270-7000, www.mauioceancenter.com, 9am-5pm daily, until 6pm in July and Aug., $25.50/adult, $18.50/child). This three-acre marine park has the nation's largest collection of live tropical coral. Children will enjoy the tidepool exhibits and the green sea turtle lagoon, but everyone comes here to experience the 54-foot-long acrylic tunnel that runs beneath a 750,000-gallon aquarium filled with dozens of rays and sharks. Stand in dry comfort and safety as a tiger shark floats right above you and contemplate how spotted eagle rays look just like underwater birds as they buzz circles a few feet from your head.

In addition to the enthralling underwater experience, there's a good chance you'll learn something (Did you know that nearly 25 percent of Hawai'i's fish and coral species are found nowhere else on earth?). The center educates visitors on our unique marine ecosystem and as well as native Hawaiian culture, with exhibits on everything from Polynesian wayfaring to ancient Hawaiian fishponds. The center is committed to providing animals with a realistic, natural environment.

This is one of the island's best family attractions and its best rainy day activity. With over

© KYLE ELLISON

Encounter sealife at the Maui Ocean Center.

SOUTH MAUI

400,000 visitors every year, it gets crowded. To avoid the crowds, visit in the morning right as the facility opens. A self-guided tour meanders through the various exhibits; head directly to the last exhibit and work your way toward the front. Allow at least two hours. Lunch is available at the Seascape Restaurant (11am-2:30pm) or the Reef Café (10am-4pm).

Ebisu Sama Shrine

Even though all of the original Ma'alaea Village has been bulldozed and rebuilt, there's still one tiny piece of history quietly sandwiched between the Harbor Shops and the Ma'alaea General Store. If you go to use the harbor restrooms next to the Coast Guard Station, and you see a lonely, out of place shrine across the street, this is the **Ebisu Sama Shrine,** a building erected by Maui's Japanese immigrant community in the early 1900s. Though most Japanese laborers ended up working in the sugarcane plantations, others opted for the job of commercial fishers, and this Shinto shrine is meant to bring safety to those venturing out

to sea. A festival is still held here on the second Sunday of January, but other than that, this small shrine is mostly closed to the public.

KIHEI

Kihei doesn't have a defined city center or any real historical sites. Historically, however, Kihei was known for being empty as opposed to full. During the days of the ancient Hawaiians the Kihei area was referred to as "Kamaole," a word which loosely translates as "barren." Even during World War II the soft, gently sloping beaches of Kihei were used by the military as practice zones for amphibious landing craft. Nevertheless, there are still a few places in Kihei to either get back to nature or catch a glimpse of the past.

Kealia Pond National Wildlife Refuge

If you drive the road between Ma'alaea and North Kihei, you'll notice that it passes through a large mudflat that parallels the shoreline. Although most of this area is dry

the boardwalk at Kealia Pond National Wildlife Refuge

© JENNA STRUBHAR

during summer, on the inland side of the highway is 200-acre **Kealia Pond National Wildlife Refuge** (www.fws.gov/kealiapond). The main reason for visiting is to catch a glimpse of native bird species such as the *a'eo* (Hawaiian stilt) and *'alae ke'oke'o* (Hawaiian coot). Even if you aren't an avid birder, the boardwalk off North Kihei Road makes for an informative place to stretch your legs and learn about the threats facing the island's native species.

The main visitor center for the wildlife refuge is off Mokulele Highway (Highway 311) near the six mile marker, and there are short hiking trails which lead from here into the flats of the preserve. If you plan on visiting Kealia Pond, morning hours are best before the wind comes up, and during the driest periods of the year (August-November) the area can sometimes reek of the fish that have died from the water level receding. It isn't unbearable, but noticeable nevertheless.

Koi'ei'e Loko I'a Fishpond

Inside Kalepolepo Beach Park in North Kihei, the **Koi'ei'e Loko I'a fishpond** is the most prominent example of ancient Hawaiian existence from Ma'alaea to Wailea. Estimated to be around 500 years old, this ancient fishpond was formed by rocks passed by hand from the *mauka* (uplands) of Haleakala all the way *makai* (toward the sea) in Kihei. The native Hawaiian people were masters of aquaculture and sustainability, and fishponds such as the one here at Kalepolepo were used to trap and farm fish reserved for Hawaiian royalty. It's believed that many generations of *ali'i*, or kings, used this fishpond prior to the arrival of Western explorers, although over a period of 150 years the pond largely fell into disrepair. Thanks to the hard work of the **Maui Fishpond Association** (726 S. Kihei Rd., 808/359-1172, www.maui-fishpond.com), however, a dedicated group of volunteers has been working since 1996 to restore the fishpond to its former glory using the same—now submerged—rocks which were placed there by their ancestors many centuries before. The fishpond is available for viewing at any time by visiting Kalepolepo Beach Park.

Or, for a unique experience, the organization offers guided cultural canoe trips on Monday, Wednesday, and Friday mornings at 8am for those who prearrange a visit.

Hawaiian Islands Humpback Whale National Marine Sanctuary

Right next door to Kalepolepo Beach Park is the headquarters for the **Hawaiian Islands Humpback Whale National Marine Sanctuary** (726 S. Kihei Rd., 808/879-2818, www.hawaii-humpbackwhale.noaa.gov, 10am-3pm Mon.-Fri., 10am-1pm Sat., free), a place which is a phenomenal educational resource for anyone with an interest in humpback whales. It's a little out of the way when compared to the rest of the action in Kihei, but everything about this compound is historic or educational in one way or another. Aside from offering exhibits about both the humpback whales and the sanctuary itself (all of the waters of Maui County are included in the sanctuary), the center also boasts some unique architecture, as evidenced by the 1940s-era, coastal, clapboard structure that seems better suited for Nantucket than North Kihei; its distinct blue color makes it easy to notice from offshore. A separate building was built by the Navy during WWII. Parts of the Koi'ei'e fishpond also run in front of the compound, and informative displays discuss not only the fishponds, but the ways in which ancient Hawaiians acted in concert with the island's marine species. Given the massive renovation which has recently been undertaken, donations are both suggested and welcomed.

MAKENA

Of all the areas in South Maui, Makena is the one with the greatest amount of ancient culture and history. This rugged, lava-strewn shoreline was historically home to a thriving population of ancient Hawaiians and believed to be the most populated region in South Maui during precontact times. When diseases and foreign plant and animal species were introduced by European explorers, however, the combination of outside forces ravaged the native population,

SOUTH MAUI

and many of the villages in Makena were subsequently abandoned. The Makena region is a trove of cultural artifacts and an open-air museum of Hawaiian history and culture. In a fitting twist to the tale, Makena is also the landing site of the first European explorer to set foot on Maui's shore—French explorer Jean Francois de Galaup La Perouse in 1786. Today, a small memorial stands in the bay which now bears his name at the place where the paved road comes to an end. Despite the amount of history in Makena, many of the archaeological and cultural remnants lie either on private land, in cordoned off sanctuaries, or scattered along the shoreline in areas such as the Hoapili Trail. Nevertheless, there is still one site which is open to visitors, and it has a history which parallels the plight of Makena's native people.

Keawala'i Church

In an area of the island that's rapidly being swallowed by luxury homes, there is something about the simple, timeless beauty of **Keawala'i Congregational Church** (5300 Makena Rd., 808/879-5557, www.keawalai.org, office hours 10am-5pm Wed.-Sat.) which gives us hope that everything is going to be okay. Set on a tranquil cove that's out of view of most modern development, Keawala'i is ringed with *ti* leaves and palms and bathed in the sounds of gentle surf. Founded in 1832 and constructed in 1855 out of *pili* grass, this Protestant church served as one of the main centers of worship for the southern coast of Maui. The grass walls were eventually replaced with those made of coral, and in 1856 the church was able to raise $70 to purchase a bell from the United States of America, the separate country which 42 years later would annex the island as its own. It took that bell almost three years to travel to Hawai'i. In February of 1862 it was lifted into the belfry where it still hangs today.

Although the Makena area housed a healthy native Hawaiian population through the mid 1800s, many of the streams began to run dry and arable land become harder to find. Much of Makena's population decided to pull up roots and move elsewhere, and Keawala'i

the historic beauty of Keawala'i Church

© KYLE ELLISON

began a long slide into disrepair. In the years after World War II Keawala'i was pillaged by thieves, and many of the original prayer books were lost. It was during this time that the fledgling community banded together and decided to breathe life back into the church, and after a

half-century of periodic renovations, Keawala'i today is as beautiful as it must have been at its height. Services are still conducted in the native Hawaiian language at 7:30am and 10am on Sunday mornings, although visits to the church grounds are possible at any time of day.

Shopping

MA'ALAEA
Ma'alaea Harbor Shops

Unless you count the boat crew in the harbor selling T-shirts out of their slips, the **Ma'alaea Harbor Shops** (300 Ma'alaea Rd.) are the only place in Ma'alaea with any shopping at all. Though small, there are still a number of stores worth poking your head into if you're killing time or the rest of your party is still inside the aquarium.

The best shopping in Ma'alaea is found at the large **arts and crafts fair** (9am-5pm daily) overlooking the harbor. Dozens of local artists cycle through here, so every time you visit there's sure to be something new springing up. Much of the artwork is ocean-themed.

The only surf shop is **Da Beach House** (808/986-8279, 10am-5:30pm daily), which has a surprisingly decent assortment of beach and surf wear to accompany a wide range of accessories. As a bonus, there are often surf videos on display.

The massive headquarters of the **Pacific Whale Foundation** (808/249-8977, pacificwhale.org, 6am-8pm daily) has a retail section with everything from OluKai slippers to marine-themed artwork and a large selection of clothing and books.

KIHEI
North End

At the far northern end of Kihei is the **Sugar Beach General Store** (145 N. Kihei Rd., 808/879-9899) within the Sugar Beach Resort. It can accommodate your basic sundry needs if you're staying at a condo in the area.

Up on Pi'ilani Highway, the **Kihei Gateway**

Plaza is a sprawling semi-industrial compound with a smattering of clothing shops that might interest visitors. Of the main stores in the plaza, the largest is **Maui Clothing Outlet** (362 Huku Li'i Pl., 808/875-0308, 9am-8pm Mon.-Sat., 10am-6pm Sun.) with an enormous selection of resort wear and island-themed clothing at discount prices. One of the sister stores in the same area is **Pretty Wahine** (362 Huku Li'i Pl., 808/879-1199, 10am-6pm daily) which focuses primarily on women's boutique clothing options.

While the **Azeka** shopping centers on South Kihei Road are mostly full of chain stores, **Paradise Sandal Company** (808/879-4884) is the exception in the Azeka Mauka Center, and across the street at the Azeka Makai shopping complex, the **Maui Quilt Shop** (808/874-8050) can provide anything you need for relaxing mornings of quilting in paradise.

If you turn up Pi'ikea Avenue between the Azeka Mauka Center and the Long's Shopping Center, you'll quickly come to the **Pi'ilani Village Shopping Center** (291 Pi'ikea Ave.), which has the most relevant shopping options for visitors to North Kihei. A big draw is the **Hilo Hattie's** (808/875-4545, 9am-9pm daily) clothing store where there's a wide range of men's and women's apparel, and if you forgot your swimsuit at home (or want another one), **Maui Waterwear** (808/891-8319, 9am-9pm Mon.-Sat., 9am-7pm Sun.) specializes in women's bikinis and beach accessories.

Central Kihei

Central Kihei is the land of the roadside shopping stall, and it seems that with every brick and mortar store that closes, a roadside "marketplace" opens up somewhere down the street. Although most stores have gone this direction, an exception is the **Local Motion** (1819 S. Kihei Rd., 808/879-7873, www.localmotionhawaii.com, 9am-8pm Mon.-Sat., 9am-5pm Sun.) surf shop inside the Kukui Mall. This is one of longest-running surf shops in Kihei and an undisputed local favorite, carrying a large collection of surf and bodyboard accessories. Across the parking lot, **The Bikini Market** (1819 S. Kihei Rd., 808/891-8700, www.thebikinimarket.com, 8am-6pm daily) not only caters to a female clientele, but prides itself on promoting high-end swimwear and pieces designed by local artists.

On the other side of the road from Kukui Mall is the **Aloha Open Market** (1794 S. Kihei Rd., 9am-7pm daily), a place which has grown over the years from some random tents and roadside crafts to a legitimate retail outlet. The most popular shop inside the marketplace is **Maui Mana** (808/875-7881), probably because it's a headshop in a laid-back, warm-weather, island destination.

The largest concentration of shopping in Kihei is in the **Kihei Kalama Village** (1941 S. Kihei Rd., 10am-7pm daily), where serious shoppers could lose themselves for hours, if not days. This shopping complex houses over 40 businesses, the most notable being **Da Beach House** (808/891-1234, www.dabeachhousemaui.com) for surf-themed apparel, **Mahina** (808/879-3453, www.mahinamaui.com) for women's apparel, **Serendipity** (808/874-8471, www.serendipitymaui.com) for fine women's clothing, and **The Love Shack Maui** (808/875-0303, www.loveshackmaui.com) for your intimate moments back at the hotel. In addition to the brick and mortar stores, there are myriad kiosks and stands where you can do anything from get henna tattoos to play with a dijeridoo. This shopping area is within walking distance of the Cove Park where most of the surf rentals take place, so if part of your group is out surfing, you can wander down here for some souvenir browsing while they finish their time on the water.

South End

As you move south from the Kalama Village area down into the Kamaole area, the strip malls get smaller but also more frequent. In the **Dolphin Plaza** you'll find **Maui Gifts and Crafts** (2395 S. Kihei Rd., 808/874-9310, 9am-9pm Mon.-Thurs., 9am-6pm Fri.-Sun.), a store which has everything from carved wood turtles and elephants to exotic imports from Indonesia and beyond.

The next shopping complex is small **Kamaole Beach Center** where the main retail outlet is **Honolua Surf Company** (2411 S. Kihei Rd., 808/874-0999). This is another surf store that focuses on high-quality surf-themed clothing and is named after Maui's legendary north shore surfing spot. What's nice about this store is that you can occasionally get the exact same Honolua brand clothing here for cheaper than you will find it at places such as Whalers Village in Ka'anapali or at the nearby Shops at Wailea. More than just a clothing brand, Honolua name aims to capture the Hawaiian lifestyle.

Rainbow Mall is home to **Maui Fine Art & Frame** (2439 S. Kihei Rd., 808/222-3055, www.mauiartframe.com, 11am-8pm daily), one of the few art galleries found anywhere in Kihei. In addition to having numerous island-themed paintings and ceramics, the frames that encompass the artwork are a separate art form unto themselves.

WAILEA
Shops at Wailea

Any longtime visitor to Maui will remember when the **Shops at Wailea** (3750 Wailea Alanui Dr., 808/891-6770, www.theshopsatwailea.com, 9:30am-9pm daily) were a plantation-style shopping complex with wide open grassy areas and free hula shows from local *halau*. These days, words such as "discount" and "affordable" rarely exist inside these walls, although there are still a few locally run stores where you can find items at a reasonable price. Once inside, you'll notice art galleries such as **Ki'i Gallery** (808/874-1181) and **Dolphin Galleries** (808/891-8000) accompanying surf shops like **Billabong** (808/879-8330) and **Honolua Surf Company** (808/891-8229). You can often spot celebrities hanging out in luxury stalwarts such as **Tiffany and Co.** (808/891-9226), **Gucci** (808/879-1060), or **Louis Vuitton** (808/875-6980).

Aside from the high-end corporate stores, you can also find a few island-themed shops offering unique and boutique souvenirs. At **Sand People** (808/891-8801, www.sandpeople.com) you can pick up coastal-inspired gifts and home decor, and **Martin & MacArthur** (808/891-8844, www.martinandmacarthur.com) showcases Hawaiian-made crafts and an assortment of koa woods. If you're in town for a wedding but you're missing something from your cosmetics kit, **Cos Bar** (808/891-9448, www.cosbar.com) carries makeup lines such as Bobbi Brown that you can't find anywhere else on the island. If you're in need of a fancy gift, **Na Hoku** (808/891-8040) offers unique Hawaiian-inspired jewelry.

Wailea Gateway Plaza

Although it doesn't have anywhere near the glitz and glamour of the Shops at Wailea, the awkwardly placed little **Wailea Gateway Center** (10 Wailea Ike Dr.) still has a couple of boutique shops worth paying a visit. There are two clothing boutiques on the lower level, one of which, **Maui Memories** (808/298-0261, www.mauiislandmemories.com, 10am-9pm daily), features locally made jewelry, fashions, and artwork. Among the two standout items in the store are Nina Kuna jewelry, which has been featured on the cover of *Sports Illustrated*, and artwork from local photographer Randy Jay Braun. Right next door, **Otaheite Hawaii** (808/419-6179, www.otaheitehawaii.com, 10am-9pm Mon.-Sat., 10am-6pm Sun.) specializes in chic beach clothing centered around the island lifestyle, which means lots of swimwear

and sundresses to accompany the gifts and accessories.

With the clothing shopping taken care of, move next door to **Jeré Diamonds and Fine Jewelry** (808/879-1967, www.jerediamonds.com, 10:30am-8pm Mon.-Sat., noon-6pm Sun.) which features an impressive range of not only diamonds, but also pearls, gemstones, and local paintings. This store holds its own with Tiffany's or Baron and Leeds down the street, and also features a lot of the artists who live on the island. The prices are more reasonable as well.

If your sweet tooth is aching after shopping, **Sweet Paradise Chocolatier** (808/344-1040, www.sweetparadisechocolate.com, 10am-8pm daily) will lure you with the scent of richly made chocolate. In addition to having an ornate spread of fine chocolates, all of the items are made right here on the island, and some of the cacao is even grown in Hawai'i—the only state which currently grows cacao.

The **Aloha Shirt Museum and Boutique** (808/875-1308, www.the-aloha-shirt-museum.com, 11am-9pm daily) above Pita Paradise is a fascinating stop if you're looking for an aloha shirt. They carry styles that haven't been seen in decades (particularly the long sleeves), and some of the collection even dates back to the 1940s. If you've ever wondered what a $2,000 aloha shirt looks like, this is the place to find out.

Wailea Town Center

Although this is mostly an office complex, there's one retail outlet worth a mention. **Wailea Wine** (161 Wailea Ike Pl., 808/879-0555, www.waileawine.com, 10am-6pm Mon.-Fri., 10am-5pm Sat.) has an exceptional selection of wines from all across the globe (and one of the largest selections on the island), and the gourmet culinary options are on par with any other fine foods mart you'll find across the state.

SOUTH MAUI

Entertainment

MA'ALAEA
Family Fun

Although the Maui Ocean Center is the un-disputed kid-favorite among all the stops in Ma'alaea, the **Maui Golf and Sports Park** (80 Ma'alaea Rd., 808/242-7818, www.mauigol-fandsportspark.com, 10am-5pm daily) is an-other option if you're trying to keep the kids entertained for a few hours. There are two 18-hole miniature golf courses, bumper boats, and a small rock climbing area, and even though the minigolf is expensive ($14) it's for as many holes as you want.

Live Music

In the downstairs section of the Ma'alaea Harbor Shops **Beach Bums** (300 Ma'alaea Rd., 808/243-2286, open until 9pm) occasionally has live music during the late afternoon and evenings to accompany periodic drink specials and a jovial sports bar atmosphere. If you're staying in one of the condos at Ma'alaea, this is your best bet for finding a happening atmo-sphere and the chance to mingle with local fish-ers and boat crews who are drinking their way through that morning's tips.

KIHEI

There aren't nearly as many entertainment op-tions in Kihei when compared to areas such as Lahaina or Ka'anapali. All of the dinner shows and lu'aus are in Wailea. Even trying to find daytime events such as free hula shows can be a fruitless search. The last bastion of family entertainment—the movie theaters at Kukui Mall—closed down at the end of 2012. Ultimately, the entertainment scene in Kihei largely centers on a cluster of bars around the Kalama Village area which are collectively known as The Triangle. Some have live per-formances and other have late-night DJs.

Events

The largest and most popular event in South Maui is the **Fourth Friday** celebration which is held—as you might have guessed—on the fourth Friday of the month 6pm-9pm at the Azeka Mauka shopping complex. The final installment in the Friday Town Parties (www.mauifridays.com), there are multiple live music performances and beer gardens scattered throughout the event. While all of this sounds like a big hot mess, it's surprisingly organized and easily provides the largest thing going on the fourth and final Friday of every month.

Live Music and Dancing
INSIDE THE TRIANGLE

Like a South Maui vortex of debauchery and sin, the majority of Kihei's nightlife takes place at The Triangle, as in, The *Barmuda* Triangle, where you could end up getting lost for days. This collection of bars within the Kihei Kalama Village can almost seem like a tropical frat row where each house on the street is having a dif-ferent sort of theme party. Don't like the music at one place? Go next door.

If you're starting your night off early, check out **Haui's Life's A Beach** (1913 S. Kihei Rd., 808/891-8010, www.mauibars.com, open until 2am), aka The Lab. This rockin' beach bar has an outdoor patio that looks out to-ward South Kihei Road and is a great place for people-watching. There is live music on most nights, or you could just shoot some pool, watch some sports, and eavesdrop on some local happenings.

The best venue within the Triangle for live music is **Three's Bar and Grill** (1945 S. Kihei Rd., 808/879-3133, www.threesbarandgrill.com, open until 1:30am), a semi-formal dining establishment that also has a VIP Surf Lounge with a built-in stage area and lighting. While there can occasionally be music earlier in the evening on weekdays, late-night shows usually begin at 10pm and run until closing time.

The most popular club in the traditional sense of the word is the **South Shore Tiki**

NO DANCING!

If you want to shake a leg and get your dance on while staying on the island's south side, the best place for doing so is in the Kihei Kalama Village, otherwise known as the Triangle. When it comes to drinking and dancing, Maui is a *very* strange place.

How so? In many of Maui's evening establishments, believe it or not, dancing is illegal. In order for an establishment to legally permit dancing, there needs to be a designated area which is either roped off or separated in some way from the designated drinking area. There are to be no drinks on the dance floor, and randomly choosing to shake your rump while waiting in line at the bar is heavily verboten and can get you thrown out.

So why the strict rules? When it comes to the law, the dancers themselves won't get in trouble, but rather the licensed establishment can potentially lose its liquor license. The strangest part in all of this is that there is no legal definition for what constitutes dancing. Consequently, anything which involves rhythmic or purposeful movement from a shoulder shake to a toe tap can be construed as illicit, dangerous, and legally unacceptable. Unless, of course, you put down your drink and make your way to the designated dance floor.

Local dance advocate groups have been recommending bills to the state legislature for years in an effort to change the law (or at least define dancing), but for reasons which continue to defy common logic, dancing remains an often forbidden pursuit.

Lounge (1913 S. Kihei Rd., 808/874-6444, www.southshoretikilounge.com, open until 2am) where resident DJs play for a small but crowded dance floor. This place gets popular on the weekends with its thumping house beats and young singles. The relaxed garden setting makes a nice juxtaposition to the throbbing humanity inside.

For a completely different and more sophisticated scene **Ambrosia** (1913 S. Kihei Rd., 808/891-1011, www.ambrosiamaui.com, open until 2am) is a small martini bar that specializes in "upscale drinking," which basically means that you'll swap your draft beer for some cutting-edge mixology. DJs spin on many nights of the week here, and the vibe is decidedly classier and more refined than at some of the neighboring venues.

One of less refined venues is **Kahale's Beach Club** (36 Keala Pl., 808/875-7711, open until 2am), a working-class dive bar that has live music, cheap drinks, and a legitimately local atmosphere. This is your classic neighborhood hangout, and you won't find any grass skirts, rented convertibles, or timeshare resales within a respectable radius.

Dog and Duck Irish Pub (1913 S. Kihei Rd.,

808/875-9669, www.theworldfamousdogandduck.com, open until 2am) offers a good old-fashioned touch of the *craic*. Throw darts, eat bangers and mash, drink Guinness, rock out to live music, or take part in one of their popular quiz nights.

OUTSIDE THE TRIANGLE

There are some scattered places outside the Triangle where you can catch some live music. In the Azeka Mauka shopping area, **Stella Blues Café** (1279 S. Kihei Rd., 808/874-3779, www.stellablues.com, open until 11pm) caters to the baby boomer generation, occasionally bringing in big names to perform. Although live performances on some evenings come without a cover, other acts such as Hapa or John Cruz can carry a $30 cover charge, or be combined with a dinner menu for $60/person.

Down at the other end of the parking lot of the Azeka Mauka is **Diamonds Ice Bar** (1279 S. Kihei Rd., 808/874-9299, www.diamondsicebar.com, open until 2am), a smaller establishment tucked in the end unit that offers live music on most nights of the week. If you have a large group or party there's a private VIP room. While it doesn't see the same amount of crowds

SOUTH MAUI

as down at the Triangle, it can still be a happening place if the right band happens to be playing.

Moose McGillicuddy's (2511 S. Kihei Rd., 808/891-8644, www.moosemcgillicuddys.com, open until 2am) harnesses the late-night crowd in South Kihei who are looking for cheap drink specials and an old-fashioned good time. This sports bar cranks up the music at 9pm, and the radio ads they run championing their late-night *pupu* menu as being your best bet for staving off the munchies should give you a general idea of the clientele.

Karaoke

Whether you're a karaoke fan or not, **Sansei** (1881 S. Kihei Rd., 808/879-0004, www.sanseihawaii.com, 5pm-10pm Sun.-Mon., 5:30pm-10pm Tues.-Wed., 5:30pm-1am Thurs.-Sat.) sushi bar in the Foodland shopping center is the hottest karaoke spot in town. Sansei is always packed on the weekends, and what draws most of the locals here is that the normally moderately priced sushi menu is discounted 50 percent after 10pm every Thursday, Friday, and Saturday night. Inevitably, you're going to end up pairing your California roll with Asahi, and what you swore to yourself was going to be a night of some casual *unagi* and a glass of water turns into you ordering another round of sake and singing Journey with a guy from Reno. Despite the fact this restaurant has been around forever, the half-price sushi karaoke nights are the most consistently popular night on the town.

Or, if you want to have multiple turns at the mike due to a reduced number of people, **Isana** (515 S. Kihei Rd., 808/874-5700, www.isanarestaurant.berrysites.net, open until 1am), a Korean bar in far north Kihei, is the only bar within a three-mile radius. As you might expect, this is a heavily local crowd that doesn't see too many tourists, which can always be part of the fun.

WAILEA
Shows

While there surprisingly aren't that many dinner shows on Maui, if you're looking for one that will completely wow you, there's no better option than the **Willie K Dinner Show** held at Mulligan's On The Blue (100 Kaukahi St., 808/874-1131, www.mulligansontheblue.com, open until 1am). Even if you've never heard of Uncle Willie K, once you see him play live you'll never forget him. An insanely talented local Hawaiian musician who grew up on Maui, Willie K's prowess stretches across a wide range of genres from blues to Hawaiian to rock and roll and opera. Yes, opera. This is your chance to hear a Hawaiian man sing opera inside an Irish pub. Tickets are $30/person, or if you want to combine it with the dinner buffet option (and thereby get a better seat), the price rises to $65/person. The show goes on several times throughout the month, but since the schedule is highly variable, the best thing to do is to check the website at www.mulligansontheblue.com.

If you're on a budget and looking for a free public show, head to **Wailea on Wednesdays** (6:30pm-8pm), held at the Shops at Wailea (3750 Wailea Alanui Dr.). Local Hawaiian artists perform live music in the lower courtyard section, and all of the surrounding art galleries and restaurants get in on the action with varying specials and festivities of their own.

All of the resorts feature a rotating schedule of live performances within the hotel grounds, so if you just take a wander through the area around sunset, you're sure to find a couple of slack key guitar players picking sweet melodies as the sun goes down or live hula performances taking place around the hotel lobbies.

Lu'au

The best lu'au on the island is Old Lahaina Luau in Lahaina, but if you're staying on the south end of the island and don't want to drive that far, there are two lu'au options in South Maui from which you can choose. The official check-in time may be quite early, but don't feel like you have to show up exactly on time. The first 1.5-2 hours of most lu'aus involves waiting in line to find out where you'll be sitting, checking out the vendors, taking photos with the dancers, and participating in "pre-game" festivities such as traditional Hawaiian games or various crafts. If you want to get the full experience, then show up at the beginning, but if your main interests are the food, the drinks, and the show, then you can easily show up an hour "late," and skip waiting in line or cutting your day at the beach short without missing much at all.

Of the two luʻaus in Wailea, my top pick is **The Grand Luau at Honuaʻula** (3850 Wailea Alanui Dr., 808/875-7710, www.honuaula-luau.com, 4pm, $105/adult, $57/child), because the show focuses more on Hawaiian history as opposed to the general South Pacific. The luʻau takes place on the grounds of the Grand Wailea, and Honuaʻula is a name given to this section of the island by the original Polynesians who migrated here centuries ago. The food and drinks are par for the luʻau course, although the main stage has a rock wall backdrop as opposed to facing out toward the ocean. Shows run on Monday, Thursday, Friday, and Saturday evenings, although call in advance to double check since the schedule can sometimes be variable.

Just a few steps down the coastal walkway is the other luʻau in Wailea, **Te Au Moana** (3700 Wailea Alanui, 877/827-2740, www.teaumoana.com, 4:30pm, $104/adult, $57/child), at the Wailea Beach Marriott. The show times overlap exactly with neighboring Grand Wailea, and take place on Monday, Thursday, Friday, and Saturday evenings. While this show focuses more on the dance and mythology of greater Polynesia than specifically on Hawaiʻi, it's still a highly entertaining performance—particularly if it's your first luʻau. As an added bonus, the stage backs up to the coastline in front of the hotel. The backdrop of the setting sun creates a panorama you would expect from a luʻau in paradise.

Live Music

For live entertainment after the sun goes down, the most popular place in Wailea is

Mulligan's On The Blue (100 Kaukahi St., 808/874-1131, www.mulligansontheblue.com, open until 1am). This Irish pub is owned by a real Irishman (which means real Guinness on draft), and aside from the Willie K dinner show, the next most popular evening is on Sunday when the Celtic Tigers Irish folk band takes to the stage. There are also periodic performances by award-winning local artists, so pick up a copy of a local entertainment catalog to see what the happenings are.

Although the live music here is only for happy hour, **Monkeypod** (10 Wailea Ike Dr., 808/891-2322, www.monkeypodkitchen.com, open until 10:30pm) restaurant in the Wailea Gateway Center has the best craft beer list in Wailea. There's also an extensive wine list.

Bars

For a traditional bar scene without the live music, head to **Manoli's Pizza Company** (100 Wailea Ike Dr., 808/874-7499, www.manolispizzacompany.com, open until midnight), where in addition to draft and bottled beers there are 20 wines which are either organic or grown in sustainable vineyards. Late-night happy hour is 9pm-midnight. It's within walking distance of many of the resorts.

Inside the Shops at Wailea the best bar scene is at **Longhi's** (3750 Wailea Alanui, 808/891-8883, www.longhis.com, open until 10pm), and you can also find cold beers and tropical drinks inside **Tommy Bahama's** (808/875-9983, open until 10pm) and **Cheeseburger Island Style** (808/874-8990, open until 10pm).

The Red Bar at **Gannon's** (100 Wailea Golf Club Dr., 808/875-8080, www.gannonsrestaurant.com, open until 9:30pm) pairs the sexiest and sleekest drinks in Wailea along with a stunning ocean view. Choose from affordable draft beers, an extensive list of over 100 wines, and enticing cocktails made with everything from sweet tea vodka to acai liqueur. There's also occasional live entertainment, usually paired with happy hour.

SOUTH MAUI

Food

MA'ALAEA
Local Style
Looking for a cheap meal on the go? You can't go wrong at the takeout counter at **Tradewinds Deli** (20 Hauoli St., 808/242-9161, 9am-6pm Mon.-Sat., 9am-4pm Sun., $6-7), inside the Ma'alaea Mermaid condominium next to Ma'alaea Harbor. Try a bowl of chili and rice, a turkey, bacon, and avocado sandwich, or daily lunch specials like beef stew or red chicken curry.

American
If your idea of the perfect lunch is clutching a pint of PBR with barbecue-covered fingers, **Beach Bums Bar and Grill** (300 Ma'alaea Boat Harbor Rd., 808/243-2286, 8am-9pm daily, $8-25), downstairs in the Harbor Shops, is the perfect spot. It's a festive open-air sports den of pulled pork sandwiches, barbecue ribs, and sweet potato fries.

Hawaiian Regional
Surrounded by boats in various stages of dry dock, **Buzz's Wharf** (Ma'alaea Harbor, 808/244-5426, www.buzzswharf.com, 11am-9pm daily, $14-18 lunch, $18-46 dinner) is the oldest restaurant in Ma'alaea. Don't let the outward appearance fool you. The atmosphere inside is classy and the menu is laden with Pacific Rim classics. Start off with an appetizer of Tahitian *poisson cru,* and either continue with the Tahitian theme or switch directions to a wasabi crusted ahi steak or their signature shrimp scampi.

Coffee Shops
Although it dates back to 1910, the **⟨ Ma'alaea General Store and Café** (132 Ma'alaea Boat Harbor Rd., 808/242-8900, www.maalaeagen-eralstore.com, 6am-7pm daily, $6-10) sat empty for years. Energetic new owners have breathed life into the old place. Pick up an acai bowl or bagel melt for breakfast. Burgers and hot sandwiches are served until 3pm, while cold deli sandwiches are available until 5pm. Nearly everything is made fresh on-site.

KIHEI
Local Style
The only true local style plate lunch in Kihei is at **⟨ Da Kitchen** (2439 S. Kihei Rd., 808/875-7782, www.da-kitchen.com, 9am-9pm daily, $8-15), toward the back of the Rainbow Mall in South Kihei. Although the restaurant itself isn't as large as its Kahului counterpart, the portions are enormous, most large enough that you could split them and still walk away full. This hole-in-the-wall, strip-mall special is one of the best deals in town. If you're looking for a place where locals eat, this is it.

Mexican
For a proper Mexican meal, Kihei locals head to **⟨ Amigo's** (1215 S. Kihei Rd., 808/879-9952, www.amigosmaui.com, 8am-9pm daily, $8-12), in the Long's Shopping Center in north-central Kihei. Like the locations in Lahaina and Kahului, Amigo's has a welcoming and cold draft beer. The California burrito ordered "wet" combats even the strongest hunger. The lively interior makes up for the mediocre view looking out onto South Kihei Road.

Another authentic option is **Taqueria Cruz** (2395 S. Kihei Rd., 808/875-2910, 11am-8pm Mon.-Sat., $9-10), tucked in the back of South Kihei's Dolphin Plaza. It's reminiscent of a roadside *taqueria* on the back roads of Baja. Mexican music emanates from the kitchen before it even opens. The BYOB option is a nice perk: Enjoy your fish tacos with a Pacifico from your cooler. There's live music 6:30pm-8:30pm on Tuesday and Saturday nights.

Seafood
Hidden back in the central Kihei industrial yard is **⟨ Eskimo Candy** (2665 Wai Wai Pl., 808/879-5686, www.eskimocandy.com,

10:30am-7pm Mon.-Fri., $10-17), Kihei's best local secret for fresh seafood and *poke*. The ocean-themed decorations (such as the massive shark coming out of the wall) show that this place means business when it comes to seafood. Try the seafood chowder, fish-and-chips, and *poke*, featuring four different styles of seasoned ahi tuna. There are only a few tables outside for dining. To find it, make the turn off South Kihei Road by Maui Dive Shop and the Avis car rental outlet, continuing on toward the end of the road; the restaurant will be on your right.

In the Azeka Mauka shopping center in central Kihei, **Coconut's Fish Café** (1279 S. Kihei Road, 808/875-9979, www.coconutsfishcafe. com, 11am-9pm daily, $14) boasts "the best tacos in the U.S.A.," which is a bit bombastic. The special coleslaw made with coconut milk makes the famed tacos unique. There's so much happening on top of the tortilla—stacked with 17 ingredients—that you need to eat it with a fork.

Pizza

Locals say the best pizza in Kihei is at the **South Shore Tiki Lounge** (1913 S. Kihei Rd., 808/874-6444, 11am-2am daily, $6-9), ensconced in the Kihei Kalama Village. Pies are handcrafted with local ingredients and wheat flour. Sit outside on the garden-view deck.

Another favorite for south shore pizza is **Fabiani's Bakery and Pizza** (95 Lipoa St., 808/874-0888, www.fabianis.com, 7am-10pm daily, $10-12) in central Kihei. Located in a strip mall, it's tough to find, but once you get there, you'll realize why it's a local hangout. Lunch and dinner are dominated by fresh, tasty pizzas and paninis crafted by a chef from Italy. There's also a decent wine selection and the atmosphere inside is much nicer than the exterior suggests. The fresh breakfast pastries are a local secret.

The south side's original pizza joint, **Shaka Sandwich and Pizza** (1770 S. Kihei Rd., 808/874-0331, www.shakapizza.com, 10:30am-9pm Sun.-Thurs., 10:30am-10pm Fri.-Sat., $7-28), by the Kukui Mall, has been around for over two decades. The homemade,

18-inch Italian pies are big enough to fill two hungry teenagers and the cheesesteak supreme hoagie is a local favorite. Pizza by the slice is the best lunch deal in Kihei.

The chefs decided to open **Maui Brick Oven** (1215 S. Kihei Rd., 808/875-7896, www. mauibrickoven.com, 4pm-9pm Mon.-Sat., $16-24) after they were diagnosed with severe wheat allergies. The result is a pizza menu that manages to be 100 percent gluten-free without sacrificing taste or selection. There are also appetizers such as shaved beef carpaccio and a *keiki* menu as well.

Irish

Kihei is sunnier than Dublin, but when you order bangers and mash and a cold Guinness at the dimly lit **Dog and Duck Irish Pub** (1913 S. Kihei Rd., 808/875-9669, www.theworld-famousdoganduck.com, 10am-1am daily, $8-20), you feel like you're dining at the famous Temple Bar. This lively pub is one of the few places you can catch that international game Americans insist on calling soccer. Located at the back of the Kihei Kalama Village, this is a great spot if you want some stick-to-your-ribs meat and potatoes washed down with good conversation and a bit of the *craic*.

Mediterranean

Pita Paradise (1913 S. Kihei Rd., 808/875-7679, www.pitaparadisehawaii.com, 11am-9:30pm daily, $9-17) serves surprisingly large gyros and falafel you might expect to find in Mykonos, a welcome surprise in Kihei. While the lamb gyro is pricey, the Mediterranean chicken pita is affordable without sacrificing quality or taste. There are also massive kabob plates. The outdoor garden patio is a peaceful place to enjoy a meal in otherwise frenetic Kalama Village.

American

Tucked away in a peaceful garden setting, **808 Bistro** (2511 S. Kihei Rd., 808/879-8008, www.808bistro.com, 7am-noon and 5pm-9pm daily, $7-15) offers some serenity from the morning bustle of South Kihei.

SOUTH MAUI'S BEST HAPPY HOURS

Take advantage of happy hour as an opportunity to dine in a venue normally out of your price range. Here are a few of options for grabbing a light dinner and a cheap drink.

KIHEI

- **Diamonds Ice Bar:** 3pm-7pm; $2 Bud Light, $3 wells, and $1 tacos until 5pm.
- **Fabiani's Bakery and Pizzeria:** 4pm-6pm; 50 percent off pizzas and draft beer when seated at the bar.
- **Haui's Life's A Beach:** 3pm-7pm; $2.50 domestic pints, $3.50 24 oz. mugs, $2.50 mai tais, $7 1-liter mai tais, $5 lunch specials until 5pm.
- **Kono's on the Green:** 2pm-6pm; $2.50 domestics, $3 drafts, Wed.-Sun. 50 percent off sushi.
- **Sarento's:** 4:30pm-6:30pm; 50 percent off all appetizers and drinks when seated at the bar.
- **Three's Bar and Grill:** 3pm-6pm; $3 mai tais and margaritas, $3 drafts and wells. 50 percent off appetizers and sushi.

WAILEA

- **Mulligan's On The Blue:** 3pm-6pm; $3 drafts, $6 wine, $6 pupus.
- **Longhi's:** 3pm-6pm; $4 drafts, $5-8 wine, $7 cocktails, pupus from $6.
- **Monkeypod:** 3pm-5:30pm; 50 percent off appetizers, $4.75 premium drafts, $9 pizzas.
- **Gannon's:** 3pm-6pm; $2 domestic drafts, $3 premium drafts, $6 wine, 50 percent off appetizers.

MAKENA

- **Café on the Green:** 3pm-6:30pm; $4 drafts, $6 wine, $5-7 pupus.

Breakfast here is tops: the relaxing surroundings just go better with a cup of morning coffee and a plate of banana bread French toast. The evening meal is still decent (consider the BYOB option). Looking across the road from Kamaole II Beach, you would never know this place was here. Walk past Fred's Mexican Café to reach the entrance, although once you find your table you'll be happy to notice there is still an ocean view.

One of the best breakfast finds on the south side is **Kihei Caffe** (1945 S. Kihei Rd., 808/879-2230, www.kiheicaffe.net, 5am-3pm daily, $7-10). It's also the earliest, perfect for a meal before an early-morning boat trip. The portions are enormous; Try a generous omelet or gargantuan breakfast burrito. Breakfast is served all day. The atmosphere can be hectic; get here early before the traffic (both human and vehicular) picks up.

Named after a Grateful Dead song, local favorite **Stella Blues Café** (1279 S. Kihei Rd., 808/874-3779, www.stellablues.com, 7:30am-10pm daily, $12-14 lunch, $15-29 dinner) serves American comfort food. It's a nice option for families looking for a mellow, quiet meal. Lunch offers sandwiches and burgers while dinner focuses on pastas, pork chops, and fish plates.

The takeout window at **Stewart Burgers** (1819 S. Kihei Rd., 808/879-0497, 11am-8:30pm daily, $8-11), in the corner of the Kukui Mall, offers 12 specialty burgers without all the added fuss. There are a few outdoor tables where you can inhale your food. Even though the atmosphere ranks zero, if you're looking for a quick, easy meal, it's the perfect stop. Try the sweet potato fries.

Japanese

Sansei (1881 S. Kihei Rd., 808/879-0004, www.sanseihawaii.com, 5pm-10pm Sun.-Mon., 5:30pm-10pm Tues.-Wed., 5:30pm-1am Thurs.-Sat., $16) has been a South Maui favorite since 2002. Award-winning dishes such as the panko-crusted ahi rolls and signature

DID MENEHUNE BUILD THE KO'IE'IE FISHPOND?

In Hawaiian lore, Menehune are the mythical little people of the Hawaiian Islands who are believed to be mysterious, mischievous, and quick in their work. While stories about Menehune abound, the most commonly told one involves the building of stone fishponds across many of the Hawaiian Islands. In a story similar to those found on Kaua'i and Moloka'i, Ko'ie'ie Fishpond in North Kihei is believed to have been built by Menehune in the course of a single night.

Don't pass this off as a playful legend, however; history supports the claim. It's believed by many scholars that the Hawaiian Islands were populated by seafaring voyagers from the Marquesas Islands around AD 400-600, and that these original, small-in-stature inhabitants were supplanted in AD 1100 by much larger settlers from Tahiti. As it turns out, the Tahitian word for commoner is *manahune*, and

it's believed that the ruling Tahitian class put the lower, Marquesan class to work on building the fishponds.

As Hawaiian society progressed and the centuries wore on, it's theorized that the *manahune* remained as lower-class citizens. Much of the evidence for this theory is derived from a census which took place on the island of Kaua'i in 1820, where, in a tantalizing fusion of history and lore, 65 citizens classified themselves as being *manahune*.

So was Ko'ie'ie Fishpond built by magical little people or was it constructed by a diminutive class of indentured workers? Since there was no written language at the time of its construction (believed to be AD 1400-1500), all we are left with are the legends, the stones… and the Menehune Shores condominium on the shoreline.

shrimp dynamite keep locals flocking to this nondescript spot. The half-priced sushi menu (Thurs.-Sat. after 10pm), with options like *unagi* and rainbow rolls, will leave sushi-lovers feeling like kids in a candy store. Late nights can be noisy, with karaoke in full swing.

If late-night karaoke isn't your scene, head for the sushi and sashimi at the more intimate **Koiso Sushi Bar** (2395 S. Kihei Rd., 808/875-8258, 6pm-10pm Mon.-Sat., $9-32), inside Dolphin Plaza in South Kihei. This corner restaurant has a solitary low-slung counter that only accommodates 12, so reservations are highly recommended.

Indian
Downstairs in the Menehune Shores condominium, **Monsoon India** (760 S. Kihei Rd., 808/875-6666, www.monsoonindiamaui. com, 11:30am-2:30pm, 5pm-9pm Tues.-Sun., 5pm-9pm Mon., $15-23) is the only Indian restaurant in the world that looks out on an ancient Hawaiian fishpond. Tandoori breads, chana masala, and chicken tikka are served in a dining room overlooking the ancient

Ko'ie'ie Fishpond, which is gradually being restored to its original splendor. The sunsets are magnificent.

Thai
The best Thai food in Kihei is found at **Thailand Cuisine** (1819 S. Kihei Rd., 808/875-0839, www.thailandcuisinemaui.net, 11am-2:30pm, 5pm-10pm Mon.-Sat., $12) inside the Kukui Mall. Its sister restaurant in Kahului has been voted the best Thai food on Maui numerous times.

Hawaiian Regional
Since most of Kihei's restaurants are in strip malls, there isn't an overabundance of fine dining. The exception, however, is **⬤ Sarento's On The Beach** (2980 S. Kihei Rd., 808/875-7555, www.sarentosonthebeach.com, 7am-11pm and 5:30pm-10pm daily, $28-49), on the water at the north end of Keawakapu Beach. You won't find a more romantic or relaxing spot in Kihei. Start off with the seared ahi or beef carpaccio before moving on to the pan-roasted island snapper or rack of lamb

Placourakis—named after the restaurant's legendary owner. Valet parking is free.

On the lower level of the Mana Kai Resort is the semi-formal **Five Palms** (2960 South Kihei Rd., 808/879-2607, 8am-9:30pm daily, $28-43) only a few feet from the water. Brunch (8am-2:30pm) includes eggs, omelets, and griddle fare, but dinner (5pm-9:30pm) is when the kitchen turns it up a few notches. Start with Pacific crab cakes and move on to slow-roasted prime rib or seafood crusted lobster in butter sauce. Come before the rush for the early-bird special.

Another local favorite is **Three's Bar and Grill** (1945 S. Kihei Rd., 808/879-3133, www.threesbarandgrill.com, 8:30am-9:30pm Wed.-Sun., 11am-9:30pm Mon.-Tues., $10-15 lunch, $20-25 dinner), inside the Kihei Kalama Village. Opened by three chefs who each boast their own culinary specialty—Hawaiian, Southwestern, and Pacific Rim—the menu at Three's can pull your palate in a direction unique even to the Hawaiian fusion scene. The lunch and appetizer items such as Hawaiian style ribs and kalua pig quesadilla are tasty and affordable. The dinner menu features entrées such as chicken roulade and a raw bar of sushi, oysters, sashimi, and *poke*. Stick around for the live performance in the Surf Lounge.

Natural Foods

The only natural foods store in town is **Hawaiian Moons** (2411 S. Kihei Rd., 808/875-4356, www.hawaiianmoons.com, 8am-9pm daily), within the Kamaole Beach Center across from Kamaole I. The food will make you feel just like home if your diet tends toward the organic, raw, or gluten-free. The hot bar serves up filling lunches.

Coffee Shops

The most modern coffee shop in Kihei is **Java Café** (1279 S. Kihei Rd., 808/214-6095, www.javacafemaui.com, 6am-9pm daily, $7-9) in the Azeka Mauka shopping center. Seventy-five percent of the coffee served is grown in Hawai'i. You can also buy bags of unground beans from coffee farms on Maui, Kaua'i,

Moloka'i, and the Big Island. Flatbreads and paninis are available for lunch; there's also a large selection of breakfast bagels.

If you need a little afternoon pick-me-up, **Lava Java Coffee Roasters** (1941 S. Kihei Rd., 808/879-1919, www.lavajavamaui.com, 6am-8pm daily) in the Kihei Kalama Village not only offers locally grown coffee and beans, they also make a coffee-flavored granite—the perfect combination of refreshing and caffeinated, served in slushie form. If you really need to get up and go, order it with an extra shot of espresso.

Shave Ice

Kihei is officially one of the hottest places on Maui, so forgive yourself for shave ice cravings. The best option for the syrupy snack is **[** **Local Boys Shave Ice** (1941 S. Kihei Rd., 808/344-9779, www.localboysshaveice.com, 10am-9pm daily) in the Kihei Kalama Village. Mix up to three flavors onto your heaping mound of thinly shaved ice flakes and add Roselani, Maui-made ice cream, Kauai cream, and azuki beans free of charge. Placing ice cream at the bottom of the shave ice and covering it in Kauai cream is the only way to go. After you try it, you'll understand.

Ululani's Shave Ice (61 S. Kihei Rd., www.ululanisshaveice.com, 11am-6pm daily) is the staple at the northern end of town. Located by the ABC store just across from the Kihei Canoe Club, it's the shave ice stand closest to Sugar Beach or the Ma'alaea area.

Food Cart

The most popular food truck in Kihei is the **Kinaole Grill** (77 Alanui Ke Ali'i Dr., 11am-7:30pm daily, $12-14) which serves plates of garlic shrimp, coconut shrimp, and chicken katsu on the road across from the north end of Kamaole I Beach. The plates are the same price (if not more expensive) than a chicken katsu plate you could get at a nearby restaurant such as Da Kitchen.

Jawz Fish Tacos (808/874-8226, 11am-4:30pm daily, $6-11) has a truck on the corner of Keonekai and South Kihei Roads, across the street from Kamaole III Beach Park. Choose from affordable burritos, nachos, quesadillas, and tacos, all on the better side of average.

Farmers Market

In North Kihei, right across from Kenolio Park and the Kihei Canoe Club area, the **farmers market** (61 South Kihei Rd., 8am-4pm Mon.-Thurs., 8am-5pm Fri.) is a great way to support local island farmers. On weekends, there's another **farmers market** (95 E. Lipoa Street, 8:30am-11am Sat.-Sun.) between South Kihei Road and the main highway.

WAILEA

Prices in Wailea are much higher than in other parts of the island. You're often paying for master chefs, exceptional service, and unparalleled ambience in world-class resorts. Prices for most meals in Wailea will be double what a similar meal might cost in Kihei. If you venture outside of the resort areas, there are numerous places for a filling and affordable meal.

Italian

The best pizza in Wailea can be found walking distance from many of the hotels at **Manoli's Pizza Company** (100 Wailea Ike Dr., 808/874-7499, www.manolispizzacompany.com, 11:30am-10pm daily, $16-22), across from the Shops at Wailea. Expect 14-inch thin crusts (with both organic wheat and gluten-free options), with toppings like shrimp, pesto, kalamata olives, artichoke hearts, and feta cheese. There are also salads and a few pasta options.

At the Shops at Wailea, **Longhi's** (3750 Wailea Alanui Dr., 808/891-8883, www.longhis.com, 8am-10pm weekdays, 7:30am-10pm weekends, $9-16 lunch, $24-36 dinner) is a sophisticated eatery with the same classic black-and-white-checkered floor of the Lahaina location. Breakfast means frittatas, quiche, or eggs Benedict, while dinner includes prawns amaretto, fettuccine Lombardi, fresh island fish Veronique, or chicken cannelloni.

Inside Hotel Wailea, **Capische?** (555 Kaukahi Rd., 808/879-2224, www.capische.com, from 5:30pm daily, $16-50) offers sophisticated Italian food accompanied by light jazz Friday-Sunday. Expect appetizers like beef carpaccio with horseradish and quail saltimbocca, aloing with entrées of seared seafood cioppino, braised lamb shank, and truffle-grilled ono.

At the luxurious Four Seasons Resort, **Ferraro's Bar e Ristorante** (3900 Wailea Alanui Dr., 808/874-8000, 11:30am-8pm daily, $30-50) has tables close enough to the ocean that you can hear the waves. Clink glasses beneath the stars and savor the aromas of authentic *cucina rustica* cuisine: classic dishes like tagliatelle, and chicken involtini, complemented by wine selections like sangiovese and chianti. Lunch is more casual, with wood-fired pizzas.

American

The first restaurant you'll encounter in Wailea approaching from Pi'ilani Highway is **Monkeypod Kitchen** (10 Wailea Ike Dr., 808/891-2322, www.monkeypodkitchen.com, 11:30am-10:30pm daily, $13-35), the brainchild of renowned Maui chef Peter Merriman. Ingredients are all sourced locally, supporting sustainable farming and ensuring fresh, healthy meals. Dinner options range from sesame-crusted mahimahi, to bulgogi pork tacos in an Asian pear aioli, or an organic spinach and quinoa salad big enough to share. Garlic truffle oil fries are one of the most popular items on the menu. Lunch options like burgers and sandwiches are less expensive. Enjoy the best craft beer selection in Wailea along with your meal.

Irish

Mulligan's On The Blue (100 Kaukahi St., 808/874-1131, www.mulligansontheblue.com, 11am-midnight Mon-Fri, 8:30am-midnight Sat.-Sun., $10-15) is Wailea's only legitimate sports bar: one of the few places to catch international events such as soccer or rugby. The ocean views, happy hour menu, Willie K dinner show, and Celtic Tigers bagpiping draw people up the hill above the Fairmont Kea Lani. Fish-and-chips and shepherd's pie, burgers, and sandwiches are all economical.

Hawaiian Regional

The Hawaiian regional restaurants in Wailea are utterly fantastic, romantic, and expensive. **Gannon's** (100 Wailea Golf Club Dr., 808/875-8080, www.gannonsrestaurant.com, 8:30am-9:30pm daily, $12-22 lunch $28-48 dinner) overlooks the Wailea Emerald golf course, has a stunning panoramic ocean view, and offers contemporary entrées such as miso-glazed Kona kampachi or Moroccan spiced lamb. Lunch and brunch options like the oven-roasted turkey club or the Greek omelet are downright affordable.

At the Four Seasons, **Duo** (3900 Wailea Alanui, 808/874-8000, 6:30am-11am Mon.-Sat., 6:30am-noon Sun., $30-50) ranks in the upper echelon of fine island cuisine. The dinner menu is dominated by steak and seafood options such as Brandt True filet mignon and shiso panko-crusted ahi. For something light, try the lobster bisque. The breakfast buffet is lauded as the best in Wailea.

At the Grand Wailea, **Humuhumunukunukuapua'a** (3850 Wailea Alaui Dr., 808/875-1234, www.wailearesortdining.com, 5:30pm-9pm nightly, $30-49) is not only one of the hardest restaurants to pronounce, it's also one of the most popular. Named after the state fish, "Humu" sits in a thatched-roof Polynesian structure afloat on its own million-gallon saltwater lagoon. Large plates include the famous Hawaiian spiny lobster as well as hoisin and pear-braised short ribs.

Seafood

In the Fairmont Kea Lani, **Nick's Fishmarket** (4100 Wailea Alanui Dr., 808/879-7224, www.nicksfishmarktmaui.com, 5:30pm-9:45pm daily, $30-50) focuses on the bounty of the sea. Whitewashed walls and vine-covered trellises give the open-air restaurant a Mediterranean ambience. Selections include opah, mahimahi Kona kampachi, and Moroccan spiced salmon, along with creative sides like wasabi mashed potatoes and mango peppercorn chutney. Reservations are recommended.

MAKENA AND BEYOND

When it comes to finding food this far south, there are three options: Grab lunch at one of the food trucks on the side of the road, eat at one of the Makena Beach and Golf Resort restaurants, or turn back around and head to Kihei or Wailea.

American

The most casual and popular spot in Makena is **Café on the Green** (5415 Makena Alanui, 808/875-5888, www.makenaresortmaui.com, 11am-6:30pm daily, $12-16). The happy hour here is one of the best in South Maui and the late-afternoon view from the outdoor patio is the best in Makena. The restaurant is by the golf clubhouse, a 10-minute walk from the main hotel. The selection of ahi sandwiches and signature cheeseburgers are affordable and tasty enough to warrant the short jaunt.

Hawaiian Regional

Using herbs and vegetables grown on-site, chef Mark McDowell at **Molokini Bar and Grille** (5400 Makena Alanui, 808/875-5888, www.makenaresortmaui.com, 5:30pm-10pm daily, $23-38) commands a menu punctuated by Hawaiian classics like macadamia nut-crusted mahimahi and pepper-seared ahi. Everything from the bread to the sauces is made in-house. The value is exceptional when compared to Wailea, for portions just as fresh and filling.

Food Cart

Usually parked a half mile from the entrance of Big Beach, **Big Beach BBQ** (10:30am-3pm, $10) offers kalua pig tacos, kalua pork sliders, and pineapple sausages. They're a little overpriced, but you're paying for the convenience of hot and tasty barbecue this far south of town.

Information and Services

MEDICAL SERVICES
Kihei
Since the main hospital for the island is all the way in Wailuku, your best option for medical services in Kihei is at the **Kihei-Wailea Medical Center** (221 Pi'ikea Ave., 808/874-8100, www.kiheiwaileamedicalcenter.com, 8am-8pm Mon.-Fri., 8am-5pm Sat.-Sun.) in the Pi'ilani Shopping Center.

Wailea
If you're bodysurfing at Big Beach and end up with a shoulder popped out of your socket (or any other sort of beach injury), head right to **Wailea Medical Center** (161 Wailea Ike Pl., 808/874-8333, www.waileamedicalcenter.com, 8am-5pm daily) where in addition to operating an urgent care clinic, they also specialize in treating a wide range of beach injuries.

BANKS
Kihei
The only banks in all of South Maui are in Kihei, and among them are **Bank of Hawaii** (808/879-5844) at Azeka Mauka, **First Hawaiian Bank** (808/875-0055) at the Lipoa Center, and an **American Savings Bank** (808/879-1977) at the Pi'ilani Village Shopping Center.

GAS
Ma'alaea
There is one **76** gas station at the only stoplight in Ma'alaea. Stop here if you're traveling to Lahaina and the gas light has already come on, since there isn't another option for a good 12 miles.

Kihei
You can find gas stations at the Kihei Gateway Plaza, Pi'ilani Village Shopping Center, Lipoa Center, Azeka Mauka, and the ABC Shopping Center. There are no gas stations in Wailea or Makena, so top off here if your tank is getting low.

POST OFFICE
The **post office in Kihei** (1254 S. Kihei Rd., 800/275-8777, 8:30am-4:30pm Mon.-Fri., 9am-1pm Sat.) is in the Azeka Makai shopping center.

LIBRARY
Kihei
The **Kihei Public Library** (35 Waimahaihai St., 808/875-6833, noon-8pm Tues., 10am-5pm Wed.-Sat.) is across and down from the Kukui Mall. In its yard is an old Hawaiian fishing shrine.

INTERNET SERVICES
Ma'alaea
The best place to pick up some free Wi-Fi around the harbor is at the **Ma'alaea General Store and Café** (132 Ma'alaea Boat Harbor Rd., 808/242-8900, www.maalaeageneralstore.com, 6am-7pm daily) which doubles as a coffee shop and can also be a good place to escape the relentless afternoon wind.

Kihei
Internet cafés are scattered all throughout Kihei, and one of the best is **Java Café** (1279 S. Kihei Rd., 808/214-6095, www.javacafemaui.com, 6am-9pm daily) within the Azeka Mauka shopping center where there is free Wi-Fi and you can use a desktop computer for 15 minutes if you didn't happen to travel with your own laptop.

In South Kihei, **Café @ La Plage** (2395 S. Kihei Rd., 808/875-7668, www.cafemaui.com, 6:30am-5pm Mon.-Sat., 6:30am-3pm Sun.) in the Dolphin Plaza across from Kamaole I has wireless as well as printing services if you need to print out a boarding pass or any other sort of important travel document.

Wailea

On the outer edge of the Shops at Wailea facing toward the north parking lot, **The Coffee Bean** (3750 Wailea Alanui Dr., 808/891-2045, www.coffeebeanhawaii.com, 5:30am-9pm daily) provides free Wi-Fi for patrons, and it even works outside in the small outdoor courtyard.

Getting There and Around

South Maui is easily navigable by car, although there are a number of parking challenges. First, anyone staying at a Wailea resort is likely to incur a daily parking fee, some of which can be upward of $20/day. Inquire if your resort has a parking fee and factor this into the cost of the rental. One perk of the Makena Beach and Golf Resort is that there isn't any parking fee. Second, when it comes to parking in Kihei, spots along the street in the Kamaole II area can be tough to come by during the middle of the day, so either arrive at the beach early or be prepared to do a little walking. Third, the only public parking lot where you will encounter a fee in South Maui is in Ma'alaea, where spaces are charged at a rate of $5 for the day. While having a car is a necessity for anyone wanting to do a lot of exploring, those who just want to relax on the beach and make sporadic ventures elsewhere can get by with a combination of walking, shuttles, public buses, and taxis.

CAR

Car Rentals

If you've already made your way to Kihei and decide you need a rental car, you don't need to go all the way back to Kahului. There are a number of local options to get you out on the road. One of the most popular services is family-owned **Kihei Rent a Car** (96 Kio Loop, 808/879-7257 or 800/251-5288, www.kihei-rentacar.com). They will even arrange a free pickup or drop-off at the Kahului Airport for rentals longer than five days. The cars are used, but that means you don't need to worry about looking like a tourist—there's less chance thieves will break into your car. Since these cars already have a few dings, you don't have to worry about scratching a shiny new Mustang.

Rates are competitive and often beat out the major corporate competitors.

If you would rather get those corporate rewards point, **Avis** (1455 S. Kihei Rd., 808/874-4077, 8am-5pm Mon.-Fri., 8am-4pm weekends) has an outlet in central Kihei right next to Maui Dive Shop and Pizza Madness.

Taxi

To have someone do the driving for you and not worry about pesky details such as parking, directions, or being sober, the best taxi service in Kihei is **MJ Taxi** (808/280-9309, mauijimtaxi@hotmail.com).

Shuttle

For those who are staying at the Makena Beach and Golf Resort, a **complimentary shuttle** (808/875-5833, 6am-9:30pm) runs on a first-come, first-served time schedule between the areas of Wailea and Makena Resort. Although the shuttle can't take you any farther than the Shops at Wailea, you can then hop on the Maui Bus if you need to connect to another location.

Anyone needing a ride to the airport can contact **Roberts Hawaii** (866/293-1782, www.robertshawaii.com/mauiexpress). Expect fares to run $13-41 per person depending on where you're staying and the number of people in your party.

Motorcycles and Mopeds

If you just want to cruise around town on a small moped or feel the wind through your hair on a steel horse, there are a number of different operators in town to choose from.

In the Azeka Makai shopping center in North Kihei, **Hawaiian Island Cruisers** (1280 S. Kihei Rd., 808/446-1111, www.

SOUTH MAUI

hawaiiancruisers.com, 9am-5pm Mon.-Sat., 10am-2pm Sun.) offers mopeds which range from $35/day to $300/week.

In the Kukui Mall in central Kihei, **Maui Boy Mopeds** (1819 S. Kihei Rd., 808/874-8811, www.mauiboymopeds.com, 8am-5pm daily) has rentals from $15 for two hours to $300/week, and they usually offer the most competitive rates around town.

In the Kamaole Shopping Center beneath Denny's, **Aloha Motorsports** (2463 S. Kihei Rd., 808/667-7000, www.alohamotorsports.com, 8am-5pm daily) rents out everything from Harleys ($119 for four hours) to mopeds ($343/week). They sometimes offer free hotel pickup.

Bus

For the most economical way to get around the island other than your two feet, the **Maui Bus** has a number of lines that operate throughout South Maui. All sections are $2/boarding, or you can also buy a $4/day pass if you know you'll be hopping on and off a lot. The Kihei Villager Route #15 runs between Ma'alaea Harbor Village and Pi'ilani Shopping Center 6:05am-8:30pm with various stops in between. The Kihei Islander Route #10 runs between Wailea Ike Drive by the Shops at Wailea and Queen Ka'ahumanu Center in Kahului 5:30am-9:30pm, and if you are trying to get to North Kihei or Ma'alaea, you can transfer at Pi'ilani Shopping Center to the Kihei Villager Route #15. For those trying to make it to the west side of the island early and quick, a commuter bus leaves from the corner of Kilohana Street and South Kihei Road at 6:15am and reaches the Ritz-Carlton in Kapalua at 7:45am, making various stops along the way. This is convenient if you have a morning boat charter out of Lahaina Harbor or need to get to Ka'anapali.

UPCOUNTRY

Upcountry is Maui's little secret. Occupying the slopes of the towering 10,023-foot Haleakala Volcano, it's a far cry from the postcard-perfect beaches and resort-lined shores so often equated with the island—although the sunsets are equally as spectacular. Here the smell of eucalyptus trees replaces the rustle of palms and ranching and farming still dominate the local lifestyle. Upcountry is where you throw on a light flannel and take a morning drive through the crisp mountain air, perhaps stopping to relax on the porch of a family-run coffeehouse where the patrons and staff all know one another by name. It's a place to hike on the forested trails of Polipoli or Hosmer's Grove, take in the view from the summit of Haleakala, or gaze all the way to the shoreline from 2,000 feet while tasting wine at Maui's only vineyard. It's also Maui's most artistic community. In the ranching town turned New Age outpost of Makawao, it's just as easy to buy a saddle as it is to purchase freshly blown glass or boutique clothing. Whether you're catching a Sunday morning polo match, eating freshly baked, homemade doughnuts, or buying farm-fresh vegetables straight from the source, you'll see a side of Maui you never expected.

© KYLE ELLISON

HIGHLIGHTS

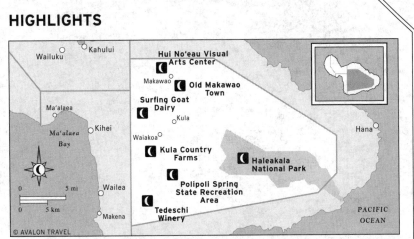

LOOK FOR TO FIND RECOMMENDED SIGHTS, ACTIVITIES, DINING, AND LODGING.

Polipoli Spring State Recreation Area: Hidden in the least-visited corner of the island, Polipoli is the only place on Maui where you can walk through a redwood forest set high up in the clouds (page 226).

Hui No'eau Visual Arts Center: This old Baldwin family mansion now houses one of the island's largest art centers, giving Makawao one of the biggest art scenes on Maui (page 239).

Kula Country Farms: Catch sweeping views over most of the island while picking up fresh produce straight from the farm (page 239).

Surfing Goat Dairy: Take the only tour on Maui where you can both snack on gourmet cheeses and hand-milk a goat (page 243).

Tedeschi Winery: Sip on either pineapple or grape wine and enjoy an elk burger at the neighboring grill (page 244).

Haleakala National Park: While sunrise gets all of the attention, sunset from atop Haleakala is just as spectacular and doesn't involve waking up at 3am (page 244).

Old Makawao Town: Linger for a while in a ranching-turned-arts town that manages to be New Age and rustic all at the same time (page 250).

Hiking and Biking

HIKING
Haleakala National Park

Anyone who hikes across Haleakala Crater will swear they could be on the moon, or Mars, but surely not Maui. The crater basin is a 19-square-mile volcanic panorama criss-crossed by colorful cinder cones and 28 miles of trails. It's a place of adventure and of silence. More important, this high-altitude moonscape is also home to the best hiking on Maui. If you're an outdoors enthusiast, no trip to Maui is complete without tackling at least one of Haleakala's trails. With that thought in mind, here's a rundown of the most popular hikes,

UPCOUNTRY

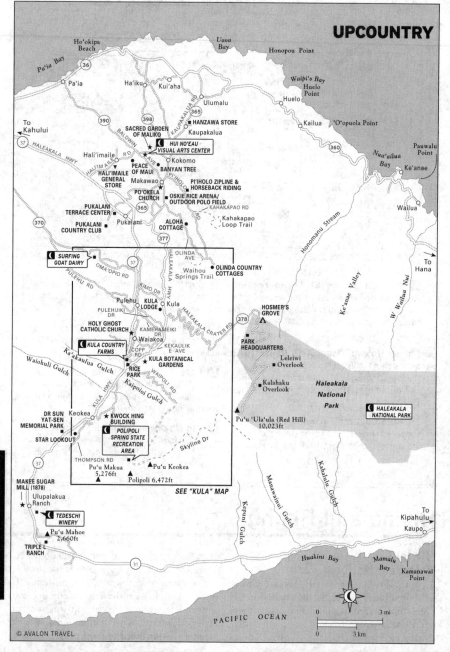

UPCOUNTRY

Ho'okipa Beach
Pa'ia Bay
Pa'ia
36
To Kahului
37
HALEAKALA HWY
390
398
Ha'iku
Kui'aha
Uaoa Bay
Honopou Point
Waipi'o Bay
Huelo Point
Huelo
'O'opuola Point
Kailua
Ulumalu
365
HANZAWA STORE
SACRED GARDEN OF MALIKO
Kaupakalua
Nua'ailua Bay
Ke'ane
Pauwalu Point
Hali'imaile
HUI NO'EAU VISUAL ARTS CENTER
360
To Hana
Kokomo
PEACE OF MAUI
BANYAN TREE
HALI'IMAILE GENERAL STORE
Makawao
PO'OKELA CHURCH
PI'IHOLO ZIPLINE & HORSEBACK RIDING
OSKIE RICE ARENA/OUTDOOR POLO FIELD
KAHAKAPAO RD
Kahakapao Loop Trail
PUKALANI TERRACE CENTER
365
PUKALANI COUNTRY CLUB
Pukalani
370
377
ALOHA COTTAGE
OLINDA AVE
SURFING GOAT DAIRY
OMA'OPIO RD
37
PULEHU RD
KIMO DR
Waihou Springs Trail
OLINDA COUNTRY COTTAGES
Pulehu
PULEHUIKI DR
KULA LODGE
Kula
HOLY GHOST CATHOLIC CHURCH
KAMEHAMEIKI DR
Waiakoa
HALEAKALA CRATER RD
378
HOSMER'S GROVE
PARK HEADQUARTERS
Leleiwi Overlook
Kalahaku Overlook
Haleakala National Park
HALEAKALA NATIONAL PARK
Ke'anae Valley
Honomanu Stream
W Wailua Nui
Wailua
KULA COUNTRY FARMS
Ka'akau'ula Gulch
COPP RD
KEKAULIK E AVE
KULA BOTANICAL GARDENS
RICE PARK
WAIPOLI RD
Waiohuli Gulch
KULA HWY
Kaipoioi Gulch
DR SUN YAT-SEN MEMORIAL PARK
Keokea
KWOCK HING BUILDING
STAR LOOKOUT
POLIPOLI SPRING STATE RECREATION AREA
Skyline Dr
Pu'u 'Ula'ula (Red Hill) 10,023ft
THOMPSON RD
Pu'u Makua 5,276ft
Pu'u Keokea
Polipoli 6,472ft
SEE "KULA" MAP
37
MAKEE SUGAR MILL (1878)
Ulupalakua Ranch
TEDESCHI WINERY
Pu'u Mahoe 2,660ft
TRIPLE L RANCH
31
Kepuni Gulch
Manawainui Gulch
Kahalulu Gulch
To Kipahulu
Kaupo
Huakini Bay
Mamalu Bay
Kamanawai Point
PACIFIC OCEAN

0   3 mi
0   3 km

© AVALON TRAVEL

listed from shortest to longest (*all mileage is round-trip*).

PA KA'OAO

If you don't feel like sharing the visitor center lookout with 400 other people at sunrise, take this five-minute trail to the top of White Hill for a little more breathing room (although you'll be huffing on the walk up there). This 0.4-mile trail departs from the parking lot at the summit visitor center and offers views down into the crater floor below.

LELEIWI OVERLOOK

This is the "secret" sunrise spot favored by locals and return visitors. Many assume that the best views will be from the top, but in some cases this just isn't true. From **Leleiwi Overlook,** the view down into the crater is the same as from the summit—but it isn't as far, and it isn't as cold. Halfway between the park headquarters and the summit, pull off into the parking lot at mile marker 17.5 (about 8,800 feet in elevation) and follow a 0.5-mile trail through the subalpine brush. At first it won't look like you're going anywhere exciting, but after a few minutes you reach the rim of the crater and are awarded with colors which spring from the earth. This is a nice option if you are running late for the sunrise, and as an added bonus there are rarely more than a handful of people watching the spectacle with you. Since this lookout faces east, however, sunset isn't as nice.

HOSMER'S GROVE NATURE TRAIL

Unlike other trails in the park, the **Hosmer's Grove Nature Trail** is at the lower park boundary just after you enter the park. This easy, 0.5-mile trail leads you through a stand of trees introduced in 1910 to see if any would be good for commercial lumber. There are more than 20 different species here. Here you'll see Jeffrey pine, ponderosa pine, incense cedar, eucalyptus, Norway spruce, Douglas fir, and Japanese sugi. Several signs are posted along the trail to explain about the trees, and this is also a good spot to look for native birds. To reach the trailhead, make a left on the road pointing toward the campground immediately after entering the park. The walk should take a half hour over mostly level ground.

KA LU'U O KA O'O

If you don't have a full day (or couple of days) to devote to a hike across the crater floor, a nice option is the 5.5-mile descent to the **Ka Lu'u O Ka O'o** cinder cone. This hike departs from the Sliding Sands trailhead and drops two miles down into the crater, or about halfway down Sliding Sands trail.

SLIDING SANDS TRAIL (KEONEHE'EHE'E TRAIL)

Starting at the summit visitors center (at 9,800 ft. in elevation) **Sliding Sands** descends 2,500 vertical feet to the crater floor below. Like a lonely vein switchbacking its way across the dark side of the moon, Sliding Sands is a barren, windswept, shadeless, and stunning conduit from the craggy summit to the cinder cone desert before you. If you just hike down to the crater floor and back, it's an eight-mile round-trip, although continuing to Kapalaoa Cabin tacks an additional 3.5 miles on to the hike. Due to the elevation, coming back up Sliding Sands can be challenging even for the fittest of hikers.

SWITCHBACK TRAIL (HALEMAU'U TRAIL)

Beginning from an altitude of only 7,990 feet, the first 1.1 miles of this trail meander through subalpine scrub brush before eventually bringing you to the edge of a 1,000-foot cliff. The view down into the Ko'olau Gap is better here than from the summit area. Although the trail is well-defined, the drop-offs can be disconcerting for those with a fear of heights. After losing over 1,000 feet in elevation, the trail passes Holua Cabin after 3.7 miles and continues on to Silversword Loop, a section of the crater floor known for its dense concentration of *ahinahina,* or endangered silversword plants. While it's possible to connect with the greater network of trails from this point, Silversword

Loop usually marks the turnaround point for this 9.2-mile round-trip hike.

SLIDING SANDS-SWITCHBACK LOOP

If you're a fit person, have an entire day to spare, and want to experience the best of Haleakala Crater, then this is hands-down the best day hike in the summit area of the park. Since this is a point-to-point trail, you're going to end up six miles from where you started, so either drive two cars up the mountain or sweet-talk a fellow visitor into letting you hitch a ride.

While the loop can be hiked in either direction, the most popular—and far less strenuous—route begins at Sliding Sands trailhead and exits via ascending the Switchback Trail. Along the path of this 12.2 mile-journey you experience the full spectrum of Haleakala wonders, from the frosty, mystical summit, to the otherworldly solitude of the crater floor.

If you're looking for an adventure, hike this trail at night under a full moon. At this altitude you're frequently above the clouds, and the moonlight reflecting off the cinder is so bright that you can walk without the use of a flashlight (though you should, of course, still carry one). If the moon rises early, depart the summit at sunset, and if the moon rises later in the evening, begin at about midnight and finish your hike at sunrise. There are few more surreal feelings than walking completely alone, bundled against the chill of the night air, hearing the crunch of volcanic cinder beneath your feet, bathed in moonlight amid a panorama of geological wonder, only to cap off the experience by watching the sun gradually set the colors of the mountain ablaze. Should you attempt to hike the crater by moonlight, it's best to be overly prepared. Bring a backpack full of extra clothing, carry extra water, pack an extra flashlight. You'll be exposed to windchills that can dip below freezing at any time of the year.

KAUPO GAP

"Shooting the gap" is the most extreme hike on the island. It takes two days, covers 17.5 miles, and has an elevation drop of 9,500 feet. In order to complete the hike you need to be in prime physical condition and comfortable in the backcountry. The majority of hikers spend the night at Paliku Cabin, which at a distance of 9.2 miles from Sliding Sands trailhead is the remotest—and lushest—of the crater's three backcountry cabins. For those without a cabin reservation there is a primitive campsite at Paliku; free permits can be arranged at the park headquarters. On the second day of the hike you'll make a steep descent from Paliku, pass through a gate that marks the park boundary, and continue across private land (which is allowed) from here until Kaupo Store. Once outside of the park boundary, keep a lookout for axis deer and feral goats, as they will occasionally leap across the trail. You finish the hike in the semi-deserted outpost of Kaupo at a distance of 53 road miles from where you started, so if you ever want to make it back to civilization, you either have to arrange a ride or convince the rare passerby to shuttle your sweaty, backcountry body all the way to the other side of the island. If you're up for the challenge, however, pack accordingly, be prepared, let someone know where you're going, and take lots of pictures. There aren't many places in America as pristine as what you'll find out here.

◖ Polipoli Spring State Recreation Area

Polipoli is an out-of-the-way, rarely visited destination offering some of the best hiking on the island. The trails at Polipoli pass through stands of old-growth redwoods, eucalyptus, ash, and pines. To reach Polipoli, drive on Highway 37 (Kula Highway) as if you were heading to Ulupalakua Ranch and the Tedeschi Winery. At the second junction of Highways 37 and 377 (just past Kula Country Farms), make a left on Highway 377 and travel for 0.3 mile until you reach Waipoli Road, where you will take a right. Follow Waipoli Road for about a mile until it crosses a cattle guard, and continue on the switchbacking road through the pastures. This is the scenic—and only—entranceway for vehicles to reach the hiking trails above.

The first hike you'll encounter in Polipoli

is the **Waiakoa Loop Trail,** which begins just after the hut at the hunter's check-in station. The trailhead technically doesn't begin for 0.75 mile down the hunter access road, but unless you have a four-wheel-drive vehicle, it's better to park at the hunter's station and walk down to the trailhead. Once you are there, a three-mile loop with a moderate elevation change of 400 feet passes through lowland brush and pines. The area around Waiakoa is also popular with hunters, so stay on the trail and wear bright clothing.

Farther up the switchbacking road, just past the cattle guard (where the road turns to dirt) is the trailhead for the **Boundary Trail,** a 4.4-mile one-way trail that descends down to the lower fence line of Polipoli before connecting with other trails. This trail offers sweeping views of South Maui and—since it's about 1,000 vertical feet lower than some of the other trails—won't leave you quite as winded. This can either be done as an out-and-back hike or combined with other trails as a loop. The shortest loop is to go up the **Lower Waiohuli Trail,** which intersects the Boundary Trail at the 2.6-mile mark. Turning left on the Lower Waiohuli Trail, it's 1.4 miles back uphill to the main road, and then a 2.5-mile trek back along the dirt road to your car.

If seven miles seems too far, most of the shorter walks in Polipoli begin and end at the campground at the end of the road. While some are only a mile long, the best hike in the park for first-time visitors is the 5.3-mile loop trail formed by connecting the **Haleakala Ridge Trail, Polipoli Trail, Redwood Trail,** and **Plum Trail.** This loop departs from the parking lot by the campground and winds its way through redwoods, pines, and plum trees which occasionally bear fruit during the summer. Bring water on the trail and pack a light jacket in case the mists roll in. Hunters sometimes patrol these same areas, so stick to the well-signed and established trails.

For those who are in good shape, it's possible to hike all the way from Polipoli to the summit of Haleakala by following the 6.8-mile dirt road known as **Skyline Drive.** This road provides a "back entrance" into Haleakala National Park that few people know about, and even fewer actually take. If it has snowed recently on top of Haleakala and the rangers have the main road closed down, this is an alternative way to hike into the park and be the only person in a tropical snowstorm. Even on regular days, however, Skyline is a strenuous hike which provides panoramic views down the southwest rift zone of Haleakala. Though Haleakala has been dormant for more than 220 years, volcanologists claim that if (and when) the mountain erupts again, magma would seep from the earth in the barren landscape that's visible from this trail.

To reach the Skyline Drive trailhead, turn left at the fork that leads down to the campground from the main dirt road. From here the road keeps climbing and begins to double back toward the north, along the way passing the trailhead for the 1.8-mile **Mamane Trail.** Eventually you'll reach a locked gate at an area known as The Ballpark; from this 7,000-foot elevation it's a 3,000-foot vertical switchback to the summit. Pack plenty of water and warm clothing and be aware of the challenges of hiking at altitude.

Makawao

While much of the land behind Makawao is either privately owned ranchland or part of the state watershed system, two well-maintained trails provide Makawao hikers with a couple of options for getting back into the forest.

In the heart of the Makawao Forest Reserve, the **Kahakapao Loop Trail** is popular with hikers, bikers, and families taking their dogs for a walk. This 5.7-mile loop trail climbs its way through the sweet smell of eucalyptus, Cook pines, tropical ash, and a handful of other native plant species in the cool air at 3,000 feet, and you would expect to find a trail like this is New England or Oregon, but not in Maui. This trail is a favorite of Upcountry locals.

To reach the trailhead from Makawao, follow Makawao Avenue toward Ha'iku for 0.3 mile before making a right on Pi'iholo Road. After 1.5 miles (just past the Pi'iholo zipline

POLIPOLI: THE LAST FRONTIER

While no official visitor statistics are kept, there's a good chance that **Polipoli Spring State Recreation Area** is the least visited corner of Maui. Even a place as desolate as Kaupo sees more people on a daily basis than the forested trails and barren slopes of Haleakala's southwestern flank. High above the protea farms, the lavender farm, the disc golf course, and even the paragliding school, the area known as Polipoli exists almost as an afterthought; so far removed from the rest of the island most visitors don't even know it's there.

As any outdoors enthusiast might expect, it's this isolation and remoteness that make Polipoli such an enchanting place. Set between 5,300 and 7,100 feet in elevation, this section of mountainside sees mists that slowly roll across it to create a panorama which at one minute can offer sweeping views down to the shorelines, and in the next completely envelop the treetops and reduce visibility to a couple of feet. Bathed in the scent of redwood and pine (yes, there are redwoods and pines on Maui), it's a magical, spooky, and refreshing place that offers visitors a literal breath of fresh air.

This 10-acre recreational area of the Kula Forest Reserve was extensively planted with nonnative trees (such as redwoods) during the 1930s as part of the Civilian Conservation Corps (CCC). A large clearing at 7,000 feet is nicknamed The Ballpark because this is where corps members would gather on their lunch break to play high-altitude games of softball and baseball. Although no more ball games take place on the mountain, Polipoli is frequented by hikers and hunters looking for wild boar, goat, and ring-necked pheasant. A massive wildfire in 2007 ignited over 1,000 acres of the mountainside, and charred stands of trees still poke out from areas of new growth. This is also the island's premier mountain biking destination, where a forested woodland of downhill and single-track provides a ride that's more akin to something you'd find in Northern California than high up on a tropical island.

Mornings offer the clearest views for hiking in Polipoli, and for anyone wanting to get an early start on the trail, there is one small campground as well as a rustic cabin which can accommodate up to 10 people (no electricity). Both are reachable by following the steep, switchbacking Waipoli Road 9.7 miles upland from Kekaulike Highway (Hwy 377), the last four miles of which are unpaved (four-wheel drive recommended). For cabin reservations ($60/night residents, $90/night nonresidents) contact the **Division of State Parks** in Wailuku (54 S. High St., Rm. 101, 808/984-8109, weekdays 8am-3:30pm). Make campground reservations ($12/night) online at www.hawaiistateparks.org.

---

tours) take a left where the road forks and follow it for 0.5 miles. Here you'll make a right onto Kahakapao Road and drive 1.5 miles on a narrow uphill until you reach a metal gate which is open 7am-7pm. From the gate, a steep asphalt road continues for another 0.5 mile until it reaches a gravel parking lot in front of the trailhead. As this is a multiuse trail network, keep an eye out for bikers.

If you don't feel like dealing with bikers on your relaxing morning stroll, you're better off heading to the two-mile-long **Waihou Spring Trail** toward the top of Olinda Road. This trail is only open to hikers and doesn't have as steep an elevation gain as the one at Kahakapao. It's uniquely situated among a pine tree experiment so that all the pines appear like towering rows of corn. While the wooded trail is nice enough for walking, the treat is at the end where a brief, steep switchback descends down into an old irrigation gulch. In the 30-foot rock face at the end of the trail you can make out tunnels bored through the rock. You can climb into the tunnels and follow them back for a bit, although it's tough to do without a light. To reach the Waihou Springs trailhead, go to the only intersection in Makawao and follow Olinda Road uphill for five miles

© KYLE ELLISON

Waihou Springs Trail

before you see the pine-needle parking lot on the right.

BIKING

With miles of open road and some of the best trails on Maui, Upcountry is the most popular part of the island for both road bikers and mountain bikers. The air up here is nice and cool, the views stretch all the way to the ocean below, and the traffic levels are lower than on many of the island's other main roads. The only rental operator Upcountry is in downtown Makawao: **Krank Cycles** (1120 Makawao Ave., 808/572-2299, www. krankmaui.com, 8am-6pm daily) specializes in mountain bike rentals ($60/day, $220/week). For road cycles, the closest options are **Haleakala Bike Company** (810 Ha'iku Rd., #120, 808/575-9575 or 888/922-2452, www. bikemaui.com, 8:30am-5pm Mon.-Sat., 9am-4pm Sun.) in Ha'iku and **Maui Cyclery** (99 Hana Hwy., 808/579-9009, www.gocycling-maui.com, 8am-6pm Mon.-Fri., 8am-4pm Sat., 8am-noon Sun.) in Pa'ia.

Road Cycling

For avid cyclists there are few better climbs in the United States than the 10,000-foot ascent up Haleakala Volcano. If biking for 36 miles straight *uphill* sounds like something only crazy people would do, consider that over 140 people took part in the 2013 Cycle to the Sun race which goes from the warm beaches of Pa'ia to the frigid air of the summit.

If, however, you want to enjoy the Haleakala panorama without having to aggressively strain your quads, a better choice is to **bike down Haleakala,** where the most strenuous thing you'll have to do is flex your fingers as you pump the brakes. One of the most popular visitor activities on the island, the "ride down the volcano" has become tamer in recent years due to the fact you can only bike from the summit on your own personal bike. Anyone on a rental is now only allowed to bike from the 6,500-foot level outside of the park boundaries. The National Park Service couldn't take on the liability of potential injuries, so touring companies cannot shuttle people with bicycles to the summit.

UPCOUNTRY

© KYLE ELLISON

Bike 6,500 feet down the side of dormant volcano Haleakala.

For those who employ basic safety, however, this ride is a great way to tour Upcountry. Since you can no longer ride down from the summit on a rental—but nearly all people want to see Haleakala Crater—tour companies will drive cyclists to the top of the mountain to view the sunrise (or simply peer into the crater if it's a later trip), and then everyone climbs back into the van to head down to 6,500 feet. While this largely detracts from what the ride used to be, the ride from the boundary of the park down to sea level still takes you through the scenic pasturelands of Kula, the cowboy town of Makawao, and finishes on the beach at Pa'ia where sea salt blows on the afternoon trade winds. Even though all companies must start at the same location, there are still a number of differences between tour groups as to where the ride finishes and how they're set up.

If you're the type of person who doesn't move with a herd, yet you still want to see the sunrise, your best bet is going to be **Haleakala Bike Company** (810 Ha'iku Rd., #120, 808/575-9575 or 888/922-2452, www.bikemaui.com,

8:30am-5pm Mon.-Sat., 9am-4pm Sun.) giving you the freedom to descend without a guide. This is the only company that has this option for a sunrise tour. The benefit is that once you're dropped off at the top you're free to make as many stops on the ride down as you'd like. Should you want to stop at a protea farm, pull over to photograph the pasturelands, peruse the shops of Makawao, or stop and get a coffee three times in an effort to wake up, you can do so. If you chose to catch the shuttle from your hotel, however, you can't linger forever because you need to be back by 11am. Alternately, you can drive yourself to the Ha'iku office in the morning. The downside of the Haleakala Bike Company tour is that since the office is in Ha'iku (at around the 1,000 feet), you don't get the opportunity to ride all the way down to the beach. If you "make a wrong turn" and decide to end up at the beach in Pa'ia anyway, they'll still come and pick you up, but it's going to cost you an extra fee. Tours available are the sunrise tour ($120), a 9am tour ($85), and an express tour which doesn't include the trip into

Haleakala National Park ($70). If you're set on biking from the summit, Haleakala Bike Company also provides rentals if you can find someone to drop you at the top.

If you would feel more comfortable biking down with a guide, companies such as **Maui Downhill** (199 Dairy Rd., 808/871-2155, www.mauidownhill.com) provide guided services down the volcano with well-trained guides who stick with you every step of the way. Tipping the guides tacks on an added expense (in addition to being far more expensive in the first place). The sunrise tours will cost more ($149), although you can shave a few dollars off the price by driving yourself to the Kahului base-yard and opting to reach the summit after sunrise ($119). They do provide warm clothing and gloves, but the lunch in Pukalani isn't included, and you finish the last 1,500 feet of the journey on a van ride back to Kahului headquarters. Other trips available are the express excursion which goes directly to the 6,500-foot starting point (and doesn't include hotel pickup) for $109 or a trip which combines the descent with a van tour out to the Tedeschi Winery ($129).

If finishing the ride next to the ocean is a must, **Cruiser Phil's** (58 A Amala Pl., 808/893-2332 or 877/764-2453, www.cruiserphil.com, 7am-7pm daily) offers riders the ability to bike from 6,500 feet all the way down to the beach in Pa'ia ($150). The section of road between Makawao and Pa'ia passes pineapple fields and historic churches, and it's a much better option than finishing in Pukalani or Ha'iku. Day trips that don't view the sunrise are also available ($135), or if you would like to ride independently with Cruiser Phil's ($99), on select days of the week you can meet a guide at 8:15am in Pa'ia and be driven up the mountain from there. Tours eat breakfast/lunch in either Kula or Pa'ia, although the cost of the meal isn't included in the trip. This is a good tour if you want to ride independently all the way to Pa'ia and don't care if you see the sunrise. Companies offering similar itineraries and services are **Maui Mountain Cruisers** (381 Baldwin Ave., 808/871-6014, www.mauimountaincruisers.com, 9am-5pm

weekdays, 10am-4pm weekends), **Mountain Riders** (15 South Wakea Ave., 808/877-4944, www.mountainriders.com), and **Bike It Maui** (808/878-3364, www.bikeitmaui.com), all of which finish in the town of Pa'ia. **Maui Easy Riders** (808/344-9489, www.mauieasyriders.com) is the island's newest bike company, with tours beginning at 9am

For regular road cyclists who aren't looking to ride down the volcano, one of the best Upcountry rides is the stretch of highway from Kula to Kanaio. Starting at Rice Park off Kula Highway (Hwy. 37), the 30-mile round-trip takes you south through the communities of Keokea, Ulupalakua, and finally to Kanaio, a dry ranching outpost on the "back road" to Hana. There's a 500-foot elevation drop from Kula to Kanaio, and the views along this ride span from the north shore all the way to Makena and Lahaina. This is a popular weekend ride where cyclists often take halftime at Grandma's Coffee House in Keokea, and the scent of eucalyptus and freshly cut grass accompany you on the entire trip.

Mountain Biking

Many people are surprised to learn that on an island best known for its ocean activities there is decent mountain biking. While it doesn't compare to places such as Tahoe or Moab, there are still downhill rides and single-track trails where even the most hard-core mountain biker can still have a good time.

The area with the most trails is the **Polipoli** section of mountainside high above the pastures of Kula. While a number of the trails in Polipoli are rated as pedestrian only, the **Waiakoa Loop Trail** is a three-mile loop with a 400-foot elevation gain which is open to both hikers and bikers. To reach Waiakoa, travel up Waipoli Road off Highway 377, go past the lavender farm, and park your car off the side of the road just past the hunter's check-in station. The trailhead is 0.75 mile down a four-wheel-drive access road. Since this is also a hunting area, wear bright clothing. Toward the top of Waipoli Road, the pavement changes to dirt, and a good ride is to park your car where the

BIKING THE VOLCANO

For those who are prepared, riding a bike down Haleakala can be one of the best days of your vacation. Those who go about it the wrong way, however, may potentially be setting themselves up for a miserable experience. Nobody wants to be miserable on vacation, so here are some tips to ensure the ride is exactly the trip you were hoping for.

- If you go with a rental company, you can no longer ride from the summit, and instead must begin biking at the 6,500-foot level. If you want to bike from the summit, you need to provide your own bicycle and transport.

- Seeing the sunrise isn't guaranteed. On 85 percent of sunrise excursions you will actually be able to see the sunrise, but on the other 15 percent of days the crater will be socked in with clouds. The variations aren't even seasonal, so all you can do is hope for the best.

- If you're planning on joining a bike tour for sunrise, be prepared to wake up *really* early. Since companies will collect guests from the farthest hotels first, if you're staying in Makena or Kapalua you can expect to meet your van driver at as early as 1:45am. Given the odd hours, try to book this excursion on the first couple days of your trip when you're still jet-lagged and waking up early. Depending on where you're coming from and the time of year, Maui is 2-6 hours behind the continental U.S., so when you factor in the natural jet lag it doesn't seem nearly as early.

- If you visit in summer, you will lose an hour of sleep because the sun is rising an hour earlier.

- If you're on a budget and don't care about the sunrise, choose a midmorning tour. It isn't as cold, you don't have to wake up as early, it isn't as crowded, and the trips are substantially cheaper, even though you're doing the exact same thing. There are only two reasons why bike companies charge more for the sunrise tours: because they're popular and because they can.

- Pack closed-toe shoes, long pants, a rain jacket, and warm clothing. Early morning temperatures can often dip below freezing at the summit, and although many tour companies provide rain gear, the more protection you have against the elements, the better.

- Ask if your company provides gloves. Even if you are wearing four jackets while riding, the wind generated from your speed will be frigid against your fingers.

- Keep your eyes on the road, and only take pictures if you are pulled over at a stop.

- Keep an eye out for cattle, other bikers, oncoming traffic, and debris in the road.

- Don't expect to get any sleep in the van ride up. The road switchbacks so many times you can never get in a rhythm, and tour bus drivers are usually entertaining the crowd with island history and jokes. It's best to just get a good sleep the night before.

- If you're a little skittish, go with a guided group. If you're an independent person, choose an independent company where you can ride down without a guide. The only option for watching the sunrise and riding independently is with Haleakala Bike Company, but know that with this company you can't ride all the way to the beach (without paying an extra fee).

- Don't schedule a ride down Haleakala on a day after scuba diving. In order to avoid decompression sickness, don't fly or travel to higher altitudes for 24 hours after diving.

- Most bike companies have age restrictions of 12 years old and weight restrictions of 250 pounds. Pregnant women cannot participate.

- Don't schedule a lu'au for the evening of the bike ride. You've been up since 2am. You're exhausted. This is a good afternoon for lounging and being lazy.

Upper Waiohuli Trail and Mamane Trail intersect the dirt road. From here you can ride a loop trail where you climb the dirt road, turn left where the road forks, and continue climbing until you reach the trailhead for the Mamane Trail, which offers a two-mile, single-track descent back down to your car. If you want to tack on a few more miles before bombing down the Mamane Trail, ride Kahua Road out to the hunting shelter and back before heading back down to your car.

While the Waiakoa Loop Trail and Mamane Trail are fine rides, the best ride in Polipoli (and the entire island) is the dirt road known as **Skyline Drive.** From the trailhead of the Mamane Trail it's about six more miles up the southwestern ridge of the mountain to the summit of Haleakala, and the switchbacking ascent is so steep in places that you'll occasionally need to get off and walk your bike. If you park your car at the Polipoli campground, it's about 8.5 miles to the summit, or, if you have four-wheel drive, you can take your car all the way up to a locked gate at area known as The Ballpark. Even if you start at The Ballpark, however, it's a 3,000-foot climb before you reach the summit of Haleakala, with the reward, of course, being the screamer of a descent you're awarded on the way down.

So how do you combine all of these trails into the ultimate, hands-down, best mountain bike ride on Maui? Begin by having someone drop you off at the summit of Haleakala and start Skyline Drive at the top! To reach the start of Skyline Drive, when approaching from the summit, drive as if you're going to the observation platform in the upper parking lot, but before you get there, take a left on the service road which leads toward Science City. On the left-hand side of this service road, you'll see a locked gate, and the dirt road that's on the other side is the start of the Skyline Trail. Beginning from this point, you'll switchback down Skyline Drive for six miles before linking up with the Mamane Trail, at which point you will enjoy the two miles of single-track down to the dirt portion of Waipoli Road. Take a right and begin riding down Waipoli Road until it turns to pavement. If you're feeling like an extra workout, you can branch off and tackle the Waiakoa Loop Trail on your way down. Ascend from the loop trail back to the main road, and then continue down Waipoli Road all the way to Highway 377. From here, go left, down to Highway 37, then left again, and finish your epic ride with a two-mile gradual descent on pavement to Grandma's Coffee House in Keokea for a celebratory lunch. Along the ride you will have dropped more than 7,000 vertical feet. Arrange to have someone pick you up here to cap off what is the best mountain descent on the island.

If you don't have a day to devote to a downhill epic, however, and are just looking to squeeze in a couple of hours on the trail, the **Kahakapao Loop Trail** in the Makawao Forest Reserve offers a 5.7-mile loop that climbs its way through eucalyptus, pine, and a handful of native plants. At 3,000 feet, the cool mountain air combined with the dense forest gives the feeling of riding in British Columbia or the foothills of Vermont, but certainly not somewhere that's only 20 minutes from the beach. From the gravel parking lot a 0.5-mile entry trail leads to a junction where bikers can choose between the east and west loops. In planning for the descent, note that the west loop has more jumps, but the east loop is a smoother ride. Granted, you could always ride it both ways and decide for yourself. Aside from Polipoli, this is going to be the epicenter of the island's mountain biking community.

PANIOLO COUNTRY

Anyone headed Upcountry is sure to hear the term *paniolo* at least a couple of times, particularly when wandering around Makawao. While most locals will tell you that *paniolo* is simply the Hawaiian word for cowboy, the term also encapsulates a unique portion of Hawai'i's heritage which continues to thrive Upcountry.

In 1793 the British explorer George Vancouver gave a few cattle to Kamehameha I on the Big Island of Hawai'i, and after a few of the cattle were killed, Kamehameha placed a *kapu*—taboo—on the slaying of all cattle so that the population would have time to thrive. By 1830, when the *kapu* was lifted, tens of thousands of wild cattle ran amok over the Hawaiian Islands to the point of being a nuisance. With wild steers destroying crops and endangering lives, in 1832 King Kamehameha III sent an adviser to California to find someone—anyone—who could find a way to deal with the cattle explosion. When the king's adviser returned with three Mexican *vaqueros*, they immediately set to work teaching the Hawaiians how to train horses and rope cattle. The strange-sounding foreign language these men spoke, *español* would be the basis for today's word for Hawaiian cowboys—*paniolo*.

With this newfound ability to domesticate wild herds, the Hawaiian *paniolos* set up ranches in areas such as Waimea on the Big Island and on the slopes of Haleakala, Maui. These Hawaiian cowboys predated those of the American West, and by the time the first U.S. ranchers were staking their claims in California, the Hawaiian cowboys were already mastering their roping and riding. Ikua Purdy, a *paniolo* from the Big Island, not only won the World Championships of steer roping at the Cheyenne Frontier Days in 1908, but he was the first Hawaiian to be elected to the National Rodeo Cowboy Hall of Fame.

This rich ranching heritage continues in Upcountry today, where *paniolos* working on Haleakala Ranch (30,000 acres), Ulupalakua Ranch (20,000 acres), Ka'ono'ulu Ranch (10,000 acres), Thompson Ranch (1,400 acres), and Pi'iholo Ranch (800 acres), are still "the real deal." One of the largest annual Upcountry events is the Makawao Rodeo held over the Fourth of July weekend, and while Upcountry is quick to celebrate its *paniolo* past, ranching and agriculture continue to be a way of life here in the pastures of Haleakala.

Horseback Riding and Bird-Watching

HORSEBACK RIDING
Makawao

Sprawling across 800 acres, **Pi'iholo Ranch** (808/270-8750, www.piiholo.com, 8:30am-1pm Mon.-Sat.) is a working cattle operation set back in the pastures above Makawao. One-hour ($75), two-hour ($120), and private rides are available for journeys across open ranchland 2,000 feet up on the mountainside. Groups are capped at six people and the one-hour and two-hour rides go at a mellow pace. Coffee is provided for the early morning rides (8:30 and 9am), and every Tuesday and Thursday at 4pm there are free roping sessions open to the public

to come and enjoy. To reach Pi'iholo Ranch go 1.5 miles up Pi'iholo Road before branching left on to Waiahiwi Road. Follow this for 0.5 mile, and the sign for the ranch will be on the left.

Kula

In addition to offering fairly standard—though enjoyable—rides across the pastureland of Haleakala Ranch ($95-110), **Pony Express** (18303 Haleakala Hwy., 808/667-2200, www.ponyexpresstour.com) is the only operation on the island that takes you down inside the crater on horseback. Saddling up from the 9,800-foot level near the summit, riders depart down Sliding Sands Trail before eventually reaching the crater floor over 2,500 vertical feet below ($182). Over the course of this 7.5-mile, four-hour excursion, you're able to descend into the backcountry of Haleakala National Park and a realm accessible only by trail. It can be cold and breezy up here, but riding in the saddle as you crunch your way across an otherworldly panorama of cinder is a riding experience unlike any other on the island. In the days of the *paniolo*, before Haleakala was a national park, cowboys and ranchers would ride all the way into the crater to round up wild cattle. Although cattle no longer roam the barren moonscape, the time-sculpted theater still looks much the same as it did when those early ranchers rode these same trails. The horses that make this run are exceptionally well-trained and sure-footed, although you should have previous riding experience to take part in this tour.

Keokea and Ulupalakua

If you want the feeling that you're riding with a genuine ranching family in their scenic backyard, then book an excursion with the folks at **Thompson Ranch** (Middle Rd., 808/878-1910, www.thompsonranchmaui.com). The rides take place in the pastures of a working cattle ranch, and there isn't one thing about this ride that feels "touristy" in any way. You meet Jerry and Toni Thompson at their ranch house and then hitch a ride with them up to the horse stables, where you are introduced to your steed for the next two hours ($100). Once saddled up, you climb up toward the uppermost edge of the ranch where the pasture bumps into the edge of the Polipoli forest. Since this is all private land—and there is no other way to access this section of the mountain—riding across these pastures provides a glimpse into one of the only places in the United States where you can ride near forests of native koa and sandalwood trees and gaze down on the clear blue Pacific. This is a fantastic ride for couples or families looking for an off the beaten path riding experience.

To ride across the back of a dormant volcano on horseback, head to **Triple L Ranch** (15900 Pi'ilani Hwy., 808/280-7070, www.triplelranchmaui.com, 8am-6pm daily). The *paniolos* out here seem a little gruffer, a little tougher, and just a little more "cowboy." Maybe it's just the isolation of Kanaio, but something about being out here makes it feel more lawless and exciting. While one-hour and two-hour rides are offered for $125 and $150 (and include a voucher for a free Bully's Burger), the real reason to choose this ranch over any other is the chance to book either a half-day ($285) or full-day ($375) ride down to a rocky beach completely inaccessible from anywhere else on the island. Centuries ago this section of mountain sported a large native Hawaiian population, and along the way the guides will point out archaeological sites dating to the days of ancient Hawai'i. Furthermore, if you are an advanced rider and want to trot, canter, or gallop your horse, there isn't anyone who's going to stop you. Four miles past the Tedeschi Winery in Ulupalakua, this is truly the "last frontier" out here, a place of rugged beauty, relentless sun, and genuine guides who have been ranching this land for more than 50 years.

BIRD-WATCHING
Haleakala National Park

The forests of **Haleakala National Park** offer the best opportunity for spotting endangered and endemic forest birds. Given the extreme isolation of the Hawaiian archipelago, 71 species of birds have been classified as being endemic to the islands, a distinction meaning they are found nowhere else on earth. Unfortunately, of those initial 71 species, 23 have already become extinct, and dozens of others are critically endangered. Due to rodents, feral cats, and mongooses, as well as the removal of the native bird's habitat, species such as the 'i'iwi, 'apapane, 'amakihi, Maui creeper, and 'akohekohe now find themselves clinging to existence on the remote slopes of Haleakala.

One of the best places for amateur bird-watchers to catch a glimpse of Hawai'i's native species is at **Hosmer's Grove** on the moderate, half-mile loop trail. Even if you don't see any of the native species of honeycreepers—birds whose bills have been specially adapted to extract nectar out of native plant species—the treetops of Hosmer's Grove chirp with a birdsong different than anywhere else on the planet. While casual hikers have a good chance of spotting an *'i'wi* or *'apapane,* the best way of spotting a rare species is to take a guided walk into the **Waikamoi Preserve** with a national park ranger. Every Monday and Thursday at 8:45am rangers lead three-mile guided walks into the preserve monitored by The Nature Conservancy which focus on the area's native flora and fauna. For more information call park staff at 808/572-4400. Reservations are essential. Although operating on a less frequent basis, hikes into the preserve are also occasionally arranged by the **Maui Forest Bird Recovery Project** (808/573-0280).

Higher on the slopes of the park, birdwatchers should keep an eye out for two endangered species, the *'u'au* (Hawaiian petrel), which burrows in areas near the summit visitor center, and the *nene* (Hawaiian goose), which can be spotted along roadways as well as the valley floor. At one time facing imminent extinction (it's estimated only 30 birds remained in 1951), the *nene* has made a moderately healthy comeback in recent years. Researchers now estimate the state's population at more than 2,000 birds in the wild. The *nene* is also the official state bird. One of the best places for spotting the rare goose is in the wet grasslands and pastures surrounding Paliku Cabin on the eastern edge of the crater floor.

Adventure Sports

PARAGLIDING

Anyone driving up the slopes of Polipoli might look out and simply see a lot of grass, but to the trained eye of a paraglider, this misty green hillside offers perfect conditions for throwing yourself off a ledge and getting a bird's-eye view of Maui. **Proflyght Hawaii Paragliding** (1598 Waipoli Rd., 808/874-5433, www.paraglidemaui.com, 7am-7pm daily) is the oldest—and only—full-fledged paragliding school in all of Hawai'i. Due to the island's optimal conditions, tandem instructors are able to help people soar above the pasturelands 330 days out of the year, and the launching and landing sites are perfectly suited to learning the sport of paragliding. Nearly all of the flights take place in the still morning hours before the clouds fill in. Tandem flights cost $95 for a 1,000-foot descent, or $185 for a 3,000-foot drop over the forest treetops and down to the landing site below. It's easy to see why people get hooked.

ZIPLINE TOURS
Makawao

The largest zipline on the island with two lines that run parallel to each other is at **Pi'iholo**

Zipline Tours (799 Pi'iholo Rd., 808/572-1717 or 800/374-7050, www.piiholozipline.com, 7am-9pm daily) in the forested uplands above Makawao. There is a 4-line course that is more economical at $140, but if you're going to spend the money and make the drive up here, you may as well spend the little bit extra to do the 5-line course ($190) where the last two lines offer a different thrill. The second to last line of the 5-line course zips for 1,420 feet to the base of Pi'iholo Hill, where you are then driven to the top for a 360° view of the surrounding Makawao and Ha'iku area. As if the view weren't enough, the final pièce de résistance is a 2,800-foot zip that leaves your feet dangling over 600 feet above the forested ravine below. This is the longest side-by-side zipline in the state and well worth the experience. In order to be eligible to zip you need to be at least eight years old and between 75 and 275 pounds. Closed-toe shoes are required. Bring a jacket for the cool early morning hours. Complimentary coffee is provided at the site, and helmets equipped with GoPro cameras are available for an additional charge. Makawao is on the windward side of the island and receives considerably more rain than Lahaina and Wailea. Trips continue to run rain or shine (and there are even small waterfalls in the ravine when it rains), so all you can do is cross your fingers and hope for the best. More than just ziplines, Pi'iholo also offers **canopy tours** (808/270/8750) where you zip from tree stand to tree stand on either a 3-line ($90), 6-line ($135), or 9-line ($165) course through the treetops. For the ultimate test of strength and agility, combine a 3-line zipline course with a climb up the 42-foot military-style **Tango Tower.**

Kula

Farther up the mountainside on the road to Haleakala, **Skyline Eco-Adventures** (12 Kiopa'a Pl., 808/878-8400, www.zipline. com, 7am-7pm daily) holds the distinction of not only being the original zipline course on Maui, but also the first one found anywhere in the United States. Here's the good news when compared to Pi'iholo: At $95 it's much cheaper and because it's on the leeward side of the island, it's less prone to rain. Although there are five lines, they are much tamer than the ones at Pi'iholo, the age limit is 10 years old (as compared to eight at Pi'iholo), you can't ride side by side, and seeing as it's located at 4,000 feet, you can't have been scuba diving the day before. The weight limit for this course is 80-260 pounds. Still, this is a good option if you're on a budget or it's your first time ziplining.

Golf and Tennis

GOLF

The lone golf course Upcountry is at the **Pukalani Country Club** (360 Pukalani St., 808/572-1214, www.pukalanigolf.com, 6:30am-6pm daily), an 18-hole, 6,962-yard course that weaves through the residential district of Pukalani. At 1,100 feet in elevation this course looks out over island's central valley. Hole #3 has a unique arrangement where you can play to one of two different greens—the only such hole in the state. Greens fees for visitors are $88 for tee times before noon, but golfers on a budget will love the $28, "super-twilight" tee times which are available to anyone teeing off after 2:30pm. There's a driving range and putting green where you can warm up before your round ($4/bucket for the range). Cart and club rentals are also available.

TENNIS

The only tennis courts are of the public variety. The best are the **Kula Tennis Courts** at the Kula Community Center. There are four courts here which stay lit until 8:30pm, it's rarely windy, and the view from 3,000 feet offers evening sunsets past the silhouette of Holy Ghost Church. To reach the Kula tennis courts, drive toward the parking lot for Holy Ghost Church (4300 Lower Kula Hwy), where you'll notice the community center on the opposite side of the road. If you reach Morihara Store you've gone too far.

In Makawao there are two public tennis courts at the **Eddie Tam** sporting complex, although they have some cracks forming in them and are more prone to wet weather than the courts in Kula. The courts are along Makawao Avenue half a mile before the intersection at the center of town, and rarely is there anyone waiting to play.

In Pukalani there is one public tennis court at the **Hannibal Tavares Community Center** (91 Pukalani St.) across the street from the Pukalani Terrace Center. This lone court is tucked away in back of the swimming pool and was built facing the wrong direction,, rur so you find yourself staring due west into the sunset during the later hours of the day.

The only other tennis court Upcountry is a concrete, cracked, rarely used court in Hali'imaile across the street from the Hali'imaile General Store (900 Hali'imaile Rd.).

Yoga, Fitness, and Spas

YOGA AND FITNESS
Makawao

Right next to Casanova restaurant, **Makawao Yoga** (1170 Makawao Ave., 808/359-2252, www.makawaoyoga.com, front desk hours 11am-2pm Tues.-Fri., 12:30pm-3:30pm Sat.) offers three-day visitor passes starting at only $45 for hour-long classes. This is a good option for vacationers who just want to pop in for a quick class and decompress. A detailed class schedule may be found on the website.

At **Yoga Awareness** (3660 Baldwin Ave., 808/280-7771, www.yogawareness.com, classes 8:30am Mon.-Sat, 4:30pm Mon. and Wed.), single classes are also offered for $15, although there is a greater focus on educating students who are looking to delve deeper into the physical and spiritual benefits of the practice. The studio is across from Rodeo General Store. Class schedules can be found on the website.

A few miles out of town on the road between Makawao and Pa'ia, **Lumeria Maui** (1813 Baldwin Ave., 808/579-8877, www.lumeriamaui.com/yoga-programs, call for class schedule) is a full-fledged, zen-inspired yoga retreat set on a beautiful rural spread of land overlooking the island's north shore. Although Lumeria specializes in multiday workshops and yoga retreats (it's also a hotel with its own restaurant), visitors are welcome to drop in for a single session. The price of $25/class is higher than some of the other options up in town, but a light organic breakfast, Wi-Fi, and access to the outdoor compound are included in the cost of the session.

Pukalani

The main yoga studio in Pukalani is **Om Maui** (95 Makawao Ave., 808/573-5566, www.mauiyogafitness.com, 6am-8pm weekdays, 8am-noon weekends), an upstairs studio next to Kojima's Sushi that also offers spinning classes and Pilates workouts. Classes start at $15/session and take place in a clean, hardwood floor studio.

SPAS
Makawao

Set in the calming uplands just above Makawao town, **Maui Spa Retreat** (Olinda Rd., 808/573-8002, www.mauisparetreat.com) offers a wide range of spa services in a relaxing rural setting. The property features an aromatic botanical garden as well as a saltwater lap pool and flower-laced hot tub which are used as part of the healing aromatherapy.

Hale Ho'omana (1150 Pi'iholo Rd., 808/573-8256, www.halehoomana.com) is another day spa in the soothing uplands above Makawao town where the services aim to combine cultural Hawaiian values with the healing properties of massage.

Within Makawao town, **Maui Ocean Spa** (1170 Makawao Ave., 808/572-7482, 8am-8pm Mon.-Thurs., 8am-2pm Fri.) next to Makawao Yoga offers a full range of spa services from massage ($80 for 60 minutes) to facials and body scrubs.

Sights

MAKAWAO

◖ Hui No'eau Visual Arts Center

About one mile downhill from Makawao is the **Hui No'eau Visual Arts Center** (2841 Baldwin Ave., 808/572-6560, www.huinoeau. com, 10am-4pm Mon.-Sat., $2 donation suggested), located on the Baldwin family's 10-acre estate. Matriarch Ethel Baldwin is described as "a child of privilege who used every gift she possessed for the creation of a more beautiful, more intelligent, and more just world." Given her commitment to education and the arts, it came as no surprise that in 1934 the resplendent neo-Spanish mansion was transformed into a sprawling arts center. Today, artisans here produce everything from ceramics to *lau hala* weaving and drawings to sculptures. The old house is home to the center office, gift gallery, periodic shows, and an informative historical museum about the estate, while the former

stable and carriage house have been changed into working studios. Classes are available for both visitors and locals. A full class schedule of everything from ceramics to felting can be found on the website.

Sacred Garden of Maliko

Swing by the **Sacred Garden of Maliko** (460 Kaluanui Rd., 808/573-7700, www.sacredgardensmaui.com, 10am-5pm daily, free admission) to deeply exhale and bring yourself back to center. In addition to being a working nursery, this quiet, forested space also offers two labyrinths and a Buddha garden for embarking on a metaphoric pilgrimage. Labyrinths differ from mazes in that mazes are meant to leave you feeling lost whereas labyrinths are designed to help you find yourself. Your feelings on alternative healing aside, this is a nice open space to relax and enjoy the natural beauty of lower Makawao.

KULA

Gentle Kula is rural and rustic, and most of the sights have agricultural ties. Occupying a swath of mountainside at 2,000-4,000 feet, Kula's bicoastal views are reason enough to visit. There's just something calming about driving a backcountry road while shopping for local produce. This is a side of Maui most visitors never see, and the infrequency with which tourists properly explore the area has inspired the country's largest travel outlets to label it as "the secret Maui." Although Kula is not intentionally secret, if you take even half a day to explore the area, you might find yourself chuckling about how you scored this place all to yourself.

◖ Kula Country Farms

The **Kula Country Farms** (Kula Hwy. past mile marker 13, 808/878-8381, www.kulacountryfarmsmaui.com, 10am-5pm Tues.-Fri., 8am-4pm Sat.-Sun.) genuinely captures the agricultural spirit of Kula, and provides a

© JENNA STRUBHAR

Hui No'eau Visual Arts Center

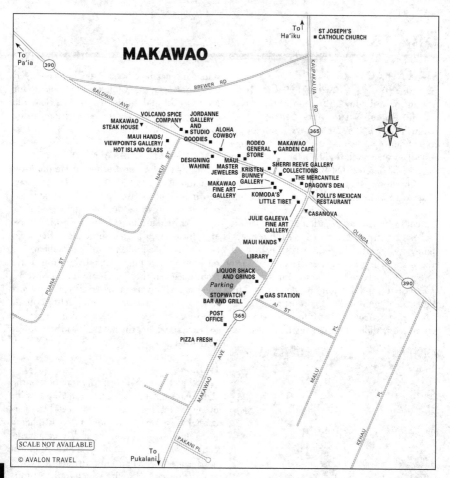

window into the locals who call this beautiful place home. This roadside farmer's market also has one of the best views on the island. It's not a trendy, New Age farmer's market, it's where farmers literally bring crops to market. Everything is locally grown, and the colors of the vegetables explode off the shelves. You can eat a box of fresh strawberries at a picnic table overlooking the southern coastline or visit the pumpkin patch and canoodle in the hay. At the end of the day, however, two of the best reasons for visiting here are that you're supporting local farmers and the prices are a fraction of what they would be at the major supermarkets.

Holy Ghost Church

On the Kula Highway you might have noticed an octagonal white church that kind of resembles a wedding cake. Easily recognizable from as far away as Ma'alaea, Holy Ghost Church is the de facto architectural monument in otherwise practically constructed Kula. Built by the Portuguese immigrant community in 1895 as a place to congregate and worship, the towering white church is the only octagonal structure

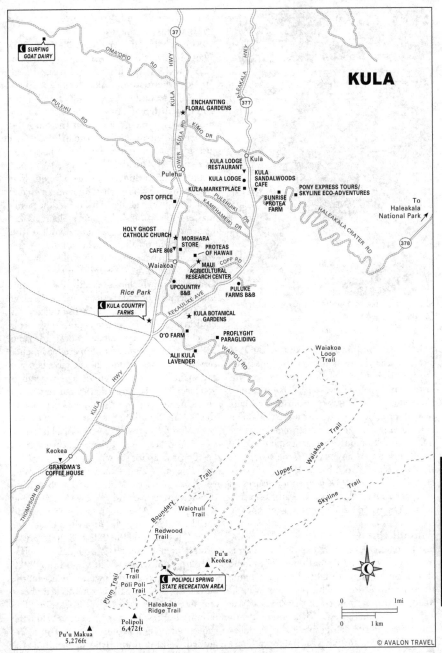

KULA

SURFING GOAT DAIRY

OMA'OPIO RD

PULEHU RD

KULA HWY 37

KIMO DR

HALEAKALA HWY 377

ENCHANTING FLORAL GARDENS

Kula

KULA LODGE RESTAURANT

Pulehu

KULA LODGE

KULA SANDALWOODS CAFE

KULA MARKETPLACE

PONY EXPRESS TOURS/ SKYLINE ECO-ADVENTURES

POST OFFICE

PULEHUIKI RD

SUNRISE PROTEA FARM

HALEAKALA CRATER RD

To Haleakala National Park

378

KAMEHAMEIKI DR

HOLY GHOST CATHOLIC CHURCH

MORIHARA STORE

CAFE 808

PROTEAS OF HAWAII

COPP RD

Waiakoa

MAUI AGRICULTURAL RESEARCH CENTER

Rice Park

UPCOUNTRY B&B

PULUKE FARMS B&B

KEKAULIKE AVE

KULA COUNTRY FARMS

KULA BOTANICAL GARDENS

O'O FARM

PROFLYGHT PARAGLIDING

Waiakoa Loop Trail

ALII KULA LAVENDER

WAIPOLI RD

KULA HWY

Waiakoa Trail

Keokea

GRANDMA'S COFFEE HOUSE

Upper

Skyline Trail

THOMPSON RD

Boundary Trail

Waiohuli Trail

Redwood Trail

Pu'u Keokea

Plum Trail

Tie Trail

Poli Poli Trail

POLIPOLI SPRING STATE RECREATION AREA

Haleakala Ridge Trail

Polipoli 6,472ft

Pu'u Makua 5,276ft

0   1mi

0   1 km

© AVALON TRAVEL

UPCOUNTRY

© KYLE ELLISON

Stock up on fresh produce at Kula Country Farms.

to have been built in Hawai'i during the 19th century. As striking as the church appears on the outside, however, the real treasure is on the inside: a nine-piece, hand-carved, hand-painted altar shipped all the way from Austria to Maui. A work of ecclesiastical art unlike any previously seen in Hawai'i, the altar remains as the finest example of museum-quality hand-crafted woodwork found anywhere in the state. The church was placed on the National Register of Historic Places in 1983, is open for visits 8am until dark, and holds mass on Saturday afternoons at 5pm and Sunday mornings at 9:30am.

Waipoli Road

Just past Rice Park and Kula Country Farms is a turnoff which heads up Route 377 to some of Kula's most popular sights. Less than a mile after the turnoff you will happen upon Waipoli Road, a steep, narrow track that leads all the way up to Polipoli forest. When you first turn onto this rural ribbon of asphalt, you'll probably wonder if you are going the right way. Don't

worry, this is it, and two of Upcountry's best sights are just up the road.

After a half a mile you'll see **O'o Farm** (651 Waipoli Rd., 808/667-4341, www.oofarm.com) on the left. This 8.5-acre natural farm provides the food for Lahaina's I'o, Pacifico, and 'Aina restaurants. Not only does it grow dozens of different crops, but *everything* on the property is home-grown, even the bugs and homemade fertilizer. Unfortunately you can't just stop in to the tour the farm, but have to do so as part of a prearranged tour. At $50/person it's pricy for lunch, but the 3.5-hour tour (10:30am-2pm Mon.-Thurs.) includes a guided walk around the garden with one of the farm's master growers, and the empty picnic basket he begins the tour with is gradually filled with produce right off the vine that a resident chef will soon prepare your lunch with. Along the way you can sample everything from purple Osaka leaves (which taste exactly like horseradish) to lemon hot chile peppers. While the air at 3,500 feet can be brisk, you're also welcome to endless cups of farm-roasted coffee to stave off the chill. After you've wandered the garden and the coffee operation, an unforgettable lunch is served on a large wooden picnic table beneath the shade of a covered grove. The vegetables you just picked in the garden are paired with an entrée made fresh in the outdoor kitchen, and this is truly Maui's finest farm to table experience. Visit on your way down from a Haleakala sunrise, or, better yet, as your lunchtime meal on your way up for sunset.

Following Waipoli Road another half-mile, you'll pass over a cattle guard and begin driving through empty pastures. Yes, you're still going the right way. After a few bends in the road you'll happen upon the **Ali'i Kula Lavender Farm** (1100 Waipoli Rd., 808/878-3004, www.aliikulalavender.com, 9am-4pm daily), a relaxing outpost of serenity. The views from 4,000 feet stretch all the way down to the ocean, the air is crisp, and the calls of ring-necked pheasants sing out over the eucalyptus and pine. The farm itself sprawls across 13.5 acres. While the general admission is only $3, the farm offers guided walking tours five times daily ($12)

© KYLE ELLISON

the octagonal Holy Ghost Church

9:30am-2:30pm on which lavender experts (yes, they exist) divulge everything you never knew about the soft purple plant. A small café serves scones and tea, and the gift shop is a great place to pick up anything from organic lavender body butter to a soft lavender eye mask. Check the event calendar on the website for special events like lavender treasure hunts or gourmet picnic lunches.

Kula Botanical Garden

The steep driveway for **Kula Botanical Garden** (638 Kekaulike Ave., 808/878-1715, www.kulabotanicalgarden.com, 9am-4pm daily, $10, children $3) is less than a mile from Waipoli Road. This 19-acre private garden was started all the way back in 1969 and has grown to include more than 2,500 species of plants. There are over 90 varieties of protea alone. The self-guided walking tour will take about 45 minutes to drink it all in. If you are on your way down from Haleakala and didn't get the chance to see a *nene,* there are two that make a permanent home in the botanical garden—which means

you can at least get your photos of Hawai'i's endangered state bird. There is also a Jackson chameleon exhibit for kids, a Christmas tree farm, three carved wooden tiki gods, and five acres of coffee trees which produce beans you can buy right from the farm.

◖ Surfing Goat Dairy

While out of the way, the eccentric **Surfing Goat Dairy** (3651 Omaopio Rd., 808/878-2870, www.surfinggoatdairy.com, 9am-5pm Mon.-Sat., 9am-2pm Sun.) is a must-see attraction because, quite frankly, where else on the island are you going to get the chance to hand-milk a goat? Three miles down Omaopio Road off Kula Highway (Hwy. 37), a line of enormous palms provides what's probably the most regal entrance to a goat dairy anywhere in the world. The palms are for a neighboring housing development, but they may as well announce the fact you're only minutes away from sampling the best (and probably only) horseradish and cayenne pepper goat cheese you've ever taken to your palate. There are more than 30 flavors of gourmet goat cheese, more than 25 types of goat cheese truffles, and an ever-changing number of goats on the property. For the up-to-the-minute number, check out the side of the red barn, where it's written in chalk. While the errant surfboards, baby goats, and cheese sampling station are nice and all, the real reason for coming here is to take the 3:15pm tour. There are tours for $10 which run every 30 minutes 10am-3pm, but for only $5 more you can take part in the only tour of the day that allows you to get in on the action and hand-milk a goat.

KEOKEA AND ULUPALAKUA

Once you pass Rice Park and the turnoff for 377, the highway begins to take on a different feel. The elevation slowly drops, the jacaranda trees provide shade over the road, and the views of South Maui begin to open up before you. Life is slow up here, and much like Kula, this is the hangout of artists, farmers, and lifelong ranchers. You'll know you've reached the community of Keokea when you see **Keokea Park**

© KYLE ELLISON

the quirky compound of Surfing Goat Dairy

to your left, a small, one-field opening that also has a playground and public restrooms.

◖ Tedeschi Winery

The expansive beauty of Ulupalakua Ranch and the winery that goes along with it alone makes a trip to this winery worth the drive. Yes, there is a winery on Maui and they serve more than just pineapple wine. While **Tedeschi Winery** (Ulupalakua Ranch, 808/878-6058, www.mauiwine.com, 10am-5pm daily) does produce three varieties of wine which are derived from pineapples, the Ulupalakua grape vines also produce grenache, malbec, syrah, viognier, and chenin blanc varietals. What makes the winery a must-see is that in addition to the complimentary tastings, the grounds and tasting room are sights unto themselves. The tasting room bar is 18 feet long and made from a single mango tree, and the tasting room itself served as the guesthouse for King David Kalakaua's visit to the ranch in April 1874. There's a small historical room attached to the tasting area that details the history of the ranch,

and free guided tours discuss how this land has gone from being a potato farm to a sugar plantation to a fully functioning cattle ranch and vineyard. Many of the trees which surround the tasting room are over 100 years old, most of them having been imported by former ranch owner Captain James Mackee—a whaling ship captain—who collected them as specimens on his ocean voyages around the globe. The cannon that rests in the yard outside the winery was fired to greet King Kalakaua upon his arrival. The combination of the history, the wine, the ranching atmosphere, and the scenery make Tedeschi Vineyards a must-stop. Or, as part of an alternate itinerary, you can visit the tasting room in the late afternoon if you are driving the back road from Hana.

◖ HALEAKALA NATIONAL PARK

Hale-a-ka-la: House of the Sun. Few places are more aptly named in the Hawaiian language than this 10,023-foot volcano. Dormant since its last eruption in 1790 (the summit area has been inactive for 600 years), Haleakala has been the site of grandiose experiences since before the arrival of humans. Bubbling over 30,000 feet from the seafloor below, only one-third of the mountain's mass exists above water, with the remaining 20,000 resting silently beneath the ocean. Along with neighboring Mauna Kea and Mauna Loa—two peaks on the Big Island which are visible from the summit—Haleakala ranks as one of the largest mountains on earth.

Stoic and spellbinding, its lofty summit was where the Polynesian demigod Maui captured the sun in mythology. Legend states that since the sun would race across the sky far too quickly to allow any crops to grow or any daily tasks to be accomplished, Maui snared the sun with his great net and only agreed to let him go if he promised to slow his path, thereby providing enough warmth for farmers to grow their crops and for life on the island to continue. Today, scores of visitors make the predawn sojourn to the summit to watch the sun illuminate the eastern horizon, squinting in excitement as it crests the clouds and bathes the crater

© HEATHER ELLISON

Tedeschi Winery

in a brilliant orange light. There is something about Haleakala which is detached, revered, and almost heavenly.

When to Visit

The biggest question surrounding Haleakala is not *if* you should visit, but when. Sunrise is the most popular option, and although everyone should experience a Haleakala sunrise at least once in their lifetime, by no means does that mean that it's the *only* time to visit. While the sunrise can indeed be spectacular, it's also crowded, tough to find parking, requires waking up at 3am, and is often near or below freezing. To see a light display nearly as colorful but without all the crowds, visit for sunset. Although you don't get the benefit of watching the sun emerge from the horizon, there are often only 20 people instead of 400. It isn't as cold (although it can still be near freezing with the windchill) and you can lay on the hood of your car (warm engine!) and watch the stars come out. Visit in the middle of the day to give yourself time to hike

down into the crater or explore the forests of Hosmer's Grove.

The largest factor, however, is working around the weather. Unfortunately, since Haleakala is a windward-facing mountain, the weather can be fairly unpredictable. Though rain (or even snow) can fall at any time of year, summers are usually a safer bet than winter when there is the chance of a big storm rolling through. Statistically, the sunrise is visible on 85 percent of days, with the other 15 percent being socked in with clouds, so at least the odds are with you. If, on the other hand, you're planning on heading up during the day or for sunset, a good rule of thumb is that if you can't see the mountain itself, then you probably shouldn't bother. On the other hand, if you can see the mountain itself, but just not the top, then you know you're going to be in for a fabulous sunset. During the midmorning to afternoon hours a cloud layer known as the *mauna lei* creeps its way across the mountain between 5,000 and 8,000 feet. Although you will be driving through the clouds on your

UPCOUNTRY

UPCOUNTRY

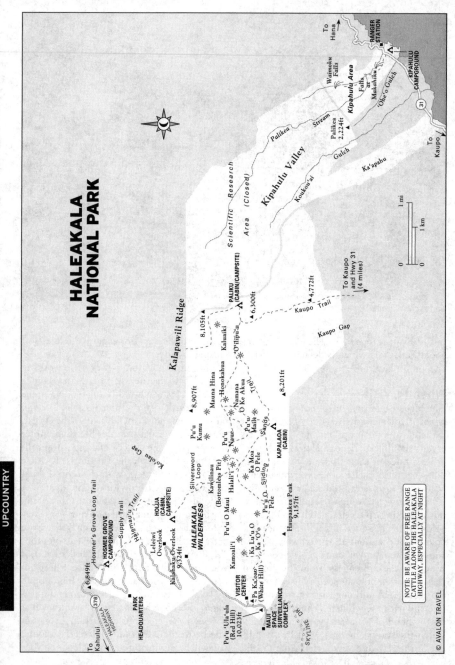

HALEAKALA NATIONAL PARK

To Kahului

378

HALEAKALA HIGHWAY

6,649ft ▲

Hosmer's Grove Loop Trail

HOSMER GROVE CAMPGROUND

Supply Trail

Halemau'u Trail

PARK HEADQUARTERS

Leleiwi Overlook

Kalahaku Overlook 9,324ft

Ko'olau Gap

HOLUA (CABIN, CAMPSITE)

Silversword Loop

HALEAKALA WILDERNESS

Kawilinau (Bottomless Pit) ☀

Pu'u o Maui Halali'i ☀

Pu'u Kumu ☀

Pu'u Naue ☀

Ka Moa O Pele ☀

Pu'u O Pele Sliding Sands

Pu'u Malie ☀

Kalapawili Ridge

8,907ft ▲

Mauna Hina ☀

Namana O Ke Akua ☀

a Honokahua ☀

O'ilipu'u ☀

Kaluaiki ☀

8,105ft ▲

PALIKU (CABIN/CAMPSITE)

6,300ft ▲

Halali'i Trail

8,201ft ▲

KAPALAOA (CABIN)

Kamoali'i ☀

Ka Lu'u O Ka 'O'o ☀

Pa Ka'oao (White Hill)

VISITOR CENTER

Pu'u 'Ula'ula (Red Hill) 10,023ft

MAUI SPACE SURVEILLANCE COMPLEX

SKYLINE DR

Haupaaka Peak 9,157ft ▲

Kaupo Gap

To Kaupo and Hwy 31 (4 miles)

Kaupo Trail

4,772ft ▲

Scientific Research Area (Closed)

Kipahulu Valley

Palikea Stream

Palikea 2,224ft ▲

Koukoʻai Gulch

Kaʻapahu

Waimoku Falls

Kipahulu Area

Falls at Makahiku

Ohe'o Gulch

KIPAHULU CAMPGROUND

RANGER STATION

To Hana

31

To Kaupo

1 mi

1 km

0

© AVALON TRAVEL

© KYLE ELLISON

Haleakala can be crowded at sunrise, but it's nearly empty at sunset.

way up to the top, on most occasions you will pop out above the clouds to watch the sunset from your own floating island, awash in a sea of white. Or, to take the guesswork out of the equation, call the National Weather Service hotline for Haleakala summit (866/944-5025, ext. 4) for an up-to-date weather forecast, or check out the website (www.ifa.hawaii.edu) for up-to-the-minute weather data (including windchill, wind speed, visibility, and rainfall) before taking off for the summit.

Headquarters and Hosmer's Grove

Admission to Haleakala National Park (www.nps.gov/hale) is $10 per car, $5 for bikers, hikers, and motorcycles, but it is good for three days. If you're driving up here for sunrise, you're going to want to drive straight to the summit to catch the show. If you're meandering up the mountain during the middle of the day (or are on your way up for sunset), take a side trip to **Hosmer's Grove,** a densely forested swath of hillside where an early 20th-century forester by the name of Ralph Hosmer experimented with over 80 species of nonnative timber in hopes of kick-starting the island's lumber industry. Though the 20 species that survived created a densely forested grove, they also invaded the hillside and destroyed the native foliage. Park rangers now work hard to keep the invasive grove in check. There is an enjoyable 0.5-mile nature hike and a campground for visitors who are just passing through. To reach Hosmer's Grove, make a left on a short access road just after entering the park.

Continuing straight past the Hosmer's Grove turnoff you'll soon arrive at **park headquarters** (808/572-4400, daily 7am-3:45pm) at an elevation of 6,800 feet. Campers can get their permits here, and others can stop for information concerning the park, gifts, water, or to use the toilet or pay phone. There are some 'ahinahina (silversword) plants outside, and a few nene can occasionally be seen wandering the area.

After you pass the park headquarters and zig and zag a couple more times, there's parking for another hiking option: Halemau'u Trail.

UPCOUNTRY

BRRRRR...

On any given morning at the top of Haleakala there always seems to be at least one unfortunate person shivering away in a tank top and boardshorts. People forget that Haleakala tops out at over 10,000 feet, which means that even though this is the tropics, the temperature can often be 30° colder than at sea level. Even though Haleakala is "The House of the Sun," the early morning windchill—particularly in the winter—will often be below freezing, and about every five years or so Haleakala will get a dump of snow (2-5 inches) that sticks around for a couple of days. Whenever it snows on Haleakala, the road to the top is usually closed due to ice, and when it reopens, hundreds of locals rush to the summit to build snowmen and take pictures with their children.

During most mornings, however, the temperature will only be in the lower 40s, but when combined with 30 mph wind gusts, that can warrant the use of gloves, a beanie, a windbreaker, and a couple of jackets. On rare mornings when the wind is light, you could probably get away with a long-sleeve shirt and jeans, but it's better to pack accordingly, lest you be the person sitting in the parking lot with the heater on while everyone else is getting pictures of the sunrise. By midmorning the temperature is usually into the mid 60s, but any sunrise or sunset visitors should be prepared to bundle up.

Following that are two overlooks, **Leleiwi** and **Kalahaku,** both offering tremendous views and different perspectives looking down into the crater basin.

Visitors Center

Near road's end is the visitors center at an elevation of 9,740 feet. It's approximately 10 miles up the mountain from headquarters or about a 30-minute drive. This is where all of the bike tour companies bring you for sunrise because you get one of the best views into the basin from here. It's open from sunrise to 3pm and contains a clear and concise display on the geology of Haleakala. Maps and books are available, and ranger talks are particularly informative. A 20-minute ranger talk takes place daily at 9:30am, 10:30am, and 11:30am at the summit observation center above the visitors center, and various ranger-led hikes are also given (Tues. and Fri. 9am for a two-mile hike on Sliding Sands Trail). By 10am, there will be lots of people at the top, so enjoy the time between when the bikers leave and the buses arrive.

Bikes going down the mountain travel about 20-25 miles per hour, sometimes faster. If you're caught behind a string of bikes on your way down, just slow up and wait for them to pull over and let you pass. On your way down, shift into a low gear to control your speed to prevent riding the brakes.

Summit Observation Building

At the road's end is **Pu'u 'Ula'ula** (Red Hill), the highest point on Maui at 10,023 feet where a glass-sided observation area is open 24 hours. From here, you have more expansive vistas than from the visitors center below, but the view into the crater isn't quite as good. This is where many people come to see the sunset. To add some perspective to size and distance, it's 100 miles from the top of Haleakala to the volcanic peak of Mauna Loa on the Big Island to the southeast.

Behind you on the slope below is **Maui Space Surveillance Complex** (www.ifa.hawaii.edu/haleakala), aka Science City, a research facility with telescopes used by the University of Hawai'i, a satellite tracking station that's staffed by the U.S. Air Force, and the largest telescope controlled by the Department of Defense. As you might expect, this complex is officially closed to the public.

Camping and Cabins

While watching the sunrise, hiking the crater floor, or looking up at the stars as they come out are great introductions to the crater, spending a night in the backcountry is the absolute best way to commune with nature on this mountain. The most accessible campground is the one at **Hosmer's Grove** where you don't even need a permit. There are only tent sites and no open fires are allowed, but there is a pit toilet, running water, and you can drive right up to the campsite. At an elevation of 6,800 feet, the nights can still get chilly (and can drop close to freezing in the winter), but the camping area is largely protected from the wind. This is a great place to camp if you're looking to make an early assault to see the sunrise, are planning to hike into the crater basin from here (a 2.3-mile supply trail connects the campground with the Halemau'u trailhead), or want to sleep among the eucalyptus for the evening.

For those who plan on backpacking with a tent, two **wilderness campsites** are located at Holua (elevation: 6,940 ft.) and Paliku (6,380 ft) campgrounds. Anyone planning on spending a night in the backcountry needs to secure a permit from the park headquarters, which is free, but requires that you watch an 8-minute orientation video and pick up the permit before 3pm. Pit toilets and non-potable water are available at both campsites, and although the sites are officially first-come, first-served, they can accommodate 25 people and are rarely full. Maximum length of stay is three nights total in a 30-day period, and no more than two nights in a row at the same site. Holua is accessible by a 3.7-mile hike down Halemau'u Trail and is set amid subalpine scrub brush looking over the Ko'olau Gap. Paliku, on the other hand, requires a 9.2-mile hike on Sliding Sands Trail (or a 10.3-mile hike on Halemau'u Trail), and is wet, lush, and surrounded by foliage. In addition to being a great place to spot *nene,* Paliku is also the preferred camping area for hikers opting to walk out the Kaupo Gap.

There are three **backcountry cabins** available at Holua, Kapalaoa (elevation: 7,250 ft.), and Paliku, although due to their popularity securing a reservation can be a little difficult. Cabin reservations can only be made up to 90 days in advance either by calling the

park headquarters at 808/572-4400, or online at https://fhnp.org/wcr. Local people are usually waiting on the 91st day to secure the reservation first thing in the morning, so if this is something you want to include on your Maui trip, plan ahead and be flexible. If you manage to reserve a cabin, however, the cost is $75/night and includes 12 padded berths, a woodburning stove, and basic kitchen utilities. Pit toilets and non-potable water are available, and all trash must be packed out.

TOURS

If you still think that pineapples grow underground or on a tree, then you will learn a lot by going out on the **Maui Pineapple Tour** (875 Hali'imaile Rd., 808/665-5491, www.mauipineappletours.com, tours 9:30am and 11:45am Mon.-Fri.). Not only do you get a free pineapple with every tour, but you also learn all about the current state of an agricultural industry fighting to stay alive. Find out about all the other uses of pineapple you never knew about such as pineapple jam, pineapple lemonade, and even pineapple wine. Tours run $65/person or $75/person if you include lunch. Seeing as the food is from the acclaimed Hali'imaile General Store, the extra $10 charge is a good deal.

For a private tour guide who delivers a cultural connection to the island, check with Pono of **Open Eye Private Tours** (808/572-3483, www.openeyetours.com). He has been a private tour guide on Maui since 1983, and communicates with the clients before the tour to get an assessment of what sort of activities might suit them best. For visitors with an interest in music or dance, he might arrange a tour on which hula dancers from a local *halau* offer a private performance with chants which relate to the land around you. If you're interested in the spirituality of the islands, Pono can plan an itinerary of places steeped in Hawaiian mythology and spirit. As a former teacher, Pono also specializes in tours with children and offers activities for kids such as making fish out of coconut leaves. Pono takes you places few other people get to go. He's built up contacts over the years that enable him to bring guests to the properties of local people who regard him as a friend. For example, a large tour bus of 45 people won't be able to stop at a taro field on the way to Hana and pull taro with the owners. You won't be disappointed.

Shopping

◖ OLD MAKAWAO TOWN

There's no faster way to make an Upcountry local cringe than by referring to Old Makawao Town as another Lahaina. The galleries and boutiques here are on par—if not better—than the shops and galleries lining Lahaina's Front Street, but you don't have the tourist kitsch, swarms of cruise ship passengers, and drum machine musicians that would mold it into "just another tourist town." Instead Makawao prefers to stay off the radar, yet accessible enough so as to attract art patrons and fashionistas who are passionate about what they're purchasing. Add in the *paniolo* ranching heritage of the town (there are still hitching posts lining the storefronts), and walking the shops of Old Makawao Town becomes a sight unto itself.

Art Galleries

Those interested in fine Polynesian jewelry will enjoy stepping inside **Maui Master Jewelers** (3655 Baldwin Ave., 808/573-5400, www.mauimasterjewelers.com, 10am-5pm Mon.-Fri., 10am-4pm Sat.), where works by over 30 local artists are consistently on display. They are the island's leading source for New Zealand bone and jade carvings and also offer Tahitian pearl jewelry and colored gemstones.

Sherri Reeve Gallery (3669 Baldwin Ave., 808/572-8931, www.sreeve.com, 9am-5pm Mon.-Fri., 10am-4pm Sat.) showcases this ebullient Makawao artist whose distinctive floral designs have graced shirts, cards, paintings, and prints for years. Despite the large number of galleries in town, no visit to Makawao would be complete without at least popping in and having a look around.

Jordanne Gallery and Studio (3625 Baldwin Ave., 808/563-0088, www.jordannefineart.com, 10:30am-5pm daily) is toward the bottom of the shops on Baldwin Avenue. This plein-air painter landed in Hawai'i when she decided at the airport during a family trip to Lana'i that she wasn't getting back on the plane. With little money and no plan, she let her painting talents pave what was once an unforeseen path.

The first store you'll notice in the Courtyard shopping area is **Viewpoints Gallery** (3620 Baldwin Ave., 808/572-5979, www.viewpointsgallerymaui.com, 10am-6pm daily), a large, clean gallery which features a rotating array of artists focusing predominantly on paintings.

Back behind the gallery next to Market Fresh Bistro is **Hot Island Glass** (3620 Baldwin Ave., 808/572-4527, www.hotislandglass.com, 9am-5pm daily), the island's most well-known glass studio where you can watch artists blow glass right before your eyes. Although the gallery is open every day, live glass blowing demonstrations only take place Monday-Saturday 10:30am-4pm.

The **Kristen Bunney Gallery** (3660 Baldwin Ave., 808/573-1516, www.kristenbunney.com, 11am-5pm daily) provides passersby with playful, animated, and inspiring artwork. The passion behind her work is evident in every piece.

In the building right next door you will find the **Makawao Fine Art Gallery** (3660 Baldwin Ave., 808/573-5972, www.makawaofineartgallery.com, 11am-5pm Mon.-Sat., noon-5pm Sun.), a gallery with a collection of over a dozen featured artists. Among the highlights of the works on display are watercolors of wine by Eric Christensen, familial portraits by Bob Byerley, and the perception-altering visual art of Andreas Nottebohm.

Right on the corner of the center of town, **Julie Galeeva Fine Art** (3682 Baldwin Ave., 808/573-4772, www.juliegaleeva.com,

Old Makawao Town is renowned for its boutiques.

10am-5pm Mon.-Sat.) showcases the highly textured paintings of this talented Russian-born artist and Maui resident.

Clothing and Gifts

Trendy boutiques and global fashions seem to pop up at every other storefront. Working your way down Baldwin Avenue from the center of town, you'll hit a number of standouts. **Collections** (3677 Baldwin Ave., 808/572-0781, www.collectionsmauiinc.com, 9am-6pm Mon.-Sat., 11am-5pm Sun.) has been providing men's and women's clothing and boutique home furnishings since opening its doors in 1975.

The Mercantile (3673 Baldwin Ave., 808/572-1401, 10am-6pm daily) specializes in boutique women's clothing. This welcoming shop always has a steady stream of customers.

Past Rodeo General Store you'll find **Aloha Cowboy** (3643 Baldwin Ave., 808/573-8190, www.alohacowboy.net, 9:30am-6pm Mon.-Sat., 10am-5pm Sun.), one of the best stores in Makawao and a place that captures the combined Hawaiian and *paniolo* spirit. Inside this old building you'll find western-themed clothing, Makawao-centric items, saddles, horse tack, a cowhide-colored surfboard, and a train going around the ceiling above the wares. If you're walking down the street and looking for the store, you don't even have to spot the sign—the smell of leather is noticeable from two storefronts down.

The collection of clanging wind chimes will announce your arrival at **Goodies** (3633 Baldwin Ave., 808/572-0288, 10am-6pm daily), an eccentric but genuinely artsy clothing boutique that caters to the female crowd.

Check out the **Volcano Spice Company** (3623 Baldwin Ave., 808/575-7729, www.volcanospicecompany.com, 10am-5pm Mon.-Sat., 11am-3pm Sun.), a small shop run by the owner and head chef, who creates handmade rubs and spices out of a kitchen right on the property. There are a few crafts in the store, such as hand-turned wood bowls, but the real stars of the show are the bottles of coffee barbecue rub and

PROTEA

Protea are large flowers that grow in a variety of colors from dark brown to brilliant orange, bright yellow, and pale pink. Natural or hybridized, some have pincushion-like heads, others have tops that resemble a bunch of wispy feathers, while others look like bottlebrushes. Originally from South Africa, these beautiful flowers have been grown on Maui since the mid-1960s and are now big business as the state's showiest of flowers. Dozens of hybrids have been created for their long stems, colors, or size and shape of petals. Kula and its environs at about 3,000-foot elevation make a perfect place to grow protea, as they need sunny days, cool crisp nights, and moderate, even temperatures that don't usually go above 80°F. Upcountry boasts numerous protea growers, some with shops, many of whom ship.

the original volcano spice blend, which goes great on seared ahi.

Designing Wahine Emporium (3640 Baldwin Ave., 808/573-0990, 10am-6pm Mon.-Sat., 11am-5pm Sun.) offers everything from locally made crafts to children's clothing to a few pieces of menswear—something rare here in Makawao.

Around the corner at Komoda Bakery is the tiny little enclave of **Little Tibet** (3682 Baldwin Ave., 808/573-2275, 10am-5pm Mon.-Sat.), where an array of ancient gemstones and crystals from all across the world warrant a peek.

At the far end of the same building is **Jewels of the White Tara** (3682 Makawao Ave., 808/573-5774, 10am-6pm Mon.-Sat., 11am-5pm Sun.), an obscure-sounding import store that features home decor and clothing items from India, Indonesia, Laos, Vietnam, and a handful of other international venues.

Adding to an array of already existing shops in Pa'ia, Lahaina, and Ka'anapali, **Maui Hands** (1169 Makawao Ave., 808/572-2008, www.mauihands.com, 10am-6pm Mon.-Sat., 11am-5pm Sun.) took over an old health food market and has transformed it into a spacious gallery of consignment craft work.

KULA
Art Galleries

It isn't possible to talk about Upcountry art without mentioning the **Curtis Wilson Cost Gallery** (15200 Haleakala Hwy., 808/874-6544, www.costgallery.com, 8:30am-5pm daily). Tucked neatly beneath the Kula Lodge Restaurant, the gallery has the feeling of a fine wine cellar, though the wine is swapped for exceptionally fine art. It's fair to say that nobody paints rural Maui better. Cost's love for the island is apparent in his innate ability to capture its fleeting magic. A recent addition to the collection are pieces by Cost's daughter Julia Cost. This gallery is a must stop for anyone with an appreciation for fine art.

If you thought the only place you could find locally made blown glass was in Makawao, then you haven't stumbled upon **Worcester Glassworks** (4626 Lower Kula Rd., 808/878-4000, www.worcesterglassworks.com, 10am-5pm Mon.-Sat., by appointment Sun.), a studio you would never know was there unless you accidentally ran into the kiln. Just twenty yards up the road from Kula Bistro and Morihara Store, the clean and well-lit gallery only occupies a small corner of the rustic studio, with the remaining space taken up by numerous heavy-industrial machines instrumental in the glassblowing process. This gallery is worth a wander in conjunction with a meal at Kula Bistro.

Gifts and Flowers

Right next to the Kula Lodge is the **Proteas of Hawaii Gift Shop** (15200 Healakala Hwy., 808/878-2533, www.proteasofhawaii.com, 8am-4pm daily) where you can pick up a bouquet of freshly cut protea ($75-140) grown only a half mile away. In addition to the flowers this small store also sells a number of other locally made crafts, artwork, and gifts.

Down the driveway and between the Kula Lodge and the Proteas of Hawaii Gift Shop, tucked just out of sight, is the larger **Kula Marketplace** (808/878-2135, www.kulamarketplace.com, 8am-7pm daily) where you could easily spend a half an hour browsing all the various local offerings. Everything from locally made jam to clothing to Hawaiian music to photography and bamboo cutting boards is on display in this store. It's a great place to wander through while digesting a Kula Lodge breakfast or making your way down from the crater.

Pick up baskets of locally grown protea at the **Upcountry Harvest Gift Shop** (638 Kekaulike Ave., 808/878-2824, www.upcountryharvest.com, 9am-4pm daily) inside the Kula Botanical Garden. The gift shop offers a full range of floral arrangements at $59-250, as well as bags of coffee beans grown right on the property ($22).

KEOKEA AND ULUPALAKUA
Ching Store and Fong's Store

Just past the park in "downtown" Keokea, you'll find **Ching Store** (9212 Kula Hwy., 808/878-1556, 7am-5pm daily) and **Fong's Store** (9226 Kula Hwy., 808/878-1525, 7:30am-5:30pm Mon.-Sat., 7:30am-3:30pm Sun.), which are one part grocery market and two parts time capsule. These stores are so old that oversize cigarette boxes still serve as the decor, and the poster in the doorway of Fong's Store from the Maui County Liquor Commission informs patrons that anyone wishing to purchase alcohol must be 18 years of age. Mrs. Fong will be quick to remind you, however, that this store is in the "new" location; though the original store opened in Keokea in 1908, the one that currently stands has only been here since 1932. Wood shelves match the wood floors, and it's as if someone forgot to tell these elderly children of the original Chinese immigrants that the rest of the world has quickened its pace a little bit.

Art Gallery

Sandwiched between Grandma's Coffee House and Fong's Store, tiny little **Keokea Gallery** (9230 Kula Hwy., 808/878-3555, 9am-5pm daily) has existed as a fully working studio since 1989. Inside the humble little gallery are a collection of linocut collages, paintings, painted surfboards, handmade frames, and of course the affable artist Sheldon and his mellow dog Ipo. It's an odd place to find a gallery, and it catches you off guard, but when you poke your head inside and have a look around, you find yourself wondering if you've stumbled into something no one else knows about. It's almost as if you say, *Wait a minute, these are good. So what are they doing way out here?*

Food

MAKAWAO
Mexican

The sign hanging on the door says, "Come in and eat or we'll both starve!" Mix some mango margaritas, a seafood burrito, and a great community atmosphere, and it will be obvious why ◖ **Polli's Mexican Restaurant** (1202 Makawao Ave., 808/572-7808, www.pollismexicanrestaurant.com, 11am-10pm daily, $11-22) is a Makawao classic since its founding in 1981. The portions are enormous: whether you order a seafood enchilada, a chicken burrito supreme, a sizzling beef fajita, or even a "Makawowie" nachos appetizer, you'll be be hard-pressed to finish. More than just Mexican, Polli's also offers Maui Cattle Company cheeseburgers, barbecue pork sandwiches, a heaping array of vegetarian options, and baby back ribs that fall off the bone. It's a true community gathering place where half the patrons know each other by name. The festive interior is decorated with photographs from Mexico, surf photography from Hawai'i, and

WELCOME TO KEOKEA, MAUI'S CHINATOWN

Ask any local how to get to Chinatown and there's a good chance they'll laugh and point you toward Honolulu. While Hawai'i's capital city does in fact have one of the oldest Chinatowns in America, few people are aware that Maui's Chinatown is on the slopes of Haleakala in the rural hamlet of Keokea. Don't expect to find any swinging red lanterns, streetside dim sum carts, or seedy back alley parlors. This Chinatown was initially founded on something decidedly un-Chinese:

Potatoes. Having arrived in the 1820s on ships engaged in the lucrative sandalwood trade, many of Maui's original Chinese immigrants would end up working in early sugar mills once the supply of sandalwood began to diminish. Laboring hard on the fledgling sugar plantations, Chinese farmers who had moved to Keokea would eventually strike pay dirt in the form of potatoes, tons of which were needed to feed the throngs of prospectors taking part in the California Gold Rush. At one point Kula farmers were shipping such a steady stream of potatoes to the ports of California that the area earned the nickname of "Nu Kaleponi," Hawaiian for "New California."

Back in China, hundreds of thousands of Chinese citizens continued to live under the system of imperial rule which had lasted for two thousand years. When the Qing Dynasty finally fell in 1911, the roots of the revolution wouldn't be traced to major cities such as Beijing or Shanghai, but instead, to the rural slopes of sleepy Keokea.

Today the remnants of this lengthy Chinese history are evident in the town's two mom-and-pop stores—Fong's Store and Ching Store—and the cashiers at either will be more than happy to talk about the unique heritage of Keokea. In addition to the general stores, sites such as the Kwock Hing Society building and St. Joseph's Church were constructed by members of the Chinese community.

authentic souvenirs from all corners of the Latin American world.

Italian

Holding down the other corner of Makawao's only intersection since 1986, **Casanova** (1188 Makawao Ave., 808/572-0220, www.casanovamaui.com, 7:30am-9:30pm Sun.-Tues., 7:30am-2am Wed.-Sat., $18-34) restaurant is a three-part establishment where you can either grab a quick deli sandwich for lunch, have a fine meal of pizza and pasta for dinner, or dance to the wee hours of the morning at Upcountry's only nightclub. While the restaurant is also open for lunch, most diners come here for the fine Italian dinner menu where authentic selections such as *linguine pescatore* and *filetto di manzo* punctuate an affordable menu. Pair Upcountry's best wine list with wood-fired pizzas baked in an Italian oven, and Casanova has all the makings of a romantic date night you might find in a big city in a town that doesn't even have stoplights.

If you're looking for Italian that's a lot more casual, **Pizza Fresh** (1043 Makawao Ave., 808/572-2000, 4pm-9pm daily, $13-29) is just a half mile down the road. Specialty pizzas such as pesto chicken or eggplant gouda are available either whole or by the slice and can be accompanied by fresh salads. There's limited seating, but ordering pizza to go is always an option.

American

The two best things about **Market Fresh Bistro** (3620 Baldwin Ave., 808/572-4877, www.marketfreshbistro.com, 9am-3:30pm Tues.-Sat., 9am-2pm Sun., dinner 6pm-8:30pm Thurs.-Fri., $12) are the courtyard setting and the salmon and tomato Benedict. Although this place is also open for lunch (and dinner two nights of the week), breakfast, served until 11am, is the meal of choice.

A true hole-in-the-wall favorite, the

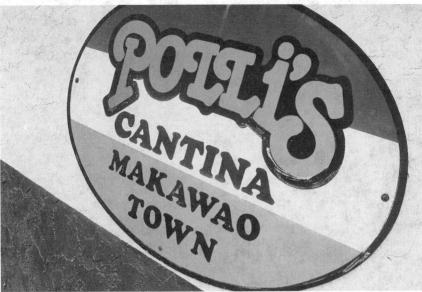

© KYLE ELLISON

Polli's Mexican Restaurant is a Makawao favorite.

Makawao Garden Café (3669 Baldwin Ave., 808/573-9065, www.makawaogardencafe.com, 11am-3pm Mon.-Sat., $6-9) is hidden in an alcove next to the Sherri Reeve art gallery. The café only offers outdoor seating, which means that when it rains, the restaurant closes. Laid-back and only open for lunch, its options include a baby brie and bacon sandwich or quinoa salad with goat cheese.

If you're in the mood for a turkey or club sandwich paired with freshly squeezed juices, the deli counter inside **Rodeo General Store** (3661 Baldwin Ave., 808/572-1868, 6:30am-10pm Mon.-Sat., 6:30am-9pm Sun., $8-10) serves filling and affordable deli sandwiches which are great for anyone on the run. Spend the extra money for a "Green Machine," an all-natural collection straight from the juicer, with celery, apple, parsley, kale, and cucumber blended into a healthy dose of energy.

Casanova (1188 Makawao Ave., 808/572-0220, www.casanovamaui.com, 7:30am-5:30pm Mon.-Sat., 8:30am-5:30pm Sun., $7) offers deli sandwiches on five different types of bread as well as a full range of affordable salads. Sit at the tables inside or on the patio stools facing the happening street corner.

If you're looking to catch the big game or craving a local draft beer, the local hangout **Stopwatch Bar and Grill** (1127 Makawao Ave., 808/572-1380, www.stopwatchmaui.com, 11am-10pm Mon.-Sat., 8am-10pm Sun., $8-10) is Makawao's token sports bar. Flat-screen TVs circle the bar, and burger and sandwich offerings round out the lunchtime menu.

Of course an authentic ranching town has its own steak house, the dimly lit, dark wood **Makawao Steak House** (3612 Baldwin Ave., 808/572-8711, 5pm-9pm Tues.-Sun., $25-30). There are few things better than hunkering down behind this old-western-style storefront with a warm bowl of Maui onion soup on a cool winter evening. The steak fillets are expertly prepared (though curiously served with a side of beans). This is a longtime local date-night venue where the price is steeper than other places around town.

UPCOUNTRY

Hali'imaile General Store offers fine dining in a casual setting.

Hawaiian Regional

The **€ Hali'imaile General Store** (900 Hali'imaile Rd., 808/572-2666, www.bevgannonrestaurants.com/haliimaile, lunch 11am-2:30pm Mon.-Fri., dinner 5:30pm-9pm daily, $22-42), serves elegant gourmet food to anyone lucky enough to find this Upcountry roadhouse. In Hali'imaile village along Hali'imaile Road between Baldwin Avenue and the Haleakala Highway, the restaurant is housed in what was this pineapple town's general store. Master chef Beverly Gannon presents creative "Hawaiian regional cuisine with an American and international twist," and while the menu changes seasonally, a sampling of what you might expect includes appetizers such as the brie and grape quesadilla, sashimi Napoleon, and Bev's crab pizza. Entrées include *paniolo* barbecue ribs, coconut seafood curry, rib eye steak, rack of lamb Hunan-style, or pan-seared scallops. The food is always healthy and fresh, and the portions plentiful. Whatever your choice, you'll leave with a full belly and a smile on your face. The setting is casual, but because of the elevation, long sleeves and pants might be in order.

Coffee Shops

The best coffee bar is inside the **Rodeo General Store** (3661 Baldwin Ave., 808/572-1868, 6:30am-10pm Mon.-Sat., 6:30am-9pm Sun.), where resident baristas sling a wide array of caffeinated cheer. It's one of the few places on the island that serves organically roasted coffee with organic milk. But if that's too "hippie" for you, rest assured that the taste is on par with, if not better, than the majority of coffee shops on the island.

Along with Komoda Bakery, **Casanova** (1188 Makawao Ave., 808/572-0220, www.casanovamaui.com, 7:30am-5:30pm Mon.-Sat., 8:30am-5:30pm Sun., $7) essentially defines mornings in Makawao. The coffee and breakfast offerings are standard fare (breakfast croissants and omelets are an affordable choice). The true color of this place in the mornings is the cast of eccentric and artsy characters. It's

Stick doughnuts from Komoda's are an Upcountry classic.

© KYLE ELLISON

a classic community meeting place in one of America's best small towns.

Bakery

You haven't officially visited Upcountry until you've stood on the corner of Makawao's only intersection and treated yourself to the doughy perfection served at **(Komoda Store and Bakery** (3674 Baldwin Ave., 808/572-7261, 7am-5pm Mon.-Tues. and Thurs.-Fri., Sat. 7am-2pm). Komoda's *defines* Upcountry. The unmistakable aroma of its "stick" doughnuts and cream puffs wafts on the predawn air each morning. Residents of Makawao have been getting their early morning pastry fix at Komoda for generations. It's where grandparents can still take their grandkids to get the same handmade pastry at the same store that they would go to when they were kids. Lines still form outside before the 7am opening, and popular items such as the baked butter rolls will often sell out within hours. The store continues to operate without computers, so expect to pay with cash.

Tours

For self-proclaimed foodies, even laid-back Makawao town has managed to get in on the recent explosion in food tours. **Local Tastes of Maui** (1079 Maohu St., 808/446-1190, www.localtastesofmaui.com, 9:30am-11:30am weekdays) offers tours of both Makawao and Pa'ia where participants hit a number of eateries across town and learn about the history and lore behind the culinary establishments. Makawao tours run Tuesday and Thursday and Pa'ia tours are on Monday, Wednesday, and Friday.

KULA
American

The **Kula Lodge** (15200 Haleakala Hwy., 808/878-1535, www.kulalodge.com, 7am-9pm daily, breakfast until 10:45am, $12-34) has been welcoming hungry patrons into its rustic interior for so long it's become synonymous with Kula dining. Set inside a private home constructed in the 1940s, this panoramic, mountainside perch maintains a pace

UPCOUNTRY

of life that hasn't changed much. At 3,200 feet in elevation, it's little bit cooler up here, and the Lodge's dark-wood interior seems a perfect fit with the low temperatures and low-hanging clouds. The entranceway is adorned with Curtis Wilson Cost paintings (his gallery is located beneath the restaurant) and the warm, welcoming atmosphere is the biggest draw for dining at the Lodge. The service can be hit-or-miss, but you'll be so full from a huge breakfast of *paniolo* steak and eggs or a dinner of kiawe-roasted prime rib to care about anything else.

Kula Sandalwoods Café (15427 Haleakala Hwy., 808/878-3523, www.kulasandalwoods. com, 7am-3pm daily, $9-11) is a laid-back venue where the owners will chat you up like an old friend. Breakfast is served until 11am, although if you're a few minutes late and hankering for an omelet, they'll probably be nice enough to let it slide. While the outdoor lanai is still a nice place to enjoy your meal, the cozy interior features a fireplace in the corner and country music on the radio. For breakfast try the Keokea omelet; at lunch go for the kalua pig sandwich.

Italian

¢ Kula Bistro (4556 Lower Kula Rd., 808/871-2960, www.kulabistro.com, 7:30am-8:30pm daily, $12-20) has infused the Kula culinary scene with new life. Upon first bite of the pesto chicken flatbread or grilled vegetable panini, it's apparent that head chef Luciano Zanon has been perfecting this cuisine since his childhood spent in Venice. The barbecue chicken and Maui onion pizza and creamy vodka pomodoro only further prove his success. As if you needed more reasons to love the restaurant, Kula Bistro also puts out desserts which are freshly baked every day, mainly uses locally sourced ingredients, and allows patrons to bring in their own beer or wine without charging a corkage fee. Forgot the bottle of wine? Morihara Store sells some right across the street.

French

To call **La Provence** (3158 Lower Kula Rd., 808/878-1313, www.laprovencekula.com, 7am-9pm Wed.-Fri., 8:45am-1:45pm weekends, $1, cash only) a hidden gem might read like a cliché, but in the case of this boutique French restaurant, it's hidden so well you could drive by without even noticing it. On Lower Kula Road just past the True Value hardware store, La Provence offers everything from flaky croissants and café au lait for breakfast to affordable and filling crepes. Order a mushroom and spinach or vegetable and goat cheese crepe accompanied by Kula greens and roasted potatoes. It's cash only; there's an ATM at the True Value.

Food Cart

Inside the gate of the **Kula Country Farms** (Kula Hwy. past mile marker 13, 808/878-8381, www.kulacountryfarmsmaui.com, 10am-3pm Tues.-Fri., 8am-3pm Sat.-Sun.) is a food truck serving $6 fish tacos and $8 Papa Rice Burgers made from beef sourced straight from Kula's Ka'ono'ulu Ranch. Lunch items can sell out early since the price is a steal for what you're getting.

Markets

If Kula were to have anything resembling a town center, the argument could be made for it being **Morihara Store** (4581 Lower Kula Rd., 808/878-2578, 6:30am-8pm Mon.-Sat., 7:30am-8pm Sun.), the main general store that services most of Kula's basic culinary needs. Pick up anything from condiments for a picnic in Rice Park, cheap to-go items for lunch, or a beer or bottle of wine for the BYOB restaurant across the street. Like many other general stores across the island, Morihara is a throwback to antiquity where the fast pace of modern life can be checked at the door.

Coffee Shops

Although the best coffee shop in all of Upcountry is out in Keokea, those in need of a quick—and early—cuppa joe can find it at the **Crater Coffee** (15200 Haleakala Hwy., 808/757-1342, 3am-7am Mon.-Sat.) truck sitting right in front of the Kula Lodge and opening at a REM-shattering 3am. The main customers here are visitors heading up to catch the sunrise at Haleakala in the morning, and seeing as it's the only place open this early that serves coffee and bagels, this is going to be a life-saver if you find yourself struggling through the early sunrise wakeup.

PUKALANI
Local Style
Inside the Pukalani Terrace Center, **Mixed Plate** (55 Pukalani St., 6am-3:30pm Mon.-Fri., 6am-2:30pm Sat., 9am-2pm Sun., $6-10) has been pumping out traditional plate lunch options for years. While it might not look like much from the outside, there's always a good-size local crowd hanging out in this funky old diner.

Italian
The best—and only—Italian food in tiny Pukalani is at **Serpico's Pizzeria** (7 Aewa Pl., 808/572-8498, www.serpicosmaui.com, 11am-10pm daily, $12-25) just off Old Haleakala Highway. If you are heading uphill, it's on your left in a standard-looking office building just past the town McDonald's. Despite its humble appearance, however, the food is anything but standard. The owners came to Maui by way of Italy, and the thin-crust, hand-tossed pizzas reflect the generations of tinkering that have gone into their pies. Beyond pizza, Serpico's also serves up calzones, lasagna, raviolis, and a range of hoagies at an affordable $7-9. If you want to pair your chicken parmesan dinner with a bottle of Italian wine, feel free to bring your own, as Serpico's is BYOB.

American
Tucked away in the residential section of Pukalani, you would never happen upon the **Pukalani Clubhouse** (360 Pukalani St., 808/572-1325, www.pukalaniclubhouse.com, 7am-8:30pm daily, $9-14) unless you were playing golf at the country club. The food here is a combination of local plate lunch and traditional American, with Maui Cattle Company burgers and deli sandwiches. If you're feeling like you could eat an entire Upcountry cow,

loosen up your belt by taking the "Loco Moco Challenge," a gluttonous undertaking which involves ingesting six beef patties, six eggs, six scoops of rice, a pint of gravy, and a cup of macaroni salad within a gut-busting time of 60 minutes. The reward? Your meal (a $35 value) is free and you get your picture on the wall!

Japanese
About the only thing that Pukalani has in common with cities such as Tokyo, New York, and Chicago is they are all places where Chef Kojima has artfully mastered his sushi trade. At the out-of-the-way **Kojima's Sushi Bar** (81 Makawao Ave., 808/573-2859, www.kojimas-sushi.com, noon-3pm Mon.-Fri., 5pm-9pm Mon.-Sat., $7-16), classic sushi options such as California rolls and rainbow rolls accompany standard plate lunch fare such as teriyaki chicken and seared ahi wraps. Come for dinner and BYOS (bring your own sake). Kojima's is just east of Pukalani Superette in the Pukalani Square shopping center. Its traditional Japanese decor gives the restaurant an air of urban authenticity you would never expect sitting across the street from an old pineapple field.

KEOKEA AND ULUPALAKUA
Continental
The **Ulupalakua Ranch Store** (Kula Hwy. 37, 808/878-2561, www.ulupalakuaranch.com/store, grill 11am-2:30pm daily, $10) is also the only place on the island where you can—believe it or not—order an elk burger for lunch. Despite the quirky signs on the walls, don't be fooled into thinking this is just some out-of-the-way tourist trap. Ulupalakua Ranch is the real deal, and the meat served here is raised right on the same pastures you were looking at when you drove in. This 20,000-acre cattle ranch has raised beef cattle since 1886, and over a hundred head of free-range elk still roam the upper pastures. Other options include the Ulupalakua beef burger, steak chili and rice, or a beef tenderloin sandwich. They also serve salads, but you don't come here to eat quinoa and kale. This is a real ranch that serves real meat, and if the cowboy vibe suddenly strikes

mid-meal you can pick up a belt buckle at the store inside.

Bully's Burgers (15900 Pi'ilani Hwy., 808/878-3272, www.triplelranchmaui.com, 11am-7pm, $9-12) is a roadside stand in the pasturelands of Kanaio where the beef is 100 percent all-natural, and you can occasionally even see the herd being driven by while you dine. This might look like little more than a wooden shack in the middle of nowhere (because that's exactly what it is), but once you chomp into a 10-ounce Double Bully, you can immediately taste the difference of eating locally sourced beef. Seeing as Bully's is only four miles past the Ulupalakua Store, this is the place to come if the Ulupalakua Grill is already closed, or if you're driving the "back road" from Hana and realize you haven't eaten since breakfast.

Coffee Shops

While most visitors are bathing on the shoreline, those in the know are having weekend brunch at (**Grandma's Coffee House** (9232 Kula Hwy., 808/878-2140, www.grandmas-coffee.com, 7am-5pm daily, $13). Most locals won't drive over an hour to get to breakfast, but this is the one exception. The gentle tunes of live slack key guitar mingle with the aroma of freshly roasted coffee, and both waft over the outdoor patio and out into the pastureland below. Doing business out of the simple, green, plantation-style building since 1988, Grandma's coffee's story dates back much further than that. "Grandma" began brewing her own coffee back in 1918, although only for herself and her friends, using locally grown beans and her own roaster. Her coffee tradition was passed down four generations through the family that still operates the restaurant today. The same strain of locally grown beans are still used in all of their coffee, and the same roaster—which is now over 100 years old—sits right there next to the kitchen and is where all the coffee is still roasted today. In addition to the coffee, Grandma's serves up delicious crepes and deli sandwiches which are best enjoyed on the outdoor garden patio overlooking

There are few things better than Sunday brunch at Grandma's Coffee House.

the pastures. On Saturday and Sunday mornings live slack key music is played out on the porch, and the screen door seems to be constantly swinging open with smiling locals who address each other by first name. It's a welcoming atmosphere in the most charming corner of Maui. And if you love the coffee, pick up a bag of beans for the road.

Information and Services

MEDICAL SERVICES

The **Kula Hospital** (100 Keokea Pl., 808/878-1221) in rural Keokea provides the most comprehensive medical care available Upcountry, although it's almost closer to rush to the island's main hospital in Wailuku. The Kula hospital offers 24-hour emergency services and has a clinic open 8am-4pm; make an appointment if it isn't an emergency. In Pukalani the **Maui Medical Center** (55 Pukalani St., 808/573-6200, 8am-5pm Mon.-Fri.) in the Pukalani Terrace Center offers an urgent care clinic, although patients can only be seen by appointment.

For prescription drugs or pharmaceutical needs the **Makawao Town Pharmacy** (1120 Makwao Ave., 808/573-9966) has a counter open 9am-6pm on weekdays and 9am-1pm on Saturday.

In Kula, **Long's Pharmacy** (55 Kiopaa St., 808/573-9300, 8am-8pm Mon.-Sat., 9am-5pm Sun.) provides a full-service pharmacy counter where you can have any prescription called in from a local doctor's office.

BANKS

Upcountry only has three banks, and all of them are in Pukalani. **First Hawaiian Bank** (67 Makawao Ave., 808/572-7238, 8:30am-4pm Mon.-Thurs., 8:30am-6pm Fri., ATM 24 hours) is right down the road from Pukalani Superette market, and the other two, **Bank of Hawaii** (808/572-7242, 8:30am-4pm Mon.-Thurs., 8:30am-6pm Fri., ATM 24 hours) and **American Savings Bank** (808/572-7263, 9am-6pm Mon.-Fri., 9am-1pm Sat.) are within the Pukalani Terrace Center on the corner of Pukalani Street and Old Haleakala Highway.

In Kula, **ATMs** may be found at **True Value Hardware** (3100 Lower Kula Rd., 808/878-2551, 7am-6pm weekdays, 8am-5pm weekends) and **Morihara Store** (4581 Lower Kula Rd., 808/878-2578, 6:30am-8pm Mon.-Sat., 7:30am-8pm Sun.). In Makawao there is an ATM inside **Rodeo General Store** (3661 Baldwin Ave., 808/572-1868, 6:30am-10pm Mon.-Sat., 6:30am-9pm Sun.).

GAS
Makawao

The only gas station in Makawao is the **Ohana Fuels** (1100 Makawao Ave., 808/573-9295, 24 hours) station across the street from Stopwatch Bar and Grill. There is also a small Minit Stop convenience store that sells standard gas station fare as well as basic auto supplies if you're in need of a quick auto fix.

Pukalani

Pukalani has two gas stations, **Shell** (3425 Old Haleakala Hwy., 808/572-3977, 24 hours) and **Ohana Fuels** (3310 Old Haleakala Hwy., 808/572-6350, 24 hours) a quarter-mile from each other along Old Haleakala Highway. While the Shell station only has a tiny walk-in concession booth, the Ohana Fuels station has a Minit Stop convenience store where you can pick up some late-night munchies or an early morning coffee if fueling up for sunrise at Haleakala.

Kula

Both the gas stations in Kula are classically "old school," and you're just as likely to see someone grabbing diesel for farm equipment as you are to see someone putting "the expensive gas" into their foreign-made luxury car. At **True Value Hardware** (3100 Lower Kula Rd.,

808/878-2551, 7am-6pm weekdays, 8am-5pm weekends) you can fill up and also shop for some basic auto supplies. The price of gas here is usually some of the cheapest on the island.

For a true Kula experience, however, why not top off with a few gallons at the historic **Calasa Service Station** (4836 Lower Kula Rd., 808/878-6461, 8am-5pm weekdays, 8am-3pm Sat.), which looks like something out of the 1930s. Attendants still pump the gas for you. To find Calasa just keep driving straight up Lower Kula Road past Holy Ghost Church and Kula Bistro.

Keokea and Ulupalakua

The only gas this far out is at the Chevron station at **Ching Store** (9212 Kula Hwy., 808/878-1556, 7am-5pm daily), although since there are no credit card readers on the pumps outside, you need to be there before the 5pm closing time.

POST OFFICE
Makawao

The **United States Post Office** (1075 Makawao Ave., 808/572-0019, 9am-4:30pm Mon.-Fri., 9am-11am Sat.) is within walking distance from the town center and provides a full range of postal services.

Pukalani

The Pukalani **United States Post Office** (55 Pukalani St., 808/572-0019, 9am-4pm Mon.-Fri.) is much smaller than the one in Makawao but still offers the same range of shipping options.

Kula

Next to Kula Elementary School, the **United States Post Office** (4450 Kula Hwy., 808/876-1056, 8am-4pm Mon.-Fri., 9:30am-11:30am Sat.) is the town's only option for packing and shipping needs.

LIBRARY

The **Makawao Public Library** (1159 Makawao Ave., 808/573-8785, noon-8pm Mon. and Wed., 9:30am-5pm Tues., Thurs., Sat.) offers a decent selection of used reading material. The convenient location in the center of town makes it a nice place to browse for some reading material after enjoying a coffee at the town's cafés.

INTERNET SERVICES

To use a desktop computer at the **Makawao Public Library** (1159 Makawao Ave., 808/573-8785, noon-8pm Mon. and Wed., 9:30am-5pm Tues., Thurs., Sat.) nonresidents need to purchase a nonresident Hawai'i library card which costs $10 for three months or $25 for five years. Wi-Fi is also available, although you still need to enter a valid library card number to access the system. For free Wi-Fi, you can also stop in at Starbucks in the Pukalani Terrace Center, or McDonald's in Pukalani.

Getting There and Around

BUS

Select parts of Upcountry are serviced by the **Maui Bus** (808/871-4838, www.co.maui.hi.us/bus), although no routes extend into Kula. The three bus stop locations which link Upcountry with Kahului are in front of the Pukalani Community Center, in front of the Makawao Library, and in the center of town at Hali'imaile. Rates are $2/person, and the bus makes stops at the Kahului Airport as well as at Queen Ka'ahumanu Mall where you can link up with other lines. The earliest bus leaves from Pukalani Community Center at 6:30am, and later buses run every 90 minutes until 9:30pm, although the last service of the day only goes as far as Kahului Airport. For buses heading farther Upcountry, the earliest departure from Kahului is 6am and the latest is 9pm. For a detailed schedule check online at www.mauicounty.gov.

EAST MAUI: THE ROAD TO HANA

East Maui is more than just a destination—it's a completely different mind-set. Lush, tropical, and laden in waterfalls, East Maui is not only the location of the famous Road to Hana, it's where Maui locals come to escape for a few days. From the windswept taro patches of the Keʻanae Peninsula to the empty pastures of Kaupo, time in East Maui ticks by at a slower place. By no means, however, does that make East Maui lazy. It's also the island's adventure center, where an average day could consist of trekking to remote waterfalls, cliff jumping in a bamboo rainforest, spelunking hidden caves on a black sand beach, or bodysurfing off sandy shores.

Many who drive the legendary Road to Hana (especially those who raced along in a "need to get there" fury) end up confused when they pull into town. Perhaps the two most commonly asked questions are *"This is it?"* and *"Where is the rest of town?"* Understand that Hana is not a destination unto itself; it's more famous for what it *isn't* than for what it is. Hana is *not* like the rest of the island. This sleepy little fishing hamlet is content to drift along at its own pace. Hana is a town where neighbors still talk to each other and wave as they pass on the street; where fishing nets hang in front yards and fish end up on the dinner table instead of hanging on the wall. You don't come to Hana to reach something; you come to leave everything else behind.

Hana was already a plantation town in 1849 when a hard-boiled sea captain named George Wilfong started producing sugar on 60 acres. Later, Danish brothers August and Oscar

HIGHLIGHTS

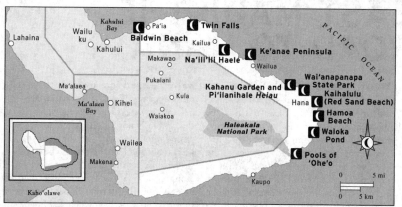

LOOK FOR **C** TO FIND RECOMMENDED SIGHTS, ACTIVITIES, DINING, AND LODGING.

C Ke'anae Peninsula: Whether photographing the mosaic of taro fields from the lookout or watching waves crash on the rocky shoreline, this fertile peninsula provides you a glimpse into one of the last holdout of an ancient way of life (page 275).

C Kahanu Garden and Pi'ilanihale Heiau: Surrounded by a grove of Polynesian plants, take a journey back to ancient Hawai'i and gaze upon the largest *heiau* anywhere in the state (page 278).

C Wai'anapanapa State Park: Swim inside hidden caves, bask on the shores of a black sand beach, and walk in the footsteps of kings at this park on the outskirts of Hana (page 278).

C Waioka Pond: This hidden pool offers some of the island's most scenic swimming and cliff jumping in a natural, oceanfront setting (page 282).

C Pools of 'Ohe'o: Pinch yourself as you explore the postcard photo of Maui you've seen 100 times before taking this trip—dubbed the **Seven Sacred Pools** by the tourism industry. Swim beneath waterfalls tumbling down to the ocean (page 284).

C Baldwin Beach: Start your journey to Hana on the right foot by enjoying an early morning stroll down this undeveloped expanse of shoreline (page 287).

C Kaihalulu Beach (Red Sand Beach): Navigate your way around a hidden coastal path to emerge at a scenic cove of red sand (page 289).

C Hamoa Beach: Bodysurf, surf, or snorkel at a beach that Mark Twain and James Michener both recognized as one of the most beautiful they'd ever seen (page 291).

C Twin Falls: Explore the recesses of this lush compound where you can swim beneath waterfalls in a family-friendly and accessible setting (page 298).

C Na'ili'ili haele: Trek through a bamboo forest punctuated by waterfalls, guava trees, and natural swimming holes along the world-famous Road to Hana (page 299).

Unna came to run the plantation. Through the years, the laborers were a mixture of Hawaiian, Japanese, Chinese, Portuguese, Filipino, and even Puerto Rican stock. The *luna* were Scottish, German, or American. All have combined to become the people of Hana. After sugar production faded out by the 1940s, Paul Fagan founded Hana Ranch, which still raises more than 1,200 head of cattle on about 4,500 acres today. Their faces stare back at you as you drive past, a standard part of Hana's scenery.

A worthwhile stopover on the Road to Hana is trendy, funky, and undeniably sexy Pa'ia (Pa-EE-ah). Nominated by *Coastal Living* magazine as one of the "happiest seaside towns in America," it's unlike anywhere else on the island. It only takes 10 minutes in town to realize that the residents of Pa'ia are stoked on life. Laid-back and worry-free, Pa'ia is a town that skanks along to the beat of its own bongo. When Jerry Garcia died, thousands of descended upon the town when it was determined that his soul had gone to Pa'ia. If you feel that a public sidewalk isn't the proper venue for dreadlocked, barefoot hippies weaving hemp bracelets, this town may not be for you.

East Maui is a pocket of serenity in a rapidly paced world, a breath of fresh air, a weight off your shoulders. Throw in some freshly baked banana bread, fresh-picked fruit from a roadside stand, tent poles or a quaint bed-and-breakfast, and you have a true getaway. Stroll barefoot down the center of the highway and forget the rest of the world even exists.

Driving the Road to Hana

Ah yes, the "Road to Hana." The most loved and loathed section of the island divides visitors into two distinct camps: those who swear it's heaven on earth and those who would rather pull their teeth out than ever drive it again. Most people who don't enjoy their excursion to Hana didn't know what they were getting themselves into. Three little words will make or break your trip:

Don't rush Hana.

Devote a full day to the experience. *Minimum.* You're visiting arguably the most beautiful place on earth; allocate at least an entire day. Two or three days are even better. Don't expect to breeze through and just see it quickly and don't expect to be back on the other side of the island to make dinner reservations. If you're staying in Ka'anapali or Wailea, it will take you 3.5 hours just to reach the Pools of 'Ohe'o (aka Seven Sacred Pools). That's not including any stops—and stops are what make the journey worthwhile.

No one should ever have to endure a journey to Hana without knowing exactly where the next waterfall, hiking trail, ATM, food cart, or restroom is going to be. Since sights can spring up in an instant—and making a U-turn just isn't possible— be prepared. A mile-by-mile rundown of what you'll see along the side of the road follows, with specific sights and places worth stopping to linger described in greater detail.

- **Mile Marker 7:** Start in the town of Pa'ia, located around mile marker 7 on the Hana Highway (Hwy. 36). It's worth stopping to see some of the sights in town, many of which are located on Baldwin Avenue.

PA'IA
Mantokuji Soto Zen Mission

On the eastern side of town—in the direction of Hana—you'll find the **Mantokuji Soto Zen Mission** (253 Hana Hwy., 808/579-8051, www.mantokujimauitemple.org) on a scenic parcel a quarter mile out of town. Established in 1906, this temple is best known for its oceanfront cemetery and the 100-year-old bell hanging out front. Both the bell and a war memorial stupa were delivered from Japan in 1912, during a time when the Asian nation was emerging from wars with both Russia and China. When

Japan went to war with the United States 40 years later, the reverend of the temple was detained as an enemy alien and sent to a Japanese internment camp on the mainland. In 1946, part of the cemetery and some of the temple grounds were destroyed in one of the largest tsunamis to ever hit Hawai'i. The temple has survived these hardships. Visitors are encouraged to attend regularly scheduled zazen meditations and periodic Obon festivals.

Maui Dharma Center

Above the parking lot by Mana Foods, perhaps the most curious of all of Pa'ia's sights is the temple at the **Maui Dharma Center** (81 Baldwin Ave., 6:30am-6:30pm daily) which rises from Pa'ia like an out-of-place white spire. The Dalai Lama himself gave his blessings to this Tibetan Buddhist compound during a visit in 2007. Visitors are encouraged to walk inside and turn the prayer wheel in a reflective and respectful manner.

Old Sugar Mill

Three quarters of a mile above town, the **Old Pa'ia Sugar Mill** is the first of a number of sights which dot the road toward Makawao. This once-thriving mill which defined Pa'ia for generations shuttered its doors in 2000 amid rising operation costs and competition from foreign markets. The massive industrial structure now sits forgotten and graffitied on the side of Baldwin Avenue. Its appearance is so eerie you almost expect to hear voices of plantation workers as they move about the empty corridors.

La'a Kea Community Farm

A half a mile up the road from the forgotten mill is the **La'a Kea Community Farm** (808/281-3463, www.laakea.org, 9am-5pm daily), a small hideaway which defines rebirth on the soil of Pa'ia's past. Started as a means of providing work for adults with developmental disabilities, this humble farm grows organic produce that nourishes your body and your soul. Through the support of the local community (and passing tourists who pop in for

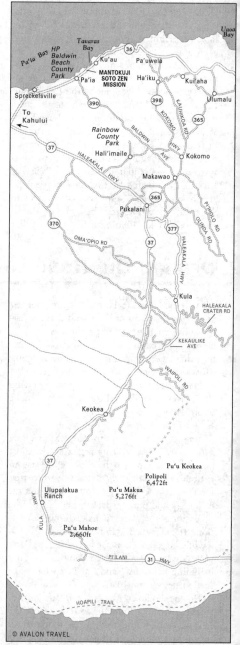

© AVALON TRAVEL

EAST MAUI

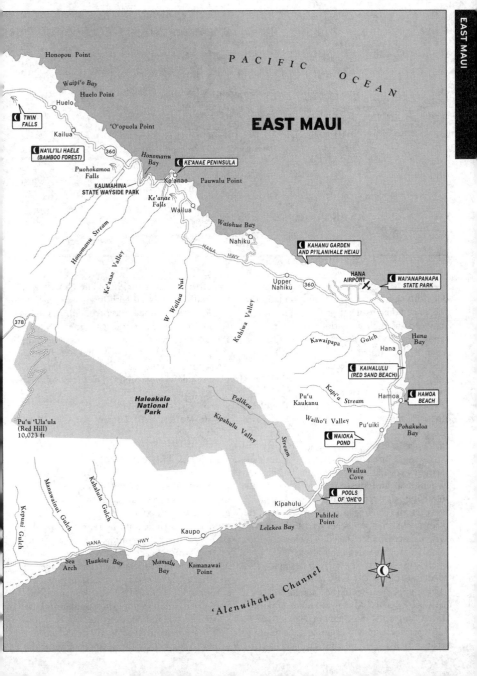

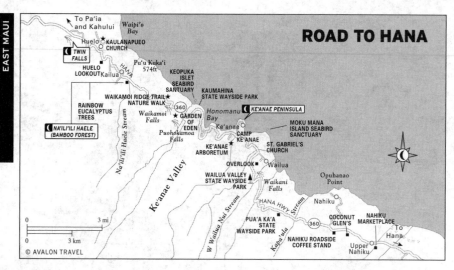

organic snacks such as apple bananas or avocados), this small farm plants crops on land that was once home to sugar plantation camps. As they expand their operations and plant more crops, workers now showcase pieces of history (such as the foundations of old homes) uncovered in the digging process.

Holy Rosary Church

Immigrant Filipino workers constructed **Holy Rosary Church** (954 Baldwin Ave., 808/579-9551, services 7am Mon.-Fri., 7:30am Sun.) in Upper Pa'ia in 1915, during the heyday of Pa'ia's sugar operations. The church dutifully served Pa'ia's Catholic community throughout its tenure as an industrial sugar town. As the sugar industry waned and the workers aged, however, the congregation thinned out. As the historic church approaches its 100th anniversary, visitors are encouraged to leave a donation to aid in much needed renovations.

Makawao Union Church

On the upper reaches of the ambiguous border between Pa'ia and Makawao stands **Makawao Union Church** (1445 Baldwin Ave., 808/579-9261, service 10:30am Sun.), a stone, Gothic-style church placed on the National Register

of Historic Places in 1985. The church was originally established within a wooden building in 1861; the stone reconstruction was overseen by renowned architect Charles William Dickey, the same man responsible for designing the expansive Hui No'eau Visual Arts Center a few miles up the road. The colorful stained glass windows were retained from the original church.

- **Mile Marker 8.5:** Turnoff for Old Maui High

Old Maui High School

Stoic in appearance (and rumored to be haunted), **Old Maui High** (www.oldmauihigh.org) is one of the last relics of Upper Pa'ia's glory days. When traveling toward Hana, by making a right onto Holomua Road and traveling 1.3 miles uphill through a tunnel of trees you'll reach what was once one of Maui's thriving educational centers. Opened in 1913 as the island's first coeducational institution, Old Maui High was the central valley's main school before the population base shifted to Kahului during the 1950s. Some 1,000 students arrived in this rural corner of Hamakuapoko by horse and buggy or the old Kahului Railroad. As plantation workers fanned out to other parts of the island, however, the population of Pa'ia dwindled. When a new Maui High School opened in Kahului in 1972, the old Hamakuapoko campus fell into disrepair. Various organizations have emerged over the last decade to preserve and maintain the 24-acre campus. Tourists rarely visit to Old Maui High, but it's a quick, scenic, and historic detour from the Road to Hana.

• **Mile Marker 8.8:** Ho'okipa Beach Park

Ho'okipa Beach Park

Two miles past the town of Pa'ia is Ho'okipa Beach Park (mile marker 8.8), with a scenic overlook for watching the surf in winter and turtles in summer. This is not only one of the best surfing spots on the island, but it's considered the best windsurfing spot in the world. On most afternoons you can find windsurfers racing through the waves on the left side of the beach. During the winter, watch from the safety of the cliffs as surfers throw themselves into waves that out at over 20 feet. On days when the surf is too big for even the most experienced surfers, Ho'okipa can be an even more dramatic spot for watching the surf than Jaws, because at Ho'okipa you're much closer to the raw power of the ocean. Massive North Pacific swells march their way across the horizon and explode on the jagged rocks with a frothy fury, like white horses galloping on the sea.

• **Mile Marker 10.3:** Maliko Gulch

• **Mile Marker 13.5:** Turnoff for Jaws

Peahi (Jaws)

This is quite possibly the most famous surf break on the planet. Scores of visitors come here hoping to say they saw 70-foot waves during their trip to Hawai'i.

• **Mile Marker 14.5:** Maui Grown Market and Deli advertises that it's the last stop for food before Hana. Don't worry. It isn't.

• **Begin Highway 360**

• **Mile Marker 0:** Note the change in mile

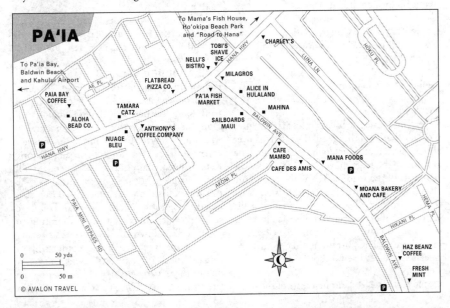

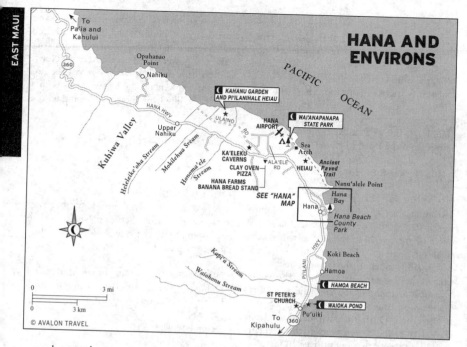

HANA AND ENVIRONS

markers at the junction of Hana Highway and Kaupakalua Road.

- **Mile Marker 0.3:** Congratulations, your first waterfall! Just joking. They get much better than this.

- **Mile Marker 2:** Twin Falls

Twin Falls

When you round the hill by mile marker 2 (remember that the mileage markers started over at the junction of Kaupakalua Road), you'll be amazed at the large gravel parking lot on the right side of the road packed with cars. Many visitors are confused because they can't see anything from the road. As it turns out, Twin Falls is the first set of waterfalls you'll encounter on the Road to Hana (and thereby the closest to many hotels). The 20-minute hike to the falls is relatively accessible for most visitors.

- **Mile Marker 2.8:** Your first taste of the turns

that you're going to experience for the next 20 miles.

- **Mile Marker 3.5:** Turnoff for Door of Faith Road and Kaulanapueo Church

Kaulanapueo Church

Fans of simple and historic churches will enjoy Kaulanapueo Church, 0.2 mile down Door of Faith Road (the one with all of the mailboxes). Don't be fooled by the modern and underwhelming Door of Faith Church on your left when you first turn down the road. Historic Kaulanapueo is around the next bend; you'll notice its green steeple poking out above the treetops. This Protestant church constructed mostly of coral has held Hawaiian language services continuously since its founding in 1853. Riding down this country road gazing out over the blue Pacific, it's comforting to think that this rural area still looks much as it did for those who worshipped here during the late 19th century. There's a small graveyard in the middle of the well-manicured lawn. If you do decide to make a side trip to Kaulanapueo, be warned that the road can often have some deep potholes; be careful if it's been raining heavily.

- **Mile Marker 4.5:** Huelo Lookout fruit stand

- **Mile Marker 4.9:** Your first narrow bridge crossing!

- **Mile Marker 6.5:** Naʻiliʻili haele hike (aka Bamboo Forest)

- **Mile Marker 6.7:** Rainbow eucalyptus trees

Rainbow Eucalyptus Trees

Just past the trailhead for the Naʻiliʻili haele hike is a grove of rainbow eucalyptus trees, silently springing from the green pasturelands. One of the most-photographed sights on the Road to Hana, these trees have bark which drips with pastel hues of red, pink, orange, green, and gray, as if a painter had taken a brush directly to the bark, with deliberate strokes running the length of each narrow tree. Unlike trees which have a cork-like bark, rainbow eucalyptus have a smooth, hard exterior which is constantly going through stages of regrowth. As a section of tree undergoes exfoliation and sheds a section of bark, the young wood exposed has a deep green hue. As the new bark ages in the sun, the wood morphs from green to blue and from purple to orange, eventually dying off once again to reveal the green growth below, starting the cycle anew. Parking can be found either at the trailhead for the Naʻiliʻili haele hike or at a small pullout for a hunting road a hundred yards past the trees.

- **Mile Marker 8.1:** First scenic view of a valley gazing out toward the ocean. Exhale deeply and remember why you drove here. The great views are just getting started!

- **Mile Marker 8.5:** Sweeping view of dense swaths of bamboo crawling their way up the eastern flank of the mountain

- **Mile Marker 9.5:** Waikamoi Ridge Trail

Waikamoi Ridge Trail

The next point of interest on your journey is the Waikamoi Ridge Trail. This small picnic area provides a relaxing place to stretch your legs or enjoy a roadside snack (although there are no restrooms or other facilities). There's a short loop trail here that gains 200 feet of elevation in the surrounding forest.

- **Mile Marker 10:** Waikamoi Falls

Waikamoi Falls

Congratulations, you've reached your first roadside waterfall and swimming hole! Simple, elegant, and easily accessible, Waikamoi Falls is a convenient place to take a dip. The refreshing, cool waters will wake up anyone who might be lagging from rising early. Be careful if you swim; the falls can be raging during or after heavy rains. A small trail leads down to the pool and a second waterfall is accessible above the first pool by wading across a streambed. The only inconvenience here is the lack of parking.

- **Mile Marker 10.5:** The Garden of Eden Botanical Garden and Garden Gourmet food cart

Garden of Eden

Half a mile up the road from Waikamoi Falls is the enticing **Garden of Eden** (808/572-9899, www.mauigardenofeden.com, 8am-3pm daily, $15/person), an ornately manicured 26-acre rainforest utopia. This flank of coastline was once little more than overgrown jungle. In 1991, Alan Bradbury, the state's first I.S.A. certified arborist, slowly but surely began clearing the hillside and replanting native trees. It was truly a labor of love: After two decades of work, the Garden of Eden now has over 600 individually labeled plants. You may recognize this view of the coastline: the opening scene of *Jurassic Park* was filmed there. Those with a keen interest in botany and landscaping will appreciate the sanctuary and it makes a great spot for

EAST MAUI

10 TIPS FOR DRIVING THE ROAD TO HANA

Perhaps one of the most beautiful—if not controversial—activities on Maui is driving the Road to Hana. Weaving its way for 52 miles around 600 curves and over 56 one-lane bridges, it's the most loved and loathed stretch of road on the entire island. Here's how to plan a visit to Hana that will leave you poring over a photo album instead of searching for a divorce lawyer.

1. Hana is not a destination, but a journey. Visitors race all the way to the sleepy village of Hana and are left saying only one thing: "This is it?" With a population of around 1,800, Hana is not big. Hana is not a destination; it's a place to get away from it all.

2. The Road to Hana doesn't actually end at Hana. Technically the famous Road to Hana is only 52 miles long and stretches between Kahului Airport and the town of Hana itself. But the actual road doesn't end in Hana. Many of Hana's natural treasures lie in the 10 miles beyond Hana town. Hamoa Beach, consistently voted as one of the top beaches in the country, is a couple of miles past Hana. So is Waioka Pond, a hidden pool on the rocky coastline. Thirty minutes beyond Hana town are the pools of 'Ohe'o (also known as the Seven Sacred Pools), with a series of cascading waterfalls and pools falling directly into the blue Pacific.

3. Don't drive back the same way you came in. Your rental car contract tells you the road around the back of the island is for four-wheel-drive vehicles only, but that's just not true. Parts are bumpy, and a few miles are dirt road, but unless there's torrential rain, the road is passable with a regular vehicle. Following the back road all the way around the island, you are graced with new views as your surroundings change from lush, tropical rainforest to windswept, arid lava flows.

4. Don't make dinner reservations. Too many people try to squeeze Hana into half a day or end up feeling rushed. Hana is a place to escape from the rush, not add to it. If you're planning a day trip to Hana, block off the entire day, leave early (7am), and see where the day takes you.

5. Stop early, stop often. Take a break for a morning stroll or for breakfast at a tucked-away café. Pick up some snacks and then watch the waves. Stop and swim in waterfalls, hike through bamboo forests, pull off at roadside stands for banana bread. If the guy behind you is on your tail, pull over and let him pass. Who cares? This is Hana, and there isn't any rush.

6. Think hard before taking a van tour. If you question your ability to drive narrow, mountainous roads, then take a guided van tour. Local guides can provide insights into Hawaiian history, culture, and personal anecdotes which add humor to the lengthy drive. The problem is that you're on someone else's schedule. If you decide you want to go bodysurfing, you can't. If you see a waterfall that you want to go swim under, you can't. You're going to be called back to the van.

7. Bring a bathing suit and hiking shoes. Hana is a land of adventure. Pack the necessary wardrobe and equipment for your activity of choice.

8. *Kapu* means keep out. If you see a sign which says *kapu*, it translates to "No Trespassing" or "Keep Out." Move along and enjoy a spot more accessible to the public.

9. Don't stay too long. While Hana can be tough to leave, don't drive home in the dark—particularly if going the back way. If you think driving on narrow, one-lane roads with precipitous drop-offs is difficult during the day, try doing it at night. Leave by 4pm to ensure a well-lit journey home.

10. Stay overnight. A day trip to Hana makes for a long day. Most locals stay overnight, either camping at the Pools of 'Ohe'o or staying in a bed-and-breakfast or the Travaasa Hana hotel. When you wake up, you'll have beaches and swimming holes all to yourself before throngs of day-trippers arrive—usually around 11am. If you've already booked a hotel stay for the entirety of your trip, but you don't want to rush Hana, stay at a bed-and-breakfast and forget about your hotel room on the other side of the island. It will be the best $200 you ever spend.

STAND-UP PADDLING THE MALIKO RUN

© HEATHER ELLISON

Paddlers race to the finish line of the famous Maliko Run.

Unless you're a world-class waterman, don't try the Maliko Run. In the same way that Jaws isn't a surf break that is accessible to visiting surfers, however, it's still interesting to know that it's there.

While most people paddle along flat, calm waters somewhere on the island's south shore, a different subgenre of the sport gets going as the wind gets stronger. "Downwinders" paddle with the breeze at their backs and ride the waves created by wind-whipped ocean swells. This involves paddling over a mile offshore in winds that can reach 40 knots on waves that grow to eight feet or higher. It's an extreme sport reserved for only the world's most competent paddlers.

Of all the places around the globe where the conditions align for an epic downwinder, the Maliko Run on Maui's North Shore is considered to be the granddaddy of them all. Beginning in protected Maliko Gulch 1.5 miles past Ho'okipa Beach Park, the 8.5-mile downwind run goes all the way to Kahului Harbor while paralleling the fabled stretch of Maui's North Shore. Along the two-hour journey (the world's best complete the feat in a little over an hour), paddlers will pass the reefs of Ho'okipa and Kanaha and view the beaches of Pa'ia from the water. In the distance, towering Haleakala stands stoically above the rows of sugarcane fields and flecks of residential homes. While admittedly challenging, the run provides an island vantage point which will only be seen by an experienced few.

While Maliko Runs are a favorite after-work or weekend activity of the island's water sports community, over 200 hundred racers will all gather in the Naish International Paddleboard championship held at Maliko every July. The event gives Maui locals the chance to compete against some of the world's biggest names in paddleboarding such as Jamie Mitchell, Dave Kalama, and Kai Lenny. It's a unique island event which embodies island resident's love for the ocean and adventure.

If you're an avid, experienced paddler well-versed in the nuances of the ocean, **Moore Water Time** (www.moorewatertime.com) can provide a shuttle that will transport you and your board from Kanaha Beach Park or Kahului Harbor to Maliko Gulch so that you can have your car waiting for you at the end of the paddle.

---

a picnic. The $15 entrance fee is a little steep. If you're traveling on a budget, you can get a similar experience at the Ke'anae Arboretum six miles down the road.

• **Mile Marker 11:** Postcard-perfect Upper Puohokamoa Falls. There is only enough parking for 10 cars, but taking the trouble to find a spot is worth it.

Upper Puohokamoa Falls

At a narrow bend in the road at mile marker

© KYLE ELLISON

Puohokamoa Falls is an easily accessible waterfall on the Road to Hana.

11 (just past the Garden of Eden), gentle Puohokomoa Falls is as scenic as they come. Unfortunately, there are only enough parking spaces for about 10 cars and you need to be agile enough to climb a small rock wall to access the trail. If you're lucky enough to find a parking spot and are fit enough, the reward is a swimming hole of tropical simplicity. On the Garden of Eden side of the bridge you'll notice a rock wall toward the back of the parking area, where you can circumvent the concrete barrier (at the time of last visit, no signs warned against entry). A short trail will bring you to the edge of the pool. Signs warn against diving or jumping into the pool, since there's no way to know the depth. Carry your camera for this one. Access to Lower Puohokamoa Falls is severely limited, in part by a concrete barrier, and is not advised.

- **Mile Marker 11.5:** Haipua'ena Falls

Haipua'ena Falls

If you couldn't find parking at Puohokamoa Falls, fear not: half a mile later is the small turnout for Haipua'ena Falls. Parking here can also be limited. The falls aren't nearly as nice as at Puohokamoa, but that may mean it will be less crowded. A swimming pool in the jungle is still a swimming pool in the jungle—you can't go wrong when surrounded by such beauty. It's a nice place to stop for a quick dip, but there's no need to linger for more than 20 minutes.

- **Mile Marker 12.2:** Kaumahina State Wayside Park. Public restrooms and a picnic area with a sweeping view of Ke'anae coastline.

Kaumahina State Wayside Park

Kaumahina State Wayside Park is known for one thing: public restrooms! If you've been holding it since the Huelo fruit stand, this is the first place you'll find any official facilities. There's also a small picnic area on the far side of the restrooms offering a sweeping view of the Ke'anae coastline. A short trail follows the metal fence uphill. Another small trail heads back into the forest, but it quickly dissipates and doesn't lead anywhere at all.

- **Mile Marker 14:** Honomanu Bay

- **Mile Marker 16.5:** Ke'anae Arboretum

Ke'anae Arboretum

Myriad species of trees, from rainbow eucalyptus to guava and sugarcane, are spread throughout the free Ke'anae Arboretum. A 30-minute, paved, wheelchair-accessible trail winds back into the lush surroundings. After 10 minutes of walking, the paved portion of the trail ends and changes to dirt as you make your way past a fence. If you make a left once inside the boundary and head toward Pi'ina'au Stream, you'll find a small hidden swimming hole. Reaching it requires a scramble down the rocks. Following the trail toward the back of the valley will once again lead over a low metal fence; although there are some small waterfalls and swimming holes further up the stream, the trail becomes muddy, narrow, and less worth the effort.

- **Mile Marker 16.6:** Turnoff for Ke'anae village

C Ke'anae Peninsula

This fertile, volcanic sprig of land jutting out from the coastline seems frozen in time. When you turn off the highway at the 16.6 mile marker you pass through a portal to a way of life you forgot existed. The peninsula itself is a mosaic of irrigated green taro fields, vital to the livelihood of Ke'anae. Legend says the soil was originally imported one basket at a time by a chief who demanded the villagers turn the volcanic peninsula into arable land. Every part of the plant is used in some type of food (including everyone's favorite, *poi*). Taro (also known as *kalo*) isn't just a crop, it's a representation of native Hawaiian heritage. In Hawaiian mythology, a child named Haloa was stillborn and, upon being buried, turned into a taro plant. Haloa's brother became the ancestor of the Hawaiian people. In this way,

native Hawaiians have a blood relationship to the plant which provides them with sustenance.

In addition to seeing the taro fields, you can watch the powerful surf crash onto the rugged, volcanic shoreline. There aren't any beaches on the Ke'anae Peninsula, although you'll often encounter locals fishing. The main sight is **Lanakila 'Ihi'ihi O Lehowa o Na Kaua Congregational Church,** constructed in 1860. The church sits right next to a softball field against the dramatic backdrop of the Ke'anae Valley. It was the only building on the peninsula to survive the devastating tsunami of 1946. While down on the peninsula, stop in at **Auntie Sandy's** (808/248-7448, www.keanae-maui.blogspot.com) for some banana bread.

- **Mile Marker 17:** Ke'anae Overlook

- **Mile Marker 17.3:** Halfway to Hana store and ATM

- **Mile Marker 18:** Turnoff for Wailua village and Uncle Harry's food stand

Wailua

While Ke'anae has some tourist draws, the adjacent peninsula of Wailua at mile marker 18 rarely sees any visitors. This is one of the few spots on the island where native Hawaiians continue to live like their ancestors. A perk of venturing down this road is that you're greeted with a view of Lower Waikani Falls you can't see from anywhere on the main road. Just follow the main, paved road all the way to the end, and you'll spot the falls tumbling down the distant hillside. The view of the falls is only a five-minute diversion. A drive down into Wailua offers a no-nonsense look at life in an authentic fishing village.

- **Mile Marker 18.5:** Taro *lo'i* (fields) and small waterfalls coming down the road

- **Mile Marker 18.7:** Wailua Valley Wayside Park

Keʻanae Peninsula, as seen from the Overlook

© HEATHER ELLISON

Wailua Valley State Wayside Park

Only 0.7 miles from the Wailua turnoff is the small parking area for Wailua Valley State Wayside Park. The dirt hunting road which runs back into the valley looks as if it might disappear, but it leads to an overlook offering sweeping coastal views. Many visitors drive right past it because you can't see the overlook from the road; you need to stop in the designated parking area and look to your right for a hidden set of stairs. Follow the stairs to the top, and you'll be rewarded with a panoramic vista from the **Keʻanae Overlook.** It's a good place to stretch your legs and get a photo that not too many others will have.

- **Mile Marker 19.6:** Upper Waikani Falls

Upper Waikani Falls

Back on the road, the next sight you'll encounter is the three-part Upper Waikani Falls, also referred to as Three Bears Falls. This is a great place to stop for a swim. There's only enough parking for a few cars. If you find a spot, look on the Hana side of the bridge for a sketchy drop-off that leads down onto the trail. Make your way down the small trail to bathe in the beauty of this roadside favorite. On days with heavy rainfall, the three-part falls can become a single torrent of angry runoff. On days like this, enjoy the falls from a distance.

- **Mile Marker 22.6:** Puaʻa Kaʻa State Wayside Park

Puaʻa Kaʻa State Wayside Park

This small roadside park sports the best name of any site along the drive: It translates as "Park of the Rolling Pigs." Most people stop for the restrooms. There are also small picnic pavilions on the *mauka* side of the highway looking out over the stream. A short, three-minute walk leads from the road up the stream to an underrated swimming pool and waterfall. This small waterfall is the most accessible along the Road to Hana. Signs warn against venturing farther than the first falls; respect them. Driving past "the park of the rolling pigs," will bring you to

© JENNA STRUBHAR

Lanakila 'Ihi'ihi O Lehowa o Na Kaua Congregational Church in Keanae

a curvy section of road, with little in the way of sights for two miles.

- **Mile Marker 24.1:** Painted Little Green Shack

- **Mile Marker 25:** Turnoff for Lower Nahiku Road and pullout for Makapipi Falls

Nahiku Village

Just before mile marker 25 you'll cross over a bridge spanning thundering Makapipi Falls. Immediately on the other side of the bridge is the turnoff for Lower Nahiku Village, a laid-back, rural outpost where agriculture and family are the pillars of existence. At the end of the road down into Nahiku you'll find a stunning overlook where multiple waterfalls cascade into the sea. If you skipped the drive on the Ke'anae Peninsula, consider making the steep, 2.5-mile descent to the shoreline for the chance to witness this pristine section of coastline. The road is narrow and at many points only a single lane, so take it slow. Since this is a small community,

be respectful of *Kapu* (No Trespassing) signs placed on private property. Park your car well off the road and pack out any garbage. Many village residents would rather go back to the days when the overlook was completely off the tourist map. As long as you respect to those who live here, you in turn will be met with respect.

Once you travel 2.2 miles, you will reach the **Nahiku Protestant Church** and a fork in the road. Go left. Continue on this road for another 100 yards to reach a rickety wooden bridge, which offer a view of the dense jungle. In another 0.2 mile the road dead-ends in a parking area which gazes back across Honolulunui Bay toward the Wailua Peninsula. Walk back uphill for about 30 yards, where you see an overlook for a small waterfall tumbling directly into the sea. Follow the small trail from the end of the parking area leading back into a cove and you'll encounter a second waterfall. There isn't much swimming here; the main draws are the coastal views and the streams which end their mountain-to-sea journey in a dramatic terminus.

- **Mile Marker 26.5:** Nahiku Roadside Coffee Stand

- **Mile Marker 27.5:** Coconut Glen's Ice Cream Stand

- **Mile Marker 28.3:** Banana bread stand

- **Mile Marker 28.7:** Nahiku Marketplace

- **Mile Marker 29.7:** View of the Hana Airport

- **Mile Marker 31:** Turnoff for Ka'eleku Caverns and Kahanu Garden

Ka'eleku Caverns

As you make your way from Nahiku Marketplace, the first set of sights you'll encounter are a few miles before "downtown" Hana. At mile marker 31 you'll see the signs for **Ka'eleku Caverns** (808/248-7307, www.mauicave.com, 10:30am-4pm daily, $12.50/person). Turn down 'Ula'ino Road to visit this subterranean network of lava tubes, the 18th largest in the world and the only lava tubes on Maui that are navigable and open to the public. You can walk upright all the way, so no kneeling or crawling is involved, and there are no mosquitoes or bats! The underground network of tunnels runs for over two miles. As lava surged through these tubes, it scored the walls. Benches and ledges were left where lava cooled faster on the periphery than in the middle. Cave explorers are given a flashlight to examine the stalactite-encrusted surroundings. On your way out, navigate your way through the maze of red *ti* leaves which create the only such maze found anywhere on the planet. Walking the caverns at an average pace will take about 30 minutes. There are no garbage cans or restrooms, so pack out your trash.

◖ Kahanu Garden and Pi'ilanihale *Heiau*

On 'Ula'ino Road, the pavement gradually gives way to dirt road leading to **Kahanu Garden** (808/248-8912, www.ntbg.org, 9am-2pm Mon.-Sat., $10). This 464-acre property is

in Honoma'ele, an area ceded in 1848 to Chief Kahanu by King Kamehameha III. The land has remained largely unchanged since the days of ancient Hawai'i. The sprawling gardens focuses on plant species that are integral parts of Polynesian culture. You're greeted by a massive grove of *ulu* (breadfruit), which come thundering to earth with a telltale crash. There are also groves of bananas, coconuts, taro, sweet potato, sugarcane, and 'awa. A self-guided tour details the history of these plants and the uses they had for native Polynesians.

Towering **Pi'ilanihale *Heiau*,** a massive, multi-tiered stone structure, is the largest remaining *heiau* in the state of Hawai'i. The walls stretch over 50 feet high in some places and the stone platforms are the size of two professional football fields. Multiple archaeological surveys have determined that the temple was most likely built in stages and dates back as far as the 14th century.

- **Mile Marker 31.2:** Hana Farms banana bread stand and clay-oven pizza

- **Mile Marker 31.4:** Turnoff for Hana Airport

- **Mile Marker 32:** Turnoff for Wai'anapanapa State Park

◖ Wai'anapanapa State Park

Rugged Wai'anapanapa State Park is often known as "black sand beach." At the beach overlook, you'll be greeted with one of the most iconic vistas on the drive to Hana. Take it slow on the 0.5-mile road down to the park; there are often small children playing. Once you reach the park, turn left at the parking lot and follow the road to the end, where you can access the black sand of Pa'iloa Beach and its freshwater caves. Comprised of crushed black lava rock, the sand is as black as Hana's gaping night sky. Lush green foliage clings to the surrounding coastline, and dramatic sea arches and volcanic promontories jut into the frothy white sea. Since it faces nearly directly east, this is a popular venue for sunrise weddings.

Across from the viewpoint you can

sometimes make out local kids cliff jumping off the various rock structures into the water. The currents here can be wicked, so it's best to stay on dry land. A small trail and set of stairs lead down to the beach itself. For the best photo-op, hike across the sand and onto the trail running out to the distant point. From this vantage, you can get a wide-angle photo of the surrounding coastline.

Back on the main, paved trail by the parking lot overlook, you'll see a trail that runs in the opposite direction of the beach; this is the beginning of a popular coastal hike. One of the more popular stops along this trail is a blowhole that erupts on days with large surf. Maintain a safe distance; visitors have been swept into the ocean here.

The other main draw of Wai'anapanapa is the system of freshwater caves hidden in a grotto not far from the parking area. Following the cave trail from the parking lot, you'll be met with a sign that details the legend of the caves. Go left at the sign and travel downhill on a short loop trail. After a three-minute walk

you'll reach the cave entrance. The clear, fresh water is crisp and cold. Back toward the right you'll find a separate cavern. The water level fluctuates with the ocean tides, so you might have to duck your head underwater to reach the opening of the second cave. Only proceed if you're comfortable with your swimming abilities and have a strong flashlight to illuminate the way. On the other side of the main cave, another narrow tunnel leads back to the left, about 15 yards into utter darkness. The cave complex is one of the true wonders of Hana.

- **Mile Marker 32.7:** Hana school

- **Mile Marker 34:** Fork in the road; stay left. Road will rejoin with main highway in 1.5 miles via a right turn at the softball field in Hana town.

HANA TOWN

Hana has deep ties to its history. Before the arrival of Western explorers, it was a stronghold that was conquered and reconquered by

© HEATHER ELLISON

freshwater caves at Wai'anapanapa State Park

EAST MAUI

the kings of Maui and those of the Big Island. The most strategic and historically rich spot is Kaʻuiki Hill, the remnant of a cinder cone that dominates Hana Bay. It's said that the demigod Maui transformed his daughter's lover into Kaʻuiki Hill and turned her into the gentle rains that bathe it to this day.

Hana was already a plantation town in 1849 when sea captain George Wilfong started producing sugar on 60 acres here. After sugar production faded out in the 1940s, San Francisco industrialist Paul Fagan bought 14,000 acres of what was to become the Hana Ranch. Today, Hana's population, at 1,200, continues to be predominantly Hawaiian. Visitors will enjoy a host of sights scattered throughout the community.

Fagan Memorial

Once you finally roll in to Hana town, one of the most prominent sights is a massive cross presiding above the village. Set on the 545-foot summit of Puʻu O Kahaula (Lyon's Hill), the **Fagan Memorial** was constructed to honor the

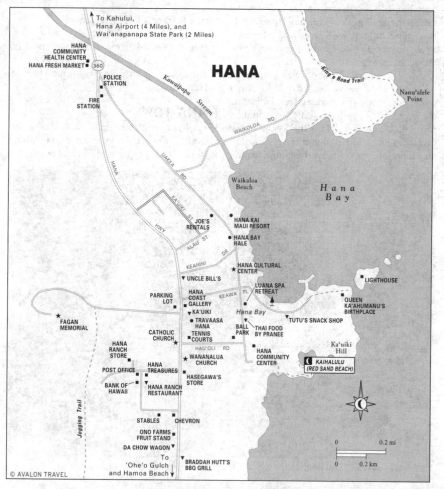

© AVALON TRAVEL

PAUL FAGAN AND HANA RANCH

After having grown to half a dozen plantations by the 1880s, sugar production faded out by the 1940s, and Hana began to die, its population dipping below 500. In 1944, San Francisco industrialist Paul Fagan bought 14,000 acres of what was to become the **Hana Ranch.** Realizing that sugar was *pau* (finished), he replanted his lands in *pangola* range grass and imported 300 Hereford cattle from another holding on Moloka'i. Today, Hana Ranch has about 4,500 acres and raises more than 1,200 head of cattle. Their faces stare back at you as you drive past.

Fagan loved Hana and felt an obligation to and affection for its people. He also decided to retire here, and with enough money to materialize just about anything, he decided that Hana could best survive through limited tourism. He built the Ka'uiki Inn in 1946, later to become the Hotel Hana-Maui, which catered to millionaires, mostly his friends. Fagan owned a baseball team, the San Francisco Seals, and brought them to Hana in 1946 for spring training. The community baseball field behind the hotel was made for them. This was a brilliant publicity move because sportswriters followed along; becoming enchanted with Hana, they gave it a great deal of copy and were probably the first to publicize the phrase "Heavenly Hana." It wasn't long before tourists began arriving.

Unfortunately, the greatest heartbreak in modern Hana history occurred at just about the same time, on April 1, 1946. An earthquake in Alaska's Aleutian Islands sent a huge tsunami that raked the Hana coast, killed a dozen, and destroyed hundreds of homes. Hana recovered but never forgot. Life went on, and the menfolk began working as *paniolo* on Fagan's ranch. Entire families went to work at the hotel and Hana lived again. This legacy of quietude and old-fashioned *aloha* has attracted people to Hana ever since. Everyone knows that Hana's future lies in its uniqueness and remoteness, and no one wants it to change.

town's modern founder—Paul Fagan—after he passed away in 1960. The memorial is accessible by following a steep walking path departing from the parking lot of the Travaasa Hana hotel. Or, if you ask at the front desk, they'll sometimes grant you the key to drive up to the top if your mobility isn't what it used to be. If you make the trek to the summit, watch out for the and the gooey presents they leave on the road. When in season, there are a number of guava trees toward the summit which can provide a healthy midday snack. Atop the summit you're treated to the best view in Hana, with a panoramic vista out over historic Hana Bay and 'Alau Island in the distance.

Wananalua Church

Across the street from the ball field at one of the only intersections in town, the **Wananalua Congregational Church** is a historic place of worship built from coral blocks in 1838. Upon its founding, missionaries deliberately and symbolically built it on top of an old *heiau* where the pagan gods had been worshipped for centuries. This small church was placed on the National Register of Historic Places in 1988. Sunday services are still held every week at 10am.

Hana Cultural Center

While it might not look like much from the outside, the humble yet informative **Hana Cultural Center** (4974 Uakea Rd., 808/248-8622, www.hanaculturalcenter.org, 10am-4pm Mon.-Thurs., $3) provides a historical backbone for the town. Over the course of Maui's history, Hana has been a unique eastern outpost, with one foot on Maui and one foot on the Big Island. Visitors to the Hana Cultural Center can not only see ancient Hawaiian artifacts excavated from the Hana region (such as stone adzes and hand-woven fishnets), but they'll also get a chance to walk around the Hana courthouse listed on the National

Register of Historic Places in 1991. Like something out of an old Western movie, the one-room courthouse still holds sessions on the first Tuesday of each month, and in a testament to the island's multicultural heritage, the proceedings can take place in no fewer than 24 languages. During the rest of the month when court isn't in session, the courthouse serves as a somber museum where Hana residents recount the morning of the 1946 tsunami which devastated the eastern end of the island. If you have an interest in the history of Hana, there's no finer place to stop along your journey.

- **Highway 330:** Technically, Highway 360 ended at Hana Bay and Highway 330 started back at the fork in the road by the fire station. Once you drive past the center of Hana town (i.e., Hasegawa General Store and the gas station), you are now traveling on Highway 330, although the mileage markers don't start again for a couple of miles, and when they do, they are now counting down

A cliff jumper takes to the air at Hana's Waioka Pond.

as opposed to up. The turnoff for Hamoa Beach and Koki Beach is at the first turnoff for Haneo'o Road about 1.5 miles past the center of Hana town, which is before the mileage markers begin again. There are two turnoffs for Haneo'o Road, and you want to make sure you take the first one because this is the direction that local traffic naturally travels.

HANA TO KIPAHULU

- **Mile Marker 51:** The mileage markers restart

- **Mile Marker 48:** Waioka Pond

Waioka Pond

Hidden at mile marker 48, Waioka Pond is a local favorite which remains controversial. Waioka Pond (often referred to as Venus Pool) is a "locals only" spot that will need to be respected to remain open. You need to cross through a private pasture to get to the ocean-front pool. Because it's such a popular spot among locals, the landowners don't want to completely restrict access—yet. An injury, a lawsuit, or other negative impacts on the environment could result in the pond being closed to visitors and locals alike. So be careful, be respectful, and tread lightly.

For responsible visitors, this is one of the most scenic spots on the island. The first challenge is finding a legal parking spot. Because the *mauka* (mountain side) of the road is lined with residential homes, the only parking is along a fence on the *makai* (ocean side) of the road. In order to park legally—facing the correct direction—you need to cross over the bridge past the 48 mile marker sign, pull off the side of the road, flip a U-turn, and then start traveling back toward Hana town. Now that you're facing the correct direction, you can find a parking spot along the grass bordering the thin metal fence. Once you've parked, follow the fence line toward the bridge where you'll notice the signs and a small but deliberate opening in the fence. Pass through this opening and then follow the thin dirt trail running

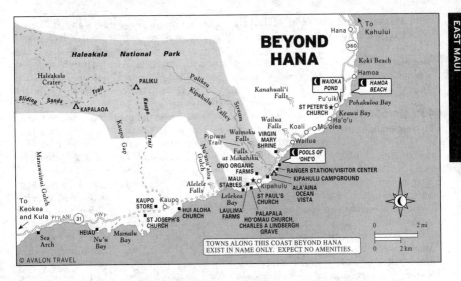

through the pasture down toward the shoreline. Make a right down through the trees at the concrete structure and you'll emerge at a cliff face peering out over a large pool. This first overlook is a popular cliff diving spot among locals. To reach the pool without jumping, clamber down the rocks off to your right. The pool is fed by both fresh stream water as well as saltwater washing in from the ocean. There's a small island in the middle of the pool; swim over for a view of the rocky shoreline.

Waioka Pond truly is special among Hana sights, and it's the type of place that locals will use as their mental happy place when hard times have them down. Waioka deserves to be experienced by all, so be respectful to help preserve access for future visitors.

- **Mile Marker 47.5:** Fruit and flower stand popular with tour buses

- **Mile Marker 46.3:** Karen Davidson Fine Art

- **Mile Marker 45.9:** Go Packers!

- **Mile Marker 45.3:** The road becomes *narrow* and offers dramatic views of coast

- **Mile Marker 45.2:** Roadside waterfall!

- **Mile Marker 44.8:** Wailua Falls

Wailua Falls

Prominently visible on the right side of the road is 80-foot Wailua Falls, a wispy cascade that could be the most photographed waterfall on Maui. Although there's no denying its beauty, the throngs of visitors and street-side merchants detract from the experience. The falls aren't that much different than the dozen or so waterfalls you've already passed on the road up to this point; what makes them so popular is that there is room for tour vans to park. The best way to experience these falls is to take the short trail down to the base and take a dip in the swimming pools, away from the crowds.

- **Mile Marker 43.2, 42.9:** Old bridges from 1910

- **Mile Marker 42.5:** Another waterfall!

- **Mile Marker 42.3:** Horses with the best view in the world

- **Mile Marker 42.2:** Start of Haleakala National Park, Kipahulu section

- **Mile Marker 42.1:** 'Ohe'o Stream and bridge looking over the incorrectly named Seven Sacred Pools

◖ Pools of 'Ohe'o

The most popular attraction in Kipahulu are the fabled Pools of 'Ohe'o inside Haleakala National Park (808/248-7375, www.nps.gov/hale). The name **Seven Sacred Pools** is the largest misnomer on the island. There are far more than seven pools and there's no record in Hawaiian history of these pools being sacred. The name likely began as a marketing ploy by the staff at a nearby hotel (now the Travaasa Hana) in the 1940s. But the name stuck and continues to be used to this day. The real name is 'Ohe'o (pronounced oh-HEY-oh); locals will appreciate you using it.

This part of the island is truly stunning. The first taste you'll get of the park is crossing over 'Ohe'o Gulch on a bridge at mile marker 42.1.

the unparalleled beauty of 'Ohe'o

There's a breathtaking view of the pools here. Try not to linger too long, as you'll stop traffic. The entrance to the park is 0.4 mile down the road. The entrance fee is $10/vehicle (If you have visited Haleakala National Park within the last three days, your paperwork will still allow you entry).

Once inside the park, you'll notice a large parking lot next to an informative visitor center. Take time to explore the visitor center because it's the best place on this side of the island to gain an understanding of the history, culture, and unique environment of the Kipahulu region. Rangers here are the best sources of information on current conditions of trails and waterfalls throughout the park.

The visitor center is also where you begin the Kuloa Point Loop Trail leading down to the famous pools. Along the 10-minute walk you'll go through groves of *hala* trees and past a number of historic sites. Eventually the trail emerges at a staircase down to the pools and one of the most iconic vistas in Hawai'i.

On most days the three main pools are open for exploring and swimming, although they're closed during heavy rains and flash floods. Reaching the uppermost pools requires some rock scaling; it's well worth the effort if you're physically fit.

- **Mile Marker 41.9:** Trailhead for Pipiwai Trail (parking for trailhead is inside park)

- **Mile Marker 41.7:** Entry to Haleakala National Park

- **Mile Marker 41.2:** Ono Organic Farms

Ono Organic Farms

The granddaddy of all the organic farms is **Ono Organic Farms** (808/248-7779, www.ono-farms.com, tours $35 adult, children under 10 free), half a mile past the entrance to Haleakala National Park. If you're a fan of exotic produce, you'll be absolutely blown away by the selection at this 50-acre farm. In addition to growing over 3,000 pounds of bananas *every week,* this farm also cultivates durian, cacao, coffee, tea, 'awa, star fruit, Surinam cherries, and 60 other types of tropical and exotic fruits. Owner Chuck Boerner recommends you come hungry. Tours run Monday-Friday at 1:30pm and last two hours. The cost of the tour more than pays for itself in food, local knowledge, and genuine island experience, offering a culinary journey of certified organic and GMO-free produce plucked directly from the land. Chuck is happy to "talk story" about everything from the history of Kipahulu to surfing (the movie *Blue Crush* was based on his daughter Lilia and her friends surfing around Maui). A genuine spirit of *aloha* permeates the compound. It's easiest to take the tour if you're staying overnight in Hana. The driveway up to the farm is part of the adventure.

- **Mile Marker 40.9:** Ho'onanea Farms fruit and coffee stand

- **Mile Marker 40.8:** Turnoff for Palapala Ho'omau Church

Palapala Ho'omau Church

This unassuming, blissfully tropical church founded in 1864 is the final resting place of historic aviator **Charles Lindbergh.** If you reach the fruit stand at Laulima Farm, you've gone too far. Once on the correct road, follow the signs which point out the church and park in the shade of an enveloping banyan. The doors of this church are often locked, but the main draws are the rural beauty and the historic gravesite. A small trail from the back of the cemetery leads to **Kipahulu Point Park** which offers a basic picnic table overlooking the coast.

- **Mile Marker 40.6:** Laulima Farm fruit stand and kitchen

Laulima Farm

Just 0.2 mile past the turnoff for the church is eccentric and welcoming **Laulima Farm** (9am-5pm Tues.-Sun.), a sprawling compound growing a wealth of organic produce. The small roadside kitchen is for a healthy afternoon snack. At one time, you could blend your own smoothie here by riding a bicycle-powered blender, but recent objections from the Health Department have discontinued that practice. Thankfully, the farm still retains its funky charm.

- **Mile Marker 39.2:** Lelekea Bay

- **Mile Marker 39:** Road begins to deteriorate and becomes narrow with precipitous dropoffs. This is where you should turn back if you don't want to drive around the "back" of the island. As a point of reference, from this point it's 50 miles to Kahului Airport going around the back side, and it will take about two hours without stopping. If you choose to return the way you came, it's 60 miles, and it will take about 2.5 hours without stopping. While bumpier, the back road is much straighter and has less traffic.

- **Mile Marker 38.8:** Alelele Falls

Alelele Falls

You've seen *a lot* of waterfalls on your journey, but 60-foot Alelele Falls truly are a beauty. Reaching the falls requires a short 10-minute hike. Although parking for the trailhead is on the Kaupo side of the bridge at mile marker 38.8, the trailhead itself is back on the Kipahulu side at the spot where the bridge begins. Following this well-defined trail, you'll crisscross the stream a couple of times and pass by ancient lava rock walls before emerging at the base of the pristine falls.

- **Mile Marker 38.5:** Highway 31 begins.

- **Mile Marker 38.4:** The scariest section of road you'll encounter. If you make it past this without a heart attack, you'll be fine the rest of the way!

- **Mile Marker 37.8:** Road turns to dirt.

- **Mile Marker 36:** Surroundings morph from tropical and lush to windswept and arid. Welcome to Kaupo!

© KYLE ELLISON

Kaupo Store

- **Mile Marker 35.5:** Overlook for Hui Aloha Church (1859). Public access is no longer possible. The best way to get a photo is from this small overlook.

- **Mile Marker 34.9:** Smile!

- **Mile Marker 34.6:** Kaupo Store

Kaupo Store

No other store on the island will amaze you quite like **Kaupo Store** (10am-5pm Mon.-Sat.). "How," you ask yourself, "can anyone live out here? How is there a store out here?" The area surrounding Kaupo Store feels like the end of the earth. It's squirreled away inside a building constructed in 1925. The property has the appearance of an American Plains town during the Dust Bowl; you could be excused for thinking this was a landlocked ghost town. Inside visitors will be happy to find cold drinks and Haagen-Dazs ice-cream bars in a freezer like the one in Grandma's basement. It won't come as a surprise that transactions are cash

only. Stock up on water and snacks because it's a long, winding, beautiful drive from here to the next place that sells anything.

- **Mile Marker 33.5:** St. Joseph's Church and view of Kaupo Gap

St. Joseph's Church and View of Kaupo Gap

St. Joseph's Church has stood in this solitary location a mile past Kaupo Store at mile marker 33.5 since 1862. One of the main reasons to stop here is the sweeping view of rugged Kaupo Gap. At the upper rim of the gap is the 6,800-foot floor of Haleakala Crater. At one time, lava spilled down this mountainside as if poured from a massive cauldron.

- **Mile Marker 31.8:** The most amazing view of Haleakala you will ever see

- **Mile Marker 31.1:** The gate which leads to Nu'u Bay

- **Mile Marker 30.1:** Huakini Bay

Nu'u Bay, Huakini Bay, and the Rugged "Back Side"

If you thought the stretch of road between Kipahulu and Kaupo was desolate, you're in for a real treat. Once you leave St. Joseph's Church, the southeastern flank of Haleakala opens up into the most dramatic panorama you'll find on the island—a pristine expanse of wide-open country. You can be excused for wanting to pull over every 5-10 minutes to gawk at the desolate beauty. The road on this section of coast is exceptionally bumpy, so give the car in front of you plenty of space. After Manawainui Gulch (with a bridge in the middle of nowhere), the road begins its gradual climb away from the coast and up to the 3,000-foot elevation of Keokea.

- **Mile Marker 29:** You survived the worst part of the road! Smooth pavement begins.

- **Mile Marker 28.7:** Beautiful view of a lava rock sea arch

- **Mile Marker 27.3:** Manawainui Bridge and gulch

From this point on, the road climbs in elevation through the rural communities of Kahikinui and Kanaio before wrapping around to the Tedeschi Winery in Ulupalakua 13 miles later. If it's before 5pm, you can toast to your success at the winery, although you won't find any real restaurants or gasoline until you get to Grandma's Coffee House in Keokea another 5.2 miles past Ulupalakua.

Congratulations! You've just survived the drive around the "back" of the island. When you make it back to your hotel at night, it will truly feel as if you've journeyed to the end of the earth.

Beaches

There isn't a single stretch of sand in all of East Maui that is home to a condo or resort. Beaches remain windswept, undeveloped, and rural. Due to the easterly trade winds, there isn't much snorkeling along east shore beaches. The water can be rough due to exposed and choppy ocean conditions. Bodysurfing replaces scuba diving, windsurfing replaces kayaking. Mornings offer the calmest conditions, perfect for a jog, a quick dip, or a chance to quiet your head and commune with nature.

PA'IA
◖ Baldwin Beach

Not enough visitors spend time at long, wide, and mostly empty **Baldwin Beach,** which is a mistake. You have a better chance of finding a drum circle or guitar jam than walking past an oceanfront lu'au. This is a popular local bodysurfing spot, although the waves can get large during winter. Baldwin is at its best in the morning before the afternoon trade winds pick up, and there's no better place on the island for enjoying a morning stroll. The best way to kick off a trip to Hana is to arrive in Pa'ia around 7am, grab a coffee in town from Anthony's, and spend 30 minutes walking the length of Baldwin, the turquoise water and white sand creating a reflective amphitheater of calm.

At the far western end of the beach (the side farthest from Pa'ia) is a small cove known as **Baby Beach,** where a fringing reef creates a natural pool perfect for wading with young ones. Instead of walking the length of Baldwin, you can also access Baby Beach by turning on Nonohe Place off Hana Highway, followed by a right on Pa'ani Place, and a quick left onto Kealakai Place. On the far eastern end of Baldwin (the side closest to Pa'ia), a small trail leads around the point and connects with a hidden beach that's next to Pa'ia Bay. This little-known stretch of sand is often occupied by sun-worshipping nudists, affable hippies, and locals passing around the *pakalolo*. If you visit during the afternoon and the wind is howling, the cove on the far eastern end of Baldwin is protected from the wind and offers calm swimming during most of the year.

Not everything here is idyllic. The parking lot can attract unsavory characters. Don't leave any valuables in your car. Respect the warning signs that lifeguards have posted. Although there are plans for restrooms in the near future, green port-a-potties are the lone facilities.

Pa'ia Bay

The closest beach to the center of town, **Pa'ia Bay** is as active as Baldwin is calm, with a basketball court in a small park area and overflow parking for the town. The skate park at the Pa'ia Youth Center teems with area youth. Bodyboarders and surfers flock here for the waves and a number of downhill bike companies finish tours here after descending 6,500 feet down the mountainside. There are restrooms, a beach shower,

and an ever-changing cast of entertaining and colorful characters.

Kuau Cove

The scenic backdrop for Mama's Fish House, where most visitors take an obligatory sunset photo, is this public beach. This small cove has a smattering of sand and an intriguing system of tidepools great for exploring with small children. The beach shrinks at high tide, so low tide is the best for poring over the rocks to take a peek at all the slippery critters. There are a few parking spots near Mama's Fish House; the spaces with blue cones are designated as beach parking.

Tavares Bay (aka Blue Tile Roof)

Barely visible from Hana Highway, the access for the sandy cove at **Tavares Bay** can be found by turning at the house with the blue tile roof. Located 0.6 miles past the stoplight in Pa'ia, this beach gets windy in the afternoon and offers marginal, shallow swimming. Tavares can get popular on the weekends, but the crowds

Black Sand Beach at Wai'anapanapa State Park

© HEATHER ELLISON

during the weekdays are usually thin. The only facilities are a couple of port-a-potties in the dirt parking lot. On occasion the parking lot can turn into a raucous local tailgate party.

Ho'okipa Beach Park

The global epicenter of the windsurfing world, **Ho'okipa** also offers a thin, sandy beach better for tanning than any form of swimming. A fringing reef creates a small pond which is nice for small children. A wide range of international visitors can usually be found sunning here. Mornings are usually calm at Ho'okipa. When the surf isn't too high, local spearfishers dive for *tako* (octopus) and you'll see numerous sea turtles coming up to breathe. There are two lifeguard towers as well as showers. A heavy local crowd usually dominates the pavilion area. The best place for visitors is on the stretch of sand on the left side of the beach. The parking can be tight.

ROAD TO HANA
Honomanu Bay

Although you don't realize it while driving, only a small section of the Road to Hana actually hugs the coastline. There are dramatic vistas out over the water, but most of the time you're looking from at least a mile inland. The only exception to this rule is **Honomanu Bay,** a deep cleft in the mountainside where a thickly forested valley gives way to a gray sand beach. Due to the rough water there isn't any swimming at Honomanu. You'll find the beach empty. Accessing Honomanu can be difficult: Keep an eye out for the hidden entryway next to mile marker 14. Caution: The access road to Honomanu is steep and only paved for the first half. Drivers with low clearance cars or those without four-wheel drive should think twice before venturing down the hill.

HANA TOWN
Pa'iloa Beach (Black Sand Beach)

The black sand beach at Wai'anapanapa State Park is the most popular in Hana—for good reason. Just a few miles before the sleepy center of Hana (and just past the turnoff for Hana

Airport), this is a place where dense foliage and black lava rock come face-to-face with crashing blue surf. The water along the shoreline is often rough, particularly in the afternoon. The result of this tumultuous wave erosion is a beach formed of crushed black lava rock. The color of the sand here is as black as the sky that envelops the town of Hana each night. To reach the shoreline you need to walk down a paved path from the parking lot of the state park. When you reach the bottom, you'll notice some sea caves you can explore at low tide. Since the sand is formed from lava rock, it isn't the most comfortable; bring a blanket or a towel if you plan on hanging out for a while. Once back at the parking lot, don't leave without checking out the freshwater caves. You can also walk the trail winding along the shoreline.

◖ Kaihalulu Beach (Red Sand Beach)

It's important to understand three things: For one, **Red Sand Beach** can be a nude beach, so if you're offended by nudity, it's best to stay away. Second, Red Sand Beach can be dangerous to access. There are rock slides, slippery scree slopes, sheer drop-offs, and an angry ocean. If you're unsure of your footing or have mobility issues, it's best not to try. Third, should you decide to venture to Red Sand Beach and end up hurting yourself, accept responsibility for your actions. A lawsuit would result in Red Sand Beach being closed to all visitors—resident or tourist. Visitor access to Red Sand Beach is already tenuous at best, so please, act responsibly and respect No Trespassing signs.

Should you feel you meet the criteria to visit Red Sand Beach, you're in for one of the coastline's most epic spots. This cavernous cove hidden in the mountainside offers decent swimming and a sandy beach the color of a cinder cone. To find the trail for Red Sand Beach, get to the legal parking area on Uakea Road by the ballpark (don't park facing the wrong direction) and walk toward an open grass field next to the community center. Walk across the grass field, keeping an eye on the bushes on your right for a couple of narrow trails. Wading for

Kaihalulu Beach

a minute through waist-high grass, you'll eventually emerge at a small dirt trail that scrambles down the roots of a tree. The footing on this trail can be slippery, so bare feet or closed-toe shoes are better than rubber slippers. The thin trail continues to the left up and over a bluff, where landslides can leave a lot of scree on the trail. Once at the top of the bluff, you'll be greeted with your first photo-op of the stunning cove. From here it's a short, one-minute walk until you emerge on the red shoreline.

Hana Bay

While anyone who frequents tiki bars will already know the name (from Hana Bay rum, of course), the real **Hana Bay** is a laid-back crescent of gray sand smack in the middle of Hana town. Tucked in the lee of Ka'uiki Head—a large promontory where Queen Ka'ahumanu was born—Hana Bay is where the town's boat ramp is located and the outrigger canoe club holds practice. This is a working-class, community bay—it's also where many confused visitors end up when they "can't find Hana."

Compared to neighboring Hamoa Beach, Hana Bay is more utilitarian: a nice area for a picnic and stretching your legs after the long drive. Swimming is calm but not spectacular.

HANA TO KIPAHULU

Visitors lament that there aren't any nice beaches in Hana. Waterfalls, yes, but beaches, no. This is a common misperception among those who made the mistake of turning around in the town of Hana, thinking they had reached the final destination. As it just so happens, a few miles past the town of Hana are two of the most stunning beaches you'll find in East Maui, including one that consistently ranks as one of the top 10 in the United States.

Koki Beach

To reach Hana's two famous beaches, travel 1.5 miles past the center of town (Hana Ballpark) and then make a left on Haneo'o Road. Going downhill, the first beach you'll come to is **Koki Beach,** a favorite hangout of local surfers. Signs warn visitors that rip currents can be strong; the

LANDING ON RED OR BLACK?

When it comes to choosing a beach in Hana, this question has nothing to do with a roulette wheel and everything to do with the color of the sand. Unlike at a casino, choosing isn't a gamble, however, since you're sure to be awed by the beauty of both. The red sand of Kaihalulu (Red Sand Beach) is formed by the crushed red cinder of towering Ka'uiki Hill, and this is one of the island's most oft-photographed and unique sections. Meanwhile, on the outskirts of town by Wai'anapanapa State Park, Pa'iloa Beach (Black Sand Beach) is formed from the crushed black lava rock from the dramatic coastline, and the sand is closer to little black pebbles than fine powder. Can't decide between the two? That's okay. Hana is small enough you can make time to visit both.

water on most days is too choppy, so heed the advice. Koki gets windy during the afternoon. On the left side of the beach, you can scramble over some rocks to reach some hidden sections of sand. Access to these smaller beaches is only possible at low tide, so most visitors stay on the main section of beach. The dark-red sand is a product of a cinder cone known as Ka Iwi O Pele ("the bones of Pele"). According to legend, this is where Pele, the volcano goddess, met her mortal end. Her bones were stacked high on the shoreline before her spirit traveled southeast to the Big Island. The Koki shoreline was hard hit during the tsunami of 1946. It makes for a great photo-op and is one of Hana's most popular beaches.

◖ Hamoa Beach

Continue along Haneo'o Road, paralleling the ocean, the snowcapped peak of Mauna Kea on the Big Island occasionally visible in the distance. At low tide you can also see the remnants of the ancient Haneo'o Fishpond, although access to the fishpond rests on private land. As the road rounds back to the right, you'll finally catch glimpses of a beach that Mark Twain considered one of the most beautiful in the world.

Before you experience **Hamoa Beach** for yourself, however, you need to find a parking spot. Parking is tight; park only on the right side of the road so that traffic flows smoothly on the left. You might have to drive past the beach before you can find a space. Access to the beach is down the stone stairway. The park area at the bottom of the stairs is property of the Travaasa Hana hotel but the sandy beach is public property.

This is the best spot in Hana for a relaxing day at the beach. On the calmest of days it's possible to snorkel along the rocky coastline, though most visitors will prefer to bodysurf the consistent, playful shorebreak. This can also be one of the best surf breaks in the area

KIPAHULU AND BEYOND

Although there aren't any beaches between Hamoa and 'Ohe'o (Seven Pools), if you're continuing around the "back" of the island the road will intersect the shoreline again at a number of rocky beaches.

Lelekea Bay

After dozens of turns and numerous roadside waterfalls, the road intersects the shoreline 2.5 miles past 'Ohe'o. At mile marker 39.2, **Lelekea Bay** is a strip of rounded boulders popular with fishers and daredevil bodyboarders. If you need to stretch your legs, this is a great place to stroll down the shore. You'll be greeted by the thunderous rumblings of stones rolling in the turbid surf. If you walk to the far eastern end of the beach and crane your neck, you can make out a waterfall tumbling into the ocean. This is an out-of-the-way beach that most Maui visitors will never see.

Nu'u Bay

Part archaeological site and part beach, **Nu'u**

EAST MAUI

© HEATHER ELLISON

Koki Beach

Bay is one of the few places on the "back" of Maui that offers a protected inlet out of the wind. Finding Nu'u can be a little tricky. Unless you're in a four-wheel-drive vehicle or a car with high clearance, park your vehicle on the side of the road by the 31 mile marker and get out and walk. Follow the road 100 yards back in the direction of Hana and you'll notice a metal gate on the ocean side of the road held in place by a metal latch (don't confuse it with the private gate which is locked with three different padlocks and leads onto private land). Once you are inside the correct gate (remember to re-latch it!), it's about a five-minute walk down to the shoreline. The rock beach has areas of black sand, with remnants of ancient Hawaiian fishing villages around the point. Just inland is the Nu'u salt pond, a naturally occurring wetland where birders might spot the native *a'eo,* or Hawaiian stilt. Set in a dry, remote area, Nu'u is only sparsely frequented by campers, fishers, and the rare scuba diver. Although some guides will mention snorkeling on the left side of the bay, the currents can be strong and the surf large, so it's best to enjoy this beach from shore.

Surfing

East Maui includes the island's fabled "North Shore," the proving ground for the world's most talented watermen. You can feel the ocean's energy permeating through the community. Surfing is reserved for only intermediate and advanced surfers. While places such as Ho'okipa Beach Park and Hamoa Bay can see surf at any time of the year, this stretch of coast roars to life October-April with massive North Pacific swells. This is some of the largest, heaviest surf on the planet. Most visitors are better off as spectators than participants. Even watching from the shoreline, you can still feel the rush of waves large enough to rumble the ground beneath you.

PA'IA
Surf Spots

Although it's rarely surfed, a break in front of the lifeguard tower at **Baldwin Beach** offers fun longboarding before the afternoon wind picks up. If the surf is too large at places such as Ho'okipa or Pa'ia Bay, there is a reform on the shallow reef here that can offer a long ride if you know where to sit. The downside to surfing here is that on your way back in, it can be a challenge to wrangle your longboard through the shorebreak. On the opposite side of the beach, down toward **Baby Beach,** there are also a couple of breaks better for shortboarding, although the rides are noticeably shorter and the entry and exit can be challenging.

If you're renting a board in Pa'ia, the closest beach break to town is **Pa'ia Bay,** where many of the island's north shore "groms" rode their first waves. While the inside section is popular with bodyboarders, there is a second peak a little farther out that is better for surfing. Mornings are best before the wind blows the wave to pieces. Since the wave can be fast and steep, it's best for intermediate surfers.

Moving east from town toward Hana, the left break at **Tavares** is popular with north shore locals, although since the wave can only handle a small crowd you need to be a competent surfer. The parking lot for Tavares is found by making a left at the house with the blue tile roof 0.6 mile outside of town and following the beach access sign to the end of the road. Paddling out from the beach can be shallow at low tide. Defer to locals on the best waves in the set.

The epicenter for surf on the island's north shore will forever be **Ho'okipa Beach Park,** three miles past the town of Pa'ia. This legendary windswept cove is a year-round playground for everyone from up-and-coming surf stars to world-champion windsurfers. For surfers, Ho'okipa is broken up into four sections: Pavilions (Pavils), Middles, The Point, and Lanes. If you are standing on the beach, Pavilions is the break that's the farthest to the right; a spot that can pick up wrapping windswell even during the summer. Since it's the most consistent, it can also be the most localized, so beginners should only paddle out on the smallest of days. In the center of the beach, Middles is a big left that breaks in deep water and can get board-shatteringly heavy during the winter. The wave can accommodate a larger crowd than Pavils, although you should still be an intermediate to paddle out. On the left side of the beach is The Point (H'poko Point), a heavy A-frame that's popular with windsurfers. Finally, Lanes is a left-hand wave that breaks in the cove to the west of Ho'okipa, but is frequently accessed by paddling around from the point. Since it's such a long paddle, not as many surfers venture out there. If you're an advanced surfer and want to escape the crowds, this can be a fun wave if you put in the effort. If you get stuck inside, however, the entry to shore can be over sharp, urchin-covered rocks. Only paddle out on days within your ability level.

The most notorious of all East Maui surf breaks is the mountain of water known as **Peahi (Jaws),** a deep-water trench where waves as large as 70 feet have been ridden by the

A surfer tears apart a wave at Ho'okipa.

world's most death-defying surfers. Jaws only breaks on a handful of days during the winter, and you can't see it from the road, so you need directions. The intersection for the road that leads to Jaws is labeled as Peahi Road, which is located 6.5 miles past the stoplight in Pa'ia, and just before mile marker 13.5. About 20 minutes east of Pa'ia, you'll notice a large cemetery named Valley Isle Memorial Park on the left side of the road on the incline of a hill. Toward the top of the hill you'll notice a small road that intersects the highway labeled as Peahi Road. Unless you have a four-wheel-drive, this is the spot where you should park your car. The road from this point on can be steep, muddy, and impassable for low-clearance vehicles, so it's best to leave your rental car parked by the highway. If there aren't any other cars parked here, it's an indicator that there aren't any waves; if the area is teeming with activity, you're in for a treat.

After parking the car you'll cross to *makai* (ocean side) of the highway, where you'll notice a road leading either right or left. Go left. After a short section of asphalt the road will turn to dirt. The walk downhill through the pineapple fields takes 20-30 minutes. Often locals who are driving down in their trucks offer rides to visitors on foot. Once you reach the bottom of the road, you'll find a bluff that overlooks the bay, offering an unobstructed view of the world-famous wave. The tow-surfers and paddle-surfers appear as little more than specks on the face of the gargantuan wave. If you want to see people riding waves, morning is best, since most surfers head back to shore once the wind picks up. If you want to make sure that you get a ride down the hill or a good vantage place on the side of the bluff, a six-pack of beer can be valuable bartering currency (and packing one for the walk down isn't a bad idea). Although the viewing area at Jaws can be a zoo, it's still a once-in-a-lifetime experience to watch surfers tackle nature's largest waves.

Surfboard Rentals

The surfboard rental scene is remarkably casual. Both **HI Tech Maui** (58 Baldwin Ave.,

"SO WHEN CAN I SEE JAWS?"

On a sunny July afternoon, I once had a conversation with a visitor that went something like this:

"So what do you have planned for the rest of your trip?"

"Well, tomorrow we're going to go and see the 70-foot waves at Jaws."

I realized not everyone understands just how Maui's waves work.

Pe'ahi (aka Jaws) is the place on Maui that can *potentially* get 70-foot waves, but this only happens a few days out of the year, if at all. The waves themselves are created by massive storms in the North Pacific that churn between the Aleutian Islands and Japan, and since the North Pacific is calm during summer, it's only October through April that you stand a chance of seeing the large surf at Jaws.

As a foolproof way of determining if Jaws is "going off," a "high surf warning" needs to have been issued for the waves to be big enough to break on the deep-water trenches of Pe'ahi. A high surf *warning* requires wave heights of 25 feet or greater on the island's north shores, and this is different than a high surf *advisory*, which only requires waves of 15 feet or greater. If you've only seen a high surf advisory, then there aren't going to be 70-foot waves at Jaws.

If, however, a warning has been posted, the next step is to ask a local, since the "coconut wireless" is always in effect whenever the surf gets huge. Thanks to the wonders of surf forecasting, surfers are able to successfully predict just when Jaws is going to be going off up to a week ahead of time. If you're visiting during the winter and you're hoping to see some big surf, ask your concierge, a surf shop staffer, or any activity or boat crew if Jaws is going to be going off at any point during the next week. Since the island surf community watches the surf forecast like a trader watches stock futures, they'll be able to pinpoint your exact chances. If Jaws is going to be breaking, get there during the morning hours, because by the time the wind comes up in the afternoon, most of the surfers have already left.

808/579-9297, www.surfmaui.com, 9am-6pm daily) and **Sailboards Maui** (22 Baldwin Ave., 808/579-8432, www.sailboardsmaui.com, 9:30am-7pm Mon.-Fri., 9:30am-6pm Sun.) offer board rental for $20/day. Both shops have a full range of longboards, shortboards, and fun boards. They are an affordable option for playing in the waves of Pa'ia Bay or a multiday safari to Hana.

Surf Schools

Given the advanced surf conditions of the island's North Shore, there aren't nearly as many surf schools in East Maui as there are on parts of the island such as Lahaina or Kihei. There are a couple of highly personalized instruction services where you can learn from the island's top surfers.

One of the best surf schools on the island is **Rivers to the Sea** (855/6284-7873, www.riverstothesea.com), a first-class operation run by local Maui surfer Tide Rivers. Two of the island's top surfers, Tide and his brother Kiva have gained a reputation for giving surf lessons to celebrities who pass through the area. All lessons are customized to the client's ability level, but before venturing out on to the North Shore, take a lesson on the user-friendly waves of the south shore to get a firm grasp of the basics. Tide will meet beginners at a predetermined spot outside of Lahaina and guarantee to have you up and standing before the end of the 1.5-hour lesson. All instructors were born and raised in Hawai'i. Lesson rates are $160 for a private lesson, $220 for two people, and $85/person for private groups of three or more. Photo packages are available.

Professional longboard surfer **Zack Howard** (808/214-7766, www.zackhowardsurf.com) also offers the opportunity to surf on the North Shore. While most of his lessons are conducted at locations on the south shore on the road to

Lahaina, advanced surfers can paddle out on the North Shore if the conditions are right. Lesson rates are $160 for a private lesson, $220 for two people, and $90/person for private groups of three or more.

HANA
Surf Spots

Although there are a number of secret spots scattered around the coastline, the two main Hana surf breaks frequented by visitors are **Koki Beach** and **Hamoa Beach,** both on Haneo'o Road 1.5 miles past the town of Hana. Due to its easterly location Hana gets waves any time of the year. Since the waves are often the result of easterly windswell, conditions can be rougher than elsewhere on the island. Koki is more exposed to the trade winds and the strong currents can often be challenging. The steepness of the wave here is better suited for shortboards than for longboards. Koki is where many of Hana's *keiki* (children) first learn how to pop up and ride.

Around the corner at Hamoa, the protected bay offers a respite from the trade winds. Whereas Koki breaks fairly close to shore, the wave at Hamoa breaks farther out over a combination of sand, reef, and rocks. On moderate days, this is a good place for riding a longboard or a stand-up board since the wave isn't as steep, but the largest waves are reserved for locals and experts. There are no lifeguards at either beach in Hana.

WINDSURFING

Despite the fact that the trade winds blow almost every afternoon for the majority of the summer, most windsurfers flock to the island's North Shore in winter. Summer windsurfing is reserved for spots such as Kanaha Beach Park in Central Maui where wind takes precedent over waves. Here on the North Shore, the world's best all flock in droves to Ho'okipa Beach Park for the chance to combine the trade winds with waves regularly reaching over 20 feet in height. Don't expect to see any windsurfers during your morning drive to Hana, however, as there is a local law that prohibits windsurfing before

11am. Seeing as the trades don't usually start blowing until noon, however, rarely is this ever a problem for those who want to get out on the water.

Windsurfing Spots

Sprecklesville is a local sailing spot that offers conditions less crowded than Kanaha or Ho'okipa. It's an advanced location, so if you're still new to the sport, it's best to stick to the area around Kanaha. If you're a competent sailor, however, the launching point at Sprecklesville can be reached by turning on Stable Road 1.4 miles past the intersection of Hana and Haleakala Highways. On Stable Road there are two main launching points known as Euro Beach and Camp One. Euro Beach (named for the number of European windsurfers who frequent the spot) is the closest to Hana Highway, and Camp One is the spot toward the end of Stable Road. Both have short access roads off Stable Road which lead down to small parking areas by the beach. There isn't any kitesurfing allowed here because the beaches are directly beneath the flight path of departing aircraft, so don't be startled when a jet engine roars over your head while you're rigging up on the sand.

If you're an avid windsurfer, you already know without reading this book that **Ho'okipa Beach Park** is the mecca for the world's best windsurfers. For visitors, the best place for watching these front-flipping professionals is from the western tip of the beach (the side closest to Pa'ia), since this is the section most frequented by the windsurfing crowd. Since Ho'okipa is a multiuse area for a variety of water sports, there is a rule that states if there are more than 10 surfers in the water at The Point then there isn't any windsurfing allowed. Conveniently, however, good windsurfing conditions make for bad surfing conditions, so on windy days most surfers will just move down to the surf break known as Pavilions slightly more protected from the wind. Parking can be tough at Ho'okipa, so if you're only coming here to watch the windsurfers, it's best to park up along the highway and leave the spots closer to shore for those who need to move their gear.

© KYLE ELLISON

A kitesurfer takes flight.

Windsurfing Rentals

Although most of the windsurfing rental shops are in Kahului, **Simmer Style** (137 Hana Hwy., 808/579-8484, www.simmerhawaii. com, 10am-7pm daily) is the closest shop to Hoʻokipa and is the best spot on the North Shore for windsurfing rentals and supplies.

KITESURFING

Since kitesurfing isn't allowed along the length of Sprecklesville, and since Hoʻokipa is dominated by windsurfers and surfers, there are only a handful of places along the island's North Shore amenable for the sport. What few spots are available, however, are only accessible to

advanced riders. If you're still relatively new to kitesurfing, it's best to stick to Kite Beach and Kanaha Beach Park in Central Maui. If you're determined to kite along this stretch of coastline, however, most kiters will launch out of the **Kuau Cove** section of shoreline between Mama's Fish House and The Point at Hoʻokipa. Parking can be found either in the beach access stalls within the Mama's Fish House parking lot or at pullouts along the highway by Hoʻokipa Beach Park. Entry from the shore, however, means tiptoeing your way across an urchin-covered reef. For the best representation of the island's allowed kitesurfing zones, check out the maps at www.mauikiteboardingassociation.com.

EAST MAUI

Hiking and Biking

HIKING
Road to Hana
C TWIN FALLS

At mile marker 2 (11.4 miles past Pa'ia), **Twin Falls** is one of the easiest and shortest waterfall hikes you'll find in East Maui. It's also the first series of waterfalls you'll encounter on the Road to Hana. Since much of the area weaves through private homes (respect the *Kapu,* or "Keep Out" signs on driveways), most of the "trail" is a gravel road that is wide and easy for strolling. Although there are a few spots where the footing can be tricky, this is the perfect choice for anyone looking for a "tame" walk into the jungle. A few sections require walking across slippery rocks or clambering over irrigation structures.

An outdoor playground peppered with waterfalls, the only downside about Twin Falls is that it's far from being a secret. During the midmorning hours as visitors make their way toward Hana, there can be well over 50 cars parked along the side of the road, and it's safe to say that you won't have the waterfalls to yourself. If you would prefer to visit without the crowds, you can either stop on your drive *back* from Hana, visit *really* early before everyone else has arrived, or make a separate trip out here in the late afternoon. Regardless of when you visit, bring mosquito repellent.

Although there are myriad waterfalls at Twin Falls, the two main ones are most accessible for visitors. For a more thorough exploration into the hinterlands of the rainforest, Hike Maui offers an informative guided tour. For casual visitors, however, the 1.3-mile trail begins in the gravel parking lot and makes its way through a small gate in a lush and forested orchard area. There are port-a-potties on the right side of the trail, and visitors are encouraged to leave a donation for their maintenance and upkeep. After five minutes of walking along the gravel road, you'll hear some waterfalls off to your left. While these are nice for a quick photo, the main waterfalls are still farther down the trail. After 10 minutes of walking, you'll come to a stream crossing that can flood during periods of high rain. If the water appears to be rushing violently, it's best to turn around. Five minutes past the stream crossing, you'll come to a three-way fork in the road: Go straight. After five more minutes you'll come to another fork, where the trail to your left has a wooden plank crossing over a small stream. Go straight, and after two minutes of clambering around an irrigation flume, you'll reach a waterfall that has a small pool for swimming. While this waterfall is nice enough, there's a second waterfall known as Caveman that is far more dramatic, although it can be a little tougher to reach.

To get to Caveman, turn around and go back to the fork in the trail where there was the wooden plank. Cross over the wooden plank, ascend a small hill, take the fork to

© HEATHER ELLISON
Cool off beneath Twin Falls.

the left, and then a take a right 50 yards later. You'll now find yourself walking downhill, and a few minutes later you'll reach a concrete irrigation structure with steps leading up and over it. From here you'll begin to see the waterfall in the distance, although to reach the base of the falls you must wade across a stream that is usually about knee-deep. If the stream is manageable, a short scramble past it will bring you to a cavernous waterfall begging you to take your photo behind it. Since the water isn't clear enough to see the bottom, don't even think about jumping off the top. Adjacent to the pool at Caveman you'll notice a thin trail which switchbacks its way up the hill. Following this trail will bring you to more pools and waterfalls, although since it's easy to get lost back here it's best to have a guide if you plan on venturing any farther. On your way out from Caveman, after you climb up and over the irrigation structure and ascend the hill, by following the trail to the right when it forks you'll end up at the three-way fork in the trail you originally encountered on your walk in, ultimately having done a full loop. From here it's a short walk back to the parking lot and the rest of East Maui's treasures.

◖ NA'ILI'ILI HAELE (BAMBOO FOREST)

There was once a time when—like many other places on Maui—this trail was known only to locals, overlooked by all but the most well-connected of island visitors. Today, the waterfalls of **Na'ili'ili haele** are one of the highlights of the Road to Hana, but it's important to understand that this hike is not for everyone. Dangers include traversing steep, slippery slopes as well as crossing streams prone to flash floods. This is truly one of the most adventurous, scenic, and unique hikes on the eastern flank of the island, but the best thing you can pack with you on this hike is a healthy dose of common sense.

At the 6.5 mile marker, you'll first know that you're approaching the trailhead when you make an enormous hairpin turn flanked on the right by a narrow rock wall. The road becomes narrow here, and parking can be difficult during the busiest times of day. As long as your

car doesn't obstruct the road, you can park on the right side against the bamboo, although the passenger will need to climb out of the driver's seat. If all these spots are taken, there are more pullouts within the next quarter mile. The first place where many visitors go wrong is in finding the correct trailhead, which is marked by a lone metal pole springing up from a break in a wire fence. On the other side of the fence, the trail will be narrow at first and wind its way downhill. After two minutes of walking you'll reach an intersection where you'll turn left and be confronted with a steep scramble down a hill. This area can become slick, so use your hands to aid against a slip or a fall.

Once at the bottom of the hill, you'll encounter a stream crossing with a wooden plank stretching over a gap. Once on the other side of the stream, you'll continue straight through a tunnel of bamboo before the path wraps around to the left and you rejoin the main trail. Make a right and follow the trail for another two minutes until you come to a major stream crossing.

The stream crossing is the second point (after the trailhead) where most visitors get turned around. Since the trail runs cold at the stream (that stream water isn't warm!), it can be confusing where to go from here. When you look across to the other side of the stream, you'll notice a downed tree on the opposite bank and slightly to the left. Follow the tree trunk to its base, and here you'll notice where the continuation of the trail is on the other side of the stream. This is where you're aiming for during your stream crossing. Once on the other side, the trail will parallel the water as you move upstream. This section has some of the densest bamboo on the whole trail, and even when the sun is high in the sky, the thick grove can nearly block out the sun. A few minutes into this bamboo trail, you'll encounter a clearing off toward your left. After a few more minutes, you'll come to a second clearing. When you come to a third clearing on your left, you should hear the rush of a waterfall. Turn left to cross the stream again here; this will bring you to the first waterfall where there's a small pool.

RESPECT

Although millions of visitors tour Maui annually and return home without incident, every year there are a handful who have regrettable experiences in the islands. Tourists get hurt and end up in hospitals. Landowners get sued and access becomes restricted. Local-visitor relations become increasingly strained, and more often than not, litigation has replaced handshakes, liability waivers become prolific, and warning signs stand where common sense once reigned.

While there is no denying the dirty underbelly of tourism, there is a single word which can do more for island relations than any lawsuit, warning sign, or waiver ever could:

Respect.

Healthy respect for the island, nature, people, and culture is essential to a meaningful and successful vacation. Just as each local is an ambassador for the state and should treat visitors with respect and *aloha*, every visitor to the island is a representative of the industry, and when visitors show respect for these islands, locals take notice. Most island visitors already practice these virtues, but for those who are first-time tourists, acquainting yourself with these general guidelines will be the best trip planning you could possibly perform.

RESPECT THE LAND

In traditional Hawaiian culture, the land is sacred above all. The earth beneath our feet and the sea in which we swim provide us with the sustenance and bounty for sustaining life. To disrespect the land is the ultimate offense. The concept of landownership is foreign to Hawaiian culture. We are instead seen as stewards of the land who have been temporarily placed here to foster it for future generations. While this might not be the same as the view where you live, you can do your part while visiting the island by showing respect for the land around. Pick up your *opala*, or trash, and stay off sensitive coral reefs. Throw cigarette butts in proper recep-

tacles, and help keep our valleys and shorelines as pristine as nature intended.

RESPECT LANDOWNERS' WISHES

Some unscrupulous travel publications encourage trespassing. As a result, far too many visitors walk across private land even when signs tell them they aren't welcome. Over the years, due to disrespect for the land (leaving trash, urinating, parking on lawns, etc.) and lawsuits, access to some formerly public sites is now restricted. If you see a sign that says *Kapu* (meaning "keep out") No Trespassing, Private Property, or Stay Out, respect the landowners' wishes and leave the place undisturbed.

RESPECT NATURE

Many visitor injuries are a direct result of failing to respect the strength of nature. Waves are stronger in Maui than other places in the world, and flash floods, high winds, rough seas, and slippery rocks all claim the lives of visitors annually. Know when the conditions might be too powerful for your control, respect warning signs and posted placards, and "if in doubt, don't go out."

RESPECT THE CULTURE

Hawai'i is blessed with a unique culture unlike anywhere else in the world. Allowing yourself to experience that culture is one of the best parts of visiting the islands. While tourism might be the state's largest industry, ultimately, these islands belong to the Hawaiian locals, and it's important to remember we are guests here. People in Hawai'i might do some things differently than the rest of the world; rather than trying to change the culture into what you're used to back home, embrace the Hawaiian way of living and slow down for a little while.

By following these few guidelines and showing respect for the island around you, not only will you enjoy a successful vacation, but you will do wonders to bridge a widening gap between visitors and island locals.

© KYLE ELLISON

waterfalls at Na'ili'ili haele

thinking there's a public bathroom, only to find the nearest facilities are three miles down the road. The 30-minute loop trail takes you just far away enough from the road that the only sound you can hear is the call of native birds and the creak of bamboo as it sways in the wind above you. The trail itself gains 200 feet in elevation and consists of two parts: the loop trail and the spur trail to the upper picnic area. Hike in a counterclockwise direction since this is the best-maintained section of trail. The second half of the loop heading back downhill toward the parking lot isn't as well maintained and is a lot muddier than the platform steps found on the way up.

If you choose to take the spur trail to the upper picnic area, you'll be rewarded with an open clearing few visitors take the time to explore. The trail to the upper picnic area will take about 10 minutes. It is covered in *lau hala* leaves and slippery roots. At the end of the trail is a simple picnic area where a covered pavilion provides a relaxing place for a snack and a rest. Pack mosquito repellent if you plan on stopping to eat here. At the edge of the clearing a sign says "End of Trail," yet the trail continues into the brush. Respect the sign and turn back. While there is a small waterfall back here, it's mediocre compared to others along the highway and involves scrambling over EMI infrastructure. The 20 minutes you save will be better spent on other adventures.

Hana Town
KING'S HIGHWAY COASTAL TRAIL
One of the few hiking options in East Maui that doesn't involve a waterfall, this three-mile trail which runs between Wai'anapanapa State Park and the northern tip of Hana Bay is one of the few navigable remnants of the ancient King's Highway which once circled the island. Commissioned by King Pi'ilani in the 15th century, the **King's Highway** (or *alaloa,* "long road") was used as a way for ruling chiefs and *ali'i* to move about the island. Before there was a paved road connecting Hana with the rest of the central valley, this footpath served as the only means for navigating treacherous ravines

Many visitors make it this far and decide that this is enough, because beyond this point the trail gets exponentially more challenging and treacherous. Should you want to continue, however, trace the edge of the pool to the far side of the streambed and you'll notice a thin rope dangling over a slippery rock face. This is where the trail continues; shimmy your way up the slick rock area (use the rope!) to rejoin the trail. Once you've successfully navigated that obstacle, the trail will flatten out and pass through more bamboo before arriving at another pool which is larger and less crowded than the first. Slip off your shoes and slide in for a dip. Unless you're a Navy SEAL, part mountain goat, or are accompanied by a local, stop here. Beyond is a "locals-only" realm; you need to have experience and familiarity with the conditions to continue farther.

WAIKAMOI RIDGE TRAIL
The **Waikamoi Ridge Trail** (mile marker 9.5) provides a calming respite to get out and stretch your legs. Most people pull over here

across some of the most inaccessible parts of the island. Today, only scarce remnants of this ancient trail are evident, but the most prominent section lies right here on the coastline leading south from Wai'anapanapa. Parking for the trailhead is in the main lot of the state park. Along the course of this three-mile trail, you'll weave around azure bays flanked by black sand, pass beneath dense groves of dry *lau hala* trees, and gaze upon lava rock arches which have been carved from the coastline by the often tumultuous sea.

Wear hiking boots, as the jagged *a'a* lava can rip rubber slippers to pieces. Carry plenty of water as there are no facilities along trail. As you get closer to Hana Bay, the trail becomes a little more treacherous, and most visitors start from the Wai'anapanapa trailhead and hike about halfway before turning back in the direction they came. To take the literal road less traveled, continue to the north of Wai'anapanapa and pass a series of smaller black sand coves before eventually emerging near the Hana Airport. Expect to devote at least three hours to this trail if hiking round-trip from the trailhead, and for maximum dramatic effect, hike this trail at sunrise

For a quick and easy hike which still offers a rewarding view, the trail leading from the Travaasa Hana parking lot up to **Fagan's Cross** will take most hikers about 20 minutes and has a steep enough grade to offer a good leg workout. Keep a keen lookout for fresh guavas growing on the trees, in addition to the fresh cow pies left by the free range cattle.

A two-mile long **walking trail** leads from the trail to Fagan's Cross south toward the beach at Hamoa. The track is little more than flattened grass running through the pasturelands, although you'll have the coastal views all to yourself.

Kipahulu and Beyond
PIPIWAI TRAIL

Hands down, **Pipiwai Trail** is the best in Maui. In the Kipahulu section of Haleakala National Park, the **Pipiwai Trail** is comprised of the upper portion of 'Ohe'o Gulch in the area known as Seven Sacred Pools. While most visitors to 'Ohe'o only pay a cursory visit to take photos, the Pipiwai Trail which runs *mauka* (mountain-side) of the highway is the undisputed highlight of the Kipahulu section of the park. The four-mile trail is just long enough to be adventurous and just short enough to be accessible, and the trail is at a moderate enough grade that most hikers should be able to reach the end. Speaking of the end, the last half mile of this trail winds its way through bamboo which is so thick it blocks out the sun, and just when you think the scenery couldn't get any more tropical, the trail emerges at the base of 400-foot Waimoku Falls. This two-hour expedition more than justifies the winding drive out here. Or, for the best way to experience the trail, camp overnight at the Kipahulu campground and hit the path before the throngs of day-tripping tourists arrive.

To find the trailhead for the Pipiwai Trail, drive 30-40 minutes past the town of Hana. At mile marker 41.7 you'll reach the entrance to the Kipahulu section of Haleakala National Park, and parking for the trailhead is within the park boundaries. You'll have to pay the park entry fee ($10/car) to hike, but since you should spend additional time exploring the pools down by the ocean, it's no different than if you were visiting the park.

Find the trailhead by walking back out to the road and going 100 yards in the direction toward Hana. Here you'll see the signs for the trailhead on your left. From the time the trail departs the road, it steeply climbs its way up a rocky slope until you are greeted with a sign offering trail distances and words of caution. Much of the Pipiwai Trail parallels 'Ohe'o Gulch, and you can hear the rush of the water as your make your way uphill toward the falls. However, it is never safe to access the pools or waterfalls located in the river. There may be days when you *can* get to the river by scrambling down a sketchy hillside or undefined trail, but a number of visitors have been swept to their death in flash floods. The National Park Service advises against any attempt to access the stream.

© MARK DRIESSEN

The Pipiwai Trail is punctuated by 400-foot Waimoku Falls.

After 10 minutes on the trail you'll reach the lookout for Makahiku Falls, a 200-foot plunge which can be anything from a trickle during drier months of the year to a torrent of violent water during the throes of a flash flood. After Makahiku Falls, the trail will begin gaining in elevation for another five minutes before emerging in the shade of one of the most beautiful banyan trees you'll ever see. Branches of sunshine burst through the canopy.

The section between "the tree" and the first bridge is one of decisions. Multiple spur trails lead to waterfall overlooks, offering views of the canyons and pools. Getting in the water from here is dangerous. Don't do it.

Ten minutes past the tree you'll reach the first of two bridges that zigzag their way across the stream. This is a great place to snap pictures of the waterfalls and your first taste of the bamboo forest. You'll notice after crossing the second bridge that when the trail turns into stairs which climb steeply toward the bamboo, there's an opening in the railing on the left side where a path leads down to a rocky streambed.

This is the Palikea Stream, and if you rock hop up the riverbed for about 15 minutes, you'll emerge at a waterfall that is less dramatic—but also less-visited—than neighboring Waimoku Falls. The waterfall here trickles its way down the towering canyon walls, and the pool at the bottom can occasionally be frequented by those who prefer to bathe *au naturel.*

Back on the main trail, by continuing up the stairs you'll find a boardwalk through the densest bamboo on the island. The sun can be shining directly overhead and yet it can be dark enough inside you would think it were sunset. Finally, as you emerge from the creaking cavern, five more minutes of rock hopping brings you to the pièce de résistance, which of course is 400-foot Waimoku Falls.

ALELELE FALLS

Most visitors never take the time to make the short hike back to 60-foot **Alelele Falls,** where there is a refreshing pool for swimming. Located on the fabled "back road" about three miles past the pools of 'Ohe'o, the trailhead is at Alelele Bridge at mile marker 38.8; park in one of the few parking spots available on the Kaupo side of the bridge. Alelele Falls are officially the last waterfalls you'll encounter on your epic East Maui journey. If you have the tiniest shred of energy left in you for a 10-minute hike through the jungle, the reward is a waterfall of just the right height which offers just the right amount of seclusion. Although parking for the trailhead is on the Kaupo side of the bridge, the trailhead itself is back on the Kipahulu side at the spot where the bridge begins. Following this well-defined trail, you'll crisscross the stream a couple of times and pass by ancient lava rock walls before emerging at the base of the pristine falls.

BIKING

The town of Pa'ia is the elbow joint for two of the most popular rides of the island: the frigid ride down Haleakala and the weaving journey out toward Hana. Many of the island's downhill bike tours finish their 6,500-foot descent on the shores of Pa'ia Bay, and many of the island's avid cyclers depart Pa'ia for the ride of a lifetime toward Hana. With East Maui's prominent location as a hub for island cycling, it should come as no surprise there are also a few bike shops sprinkled around town.

Pa'ia

Far and away one of the most comprehensive cycling experiences on Maui is found at **Maui Cyclery** (99 Hana Hwy., 808/579-9009, www.gocyclingmaui.com, 8am-6pm Mon.-Fri., 8am-4pm Sat., 8am-noon Sun.), a small but thorough shop in the heart of Pa'ia. In addition to offering rentals, parts, services, and sales, the staff at Maui Cyclery offer a "fantasy camp for cyclists." This is the only place on the island that offers a tour for visitors who are avid about cycling. Rentals range from $30/day for a single day and go up from there for elite performance bikes. Group rides begin at $140 for a four-hour riding experience.

Ha'iku

Over in the Ha'iku Cannery, **Haleakala Bike Company** (810 Ha'iku Rd., #120, 808/575-9575 or 888/922-2452, www.bikemaui.com, 8:30am-5pm Mon.-Sat., 9am-4pm Sun.) mainly specializes in tour groups making the ride down Haleakala Volcano. In addition to the volcano run, you can also rent your own bike from $35/day, and as long as you arrange your own transportation to the top, you'll be able to ride from the summit of the volcano. If you do rent a bike from Haleakala Bike Company and are making your way back to the shop from the town of Makawao, be aware that Kokomo Road has uneven pavement and potholes, so it's a good idea to temper your speed.

Adventure Sports

ZIPLINING
Ha'iku

Even though most of the adventure sports along Maui's North Shore take place in the water, **North Shore Zipline Company** (2065 Kauhikoa Rd., 808/269-0671, www.nszipline.com, closed Sun.) provides a course of seven ziplines that weave their way through the trees of a rural Ha'iku location that at one time served as an island military base. The course here is family-friendly and caters mainly to first-time zippers. Children as young as five

are welcome to participate as long as they're accompanied by a paying adult. Don't think that you won't still get a rush, however, as you can hit speeds of up to 45 mph on the last line of the course, and the viewing platforms provide a unique vantage point for peering out over the rural section of mountainside.

SOARING AND HANG GLIDING
Hana

Those who feel that helicopters tours are *way* too cliché will enjoy two adventures that push them outside their comfort zones to see the beauty of Hana from the air.

Skyview Soaring (Hana Airport, 808/244-7070, www.skyviewsoaring.com, $165 and up) is a self-powered glider where your pilot, Hans, will take you as high as 10,000 feet before killing the engines and gliding all the way back to your starting point at the airport. As you can imagine, this isn't for the faint of heart, although the views afforded of Haleakala Crater and the eastern flank of mountainside far surpass any you could ever get from driving along the highway. Bring your camera as you glide silently past towering waterfalls and above the shoreline of Wai'anapanapa State Park. Flights last for either 30 minutes or an hour, and if you decide to go for the full hour, you'll be able to soar all the way to the rim of Haleakala Crater and reach speeds of 50-100 mph on the ride down.

Despite some similarities, **Hang Gliding** Maui (808/572-6557, www.hanggilidingmaui.com) offers a different experience. The flight is an instructional lesson which can go toward earning a certification in sport flying. You won't travel nearly as high as you would with soaring, although this ultra-light "trike" places you in an exposed outdoor seating arrangement open to the winds. Consequently, you feel as if you're one step closer to flying. The time in the air is a one-on-one instructional period with your pilot, Armin, so this isn't an experience you can share as a couple. In all his years of piloting hang gliders on Maui, Armin boasts a 100 percent safety record, and the aircraft is equipped with backup parachutes for added safety. You can also purchase still photos or video of your experience from a camera fixed to the wing. Rates for the hang gliding experience range from $170 for a 30-minute lesson to $280 for a full hour.

Yoga, Fitness, and Spas

YOGA AND FITNESS

East Maui is the island's epicenter for yoga and alternative health practices, and the prevalence of yoga instructors is evident by perusing a community bulletin board. Yoga in East Maui isn't so much a fad or hobby, but part of a lifestyle devoted to wellness, spirituality, and health.

Pa'ia

The most popular place for yoga in Pa'ia is the **Maui Yoga and Dance Shala** (381 Baldwin Ave., 808/283-4123, www.maui-yoga.com) at the historic Pa'ia Train Depot just below the abandoned sugar mill. Class times vary greatly, so check the schedule online. Drop-in rates are $20/class for visitors or a five-class pass for $75. In addition to yoga classes such as Vinyasa yoga, prenatal yoga, and Iyengar, there are also periodic dance classes which range from West African dance and belly dancing to modern jazz and ballet. Massages can also be arranged

by talking with the front desk staff. You can grab a bite on most days at the One Love Café right next door.

Ashtanga Yoga Maui Mysore Style (137 Hana Hwy., 808/463-7293, www.mauimysorestyle.com, 7:30am-9am Mon.-Fri.) is smack in the center of town in the heart of all the action. Drop-in classes are $20/session, and a package of 10 sessions is $140. No classes are offered on the days of the new and full moon.

For those who prefer to practice Taoist arts, **Maui Movement Arts** (808/268-7913, www.mauimovementarts.com) in the Pa'ia Plaza offers a full range of classes on everything from tai chi to Tiger qigong. Rates for drop-in classes are only $15 for classes on Tao yoga, meditation sessions, and the foundations of qigong practices.

Ha'iku

For a full range of fitness activities, **Upcountry Fitness** (810 Kokomo Rd., 808/575-7334, www.upcountryfitness.com, 6am-9pm Mon.-Fri., 8am-8pm weekends) is Ha'iku's go-to spot for working up a sweat. In addition to the standard gym equipment, there are also daily classes in everything from yoga and Pilates to belly dancing and fire dancing. Classes are free for gym members. Inquire with the front desk staff about short-term membership specials during your time on the island.

If you would rather practice yoga in a scenic retreat in the jungle, single-session classes are offered for $17 at **Maya Yoga Studio** (808/268-9426, www.mayayogastudio.com), a calming yoga center on a remote back road of Ha'iku not far from Twin Falls. For specific directions it's best to either call or view the website, and since class schedules can sometimes be variable, it's best to inquire ahead of time.

Hana

Daily yoga classes are available at the **Travaasa Hana** hotel (5031 Hana Hwy., 808/270-5290, www.travaasa.com/hana), although the classes are only for registered guests of the hotel. If you're staying at the hotel, inquire with the concierge about the class schedule, although most classes are usually in the early morning hours.

If you don't happen to be staying at the hotel, you can inquire about classes at **Ala Kukui** (4224 Hana Hwy., 808/248-7841, www.alakukui.org), a nonprofit establishment which uses a 12-acre Hana retreat to provide healing pursuits for those seeking personal enlightenment and reflection. Special retreats have been arranged to bring returning U.S. veterans to the tranquil surroundings of Hana. This retreat center is a welcoming collective of interfaith initiatives and focuses on not only yoga, but also meditation, writing, cultural workshops, and creative arts. The schedule is constantly changing, so call ahead or inquire online about ways you can be involved during your relaxing stay in Hana.

SPAS
Pa'ia

If your back muscles are tight from three straight days of surfing Pa'ia Bay, **North Shore**

Chiropractic and Massage (16 Baldwin Ave., 808/579-9134, www.northshorechiropracticandmassage.com) in the heart of town offers 60-minute massages from $70. The massage schedule can sometimes be variable, so call ahead and inquire about specific arrangements.

You can also find massage services up the street at **Thee Salon** (109 Baldwin Ave., 808/579-6333,www.theesalonmaui.com, 10am-5pm Tues.-Fri., 9am-4pm Sat., by appointment Sun.-Mon.), where resident massage therapists offer 60-minute massages starting at $75.

Grace Beauty Day Spa (62 Baldwin Ave., 808/579-9779, www.dayspasmaui.com, 10am-6pm Mon.-Sat.) specializes in bikini waxes and offers a full range of additional wax and nail treatments in a casual setting. The spa itself is across the street from Mana Foods, ensconced within a clothing boutique. The friendly staff will answer any questions about spa services, clothing, or general tips about town.

Hana

The services at **The Spa at Travaasa Hana** (5031 Hana Hwy., 808/270-5290, www.travaasa.com/hana, 9am-7pm) go far beyond a massage. This isn't a place you come for a single treatment; it's a sanctuary of calm for an experience that will leave you blissfully renewed and on the verge of floating. If you've always dreamt of pampering yourself in the peaceful surroundings of a tropical island, this spa is the incarnation of the image you hold in your dreams. Arrive ahead of time to loosen up your muscles in the outdoor lava-rock whirlpool, or enjoy an herbal tea in the soothing relaxation lounge. Let your muscles embark on a journey of temperature as you slink your way into the cold plunge pool before decompressing in the comfort of the welcoming steam room. Having shed all your stress during the relaxation process, it's almost easy to forget that you still get to experience the actual massage. The treatment options here run the gamut of services from aromatherapy to deep tissue to *pohaku* hot stone. The starting rate for a 60-minute massage is $130. The price, of course, includes access to all the aforementioned amenities, and you're free to relax in the garden setting even once your massage is through.

The **Luana Spa Retreat** (5050 Uakea Rd., 808/248-8855, www.luanaspa.com), on the slopes of Ka'uiki Hill right behind Pranee's Thai food restaurant, offers a more low-key experience. Services such as massages, scrubs, and facials take place in their secluded garden yurt, although for an additional $10 you can upgrade to the thatched roof *hale* with a view gazing out

over Hana Bay. The vibe here is more organic than at the Travaasa Hana Spa across the ballpark, and at only $80 for a 60-minute massage, you can soothe your spirit without having to open your pocket nearly as wide.

If you're staying in a bed-and-breakfast and are looking for a mobile massage therapist, Cynthia at **Hana Massage** (808/268-6888, www.hanamassage.com) is a licensed masseuse well-versed in multiple areas of massage and recommended by locals.

Shopping

PA'IA
Once known only for hippies, surf culture, and sugarcane, Pa'ia now features some of the island's trendiest boutiques. The bikini shops, beachwear boutiques, and craft galleries populating this one-stoplight town keep serious shoppers occupied for hours.

Art Galleries
One of the only art galleries in town is **Turnbull Fine Art** (137 Hana Hwy., 808/579-9385, www.turnbullfineart.com, 11am-7pm Mon.-Sat.) on the Hana side of the intersection. This store is an extension of the rural showroom on the twisting road to Kahakuloa. Art aficionados will appreciate the creative style of these longtime local artists.

Surf Shops
It should come as no surprise that Pa'ia has its fair share of surf shops. If you're in need of any surf, skate, or even snowboard wear, you'll find **HI Tech Maui** (58 Baldwin Ave., 808/579-9297, www.surfmaui.com, 9am-6pm daily), **Sailboards Maui** (22 Baldwin Ave., 808/579-8432, www.sailboardsmaui.com, 9:30am-7pm Mon.-Fri., 9:30am-6pm Sun.), **Hana Highway Surf** (149 Hana Hwy., 808/579-8999, www.hanahwysurf.com, 10am-7pm daily), and **Honolua Surf Company** (115 Hana Hwy., 808/579-9593, 9am-9pm Mon.-Sat., 9am-7:30pm Sun.) all offer island surf apparel for

looking the part in one of the happiest surf towns in the United States.

Clothing and Swimwear
The only genre of shopping which rivals surf gear in Pa'ia is women's clothing boutiques and bikini stores. Along Baldwin Avenue, **Alice in Hulaland** (19 Baldwin Ave., 808/579-9922, www.aliceinhulaland.com) offers a snarky range of clothing and accessories, and **Mahina** (23 Baldwin Ave., 808/579-9132, www.shopmahina.com, 9:30am-8pm Mon.-Sat., 10am-6pm Sun.) offers trendy women's clothing which can also be found in its sister stores all around the island. On the finer end of apparel is **Nuage Bleu** (76 Hana Hwy., 808/579-9792, www.nuagebleu.com, 9:30am-6pm daily) and **Tamara Catz** (83 Hana Hwy., 808/579-9184, www.tamaracatz.com, 10am-6pm daily) which sit along Hana Highway toward the entrance to town. These are two of the more popular clothing boutiques among elegant and fashionable locals.

When it comes to bikinis, sun-seekers will love bouncing around between **Pakaloha** (151 Hana Hwy., 808/579-8882, www.pakalohamaui.com, 10:30am-6pm daily), **Maui Girl** (12 Baldwin Ave., 808/579-9266, www.maui-girl.com, 9am-6pm daily), and **Letarte** (24 Baldwin Ave., 808/579-6022, www.letarteswimwear.com, 10am-6pm daily), the latter two advertising that their bikinis were featured in the 2013 *Sports Illustrated* magazine shoot.

Jewelry

While Pa'ia doesn't boast nearly the same number of jewelry stores as Lahaina, **Studio 22K** (161 Hana Hwy., 808/579-8167, www.studio22k.com, 10am-6pm Tues.-Sat.) on the far Hana side of town is a small studio that specializes in handmade 22 karat gold items with metal malleable enough to morph into all sorts of twisting shapes and designs.

If sterling silver is more of what you're looking for, **Oceania Maui** (120 Hana Hwy., 808/579-6063, www.oceaniamaui.com, 10am-6:30am daily) operates a gallery between Charley's restaurant and the Da Kine surf shop that has a wide range of over 400 sterling silver jewelry designs.

If you would prefer to make your own jewelry, **Aloha Bead Company** (43 Hana Hwy., 808/579-9709, www.alohabead.com, 10:30am-5:30pm Mon.-Sat., 11am-5pm Sun.) right next door to Pa'ia Bay Coffee has a huge selection of beads and glass for creating unique island-inspired accessories.

Furnishings

Although you probably aren't looking for much furniture while on vacation, **Indigo** (149 Hana Hwy., 808/579-9199, www.indigopaia.com, 10am-6pm daily) is still an eclectic and fascinating store that also has a large displays of photography, rugs, and jewelry from the owner's travels all over the globe. There are heavy Asian and African influences in a lot of the pieces. If you're always on the hunt for intriguing international souvenirs and crafts, this is where you're going to find them.

ROAD TO HANA
Gifts and Souvenirs

The best place to do any real shopping along the Road to Hana is at **Nahiku Ti Gallery** (mile marker 28.7, 808/248-8800, 10am-5pm daily), a small gallery within the Nahiku Marketplace. This curious "strip mall in the jungle" is already strange enough in that it offers legitimate

food options in the middle of nowhere. The curiosity is only amplified by the fact that there's an actual art and souvenir gallery that rivals any you might find in the tourist enclaves of Ka'anapali or Wailea. While nowhere near as large as the south shore shopping venues, the Nahiku Ti Gallery still has a varied selection of jewelry, crafts, paintings, pottery, and a surprising collection of art you wouldn't expect to find in this part of the island.

HANA TOWN
Art Galleries

By far the most comprehensive gallery in all of Hana, the **Hana Coast Gallery** (5031 Hana Hwy., 808/248-8636, www.hanacoast.com, 9am-5pm daily) could be the nicest art gallery on the island. A freestanding building within the Travaasa Hana hotel, the Hana Coast Gallery features fine works by Hawaiian artists and is a must-stop for anyone who appreciates fine art. Everything from oil paintings to ceramics and wooden sculpture is on display in this sophisticated space, and the depth of knowledge of the staff on the intricacies of individual pieces provides an educational component to this fine art experience.

Gifts and Souvenirs

Within the same complex as the post office and the Hana Ranch Restaurant is the small **Hana Treasures** (5031 Hana Hwy., 808/248-7372, 10am-5pm Mon.-Sat., 10am-3pm weekends) souvenir store which sells everything from clothing and trinkets to "Thank God for Hana" bumper stickers. Most visitors end up wandering into this shop while they're waiting for their lunch order at the restaurant takeout window. While it has the appearance of classic tourist kitsch from the outside, you might be surprised when you end up walking out with something.

For Hawaiian-themed souvenirs and resort wear, visit **Noe Noe** gift shop inside the Travaasa Hana hotel (3501 Hana Hwy., 808/359-2401, 9am-7pm daily). It has a selection of island-infused apparel to help you look fashionable down at Hamoa Beach. For a full-range of Hawaiian beauty products, continue on a short walk down to the spa.

Although the selection is more utilitarian than artistic, you can also pick up some basic gifts and souvenirs at the **Hasegawa General Store** (5165 Hana Hwy., 808/248-7079, www.hanamaui.com, 7am-7pm Mon.-Sat., 8am-6pm Sun.) in the center of town. Here you'll find everything from tank tops and hats to Hana-themed stickers and merchandise. You just never know when that perfect gift is going to pop up in the most unlikely of venues.

HANA TO KIPAHULU
Art Galleries
For a gallery that focuses on the unique art of handcrafted paper, stop into **Karen Davidson Fine Art** (mile marker 46.3, 808/248-4877, www.karendavidson.net) tucked along the road between Hana and Kipahulu on the ocean side of the highway. Many of the works here are either oil paintings on handmade paper or an array of paper collages. There's a Hawaiian/Polynesian theme coursing through much of the artwork unique and relevant to Hana. The studio itself is a work of art in that it opens out to the Hana coastline. If you are more interested in fine art than tumbling waterfalls, call ahead to arrange a visit.

Ark Ceramics studio and gallery (808/344-3885, www.arkceramics.net, 11am-4pm) is nestled eight miles past Hana in a section known locally as Koali. You'll need to call ahead and arrange an appointment, but if you're a tea-lover, you'll be amazed at artist Arrabella Ark's pottery prowess in creating teapots in the traditional *raku* form.

Entertainment

LIVE MUSIC
Pa'ia
The de facto late-night watering hole for all of the North Shore continues to be **Charley's** (142 Hana Hwy., 808/579-8085, www.charleysmaui.com, open until 2am), where there's live music on most nights of the week. Charley's is the only place in Pa'ia where you can dance. There can also occasionally be live music in the courtyard of **Café des Amis** (42 Baldwin Ave., 808/579-6323, www.cdamaui.com, open until 8:30pm), which is an intimate venue for taking in some tunes.

Hana
The most happening show in town is at the **Travaasa Hana** hotel (5031 Hana Hwy., 808/359-2401, www.travaasa.com/hana) every Sunday, Monday, and Thursday evening in the dining room. Thursday is usually the most eventful, when local people will put on their finest wear and head out on the town for a drink and entertainment. You never know the local talent that might roll through the dining hall. Many famous Hawaiian artists have Hana roots either in that they were raised here or have family who live here. It isn't uncommon for the regularly scheduled performer to be joined by a visiting musical artist who just happened to be in town for the week. It also isn't uncommon to have a local person jump out of a chair mid-meal and dance hula to a favorite song before sitting back down to finish the meal. More so than at any other establishment on the island, the evening entertainment is rich with community and a feeling of *aloha*, and an evening experiencing the live entertainment at the Travaasa can be more of a cultural experience than any resort lu'au or show.

Live music can also be found at the **Hana Ranch Restaurant** (5031 Hana Hwy., 808/270-5280, 7:30pm-9:30pm Tues.) one night a week. A scheduled band will usually provide the entertainment for the first hour, followed by a second hour of open-mic night. When it comes to open-mic night in Hana, you'd be surprised how much talent a small community can foster when you eliminate the so-called conveniences of the modern world. Ukulele, hula, music, and song are ways of life when living in Hana, and the artistic talent which courses through this community is inspiring.

Food

PA'IA
Local Style
The budget midday crowd enjoys the plate lunches at **Nellie's Bistro** (126 Hana Hwy., 808/579-8252, 7am-7pm Mon.-Sat., 7:30am-3pm Sun., $8), which can be eaten on the outdoor patio. There's talk of converting the bistro (which is more of a coffee shop and deli) into a larger restaurant and bar. For now, enjoy the relaxing spot to grab a lunch that won't break the bank.

Seafood
🄲 Mama's Fish House (799 Poho Pl., 808/579-9764, www.mamasfishhouse.com, 11am-2:30pm and 4:15pm-9pm daily, $20-40 lunch, $28-55 dinner) has become synonymous with Maui dining. Many in its cult-like following claim that if you haven't been to Mama's, you've never been to Maui. The oceanfront location is unbeatable, the romantic ambience is better than anywhere on the island, and the fish is so fresh that the menu not only tells you where your fish was caught that morning, it tells you who caught it. Prepare for a meal where the beauty of Polynesia is evident in every bite. It's a once-in-a-lifetime splurge that's well worth it. Call well in advance for reservations (timing your meal for sunset is best). To get there, travel a mile past the town of Pa'ia as if headed to Hana; just as the road meets up with the ocean again, you'll see the Mama's Fish House sign and the entry to Kuau Cove.

While your hotel concierge will recommend Mama's, the local surfer will point you to **🄲 Pa'ia Fish Market** (100 Baldwin Ave., 808/579-8030, www.paiafishmarket.com, 11am-9:30pm daily, $10), on the corner of the only stoplight in town. Lines stretch out the door for the popular ono and mahi burgers.

My personal favorite is the ahi burger. Pair your fish with a draft Hefeweizen, locally canned Bikini Blonde lager, or maybe even a glass of wine.

Mexican
On the *other* corner of Pa'ia's only stoplight, separated by the bustling crosswalk, **🄲 Milagros** (3 Baldwin Ave., 808/579-8755, www.milagrosfoodcompany.com, 11am-10pm daily, $10-18) is known for Mexican fare with a funky island twist, enormous portions, and the best happy hour in town. The black bean nachos, ahi burrito, and blackened ahi tacos are all local favorites. Get a seat at the outdoor patio, which has some of the best people-watching in Pa'ia.

Get the easiest and most affordable meal in town at family-run **Tortillas Burrito Company** (149 Hana Hwy., 808/579-8269, 7:30am-8pm daily, $5-8). Burritos are served with locally sourced meat, organic black beans, Spanish rice, fresh vegetables, and a squeeze of lime. The tacos are even more affordable, although the size pales in comparison to the bulging burritos. It's in a small strip mall on the Hana side of the stoplight, on the *makai* (ocean side) of the highway.

Italian
As the name of **🄲 Flatbread Pizza Co.** (89 Hana Hwy., 808/579-8989, www.flatbreadcompany.com, 11am-10pm daily, $16-22) implies, you won't find any Chicago-style deep dish here. All of the pizzas use organic, locally sourced ingredients and are fired in an open kiawe (mesquite) wood oven. Try the Mopsy (free-range kalua pork, organic mango barbecue sauce, organic red onions, Maui pineapple, and goat cheese from Surfing Goat Dairy),

or Coevolution (kalamata olives, organic and local rosemary, red onions, goat cheese from Surfing Goat Dairy, sweet red peppers, and organic herbs), both made with organic dough. A lively bar scene fills up nightly; get there early or expect a wait. Tuesday nights, the restaurant hosts benefits for the local community.

American

Charley's (142 Hana Hwy., 808/579-8085, www.charleysmaui.com, 7am-10pm daily, $8-14) is as integral a part of town as a dawn patrol at Ho'okipa or a bodysurfing session at Baldwin Beach. Known as "Willie's Place" because Willie Nelson frequently dines here, Charley's breeds a colorful cast of characters. You may find yourself dining next to a famous celebrity on an incognito North Shore vacation. The run-down exterior of the wooden saloon exudes a gritty, no-nonsense vibe. On the inside, it's a jovial, comfortable sports bar and bistro that offers healthy menu options with locally sourced ingredients. Top off an early morning surf session with macadamia nut pancakes. Classic burgers such as a "bacon and blue" are filling and won't break your budget.

At colorfully decorated **Café Mambo** (30 Baldwin Ave., 808/579-8021, www.cafemambomaui.com, 8am-9pm daily, $10-21), options range from organic tofu to a Mambo Bacon burger served with a slice of Spanish omelet. All beef is from grass-fed Maui Cattle Company cows. There's also a full range of sandwiches, fajitas, tapas, and breakfast options. Expect a comfortable, open-air atmosphere where locals come to linger.

Natural Foods

Natural foods enclave **(Mana Foods** (49 Baldwin Ave., 808/579-8078, www.manafoodsmaui.com, 8am-8:30pm daily) is the epicenter of the island's health-conscious community, with a selection of organic and natural offerings so comprehensive and affordable that shoppers come from as far away as Napili to stock up. For quick meals there's a hot bar as well as a deli section where you can build your own health-conscious picnic lunch for the

Road to Hana. The aisles also provide some great people-watching.

Mediterranean

Culinary hideaway **(Café des Amis** (42 Baldwin Ave., 808/579-6323, www.cdamaui.com, 8:30am-8:30pm daily, $9-18) specializes in crepes and curries. Enjoy Italian coffee and crepes stuffed with vegetables, chicken, and cheese (or all of the above) in the outdoor courtyard. There's also a wide range of sweet crepes and a full menu of curries, best when paired mango chutney.

Vietnamese

For all the health-conscious restaurants in town, the only one that is entirely vegan is tiny **Fresh Mint** (115 Baldwin Ave., 808/579-9144, 11am-9pm Wed.-Sun., $9-14), toward the top of Pa'ia. This mom-and-pop hole-in-the-wall runs thin on decor and heavy on portions. Soy fish in a clay pot and pho are popular items. A bonus: You can bring in your own bottle of wine.

Coffee Shops

If you've dreamed of being a professional surfer like Laird Hamilton, start your day off at **(Anthony's Coffee Company** (90 Hana Hwy., 808/579-8340, www.anthonyscoffee.com, 5:30am-6pm daily). This legendary Pa'ia mainstay is known as the refueling center for some of the North Shore's biggest names. You just might catch sight of a passing celebrity as you slurp up the last of your eggs Benedict or acai smoothie. A full espresso bar adds a jolt into your morning. Twenty different varieties of freshly roasted beans (including those from Kona, Moloka'i, and Ka'anapali) are on sale. As the sign says, it offers the "last Wi-Fi before Hana," in case you need to fire off a final TPS report before disappearing into the vine-dripping hinterlands beyond.

If you would rather enjoy a casual coffee in a garden setting, **Pa'ia Bay Coffee** (43 Hana Hwy., 808/579-3111, www.paiabaycoffee.com, 6:30am-6pm Mon.-Sat., 7am-6pm Sun.) is steps away from the bay on the ocean side of the highway. Enjoy a small selection of sandwiches, croissants, salads, and bagels in the shaded grove along with free Wi-Fi.

Counter-culture is served daily, along with organic coffee, at quirky **Haz Beanz** (113 Baldwin Ave., 808/268-0149, 6am-2pm Mon.-Fri., 6am-1pm Sat., 6am-noon Sun.), toward the top of Pa'ia. The shop is best known for its "orgasm" drink, a chocolate and peanut butter concoction. (Note the oft-photographed sign in the window: "Have you had an orgasm today? Come on in...we can help!").

Shave Ice

Nothing caps off a day at the beach like a visit to **Tobi's Shave Ice** (137 Hana Hwy., 808/579-9745, 11am-6pm daily). Get the Kauai cream drizzled on top of the syrupy mound (it goes best with blue vanilla) and add azuki beans and ice cream to the bottom.

HA'IKU
Local Style

French stalwarts like *croque monsieur* sit on the same menu as gravy-covered loco moco at **Hana Hou Café** (810 Ha'iku Rd., 808/575-2661, www.hanahoucafe.com, 9am-9pm Wed.-Mon., 4:30pm-9pm Tues., $13-23), offering a garden setting in the Ha'iku Cannery. Choose from affordable plate lunch favorites such as chicken katsu and hamburger steak. It's also one of the few places on the island where you can order a lu'au-style dinner without actually being at a lu'au. Go all in with Hawaiian classics such as lau lau, kalua pig, lomi salmon, and squid lu'au. Top it all off with coconut haupia pudding.

Mexican

A pop-up tent in the parking lot of the Ha'iku Cannery, **Island Taco** (810 Ha'iku Rd., 10am-4pm Mon.-Fri., $5) serves chicken, pork, and fish tacos at a wallet-friendly price. Dig into a fresh fish taco at one of picnic tables where the cheery staff are happy to "talk story."

American

Colleen's (810 Ha'iku Rd., 808/575-9211, www.colleensinhaiku.com, 6am-10pm daily, $7-14, dinner $18-30) has become synonymous with Ha'iku dining. Expect heaping plates of omelets, eggs Benedict, and breakfast burritos. Pizzas, fish tacos, and Maui Cattle Company cheeseburgers dominate the lunch menu. Pair your portobello mushroom burger with locally brewed beer on tap. For dinner, enjoy island favorites like pan-seared ahi or wild mushroom ravioli. Stop in after biking down Haleakala with Haleakala Bike Co., which is right next door.

Thai

Heaping portions come from the window of the **Tuk Tuk Thai** (810 Ha'iku Rd., 11am-6pm Tues.-Sat., 11am-4pm Sun., $9-12) food truck, in the parking lot of the Ha'iku Cannery. The chicken satay, yellow curry, and pad thai are as authentic as they come.

Vegetarian

In the back of the Aloha 'Aina Center, **Maui Kombucha** (810 Kokomo Rd., 808/575-9233, www.mauikombucha.com, 8am-8pm Mon.-Fri., 10am-5pm Sat.-Sun., $7-12) is a happening place devoted to healthy living. Kombucha is an acquired taste, but the health benefits of the effervescent, fermented tea are believed to be far reaching. Maui Kombucha offers three different flavors on tap, which can change by the hour, as well as raw desserts and vegetarian meals. Everything is made in-house at this humble little hideaway.

Just a few doors down, health food stalwart **Veg Out** (810 Kokomo Rd., 808/575-5320, www.veg-out.com, 10:30am-7:30pm Mon.-Fri., 11:30am-7:30pm Sat.-Sun., $8-10) offers affordable falafel wraps, vegetarian burritos, pad thai, and vegan pizzas. It's a budget-friendly and tasty way to fill up.

ROAD TO HANA

Seemingly every store in Pa'ia (and even some as far away as Ka'anapali) offers "Road to Hana picnic lunches" as a means of staving off starvation, even though the longest stretch without any food options is a little under seven

© KYLE ELLISON

Huelo Lookout fruit stand

miles. There are plenty of places to pull over and enjoy an outdoor meal, but don't settle on a picnic lunch out of desperation. A better plan is a hearty breakfast in Pa'ia followed by occasional stops at the roadside food trucks and fruit stands to get some local flare along with your snacks. Once you reach the Nahiku Marketplace (39 miles past Pa'ia and six miles before Hana) you're presented with more options, ranging from coffee shops to barbecue to freshly made Thai. So when setting out for Hana, the question shouldn't be whether you're going to starve, but rather, *which* place to stop to eat! Go slow, "talk story" with those serving your food, and sample the local flavors of the East Maui jungle.

Fruit Stands

The first fruit stand on the road is **Huelo Lookout** (7600 Hana Hwy., 808/280-4791, www.huelolookout.coconutprotectors.com, open daily), just past mile marker 4. Enjoy your fresh fruit, smoothies, and coconut candies

at the coastal lookout a few steps behind the stand. They also sell local arts and crafts.

Other fruit stands may appear along the roadside. Make your next stop at **Uncle Harry's** (808/633-3129, 10am-3pm daily, hours vary), which offers intriguing conversation with locals along with basic snacks and drinks. The yellow plywood stand is toward the top of the road leading down to Wailua. You'll see more fruit stands at mile markers 28.3 and 30.7.

Food Carts

Inside the Garden of Eden is the aptly named **Garden Gourmet Café** (10600 Hana Hwy., 808/269-4060, 9am-3pm daily, $8-12), a simple food truck serving fish tacos, pizzas, spring rolls, and coffees. There's no arguing with the tranquil surroundings or the impeccably manicured grounds. While the plates aren't filling enough for a full meal, they're a welcome hunger-buster if you haven't eaten since breakfast. Expect to wait a little while since it's all prepared fresh. The outdoor setting is worth the wait. You also need to pack out your trash.

Market

As you pass the turnoff for Jaws and make your way deeper into Ha'iku, at mile marker 14.5, you'll see run-down little **Maui Grown Market and Deli** (6:30am-6pm) which advertises itself as the "Last Stop Before Hana." Although this may have been true at one time, there are now a number of stops between here and Hana, so don't worry about impending starvation. The small store is a convenient place for a sandwich, snacks, or cold drinks. It's almost worth a stop to experience its old-school existence.

The accurately named **Halfway to Hana** (www.halfwaytohanamaui.com, 8:30am-4pm daily, $2-6, cash only) is located at the 17.3 mile marker between the Ke'anae Overlook and the turnoff for Wailua. It's basically a hot dog, sandwich, and shave ice stand with an ATM around the corner, making it the closest thing to a store around Ke'anae. Ask about the fresh baked banana bread.

Thai

You'll be blown away by **My Thai** (mile marker 28.7, variable hours, $10-13) food stall, in the Nahiku Marketplace. Their steaming plate of chicken pad thai is fresher and tastier than anything in the city. Other options include tofu, chicken, or shrimp, and massive plates of fried rice, green curry, or pork and vegetable stir-fry.

Local Style

Also located in the Nahiku Marketplace, quick and convenient **Up In Smoke BBQ** (mile marker 28.7, 10am-5pm daily, $5-9) serves lunch plate classics alongside a taco menu featuring shrimp, pork, chicken, and steak. The chili and rice is the best bang for your buck, but it's hard to argue with the kalua pig.

Coffee Shop

For an afternoon pick-me-up, the **Nahiku Roadside** stand (mile marker 26.5, 10am-4pm Sun.-Thurs.) offers fruit, coffee, tea, banana bread, and patio seating that looks out over the highway.

The best-and earliest—cup of coffee on the east end of the island is served at **(Nahiku Café** (mile marker 28.7, 6am-5pm daily), inside the Nahiku Marketplace. Choose from multiple flavors of Maui-grown coffee as well as espresso drinks. There is also a decent array of food options such as toasted bagels and pastries.

Ice Cream

One of the last roadside stands you'll encounter before the town of Hana is **Coconut Glen's** (mile marker 27.5, 808/248-4876, www.coconutglens.com, 10:30am-5pm daily). "Coconut Glen" is the Willy Wonka of Maui, a chef from Boston who moved to the island in 2006. Once he realized the culinary possibilities of the coconut, he constructed this roadside stand as a means of sharing coconut concoctions sourced directly from the land, most notably vegan ice cream made with fresh coconut milk. Much of the building itself is made from recycled materials gathered around East Maui.

HANA

In the last few years, Hana has seen a huge proliferation of food options. However too many visitors continue to drive to Hana Bay thinking it's the end of the road and don't take the time to look around. Spend the day in Hana and you'll be rewarded with a tasty cornucopia.

Local Style

Set on the shores of Hana Bay, popular **Tutu's Snack Shop** (Hana Bay, 9pm-4:30pm daily) is frequented by visitors who have driven to Hana and are still searching for the actual town (*This is it?!*). They settle for moderately overpriced hot dogs and plate lunches at this oceanfront takeout window. The plates themselves are fine and you can't beat the bay view setting.

American

A longtime staple of the town's restaurant scene, the **Hana Ranch Restaurant** (5031 Hana Hwy., 808/270-5280, 11am-8:30pm daily, $8-10) is located on the mountain side of the road in the "center of town" (if the bank and post office are there, it's the center of town). There are shoyu chicken plate lunches, fish and chicken sandwiches, and soothing bowls of saimin noodles to calm your upset stomach. The takeout window is open from 11am-4pm; the inside seating area stays open for dinner.

Hawaiian Regional

If you're craving is a proper meal in a resort setting, the **(Ka'uiki** (5031 Hana Hwy., 808/359-2401, 7:30am-9pm, $20-40) restaurant and **Paniolo Lounge** (11:30am-9pm daily) inside the Travaasa Hana hotel are the best (and only) options in Hana. This is hands-down the town's best breakfast option (think French-pressed coffee and eggs Benedict). The lunch options of fish tacos, grilled vegetable pitas, and ahi nicoise salad provide a solid dose of civilization. Dinner means risottos, fish, steak, and chicken dishes that coddle your taste buds. The entrée menu uses locally sourced ingredients. A full-service bar and wine list add some libations to a romantic meal in paradise. Prices are higher than a food cart on the road, but you're getting a relaxing respite in one of the nicest hotels in the state.

Fruit Stands

Only a few miles before the town of Hana, the legendary ◖ **Hana Farms Banana Bread Stand** (mile marker 31.2, 8am-7pm daily) features six different types of banana bread, as well as a full range of fruits, coffee, sauces, and flavorings. There will be more fruit stands as you wrap your way between Hana and Kipahulu, but none of them are like this. Do yourself a favor and stop for a coffee, banana bread (get a loaf with chocolate chips), and advice on your Hana adventure.

Farmers Market

One of the best Hana lunch options, and one of the few actually open on Sunday, is **Hana Fresh Market** (4590 Hana Hwy., 10am-4pm Mon., 10am-2pm weekends, $8), in the parking lot of the Hana Health Clinic between the town of Hana and the turnoff for Wai'anapanapa. Not only do the proceeds support the Hana Health Clinic, but many of the vegetables and fresh produce are grown in a greenhouse on the property. There is also an ample selection of filling lunch options such as ham apple brie paninis, Italian sausage pasta, and lemon caper mahimahi. Wash it all down with a fruit smoothie or freshly brewed coffee.

Italian

Right next door to the Hana Farms fruit stand, ◖ **The Clay Oven** (4pm-8pm Fri.-Sat, $14-17) is the best thing to happen to the Hana dinner scene in a long time. Don't be fooled by the appearance of this outdoor pizza kitchen in the jungle or the "pizza box" of fresh banana leaves. You'll be surprised to find a full menu of seven different pizza options ranging from classic margherita to creative potato and pesto. The pizzas are filling enough for two. Large groups can enjoy sitting in "the fireside lounge," a tent behind the open-air kitchen. It's at mile marker 31.2 (a few miles past Wai'anapanapa if heading back toward Kahului).

Thai

◖ **Thai Food by Pranee** (5050 Uakea Rd., 10:30am-4pm Mon.-Fri., 10:30am-6pm Sat.-Sun., $10-12) has diversified the town's culinary scene for the better. Located on Uakea Road, smack in the center of town between Hana Ballpark and Hana Bay, this open-air restaurant gets packed for lunch. The filling portions of pad thai and green curry are worth the wait. The cooks aren't messing around: The curry is served with sweat-inducing spice. Ask them to pour a ladle of coconut milk over the fiery dish. Parking can be tough; If you park along Uakea Road, be sure to face the correct direction to avoid a ticket.

Food Carts

Hana's food trucks park in a semi-permanent location, catering to visitors passing through for the day. All are worth a stop. The main distinctions between them are slight variations in the menu and how long you expect to wait.

As you first drive into town on the "upper road," longtime classic **Uncle Bill's** (808/264-1731, 6am-1pm Mon.-Fri., $5-12) runs in the driveway of a residential home. Hana's most laid-back breakfast spot serves heaping veggie omelets, stacks of pancakes, and refillable cups of coffee. You may end up "talking story" with whoever runs the window. To find Uncle Bill's, go to the two churches in the center of town and drive half a mile back toward Kahului; you'll see the sign on the ocean side of the roadway.

On the right side of the highway past the gas station is **Da Chow Wagon** (10am-4pm Mon., Wed.-Fri., $9-10), serving local classics like roast pork, loco moco, and hamburger steak. Seating is limited and the setting is little more than a parking lot, but this is a good place to pick up a meal to enjoy at nearby Hamoa Beach.

Fifty yards farther down the road on the ocean side of the highway is the **Braddah Hutt's BBQ Grill** (11am-2:30pm Mon.-Sat., $8-14). The portions are filling and the plates are *ono*, but this food truck is popular with tour groups. Don't stop if you're in a rush (or just don't be in a rush anyway, because this is Hana!). Plates range from fish tacos to grilled steak or mahimahi.

Cool down with a unique and fruity treat at **Shaka Pops** (5240 Hana Hwy., 808/344-1245, www.shakapopsmaui.com, 10am-4pm most days), in the general vicinity of the gas station. These gourmet ice pops use ingredients like Maui pineapples and Kula strawberries for a fresh taste far better than any mass-produced popsicle.

KIPAHULU AND BEYOND

If you plan on driving "the back road" all the way to the other side of the island, don't expect many food options. In nearly 35 miles of roadway between Hasegawa General Store and Kanaio, there are exactly three—one of which is only open on Sunday nights. The other two are known to close without warning. If you're planning on venturing from Hana to 'Ohe'o (Seven Pools) and then continuing around the back side of the island, stock up on water and snacks at Hasegawa General Store or a fruit stand, lest you get marooned with a rumbling stomach and parched lips.

Fruit Stand

The most consistent fruit stand is quirky **Laulima Farm** (9am-5pm Tues.-Sun.) at mile marker 40.6, just past the turnoff for Maui Stables and Palapala Ho'omau Church. Laulima specializes in certified organic, GMO-free produce which they craft into salads and roadside cuisine. Everything is plucked straight from the earth. The staff here are all stoked to be alive; a spirit of community permeates the jungle compound.

Ho'onanea Farms (mile marker 40.9) operates a small roadside stand that starts serving coffee as early as 7am. A few store-bought pastry items accompany the cuppa (expect to pay more since you're in the middle of nowhere).

The stand usually only stays open for a couple of hours in the morning and operates on a variable schedule. Nevertheless, if it's a Monday morning and Laulima Farm is closed, this small outpost will save you from driving 30 minutes back to Hana just for coffee.

Vegetarian

Spunky **Café Attitude** (6:30pm-10pm Sun.) only operates on Sunday nights and is closer to a community potluck than an actual restaurant. Organic farmers gather on Sunday evenings and take turns preparing a weekly meal, which is open to all who care to attend. Guests are suggested to trade a donation ($15) for a large plate of freshly prepared vegetarian cuisine. There are usually exotic teas, homemade kombucha, and all-natural popsicles available by small donation as well. More important than the food is the open-mic jam session which takes place on the small stage. Sit around the communal fire pit and listen to local artists perform everything from acoustic guitar and harmonica to lyrical spoken word. A strong sense of *aloha* permeates the rural setting: As the banner hanging from the dining area says, "Be grateful, or get out." To find Café Attitude, travel past the Laulima Farm stand in the direction of Kaupo and keep an eye out on the *makai* (ocean side) of the road for a driveway with two pillars of a sun and a moon. Follow the steep driveway down into a grassy parking area and listen for the sound of laughter and bongos.

Market

Six miles past Kipahulu at mile marker 34.6 is the historic **Kaupo Store** (808/248-8054, 10am-5pm Mon.-Sat.), a welcome stop for those in need of a cold drink, a bag of chips, or an ice-cream bar pulled out of the old-fashioned freezer. You have to go another 20 miles to find a real restaurant.

Information and Services

MEDICAL SERVICES

The medical services in East Maui are limited. You'll need to go the Maui Memorial Hospital in Kahului for any serious injuries or an emergency. Nevertheless, there are still a few small clinics and pharmacy options for picking up prescriptions.

Pa'ia

The best place for picking up any prescriptions or over the counter medications is the **Pa'ia Pharmacy** (9am-6pm Mon.-Sat., 10am-4pm Sun.) smack in the heart of town.

Ha'iku

For anyone experiencing ailments in Ha'iku, the **Ha'iku Medical Clinic** (8am-noon and 2pm-6pm Mon.-Fri.) inside the Ha'iku Cannery Marketplace offers a basic range of medical needs.

Hana

Clearly marked on the right just as you enter town is **Hana Community Health Center** (808/248-8294, 8:30am-4:30pm weekdays). If you're Hana and in need of medical services, walk-in, nonemergency treatment is available.

BANKS
Pa'ia

The largest bank in East Maui is here in Pa'ia: the **Bank of Hawaii** (35 Baldwin Ave., 808/579-9511, 8:30am-4pm Mon.-Thurs., 8:30am-6pm Fri.) between Milagros and Mana Foods. In addition to the bank, you'll also find ATMs at numerous gas stations and restaurants across town.

Ha'iku

While there aren't any official banking branches in Ha'iku, you can find an ATM at the **Ha'iku Grocery Store** (810 Ha'iku Rd., 808/575-9291, 7am-9pm daily) inside the Ha'iku Cannery Marketplace.

Road to Hana

While it probably won't come as any surprise that there aren't any banks on the Road to Hana, it might come as a surprise that there is actually an ATM. The lone functioning ATM is currently at the **Halfway to Hana** store (mile marker 17.3, www.halfwaytohanamaui.com, 8:30am-4pm daily), where, not surprisingly, everything must be paid for in cash.

Hana

The **Bank of Hawaii** (808/248-8015, 3pm-4:30pm Mon.-Thurs., 3pm-6pm Fri.) is open for cash advances on Visa and MasterCard across from the Hana Ranch Restaurant. (Notice the hours!) For an ATM, go to Hasegawa's store.

GAS
Pa'ia

There are three gas stations within walking distance of each other in Pa'ia; be sure you have close to a full tank if you're going to be taking the long, winding journey out to Hana. None of the stations offer a public restroom (the closest ones are at Pa'ia Bay).

Ha'iku

Tucked away on a back road that visitors only end up on if they're lost, the only gas station in Ha'iku can be found at **Hanzawa's** (1833 Kaupakalua Rd., 808/298-0407, 6am-8pm Mon.-Sat., 7am-7pm Sun.) store about halfway between Hana Highway and the town of Makawao.

Hana

In all of Hana there is only one gas station: the **Chevron** (808/270-5299, 7am-8:30pm Mon.-Sat., 7am-6pm Sun.) on the highway next to the horse stables. It has a few auto supplies, snacks, and a telephone, although for a public restroom you're better off going down to the Hana ball field. Gas in Hana is expensive, roughly $0.50 per gallon higher than the already high prices elsewhere on the island. Fill up before leaving town because the nearest gas station west is in Pa'ia; going south around the bottom, the closest is in Keokea in Upcountry, and it isn't open in the evening hours.

POST OFFICE
Pa'ia

If you want to mail home that new Technicolor outfit you picked up in town, the **U.S. Post Office** (120 Baldwin Ave., 808/579-8866, 8:30am-11am, noon-4:30pm Mon.-Fri., 10:30am-12:30pm Sat.) is modern, convenient, and the only option in town.

Hana

The **Hana post office** (808/248-8258, 11am-4pm weekdays) is a tiny station across from the Hana Ranch Restaurant, and there is a community bulletin board is posted outside.

LIBRARY
Hana

The excellent Hana School public library (808/248-4848) is on the western edge of town. The library is open Monday and Friday 8am-4pm, Tuesday 9am-4pm, Wednesday-Thursday 11am-7pm.

INTERNET SERVICES
Pa'ia

Although there isn't anywhere in Pa'ia with truly "free" wireless, if you make a purchase at either **Haz Beanz** (113 Baldwin Ave., 808/268-0149, 6am-2pm Mon.-Fri., 6am-1pm Sat., 6am-noon Sun.) or **Anthony's Coffee Company** (90 Hana Hwy., 808/579-8340, www.anthonyscoffee.com, 5:30am-6pm daily), you are welcome to use the Wi-Fi provided for guests.

Ha'iku

One of the only places in Ha'iku with formal Internet and printing services for those without their own computer is the **Postal Shop Ha'iku** (810 Ha'iku Rd., 808/575-2049, 9am-5pm Mon.-Fri., 10am-2pm Sat.) inside the Ha'iku Cannery Marketplace.

Hana

If you're truly in dire need of the Internet and are only a day trip to Hana, you can try your chances at the **Hana Library** (808/248-4848) at the Hana School on the western edge of town. The library is open Monday and Friday 8am-4pm, Tuesday 9am-4pm, Wednesday-Thursday 11am-7pm. Otherwise, if you're staying overnight at a resort or a bed-and-breakfast, most places will offer free Wi-Fi as part of the accommodation.

Getting There and Around

CAR
Rental Car

The only rental car operator is East Maui is **Manaloha Rent a Car** (375 W. Kuiaha Rd., 808/283-8779, www.manaloharentacar.net, 9am-5pm daily) in Ha'iku. Since it's in a rural location, they'll offer to pick you up at the airport for free (with a minimum one-week rental). The rates that you'll find here are some of the best on the island. If you're flying into Hana Airport, you'll need to arrange for a pickup at the airport (although wherever you are staying will almost assuredly have it arranged for you).

TAXI

All taxis across the island will gladly take you on a tour of Hana (it's like hitting the lottery for them). This, of course, is not by any means the economical way to experience Hana, but some people can't be bothered with driving or with joining a group tour. If you're just looking for a taxi to get you from A to B on the island's North Shore, **Paia Taxi** (808/298-6390, www.paiataxi.com) is one of the few operators based here and will offer the quickest response time for where you need to go. They can also arrange tours to Hana or anywhere else in Upcountry.

UNDERSTANDING "THE BACK ROAD"

© HEATHER ELLISON

The "back road" from Hana is a journey into another world—and it's more accessible than you would think.

The back road from Hana is truly unlike any other stretch of road on the island. It feels as if you've journeyed to the edge of the earth. Panoramic views stretch out to the blue horizon and the back of Haleakala opens up before you in a rugged swath of mountainside plunging from summit to sea. Waterfalls tumble directly into the ocean and the noises of the modern world are given over to the sound of the wind.

At the beginning of the drive, the terrain changes from a lush paradise laden with waterfalls to windswept grasslands. Past Kaupo Store, the road straightens out. The last half of the drive, between Manawainui and Kanaio, is one of the nicest stretches of pavement on the island. There's a good chance you'll like this section of road better than even the more famous front section.

The biggest misconception about the Road to Hana is that the "back road" around the Kaupo section of the island is only accessible with four-wheel drive. You'll be told that driving this section of road violates your rental car policy. Neither of these commonly held opinions is accurate. Driving the full loop around the entire east end of the island is by far the best way to experience Hana.

On virtually all days of the year the back road (which is technically Highway 31) is passable in any form of vehicle, including a regular rental car. The road is unpaved, well-graded dirt for five miles. At some points it is only one-lane wide and has precipitous drop-offs, but at no point is four-wheel drive essential. The only time you would need four-wheel drive would be during a torrential rainstorm—and in that situation, you should just stay off the road altogether. Your rental car company won't penalize you just because you drove out here, but if something goes wrong, you're liable for any damage, injury, or inconvenience. Luckily, island locals are some of the friendliest people you'll meet. If anything were to go wrong, you won't have any trouble flagging someone down for help.

Preparation is key to enjoying a drive around the back side. Make sure that you have plenty of gas. If you have half a tank or less when leaving Hana, you're cutting it too close and should stop for gas. Driving this road at night can be dangerous—and is pointless since you miss the expansive views. Keep an eye out for free range cattle on the road. Other than Kaupo Store there isn't anywhere to get food or water, so be sure that you have enough water and snacks—it's a long way back to civilization. If you're not a confident driver, the narrow sections and steep drop-offs mean this isn't the road for you. The back road can be closed due to a landslide or overflowing streams. Call 808/986-1200, ext. 2, for the latest information.

GUIDED TOURS

Despite how much fun it is to craft your own Hana adventure, a surprising number of visitors decide to visit Hana as part of a private tour.

Temptation Tours (808/877-8888, www.tempatationtours.com, $219 and up) offers small group tours in "limo vans" and has a number of different tour options for visiting Hana. One of the tours spends time exploring the recesses of Ka'eleku Caverns, while there is also a Hana picnic tour similar in itinerary to the other options but with much nicer vans. The top choice, however, is to drive the Road to Hana and then hop aboard a helicopter at the Hana Airport for a ride back to Kahului. During the flight you'll zip by towering waterfalls you would never see from the road, and also buzz over the multihued cinder cones of Haleakala Crater. Prices for this Hana Sky Trek option are understandably higher at about $345/person.

Valley Isle Excursions (808/661-8687, www.tourmaui.com, $132/adult, $94/child), **Roberts Hawaii** (800/831-5541, www.robertshawaii.com, $124/adult, $74/child), and **Mahalo Tours** (877/262-4256, www.mahalotoursandtrans.com) also offer tours in larger vans that make all of the usual stops, and you'll wrap all the way around the back of the island and make a stop at the Tedeschi Winery in Ulupalakua.

For smaller, private, more customizable tours, **Awapuhi Adventures** (808/269-6031, www.awapuhiadventures.com), **Open Eye Tours** (808/572-3483, www.openeyetours.com), and **Maui Easy Riders** (808/344-9489, www.mauieasyriders.com) provide personalized experiences which—if you are going to choose a guide trip for Hana—are the best, albeit most expensive ways to go.

BUS

The **Maui Bus** provides regular service between Pa'ia, Ha'iku, the Kahului Airport, and Queen Ka'ahumanu Center in Kahului (where you can connect with buses to anywhere else on the island). The rate is $2/boarding or $4 for a day pass, and pickup begins in Pa'ia at 5:53am if headed toward Ha'iku and 6:29am if headed toward Kahului. The route also makes stops at the Ha'iku Marketplace and Ha'iku Community Center, with the final bus going from Ha'iku to Kahului departing the community center at 7:47pm.

FLIGHTS
Hana

At the small airport in Hana, you can swap the nausea of a three-hour drive for the convenience of a 20-minute flight. Of course, you'll miss out on all the sights along the Road to Hana, but if your focus is on getting to Hana and relaxing at the resort, then **Mokulele** (866/260-7070, www.mokuleleairlines.com, 7am-7pm daily) operates flights twice daily between Kahului Airport and the landing strip in Hana. Often the Travaasa Hana hotel will run specials in which you can bundle airfare with a stay of three nights or more, and occasionally the airfare will actually be free. If you fly to Hana, however, remember that there aren't any rental cars here, so you'll need to have your airport transport arranged before you get on the flight.

LANA'I

It's hard to find an outdoor playground more stunning than Lana'i, home to a mere 3,300 residents and crisscrossed by just over 30 miles of paved roads. The late 1980s saw this island's cash crop transition from the world's largest pineapple plantation to tourism. With the construction of two luxurious resorts, Lana'i was instantly transformed into one of the Hawaiian Islands' most exclusive getaways. Recently, 98 percent of the island was purchased by Oracle CEO Larry Ellison; the lavish amenities appear set to continue.

There's far more to Lana'i than sitting in a lawn chair and being spritzed by an Evian bottle. Typical visitors come to enjoy the snorkeling at Hulopo'e Beach Park, the plantation-era charm of Lana'i City, and tackling the greens at one of the island's two championship golf courses. Choose to explore a little deeper, however, and you will find yourself enjoying morning hikes on pine-shrouded mountain trails, off-roading through otherworldly moonscapes, or surfing empty waves along a beach you will have all to yourself.

Lana'i is an island of unparalleled luxury and oceanfront massages, but it's also an island of four-wheel-drive trucks with deer skulls mounted to the bumper, aging Filipino plantation workers "talking-story" in Dole Park, and historic petroglyphs scattered across rock faces which predate any of the island's multiple phases. It's a tight-knit community where everyone knows everyone else's business and townsfolk greet each other with first names and a smile. It truly is like nowhere else—and the people who live here want to keep it that way.

© HEATHER ELLISON

HIGHLIGHTS

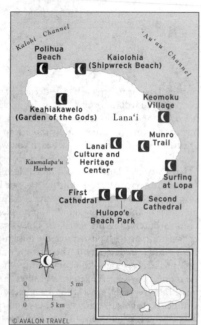

© AVALON TRAVEL

LOOK FOR ◖ TO FIND RECOMMENDED
SIGHTS, ACTIVITIES, DINING, AND
LODGING.

◖ **Hulopo'e Beach Park:** This crescent of
white sand was voted the number one beach in
the United States in 1997. It has the island's best
snorkeling when the ocean is calm and its best
surf on a southern swell (page 323).

◖ **Kaiolohia (Shipwreck Beach):** The
fringing reef ringing the island's northwest

coastline has been the demise of dozens of
ships, including the WWII Liberty ship that provides a dramatic backdrop for this windswept
beach (page 324).

◖ **Polihua Beach:** Get lost on Lana'i's remotest beach. The only footprints will be yours
(page 327).

◖ **Scuba Diving Cathedrals:** These underwater caverns are two of the top dives in all of
Hawai'i—and have even been the site of underwater weddings (page 329).

◖ **Surfing at Lopa:** Protected from the wind,
the waves a this remote beach are perfect for
beginning surfers (page 331).

◖ **Munro Trail:** This 12.8-mile hiking trail
winds its way to the island's 3,370-foot summit and serves as the main vein for exploring its
cloud forest watershed (page 333).

◖ **Lana'i Culture and Heritage Center:**
Everything from wooden spears used in ancient
battles to old photographs of Lana'i's plantation days adorn this informative and authentic
cultural resource (page 340).

◖ **Keahiakawelo (Garden of the Gods):**
This otherworldly landscape of tortured earth
is dotted with red boulders which appear to
have fallen from the sky (page 342).

◖ **Keomoku Village:** With a collection of old
homes and a haunting, abandoned church, this
stretch of shoreline exhibits what life on Lana'i
must have been like a century ago, when the
population numbered fewer than 200 people
(page 344).

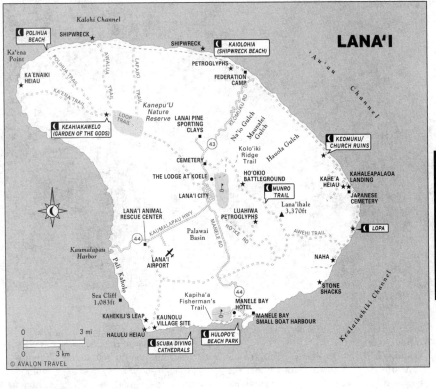

LANA'I

Beaches

Unless you have a four-wheel drive or high-clearance vehicle, Lana'i only has one accessible beach. That beach has been voted one of the best in the country; it's also the only beach with any sort of facilities. If, however, you happen to procure a Jeep or a local's truck, there are a number of undeveloped beaches where you could run around naked and there would be no one there to care. It's rare in modern day Hawai'i to walk down an empty stretch of sand that isn't lined by any sort of development. When you're the person leaving the only set of footprints in the sand, you realize just how secluded this island is.

◖ HULOPO'E BEACH PARK

Hulopo'e Beach Park is the undisputed hangout for island locals. It was crowned number one beach in America in 1997. Within walking distance from the Manele small boat harbor, Hulopo'e is the only beach on the island with restrooms and showers, and despite being the island's most popular beach, it's a far cry from crowded. The right side of the beach is used by guests of the Four Seasons Manele Bay Hotel who have access to the white umbrellas and lounge chairs. Similarly, Monday-Friday, guests of Trilogy Excursions' snorkel tour from Maui inhabit the left-hand side of the beach, thereby leaving the middle section of the beach

© HEATHER ELLISON

Hulopo'e Beach Park

as the place for visitors to relax in the shade or bake out in the sun.

Hulopo'e Bay is a marine reserve and home to one of the few reefs in Maui County that isn't in a state of decline. The reef extends over the left side of the bay, where colorful parrotfish the size of your forearm can easily be spotted (and heard) nibbling on the vibrant corals. Hulopo'e is also famous for the Hawaiian spinner dolphins which enter the bay on a regular basis. In an effort to protect the natural sleep cycles of the dolphins, swimmers are asked to not aggressively encroach on them in any way. If dolphins just happen to swim toward you, consider yourself lucky.

In addition to the sugary sands and perfectly placed palm trees, there are also two nature trails on each side of the beach. The Kapiha'a Trail departs from the right side of the bay, whereas the trail to the Pu'u Pehe Overlook and Shark's Bay winds its way from the left side. There is also a fantastic system of tidepools stretching around the left point of the bay, and one is even deep enough to snorkel in

(which is great for teaching young kids). The easiest way to get to the tidepools is to use the stairway found on the trail to Shark's Bay.

Although most days are calm at Hulopo'e, the southern-facing shoreline can be prone to large surf in the summer, which makes entering and exiting the water a challenge.

KAIOLOHIA (SHIPWRECK BEACH)

Other than Hulopo'e, **Shipwreck Beach** is the most popular beach among island visitors. To get to Shipwreck, drive past the Lodge at Koele and drop down Lana'i's windswept "back side" by following the switchbacking—but paved—Keomuku Highway. The views as you descend this winding road stretch all the way to neighboring Maui. A favorite pastime of island teenagers during the plantation days would be to flash their headlights at family members on Maui at a prearranged time, and then wait in eager anticipation for their cousins to flash them back (Did I mention Lana'i can be *slow?*). Once you reach the

© KYLE ELLISON

the shipwreck at Kaiolohia Beach

bottom of the paved highway, a sign points left toward Shipwreck Beach. Follow the sandy road (four-wheel drive recommended) for 1.5 miles before it dead-ends in a parking area. When you pass the shacks constructed out of driftwood and fishing floats, you'll know that you've arrived.

Traditionally this area was known as Kaiolohia. The current moniker only stuck due to the World War II Liberty ship which was intentionally grounded on the fringing reef. Though numerous vessels have met their demise on this shallow stretch of coral, this concrete oil tanker has rotted slower than most. Stoic in its haunted appearance, the ship remains firmly lodged in the reef as a warning to passing vessels of the dangers.

Due to the persistent northeasterly trade winds Kaiolohia rarely offers anything in the way of snorkeling or swimming. Your time here is better spent combing the beach for the flotsam and jetsam which finds its way to shore, and Japanese glass balls used as fishing floats are the ultimate beachcomber's reward. To reach the Liberty ship it's about a mile walk along the sandy coastline, although numerous rocks interrupt the thin strip of sand to give the appearance of multiple beaches. From here it's technically possible to walk all the way to Polihua Beach, although unless you have a ride arranged at the other side it's a 16-mile round-trip venture in an area with no services or shade.

Walking as far as the ship gives you ample time to explore, although make a side trip to visit the **petroglyphs** on your way back to the car. About a quarter of a mile after the road ends, you'll encounter the concrete base of what was once an old lighthouse, and if you're uncertain of whether or not you're at the right place, check the concrete base where names were inscribed in 1929. From the base of the lighthouse turn directly inland and rock-hop for 300 yards before you'll see a large rock with the words "do not deface" written on it. A white arrow points to a trail behind the rock which leads to petroglyphs of dogs, humans, and a drawing known as "The Birdman."

LANA'I'S OTHER SHIPWRECK BEACH

There's a good chance you're already familiar with Lana'i's famous Shipwreck Beach, but did you know there is a second shipwreck off Lana'i which is hardly ever visited? To reach the rarely frequented YO-21 Navy ship, take your four-wheel-drive vehicle out Polihua Road seven miles to the Garden of the Gods and make a right onto Awalua Road. This steep, eroded trail offers sweeping views across the Kalohi Channel to neighboring Moloka'i before depositing you three miles later at a coastal outpost known as Awalua. The Dollar Jeep rental company doesn't recommend going down this road, so should you choose to drive to Awalua, stay out of any deep sand and know that you're doing so at your own risk. There are multiple pullouts on the side of the road should you want to drive only part of the way and walk the rest down to the beach. The rewards for your efforts, however, are a narrow stretch of coastline where you're guaranteed to be the only person there and the chance to view a rusting ship which was stationed at Pearl Harbor on the morning of the Japanese bombing. As at the more well-known shipwreck beach, however, photographing the ship and beachcombing are much safer options here than trying to swim.

Aside from the wrecks at Awalua and Kaiolohia, hundreds of ships have met their final demise on this remote stretch of reef. In 1826 the U.S. ship *The London* sank here with a large amount of gold and silver, only an unknown portion of which was ever recovered. No lobster divers have ever come back holding gold bullion, however, so whatever treasure may remain has seemingly been lost to the mystery of the sea.

KAHALEPALAOA

When you reach the bottom of Keomuku Highway (where the pavement ends), taking a right at the fork in the road will lead you on a rugged coastal track that ranks as one of the best drives on the island. Four-wheel drive is recommended as the deep sand patches can often drift onto the road, and depending upon the recent rain activity, the road can become rutted and rough. Nevertheless, some of Lana'i's nicest beaches lie down this road, and anyone with a Jeep or SUV should be able to navigate the road just fine.

While there are a number of small pullouts along the side of the road leading to narrow, windswept sand patches, the first beach of any real size is **Kahalepalaoa**, 7.5 miles from where the pavement ended. This Hawaiian name translates to "House of the Whale Ivory" (whale bones are rumored to have once washed ashore here). In more recent times this spot was also the site of a now-defunct, Club Med-style day resort named Club Lana'i. Though the booze-fueled excursion from Maui no longer operates, the coconut grove which once housed the venue marks the start of a long white beach that's perfect for casual strolling. This is the site of the proposed hotel new owner Larry Ellison envisions, so within the next couple of years there is a high likelihood that high-end bungalows will be lining the eastern shore.

LOPA

A little over a mile past Kahalepalaoa lies **Lopa,** a protected stretch of sand which is the nicest on Lana'i's back side. Although the beach here isn't all that different from Kahalepalaoa, the fact that Lopa faces south means it's more protected from the northeasterly trades, a geographic benefit which makes reading a book in a beach chair infinitely more enjoyable. Lopa is a popular camping spot for locals and a couple of picnic tables have been placed beneath the thorn-riddled kiawe grove lining the beach. Although the swimming and snorkeling are nothing compared to Hulopo'e Beach Park (and can sometimes be rough), Lopa is the perfect place for longboard surfing or paddling along the shore in a kayak (if you brought your own). The chances of encountering anyone else on Lopa are higher on the weekends when locals come to camp and fish, but as at many of Lanaʻi's beaches, if there happens to be anyone else there it's justified in calling it crowded.

There's more to Lopa than just a beautiful and protected beach. Historically this was also the site of a *loko ʻia* fishpond which is barely visible today. Although the fishpond has fallen into disrepair, the waters offshore still teem with schools of fish that locals now collect by casting from shore. Pack out what you pack in.

NAHA

Even though the dirt road along the coastline seems like it's going to wrap back around toward the harbor at Manele Bay, eventually even dirt roads come to an end. In this particular instance the end of the road is a beach known as **Naha,** and while it looks like there is hardly anything there, Naha—like Lopa—was once the site of ancient fishponds which supported a native Hawaiian village. Unlike at Lopa, however, at low tide the fishponds are still visible, little changed from their original construction centuries ago.

The swimming at Naha isn't very good and the beach isn't as nice as Lopa, but given the historical significance of the ancient village site it's worth checking out if you've already driven all the way. Other than the fishponds, however, don't expect to reach the end of the road and see anything markedly different than what you've already been driving past. Naha is a favorite of local fishers as well as surfers who park their cars here to hike the thorny trail down to the break known as Stone Shacks. To reach Naha continue for two miles past Lopa, and at this point you should be about 11 miles from when you turned right at the end of the paved road.

◖ POLIHUA BEACH

Polihua is so remote that even Lanaʻi residents consider it "out there." A vast, windswept, and often empty stretch of sand, Polihua is unrivaled in its seclusion. If you've ever fantasized about placing the only set of footprints on a deserted Hawaiian beach, this the place. Although the area is occasionally frequented by fishers, unofficial campers, or the rare surfer, Polihua is a place you go to collect your thoughts, beachcomb, or run around naked simply because you can. The name is derived from a Hawaiian term for "eggs in the bosom," a reference to the green sea turtles which haul out on the sand and bury eggs on the isolated shore.

Unfortunately the strong currents at Polihua make the water unsafe for swimming, and often the afternoon trade winds turn the beach into a curtain of blowing sand. The morning hours are best for taking a relaxing stroll through the dunes, and by sunset the winds have usually died down enough to watch the sun slink behind the northwest horizon. The views stretch across the Kalohi Channel toward Molokaʻi.

Access to this area is threatened by a plan to place dozens of windmills on the northern slope of Lanaʻi, a project which has received formidable criticism from the community (the power generated would run in an undersea cable to Honolulu). It appears on the verge of being abandoned.

While Polihua remains in the public realm, reaching it requires the use of four-wheel drive. To find the beach, travel seven miles from Lanaʻi City on Polihua Road to the Keahiakawelo. From here you'll continue on the same road for another 25 minutes as it switchbacks down the rutted dirt track before reaching a terminus a few yards short of the beach. There are no facilities or services this far outside of town, so pack water and food. Pack out everything you brought with you.

LANAI

LANA'I

© KYLE ELLISON

the empty expanse of Polihua Beach

Snorkeling and Diving

SNORKELING

When it comes to snorkeling, **Hulopo'e Beach Park** easily trumps any other place on the island for the health of the reef, clarity of water, and variety of fish. Thanks to its protected status as a marine preserve, the reef here is in better shape than other places on the island, and snorkelers will revel in the large schools of *manini* (convict tang) and vibrant *uhu* (parrotfish) which flit around the shallow reef. The best snorkeling within the bay is on the left side of the beach. Since Hulopo'e faces south, it can be prone to large surf and shorebreak April-October. The shorebreak can make entry and exit into the water a little challenging, and the visibility won't be as good as it is on days which are as calm as a swimming pool. If you see surfers on the left side of the bay, use caution when entering the water and expect visibility to be reduced.

Nevertheless, even a mediocre day at Hulopo'e is better than a good day many other places. The reef here never gets deeper than 25 feet. It's also a good idea to stay within the bay and not venture halfway to Tahiti. Occasionally the Hawaiian spinner dolphins will venture into this bay, although they usually hang out over the sand on the right closer to the hotel.

Not far from Hulopo'e but equally as gorgeous is the vibrant reef at **Manele Bay.** Don't confuse this with snorkeling in Manele Harbor, because that would be disgusting. Instead, the reef at Manele Bay is on the opposite side of the breakwall set between the harbor and the cliffs. Entry from shore can be tricky since you have to come off the rocks, but if you follow the driveway of the harbor all the way to the far end, there is a little opening in the rocks where it's possible to make a graceful entry.

Schools of tropical reef fish gather in abundance here, and the same school of spinner dolphins can sometimes hang out in this area as well. Although Manele Bay is a good quarter mile from Hulopoʻe Beach, it's still part of the marine preserve, so the same rules apply: Don't stand on the coral, don't feed the fish, and you're best off just not touching anything at all.

There isn't anywhere on Lanaʻi to rent snorkeling equipment for the day, so your best bet is to have your own before you get on the ferry or plane. The snorkeling equipment at Hulopoʻe Beach is privately reserved for Trilogy's day guests who come over from Maui, and the gear at the Four Seasons beach kiosk is exclusively for hotel guests.

Technically it's possible to snorkel at other island locations such as **Lopa, Kahalepalaoa,** and **Shipwreck Beach,** but the wind and currents are usually a factor. For what you're going to see you're better off just working on your suntan.

If you want to explore the island's remoter reefs which are only accessible by boat, **Trilogy Excursions** (1 Manele Harbor Dr., 808/874-5649, www.scubalanai.com) provides the best (and only) snorkel charter service operating out of Lanaʻi. Aboard their 51-foot sloop rigged sailing catamaran *Trilogy III,* Trilogy offers a 3.5-hour snorkeling and sailing excursion which usually heads around the southwestern coastline of the island to the towering sea cliffs of Kaunolu. There can occasionally be other boats from Maui back here, but more often than not this trip provides the opportunity to snorkel the waters of the historic fishing village with only a handful of other passengers. Given that Kaunolu (also known as Shark Fin Cove due to the dorsal fin-shaped rock in the middle of the bay) is exposed to the deeper waters offshore, sightings of pelagic species such as spinner dolphins, bottlenose dolphins, eagle rays, manta rays, and whale sharks have been known to occur on an intermittent basis. The captain and crew aboard Trilogy's catamaran were born and raised on Lanaʻi, and if you snorkel close to one of the crew members, there's a good chance

they can find you an elusive *tako* (octopus). If there's wind to sail on the way back to Manele, the crew will hoist the sails. The views afforded of the coastal cliffs make this the best way for exploring the southwestern coastline.

During whale season, Trilogy also offers two-hour long **mammal searches** which depart from Manele Harbor on a jet-propelled inflatable raft for a high-paced marine safari focused on finding humpback whales, green sea turtles, the occasional Hawaiian monk seal, and various species of resident dolphins. The high-speed cruise of the coastline alone is worth the trip, and the crew on this trip are some of the friendliest and most knowledgeable in the industry.

◖ SCUBA DIVING

Those familiar with Hawaiʻi diving will know that Lanaʻi has some of the best diving in the state. While there are no fewer than 14 named dive sites along the southwestern coastline, the two which make Lanaʻi famous are **First and Second Cathedrals.** At First Cathedral, just offshore from Manele Harbor, the cavern entrance sits at 58 feet. Inside, beams of sunlight filter down through the ceiling looking exactly like light passing through a stained glass window. There have even been a few underwater weddings here. The best way to exit the cathedral is via a hole in the wall known locally as The Shotgun, where divers place their hands on the sides of the cathedral and allow the current to wash through a narrow opening. In addition to the main cathedral there are a number of other swim-throughs and arches where you can catch a glimpse of spiny lobsters, frogfish, colorful parrotfish, and if you're lucky, a pod of spinner dolphins passing overhead.

Down the coast at Second Cathedral, the underwater dome is about the same size but intersected by so many openings it looks like Swiss cheese. Divers can pass in and out of the cathedral from a variety of different entry points. The highlight of the dive is a rare black coral tree that dangles from the cathedral ceiling. Large schools of *taʻape* (blue striped snapper) congregate on

© KYLE ELLISON

scuba diving Second Cathedral

the back side of the cathedral, and you can swim through a school that numbers in the hundreds. Visibility at both of these sites regularly stretches 80-120 feet, and the water can often be so clear that you see most of the dive site just standing on the pontoon of the dive boat.

While a few dive boats from Maui make regular morning trips to Lana'i, the only scuba outfit operating out of Lana'i is **Trilogy Excursions** (1 Manele Harbor Dr., 808/874-5649, www.scubalanai.com), which offers two-tank dives for certified divers Monday-Friday off its inflatable jet boat raft, *Manele Kai*. Trilogy also offers introductory beach dives off Hulopo'e Beach for divers who aren't yet certified or are working on their certification courses. Another option is **snuba** diving off Hulopo'e Beach, a hybrid between snorkeling and scuba diving. The only gear that the diver has to wear is a weight belt (to sink) and a light shoulder harness (which attaches to the scuba regulator). With this basic gear, divers are able to breathe and stay underwater for just over 20 minutes. Snuba is available to divers ages 8 and up.

Surfing

SURF SPOTS
Hulopo'e Beach Park

Given that **Hulopo'e Beach** is the island's most popular beach, it should come as little surprise that it's also the island's most popular surf spot. Since Hulopo'e faces south, it's exposed to southerly swells, which means that the months of April-October are going to be the best for finding surf. This left pointbreak can be challenging, however, and it's not a spot for beginners. The wave breaks over a shallow coral reef and the takeoff can be steep, although when Hulopo'e is firing it can be one of the best summer waves in Maui County. The long lefthander will hold its size 2-12 feet, and you have to be careful of the inside section which can carry you straight into the shorebreak. If the angle of the swell isn't quite right, you can occasionally find a better wave by walking the nature path for 200 yards to the next bay over.

A short scramble down the rocks will bring you to a hidden, sandy cove, although the wave here is more of a beach break which pales in comparison to the quality of Hulopo'e. To reach Hulopo'e Beach Park, drive a quarter mile past the small boat harbor on Manele Road until the pavement ends in a parking lot.

◖ Lopa

Lopa is the island's preeminent beginner wave. But just because it's user-friendly doesn't mean that it can't be a great wave. A beach break with multiple peaks, the waves at Lopa aren't usually as steep and are better suited for longboards and noseriding. This is where the island's lone surf school takes its students, although on most days—due to the difficult, four-wheel-drive access—you will have Lopa all to yourself other than a handful of fishers or campers. To reach Lopa, take Keomuku Highway over to the back

© HEATHER ELLISON

kayak surfing at Lopa

of the island to the end of the paved road, then take a right and proceed for nine miles.

Stone Shacks

Bring your hiking boots for this spot, because the only way to surf **Stone Shacks** is to walk a half-mile-long, kiawe-riddled trail to a remote and rocky beach. The name refers to two rudimentary stone structures which have been constructed on the shoreline as a place where campers can stay out of the wind. The walk is worth it, however, as Stone Shacks offers one of the best right- and left-hand waves anywhere on the island. The surf can be bigger here than at nearby Lopa, and it can pick up more of a southerly angle, whereas Hulopo'e faces southwest. To reach Stone Shacks, take Keomuku Highway over the back side of the island to the end of the paved road, then take a right and proceed for 11 miles until the dirt road ends at Naha. Then park the car and start walking. Hazards include locals, sharks, and making your way out through the rocky entry.

Polihua

Polihua is the island's lone wintertime wave, as this stretch of shoreline produces some fickle waves which only turn on during northeasterly swells. Or, if a large west-northwest swell comes barreling down the channel and has enough of a westerly direction to squeak around O'ahu, then Polihua can also see surf. The currents here can be extreme, however, and the waters offshore are jokingly referred to as "the Tahitian Express." Sharks are also a concern around Polihua. Only the most competent, confident—and slightly crazy—surfers even consider chasing waves along this desolate stretch of coast. To reach Polihua, follow the signs from Lana'i City for the Garden of the Gods, and once you've reached it, proceed for another 25 minutes until the road runs straight into the beach.

RENTAL OPERATORS

Having grown up on Lana'i but perfected his surfing skills on the North Shore of O'ahu, owner Nick Palumbo now runs **Lana'i Surf Safari** (808/565-9283, www.lanaisurfsafari. com), your one-stop outfit for all things surf-related on Lana'i. Rentals are arranged off Hulopo'e Beach and include longboards ($58 for 24 hours), shortboards ($58 for 24 hours), bodyboards ($30 for 24 hours), and stand-up paddleboards ($150 full day/$75 half day).

While renting a board and surfing the wave at Hulopo'e are great for the intermediate surfer, for those who are looking to take actual surf lessons and explore the back of the island there's no better option than booking a half-day surf safari (9am-2pm, $200) to pristine and isolated Lopa Beach. Tours include pickup and drop-off from the harbor or your hotel as well as all gear, instruction, drinking water, and transport to Lana'i's rugged back side. Unlike the surf schools of Waikiki or Lahaina where you can find yourself fighting to catch a wave amid 50 other students, guests here on Lana'i are treated to a private session on a beach which is almost guaranteed to have nobody else on it. Even if you aren't staying on the island, day trips from Maui can be arranged.

Hiking and Biking

HIKING
◖ Munro Trail

Munro Trail doesn't look like anywhere else on Lana'i—or anywhere else in Hawai'i. Anyone who ventures out on this 12.8-mile dirt road might swear they are in the Pacific Northwest instead of the tropics. When you think about Hawai'i, you think about palm trees, not pine trees, and yet wandering around the stands of Cook pines is one of Lana'i's most iconic adventures. There are few better ways to spend a morning on Lana'i than by rising early, throwing on a light jacket, and heading into the uplands where the smell of eucalyptus wafts through an understory of ironwoods and pines. For clear skies and dry conditions, it's best to hike Munro Trail in the morning hours before enveloping clouds blow in on the trades.

To reach Munro Trail, travel past the Lodge at Koele on Keomuku Highway until you reach

© KYLE ELLISON
the forested uplands of the Munro Trail

a sign for Cemetery Road, where you will make a right just before the first mile marker. On Cemetery Road the pavement turns to dirt and then branches off to the left, bringing you to the start of the trail. Technically Munro Trail is a single-lane, dirt road which is navigable by anyone with four-wheel drive. The Dollar Jeep rental company doesn't allow its Jeeps to go on the steep and potentially muddy track, and even those who have rented a Hummer have occasionally gotten stuck. The other option is to park your car at the trailhead and make the 5.5-mile hike to the summit (one-way), choosing to stop at lookouts along the way.

The first such lookout if starting from Cemetery Road is the **Koloiki Ridge** about 2.5 miles into the trail. A small red and white sign on the left side of the trail points the way to the ridge, and after a brief quarter mile jaunt you are rewarded with grandiose views peering back into Maunalei Gulch and out to the islands of Maui and Moloka'i. This lookout is also accessible as part of the **Koloiki Ridge Trail** hike which departs from behind the Lodge at Koele.

Back on the main trail you'll continue for a couple miles beneath a shroud of forest until you pass some communication towers. Just past the towers is **Ho'okio Gulch,** a place of historical significance that forever transformed the island of Lana'i. In 1778, Kahekili, ruler of Lana'i and Maui, was besieged by Kalaniopu'u, a powerful chief from the Big Island whose army featured a fearless young warrior by the name of Kamehameha. In the battle at Ho'okio, Kahekili and his warriors attempted to defend the island from the invading warriors by slinging stones down from the hilltop and hiding in crevasses carved into the cliff face. Ultimately, however, Kahekili and his men would emerge defeated, and the ensuing occupation of Lana'i by Kalaniopu'u and his army drove the resource-strapped island into a famine which decimated much of the native population. It's said that the spirits of

LANA'I

© KYLE ELLISON

the view up Maunalei Gulch from the Koloiki Ridge Trail

those who perished in the battle still reside in the cool forests and keep watch over the eroded gulches and canyons.

Finally, after you've climbed an uphill section of trail, 5.5 miles from the end of Cemetery Road you'll find the 3,370-foot summit of Lana'ihale—or the Hale, as it's known to locals. This is the only point in all of Hawai'i where it's possible to see five other islands on the clearest of days, and during winter even the snowcapped peaks of Mauna Kea and Mauna Loa on the Big Island can be clearly seen over 100 miles to the southeast. Should you decide to continue the length of the trail you'll descend for seven miles down the southern side of the ridge, past turnoffs for the Awehi and Naha trails, and eventually emerge in the remains of old pineapple fields at Highway 440 (Manele Road). Though properly exploring Munro Trail takes the better part of a day, it's one in which you're able to step out of the tropical "norm" and breath the fresh air of one of Hawai'i's most scenic and storied places.

Pu'u Pehe Overlook

This oft-photographed sea stack is an iconic symbol of the island of Lana'i and is easily one of the most scenic sites on the island. Though it's not possible to climb onto Pu'u Pehe itself, the **Pu'u Pehe Overlook Trail** offers hikers a sweeping panorama of the rock and the surrounding coastal area. To reach the overlook, take the dirt road on the south end of Hulopo'e Beach Park (the side opposite the resort) and follow it for 100 yards until it reaches a set of stairs leading down to the tidepools. From here the road becomes a trail which wraps its way left across the headland before reaching a hidden, sandy cove popular with bodyboarders and topless sunbathers. To get down to this sandy cove, known as Shark's Bay, requires a scramble through a chute in the rocky cliff that is "at your own risk." To reach the overlook, safely follow the edge of the cliff until it reaches a promontory about 100 feet above the shimmering reef below. Aside from the sweeping vista it's also possible from here to get a good view of the *heiau* that stands atop Pu'u

© KYLE ELLISON

Pu'u Pehe, as seen from Shark's Bay

LANA'I

Pehe, an archaeological site which is a mystery given the near-impossible access to the top of the rock.

Kapiha'a Fisherman's Trail

The **Kapiha'a Fisherman's Trail** begins on the side of Hulopo'e Beach right in front of the Four Seasons Hotel and meanders past the mega-mansions set out on the point. Well-marked by a natural stone walkway, this 1.5-mile trail hugs the rocky coastline as it weaves its way through the ancient village of Kapiha'a. Though little remains of the village today (it allegedly was abandoned around 1840), various historical markers point out the location of *heiau* still visible in the area. Even though this trail catches the coastal breezes off the surrounding water, there is laughably little shade, and the midday sun warrants at least one bottle of water. Given the rugged nature of the path, wear closed-toe shoes. After the trail reaches a dramatic terminus atop sea cliffs on the back nine of the golf course (which is also where Bill and Melinda Gates were married), an easier

return route is to follow the cart path back to the golf clubhouse.

Koloiki Ridge Trail

An offshoot of the Munro Trail, the **Koloiki Ridge Trail** is a five-mile out and back hike which begins directly behind the Four Seasons Koele Resort. On a nice day this is the perfect way to spend 2-3 hours. Walking the trail is like taking a historical tour through Lana'i's past.

To reach the start of the Koloiki Ridge Trail, head to the main entrance of the Four Seasons Koele Resort and then follow the service road toward the golf clubhouse. Along the way you'll pass what is probably the nicest miniature golf course in Hawai'i. Once you reach the main clubhouse, another paved service road running behind the fairway ultimately leads to the trailhead. Along the walk you'll encounter white and red signs which have been placed on the trail as part of an interpretive map available at the hotel's concierge desk. A number of these are scattered along the initial paved section of trail.

LANA'I

Once the dirt trail begins, you'll find yourself walking beneath a canopy of ironwood trees and Cook pines which predate the luxurious hotels. Planted in 1912 by the botanist George Munro, the pines were used as a means of securing water by way of trapping moisture from the passing clouds, and even today they still play a major role in providing water for the island's residents.

Making a right at the red and white sign marked "10" places you directly on the Munro Trail. The road is frequented by tourists and hunters. About a half mile down Munro Trail at sign number 17, an arrow points the way down to the dramatic Koloiki Ridge. Once out from beneath the canopy of trees, you'll notice that the ridge is flanked on both sides by gulches which have been dramatically carved by the elements and time. From this (often windy) vantage point at the end of the trail, the islands of Moloka'i and Maui spring up on the horizon above the deep blue Pailolo Channel. When facing the islands, the gulch on your left is Naio Gulch, a dry and rock-strewn canyon where you can occasionally catch a glimpse of the island's elusive mouflon sheep. On the right side of the ridge is Maunalei Gulch, a deep cleft in the island which at one point was home to the island's only free-flowing stream. If you look closely on the valley floor, you can still notice an old service road leading up to a pump house. Water from Maunalei once serviced the island's sugar plantation.

Awehi Trail

Technically the **Awehi Trail**—like the Munro Trail—is a road and not a hike. You wouldn't want to try and drive this in a rental though, given that the road is steep, eroded, and a long way from help. The cool canopy of pine trees on the Munro Trail is swapped on the Awehi for thorny kiawe trees offering no shade. Nevertheless, the rewards for hiking the Awehi Trail are sweeping views stretching toward the island of Kaho'olawe and the ability to walk from the eucalyptus and pine tree laden summit to an empty white sand beach.

Over the course of three miles the Awehi Trail switchbacks its way down the barren slope of Lana'i's southeastern flank, eventually reaching a terminus on the shoreline not far from Lopa Beach. Unless you have arranged for a car to pick you up at the bottom, however, it's going to be a long and dusty climb back up. The start of the Awehi Trail is a dirt track on the left side of the Munro Trail 1.2 miles south of the summit. You can either park your car at a pullout off Munro Trail, or drive on the Awehi Trail until it gets too sketchy to navigate safely. Good luck.

Naha Trail

Not too different from the Awehi Trail, the **Naha Trail** branches off the Munro Trail and switchbacks down the back of the mountain to the remote southeastern shoreline. It's three miles long, dusty, thorny, and has a terminus not far from Naha Beach. The start of the Naha Trail is two miles south of the summit on Munro Trail. Bring plenty of water and a sturdy pair of shoes capable of handling the vicious kiawe thorns.

Hiking Groups

If you would prefer to hike with a guide, contact **Hike Lana'i@** (808/258-2471, www.hikelanai. com). Guided hikes are offered to the shoreline of Kaunolu, the shoreline of Kaiolohia, and the ridges and uplands that branch out from the Munro Trail. Most hikes are a little over two hours. The hike along the shoreline at Kaiolohia is the easiest. Depending on the hike, prices vary between $90 for children (ages 10-12), to $125 for adults. The guides are happy to "talkstory" about the island and its history.

BIKING

Companies have rented out bikes to island visitors in the past, but currently the only way to procure a bike is to either know someone locally or bring one over on the ferry from Maui. Seeing as there are only 30 miles of paved road on the entire island (compared to over 400 which are unpaved), Lana'i is an island more suited to mountain biking than road cycling. Although there isn't any single-track, the hunting roads and old pineapple roads crisscrossing the island are a mountain biker's dream terrain. Intermediate riders can pedal the seven miles of dirt road leading out to the Garden of the Gods, or more advanced riders can make the 3,300-foot descent from the summit of Lana'ihale down the Munro Trail, hook up with the Awehi Trail, and end at a deserted white sand beach. Logistics are always an issue with Lana'i mountain biking, however, and unless you're into a leg-burning ascent after your downhill ride, a one-way transport will need to be arranged. If riding on the Awehi Trail, Naha Trail, or anywhere on the island's "back side," tire-puncturing kiawe thorns can be a pesky issue, so pack a pump and an extra tube.

Outdoor Adventure

FISHING

Fishing is the most popular pastime for Lana'i locals. While spearfishing is common among island locals, many people still choose to fish either by net or by rod and reel. Favorite places for shorecasting include Kaunolu, Ka'ena Point, Shipwreck Beach, and off the beach at Naha, and even though Hulopo'e Beach is a marine life conservation district, casting from shore is still allowed. When the *halalu* (juvenile bigeye scad) are running, it isn't uncommon to see up to 40 fishers plucking the small fish out of the harbor basin down in Manele as they chum the water with *palu,* a concoction of bread, flour, sardines, and squid belly. While it's possible to get good-size *kawakawa* or *papio* when fishing from shore, to land a mahimahi, ono, or marlin, you're going to have to get out on a boat and troll the deeper waters.

For sportfishing charters, the 36-foot **Fish N Chips** has been taking Lana'i anglers out for years to troll around the buoys and ledges along the southwestern coastline. The captain and crew are longtime residents of the island who are intimately acquainted with the environmental nuances of Lana'i's waters, and this is going to be your best chance for reeling in a huge *ahi* (yellowfin tuna) or a trophy marlin.

HORSEBACK RIDING

Lana'i is steeped in its ranching heritage as anywhere else in Hawai'i. Many forget that this island was one huge sheep and cattle ranch where *paniolos* on horseback roamed the terrain. Though cattle no longer roam free on the island's barren slopes, the island's ranching heritage lives on at the **Stables at Koele** (1 Keomuku Hwy., 808/563-9385, www.lanaigrandadventures.com) where local guides who are the "real deal" offer guided trail rides through the Lana'i City hinterlands. Keep an eye out for axis deer or mouflon sheep as you ride at your own pace on excursions geared to your skill level. The knowledgeable guides fortify the excursion with tales of the island's history and inside local info.

ADVENTURE SPORTS
UTV Rides

There are no guided ATV tours on Lana'i, but don't get bummed out. Lana'i actually offers something far more comfortable, practical, and better-suited to the terrain: UTV tours. Whereas ATVs have handlebars like a motorcycle, UTVs feature a steering-wheel similar to a Jeep, although unlike a Jeep, it's virtually impossible to get a UTV stuck in the mud. They are the perfect way to see rugged areas such as Munro Trail. **Hawaii Western Adventures** (1 Keomuku Hwy., 808/563-9385, www.lanaigrandadventures.com) operates guided UTV tours from its scenic Koele headquarters where you can either navigate your own vehicle or enjoy a leisurely, guide-driven expedition in vehicles which can hold up to six people. Choose from either a 1-hour scenic ride through the uplands ($75), or a 1.5-hour ($100) or 3-hour ($200) foray onto the Munro Trail.

LANA'I

© KYLE ELLISON

a local fishes for *halalu* at Manele Harbor

Hunting

There is a joke among Lana'i locals that the only groceries you ever need to buy on Lana'i are beer and ingredients. Despite the fact that the island has a number of small supermarkets, a large percentage of Lana'i's population still puts food on the table by hunting, farming, and fishing. While fresh fish is something to be expected on a tropical island, many people are surprised to find out just how much hunting takes place here.

Although there are no wild boar or goats, one of the main prizes would be the island's large population of axis deer. Smaller in size than many North American species, these 100-200 lb. deer were introduced to the island of Moloka'i in the 1860s as a gift from Hong Kong to King Kamehameha V. Over time the deer were also introduced on Lana'i and Maui. With no natural predators the population has exploded to the point of a being a nuisance. Lana'i is also home to a healthy population

of mouflon sheep, a species native to the Caucasus Mountains, introduced in Hawai'i in the 1950s. For bird hunters, various species such as Rio Grande wild turkeys, ring-necked pheasant, Chukar partridge, and California quail are all found on the island, though rarely hunted in the same quantities as the axis deer and mouflon.

Anyone wanting to try their hand at hunting while on Lana'i can arrange a private safari through **Hawaii Western Adventures** (1 Keomoku Hwy., 808/563-9385, www.lanai-grandadventures.com) where out of state licenses, gear, and protective gear are included in the two-day hunt ($2,600, hunter safety card required). Anyone who wants to practice their shot with sporting clays can also visit the Hawaii Western Adventures' range on the scenic stretch of Keomuku Highway. Near the turnoff for Munro Trail, this challenging sporting clays course is worth the experience for the views alone, although the expert instruction and user-friendly gear make this the perfect outing for someone new to shooting a gun. Even experienced gunners will appreciate being able to fire off rounds in this dramatic and private landscape, and each station has been purposely planned to mimic the flight pattern of pheasants, duck, quail, or even running rabbits.

Golf and Tennis

GOLF

If you find yourself walking around Maui's Lahaina Harbor around 6:30am you'll notice a curious sight: A bunch of nicely dressed people walking around with golf clubs in the middle of a dingy harbor basin. No, they aren't planning on using their seven-iron as a gaff while sportfishing, they're taking the 6:45 AM ferry to Lana'i for the day to tackle one of the island's two championship golf courses. Although the courses are obviously open to guests of the Lana'i resorts, they're also open to golfers from the general public—many of whom choose to commute from Maui for the day.

At the 7,039-yard, Jack Nicklaus-designed

Challenge at Manele (1 Manele Bay Rd., 808/565-2000, $210 resort guests, $225 day guest), the course lives up to its name by forcing golfers to tee-off across natural ravines which use the Pacific Ocean as a water hazard. There are five different tees which you can choose from, although pack a few extra balls in your bag, as playing from out of bounds on this course would involve a wet suit and some scuba gear.

Whereas the Challenge at Manele can take your breath away with its panoramic vistas, the **Experience at Koele** (1 Keomuku Hwy., 808/565-4000, $125 resort guest, $185 day guest) course might literally take your breath

© KYLE ELLISON

the oceanfront greens of the Challenge at Manele

away with its 2,000-foot elevation. Set among ironwood trees and Cook pines, this 7,014-yard, Greg Norman-designed masterpiece weaves its way through Lana'i's cool and forested uplands, and the signature 17th hole drops 250 feet from tee to green in the heart of a wooded ravine. On a morning when low-hanging clouds usher in a mist, this is truly a course where your competitive spirit is dampened by relaxation.

While the two courses mentioned above have been the recipients of international fame, there's actually a *third* course on the island of Lana'i, which comes with a price tag much easier to stomach. More of the no-shirt, no-shoes, beer-a-hole type of course, the nine-hole **Cavendish Golf Course** is better suited for recreational golfers who either want a quick practice round or haven't quite figured out how to break 100. Best of all, the course is free. Constructed in 1947 as a recreational option for island pineapple workers, the Cavendish still operates as a place for island locals to practice their game and casually unwind. Although the fairways and tee boxes can be speckled with crabgrass and patches of dirt, the greens are still properly maintained. As there are no carts or cart paths, you also get a good workout walking the course's moderate elevation changes. To reach

the first tee box for the Cavendish course, make a right as if going to the Koele golf clubhouse off Keomuku Highway. Just after the turn you will notice an open field on the right side of the road with a small flag fluttering in the distance. Welcome to the Cavendish, although you're going to have to supply your own clubs, balls, tees, and beer.

TENNIS

Much like the golf options, you can choose to either pay to play at the Four Seasons or knock a few balls around at the community courts for free. Both of the Four Seasons hotels have tennis courts available to guests, although the main pro shop and all clinics, lessons, and equipment rentals are down at the **Four Seasons Manele Bay** (808/565-2000, 8am-6pm) resort. The tennis program at the resort is administered by Peter Burwash International, a company which excels in providing top-level tennis services for resorts all over the world. If private lessons or clinics aren't in the budget, however, there are also three **public tennis courts** in Lana'i City right next to Lana'i High and Elementary School (711 Fraser Ave.), which are available for public use, although the quality of the courts isn't nearly as high as at the resorts.

Sights

◖ LANA'I CULTURE AND HERITAGE CENTER

There's no better place to learn about the history of Lana'i than at the **Lana'i Culture and Heritage Center** (730 Lana'i Ave., 808/565-7177, www.lanaihc.org, 8:30am-3:30pm Mon.-Fri., 9am-1pm Sat.). Started in 2007 in a building adjacent to the Hotel Lana'i, the exceptionally informative little museum features displays pertaining to the days of ancient Hawai'i all the way up through the end of the Dole plantation. Black-and-white photos from Lana'i's ranching days are joined by stone adzes, poi pounders, and a 10-foot-long *'ihe*

pololu wooden spear used as a weapon similar to a jousting lance. More than just a collection of historical photos and artifacts, the center also highlights how the culture of the people of Lana'i has been influenced by the coming and going of historical events.

KANEPU'U PRESERVE

Six miles down Polihua Road just before reaching the Garden of the Gods, **Kanepu'u Preserve** is the only remaining dryland forest of its kind found anywhere in Hawai'i. Thanks to a fence erected in 1918 by Lana'i Ranch manager George Munro, this 590-acre preserve

LANA'I

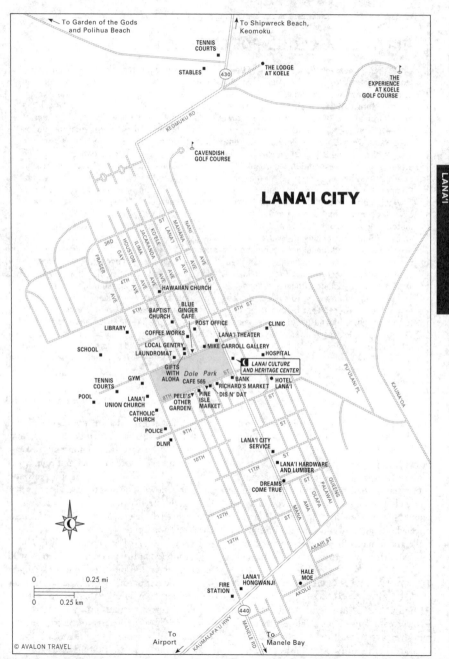

LANA'I CITY

→ To Garden of the Gods and Polihua Beach

↑ To Shipwreck Beach, Keomoku

TENNIS COURTS

STABLES

430

THE LODGE AT KOELE

THE EXPERIENCE AT KOELE GOLF COURSE

KEOMUKU RD

CAVENDISH GOLF COURSE

3RD ST

FRASER

GAY

HOUSTON

ILIMA AVE

JACARANDA AVE

KOELE AVE

LANA'I AVE

MAHANA AVE

NANI AVE

4TH AVE

5TH AVE

6TH ST

HAWAIIAN CHURCH

BLUE GINGER CAFE

BAPTIST CHURCH

COFFEE WORKS

POST OFFICE

LIBRARY

LANA'I THEATER

CLINIC

LOCAL GENTRY

MIKE CARROLL GALLERY

SCHOOL

LAUNDROMAT

HOSPITAL

LANAI CULTURE AND HERITAGE CENTER

Dole Park

GIFTS WITH ALOHA

GYM

TENNIS COURTS

CAFE 565

8TH ST

BANK

RICHARD'S MARKET

HOTEL LANA'I

PINE ISLE MARKET

PELE'S OTHER GARDEN

DIS N' DAT

POOL

LANA'I UNION CHURCH

CATHOLIC CHURCH

8TH ST

POLICE

9TH ST

DLNR

LANA'I CITY SERVICE

10TH ST

PU'ULANI PL

KAUNA'OA

11TH ST

LANA'I HARDWARE AND LUMBER

DREAMS COME TRUE

MANA

AHA

OKAPA

QUEENS

PALAWAI

12TH ST

13TH ST

AKAHI ST

LANA'I HONGWANJI

HALE MOE

AKOLU

FIRE STATION

440

KAUMALAPA'U HWY

MANELE RD

→ To Airport

→ To Manele Bay

N

0   0.25 mi

0   0.25 km

© AVALON TRAVEL

BIRTH OF A CLOUD FOREST

Other than James Dole (pineapples) and David Murdock (hotels), few men have been more integral to the modern development of Lana'i than George Munro (1866-1963). A New Zealand-born botanist and ornithologist, Munro first journeyed to Hawai'i in 1890 as a member of Lord Walter Rothschild's expedition documenting the birds of the islands. Choosing to stay after the end of the expedition, Munro would be hired in 1911 as the ranch manager for the Lana'i Company's cattle operation.

When Munro arrived on Lana'i, he found a dry island which had been completely decimated by overgrazing. Cattle and sheep ran amok through the uplands, the watershed had been depleted, and the island's population of native birds had all but completely vanished. With Lana'i in a sorry state of affairs, Munro walked the entire island with bags full of seeds and clippings in an effort to solve the problem. He also ordered that fences be erected to protect what few native plants remained. The Kanepu'u Preserve owes its existence to a fence put up here in 1918 by the forward-thinking Munro.

Despite Munro's efforts at replanting, Lana'i's watershed continued to suffer.

Strangely enough, the answer would ultimately manifest itself not in fences or seeds, but in an annoyance on Munro's tin roof. As ranch manager, Munro enjoyed a modest dwelling in the upland pastures of Koele beneath the shade of a Norfolk pine. On evenings when the clouds would roll across Koele, moisture from the passing cloud vapor would gather in the pine needles and ultimately drip onto Munro's tin roof in a rhythmic—and bothersome—tapping. Instead of putting the pillow over his head, Munro realized that the pine tree was extracting water directly from the clouds, and he soon thereafter ordered hundreds of pines to be planted on Lana'i. Due to the fact that pine needles have a surface area much larger than regular leaves, it's believed that each pine tree can provide up to 200 gallons of freshwater per day by trapping the passing fog. Today there are thousands of Cook Island pines foresting Lana'i's uplands, and a century later the health of the watershed is slowly being restored. The best place to immerse yourself in this cloud forest is on the dirt road heading to Lana'i's summit, a four-wheel-drive track aptly named the Munro Trail.

---

is home to 48 species of native Hawaiian plants which used to cover most of the island prior to the arrival of the invasive kiawe tree and root-destroying goats and sheep. Managed by the Nature Conservancy, the preserve features a short, self-guided trail where visitors can get a rare chance to see native hardwoods such as *lama* (Hawaiian ebony) and *olopua* (Hawaiian olive). The trail only takes about 15 minutes to walk, and it makes for a nice stopping point before exploring the Garden of the Gods.

◪ KEAHIAKAWELO (GARDEN OF THE GODS)

Although we've successfully put a rover on Mars, Keahiakawelo is the closest most of us will ever get to walking on the red planet. Despite being only seven miles from the pine-lined streets of Lana'i City, the moonscape known as the Garden of the Gods may as well be a universe away. Thousands of years of erosion have created ravines and rock spires which are bathed in deep reds, purples, and sulfuric yellows. The best time to visit this dry, dusty, and often windswept area is at sunset, when the rich palette of color is enhanced by the afternoon light.

Keahiakawelo is almost completely devoid of vegetation (what little remains is eaten by wild axis deer and mouflon sheep), but the strangest part of the panorama is the expanse of boulders which tumble over the barren hillside. While it's anyone's guess just how exactly this otherworldly scenery came to be, the ancient Hawaiians have a number of theories.

According to legend, two *kahuna* (priests)

LANA'I

© KYLE ELLISON

the otherworldly landscape of the Garden of the Gods

from Lana'i and neighboring Moloka'i were engaged in a fierce competition as to who could keep a fire burning the longest. The winner, it's believed, would see his island showered in great abundance, and Kawelo—the *kahuna* from Lana'i—plucked every piece of foliage in the area for fuel to further the fire. The name of the area—Keahiakawelo—translates as "the fire of Kawelo," and with Moloka'i looming large across the whitecapped Kalohi Channel it isn't hard to imagine Kawelo's fire burning bright on the hill.

This still does nothing to describe how boulders that weigh thousands of pounds came to exist on a hillside that is otherwise devoid of boulders. According to legend, these rocks were dropped here by gods as they tended to their heavenly gardens, providing the basis for the site's English name, "Garden of the Gods," by which it is regularly known today.

Regardless of name or legend or erosion or lore, Keahiakawelo remains a must-see location for Lana'i visitors if for no other reason than the consuming sense of seclusion. The road

out here can be rutted and rough, and four-wheel drive is needed if visiting after a heavy rain. To reach the site, take a left just after The Lodge at Koele and travel seven miles on Polihua Road, veering right at the fork after the Koele Stables.

KA'ENA IKI *HEIAU*

On the dusty stretch of road between the Keahiakawelo and Polihua Beach, a side road branches off to the left and leads to the island's westernmost promontory, Ka'ena Point. The deep waters off Ka'ena make this a favorite among island fishers. Also from 1837-1843 Protestant missionaries used this desolate stretch of shore as a penal colony for adulterous women. The main reason for venturing down Ka'ena Trail, however, is to get a look at Ka'ena Iki *heiau,* the largest remaining *heiau* on the island of Lana'i. This large stone platform was constructed in the 17th century. While it doesn't take much time to explore the area around the *heiau,* this makes a nice side trip.

© HEATHER ELLISON

Ka Lanakila Church in abandoned Keomoku Village

KEOMOKU VILLAGE

Technically there isn't much to see in the abandoned village of Keomoku, but rather, you drive through this coastal ghost town as a means of feeling Lana'i's recent past. It also makes a great stop if you are heading out to the beaches at Lopa or Naha.

Before the arrival of Europeans, it's believed there were thousands of native Hawaiians living along Lana'i's eastern shoreline. Fish were gathered from the offshore reef, taro was cultivated in the deep valleys, and a freshwater stream flowed freely in the verdant gulch at Maunalei. *Heiau* were constructed as places of worship, and petroglyphs such as those found at Kaiolohia depict basic scenes from this ancient way of life. By the time Frederick Hayselden chose Keomoku as the site for his Maunalei Sugar Company in 1899, however, the island's population had dwindled to fewer than 200. Lacking an ample labor force to run his sugar operation, Hayselden set about importing laborers from Japan, and within a year the population of Keomoku had surged to as high as

800 people. Keomoku, it would seem, had become Lana'i's "capital." Water was routed from Maunalei Valley, a locomotive was installed to move cargo, and Keomoku bustled like any other Hawaiian plantation town. The problem, however, is that the water around it soon turned brackish and the supply at Maunalei quickly dried up. In what is known as one of the state's shortest sugar ventures, the Maunalei Sugar Company closed in 1901 after only two years in operation. Native Hawaiians living in the area attribute the company's demise to the fact that the stones from ancient *heiau* were used in constructing the plantation. This, it would seem, did not sit well with Hawaiian deities.

With the laborers needing to find work elsewhere, the island's population again plummeted to 125, with the majority still choosing to live at Keomoku. With the purchase of the island by James Dole, however, many of Keomoku's residents would move into the uplands of newly constructed Lana'i City and leave the shoreline of Keomoku behind. In 1951, the last resident of Keomoku—Daniel

Kaopuiki—begrudgingly moved his family into the uplands, and Keomoku, once the pulse of the island of Lana'i, was officially abandoned.

Keomoku remains almost abandoned to this day. Driving the sandy four-wheel-drive road through the former plantation town is like taking a tour through Lana'i's ancient history. Simple beachfront fishing shacks dot the sandy road, their yards ringed with fishing nets and the memories of years passed. The number one attraction in Keomoku is **Ka Lanakila Church,** 5.5 miles from where the pavement ends on Kemoku Highway. The hauntingly beautiful wooden structure constructed in 1903 to house a Hawaiian-speaking congregation. Abandoned for years, the church is currently in the process of being restored, and special sermons are still conducted in Hawaiian intermittently throughout the year. A small shrine 1.5 miles past the church honors the Japanese field laborers who died on Lana'i in the few short years of the sugar plantation's existence, and a half mile beyond the shrine is the abandoned pier at Kahalepalaoa which offers good fishing, sweeping views of neighboring Maui.

THE MYTH OF THE "PRIVATE ISLAND"

A pesky myth needs to be dispelled: Lana'i is not a private island. It's true that the island has historically had only one main landowner (today, 98 percent of the island is owned by a single landowner Oracle CEO Larry Ellison). However, the state of Hawai'i retains ownership of certain parcels such as Manele Small Boat Harbor and many local families own their own homes. You do not need to ask permission from the primary landowner to come here: It has an airport and regular ferry service, and there are 3,300 full-time residents.

Imagine that you live in a neighborhood where there are 100 homes in a 10x10 grid. Let's say you own your home, and then you buy your neighbor's, and then you find a suitcase full of cash one day and buy 96 more. Despite the fact that you still own 98 of the 100 homes in your neighborhood, you still live in a neighborhood which is in a U.S. state, and in U.S. states there are laws. It's not just a private island where you can do whatever you want. There are police officers, firefighters, a public school, a county council member, and myriad state laws that accompany your "private island." Under Hawai'i state law, all shoreline which extends from the ocean up to the line of vegetation is available for public use. Consequently there is no such thing as a private beach in Hawai'i. This is one "private island" where you are free to walk ashore.

KAUNOLU VILLAGE

It's unfortunate Kaunolu is so difficult to reach because it's one of the most historically significant and culturally rich parts of the island. Then again, it's probably this level of remoteness which has kept Kaunolu undeveloped and virtually untouched.

The road down to Kaunolu is steep, eroded, and often bumpy and rough. It isn't even listed on the map provided with a Jeep rental. There are three options for reaching the historic outpost: Chance it with the Jeep and hope for the best (although your rental company will frown on this), procure a private vehicle which has no restrictions, or drive until the road gets too sketchy and then get out and walk, which is probably the best option.

To reach Kaunolu, follow Highway 440 south from Lana'i City and head toward the airport. Just past the airport turnoff you will notice a large boulder with the name Kaunolu inscribed on the side. Turn left off the highway and travel along a smooth, dusty, former pineapple road which is fine in any two-wheel drive vehicle (provided it hasn't rained heavily), avoiding turning off on anything that appears to be a side road. After two miles you'll notice a historical marker in the shape of King Kamehameha and another sign pointing toward Kaunolu. Make a right down this road, and travel by vehicle as far as you feel

LANA'I

comfortable. It's three miles from here to the shoreline, and although the first mile is innocent enough, the last two can be steep and heavily eroded.

Once at the bottom of the road you'll reach a Y-junction. The road to the left leads to a set of fishing shacks used by locals who come down here to drink beer and fish, often in that order. The shacks are rudimentary and nice enough, and there even is an outhouse which has been constructed recently. By turning right at the Y, however, you are instantly transported into what is one of Lana'i's most storied places.

The dirt road abruptly comes to an end at a wooden picnic table set serenely beneath a tree. This picnic table marks the entrance to historical Kaunolu. One of the first sensations you'll have is of total emptiness. Save for the rustle of the breeze and crash of the waves, Kaunolu is completely silent.

For nearly 400 years, however, Kaunolu did not feel as empty as it does now. This dry shoreline was home to a thriving population from the 15th century to the time it was abandoned during the late 1800s. Under the rule of King Kamehameha, Kaunolu was known as the king's favorite fishing spot. The sandy ravine fronting the beach is the only place to successfully launch a canoe between here and Hulopo'e.

To reach the remains of the ancient canoe *hale* (house), walk for 10 yards past the picnic table and look for a trail which switchbacks to the right. Proceed down the rocky scramble until you come to the dry riverbed where the thin trail continues on the other side. After a few more yards you will reach an interpretive placard which points out the canoe *hale*. You are now standing at the base of Halulu *heiau*, a religious place of worship which remains one of the best preserved *heiau* on the island of Lana'i today. The trail bends again to the right as it climbs up away from the base of the dry stone rocks, and it's important to ensure that you stay to the trail and don't start scrambling up the rock base itself. Remember that Kaunolu is a spot of immense cultural significance to native Hawaiians; leave the site as you found it.

After climbing up a short hill, you reach another Y-junction in the trail where you can go left to find some petroglyphs carved in the rocks or right to reach a viewpoint of the Kaholo Pali. These sea cliffs are the tallest on Lana'i, with a few topping out at just over 1,000 feet. From here you'll also notice a notch in the cliff which is labeled as Kahekili's Leap. A fearless warrior chief from the late 1700s, Kahekili is reputed to have been tattooed black over the entire right half of his body, eyelids and tongue included. He's also reputed to have brought his warriors to this spot on Lana'i where they would throw themselves into the sea as a means of proving their valor. The 80-foot height from which the *lele kawa*—cliff jumping—took place, however, wasn't the tricky part; it was clearing the 15-foot rock ledge that protrudes from the base of the cliff and breaks the feet and legs of those who underestimate the distance. This spot is so revered as a historic cliff jump that Red Bull included Kaunolu on the world tour of the cliff diving circuit and a few daredevil visitors still continue to make the leap today. Since medical help is so far removed, however, leave the cliff diving to the professionals.

LUAHIWA PETROGLYPHS

The good thing about the **Luahiwa Petroglyphs** is they are only 10 minutes from Lana'i City and accessible with two-wheel drive. The bad part is they have been permanently scarred by modern graffiti (such as people scratching their names into the rocks— I'm talking about you, "Keoki"), and they no longer resemble the rock art they originally must have been. The petroglyphs at Kaunolu and Kaiolohia are in better shape but require a two-hour round-trip drive from Lana'i City. There are also a greater number of petroglyphs at Luahiwa—nearly 1,000 drawings—and bouncing from one rock to the other will reveal a different tale emblazoned on the out of place boulder formations. While 95 percent of the drawings are believed to be from pre-Western times, some etchings, such as those featuring horses, suggest that the petroglyphs offered a multigenerational canvas for recording Lana'i's varied history.

To reach the Luahiwa Petroglyphs, head south on Manele Road from Lana'i City as if you're driving down toward Hulopo'e Beach Park. After 1.5 miles turn left at a small building on the left side of the road. If you notice a locked gate, then proceed to the dirt road which immediately parallels it on your left-hand side. Head down this road for 0.7 miles until you reach a Y-junction, at which point you will go left again. After 0.3 miles you will make an extreme right-hand turn (almost doubling back the way you came) up onto a higher road. If you're unsure if this is the correct turn, look for a rock just after the intersection which has the name "Luahiwa Petroglyphs" emblazoned on it facing the opposite direction. Proceed for 0.4 miles on the upper road until you reach another rock which says "Luahiwa," and park in the small dirt pullout. The petroglyphs are on the large boulders at the base of the hill, and a thirty-second scramble through the bush will bring you face-to-face with the ancient rock carvings.

Shopping

Lana'i officially takes the cake for being the only Hawaiian Island where you could potentially visit every store on the island without having to repark the car. With the exception of the small stores within the Four Seasons resorts, every single venue on the island is within walking distance of the parking area around Dole Park.

CLOTHING AND SOUVENIRS

The nicest gas station on the island (also the *only* gas station), the **Lana'i Plantation Store** (1036 Lana'i Ave., 808/565-7227, 6:30am-10pm daily) offers a great selection of island souvenirs and clothing items to go along with the usual snacks and beverage options. Plus, it's open later than nearly every other store on the island, so if you're in need of anything from a T-shirt to a six-pack, this is going to be the place to go.

Just down the street, the aptly named **Dis N' Dat Shop** (418 8th St., 808/565-9170, 10am-5:30pm Mon.-Sat.) sells everything from hand-painted ceramic ornaments to women's jewelry to the wind chimes which dangle from the ceiling (duck!). The Balinese woodwork gives an exotic feel to the interior. To find the store, just look for the old yellow car on the lawn.

Tucked away just one block back from Dole Park is **Lana'i Beach Walk** (850 Fraser Ave., 808/565-9249, 10am-6pm Mon.-Sat.), a clean and modern boutique selling women's clothing. There are a number of Lana'i-centric clothing options, and the selection is so trendy you'd expect to find the store in Pa'ia instead of Lana'i City.

Facing the park, **The Local Gentry** (363 7th St., 808/565-9130, 10am-6pm Mon.-Fri., 10am-5pm Sat., 9am-1pm Sun.) offers a larger men's selection as well as a full range of women's clothing and Olu Kai shoes.

ART AND JEWELRY

The most prominent gallery on the island is the **Mike Carroll Gallery** (443 7th St., 808/565-7122, www.mikecarrollgallery.com, 10am-5:30pm Mon.-Sat., 9am-2pm Sun.) set right between Canoe's restaurant and the Lana'i City theater. There's a good chance that you'll find Mike painting right there in the store, and many of his pieces focus on the simple yet captivating beauty of Lana'i. He is an in-demand artist who is constantly crafting original works. The gallery will occasionally feature visiting artists who come to relax and hone their craft in this charming, plantation-style studio.

For a look at artwork which has been hand-crafted by the local community, visit the **Lana'i Art Center** (339 7th St., 808/565-7503, www.lanaiart.org, variable hours) to see just how much talent exists on an island of only 3,300 people. Fine photography and handmade jewelry accompany paintings and woodworking. A portion of all proceeds from this nonprofit go toward funding local art programs for Lana'i's youth. This gallery is a worthwhile stop either after the Saturday Farmer's Market or while walking off a Blue Ginger cheeseburger.

Food

FARMERS MARKET

Even though it's no longer a sprawling pineapple plantation, the red dirt of Lana'i still manages to produce some locally grown crops. The **Lana'i City Farmer's Market** (Dole Park and behind Richard's Supermarket, 6am-11am Sat.) is the best place for grabbing fresh items such as corn, papaya, and pineapple. It's a great weekend activity for putting your finger on the pulse of the island's only town.

LOCAL STYLE

While the outside decor might not look like much, at **⟨ Blue Ginger** (409 7th St., 808/565-6363, www.bluegingercafelanai.com, 6am-8pm Thurs.-Mon., 6am-2pm Tues.-Wed., $6-11), the swinging screen door and funky, plantation-style appearance are all part of the hole-in-the-wall charm. The number of elderly people hanging out on the front porch "talking story" are a testament to the benefits of down-home cooking. Breakfast is categorized by heaping loco moco plates comprised of fried eggs, hamburger meat, rice, and gravy, and the homemade hamburger patties (secret recipe, of course) are the lunchtime draw which have kept patrons funneling in from Dole Park since the restaurant's founding in 1991. A true local hideout. Cash only.

Not to be outdone, neighboring **Canoes** (419 7th St., 808/565-6537, 6:30am-1pm Sun.-Thurs., 6:30am-8pm Fri.-Sat., $6-10) also offers up its own special hamburger recipe, a staple of Lana'i cuisine since 1953. Canoes provides the usual selection of local plate lunches and items off the grill, although a special treat is the heaping breakfast portions available until 1pm.

When you've had your fill of plate lunches, infuse your diet with some fresh fish at the **⟨ Lana'i Ohana Poke Market** (834 Gay St., 808/559-6265, 10am-3pm Mon.-Fri., $7-17, cash only), which in classic Lana'i fashion is either open until 3 o'clock or until they run out of fish. Local people feel the same way about *poke* that Bubba in *Forrest Gump* felt about shrimp: There's shoyu *poke*, limu *poke*, *poke* Hawaiian style, kimchee *poke*, furikake *poke*... the list goes on. While the *poke* alone can be expensive, your best bet for a cheap and filling lunch is a *poke* bowl: one-third pound of fish

---

WHERE IS ALL THE PINEAPPLE?

More than 20 years have passed since the last pineapple was picked on Lana'i, but some visitors still think of it as "Pineapple Island." Although Lana'i once boasted a 16,000-acre pineapple plantation (which, as the world's largest, supplied nearly 75 percent of the world's pineapple), rising production costs caused Dole to close its Lana'i operation and focus on the Philippines and Thailand. The only remnants still visible of the Dole plantation days are the ubiquitous scraps of black plastic found sprouting from the red dirt and fluttering in the breeze, pieces of which are believed to go down as far as six feet into the dry and dusty ground. So even though the men's high school basketball team is still known as "The Pine Lads," Lana'i has shifted from an agricultural economy to a tourism-based one. For an in-depth look at the history of the pineapple on Lana'i, and to see some of the island's lone remaining pineapple plants, visit the Lana'i Culture and Heritage Center in sleepy Lana'i City.

served with two scoops of either white or brown rice. Simple outdoor picnic tables provide the seating for this hole-in-the-wall takeout stand.

AMERICAN

Just down the road from Richard's Supermarket, **Café 565** (408 8th St., 808/565-6622, 10am-3pm and 5pm-8pm Mon.-Sat., all day Tues.-Wed., $6-22) is a great option for a group that can't decide on a single taste. This hole-in-the-wall offers a culinary combo of Italian, American, and standard local fare where calzones, pizza, and sub sandwiches comprise the Italian portions, while burgers and plate lunch options round out the rest of the menu. The interior atmosphere can be a little drab, so the picnic tables on the front lawn are the place to be. Plus, you can still pick up the free wireless signal from out here, or if you want to go the old-fashioned route, people-watch as locals go about their daily routine.

Pele's Other Garden (811 Houston St., 808/565-9628, www.pelesothergarden.com, lunch 11am-3pm Mon.-Fri., dinner 4:30pm-8pm Mon.-Sat. $7-19) is the de facto hang-out of anyone hankering for a good sandwich or a cold draft beer. Why do I mention beer? Because outside of the hotels, this is the only restaurant on the island where you can get beer on tap with a decent selection of the imports as well. The bistro also whips up healthy and affordable food options, ranging from avocado and feta wraps to chicken parmesan. The place is so popular that it accepts online reservations for dinner. Wednesday nights, when the live band starts playing (7pm-10pm), are the closest Lana'i City gets to nightlife.

HAWAIIAN REGIONAL

Despite its location in what is often regarded as Lana'i's "third hotel," the ◖ **Lana'i City Grille** (828 Lana'i Ave., 808/565-7211, www.hotellanai.com/grille, 5pm-9pm Wed.-Sun., $15-38) takes the cake for the island's finest restaurant. Under the direction of award-winning chef Bev Gannon (of Hali'imaile General Store fame), Lana'i City Grille puts out a fine dinner menu that is usually reserved for birthdays, anniversaries,

proposals—or a special vacation. The fare here is going to be more expensive than at the hole-in-the-wall plate lunch stands, of course, but when the waiter serves you a plate of pan-roasted venison loin with a mushroom risotto, cost gets thrown to the wind, and you become wrapped up in culinary splendor. It's paired with the island's most comprehensive wine list. Reservations are highly recommended, particularly on Friday evenings when the live jazz band provides the best entertainment anywhere in town.

COFFEE SHOPS

Even sleepy Lana'i City needs some help waking up in the morning, and **Coffee Works** (604 Ilima Ave., 808/565-6962, 7am-3pm Mon.-Sat.) is the island's only full-time java establishment catering to the under-caffeinated. Breakfast bagels and lunch sandwiches accompany the usual range of coffee offerings, and

LANA'I NIGHTLIFE

You don't visit Lana'i for the nightlife. Evening is that inconvenient stretch of darkness which brings outdoor adventure to a halt. There are no nightclubs or dinner shows on Lana'i, and outside of the hotels there is only one place you can even order a beer (Pele's Other Garden). Nevertheless, there is still a semblance of activity on certain nights of the week—just don't expect it to stretch past 10 o'clock. On Wednesday the party is at **Pele's Other Garden** (811 Houston St., 808/565-9628, www.pelesothergarden.com), where live music rocks the bistro 7pm-10pm, and on Friday 6:30pm-9:30pm there is live island music featured at the **Lana'i City Grille** (828 Lana'i Ave., 808/565-7211, www.hotellanai.com/grille). Occasionally music will also be featured on Saturday at the Grille, although the schedule is intermittent. Also on Friday evenings 7pm-10pm there's live music at **The Lodge at Koele** in the Great Hall. It's nice to know that even on tiny Lana'i you still have choices as to where to spend a Friday night.

the outdoor porch is a great place for watching the mellow town slowly spring to life.

RESTAURANTS AT THE FOUR SEASONS LODGE AT KOELE

There are few more enjoyable dining experiences on Lana'i than eating a plate of warm, hearty food while nestled by one of the roaring fireplaces at **The Four Seasons Lodge at Koele** (1 Keomuku Hwy., 808/565-4000). The dining atmosphere is relaxed yet regal, and don't expect the food to come cheap.

Of the two main restaurants, **The Terrace** (7am-2pm and 6pm-9:30pm daily, $18-23) is more relaxed and informal. This American bistro looks out over the reflecting pool and well-manicured croquet lawn. Order an ahi tuna wrap or combat the evening chill with a bowl of venison chili.

Adjacent to The Terrace, the **Dining Room** (6pm-9:30pm daily, $59) is an immaculate and sophisticated venue offering a grandiose experience. For those into serious fine dining, the multi-course offerings, with entrées like beef tenderloin and *keahole* lobster, don't disappoint. Reservations are recommended. Ditch the tank top and rubber slippers for a nice shirt and pair of slacks.

Other places to pick up a quick bite in the hotel include the **Trophy Room** (11am-11pm daily), **Great Hall** (3pm-5pm daily, brunch 10am-2pm Sun.), and **The Bar** (11am-9pm daily) where *pupus*, drinks, and light snacks are available in a casual setting. Mini Kobe burgers and bruschetta anyone?

RESTAURANTS AT FOUR SEASONS MANELE BAY HOTEL

Swap the fireplace for the sunshine when you head down to the **Four Seasons Manele Bay Hotel** (1 Manele Bay Rd., 808/565-2000), and instead of eating a rack of lamb in an over-stuffed chair, go ahead and order some smoked *ono* (wahoo) as you sit by the pool.

One Forty (6:30am-10:30am, 6pm-9:30pm daily, $12-20), an oceanview restaurant on the lobby level, is one of the best places to get breakfast on the island. There's also fine dinner service.

If you've only made it as far as the pool by lunch and have no real intentions of leaving, order some food poolside from **《 Kailani** (11am-4pm and 6pm-9:30pm daily, $18-29), where you can get a Mediterranean seafood salad or rock shrimp and bay scallop ceviche. Having at least a drink or appetizer alongside one of the world's most scenic swimming pools is worth the price. Or, if you spent the morning hitting the golf course and are looking to replenish at the 19th hole, **The Challenge at Manele Clubhouse** (11am-3pm daily, $21) has the most reasonable lunch options with burgers, club sandwiches, and local beer.

To catch the big game, head down to **The Sports Bar** (5pm-11pm Mon.-Fri., 11am-11pm Sat.-Sun.) for light fare, a variety of drinks, and a casual social option during the often-slow evening hours.

Splurge and reserve a table at **《 Nobu Lana'i** (6pm-9:30pm daily, $30), the island's most highly anticipated restaurant in recent memory. As at other fine Nobu locations around the globe, the selections of yellowtail sashimi with jalapeño, lobster ceviche, rock shrimp tempura with butter ponzu sauce, and sushi are some of the freshest and most creative seafood offerings you'll find on the island. Expect to spend at least $50 per person.

Information and Services

INFORMATION

For general information about Lana'i and activities and services on the island, either contact **Lana'i Visitors Bureau** (808/565-7600, www.visitlanai.net) or visit **Lana'i Online** (www.lanaionline.com). For a great resource about what it's like to relocate to Lana'i, **Explore Lana'i** (www.explorelanai.com) is a site dedicated to daily life on the former pineapple isle.

MEDICAL SERVICES

Given its small population, Lana'i doesn't have the same medical services available as neighboring Maui or O'ahu. Anything requiring immediate or life-threatening attention will require a brief—yet expensive—helicopter ride to a neighboring island, so it's best to stay safe and in good health while enjoying your time on Lana'i. For minor emergencies or general care, the **Lana'i Community Hospital** (628 7th St., 808/565-8450, www.lch.hhsc.org) can provide services such as x-rays or lab work. During daytime hours there is also the **Straub Lana'i Family Health Clinic** (628-B 7th St., 808/565-6423, 8am-4:30pm Mon.-Fri.) which provides a decent range of medical services.

NEWSPAPERS

To put your finger on the pulse of the local Lana'i happenings, pick up a copy of *The Lana'i Times* for information on upcoming events.

BANKS

Lana'i City has the two banks on the island: **First Hawaiian Bank** (644 Lanai Ave., 808/565-6969) and **Bank of Hawaii** (460 8th St., 808/565-6426). Both are open 8:30am-4pm Monday-Thursday and 8:30am-6pm Friday, but they may be closed for lunch. Both have ATMs outside their offices for after-hours banking.

GROCERIES

While the supermarkets on Lana'i are much like the supermarkets in any other part of the state, there is one notable quirk which reminds you that you're still on a very small island. Of the three markets in town, two close Wednesday noon-1:30pm for "Barge Day," which is when they restock the shelves with all the new foodstuffs which arrived on the barge from Honolulu that morning.

The markets are right next to each other and for pretty much the same. **Richard's Supermarket** (434 8th St., 808/565-3780, 8am-7pm Mon.-Sat., 10am-5pm Sun.) is officially the largest store on the island and the supermarket choice of most island visitors. In addition to basic groceries it also serves as a hardware store, souvenir stop, and general sundry store. Right inside the door there is an informative community bulletin board (lost dog, weedeater for sale, yoga classes available). And this is a good place for picking up some local clothing items that don't look like souvenirs. Basic camping supplies, beer, wine, and ice are also available.

Much the same can be said for the **Pine Isle Market** (356 8th St., 808/565-6488, 8am-7pm Mon.-Sat.) right next door to Richard's. It offers more or less the same selection of everything.

GAS

There is only one station on the entire island: The **Lana'i City Service** station (1036 Lana'i Ave., 808/565-7227, 6:30am-10pm daily) supplies fuel for all 3,300 residents. Don't worry about the price; you're better off just not looking (often $1-1.50 more per gallon than on Maui). Then again, with only 30 miles of paved roads here, it isn't uncommon for a tank of gas to last a month or more.

POST OFFICE

The **Lana'i post office** (620 Jacaranda St., 808/565-6517, 9am-3pm weekdays, 9:30am-11:30am Sat.) is just a few steps off the city park. You can find boxes and padded mailers for your beachcombing treasures at the two general stores in town.

LIBRARY

At 6th Street and Fraser Avenue next to the school, the public library is open 9am-4:30pm Monday, Tuesday, Wednesday, and Friday, and 2pm-8pm Thursday.

Getting There and Around

GETTING THERE

Plane

Flying into Lana'i requires a jump from neighboring Honolulu or Maui. **Island Air** (800/652-6541, www.islandair.com) operates turboprop planes with four flights between Honolulu (HNL) and Lana'i (LNY) on weekdays and five flights on weekends. Island Air also flies to Lana'i from Maui, but you're going to have to make a stopover in Honolulu. **Mokulele Airlines** (866/260-7070, www.mokuleleairlines.com) also offers nonstop service between Honolulu and Lana'i with two direct flights per day, and one direct flight every afternoon from Kahului to Lana'i.

Ohana (800/367-5320) is an airline that will be operated by Hawaiian Airlines set to begin flying in late 2013. There are plans to increase service from Honolulu to Lana'i. If anything, getting to Lana'i by air will only become easier with all of the new services being offered.

Ferry

If you are traveling from Maui, the easiest and most practical way to get to Lana'i is by taking the **Expeditions Ferry** (808/661-3756 or 800/695-2624, www.go-lanai.com, $30/adult, $20/child one-way) which runs five times daily between Lahaina and Manele harbors. Travel time between the two islands is usually about an hour, and during whale season December through April, you can frequently spot humpback whales from the outdoor seating of the upper deck. Expeditions can also arrange golf, Jeep, and activity packages at a slight discount if you are planning a Lana'i day trip from Maui. Although you can buy tickets at the harbor kiosk in Lahaina the morning of your journey, make reservations ahead of time, particularly for the early morning trip. Don't be late. This is one ferry that doesn't wait around.

GETTING AROUND

Moving from point A to point B on Lana'i works a little differently than on the other Hawaiian Islands, and Lana'i has some options you won't find elsewhere in the state. In lieu of renting a car, guests at the Four Seasons can pay a one-time fee of $47.50 per adult ($23.75 per child) for all-inclusive access to the resort's shuttle for the duration of their stay. Resort

---

LAHAINA-LANA'I FERRY SCHEDULE

Depart Lahaina Harbor (Maui)
- 6:45am
- 9:15am
- 12:45pm
- 3:15pm
- 5:45pm

Depart Manele Harbor (Lana'i)
- 8am
- 10:30am
- 2pm
- 4:30pm
- 6:45pm

shuttles run every 30 minutes to destinations such as the harbor, airport, Lana'i City, and between the two resorts. The shuttle also makes a stop at Hotel Lana'i, although the onetime shuttle fee for Hotel Lana'i guests is only $35.

Visitors to the island who aren't staying at the Four Seasons are still welcome to use the resort shuttle at a cost of $10 per person/trip. If you have made reservations for a Jeep from **Dollar Lana'i Rent a Car,** a company shuttle will meet you at the harbor and provide complimentary transportation to the shop in Lana'i City (20 minutes) for the driver, although all other passengers will be charged $10/person. If you are traveling with a group of four, depending upon your budget, it's probably a better bet to have three of your party walk five minutes to Hulopo'e Beach from Manele Harbor while the driver goes "up-city" to procure the Jeep and then comes back down to scoop up the rest of the group.

Jeep Rentals

The longest running and most reputable Jeep rental company on the island, **Dollar Lana'i Rent a Car** (1036 Lana'i Ave., 808/565-7227 or 800/JEEP-808, www.dollarlanai.com, 7am-7pm daily) provides minivans ($129/day), four-wheel-drive Jeeps ($139/day 2dr, $169/day 4dr), and Hummers ($189/day). The company requests that the vehicles be returned by 3:30pm, so if you come over from Maui on the early morning ferry, you will arrive at the harbor by 7:45am, be at the rental car counter by 8:15am, and on your way with your Jeep by no later than 8:45am, thereby giving you more than six hours to explore the island. The rental company provides you with a map of the island and

clearly lays out which roads are off limits. If you end up requiring a tow from someplace "out of bounds," it's going to cost you $500.

A second, albeit smaller option for Jeep rentals on the island is **Lana'i Jeep Rental** (808/280-7092, www.**lanaijeeprental**.net) where the owner, John, has two Jeep Wranglers ($120/day 2dr, $135/day 4dr) he rents out to island visitors. Rather than you taking a shuttle up to Lana'i City, John will come and meet you at the harbor or the airport and hand over the keys after some basic formalities, so you can get going on your Lana'i adventure that much quicker. There are no official rules on where you can and cannot go, although he'd prefer you defer to common sense.

Hummer Rentals

In addition to those available from Dollar Lana'i, **808 Hummers** (808/286-9308, www.808hummers.com, 8am-8pm, $199/day) has a fleet of the famous off-road vehicles which are perfectly suited for Lana'i's rugged terrain. The company will arrange to pick you up. Just remember—it *is* still possible to get a Hummer stuck, so don't throw caution to the wind.

Private Car

If you're looking to cruise in style in a limousine or a private car, **Rabaca's Limousine Service** (808/565-6670, rabaca@aloha.net) can provide limos and private vans to get you around town in style. Also, if all the Jeeps are in use and you didn't make a reservation, ask around town. Somebody may agree to rent the 4x4 truck out of their driveway (cash only, of course).

LANA'I

MOLOKA'I

The island of Moloka'i is shrouded in mystery and misconceptions. While the Kalaupapa Peninsula was once the site of a leper colony, a visit to Kalaupapa is now one of the island's most revered historical and cultural experiences. And while there are no resorts on Moloka'i, there are plenty of bed-and-breakfasts, condominiums, and easygoing inns that serve as a relaxing base for exploring the island's valleys, waterfalls, and beaches.

Regarded as the birthplace of the hula, Moloka'i is a time capsule of Hawaiian history and culture. Visiting the island is an enlightening journey into a culture straddling the divide between modernity and tradition. It's one of the few places in Hawai'i where it's still possible to hear people speaking the Hawaiian language—possibly while stopped in the middle of the road, "talking story" in a "Moloka'i traffic jam." That may be the only cause of traffic on the island: its 7,500 residents still don't have to worry about stoplights.

From the east end of the island, the highrise resorts of Ka'anapali can be seen glittering at night, a floating sea of lights. From the empty beaches of the island's west end, the lights of Hawai'i's capital city of Honolulu shine brightly behind Diamond Head crater. In the middle, between the two, Moloka'i hides beneath a blanket of stars, already asleep while its neighbors stay awake late into the night.

Moloka'i has a slow pace of life, but by no means is it boring. On the contrary, this island is a tropical playground where the volume of adventure opportunities can keep outdoor

© MARK DRIESSEN

HIGHLIGHTS

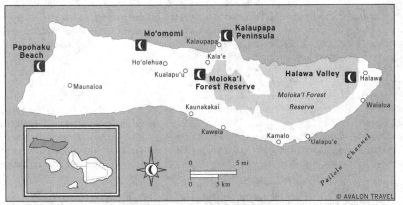

© AVALON TRAVEL

LOOK FOR 【 TO FIND RECOMMENDED SIGHTS, ACTIVITIES, DINING, AND LODGING.

【 Papohaku Beach: Six people are considered a crowd on western Moloka'i's Papohaku Beach, an outpost three miles long and nearly 100 yards wide where the solitude is trumped only by the sunsets (page 356).

【 Mo'omomi: Wild and secluded, Mo'omomi is Moloka'i's lost coast. In this undeveloped and culturally rich area, the sand dunes are meant to be shared with only the wind (page 358).

【 Moloka'i Forest Reserve: In the upper reaches of this reserve, nearly 98 percent of the plant species are indigenous to Moloka'i.

It's one of the few places in the state with an ecosystem identical to the one the Polynesians first found over 1,500 years ago (page 369).

【 Kalaupapa Peninsula: The Kalaupapa Peninsula fuses some of Moloka'i's darkest moments with its most dramatic surroundings. The former leper colony is now home to the most scenic mule ride on the planet (page 373).

【 Halawa Valley: Families have inhabited these same plots of land for centuries. A guided hike through the valley is as close to "old Hawai'i" as you can possibly get (page 378).

lovers busy for days. Imagine surfing perfect waves, scuba diving the longest fringing reef in the Hawaiian Islands, or hiking through rainforests inhabited by 219 species of plants found nowhere else on the planet. If all of the adventure is too much for you, relax on a westward-facing beach watching the sun sink into the horizon.

While the other islands dance to a different, faster drumbeat, Moloka'i is content to remain forgotten, slowly ambling along at whatever rhythm it pleases.

MOLOKA'I

Beaches

Empty and remote, only a few Moloka'i beaches are good for snorkeling or casual swimming. North- and west-facing beaches are prone to rough surf and hazardous shorebreak in winter, while south shore beaches are ringed by the long fringing reef. If having an entire beach to yourself and listening to nothing but the crashing surf seems like your kind of afternoon, then pack a beach chair and a good book to tune out the rest of the world. No beachside tiki bars, no pesky activity agents—just you, the sand, and the vast blue Pacific stretched out before you.

WEST MOLOKA'I

The west end of the island has the best beaches on all of Moloka'i, although your beach experience out here will largely be determined by the season. Summer is best for swimming. The beaches are usually spared the relentless northeasterly trade winds which frequently crank on the eastern half of the island. During winter, however, western Moloka'i catches the full brunt of the winter swells that turn the coastline into a dangerous stretch of high surf and rip currents. Regardless, the dry, empty shorelines are always good for sunbathing, and the sunsets from this western-facing vantage point are among the best in the state. If a bottle of wine, a beach chair, a fiery sunset, and a beach you have all to yourself sound like something you could get in to, then pick your spot out on the west end of the island and sit back and enjoy the show.

◖ Papohaku Beach

At over two miles long and nearly 100 yards wide, **Papohaku Beach** is where most visitors who drive out to the west end of the island will end up. Despite being the most heavily visited beach on the island, Papohaku rarely

© KYLE ELLISON

Papohaku Beach is one of the largest beaches in the state.

MOLOKA'I

THE BIRTHPLACE OF THE HULA

Although not much remains on the windswept plains of western Moloka'i, there is nevertheless a history along these arid slopes going all the way to the roots of Hawaiian culture. Not far from Maunaloa in an area known as Ka'ana, legend speaks of the goddess Laka being the first person to dance the hula, having "given birth" to the dance at a hill known as Pu'u Nana. Fanning out from Ka'ana, Laka subsequently journeyed throughout Hawai'i, teaching the dance to anyone who wanted to learn. To this day traditional *hula halau* (hula schools) will prepare an offering or altar to Laka, the goddess of hula, as part of their performance and ceremony. It's believed that after sharing her dance with the people of Hawai'i, Laka returned to the island of Moloka'i, where her remains are buried at Pu'u Nana overlooking Moloka'i's western shores. Given the cultural significance of the area, each May the *Moloka'i Ka Hula Piko* (Moloka'i Center of the Dance) festival is held at western Moloka'i's Papohaku Beach Park.

sees more than six or seven people at a time. Though smatterings of private homes adorn the southern portion of the beach, the majority of Papohaku is still undeveloped shoreline with empty sand made for strolling. Swimming is a terrible idea here as the rip currents and undertow can be overwhelming during any part of the year. Your time at Papohaku is better spent taking a morning jog or watching the sun set over the distant lights of Honolulu. To get here, follow Highway 460 toward the town of Maunaloa until you take a right on to Kaluakoi Road. Follow Kaluakoi down to sea level and until it wraps around to the left. The beach park will have multiple entrances on the right side of the road. Camping is possible at Papohaku if you obtain a permit from the County Parks Department (808/553-3204). The only time of year when this beach is truly hopping is during the annual **Moloka'i Ka Hula Piko** festival each May which celebrates the area as the birthplace of the hula.

Kepuhi Beach

Kepuhi Beach fronts the Kaluakoi Villas and the abandoned structures which once formed the Sheraton resort. It's an ideal beach for swimming during the summer; winter can see large swells much better suited for surfing. To reach Kepuhi Beach, follow the signs for Kaluakoi Villas off Kaluakoi Road. Public beach parking is available within the complex.

Just as at neighboring beaches, the sunsets from here are the kind that end up on your refrigerator.

Dixie Maru (Kapukahehu)

Named after a fishing boat which sank near the bay, **Dixie's** is as far south as the road will take you. From Papohaku Beach Park follow Kaluakoi Road until it reaches Pohakuloa, turn *makai* (toward the sea), and follow it to the end of the cul-de-sac. The narrow alleyway that looks like a driveway is the beach access, and there's a small parking area about 100 yards down. In the kiawe trees behind the beach you'll notice a hidden trail which leads back through the scrub brush and eventually over a fence. Follow this trail for 10 minutes and it will bring you a to a sandy cove frequented by surfers and nudists, but more often than not you'll be the only person there.

Kawakiu

Heading north from Kepuhi, the coastline becomes wild, scraggy, and utterly deserted. The far northern tip of the island—'Ilio Point—at one point served as a target area for the military, although now all that remains are empty bullet casings and the howl of the northeasterly trades. Between Kepuhi and 'Ilio, however, a number of hidden, sandy coves tucked out of the wind provide perfect swimming and splendid isolation. You

MOLOKA'I

MOLOKA'I

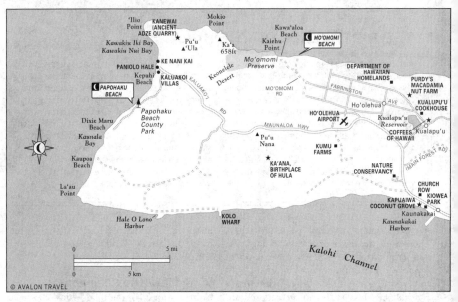

© AVALON TRAVEL

would never even know that **Kawakiu Beach** was here unless someone told you. It's that remote. To reach Kawakiu, follow the signs to the Paniolo Hale condominium complex from Kaluakoi Road by making a right on Kaka'ako and then turning left down Lio Place, where you will follow the pavement to the end. From here you'll notice a rudimentary sign pointing the way toward the beach. When the dirt road ends in a parking lot, it's only a short walk to the shore. While the beach you come to first is nice enough, it's nothing compared to Kawakiu. Keep heading north along the shoreline and scramble over some rocks until you cross a stretch of sand known as **Make Horse Beach** (Dead Horse Beach). You'll notice a dirt road running along the top of the bluff which will lead you all the way to Kawakiu. Or, if the tide is low and the surf calm, meander your way along the shoreline. The protected cove is idyllic in summer, tumultuous in winter, and almost always empty. If you prefer to bathe in the buff, then this is the place. Bring lots of water, as well as proper footwear capable of withstanding sharp lava rocks and kiawe thorns.

Hale O Lono

Hale O Lono is not a place that many visitors go. Not because it isn't beautiful, but because it's incredibly remote. With the closing of Moloka'i Ranch, the dirt roads once plied by ranch guests now are sporadically used by fishers, canoe racers, or no one at all. Known for its sunsets and solitude, **Hawela Beach** on the east side of the old harbor entrance is the most accessible and most protected. Rough conditions can persist at any time of the year, but on days with light winds and flat surf, the swimming and sunbathing at Hawela can be on par with anywhere else on the island. To find Hale O Lono follow Highway 460 until its terminus in the town of Maunaloa. From here Mokio Street will lead to a sloping, rutted, seven-mile dirt road running down to the shoreline. Two-wheel drive vehicles with high clearance can make this if it hasn't been raining. A 4WD is recommended in the event that it has.

Mo'omomi

Although **Mo'omomi** is technically on the northern coast of the island, it fits in with the "Wild West" conditions found on the western

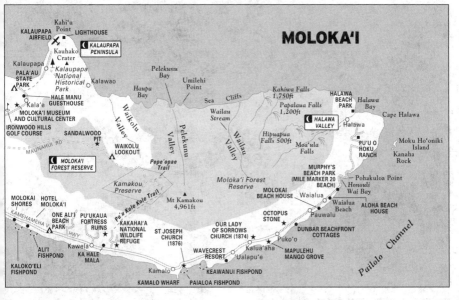

half. With numerous beaches and windswept dunes, **Mo'omomi** holds incredible cultural significance for native Hawaiians, particularly those living in the Hawaiian Homesteads of nearby Ho'olehua. Mo'omomi is a controversial spot to visit because it's on private property administered by Hawaiian Home Lands, although access has fluctuated from freedom of exploration to talk of erecting a locked gate. While enforcement is rare and the area is usually deserted, anyone wanting to visit should first get permission by contacting **The Department of Hawaiian Home Lands** (600 Maunaloa Hwy., 808/560-6104) to enquire about any current restrictions. As with anywhere in Hawai'i, respect and preservation are key.

Untouched save for the marine debris which washes onto the shores, Mo'omomi is a place for fishing, lobster diving, and soul-searching. The western portions of Mo'omomi are part of The Nature Conservancy, and visitors are asked to stay out of the sensitive ecosystem in the dunes. All hikers are advised to stick to established trails or follow the shoreline. To reach the Mo'omomi pavilion, follow

Farrington Avenue until the road becomes dirt and veer to the right at the fork in the road. Walking along the shoreline takes you to a series of underwhelming beaches, but once you hook back up with the dirt road, the beauty of windswept **Kawa'aloa Beach** opens up before you in what is potentially one of the most scenic stretches of coastline on the island. Though it's possible to hike the shoreline for miles, there are zero facilities, no places to procure water, and it all looks the same. Swimming at Kawa'aloa can be rough during almost all parts of the year. The chief benefits are scenery and isolation.

EAST MOLOKA'I

The eastern beaches are the most popular among locals despite being heavily exposed to the northeasterly winds. Morning hours are best. Like scenes out of a South Pacific postcard, white sand coves ringed by lazy palms are dotted by fishing boats of varying colors and styles. More than anywhere else on the island, a sense of calm envelops this shore. The swimming and snorkeling are best at high tide, the beachcombing and sunbathing better at low

© KYLE ELLISON

the windswept beaches of Mo'omomi

MOLOKA'I

tide, and everything is better before the afternoon wind.

Puko'o Beach

Just east of the Mana'e Goods & Grindz a small beach access sign points down a dirt driveway to the tucked away **Puko'o Beach.** Despite being only 50 yards long, this sliver of a beach is protected from the wind and offers calm swimming most times of the year. The water isn't as murky as spots closer to town. This is a good spot for eating a plate lunch beneath the shade of a tropical palm or taking a quick dip to cool off from the island heat.

Waialua Beach

Waialua Beach is a narrow ribbon of sand 18.5 miles east of Kaunakakai with some the island's best swimming, snorkeling, and small waves for learning to surf. As at other beaches in the area, the wind gains in strength throughout the day, and at high tide the sand almost disappears completely. This is a great spot for taking a dip, although when you jump in the water,

watch out for coral heads that are exposed during low tide.

Murphy's Beach

Known as "Twenty Mile Beach" to locals, **Murphy's Beach** is by the 20-mile marker of Highway 450 and the last stretch of sand before the road narrows to one lane. While the swimming here isn't as nice as at Waialua, the beach is a little larger, making it a good option for laying a blanket down. In the afternoon hours you might see kitesurfers running laps down the coast. From this vantage point the views of West Maui provide a scenic backdrop for the most popular beach on the island's east end.

Sandy Beach

Although parking can be an issue, **Sandy Beach** is a simple cove tucked into a bend in the road on the drive to Halawa. The beach is protected from the trade winds and, most of the time, from the surf. Although the beach is small, there's just enough room to lay a towel down. You might also share space with kids wading in the shallows or locals selling bananas out of the back of a truck.

Halawa Bay

After weaving your way 10 miles over the rocky coastline and down through the lush eastern valleys, the two beaches which form **Halawa Bay** appear like the gold at the end of a rainbow. At the terminus of Highway 450, Kama'alaea Bay is the more protected beach on the far side of the stream. This is the best option for swimming and escaping the wind. Kawili Beach at the bottom of the cliff is more exposed to the currents and trade winds. The surf here can get rough in winter; never attempt to swim outside of the bay. The sand here is darker than the white sand of Waialua, and it's a surreal feeling to hang out on the shores of a place considered to be one of the oldest settlements in the state of Hawai'i.

Snorkeling and Diving

Shhh—don't' tell anybody, but Moloka'i has some of the best snorkeling and diving in all of Hawai'i. The only reason you haven't heard about it is because—with the exception of a few protected areas—the majority of Moloka'i's dive and snorkel spots are best accessed from a dive boat or charter. **Dixie Maru Beach** on the west shore and **Waialua Beach** on the east shore (accessible for snorkeling only at high tide) are the only two bays where you could snorkel from the shoreline without getting caught in a rip current or scraping your stomach on the shallow reef. Moloka'i is still home to the longest fringing reef in Hawai'i, and dive outfitters have no less than 20 spots along the outer edge of the reef.

MOKU HO'ONIKI

Moku Ho'oniki on the eastern tip of the island is home to a population of scalloped hammerhead sharks, a vibrant coral reef, and occasionally some larger species with the ability to get your heart racing. While it's for advanced divers only, Moku Ho'oniki is the crown jewel in most charter boat offerings. The water is too deep here for any sort of mooring system, so often divers will shave to flop backward off the drifting boat for a Navy SEAL-style entry into the rough waters of the Pailolo Channel. At the rock's most popular dive site—**Fish Rain**— divers usually descend 100 feet or more along a sloping reef where myriad species of tropical fish appear to rain down from above.

Once at your bottom depth, your heart rate really picks up as you head out into the open blue in search of scalloped hammerheads. Other sightings have included whale sharks, tiger sharks, mahimahi, and even humpback whales during the winter season. Dive charters visit the rock from both Maui and Moloka'i.

CHARTERS AND TOURS

With an office right on the corner of Kaunakakai's main thoroughfare, **Moloka'i Fish and Dive** (61 Ala Malama Ave., 808/553-5926, www.molokaifishanddive.com, 7:30am-6pm Mon.-Sat., 8am-2pm Sun.) operates its own charter boat departing out of Kaunakakai wharf and offers three-hour snorkeling trips for $79. Scuba diving trips visit either the south shore's fringing reef for $145 or locations farther afield (such as Moku Ho'oniki) for $295. This shop is the premier (and only) PADI operation on the island and can accommodate whatever snorkel or dive excursion you're hoping to sort out. Prices and times can vary, so it's best to contact the dive shop directly about current rates and availability

Operating the 40-foot catamaran *Manu Ele'ele,* **Moloka'i Ocean Tours** (808/553-3290, www.molokaioceantours.com) can accommodate up to six passengers and offers snorkeling excursions out of Kaunakakai. Like other operators, this boat mostly travels the 30 miles of fringing reef along the south shore in front of Kaunakakai. Prices vary depending on the

© KYLE ELLISON

The island's most extreme scuba diving is at Moku Ho'oniki.

number of people on the boat, from $240/person for two people to $90/person for six people.

For a private sea tour of the northern sea cliffs—something which is only possible when the conditions allow—local adventure guide Walter Naki runs **Moloka'i Action Adventures** (808/558-8184) and is one of the few people you will find who can take you to remote valleys and the dramatic coastline of the world's tallest sea cliffs. Because conditions are variable, inquire directly about rates and availability, although if all aligns correctly, it's guaranteed to be the most memorable day of your vacation.

Surfing

To say that the surf spots on Moloka'i are empty would be a lie, but a crowded day by Moloka'i standards would be considered almost empty in Maui. If there are more than three people, maybe four, just go somewhere else. With a little walking (or a high clearance vehicle), it's still possible to find spots where there's a good chance you'll have the waves all to yourself. Since finding surf spots like this is such a rarity in Hawai'i, however, it's not surprising that Moloka'i locals can be protective of their surf breaks, so following basic surf etiquette here can go a long way. Share the waves. Don't drop in on anyone. Don't paddle in front of anyone. Smile. And if you're just learning and the waves are above your ability level, perhaps paddle out at a smaller, more manageable spot. If there were ever the venue for an *Endless Summer* surf safari where the waves are mixed with adventure, then Moloka'i is the spot.

WEST MOLOKA'I

Remote and empty, West Moloka'i is the best in winter for mixing big surf with fiery sunsets. The same swells which send waves to the North Shore of Oʻahu come crashing into western Molokaʻi, the differences being that there aren't 200 people vying for the same wave and traffic on the highway consists of a deer crossing the road. While the quality isn't the same as at Sunset Beach, the surf in western Molokaʻi can still get heavy, and only experts and advanced surfers should paddle out on the bigger days.

The most well-known (and consequently, most crowded) spot on this end of the island is **Sheraton's** at Kepuhi Beach, named after the now-defunct resort which fronts the beach. The access at Sheraton's is sandy and easy, although you have to be careful of a few shallow boulders while paddling out. The wave is on the left side of the beach, and on its better days can be an A-frame which holds its shape in faces exceeding 10-15 feet. Sheraton's is a decent spot for intermediate surfers if it's small, and is an experts-only venue if really pumping.

If Sheraton's is too big, drive south to **Dixie Maru's** where a right pointbreak wraps into the bay at sizes often half that of Sheraton's. If Dixie's is crowded (i.e., more than three people), or you're up for a little adventure, a goat trail leading from the center of the beach back through the kiawe trees (don't go barefoot!) brings you to a sandy cove where another right pointbreak bends into the often empty beach. The takeoff can be a little sketchy as you have to sit just off the rocks, but it's a fun wave to get a few turns in when Sheraton's is a cauldron of white water.

Even though the beaches around **Hale O Lono** harbor face south, they're still able to pick up swells during all parts of the year, which can often be heavy during the winter. The wind can be fierce in the afternoon, and the murky conditions conjure images of toothy predators. Plus, there's a 95 percent chance you'll be the only one surfing there. If everything comes together though, and the wind is down, the waves are up, and the water is clear, the beaches off Hale O Lono can offer some of the most adventurous surf on Molokaʻi. Just follow the dirt road from Maunaloa town and take it straight downhill until you reach the shoreline seven miles later.

KAUNAKAKAI

Since Kaunakakai faces directly south, the best time of year for scoring waves in town is May through September. Despite the fact that the area surrounding Kaunakakai boasts miles of shoreline, the majority of it is blocked by the fringing reef which makes paddling out virtually impossible. Nevertheless, locals still flock to **Kaunakakai Wharf** during the big swells of summer. Anyone surfing here can expect a long paddle since you need to head out past the reef to get to the waves, but the long paddle is rewarded by Molokaʻi's best summer wave. Given its popularity, expect a very local crowd.

EAST MOLOKAʻI

Technically, East Molokaʻi is the most consistent place to find surf year-round. It might not be *good* surf, but when there's nothing else to ride, this is where you head. Winter months pick up wrapping north swell, and if a northeast swell comes barreling down the Pailolo Channel, then this is the place to be. During summer this same stretch of rural coastline is able to pick up windswell generated by the trades, but on the flip side this means that it's often blown out and completely unrideable. Morning hours are always best, and although there are ample waves along this coastline, accessing them isn't always the easiest.

For beginner surfers the easiest waves can be found at **Waialua Beach,** where gentle rollers provide enough of a push to practice getting up on two feet. While the waves can be fun, it can be shallow at low tide.

Just past Murphy's Beach (mile marker 20) where the road turns to a single lane sits one of Molokaʻi's most well-known surf spots, **Rock Point.** This local's favorite can be a tricky place to surf for a number of reasons: finding the spot in the first place, figuring out where to park, getting it when the wind isn't up, and trying to figure out how to paddle into a wave which breaks in knee-deep water. For the advanced surfer trying to chase down an easterly swell, however, this is one of the island's best waves.

At the end of the road, **Halawa Bay** can also be one of the best waves on the island, although often this is an "experts only" spot due to strong rips and large waves. If the waves are at a manageable level and you have the ability to handle strong ocean currents, then the wave at Halawa can end up being the pot of gold at the end of the road.

RENTAL SHOPS

Your best bet is to bring boards over from Maui on the ferry, but if you're in need of a rental board on the island, there are a couple of outfitters to help you out. **Moloka'i Fish and Dive** (61 Ala Malama Ave., 808/553-5926, www.molokaifishanddive.com, 7:30am-6pm Mon.-Sat., 8am-2pm Sun.) is the only retail store in downtown Kaunakakai openly renting out surfboards. Although the selection isn't huge, for $25/day they can get you a board and provide tips on the best places to check out.

While they don't have an actual shop and are only accessible by phone or online, the staff at **Moloka'i Outdoors** (808/553-4477, www.molokai-outdoors.com) can similarly get you in the water and give you inside info on where—and when—to embark on your Moloka'i surf excursion. Rates are usually a few dollars cheaper than at Moloka'i Fish and Dive, and they currently are the only company that also rents out other water sports equipment such as stand-up paddleboards or windsurfing boards. **Moloka'i Outdoors** also offers guided kayak tours of the waters inside the fringing reef or the more high-speed option of a "downwinder" if the northeasterly trades start blowing at your back. Regular kayak rentals are also available ($42/day) and include all the necessary safety items.

Hiking and Biking

Even for Maui locals, the hiking trails of Moloka'i are shrouded in mystery. Often the trails require either four-wheel drive access or permission from private landowners, although there are still a number which are accessible to the general public. You're rewarded for your effort with sweeping views of the entire island.

HIKING
Topside

Bathed in the scent of eucalyptus and pine, the "topside" of central Moloka'i is where you truly feel as if you're in the mountains. With trails ranging in elevation from 1,500 to 4,000 feet, the air is cooler up here, and once you enter the Kamakou Preserve, the weather turns wetter and the surroundings lush. Songs of the native *i'iwi* birds ring from the treetops while mists hang in the silence of deeply carved valleys. This is where Moloka'i gets wild.

KALAUPAPA OVERLOOK

The easiest walk is the 1,500-foot paved walkway leading to the **Kalaupapa Overlook** starting at the end of the road in Pala'au State Park. Take Highway 470 past the mule barn for the Kalaupapa trail rides and continue until it dead-ends in a parking lot. Here you'll find some basic restrooms but no potable water. Be prepared for high winds that can blow your hat off, and get your camera ready for a view of the Kalaupapa Peninsula which is the best you're going to find short of actually hiking down there. At the end of the walkway you'll notice some trails leading through the pine needles and paralleling the cliff. The combination of loose needles, high winds, and steep cliffs make for dangerous, uncertain footing that isn't worth the reward.

KALAUPAPA TRAIL

The **Kalaupapa Trail** is the most popular hike on Moloka'i. Descending over 1,700 vertical

DON'T CHANGE MOLOKA'I

MOLOKA'I . . . . . NOT FOR SALE
"Just Visit"
OUR LIFESTYLE & ECONOMY DEPENDS ON IT!!!
MOLOKA'I . . . . NOT FOR SALE
"Just Visit"
OUR LIFESTYLE & ECONOMY DEPENDS ON IT!!!
MOLOKA'I . . . . NOT FOR SALE
"Just Visit"

© KYLE ELLISON

MOLOKA'I

Nowhere in the islands do the war drums against development beat louder than on Moloka'i. There is a preconception among visitors to Hawai'i that the people of Moloka'i are against tourists, which isn't exactly accurate. While it's a complex and sensitive issue, a popular bumper sticker seen around town may describe it best: Moloka'i not for sale. Just Visit. Our lifestyle and economy depend on it. As the bumper sticker says, Moloka'i vendors realize that tourist dollars are an integral part of what is usually a struggling economy, but at the same time, it only takes one glance across the Pailolo Channel to the resorts of Ka'anapali to see what Moloka'i wants to avoid turning into. With the exception of Ni'ihau, Moloka'i remains the only island where over 50 percent of the population is of Native Hawaiian descent, and in many ways it truly is the last holdout of ancient Hawaiian culture.

With development comes modernization, and with modernization comes loss of culture.

It's a swan song which has been played again and again in countless indigenous societies across the globe. Given the dispute, it's important to remember that the concept of land ownership has never existed in Hawaiian culture. Hawaiian wisdom holds that the land gives life, and we must therefore take care of it; we are stewards of the land, not owners. Given this belief, Western concepts such as property rights, real estate, development, and wealth are ideals which the people of Moloka'i want no part of, largely to the consternation of folks who weren't raised with the same beliefs.

The people of Moloka'i are all too happy to welcome visitors to the island and share with them their culture and aloha. It's just that when outside visitors want to put up housing developments, wind farms, or piers to accommodate a cruise ship, the weapons of cultural defense are unsheathed for all to see. As another popular bumper sticker says, Don't change Moloka'i, let it change you. That says it all.

feet over the course of 3.2 miles and 26 switch-backing turns, this trail was hand-carved into the mountain in 1886 by Portuguese immigrant Manuel Farinha as a way to establish a land connection with the residents living topside. The trail today remains in good shape, although you do need to be physically fit and keep a keen eye out for the "presents" left on the trail by mules. Since this is part of the National Historic Park, reservations are required to tour the peninsula, and those who try to sneak into Kalaupapa could end up facing possible prosecution. Those wanting to hike the trail instead of riding a mule can contact **Damien Tours** (808/567-6171), which, for the cost of $50/person, will meet hikers at the bottom of the trail at 10am and provide a four-hour guided tour of the Kalaupapa Peninsula. To reach the trailhead, drive 200 yards past the mule barn on Highway 470 and park on the right side of the road.

PEPE'OPAE BOG

Constantly shrouded in cloud cover and dripping in every color of green imaginable, if ever there were a place to visualize Hawai'i before the arrival of humans, then that spot is the **Pepe'opae Bog.** Ninety-eight percent of the plant species here are indigenous to the island of Moloka'i, and 219 of the species in this preserve are found nowhere else on earth. Following Highway 460 from Kaunakakai, make a right before the bridge at the Homelani Cemetery sign and follow the dirt road for 10 miles all the way to the parking area at Waikolu Overlook. Even making it this far in a two-wheel-drive vehicle requires high clearance and the best road conditions. Trying to go any further will just get you stuck. Those with four-wheel drive can knock 2.6 miles one-way off the journey by continuing to the trailhead, but even this is precarious at best and the driver needs to know what they're doing behind the wheel.

Look for the signs for Pepe'opae Bog and follow them. Once the trail begins, it's imperative you stay on the metal boardwalk. If you accidentally step off, you can expect to sink shin-deep into the soggy moss and mud. The boardwalk runs for 1.5 miles through some of the most pristine rainforest left in the state. Hikers who make it to the end are rewarded with a view into Pelekunu Valley which plunges 4,000 feet through the uninhabited, untouched wilderness below. Hikers are free to attempt the climb on their own, or the **Nature Conservancy** (808/553-5236, hike_molokai@tnc.org) leads hikes into Pepe'opae once per month March through October. Due to high demand, advance reservations are suggested.

PU'U KOLEKOLE

On the same 4WD road leading to the Pepe'opae trailhead, hikers who take the fork to the right will instead reach the start of the **Pu'u Kolekole trail.** This two-mile trail leads you to the 3,951-foot summit of Pu'u Kolekole. From here the view overlooks the southern shoreline and fringing reef to offer the best view of southern Moloka'i.

West Moloka'i

Given the lack of mountains in western Moloka'I, most of the hikes on this side of the island follow the coastline.

KAWAKIU

A nice walk from the condo complexes of Kaluakoi is to follow either the coastline or a dusty dirt road to the secluded beauty of **Kawakiu Nui Beach.** From Maunaloa Highway (Hwy. 460) take the Kalukaoi Road exit and follow it to the bottom of the hill before making a right on Kaka'ako Road. Finally, a left on Lio Place brings you to the Paniolo Hale parking lot, where you can follow the signs for the beach, crossing over the fairway of the old golf course before you reach the shoreline. Make a right, and 45 minutes of walking along the coastline will bring you to Kawakiu. Or, if the tide or surf is too high to walk along the coastline, turn inland past Make Horse Beach. After a few minutes, you'll meet up with a dirt road which leads north and deposits you at Kawakiu. About 100 yards before the road drops onto the sand at Kawakiu, there's an ancient Hawaiian *heiau* out on the rocky point. Show respect for this centuries-old site; don't remove any rocks.

East Moloka'i

Deeply carved down from the 4,961-foot summit of Kamakou, the valleys of eastern Moloka'i beckon to be explored. Despite being beautiful, forested, and laden with waterfalls, many of the valleys are cut off from public use. Liability concerns have forced landowners to restrict access to many valley trails, although some are still available by taking part in a guided tour.

PU'U KOLEKOLE

The only hike on this side of the island realistically available to casual hikers is the **Pu'u Kolekole trail** which leads to the same summit as the one accessed from Pepe'opae Bog. If you still want to see the views from Pu'u Kolekole but don't have a four-wheel drive to get you into the forest reserve, an alternate route is to follow Highway 450 east of Kaunakakai until you reach the left turn into the Kawela I housing development. Once you pass the rows of plumeria trees, take the first left leading uphill and ascend a steep road until it ends in a cul-de-sac. The dirt road behind the locked gate is the start of the trailhead for hikers. Leave your vehicle parked off the side of the road. To reach the summit of Pu'u Kolekole from here is a two-hour, strenuous uphill climb with minimal shade, so be sure that you are in proper physical condition and that you pack ample amounts of water and snacks. Save your camera battery when starting the hike since the view gets better with every step.

Halawa Valley

Ah, Halawa, the most controversial hike on the island. It used to be that anyone who visited "the end of the road" could park down by the beach park and enjoy the two-hour stroll up to 250-foot **Moa'ula Falls.** Rumor has it lawsuits following injuries sustained led the landowners of the valley to keep *everyone* out. While the trail to the falls is once again open, it can only be accessed by going through a local company and paying to hire a local guide. Bookings to hike into Halawa Valley can be made through either **Moloka'i Outdoors** (808/553-4477, www.moloka-outdoors.com) or **Moloka'i Fish and Dive** (61 Ala Malama Ave., 808/553-5926, www.molokaifishanddive.com).

BIKING

All of the best mountain biking in Moloka'i is found on the roads of the **Moloka'i Forest Reserve.** Road cyclists can enjoy miles of open road with minimal traffic. The ride east from Kaunakakai to Halawa Valley is comparable to Maui's ride to Kahakuloa.

In downtown Kaunakakai, **Moloka'i Bicycle** (80 Mohala St., 808/553 5740 or 808/553-3931, www.mauimolokaibicycle.com, 3pm-6pm Wed., 9am-2pm Sat.) can cater to every bike need, whether it's rentals, parts, or just advice on good rides. The company can arrange free pickups and drop-offs from a number of Moloka'i hotels, with a $20-25 surcharge for the airport and hotels which are farther afield, such as Wavecrest or Kaluakoi. Rentals begin at $32/day, $20/day thereafter, or $120 for the week.

MOLOKA'I

Other Recreation

BIRD-WATCHING

Although many of Hawai'i's original bird species have gone the way of the dodo, there are still a number of rare and critically endangered native bird species which cling to existence high in the Moloka'i forests or down on the protected seashore. Anyone interested in volunteering in one of Moloka'i's wetlands or learning more about the island's endangered bird species is encouraged to contact **Nene O Moloka'i** (808/553-5992), a nonprofit organization dedicated to protecting Moloka'i's endangered waterfowl.

For mountain species, the last known sightings of the Moloka'i thrush (*oloma'o*) and Moloka'i creeper (*kakawahie*) were both in the **Kamakou Preserve,** a rugged and wet mountain area which requires four-wheel drive to access. In this protected area home to 219 endemic species of plants, the trademark calls of honeycreepers (*i'iwi*, '*apapane*, '*amakihi*, and the Hawaiian owl (*pueo*) can still be heard resonating through the lush green treetops. The Nature Conservancy leads trips into the preserve once per month March through October. Find out more by calling 808/553-5236.

Although not open to the public, the **Kakahai'a National Wildlife Refuge** 5.5 miles east of Kaunakakai can be visited by arranging a tour through the Maui County National Wildlife Refuge office at 808/875-1582. This 45-acre protected area five miles east of Kaunakakai is home to endangered Hawaiian stilts (*a'eo*) as well as endangered Hawaiian coots (*'alae ke'oke'o*).

During the fall and winter months it is common to see Pacific golden plover (*kolea*) scuttling their way across the shorelines and grassy areas of the island. These birds migrate all the way to the Arctic Circle during summer before returning to Hawai'i for the long, cold winter. Once the *kolea* are seen in the islands, locals know that the humpback whales aren't far behind.

FISHING

To say that fish play a large role in Moloka'i culture would be a big understatement. The southern coast of the island is ringed with dozens of fishponds, and seemingly every third house you pass has long bunches of fishing nets drying in the yard. The Penguin Banks between Moloka'i and O'ahu are considered to be some of the most fertile fishing grounds in the state, although even if you stay near shore the chances of hauling in a fresh catch are still good. As with other locations, the earlier you depart the better chance you'll ultimately have for success.

Charters

The best place in Kaunakakai for buying fishing accessories, **Moloka'i Fish and Dive** (61 Ala Malama Ave., 808/553-5926, www.molokaifishanddive.com, 7:30am-6pm Mon.-Sat., 8am-2pm Sun.) also operates its own charter service offering both half-day ($500) as well as full-day trips ($650) aboard the 38-foot Delta cruiser *The Coral Queen*.

Not only is owner and captain Mike Holmes of **Fun Hogs Fishing** (808/567-6789 or 808/336-0047, www.molokaifishing.com) an accomplished waterman and avid canoe racer, but he also runs one of the best operations for deep-sea fishing available for visitors. Aboard the 27-foot *AHI* Holmes can take guests trolling for blue water game fish such as mahimahi, ono, ahi, and marlin. Four-hour charters run $450, while a full-day, eight-hour charter can be booked for $600. Fun Hogs can also arrange seasonal whale-watching trips for $70/adult, private snorkeling charters, or any other sort of outing provided there are six passengers or fewer.

Based out of Kaunakakai, Captain Joe Reich of **Alyce C. Sportfishing** (808/558-8377, www.alycecsportfishing.com) similarly offers half-day, three-quarter-day, and full-day charters aboard his 31-foot cruiser. A knowledgeable fisher who will go wherever the fish are biting, Captain Joe's goal is to send you home with as much fresh fish as you can possibly make use of.

GOLF

Now that the fairways of the Kaluakoi Golf Course have reverted back to dirt, the lone remaining course on the island is the 9-hole **Ironwood Hills Golf Club** (Kalae Hwy., 808/567-6000, www.molokaigolfcourse.com, $36) in the cool eucalyptus groves of Kala'e off Highway 470. Set at a 1,200-foot elevation and not far from Pala'au State Park, this course is easy on the pocketbook and the only option for breaking out the clubs while in town. Clubs and carts are available for rent.

Sights

People who claim that there isn't a lot to *do* on Moloka'i have most likely never even scoured the island to see what's out there. Although Moloka'i is a place you go to decompress, there are still a healthy number of visitor sites relating to the island's history, culture, and agricultural heritage.

KAUNAKAKAI
Kapuaiwa Coconut Grove

Situated right on the side of Highway 450, **Kapuaiwa Coconut Grove** is impossible to pass without noticing the cluster of palms. Planted in 1860 for Kamehameha V, this grove once sported 1,000 palms, although the number remaining has diminished. Despite the urge to go frolicking through the palm grove, heed the warning signs and stay out from beneath the trees, lest you get bonked on the head.

Church Row

If you're into visiting old churches, then **Church Row** across the street from Kapuaiwa Coconut Grove has seven to choose from. Most of the churches are simple and don't offer much in the way of architecture, but it's fascinating to see how many different denominations still practice devotions on a weekly basis. Some of the sermons are still conducted in the Hawaiian language. You can stand in the parking lot outside and listen to hymns being sung in Hawaiian while gazing across the street and almost see Kamehameha V relaxing in his grove of 1,000 palms.

Moloka'i Plumeria Farm

Just west of town on Highway 460 as the road starts heading uphill sits the **Moloka'i Plumeria Farm** (808/553-3391, www.molokaiplumerias. com, 9am-12pm Mon.-Sat., free) where you can tour the 10-acre property and even make your own lei.

TOPSIDE
◀ Moloka'i Forest Reserve

As you head west from Kaunakakai, slowly gaining in elevation, the turnoff for the **Moloka'i Forest Reserve** is just before mile marker 4. Turn right before the bridge, and after a few hundred yards you'll pass the Homelani Cemetery. Here, red-dirt Maunahui Road winds its way into the mountains. Your car-rental agency will tell you that this road is impassable except in a four-wheel drive, and it's right—if it's raining or has rained recently. The road is rough even when it's dry; anyone without a high-clearance truck or jeep shouldn't even consider it. If you have the proper vehicle, however, follow the rutted road up into the hills and you'll soon be in a deep forest of 'ohi'a, pine, eucalyptus, and giant ferns which have thrived since their planting in the early 1900s. The cool, pleasant air mixes, with rich earthy smells of the forest, and at 5.5 miles you enter the Moloka'i Forest Reserve.

After nine miles, you'll come upon the **Sandalwood Measuring Pit** (Lua Na Moku 'Iliahi), a depression in the ground in the shape of a ship's hull. Now bordered by a green pipe

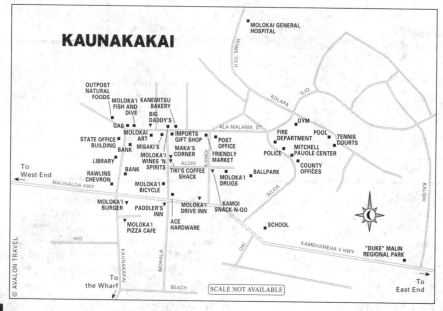

KAUNAKAKAI

OUTPOST NATURAL FOODS
KANEMITSU BAKERY
MOLOKA'I FISH AND DIVE
BIG DADDY'S
GAS
MOLOKAI ART
STATE OFFICE BUILDING
BANK
MISAKI'S
MOLOKA'I WINES 'N SPIRITS
LIBRARY
RAWLINS CHEVRON
BANK
MOLOKA'I BICYCLE
MOLOKA'I BURGER
PADDLER'S INN
MOLOKA'I PIZZA CAFE
IMPORTS GIFT SHOP
MAKA'S CORNER
TIKI'S COFFEE SHACK
MOLOKA'I DRIVE INN
ACE HARDWARE
POST OFFICE
FRIENDLY MARKET
MOLOKA'I DRUGS
KAMOI SNACK-N-GO
BALLPARK
SCHOOL
FIRE DEPARTMENT
POLICE
MITCHELL PAUOLE CENTER
COUNTY OFFICES
GYM
POOL
TENNIS COURTS
MOLOKAI GENERAL HOSPITAL
"DUKE" MALIN REGIONAL PARK

To West End
MAUNALOA HWY
To the Wharf
KAMEHAMEHA V HWY
To East End

SCALE NOT AVAILABLE

© AVALON TRAVEL

fence, it's not spectacular. This is a long way to go over a rough road just to see a shallow hole in the ground. Nevertheless, the Sandalwood Pit is a permanent reminder of the days of mindless exploitation when money and possessions were more important than land or people. Hawaiian chiefs had the pit dug to measure the amount of sandalwood necessary to fill the hold of a ship, and they traded the aromatic wood to Yankee captains for baubles, whiskey, guns, and tools. The traders carried the wood to China, where they made huge profits. The trading was so lucrative that the men of entire villages were forced into the hills to collect it, even to the point that the taro fields were neglected and famine gnawed at the door. It only took a few years to denude the mountains of their copious stands of sandalwood, which is even more incredible when you consider that all of the work was done by hand.

One mile after the Sandalwood Pit you'll reach the **Waikolu Overlook,** a precipitous, 3,700-foot drop-off where jagged cliff faces give way to the distant sea. In the days following a heavy rain the walls of the valley can explode with dozens of waterfalls, although you don't want to come up here during a heavy rain, since the valley will be socked in with clouds and you'll probably get stuck in the mud.

For most visitors, Waikolu Overlook is going to be as far as their vehicle will take them. To go farther is to head into the **Kamakou Preserve,** an incomparably lush jungle of ferns and native plants where 98 percent of the species are thought to be indigenous to the island. You're more than welcome to hike into the preserve; it's just that the road is so bad you not only need to have four-wheel drive, but you also need to be well-versed in using it. If you even attempt to drive this road in a 2WD vehicle, not only will you immediately get stuck, but your day will be ruined. It's 2.6 miles to the trailhead for the Pepe'opae Bog Trail, and despite the tough access, the best hiking and biking on the island is found high up in the hills.

Purdy's Na Hua O Ka 'Aina Farm (Macadamia Nut Farm)

One of the most popular visitor stops on the island is **Purdy's Na Hua O Ka 'Aina Farm**

© KYLE ELLISON

Kapuaiwa Coconut Grove in Kaunakakai

(808/567-6601, www.molokai.com/eatnuts, 9:30am-3:30pm Tues.-Fri., 10am-2pm Sat., free) behind the public high school on Lihi Pali Avenue near the homesteads of Ho'olehua. This is the only macadamia nut farm on the island. If there was ever anything you wanted to know about a macadamia nut, then you're going to learn it here. An informal tour led by the jovial owner will teach you not only how to crack open the hard nut, but also how the nuts are grown and how to pick out the good ones. Plus, there are no pesticides, herbicides, or any other chemicals coursing through this grove of 50 trees. Everything is all natural. Once the nuts drop down to the ground, it means it's time for roasting. While samples are included with the free tour, a small gift shop sells everything from macadamia nut honey to mac nut-themed clothing.

Ho'olehua "Post-A-Nut"

Never have kids loved going to the post office more than they do in Ho'olehua. A simple, one-room building in the middle of arid homesteading land, the **Ho'olehua Post Office** (Pu'u Pila Ave., 808/567-6144, 8:30am-4pm Mon.-Fri.) looks like something out of the days of the old Wild West. Seeing that there is a post office in neighboring Kualapu'u, you wonder what keeps this tiny outpost in business. The answer lies in something called the "Post-A-Nut," an artistic process whereby you can go to post office, decorate a dried out coconut, and then ship it off to anywhere across the globe where you think your art will be appreciated. The postmaster, Gary, is a certified agricultural inspector, making it legal for him to inspect and ship your nut. Rates to the mainland run $10-14, although the brown canvases have allegedly been shipped as far away as Kyrgyzstan, Namibia, and even the Antarctic.

Kumu Farms

Given the recent explosion of farm to table cuisine, you could be forgiven for thinking that **Kumu Farms** (Hua Ai Rd., 808/351-3326, www.kumufarms.com, 9am-4pm Tues.-Fri., free) is Moloka'i's "latest thing." On the

©KYLE ELLISON

Purdy's Na Hua O Ka'Aina Farm

small exhibit on Hawaiian artifacts as well as a basic gift shop, but where you're going to get your money's worth is watching the documentary videos and reading through old newspaper articles pertaining to life on the Kalaupapa Peninsula. On the same grounds behind the museum sits the **R.W. Meyer Sugar Mill,** which was constructed in 1878 during the island's short-lived sugar era. Although the former mill is listed on the National Register of Historic Places, creaky floors and rusted machinery add to the creepy atmosphere. It's a good thing this place closes at 2pm, because you wouldn't want to be stuck here at night.

Pala'au State Park

Above the residential town of Kala'e and past the mule barn, Highway 470 eventually dead-ends in the parking lot of **Pala'au State Park.** The park offers decent camping, and there are public restrooms available at the parking lot, although there is no potable water and very basic facilities. The air up here is noticeably cooler than down on the shoreline, and by the mid-morning hours the northeasterly trade winds are usually blowing when you head out toward Kalaupapa Overlook. To reach the lookout, follow the paved path at the edge of the parking lot until it reaches a terminus at a low rock wall perched at the edge of a cliff. From this vantage point you can take in unobstructed views of the town of Kalaupapa, the former leper settlement, which still houses a handful of patients. Unless you have booked a mule ride or plan to hike in to meet a tour group, this is the closest to Kalaupapa that you can get, so drink in the view and take a moment to reflect on what life on the peninsula must have been like.

Back at the parking lot, an unpaved trail leads 200 yards through a cool canopy of trees before emerging at a sacred spot by the name of **Ke Ule O Nanahoa,** also known as "Phallic Rock" for obvious reasons. According to legend, Nanahoa, the male god of fertility, once lived nearby in the forests surrounding Pala'au. One day when Nanahoa sat to admire a beautiful young girl who was looking at her reflection in a pool, Kawahua, Nanahoa's wife, became

contrary, this fully working farm has been growing crops in the Moloka'i dirt since 1981 and is the best place on the island to pick up a haul of fresh veggies straight from the *kumu,* or source. Not only can visitors peruse the outdoor market for certified organic and non-GMO produce, but you can also glean some expert culinary advice free of charge from recipes and cookbooks found sprinkled around the shop. Five minutes west of the airport on Hua Ai Road, an easy turn off Highway 460, this rapidly expanding farm now puts out over 20,000 pounds of papaya every week. Pick up a bag of frozen basil and macadamia nut pesto for a homemade pasta dinner unlike any in the islands.

Moloka'i Museum and Cultural Center

Off Highway 470, two miles north of Kualapu'u sits the **Moloka'i Museum and Cultural Center** (808/567-6436, 10am-2pm Mon.-Sat., $5 adult, $1 student), a simple museum predominantly focused on the history of Kalaupapa. There's a

© KYLE ELLISON

Pick up fresh produce at Kumu Farms.

so jealous that she attacked the young girl by yanking on her hair. Nanahoa became outraged in turn and struck his wife, who rolled over a nearby cliff before finally turning to stone. Nanahoa also turned to stone in the shape of an erect penis, and there he sits today still pointing toward the sky.

◖ KALAUPAPA PENINSULA

There was once a time when Kalaupapa wasn't shrouded in the stigma of leprosy. During the days of ancient Hawai'i, this northern peninsula was occupied by original settlers who lived in much the same way as those elsewhere in the state. All of that changed, however, when the first confirmed case of Hansen's disease was reported in Honolulu in 1848. Although those living in Kalaupapa at the time didn't know it, this remote peninsula on Moloka'i's northern shore would become an outpost of desperation and a place where the human spirit was tested on a daily basis.

Now registered as a National Historic Park, Kalaupapa is one of the most powerful day

trips you can take in the islands. There are three ways in to Kalaupapa (hike, mule ride, or fly). All require the services of **Damien Tours** (808/567-6171, 10am Mon.-Sat.) as your guides around what remains of the settlement. The cost of $50 is for those who choose to hike in on their own, and the fee is incorporated into the prices of the mule ride and air tours. All participants will spend a couple of hours learning the history of the isolated peninsula, and lunch is enjoyed at Kalawao—the first landing site of the original lepers at the base of Hawai'i's tallest sea cliffs. Visitors will also get the chance to visit **St. Philomena Church,** the house of worship from which Father Damien displayed his overwhelming courage in the face of insurmountable odds. From this humble Kalaupapa house of worship, you'll learn the story of how this Belgian-born priest improved the living conditions of patients and dedicated his life to their salvation and betterment.

Those wanting to ride in on a mule can contact **Moloka'i Mule Ride** (808/567-6088, www. muleride.com, 8am-3pm Mon.-Sat., must be over 16 years old and under 250 lbs., $199) for a switchbacking tour down the sea cliffs that ranks as one of the best adventures on the island.

For those who would prefer to fly in, **Pacific Wings** (808/567-6381 or 888/575-4546 toll free, www.pacificwings.com) and **Mokulele Airlines** (808/567-6381 Moloka'i or 866/260-7070 toll free, www.mokuleleairlines. com) offer flights connecting Honolulu and Kahului with topside in Ho'olehua, where you can catch a connecting flight with **Makani Kai Air Charters** (808/834-1111 or 877/255-8532, www.makanikaiair.com). If you are traveling from Honolulu, Makani Air offers flights directly to Kalaupapa. Space is limited on flights to Kalaupapa and prices and schedules change regularly, so inquire directly about current availability and rates. When booking a tour from an outer island, air tickets are often included as a package tour bundle. Unfortunately, it isn't possible to visit Kalaupapa as part of a day trip on the Lahaina to Moloka'i ferry.

Finally, hikers can drive 200 yards past the

MOLOKA'I

© KYLE ELLISON

Kalaupapa Peninsula

mule barn on Highway 470 past the town of Kala'e, and park on the right side of the road next to a locked metal gate. While you can arrange a permit in advance with Damien Tours for $50 (or potentially even pay cash at the bottom when you meet the tour guide at 10am), you can also play it safe and arrange a permit with Moloka'i Mule Ride, which will also include a light lunch for $69.

WEST MOLOKA'I

Ever since a group of wealthy Honolulu businesspeople purchased 70,000 acres of land in 1897, the western half of Moloka'i has been known as Moloka'i Ranch. Never completely steady, the ranch tried its hand at a number of different ventures for the next 111 years until finally succumbing in 2008 to public pressure over proposed development. The closing of the ranch's hospitality operations did away with 120 jobs, and in the years since, the area has yet to recover. During its tenure, the ranchland supported sugarcane, pineapples, sweet potatoes, wheat, cattle, safari tours, a luxury lodge,

an 18-hole golf course, a movie theater, and rustic accommodations on Kaupoa Beach colloquially known as "tentalows."

EAST MOLOKA'I

Since the arrival of the original Polynesians, the fertile valleys and shorelines of eastern Moloka'i have supported the majority of the island's population. The mountains provide freshwater for farming and pigs and deer to put on the dinner table. The lowlands and river valleys provide fertile ground for planting crops such as taro. The fishponds lining the shoreline provide a bounty from the sea which has been sustainably managed for more than 1,000 years. Many of the residents of eastern Moloka'i still maintain this subsistence-based lifestyle: the people serve as the stewards of the land and it, in turn, provides the people with the nourishment to live.

Given that eastern Moloka'i has historically been the population center, there are also a number of visitor sites which are worth your time. Many of the historical sites in this area have limited access due to their being situated

EXILES IN KALAUPAPA

With leprosy spreading at an alarming rate throughout the Hawaiian Islands, Kamehameha V in 1865 signed into law the Act to Prevent the Spread of Leprosy. Initially patients where quarantined at a hospital in Kalihi on the island of O'ahu, but it became evident that more space would be needed.

The remote Kalaupapa Peninsula –separated from the rest of Moloka'i by towering *pali* (cliffs) and buffeted on three sides by heaving surf– offered an isolated space to send the tortured souls rotting away from the horrible affliction. In 1866, the first leprosy patients were brought to the town of Kalawao on the peninsula's eastern shore. Those already living in Kalawao were told to vacate the area. Kalaupapa was never viewed as a place for lepers to live out their lives—it was a place for them to die.

Once someone was sent to Kalaupapa, there would be no return. The afflicted hid rather than be shipped away. Bounty hunters roamed the countryside. Babies, toddlers, teenagers, wives, grandfathers—none were immune. Anyone with any skin ailment was hounded, captured, and sometimes killed. Suspected lepers were torn from their families and villages and loaded onto a ship, where they were kept in cages open to the elements. They were allowed only one small tin box of possessions. When the ship anchored in the choppy bay at Kalawao, the victims were tossed overboard, followed by a few sealed barrels of food. Those too weak or sick to stay afloat drowned; the others swam to shore. The crew waited nervously with loaded muskets in case anyone attempted to return to the ship.

For the exiles who made landfall, life wasn't any easier. Women were raped. The elderly were beaten. They could try to escape over the mountains, but if they were caught, they would be sent back. Many unable to cope with the hellacious reality their life had become swam into the ocean clutching stones to carry them to the bottom.

Gradually life in Kalawao improved, but ever so slightly. Another settlement was established on the peninsula's western shore about a mile from Kalawao. A few volunteers who had not contracted leprosy served as *kokuas*, or caretakers, but some were so appalled by the living conditions that they turned back, leaving on the next steamship.

That is, until the arrival of Father Damien. The Belgian-born priest himself over to the betterment of living conditions for the exiles. Though he would eventually succumb to leprosy himself, Father Damien brought hope to a dark place.

In the 150 years which have passed, a treatment has been found for Hansen's disease which renders the afflicted noncontagious. In 1946, after 80 years of banishment to Kalaupapa, patients were free to leave. Most, however, chose to live out their years on the only sliver of land they had ever known. A handful of patients remain in Kalaupapa today. Many contracted the disease as children and are now advanced in years. It's likely that the last of the exiles will leave Kalaupapa in the next decade.

on private land. Out of respect for the landowners, places such as 'Ili'iliopae *heaiu* (the largest *heiau* on the island once used for human sacrifice) are not included here so as not to be disturbed.

Nevertheless, a day trip to the sites along the eastern end of the island can still be one of the best ways to spend a day on Moloka'i, as the views stretching back toward Maui are only amplified by the "main highway," which at some points nearly crumbles into the sea.

Life in eastern Moloka'i is relaxed, friendly, and refreshingly isolated, ticking along at its own slow place.

Ali'i Fishpond

Driving east from Kaunakakai, one of the first sites you will come to is **Ali'i Fishpond,** at mile marker 3 just before One Ali'i Beach Park. This 35-acre fishpond was originally constructed with rocks which had been hand-carried 10 miles over the adjacent mountain.

MOLOKA'I FISHPONDS

At one point in time there were no fewer than 60 stone fishponds lining the shoreline of Moloka'i's southern coast. Some of these have been restored and are in modern use. The locals who inhabit this area still fortify their diet in the same ways their ancestors have done for centuries. Constructed out of lava rock and large blocks of coral, the fishponds represent a system of aquaculture which serves as one of early Hawai'i's greatest feats of engineering. Most of the fishponds are believed to be between 700 and 800 years old, and although some have been overtaken by coastal mangroves, there are still a few which are open for public viewing. If you visit any fishponds during your time on Moloka'i, please be respectful of the cultural heritage they represent and don't walk on the walls or remove stones from the structures.

Having fallen into disrepair, the Ali'i Fishpond has been painstakingly brought back to life by *Ka Honua Momona,* a nonprofit organization dedicated to sustainable land practices on the island of Moloka'i. If you pull in to the parking lot and staff members are working on the property, they will be more than happy to show you around. Workers are usually here in the morning hours before the wind picks up, although if no one is around, it's best to admire the fishpond from afar.

View from the Heights

Even though the road parallels the southern coastline, from the vantage point of sea level it's difficult to find a good view. For a panoramic photo of the island's fringing reef, one of the best views is a few minutes east of One Ali'i Beach Park by driving to the top of Kawela Plantation, located on the *mauka,* or mountain side of the road. After turning into the Kawela Plantation I development, make your way down a plumeria-lined street. Take your first left and follow it until it dead-ends in a cul-de-sac. From this vantage point you can make out a large swath of the coastline, and this is your best coastal photo-op until you reach mile marker 20, where the road gets narrow and curvy.

St. Joseph's Church

For the seven-mile stretch past One Ali'i Beach Park along Highway 450, there are a number of historical sites such as Kawela (site of King Kamehameha's Moloka'i conquest) and Kamalo (the island's original wharf), but standing in them now, you would never know there was anything there. Plus, access is difficult, and unless you had someone pointing out the exact turn, you most likely would drive right by them. Small Kakahai'a Beach Park is little more than a picnic table on the shoreline. The first noticeable sight you will reach is **St. Joseph's Church** right around mile marker 10. Although Father Damien is famous for having reached out to the patients of Kalaupapa, he would also frequently make the arduous trek over the mountains down to the southern coastline where, in 1876, he constructed St. Joseph's Church as a place of Christian worship. There is a statue of Damien standing outside this small, recently restored building. Given the general lack of modern development, it isn't hard to imagine what the area would have looked like when the first nails of the church were pounded in 135 years ago. For a quick peek inside, check the doors; they are often unlocked. In an effort to convert Hawaiians to Christianity, it's believed that Father Damien purposely chose this spot in Kamalo to provide an alternative to the Puili *heiau,* which lies just inland.

Our Lady of Seven Sorrows Church

Also constructed by Father Damien in 1874,

FATHER DAMIEN

© KYLE ELLISON

By accident or miracle, Catholic priest Joseph de Veuster, Father Damien, came from Belgium to Hawai'i. His brother, also a priest, was originally slated for the trip, but he became ill and Father Damien took his place. Damien spent several years on the Big Island of Hawai'i, building churches and learning the language and ways of the people, before traveling to Kalaupapa in 1873.

What he saw touched his heart. Damien saw the lepers at Kalaupapa as children of God who deserved life and comfort. When they hid under a bush at his approach, he picked them up and stood them on their feet. He carried water to the sick and dying, bathed their wounds, and built them shelters with his own hands. When clothes or food or materials ran short, he walked topside to beg for more. Other church groups were against him and the government gave him little aid, but he persevered. Working long days alone, he collapsed exhausted at night.

Father Damien modified St. Philomena Church, originally built in Honolulu in 1872, and shipped it to Moloka'i in segments. He invited his charges inside, but those grossly afflicted could not control their mouths, so spittle would drip to the floor. They were ashamed to soil the church, so Damien cut squares in the floor through which they could spit onto the ground. Slowly, the authorities began to take notice. Damien eventually contracted leprosy himself, but he died in 1889 at age 49 knowing his people would be cared for. In 1936, Damien's native Belgium asked that his remains be returned. His body was exhumed and sent home, but a memorial still stands where he was once interred at Kalaupapa. After lengthy squabbles with the Belgian government, Father Damien's right hand was returned to Kalaupapa in 1995 and has been interred as a religious relic. He was beatified by Pope John Paul II in 1994 and canonized by Pope Benedict XVI in 2009.

Our Lady of Seven Sorrows Church sits on the inland side of Highway 450 14.5 miles east of Kaunakakai in the middle of an expansive field of finely cut grass. This is the more scenic of the two famous churches. Deep valleys form a rugged backdrop for the steeple, and coastal views stretch across the Ni'aupala fishpond to the island of Maui in the distance. Mass is still held on Sundays at 7am.

Pu'u O Hoku Ranch

Past the beaches of Waialua and Murphy's the road gets narrow and nearly runs into the sea. There are plenty of places along this ribbon of asphalt where it's a good idea to blow your horn as you come around a tight corner, and if you're ever feeling a little on the queasy side, there are a number of sandy coves perfect for pulling over and centering for a minute. It is true country living this far out on the island, and often you'll encounter groups of locals just hanging out, cruising, and taking life easy. Be sure you have more than a quarter tank of gas if you plan to venture farther, as there are no facilities as you continue heading east and it's a long hitch-hike if you run out of gas.

Once Highway 450 starts gaining in elevation, the sweeping pasturelands of **Pu'u O Hoku Ranch** (808/558-8109, www.puuohoku.com) begin coming into view. At this point you have driven so far north and east that it's possible to see the northern coastline of Maui. This 14,000-acre working ranch and farm dominates the eastern flank of the island. Although there used to be horseback riding at the ranch, too many liability claims have rendered the service inactive, although that doesn't mean the ranch doesn't still raise free-range cattle and embody the true *paniolo* lifestyle. There's a basic store at the ranch headquarters that sells local, organically grown produce and herbs such as kale, chard, eggplant, cherry tomatoes, and sweet apple bananas tiny enough to fit in the palm of your hand. The ranch is also one of the only places which grows and sells *'awa,* a traditional Polynesian herb known for its medicinal and painkilling properties. The ranch also has a number of accommodation options for couples looking to get away from it all or large groups in search of a team-building retreat.

◀ Halawa Valley

At the end of Highway 450, after utopian plantation homes, single-lane turns, the bluffs of the ranchlands, and heavily forested valleys, the road reaches a left hairpin turn where a cleft in the mountainside opens up like an amphitheater before you. This is **Halawa Valley.** Congratulations. You've made it. At the lookout, try to snap a shot of Moa'ula Falls toward the back of the valley, because this is the best view of it that you're going to have unless you're part of a guided hike.

This is believed by many to be the original landing site of Polynesians inhabiting Moloka'i (circa AD 650). There are some who say that visiting Halawa is like visiting another country, and in a lot of ways, they're right. This truly is the "old Hawai'i" out here, a place where mythology, lore, nature, and people all commune in a way not found back in "modern society." The handful of residents who still inhabit this valley live a subsistence-based lifestyle which in many ways parallels that of their original ancestors. Electricity is scarce, and taro *lo'i* (fields) weave their way up the verdant valley floor.

The two beaches in Halawa Bay are suitable for swimming. The cove accessed by walking across the streambed offers more protection and a soft, sandy bottom. Other than snapping photos and walking barefoot down the beach, the main visitor attraction in Halawa Valley is taking part in a guided hike to Moa'ula Falls. Permits are stringently required for hiking, and conversing with the local guides is the best (and only) way to feel the *mana,* or strength, of this valley.

Shopping

If your idea of a vacation well-spent is a day at the mall, jump off the ferry and start swimming back to Maui. Most shops on Moloka'i are utilitarian general stores, although there are some shops with worthy souvenirs.

KAUNAKAKAI

The good news about shopping in Kaunakakai is that you don't have to go far. All of the stores are on the same street, which means you can park your car on Ala Malama Avenue and use it as a base for scouring every shop in town.

As the name implies, **Imports Gift Shop** (82 Ala Malama Ave., 808/553-5734, 8am-6pm Mon.-Sat., 8am-1pm Sun.) offers a small selection of imported gifts and locally made items in addition to clothing, souvenirs, and snacks. **Kalele Bookstore and Divine Expressions** (64 Ala Malama Ave., 808/553-5112, www.molokaispirit.com, 10am-5pm Mon.-Fri., 9am-2pm Sat.) offers not only books, but also locally crafted artwork, jewelry, wooden bowls, and even just advice on touring Moloka'i. It's an eclectic and worthwhile stop if you are killing time while in town.

Moloka'i Art from the Heart (64 Ala Malama Ave., 808/553-8018, www.molokaigallery.com, 10am-5pm Mon.-Fri., 9am-2:30pm Sat.) is a consignment boutique where over 136 local artists are able to showcase and sell their products. You can find anything in here from sarongs to CDs to original paintings. It's a great stop for supporting the local community.

Across the street, **Moloka'i Fish and Dive** (61 Ala Malama Ave., 808/553-5926, www.molokaifishanddive.com, 7:30am-6pm Mon.-Sat., 8am-2pm Sun.) provides any basic gear you might need for the beach, as well as clothing, gear rentals, maps, or anything that has to do with a day in the sun.

Toward the wharf, upstairs from the American Savings Bank is **A Light from Heaven** (40 Ala Malama Ave., 808/553-3332,

9am-2pm Mon.-Sat.), a store specializing in any gear related to camping, hunting, fishing, or the outdoors.

On the more practical side, **Moloka'i Drugs** (28 Kamoi St., 808/553-5790, 8:45am-5:45pm Mon.-Fri., 8:45am-2pm Sat.) in the Kamoi Professional Center has you covered for any medicinal or prescription needs while on the island.

TOPSIDE

When it comes to shopping up on the topside of the island, there are only two options. Across the street from the Kualapu'u Cookhouse in the Kualapu'u Business Center is **Moloka'i Furniture and Denise's Gifts** (100 Kalae Hwy., 808/567-6083, 10am-4pm Mon.-Fri., 9am-2pm Sat.) which sells, as you might expect, fine wooden furniture as well as jewelry, women's clothing, and locally made crafts.

Adjoining the Coffees of Hawaii Espresso Bar across the street, the **Blue Monkey** (1630 Farrington Ave., 808/567-6776, 10am-4pm Mon.-Sat., 1pm-5pm Sun.) gift shop sells a fun-loving mix of everything from ukuleles to photography to handmade jewelry or hats.

WEST MOLOKA'I

With the 2008 closing of Moloka'i Ranch, a lot of Maunaloa businesses just up and closed with them. Given the commercial exodus from the western half of the island, the options for shopping are limited.

A Maunaloa staple which has been around since 1980, the **Big Wind Kite Factory** (120 Maunaloa Hwy., 808/552-2364, www.bigwindkites.com, 8:30am-5pm Mon.-Sat., 10am-2pm Sun.) is an eclectic hodgepodge of everything from handmade kites to woodwork from Bali. Plus, it's the only store left in this town, so by process of elimination it's well worth a look. The owner Jonathan is only too happy to give free factory tours of where the kites are made, help you fly a kite in the park, or even make a free kite for any children you may be toting along with you. The store also sports the largest collection of book titles found anywhere on the island. It's possible to visit this place four times over and still find something new. Just look for the rainbow stairs in what little is left of downtown Maunaloa.

Curiously ensconced among the abandoned buildings of the former Sheraton right next to the Kaluakoi Villas, **A Touch of Moloka'i** (1121 Kaluakoi Rd., 808/552-0133, 9am-5pm daily) is a basic sundry store good for procuring a few postcards, some snacks, various clothing items, but nothing of immense value. Nevertheless, seeing as it's the only store in the Kaluakoi complex, it's better than driving into town.

More of a grocery market than anything else, **Maunaloa General Store** (200 Maunaloa Hwy., 808/552-2346, 9am-6pm Mon.-Sat.,

9pm-noon Sun.) does sell a few basic clothing items such as vintage boardshorts made out of rice bags and any basic hardware supplies you might need. The pickings are slim inside this one-room market, and if there's anything specific you're looking for, there's a good chance you'll need to find it back in town.

EAST MOLOKA'I

The pickings out here can be remarkably slim. If you need any basic item, general store **Mana'e Goods & Grindz** (mile marker 16 on Hwy. 450, 808/558-8498, 6:30am-4pm Mon.-Fri., 7:30am-4:30pm Sat.-Sun.) is your only option. Farther up the road toward Halawa Valley, you need to be in dire need to warrant shopping at the **Pu'u O Hoku Ranch Store.** Not that it's bad by any means, just that the selection can be random and thin.

Entertainment

You know where most of the local people go to get their fix of nightlife? Las Vegas. After that it's Honolulu, then Maui. Most of the entertainment on Moloka'i is of the live music variety, and that usually means that it's going to be traditional island music played in a *kanikapila* style (island jam session, get-together, talk story, etc.). Witnessing a live jam session can be captivating and a true island experience.

DAYTIME ENTERTAINMENT

While there can often be impromptu ukulele sessions which pop up during the weekdays on the porch outside of the **Coffees of Hawaii Espresso Bar** (1630 Farrington Ave., 6am-5pm Mon.-Fri., 8am-8pm Sat., 8am-5pm Sun.), Sunday afternoons are when things on this laid-back wooden deck get hopping. Hawaiian and contemporary music is played live 3pm-5pm, so this is the de facto social gathering for a late Sunday afternoon.

The **Kualapu'u Cookhouse** (102 Farrington Ave., 808/567-9655, 7am-8pm Mon.-Sat.,

9am-8pm Sun.) also has live music on Thursday afternoons at 5pm to accompany the weekly dinner specials.

EVENING SHOWS

The longest running and most iconic show on the island is the performance of Na Kupuna 4pm-6pm on Friday afternoons at **Hotel Moloka'i** (1300 Kamehameha V Hwy., 808/660-3397, www.hotelmolokai. com). *Kupuna* is a Hawaiian word meaning elder, and children are taught that *kupuna* are to be revered and treated with respect—something easy to do when it comes to the musical capabilities of the island's most well-known band. Sit out on the well-manicured grounds of the hotel and enjoy a mai tai or a Longboard Lager while listening to these guys play. They offer more than simply music; the personal anecdotes, humorous stories, and island-style banter that accompany the songs all combine to make a Na Kupuna performance the best evening on Moloka'i.

BARS

Even on sleepy Moloka'i there is still "ladies night." Once the late afternoon ukulele performances are through and you feel like a few more beers, **Paddler's Inn** (10 Mohala St., 808/553-3300, 11:30am-11pm Mon.-Sun) is the closest thing that you're going to get to a sports bar or a dance hall on all of Moloka'i. On the side of the highway in downtown Kaunakakai, you'll find this place with a couple of pool tables occupying the interior while a full-service bar sits in the outside lanai. There

are live bands some nights of the week, top 40 music on others.

Other than Paddler's, the only other option in town is the bar at **Hotel Moloka'i** (1300 Kamehameha V Hwy., 808/660-3397, www.hotelmolokai.com). While a kitchen fire closed the restaurant for 2013 and the bar currently closes early, once the restaurant reopens in 2014, the bar will be moved to the ocean side of the resort and potentially stay open until 2am. Inquire with the hotel about the current status.

Food

Kaunakakai has a varied selection of food. The same can't be said once you get outside town: there are only three restaurants outside the main drag.

KAUNAKAKAI
Local Style

As a restaurant, **C Kanemitsu Bakery** (79 Ala Malama Ave., 808/553-5855, 5:30am-6:30pm Tues.-Sun., $5-9) is no better or worse than anywhere else in town. Breakfast consists of fried eggs, spam, and rice, and lunch includes standard plate lunch fare such as chicken katsu or hamburger steak. All plate lunches are of course served with the staple sides of two-scoop rice and macaroni salad in an aging interior. The best part of this hole-in-the-wall eatery isn't the food that's served during the day, however, it's what comes hot out of the oven late at night. Like some sort of crazed drug fiend, once you've had a taste of Kanemitsu's famous "hot bread" you, too, will find yourself walking down the dark alleyway at 9 or 10pm to the back door of the shuttered restaurant. Here, assembled in the dark, a crowd of local people vie nightly for their fix of Kanemitsu's addictive hot bread, so much so that the dingy alleyway is known as "Hot Bread Lane." Taking a trip down Hot Bread Lane is one of the most authentic local experiences on the island.

Elsa's Kitchen (17 Ala Malama Ave.,

808/553-9068, 11am-8:30pm Mon.-Fri., 11am-9pm Sat., $9-11) serves up local favorites such as a shoyu chicken plate lunch, vegetable stir-fry, or a popular Filipino noodle dish known as *pancit*. Eat in or takeaway.

On the corner of the Highway 450, **Moloka'i Drive Inn** (857 Ala Malama Ave., 808/553-5655, 6am-10pm daily, $5-9) serves up budget, local-style meals for breakfast, lunch, and dinner. Need a heaping breakfast mound of spam, eggs, and rice? This is your place. Lunch items such as chicken sandwiches, plate lunches, or any other of your moderately unhealthy but oh-so tasty local food options are also available.

American

After the kitchen fire that broke out at the Hula Shores Restaurant at Hotel Moloka'i, **C Paddler's Inn** (10 Mohala St., 808/553-3300, 11:30am-9pm daily, $10-18) for the foreseeable future is about the only place you can go for dinner and also shoulder up to the bar. Strip steaks, rib plates, and salmon or mahimahi filets round out the entrée menu, and the Mexican Mondays are as close as you're going to get to Mexican food anywhere on Moloka'i. This place has nightly music on the patio, pool tables inside, and good vibes all around.

Even sleepy Kaunakakai has to have its token burger joint, and the patties at **Moloka'i Burger**

(20 Kamehameha V Hwy., 808/553-3533, 7am-9pm daily, $5) don't disappoint. Little more than a drive-through shed right next door to Moloka'i Pizza Café, this place has budget burgers big enough to properly fill you up. For a local treat, skip the bun and instead spring for a loco moco, a hamburger patty served with two eggs, white rice, and gravy.

And just as every town has to have its token burger joint, every town has to have a *second* burger joint so people can banter about which is better. Only two blocks away from Moloka'i Burger, **Maka's Korner** (35 Mohala St., 808/553-8058, 7am-9pm Mon.-Fri., 9am-1pm Sat., $5-8) is a hole-in-the-wall takeout counter serving up burgers which melt in your mouth. Try the mushroom burger. It's *mo' bettah*. Though the $5 burgers are a great choice, the saimin noodle bowls are a hearty alternative perfect on a cool Kaunakakai night.

Kamoi Snack-n-Go (28 Kamoi St., 808/553-3742, 11am-9pm Mon.-Fri., 9am-9pm Sat., noon-9pm Sun.) has made a name for itself with the best ice cream you're going to find anywhere in town: Heaping double scoops of flavors such as coconut and macadamia nut. There's also free Wi-Fi.

Natural Foods

If you're in need of a little health in your diet after all of the plate lunches and spam musubis, **Outpost Natural Foods** (70 Makaena Pl., 808/553-3377, 9am-6pm Sun.-Fri.) offers a basic selection of fresh produce, energy bars, bulk grains, healthy lunch options, or a cold drink. This is also a great place to pick up some all-natural ginger candies for what is usually a stomach-churning ferry ride back to Maui.

Pizza

The undisputed place where Moloka'i heads for a slice is **Moloka'i Pizza Café** (15 Kaunakakai Pl., 808/553-3288, 10am-10pm Mon.-Thurs., 10am-11pm Fri.-Sat., 11am-10pm Sun., $10-16), in the last building before you start heading down the road to the ferry dock. Pizzas are served either whole or

by the slice ($2.50). There's also a decent selection of pasta dishes.

Filipino

Big Daddy's (67 Ala Malama Ave., 808/553-5841, 8am-6pm daily, under $9) along the main strip of Ala Malama serves a variety of inexpensive Filipino food and Hawaiian fare, in addition to the eggs and omelets for breakfast and local-style plate lunches. Next door is Big Daddy's Market for a limited selection of groceries, some prepared foods, and a few true Filipino delicacies such as *balut*.

Coffee Shop

Anyone visiting **Tiki's Coffee Shack** (35 Mohala St., 808/553-3488, 6:30am-6pm Mon.-Fri., 8am-2pm Sat., 9am-noon Sun., $6-10) will find a casual blend of metropolitan sophistication with the laid-back island flavor of Moloka'i. Relax in the downtown parlor with free Wi-Fi while sipping on coffee grown just up the road in Kualapu'u. Gourmet sandwiches and paninis are popular lunch items with as many ingredients as possible sourced here on island.

Markets

Given the lackluster evening activities on the island, there's a joke among locals that if you're looking for a place to hang out at night just go down to the **Friendly Market** (Ala Malama Ave., 8:30am-8:30pm Mon.-Fri. 8:30am-6:30pm Sat.), because everyone is going to be there anyway. It's stays open later than most places on the island.

If for some reason the Friendly Market doesn't have what you need, then **Misaki's Groceries and Dry Goods** (Ala Malama Ave., 8:30am-8:30pm Mon.-Sat., 9am-noon Sun.) a few doors down should be able to fill the gap.

FARMERS MARKET

If you're in town on Saturday morning, visit the **farmers market** held 7am-noon on the sidewalk in front of the bank buildings for local produce and craft items. This seems as much of a social event as a shopping exercise for locally grown food.

TOPSIDE
Local Style
The biggest culinary staple on the topside of the island, **(** **Kualapu'u Cookhouse** (1700 Farrington Ave., 808/567-9655, 7am-2pm Mon., 7am-8pm Tues.-Sat., 9am-2pm Sun., $8-11) is a plate-lunch institution where the going is easy and life moves nice and slow. Order inside at the drab counter, but go ahead and sit outside on the open-air lanai. When your food is ready, that's when you're going to get it. No sooner. No later. No worries. Try the chicken katsu or hamburger steak. Live Hawaiian music on Thursday evenings at 5pm fills out the area's lone entertainment, and on Thursdays it isn't uncommon to have a prime rib special suddenly spring on to the menu.

Coffee Shop
Although the Coffees of Hawaii plantation

© KYLE ELLISON

Mana'e Goods & Grindz is one of the only stores on the east end of the island.

used to have a bustling operation which included tours of the plantation and the coffee making process, all that remains now is the **Coffees of Hawaii Espresso Bar** (1630 Farrington Ave., 6am-5pm Mon.-Fri., 8am-8pm Sat., 8am-5pm Sun.) and the self-guided informative tour on the outdoor deck. By process of elimination this is the happening spot to grab a coffee, mocha, guava pretzel, baked item, ice cream, or any other sort of snack you could possibly be craving. The coffee here is grown right across the street, and the sprawling front porch has been known to host impromptu ukulele jam sessions among the affable island locals.

WEST MOLOKA'I
The good news when it comes to finding food in western Moloka'i is that you don't have to think hard about where you want to go. To be fair, even the **Maunaloa General Store** (200 Maunaloa Hwy., 808/552-2346, 9am-6pm Mon.-Sat., 9am-12pm Sun.) is a stretch in that it's just a supermarket. With the Moloka'i Ranch having shuttered its operations, there's nothing on this side of the island which could be considered an actual restaurant, but if you want to put together a picnic for the beach, then the general store will more than suffice.

EAST MOLOKA'I
The only restaurant on the east end, the **(** **Mana'e Goods & Grindz** (mile marker 16 on Hwy. 450, 808/558-8498, 6:30am-4pm Mon.-Fri., 7:30am-4:30pm Sat.-Sun., $6-9) takeout window which accompanies the general store serves up everything from chicken katsu plates to freshly made fruit smoothies. If the banana pancakes happen to be on the menu, don't even hesitate. Just order them.

While the selection is thin, in addition to the random articles of clothing and various sundries, the **Pu'u O Hoku Ranch Store** (mile marker 25 off Hwy. 450, 808/558-8109, 9am-5pm Mon.-Fri.) sells a slew of organic fruits and vegetables as well as locally grown beef raised right on the ranch.

MOLOKA'I

Information and Services

IMPORTANT PHONE NUMBERS

Telephone numbers for service agencies that you might find useful while on Moloka'i are emergency: 911; police: 808/553-5355; County Parks and Recreation: 808/553-3204; State Parks: 808/567-6923; and the State Division of Forestry: 808/553-1745.

INFORMATION

The **Moloka'i Visitors Association** (2 Kamoi St., 808/553-5221, mvafrontoffice@gmail.com, 9am-noon Mon.-Fri.) can help with every aspect of your trip to Moloka'i. From its office along the main highway, it dispenses up-to-the-minute information on accommodations, transportation, dining, activities, and services, and some brochures and island maps. For additional general and specific information about the island, try the following private websites: www.molokai-aloha.com, www.molokai.com, and www.visitmolokai.com. Also see the Moloka'i Chamber of Commerce website at www.molokaichamber.org.

MEDICAL SERVICES

Moloka'i is a small place with a small population, so there is not as much available here in the way of medical treatment as on Maui or the other larger islands. **Moloka'i General Hospital** (808/553-5331) is at the end of Home' Olu Street just above Ala Malama Avenue in Kaunakakai, and there are half a dozen doctors on the island and half as many dentists.

For prescription drugs, first-aid items, potions, lotions, and sundries, try **Moloka'i Drugs** (808/553-5790, 8:45am-5:45pm Mon.-Fri., 8:45am-2pm Sat.) in the Kamoi Professional Center, one block off the main drag in Kaunakakai.

NEWSPAPERS

For a local look at what's happening on Moloka'i, check out the island's weekly newspaper *The Moloka'i Dispatch* (www.themolokaidispatch.com). Those looking for an online source can find the frequently updated news blog *The Moloka'i News* (www.themolokainews.com).

BANKS

There are only two banks on the island, and they are right next to each other in downtown Kaunakakai. **Bank of Hawaii** (8:30am-4pm Mon.-Fri., 8:30am-6pm Sat.) on the corner across from the Chevron station has an ATM; **American Savings Bank** (8am-5pm Mon.-Thurs., 8am-6pm Fri., 8am-noon Sat.) downstairs in the Moloka'i Center also has an ATM.

GAS

There are only two gas stations on the island—right next to each other in Kaunakakai. Be sure you have at least half a tank of fuel before heading out on an adventurous day trip to Halawa or Papohaku. Of the two stations, **Rawlins Chevron** (Hwy. 450 and Kaunakakai Pl., 6:30am-8:30pm Mon.-Thurs., 6:30am-9pm Fri.-Sat., 6:30am-6pm Sun.) has longer hours and more supplies, though it still will cost you more per gallon than back on Maui.

POST OFFICE

The main post office in Kaunakakai is at 120 Ala Malama Avenue on the far eastern end of the downtown strip. It's open Monday-Friday from 9am-3:30pm and on Saturday from 9am-11am. There are also small post offices in Maunaloa, Kualapu'u, and the famous "Post-A-Nut" office in Ho'olehua.

LIBRARY

The **Moloka'i Public Library** (808/553-1765, noon-8pm Mon. and Wed., 9am-5pm Tues., Thurs., and Fri.) is next to the Chevron station in Kaunakakai across the street from the Bank of Hawaii.

LAUNDRY

Friendly Isle Laundromat (15 Kaunakakai Pl., 808/553-5177, 7am-9pm daily) in Kaunakakai is right next to Moloka'i Pizza Café in the last building before the wharf.

Getting There and Around

GETTING THERE
Plane
When flying to Moloka'i there are two things you shouldn't expect: a big plane and a smooth ride. Most airlines employ either 9- or 37-seat aircraft vulnerable to the brisk trade winds, although what the flights lack in size they make up for in scenery. Often flights from Maui will treat visitors to views of Moloka'i's dramatic northern sea cliffs as well as aerial views of the Kalaupapa Peninsula. Sit on the left side of the aircraft for the best chance of waterfall photography and coastal views. These flights may require you to step on a scale with your bags, so leave the five-piece luggage set at home.

Mokulele Airlines (808/567-6381 Moloka'i or 866/260-7070 toll free, www.mokuleleairlines.com) offers direct flights to Honolulu and Kahului, although any other city will require a connecting flight. **Pacific Wings** (808/567-6381 or 888/575-4546 toll free, www.pacificwings.com) offers direct flights from Honolulu and Kahului to Ho'olehua and can also provide connecting service to cities farther afield. In addition to providing direct service to Kahului and Honolulu, **Island Air** (808/567-6840 Moloka'i or 800/652-6541 toll free, www.islandair.com) is the only commercial airline also offering direct service between Ho'olehua and the island of Lana'i. Of the three operators, Island Air employs the largest airplanes and is less likely to be fully booked.

In late 2013, **Ohana** (800/367-5620, www.hawaiianairlines.com/ohana), a new airline operated by Hawaiian Airlines, plans to increase service to both Lana'i and Moloka'i. No time tables were available at the time of publication, but travelers in 2014 and beyond should benefit from this additional option.

For private flightseeing and helicopter flights, **Makani Kai Air Charters** (808/834-5813 or 877/255-8532, www.makanikaiair.com) operates between Moloka'i, Lana'i, and O'ahu, and also has service between Kalaupapa and Ho'olehua. **Kukui Air** (808/558-8407, www.kukuiair.com) focuses exclusively on Moloka'i and runs hour-long scenic flights departing out of Ho'olehua Airport.

Moloka'i Airport
The airport at Ho'olehua is a small, open-air facility where you still walk out on the runway to board your plane. It's a throwback to what the larger airports of Kahului and Kona once were. Here in Ho'olehua many airlines still opt for calling roll by first-name rather than handing out tickets. There is one small gift shop and a small coffee shop selling snacks and locally grown coffee, though I wouldn't plan on showing up three hours before my flight and having many things to do. There is an Alamo rental car counter at the terminal, taxis patrol outside, and tour companies all offer pickup for those arriving with a previously scheduled reservation.

FERRY
Compared to flights from Kahului, the **Moloka'i Ferry** (877/500-6284, www.molokaiferry.com) is often slightly less expensive but takes longer—and there is a greater chance that you'll throw up in a bag. Due to a recent approval of a fuel surcharge, one-way fares are now $64 for adults and $32 for children. Usually discounts can be found when buying tickets in batches of six.

Bad news aside, the ferry is a more economical option when traveling with children and allows you to bring on more luggage. Running twice-daily between Kahului and Kaunakakai

MOLOKA'I

Harbors, the boat most often used is the *Moloka'i Princess,* a 100-foot-long, two-story vessel capable of navigating the brutally rough Pailolo Channel, a name which directly translates to "crazy fisherman" in reference to those who voluntarily head out into the channel. The ride takes 1.25 hours and may be rough, but it's safe and it will get you there. To avoid seasickness, take preventative medication or a natural remedy such as ginger candy. Ferries depart from Kaunakakai Monday-Saturday at 5:15am and 4pm, with Lahaina departures running Monday-Saturday at 7:15am and 6pm. A Sunday crossing departs Moloka'i for Lahaina at 4pm and departs Lahaina for Molokai at 6pm.

For those only visiting for the day, rental cars can be combined with a round-trip ferry ticket through the **Moloka'i Ferry** (877/500-6284, www.molokaiferry.com) Cruise and Car Package with a shuttle transporting you from the Kaunakakai Wharf to your rental vehicle. Rates run $245 for a driver 25 years of age or older, and $145 for each additional adult. Children are $55 from 4-12 and under 4 is free.

Moloka'i Outdoors (808/553-4477, www.molokai-outdoors.com) also offers an Ali'i Tour package which includes a round-trip ferry ticket from Maui and a six-hour guided tour in an air-conditioned van once on the island. Rates for adults are $190 and $127 for children.

GETTING AROUND
Car Rental
The only rental car agency with a booth in the airport is **Alamo** (808/567-6381 or 888/826-6893 toll free, www.alamo.com, 6am-8pm daily), which also has the largest fleet of cars on the island. For those staying a minimum of three days, **Moloka'i Outdoors** (808/553-4477, www.molokai-outdoors.com) rents SUVs, cars, and vans, and can provide cheaper rates for extended stays. If you've taken the ferry, check the Cruise and Car Package deal offered by the **Moloka'i Ferry** (877/500-6284, www.molokai-ferry.com).

Taxi
Best known as a conduit between the airport, ferry, and wherever it is you're staying, **Hele Mai Taxi** (808/336-0937 or 808/646-9060, www.molokaitaxi.com) also offers private tours of the island and will get you wherever you need to go 24 hours a day, seven days a week. Also available is **Mid-Nite Taxi** (808/658-1410 or 808/553-5652), although the service can be a little spottier at times.

Shuttle Bus
The closest thing to public transportation on all of Moloka'i, the **MEO public shuttle bus** operates three routes throughout the island at times which are just frequent enough to make it convenient. Service in Kaunakakai originates in front of Misaki's Market on Ala Malama Street and runs six times daily to Maunaloa and eight times daily to Puko'o in East Moloka'i. Along the routes the driver will usually let you stop off wherever you please. Though the service is technically free, donations to keep the shuttle going are graciously accepted. Exact schedules can be found by visiting http://meo-inc.charityfinders.org.

Tours
For visitors staying on the island without their own transportation, **Moloka'i Outdoors** (808/553-4477, www.molokai-outdoors.com) offers an Island Tour package which scours the island from Halawa Lookout all the way to Papohaku Beach. Operating three times per week, these tours cover the island in an air-conditioned van and usually carry a small group of only 4-8 people. Rates for the island tour run $150 for adults and $78 for children.

WHERE TO STAY

With so many options, finding accommodations in Maui can be overwhelming. If you're planning on doing a lot of activities and spending most of your time away from the hotel, it might be worth basing yourself in something more moderately priced to free up some budget for activities. On the other hand, if all you want to do is relax by the pool for a week, then by all means splurge on a fancy resort. Understand, however, that when looking at prices, rates will also include state taxes of 13.42 percent when you go to check out, and some larger resorts can also charge a resort fee. Condos are great because you can cook your own meals, but read the fine print to see if there is an additional cleaning fee. Since Maui is spread out, consider spending your time in two separate accommodations instead of being tied to one area.

CONDOS AND VACATION RENTALS

Condos, more so than any other option, comprise the largest percentage of island rooms and vacation rental options. Condos are great because they provide the opportunity to cook your own meals. While they often appear to be affordable at first, pay attention to the fine print regarding **cleaning fees, parking,** and **minimum stays.** Rates fluctuate with seasons: during the slower season (usually April 16-December 14), prices can often be 20-40 percent lower than during the high season.

In a search for a condo or vacation rental home, there are dozens of island rental agencies that will help you find the right spot. Before you make the call, however, **www.vrbo.com** should be your first stop for researching condo

© HEATHER ELLISON

options. Most condos on the island are listed on the site, and you can often find better rates by booking directly through the owners. Other useful resources are **www.vacationrentals.com** and **www.mauiaccommodations.com.,**

That said, rental agents can offer deals that online websites can't. In South Maui, **Condominium Rentals Hawaii** (362 Huku Li'i Pl., 808/879-2778, www.crhmaui.com) can arrange your stay in nine different condos across Kihei. For more options, **AA Oceanfront Condo Rentals** (1279 S. Kihei Rd., 808/879-7288, www.aaoceanfront.com) manages properties from North Kihei to Makena, economy to deluxe. For even more options, **Kumulani Vacations and Realty** (115 E. Lipoa St., Ste #205, 808/879-9272, www.kumulani.com) handles rentals in more than a dozen condos in Kihei and Wailea. **Ali'i Resorts** (128 Kio Lp., 808/879-6284, www.aliiresorts.com) matches visitors to condo units from Kihei to Makena, basic to luxury.

In West Maui, one of the best rental agencies to check out is **Maui Travel Partners** (808/665-3345, www.mauicondo4rent.com) who can help you book a room at one of over 40 different West Side condo complexes. Owners Marie and Terry are active in the local environmental community and exhibit a care for the island, and this is a great first resource for talking with someone about finding the perfect Maui rental. Other reputable agencies that can help you find a West Side condo include **Maui Beachfront** (256 Papalaua St., 808/661-3500, www.mauibeachfront.com), **Sullivan Properties** (10 Ho'ohui Rd., 808/669-0423, www.mauiresorts.com), and **Chase'N Rainbows** (118 Kupuohi St., 808/667-7088, www.westmauicondos.com).

In East Maui, **Hana's Finest Rentals** (www.hanasfinestrentals.com) is a group of Hana vacation rental owners who provide a number of different options, and **Island Style Vacations** (808/264-2302, www.islandstylevacations.com) can help you find a vacation rental house in Pa'ia or Ha'iku.

Lana'i and Moloka'i similarly offer vacation agencies who are a great source of finding local accommodations. On Lana'i, inquire with **Okamoto Realty** (808/559-0200, www.homesonlanai.com) about any of their homes which are open for short-term rentals. On Moloka'i, **Moloka'i Vacation Properties** (808/553-8334, www.molokai-vacation-rental.net) is one of the island's best resources for managing condo rentals. For another option, inquire with **Friendly Isle Realty** (808/553-3666, www.molokairealty.com) about their large selection of vacation rentals across the island.

CAMPING

While there are a number of "unofficial" camping spots frequented by locals, I only list those spots where it's legal to camp. Anyone can camp anywhere at any time as long as they are fishing. If you throw a fishing line in the water, you can pitch a tent along much of the shoreline free of charge.

For proper campgrounds with facilities, however, county park camping permits are obtained through the **Department of Parks and Recreation** (808/270-7389), and contact information for each office is available on the website at www.co.maui.hi.us. Fees are $5 per adult per night ($2 per child per night), and camping permits are issued for the parks found below. Papalaua and Papohaku are the only two I recommed; Papalaua is closed for camping on Thursdays.

- Kanaha Beach Park

- Papalaua Beach Park

- One Ali'i Beach Park (Moloka'i)

- Papohaku Beach Park (Moloka'i)

Camping is also available at various locations inside **Haleakala National Park** (808/572-4400, www.nps.gov/hale). In the summit section of the park, no permits are needed for camping at Hosmer's Grove, and within the crater itself, camping is available by free permit at Holua, Kapalaoa, and Paliku wilderness campgrounds. Permits are to be picked up at the Haleakala visitor's center, and all wilderness campers will need to watch an 8-minute orientation video. For all campers, there is a maximum of three nights in each 30-day period. In the Kipahulu section of the park, camping is available for $10 per vehicle.

Camping within state parks is also available at the following locations:

• Wai'anapanapa State Park

• Polipoli Spring State Recreation Area

• Pala'au State Park (Moloka'i)

• Waikolu (Moloka'i)

Fees for camping in state parks are $18/campsite for nonresidents and $12/campsite for Hawai'i residents. Permits can be obtained either by calling 808/984-8109 or making a reservation online at www.camping.ehawaii.gov, though you will need to create a free account. Print out your permit and bring it with you, as some of the parks won't accept electronic copies.

For camping on Lana'i at Hulopo'e Beach Park, permits are available from the ranger at park. Fees are $30 for the campsite and $15 per person per night, with a maximum stay of three nights.

West Maui

KAPALUA, NAPILI, AND HONOKOWAI
Over $150

The largest, most well-known resort on the northwestern side of the island is the lavish **Ritz-Carlton Kapalua** (1 Ritz-Carlton Dr., 808/669-6200 www.ritzcarlton.com, $400), an exquisitely manicured luxury resort set back from D.T. Fleming Beach. The resort offers what you've come to expect of a Ritz-Carlton, and there are also a number of cultural and environmental programs such as the acclaimed Ambassadors of the Environment. While it can often be windy and wet here, many of the showers pass quickly, although it is still wetter than downtown Lahaina. Rates begin around $400 and work their way up from there.

Condominiums

Occupying much of the point between Napili and Kapalua Bays, the **C Napili Kai Beach Resort** (5900 Lower Honoapi'ilani Rd., 808/669-6271, www.napilikai.com, $270-500) is a West Side classic that offers individually owned condos in a family-friendly resort setting. Since the rooms are pricey, this is a great option for families whose goal is to largely stay in one place and do little more than play on the beach. The resort is steps from Napili Bay, there is a miniature putting course, multiple swimming pools, and weekly mai tai parties. The Sea House restaurant has one of the best breakfasts and happy hours on the island. Many of the units have been recently renovated and are the nicest they've ever been.

If the price of the Napili Kai is too steep, yet you still want to be on Napili Bay, the **Napili Village** (5425 Lower Honoapi'ilani, 808/669-6228, www.napilivillage.com, $149) offers condos within walking distance that are the best value in Napili. Rates can be as low as $99/night during slower seasons of the year (but are regularly $149), and these studios and one-bedroom apartments include air-conditioning, maid service, and full kitchens for those who want to cook their own meals. The rooms aren't as luxurious as some of the other options on the beach, but it's hard to argue with the price for being steps from Napili Bay.

In Kahana, **Kahana Falls** (4260 Lower Honoapi'ilani Rd., 808/669-1050, www.thesandsofkahana.com, $99-250) is one of the largest complexes in the area and features a large fitness center, spacious rooms, and hot tubs with sandy bottoms. It's only a five-minute drive to Napili or Kapalua Bay, and the small

WHERE TO STAY

© KYLE ELLISON

Napili Kai Beach Resort

beach at Pohaku Beach Park is walking distance away.

In Honokowai, the **Maui Kai** (106 Ka'anapali Shores Pl., 808/667-3500, www.mauikai.com, $200-400) is at the edge of Honokowai and Ka'anapali, so it's possible to take a long morning stroll down the beach to the center of the Ka'anapali strip. All units have full kitchens, free parking, free Wi-Fi, gas barbecues, and the convenience of being just steps from the beach. This is a good place for families who want to base themselves near Ka'anapali but save a few dollars from the steep resort prices.

Camping

Camping is permitted at **Punalau Beach,** just north of Honolua Bay on the northwest coast on land owned by Maui Land and Pineapple Company. This is primitive camping—there are *no* facilities, and while no reservations are necessary, a permit is. Camping permits are issued by the company office (4900 Honoapi'ilani Hwy., 808/669-6201, Mon.-Fri. 6:30am-2:30pm), which is across the highway

from Napili Plaza and Napilihau Street. Fees are $5 per party with a three-night maximum. I've never heard of anyone actually getting a citation, but it's always best to be on the right side of the law.

KA'ANAPALI
Over $150
All hotels in the Ka'anapali resort fit in the luxury category.

As their slogan says, (◖ **Ka'anapali Beach Hotel** (2525 Ka'anapali Pkwy., 808/661-0011, www.kbhmaui.com, $165-325) is truly Maui's most Hawaiian hotel. A genuine feeling of *aloha* permeates this laid-back resort, and while nowhere near as lavish as its fellow Ka'anapali neighbors, KBH occupies prime oceanfront real estate a two-minute stroll from Pu'u Keka'a (Black Rock). The open lawn is the perfect place to relax in the shade of an *ulu* tree, and while there is no hot tub, there is a swimming pool next to the popular tiki bar which is a welcoming place for families. On the lawn, there is an outrigger sailing canoe crafted by the employees of the resort, and free hula shows are held each night on the hotel's outdoor stage. Guests are made to feel like *ohana,* and the rates are much more affordable than larger resorts along the strip.

Right in front of Pu'u Keka'a is the 510-room **Sheraton Maui Resort** (2605 Ka'anapali Pkwy., 808/661-0031, www. sheraton-maui.com, $400-700), the original Ka'anapali resort which celebrated its 50th anniversary in 2013. This luxurious beach resort is tucked into the sacred cliff face, and despite being the "oldest" hotel on the strip (though renovated numerous times), the Sheraton doesn't skimp on any of the modern amenities. There is a large oceanfront pool, tennis courts, spacious rooms, spa, and a few of the rooms are set on top of the legendary Ka'anapali promontory. This is your classic Maui beach resort experience.

On the far southern end of the Ka'anapali strip is the **Hyatt Regency** (200 Nohea Kai Dr., 808/661-1234, www.maui.hyatt.com, $375), listed here for having the best pool system in all of Ka'anapali. This is a favorite of families who want to spend the day by the pool and the best place along the strip to grab a drink from a bar tucked behind a waterfall or ride down a twisting waterslide. This southern end of the beach is also sheltered from the afternoon trade winds, although the sand immediately in front of the resort has been steadily eroding for years. Rates begin around $375 and work their way up depending on view and size.

For those on a tighter budget, the **Royal Lahaina** (2780 Keka'a Dr., 808/661-3611 www.royallahaina.com, $189-over 500), on the northern side of Pu'u Keka'a offers affordable rooms. Rates can begin as low as $189 for a standard room. In addition to the oceanfront tower there are a number of individual cottages scattered around the property, where the Ka'anapali golf course runs right through the resort. A little more laid-back than some of the glitzier resorts, this is one of Ka'anapali's best oceanfront values.

On the far northern end of Ka'anapali North Beach, **Honoua Kai** (130 Kai Malina Pkwy., 855/718-5789, www.honuakai.com, $300-900) offers palatial suites with all the amenities and the island's largest balconies.

Condominiums

While there are a handful of condos in Ka'anapali, one of the best values is the **Maui Eldorado** (2661 Keka'a Dr., 808/661-0021, www.outrigger.com, $199-369), managed by Outrigger Resorts. The condos are only a three-minute walk to the beach but don't have the prices of an oceanfront resort. Plus, you can cook your own meals. The golf course cuts right through the property, there are a number of small swimming pools, and discounts are fairly common.

LAHAINA

While there are no large resorts in Lahaina, the town's accommodations range from historic inns and modern condos to a handful of budget options.

$100-150

The **Pioneer Inn** (658 Wharf St., 808/661-3636, www.pioneerinnmaui.com, $159-175, suites $165-200) is the oldest hotel on Maui still accommodating guests, and it was the only hotel in West Maui until 1963. Now a Best Western hotel, the P.I. is across the street from Lahaina Harbor and right in the center of the action. Food, drinks, and live music are served downstairs at the popular local bar.

On the northern end of the town, one of Lahaina's most basic but affordable oceanfront accommodations is the **Makai Inn** (1415 Front St., 808/870-9004, www.makaiinn.net, $110-190), an old concrete apartment building which was turned into vacation rentals. The garden setting is surprisingly pleasing, oceanfront rooms have their own private lanai, and you're right on the water for watching for the sunset either from your balcony or the inn's open courtyard. Rates are affordable considering you're on the oceanfront, and this laid-back Hawaiian setting is a practical option for basing yourself near Lahaina.

WHERE TO STAY IN WEST MAUI

Name	Type	Price
'Aina Nalu Resort	condo	$285-400
Camp Olowalu	camping	$15
Garden Gate B&B	B&B	$119-169
Ho'oilo House	B&B	$329
Honoua Kai	hotel	$300-900
Hyatt Regency Maui Resort & Spa	resort	$375-900
☾ Ka'anapali Beach Hotel	hotel	$165-325
Kahana Falls	condo	$99-250
Lahaina Shores Beach Resort	condo	$225-300
Makai Inn	inn	$110-190
Maui Eldorado	condo	$199-369
Maui Kai	condo	$200-400
☾ Napili Kai Beach Resort	condo	$270-500
Napili Village	condo	$99-149
Pioneer Inn	hotel	$159-200
☾ Plantation Inn	B&B	$158-265
☾ Puamana	condo	$200-600
Ritz-Carlton	resort	$400-999
Royal Lahaina	hotel	$189-550
Sheraton Maui	resort	$400-700

Bed-and-Breakfasts

Couples looking for a romantic retreat will love the ☾ **Plantation Inn** (174 Lahainaluna Rd., 808/667-9225, www.theplantationinn.com, $158-265), a hidden little pocket of calm in otherwise frantic Lahaina. On Lahainaluna Road just a one-minute walk from Front Street, this 19-room getaway has a swimming pool, free parking, free Wi-Fi, and daily maid service, and manages to retain its 19th-centuy charm. Breakfast is served daily until 9:30am and features French-inspired cuisine from chef Gerard Reversade, whose acclaimed restaurant on the same property gives hotel guests a discount.

For a bed-and-breakfast outside of downtown, try the **Garden Gate Bed and Breakfast** (67 Kaniau Rd., 808/661-8800, www.gardengatebb.com, $119-169) set between Lahaina and Ka'anapali in a quiet, residential area. All of the rooms are comfortable and well worth the price considering the cost of lodging in Lahaina. Breakfast is often served on the lanai, although not on Sunday.

Condominiums

Right on the water by 505 Front Street, the **Lahaina Shores Beach Resort** (475 Front St., 808/661-4835 or 800/642-6284, www.lahainashores.com, $225-300) is a six-story condo with individually owned units which has just undergone a major renovation. This is a convenient base for those who want to take a surf lesson, stroll down the beach, access Lahaina Harbor, or be walking distance from town. Rates vary considerably, but most studios and once bedrooms will be $300 and under.

Smack in the center of town a block off Front

Features	Why Go Here	Best Fit For
pool, kitchen	location	couples
restrooms, oceanfront	location, affordable	budget travelers
gardens, breakfast	location, quiet	couples, solo travelers
pool, breakfast	quiet, view	couples, honeymooners
suites, oceanfront balconies	location, amenities	couples, families
waterslides, oceanfront	location, pools	families
free hula show	location	families, couples
fitness center, hot tub	amenities	families, couples
pool, oceanfront	location	couples
oceanfront, gardens	location, affordable	budget travelers
kitchens, golf	location	families, couples
kitchens, oceanfront	location	families, couples
pool, oceanfront	full amenities	families, couples
oceanfront	location, price	families, couples
garden, pool	location	couples, budget travelers
pool, breakfast	location, quiet	couples, honeymooners
pool, oceanfront	location, quiet	families, couples
golf, spa	full-service resort	luxury-lovers, honeymooners
oceanfront, tennis	location	couples
pool, oceanfront	full-service resort	families, honeymooners

Street is the 188-room **'Aina Nalu Resort** (660 Waine'e St., 800/367-5226, fax 808/661-3733, www.outriggercondominiums.com, $285-400), a modern condo complex in a garden atmosphere that has the benefit of being right in town. Rooms are spacious and recently renovated, and a swimming pool provides a respite from the heat.

While the above two options are perfectly acceptable, the best condo complex in Lahaina is **❰ Puamana**, a 28-acre private community on the southern edge of town. There is a sandy beach in front of the complex good for swimming, and a luxurious pool sits out on a point surrounded by the ocean. There are tennis courts and a beautiful old clubhouse. It's just a 10-minute stroll into downtown Lahaina. Oceanfront rentals are much nicer than those along the highway, and reservations

are available through various West Side rental agents such as www.puamanavacations.com.

SOUTH OF LAHAINA
Bed-and-Breakfasts

Set in the residential community of Launiupoko above the beach park by the same name, the **Ho'oilo House** (138 Awaiku St., 808/667-6669, www.hooilohouse.com, $329) is one of the most luxurious B&Bs on the island's West Side. The views from this vantage point are out toward Lana'i and offer panoramic sunset views on a nightly basis. Everything about this house, from its Thai-inspired architecture to its furnishings and outdoor garden area, says comfort and relaxation. Six suites are decorated in unique style, a continental breakfast is served daily, and guests can make use of the swimming pool and lounge area with a view over

WHERE TO STAY IN CENTRAL MAUI

Name	Type	Price
☾ Banana Bungalow	Hostel	$32-98
Courtyard Marriott	Hotel	$200-250
Maui Beach Hotel	Hotel	$89-150
Maui Seaside Hotel	Hotel	$105-129
Northshore Hostel	Hostel	$29-89
☾ Old Wailuku Inn	B&B	$165-190

the water. There is a three-night minimum, and only two adults per room.

Camping

The best, legal, camping on the West Side of the island is at **Camp Olowalu** (800 Olowalu Village Rd., 808/661-4303, www.campolowalu.com, $15/person, $5/child), about 10 minutes south of Lahaina. The facilities have been majorly spruced up in the last year, and tent camping is available. Showers, drinking water, toilets, and picnic tables are on the property, as are water sports rentals for exploring the famous Olowalu reef which is right outside your front door.

Central Maui

If the vision you've always had of your Maui vacation was a luxurious resort on a world-famous beach, you'll be disappointed if you stay in Central Maui. Most of the options here are of the budget variety, and while the Old Wailuku Inn has some privacy and charm, all other options are utilitarian, cheap, and frequented by travelers who simply need a shower and four walls. If your main reason for being in Maui is to explore the island, you'll be happy to stay in Central Maui so you can save your dollars for activities and adventure.

WAILUKU
Hostels

The most affordable places to stay in Wailuku are the two hostels in the funkier, older part of town. While they are by no means a beach resort, they are practical, centrally located, and provide an affordable base for exploring the island. All hostel guests must display a valid passport and ticket off the island as a prerequisite for booking a bed.

If you're on a budget, the ☾ **Banana Bungalow** (310 N. Market St., 808/244-5090, www.mauihostel.com, $32-98) offers free adventures around the island. While it's expected that you tip the guides, tours to Hana, Haleakala, 'Iao Valley, Pa'ia, or Little Beach just for the cost of a tip is a nice perk. The rooms are clean and basic (there are private as well as shared dorm rooms) and the garden surroundings are relaxing, but the hostel is in an unattractive part of the island and can often be a party scene (although "quiet hours" go into effect at 10pm). Rates range from $32/night for a dorm bed to $75/night for a private single, $84 for a double, and $98 for a triple. Linens are included, towels aren't, and surfers are always welcome.

Closer to the center of Wailuku is **Northshore Hostel** (2080 W. Vineyard St., 808/986-8095, www.northshorehostel.com,

Features	Why Go Here	Best Fit For
free tours	affordable	budget travelers
modern fitness room, swimming pool	business travelers	
airport shuttle	affordable	budget travelers
swimming pool	affordable	budget travelers
quiet	affordable	budget travelers
breakfast, quiet	historic	couples

$29-89), which is great if you're looking to be centrally located, save some cash, and get some sleep. The rooms are clean, there is free breakfast, free Wi-Fi, free airport transfers, free shuttles to Kanaha Beach, and linens are included. There aren't any private bathrooms, but the rates are reasonable at only $29/night for a dorm bed and $69-89 for a private room. While Vineyard Street is a funky and slow-going part of town, you can't argue with the price for a clean, safe, and welcoming place.

Bed-and-Breakfasts

The nicest place to stay in Wailuku is the C **Old Wailuku Inn at Ulupono** (2199 Kaho'okele St., 808/244-5897, www.mauiinn. com, $165-190), listed on the Hawai'i Register of Historic Places. Built in 1924, there are 10 rooms, and all are filled with period furniture that evokes the feeling of grandma's house. Although it sounds like a slogan, this truly is Maui's most Hawaiian bed-and-breakfast. Free Wi-Fi is available, and each room has a private bath. A filling gourmet breakfast is served at 8am. There is a two-night minimum stay and most rooms are set up for double occupancy.

KAHULUI
Under $100

You would figure a hotel with the name **Maui Beach Hotel** (170 Ka'ahumanu Ave., 808/954-7421, www.mauibeachhotel.net, $89) would be the epitome of paradise. It's a hotel, on Maui,

on the beach. What else could you need? The reality, however, is that the beach is on the inside of Kahului Harbor and you're in an industrial part of town. At $89 for a standard room, however, the price is right, and there is free Internet, a free airport shuttle, and a $5 parking fee.

$100-150

In the same area is the 200-room **Maui Seaside Hotel** (100 W. Ka'ahumanu Ave., 808/877-3311, www.mauiseasidehotel.com, $105-129), which is of the same older ilk as its neighbor. There is a swimming pool in the central courtyard, access to the beach, and continental breakfast. While more motel-like than its neighbor, the Maui Seaside is clean and well cared for. This is a utilitarian yet affordable option for basing yourself in the center of the island.

Over $150

The **Courtyard Marriott** (532 Keolani Pl., 808/871-1800, $200) is the newest and nicest hotel in Kahului. Granted, it's just an airport hotel, but if that's what you're looking for, then this is your best option. Rates that hover around $200/night are expensive for a view of Costco. Nevertheless, the hotel is modern, new, and conveniently located near the North Shore as well as the airport. There is also a large swimming pool, a fitness room, and a trendy bistro, although there is a $10 parking fee if traveling with your own car.

WHERE TO STAY

South Maui

South Maui is the island's sunniest area and one of its most popular tourist zones. Ma'alaea and Kihei are dominated by condos with few hotels or cottages. Wailea offers the island's most luxurious resorts, although there are still some moderately priced condos. In the deep south, Makena has one of the island's most affordable resorts as well as some oceanfront condos.

MA'ALAEA

The only accommodations in Ma'alaea are condos, all of which are found along Hauoli Street. Although the afternoons can be windy and the swimming is marginal, the benefits of staying in Ma'alaea are the central location, being walking distance to Ma'alaea Harbor, the ability to cook your own meals, and some of the most affordable ocean views on the island. For rooms, check with **Maalaea Bay Rentals** (808/244-5627, 808/244-7012, or 800/367-6084, www.maalaeabay.com). This agency has an office at the Hono Kai Resort (280 Hauoli St., Ma'alaea) and handles more than 140 units in a majority of the condos along this road. All units are fully furnished with complete kitchens, TVs, telephones, and a lanai, and each property has a pool and laundry facilities. Rates range from $150-300 mid-December-mid-April, but summer and fall rates can be as low as $100. Many of the condos have a three-night minimum, or longer during the Christmas holidays. For monthly stays, rates are reduced by 10 percent.

KIHEI
Under $150

Set in an old coconut grove, the **Aston Maui Lu** (575 S. Kihei Rd., 808/879-5881, www.astonmauilu.com, $119-232), is an older 28-acre property at the north end of Kihei. The Maui Lu is not designed as an ordinary hotel—it looks more like condo units—but none of the rooms has a kitchen. All include TV,

air-conditioning, refrigerator, and daily maid service, while other amenities include an activities desk, tennis courts, a Maui-shaped swimming pool, two small beaches, and free Wi-Fi in the lobby. Room prices vary according to season. Special rates as low as $99 are sometimes available, and you can find discounts for longer stays.

The most affordable hotel option in South Kihei is the **Days Inn** (2980 S. Kihei Rd., 808/879-7744, www.daysinn.com, $83-200), which sits on the north end of Keawakapu Beach. Rooms are small, there is air-conditioning and a small refrigerator, and while it might be basic, it's tough to argue with the price, considering the location. There is free Wi-Fi, free parking, and outdoor grills. As expected, oceanfront suites can stretch upward to $250.

Over $150

On the northern edge of South Kihei is the **((Maui Coast Hotel** (2259 S. Kihei Rd., 808/874-6284, www.mauicoasthotel.com, $169), a 265-room high-rise hotel a three-minute walk from the beach. You'll find tennis courts, a fitness room, and a swimming pool. Rooms have free Wi-Fi and air-conditioning. There is free parking, as well as a free resort shuttle for transport around the South Kihei and Wailea area. Rates begin at around $169, although there are frequently a number of specials including AAA discounts and weekly rates. There is also a $17.50 resort fee.

Condominiums

One of the several condos at the far north end of Kihei is **Sugar Beach Resort** (145 N. Kihei Rd. 808/879-2778, www.crhmaui.com, $150-425), an oceanfront building with individually owned units as well as a swimming pool, spa, and sundries shop. Rates often vary depending upon the rental agency and time of year.

Across from the south end of Mai Poina 'Oe Ia'u Beach Park is the **Maui Sunseeker** (551 S.

Kihei Rd., 808/879-1261, www.mauisunseeker. com, $120-190) resort, a gay-friendly, adult-only property featuring 16 rooms in a small and quiet setting. A sundeck with a hot tub is on the roof, there are kitchenettes in the rooms, and laundry facilities are available on-site.

Menehune Shores (760 S. Kihei Rd., 808/879-3428, www.menehunereservations. com, $200-310) is a huge, family-oriented, and moderately priced high-rise condo on the beach overlooking an ancient fishpond. All units have an ocean view, and although the ocean swimming is poor, there is a swimming pool. Rates range from $150-275 during slower season and $200-310 in the high season. There is a three-night minimum and discounts for longer stays. This is an affordable setting just slightly removed from town.

Sandwiched between the Cove and Kamaole I, **Maui Vista** (2191 S. Kihei Rd., 808/879-7966, www.mauivistacondo.com, $210-230) is a 10-acre condo complex on the *mauka* side of South Kihei Road. There are three swimming pools, six tennis courts, and barbecue grills, and most rooms have kitchens and air-conditioning. Units are individually owned, so rates vary, but expect studios which are $189, one-bedroom suites $210-230, and two-bedroom suites $280.

Right on the sands of Kamaole II, the **Hale Pau Hana** (2480 S. Kihei Rd., 808/879-2715, www.hphresort.com, $240-350) is one of the best options for condos right on the water. There is free parking, free Internet, grilling facilities, a full kitchen, a swimming pool, and a private lanai in each room. Rates vary by season. This is a good location in a happening part of town.

Within walking distance of Kamaole III, Kihei Boat Ramp, and Keawakapu Beach is the **Aston Maui Hill** (2881 S. Kihei Rd., 808/879-6321, www.astonmauihill.com, $165-400), an upbeat condo with a Spanish motif. This quality condo resort sits high on a hill and is a nice alternative to expensive Wailea. There is a tennis court, swimming pool, putting green, and Wi-Fi, and each room comes equipped with a kitchen.

Closer to the water, the eight-story **Mana Kai Maui** (2960 S. Kihei Rd., 808/879-1561, www.manakaimaui.com, $240-500), offers the nicest resort accommodations in South Kihei. This 50-unit complex is on the north end of Keawakapu Beach and offers snorkeling and water activities right out the front door. The Five Palms restaurant is one of Kihei's best, or there are full kitchens for those who would rather cook. Expect rates of $240 for a standard hotel room to $500 for suites with private balconies.

Cottages

Cottages provide an affordable charm not found at large condos or hotels. On the north end of Kihei, **Nona Lani Cottages** (455 S. Kihei Rd., 808/879-2497 www.nonalanicottages.com, $150) has eight cottages in a garden setting across the street from the beach. The property has a refreshing throwback to the simpler times of yesteryear. There is an Internet surcharge.

WAILEA
Over $150

Wailea hotels are expensive, fancy, and meant to provide indulgence. The northernmost of the Wailea resorts is **The Wailea Beach Marriott** (3700 Wailea Alanui Dr., 808/879-1922, www.marriott.com, $340), a 497-room oceanfront resort that is the oldest in Wailea (although it's been extensively restored). Families will enjoy the large system of pools, and the snorkeling and sand of Ulua Beach is only a few steps away. Parking is $25/day, Internet is $15/day, and rates begin around $340 during the slower seasons of the year.

Not far from the Marriott are the ultra-luxurious **Wailea Beach Villas** (3800 Wailea Alanui Dr., 808/891-4500, www.drhmaui.com, $850), directly fronting the beach and steps from the Shops at Wailea. Grab a private cabana overlooking the shoreline, relax in the oceanfront infinity pool, and bask in the aura of extravagant luxury at Wailea's nicest accommodations. Parking is free of charge, although as you can imagine, these rooms don't come cheap.

WHERE TO STAY IN SOUTH MAUI

Name	Type	Price
Aston Maui Hill	condo	$165-400
Aston Maui Lu	hotel	$119-232
Days Inn	hotel	$83-250
◖ Fairmont Kea Lani	resort	$550-1,200
Four Seasons	resort	$600-1,500
Grand Wailea	resort	$564-1,200
aoundHale Pau Hana	condo	$240-350
Hotel Wailea	hotel	$359-500
◖ Makena Beach and Golf Resort	resort	$210-600
Makena Surf	condo	$600-800
Mana Kai Maui	condo	$240-500
◖ Maui Coast Hotel	hotel	$169-275
Maui Sunseeker	LGBT resort	$120-190
Maui Vista	condo	$189-280
Menehune Shores	condo	$150-310
Nona Lani Cottages	cottages	$150
Sugar Beach Resort	condo	$150-425
Wailea Beach Marriott	resort	$340-550
Wailea Beach Villas	condo	$700-1,500
◖ Wailea Ekolu Village	condo	$260-350

Directly in front of Wailea Beach are two of Wailea's largest resorts, the sprawling, pink **Grand Wailea** (3850 Wailea Alanui Dr., 808/875-1234, www.grandwailea.com, $565) and the ultra-luxurious **Four Seasons Resort** (3900 Wailea Alanui Dr., 808/874-8000, www.fourseasons.com, $600). While both resorts offer the highest quality, the Grand Wailea is famous for its pool system. Families will enjoy navigating the waterslides, rope swings, and the water elevator. Next door, at the Four Seasons, the pool scene is much more reserved, but the cream villas looking out over the water redefine island luxury. Rooms are expensive and amenities lavish.

Around the southern end of Wailea Point are

the twirling white spires of the ◖ **Fairmont Kea Lani** (4100 Wailea Alanui, 808/875-4100, www.fairmont.com, $550). Located on the sands of Polo Beach, the property has undergone extensive renovations and appears nicer now than ever before. Each room is arranged like a one-bedroom suite, and the resort is involved in a number of ecoconscious initiatives to help protect the island environment. The resort has more of an exclusive feel since it's set off on its own.

If you'd rather have a boutique hotel experience instead of an oceanfront mega-resort, the **Hotel Wailea** (555 Kaukahi St., 808/874-0500, www.hotelwailea.com, $359) is tucked away up on a hill with views looking over the coastline. There is a spa, swimming pool, and fine dining

Features	Why Go Here	Best Fit For
pool, kitchen	location, amenities	couples, families
pool, quiet	affordable	budget travelers
oceanfront, barbecue	affordable, location	budget travelers
pool, oceanfront	romantic, luxury	families, couples, honeymooners
pools, spa, oceanfront	romantic, luxury	couples, honeymooners, luxury-lovers
waterslides, spa, oceanfront	romantic, luxury, pools	families, couples, honeymooners
oceanfront, kitchen	location, amenities	couples, families
pool, spa, amenities	boutique, romantic	couples, luxury-lovers
pool, activities, oceanfront	location, great value	couples, families, honeymooners
oceanfront, kitchen	location, luxury	families, couples
kitchen, oceanfront	location, water sports	couples, families
pool, fitness center, shuttle	full amenities	couples, business travel
kitchenette, hot tub	quiet, location	couples
pool, tennis, kitchen	location, practical	couples, families
pool, lanai, oceanfront	affordable	couples
gardens, kitchenette	quiet, affordable, location	couples
pool, spa, kitchen	oceanfront	couples, families
pool, spa, luau	oceanfront, watersports	families, couples
pool, oceanfront	romantic, luxury	luxury-lovers
kitchen, amenities	location, affordable	couples, families

on property. This is Wailea's most intimate option for luxury boutique hotels.

Condominiums

Those who want to be walking distance from the beaches of Wailea without the hefty price tag can look into some of the affordably priced condos on the northern edge of the resort. The **《 Wailea Ekolu Village** (808/891-6200, www.drhmaui.com) offers one- and two-bedroom condos with free parking, free Internet, kitchens, and rates that start around $260.

MAKENA
Over $150

A gleaming, wing-shaped building where every room has at least a partial ocean view,

the **《 Makena Beach and Golf Resort** (5400 Makena Alanui, 808/874-1111 www.makenaresortmaui.com, $210-275) offers South Maui's best resort value. Recent renovations have spruced up everything from the rooms to the exterior, and activities to dining. The resort offers free bicycles and a shuttle to Wailea. Parking is free, Internet is free, there is no resort fee, and all of the activities of Maluaka Beach are right out the front door. There are six tennis courts, a relaxing swimming pool, and the golf course will reopen in the beginning of 2014 after a massive series of improvements. What's best, rates at Makena are far more affordable than at neighboring Wailea, with rooms as low as $210-275 during slower times of the year.

© KYLE ELLISON

the Grand Wailea

Condominiums

While there aren't too many condos in Makena, the luxurious **Makena Surf** (808/879-6284, www.makenasurfresort.com) is directly on the beach and looks straight out at Molokini Crater. These units are individually owned and rented, although rates usually hover in the $600 range. This is the perfect spot to escape the crowds and have a sliver of South Maui nearly all to yourself.

Upcountry

Upcountry is completely free of resorts and different than most Maui experiences. Peace and tranquility replace mai tais and swimming pools, and the cool mountain area is a refreshing change from the sun-baked shorelines below. Most accommodations are 20 minutes from the beach, although most are also conveniently located within an hour of Haleakala Volcano. Rustic, cool, and blissfully laid-back, Upcountry is where visitors come to relax.

MAKAWAO
Over $150

Unlike any other accommodation option on the island, **(Lumeria** (1813 Baldwin Ave., 855/579-8877, www.lumeriamaui.com, $300) is a holistic retreat center set between Makawao and Pa'ia. Housed within a brilliantly restored plantation building and home to its own organic garden, Lumeria focuses on providing an educational vacation experience that centers on rejuvenation and wellness. All of the 24 rooms are decorated differently, and Asian accents punctuate the courtyard. Lumeria is popular with yoga retreats, and there are regularly-scheduled classes and workshops.

Bed-and-Breakfasts

Built in 1924 and used by a Portuguese family to raise 13 children, the five-bedroom plantation house **(Hale Hoʻokipa Inn** (32 Pakani Pl., 808/572-6698, www.maui-bed-and-breakfast. com, $138-173) has been turned into a lovely B&B within walking distance from Makawao town. While improvements are constantly made, this still has the feel of an old-fashioned country home, and the accommodating owners provide local tips and insight into everyday Maui life. Organic fruits are served from the garden, rates for the one-bedroom rooms are $138-158, and the two-bedroom suite is $173.

Half a mile down the hill from Makawao town, the **Banyan Bed and Breakfast** (3265 Baldwin Ave., 808/572-9021, www.bed-breakfast-maui.com, $165-190) is an old plantation bungalow with adjoining cottages that provides laid-back accommodations in a country setting. The complex is shaded by a monkeypod and banyan, where swings hang from the wide boughs to complete the rural feel. All cottages and suites have kitchens or kitchenettes, breakfast is included, and Makawao town is a short walk away.

Down near the intersection of Haliʻimaile Road and Baldwin Avenue is the **Peace of Maui** (1290 Haliʻimaile Rd., 808/572-5045, www. peaceofmaui.com, $85-95 main lodge, $185 cottage) guesthouse, which is centrally located between Makawao and Paʻia. Peace of Maui overlooks the pineapple fields, and while the rooms aren't extravagant, they are clean and affordably priced. Rooms in the main lodge share a kitchen and bathrooms. For your own bathroom and more privacy, the two-bedroom cottage also provides access to the property Jacuzzi.

In the forest above Makawao town, you will find **(Aloha Cottage** (808/573-8555, www. alohacottage.com, $199-299) down a quiet country lane off rural Olinda Road. As quiet as quiet can be, its only neighbors are the horses in the pastures beyond the distant fence. This intimate venue sits on a five-acre estate and offers panoramic views from the deck of the octagonal structure. Slink into the two-person hot tub on the cool Olinda nights, and wake each morning to the chirp of the birds as they sing from the surrounding forest. Rates vary depending on length of stay, and there is $100 cleaning fee added to the total cost.

KULA
$100-150

The **(Kula Lodge** (15200 Haleakala Hwy., 808/878-1535, www.kulalodge.com, $125-195) is Upcountry's most popular accommodation option. On Route 377 at a 3,200-foot elevation, the air is crisp and cool up here and much more comfortable than down on the coastline. There are five detached chalets that all feature private lanais, and two of which have woodburning fireplaces. The rustic yet comfortable setting makes the perfect base for visiting Haleakala Crater.

Just up the road, the **Kula Sandalwoods** (15427 Haleakala Hwy., 808/878-3523, www. kulasandalwoods.com, $149-159) is another Kula classic that is far more laid-back than its popular neighbor. These stand-alone cottages sit up on a hillside and offer sweeping views of the island's central valley. While there is complimentary Wi-Fi as well as morning coffee, the cottages are otherwise free of appliances. This is a place to just kick back and relax. The summit of Haleakala is only a 45-minute drive from this 3,300-foot location.

Bed-and-Breakfasts

In Lower Kula on the drive out toward Keokea, **Upcountry Bed and Breakfast** (4925 Lower Kula Rd., 808/878-8083, www.upcountry-bandb.com, $150) has rooms in a relaxing Upcountry setting. The owner is a wealth of information on everything island-related, and locally grown Upcountry fruit is served with each morning's breakfast. There is also free Wi-Fi, fireplaces in winter, and sweeping sunset views.

Above Highway 377 is **Puluke Farms B&B** (26 Wahelani Rd., 808/878-3263, puluke@ maui.net, $95). Attached to the main house,

WHERE TO STAY IN UPCOUNTRY

Name	Type	Price
◖ Aloha Cottage	cottage	$199-299
Banyan Bed and Breakfast	B&B	$165-190
Haleakala National Park	camping and cabins	$10-75
◖ Hale Ho'okipa Inn	B&B	$138-158
◖ Kula Lodge	Inn	$125-195
Kula Sandalwoods	cottage	$149-159
◖ Lumeria	Hotel	$300
Peace of Maui Guesthouse	Inn	$85-95
Polipoli Springs State Recreation Area	camping	$18
Puluke Farms B&B	B&B	$95
◖ Star Lookout	vacation rental	$200
Upcountry Bed and Breakfast	B&B	$150

this one-room hideaway has great views over the isthmus. The studio has a kitchenette and full bath, and continental breakfast is included with the stay. Sunset and early-morning hours are best appreciated on the deck. Since the house is at 3,500 feet, winter nights can be refreshingly cool.

Camping
For the truly rugged, camping is available in **Polipoli Spring State Recreation Area** high on the slopes of Haleakala. The grassy camping area is small, basic, and down a lengthy dirt road. The reward, however, is waking in the heart of the Polipoli forest and having the morning all to yourself. Fees for camping are $18/campsite, and permits can be obtained either by calling 808/984-8109 or online at www.camping. ehawaii.gov. Print out your permit and bring it with you, as some of the parks won't accept electronic copies, and pack in plenty of water and food since it's long way back to civilization. You can also book a backcountry wilderness cabin for $90/night. This is sure to be an accommodation option that no one you know has taken.

KEOKEA AND ULUPALAKUA
Those looking for rural tranquility in a cool Upcountry setting need look no farther than the ◖ **Star Lookout** (622 Thompson Rd., 907/346-8028, www.starlookout.com, $200). On Thompson Road just minutes from Grandma's Coffee House, this single cottage provides a ranch-style retreat with views over the Keokea pastureland down to the shoreline of South Maui. A two night minimum is required. Perhaps Upcountry's best-kept secret.

HALEAKALA NATIONAL PARK
Camping
Spending a night in Haleakala Crater is one of the most unique adventures on Maui. Cold, arid, and beneath a blanket of stars, it's a foray into a backcountry world you'd never expect on a tropical island. The warmest and most accessible of all the campsites is **Hosmer's Grove,** at the 6,800-foot level just as you enter the park. No permit is necessary for camping in Hosmer's Grove, so you can drive your vehicle into the parking lot that sits adjacent to the

Features	Why Go Here	Best Fit For
hot tub, kitchen, lanai	quiet, peaceful, romantic	couples
kitchen, breakfast	quiet, location	couples
pit toilets, kitchen	quiet, adventurous, backcountry	couples, groups, families, budget travelers
breakfast, garden	quiet, historic	couples
fireplace, lanai	location, romantic, quiet	couples, hikers
lanai, views	quiet, location, retreat	couples
yoga classes, garden courtyard	meditative retreat	solo travelers, couples, groups
kitchen	affordable	budget travelers
none	quiet, wilderness	budget travelers, adventure travelers
kitchenette, breakfast	quiet, affordable	budget travelers, couples
kitchen, views	location, quiet, romantic	couples
fireplace, views, breakfast	quiet, peaceful	couples

grassy campground. For the three backcountry campsites within the park, you must obtain a free permit from the park headquarters and watch a short safety video. All gear must be packed in and out over a long and arduous trail, and while Holua campsite is cold and dry, Paliku campsite is a few degrees warmer and set in forested surroundings. There are also three **backcountry cabins** available which have basic cooking facilities and bunk beds. Rates for the cabins are $75/night, and bookings open up exactly 90 days in advance. To make a reservation for a cabin, either call 808/572-4400, or visit www.nps.gov/hale.

East Maui

PA'IA
Under $150
For travelers on an exceptionally tight budget, the **Rainbow Surf Hostel** (221 Baldwin Ave., 808/579-9057, www.mauirainbowsurfhostel. com, $30-100) is a short walk above Pa'ia and offers dorm rooms for $30 or private rooms for $80-100. There is a communal kitchen and free Wi-Fi, but those who can spend a few dollars more should seek out better options.

Over $150
Smack in the center of town, the (**Pa'ia Inn** (93 Hana Hwy., 808/579-6000, www.paiainn. com, $189-999) is a trendy, chic, boutique hotel just steps from the beaches of Pa'ia. All the decor within this relaxing compound has a dark wood, Balinese, tropical tone, and each individually designed room offers a luxurious and private getaway in the center of Pa'ia bustle. Sip a coffee in the outdoor courtyard or take a morning stroll along Pa'ia Bay. Rates for standard rooms begin at $189 and go all the way up to $999 for the swanky, oceanfront, "I wish I lived here" beach house, and this is a pleasing and welcoming lodging option in Maui's happiest town.

WHERE TO STAY IN EAST MAUI

Name	Type	Price
Ala 'aina Ocean Vista	B&B	$198-218
◖ Bamboo Inn	B&B	$195-265
Ekena	vacation rental	$245-400
Guest Houses at Malanai	vacation rental	$245-290
Haiku Plantation Inn	B&B	$129-159
Haleakala National Park-Kipahulu	camping	$10
Hana Bay Hale	vacation rental	$145-245
Hana Kai Maui Resort	condo	$200-300
Hana Lani Treehouses	treehouse	$135-210
◖ Huelo Point Lookout	vacation rental	$215-405
Joe's Rentals	Inn	$50-60
Kuau Inn	B&B	$125-145
◖ Pa'ia Inn	inn	$189-999
Nalu Kai Lodge	inn	$125-175
Rainbow Surf Hostel	hostel	$30-100
Tea House Cottage	B&B	$130-150
The Inn at Mama's Fish House	inn	$175-575
Travaasa Hana	resort	$400-700

Also in the center of town is the **Nalu Kai Lodge** (18 Nalu Pl., 808/385-4344, www.nalukailodge.com, $125-175) offering simple and comfortable accommodations just steps from Pa'ia Bay. There is a second-story deck with ocean views, as well as outdoor showers and a tiki bar. While you can't beat the location and the price, the area can sometimes be prone to road noise.

For an all-time classic North Shore accommodation right on Kuau Cove, **The Inn at Mama's Fish House** (799 Poho Pl., 808/579-9764, www.mamasfishhouse.com, $175-575) provides the warmth of Polynesia that the famous restaurant is known for, and this is one the island's best boutique hotels. The suites, studios, and cottages feature amenities such as full kitchens, maid service, and 15 percent off at the restaurant. The real perk, however, is the location; there is nothing like watching the sunset from beneath a rustling palm as you get the benefit of staying in this secluded cove that most visitors can only enjoy for the length of a meal.

Bed-and-Breakfasts

Between Pa'ia and Ho'okipa Beach Park, the **Kuau Inn** (676 Hana Hwy., 808/579-6046, www.kuauinn.com, $125-145) is a four-room house that offers clean B&B accommodations just minutes from the shoreline. Breakfast and Wi-Fi are both included. There is a full kitchen, covered lanai, and communal living room area. There is a minimum three-night stay.

HA'IKU
Bed-and-Breakfasts

While there are a number of small B&Bs in Ha'iku, one of the best is the **Haiku Plantation Inn** (555 Haiku Rd., 808/575-7500, www.haikuplantation.com, $129-159),

Features	Why Go Here	Best Fit For
gardens, hot tub, barbecue	quiet, peaceful	couples
oceanview lanai, breakfast	location, romantic	couples
kitchen, amenities, ocean view	location, quiet	couples
kitchen, gardens	location, amenities	couples, families
gardens, historic	quiet, affordable	couples, budget travelers
pit toilets, barbecue	location, affordable	budget travelers
kitchens	location, amenities	couples, families, groups
kitchen, lanai, oceanfront	location, quiet	couples
gardens, cooking facilities	quiet, unique	couples
hot tub, ocean view	location, quiet, peaceful	couples
kitchen	location, affordable	budget travelers
kitchens, lanai	location, affordable	couples, budget travelers
oceanfront, gardens	location, boutique	couples
oceanfront, tiki bar	location, affordable	couples
kitchen	affordable, location	budget travelers
off the grid, gardens	location, quiet, peaceful	couples
kitchens, oceanfront	location, romantic	couples, honeymooners
spa, pool, activities	location, luxury, amenities	couples, honeymooners

about a half-mile below the center of town. Under its canopy of tall and stately trees, this dignified rural bed-and-breakfast was established in the 1870s and became the island's first official B&B in 1986. The inn has four comfy bedrooms, each with its own shower, and breakfast and Internet are included—three-night minimum. This is the perfect place for stepping back to a time that was simpler and slower.

ROAD TO HANA

Down at the end of a road near Twin Falls is the **Tea House Cottage** (808/572-5610, www.mauiteahouse.com, $150 d, $130 s). This B&B is "off the grid," generating its own power by photovoltaic cells and collecting its own water. It's quiet, with no distractions, and from here you have broad views of the ocean. The room rates are $150 and $130, with a two-night minimum, and breakfast is

provided on the first day. A tunnel through the trees leads you to the house, and walkways run throughout the property, one to a small stupa built in 1976 by a Tibetan monk. The private Tiara Cottage, also on the property, can be rented by the week for $500. Breezy and light, it has a full kitchen and a bathroom and shower in an adjacent building.

In the community of Huelo you'll find the (Huelo Point Lookout (808/573-0914, www. mauivacationcottages.com, $215-405), a collection of five vacation rentals in a lush and heavenly section of the island not for the resort-loving crowd. These five separate vacation rentals provide sweeping views of the Huelo coastline and are truly a place to escape from it all. While there is no white sand beach outside your front door, there is a blanket of stars every night, and outdoor hot tubs from which to enjoy them. Discounts are given for weekly stays.

WHERE TO STAY

HANA

There are two completely different ways of experiencing Hana: trying to see it all in one day or making the smart move to spend a night and enjoy the beauty at a relaxed pace. For those who want to really relax, two or three nights in Hana are best. For those who want to experience the Road to Hana without the rush and the stress, choosing to spend a night in Hana—even if it means paying for two hotels in one night by not checking out of the other one—is the best $200 you'll spend on vacation.

Under $100

Basic, practical, and perfect for those on a steep budget, **Joe's Rentals** (4870 Uakea Rd., 808/248-7033, www.joesrentals.com, $50-60) is close to the entrance to Hana Bay and walking distance from the center of town. This home has been split into eight guest rooms, and rates are $50 for a shared bathroom or $60 for a room with a private bath. You'll find kitchen access, a communal TV room, and daily towel change, but if a little dirt and the occasional bug bother you, then you might want to look somewhere else. Cash or travelers checks only, and if no one is in the office, just ring for assistance.

Over $150

There are places to stay during your time in Hana, and then there is the ◖**Travaasa Hana** (5031 Hana Hwy., www.travaasa.com/hana, $400-650). This luxurious compound in the center of town was the island's first resort hotel when it opened in 1946, and since that time the boutique hotel has continued as the island's best resort. In addition to the standard amenities of tennis courts, a swimming pool, a fitness center, and spa, the Travaasa makes a conscious effort to help guests forge a meaningful connection with the Hawaiian culture of Hana. Resort experiences include throw net fishing, coconut husking, lei making, hula dancing, and ukulele classes, and adventure activities such as horseback riding and gliding can be booked through the resort's concierge. Wellness and culture permeate the resort, and for a real splurge, base yourself in one of the Sea Ranch cottages with its own private lanai and romantic two-person hot tub. Rates for standard rooms begin at $400, with Sea Ranch cottages ranging from $450-650.

Vacation Rentals

Set high above the west end of town, the luxurious **Ekena** (808/248-7047, www.ekenamaui.com, $245-400) vacation rental offers arguably one of the best views in Hana. This large pole house has an upper and lower unit which are each spacious enough to easily be shared by two couples. Both floors have large living rooms, fully equipped kitchens with all modern conveniences, two master bedrooms, and spacious bathrooms. There are private hiking trails departing from the property, and the on-site caretakers can provide all the info on Hana you could possibly need. The Jasmine level with one bedroom goes for $245 per night; with two bedrooms for $320. The Sea Breeze level is $350 for a couple and $400 for four people. There's a three-night minimum; no kids younger than 14.

For a truly unique accommodation option in Hana—and one that isn't for the finicky—the **Hana Lani Treehouses** (808/248-7241, www.hanalani.maui.net, $135-210) are exactly what they sound like: real treehouses inside a real jungle. Imagine sleeping beneath the stars in a screened-in bungalow set up in the trees, the path to your jungle chalet lit only by tiki torches. This "camping with a roof" is available in a number of forms, from the three-level "treetop" house to the more traditional bed-and-breakfast cottage that has its own electricity. There is also a five-person tree pavilion with views looking out at the ocean. Flowers abound everywhere you look. Rates are $135 for the treetops house, $145 for the tree pavilion, and $210 for the entire cottage. Two-night minimum usually required, but one-night stays will also be accepted for an additional $20 cleaning fee.

Closer to town, the funky, ultra-relaxing ◖ **Bamboo Inn** (www.bambooinn.com) offers three oceanfront accommodations that

©KYLE ELLISON

Be sure to book ahead for Hana Kai Maui Resort.

look out over the water toward Waikoloa Beach. A thatched roof hut serves as the centerpiece for the property. The owner, John, is a wealth of information on Hana history and culture, and this is a modern, soothing place to base yourself in Hana town and fall asleep to the crash of the waves. The one-story Honu and ʻIwa suites are $195 and $210/night, and each features its own private lanai gazing out over the calming bay. The two-story Naia suite is $265 with another private lanai. Wi-Fi is available in the courtyard and breakfast is included.

The **Hana Bay Hale** (808/248-4999, www. hanabayhale.com, $145-245) looks out over Hana Bay and features three separate suites. The Kauiki and Waikoloa one-bedroom units are $145/night plus a $25 cleaning fee for one-night stays, and the two-bedroom Hana Bay suite is $245/night plus a $35 cleaning fee for one-night stays. One-bedroom units have kitchenettes whereas the two-bedroom suite has a full kitchen, and the units can all be combined into a single large house for anyone traveling in a large group.

On the southern end of town between Hana and Kipahulu are the **Guest Houses at Malanai** (808/248-8706, www.hanaguesthouses.com, $245-295). This lush property features the one-bedroom Hale Ulu Ulu guesthouse and the larger, two-bedroom Hale Manu, both of which rent for the same rate depending upon length of stay. These two separate houses are located a 15-minute stroll from Hamoa Beach and Waioka Pool, and the owners can provide basic accessories you might need for the beach as well as insight on the area.

Condominiums

The **Hana Kai Maui Resort** (1533 Uakea Rd., 808/248-8426, www.hanakaimaui.com, $200-300) is the only condo rental in town. All units are well maintained and offer a lot for the money. Because there are only 18 rental units, you know this is an intimate place. The condo is set right on the water looking out over Hana Bay, each unit has a private lanai, and you fall asleep every night to the gentle lap of the waves. Rates vary depending on size and location of the unit but often run between $200-300.

KIPAHULU
Over $150

One of the best parts of staying in Kipahulu is the relaxing nature of the remote community and the ability to wake up in the morning and have the Pools of ʻOheʻo walking distance away. One of the most peaceful accommodations in this area is the **Alaʻaina Ocean Vista** (808/248-7824, www.hanabedandbreakfast. com, $198-218), a tropical bed-and-breakfast on four lush acres that is the exact opposite of the Kaʻanapali resort experience. Here you are bathed in a forest of mango trees that gaze over the blue Kipahulu coastline. Birds chirp in the nearby treetops, there is a barbecue area for those who want to cook their own dinner, and a large assortment of various fruit trees sustain the daily breakfast. The bamboo forest of the Pipiwai Trail is only a short walk away, and this is a romantic getaway set out in the country for those who just want to unwind. Rates vary depending on length of stay, but there is no cleaning fee.

Camping

Some of the best legal camping on the island can be found in the Kipahulu campground of **Haleakala National Park.** There are few things better than falling asleep to the sound of crashing surf, only to wake up in the morning and walk to pools before a single visitor has arrived. This is a truly a campground for getting back to center and tuning the rest of the world out for a while. There are pit toilets at the campground and grassy campsites, or, if one is available, carry your gear out to a distant *lau hala* tree and set up camp beneath its shade. Rates for camping are $10 for each vehicle in your party, which also counts as your entry fee to the park.

Lana'i

While Lana'i is home to two of the most luxurious resorts in the state, there are a handful of more affordable options for those on more of a budget.

$100-150

Small and historic ◖ **Hotel Lana'i** (828 Lana'i Ave., 808/565-7211 or 877/665-2624, fax 808/565-6450, www.hotellanai.com, $119-219) sits in the center of tranquil Lana'i City. This was the island's first hotel, built in 1923 for visiting guests of the ruling Dole Pineapple Company. While you won't find the same amenities as at the more expensive and posh resorts, the 10 rooms of this plantation-style building retain a historic feel without sacrificing comfort. The best rooms are those with their own private lanai, and there is also a cottage removed from the main building. Wi-Fi and breakfast are both complimentary, rates range from $119 for a standard room to $219 for the cottage, and shuttle service down to the beach is available for a fee of $36, which is good for the duration of your stay.

OVER $150

Lavish, luxurious, and delightfully over the top, the Four Seasons resorts on the island of Lana'i are two of Hawai'i's best. New owner Larry Ellison devoted millions of dollars to major renovations when he took over from David Murdock, and the Asian decor that once dominated the hotels has been replaced by Hawaiian designs. The resorts look better now than they ever have, and if it was even possible to make these resorts nicer, it's recently been accomplished. While both hotels are the pinnacle of luxury, each, however, offers a completely different experience although the amenities are interchangeable. Which resort you choose to stay in depends on the vacation you're looking for.

Offering an iconic beach resort experience, the ◖ **Four Seasons Manele Bay** (1 Manele Dr., 808/565-2000, www.fourseasons.com/manelebay, $450-up) is set stunningly above the cobalt waters of protected Hulopo'e Bay. The immaculate pool area sparkles in the sun and half of Hulopo'e Beach is reserved for hotel guests. You feel like a celebrity when staying here. Expect rates to begin around $450 during slower times of the year.

Above Lana'i City on the edge of open pastureland, the **Four Seasons Lodge at Koele** (808/565-4000, www.fourseasons.com/koele, $350-up) is a mist-shrouded mountain lodge where you're struck with the urge to trade the freedom of a bathing suit for the comforting warmth of a robe. While staying at Koele, play a round of croquet on the private course or stroll through the manicured gardens. Hunker down with a newspaper in the Grand Hall and pair it with a nice warm drink. Take a horseback ride through the surrounding countryside, or try your hand at skeet shooting. Marvelously

© KYLE ELLISON

Hotel Lana'i

dignified and impossibly romantic, rates at the Lodge are more affordable than Manele and begin as low as $350 during slower times of the year.

At the time of publication, a third resort was under construction on the east-facing Kahalepalaoa shoreline, with the vision being of private beach bungalows at the site of the abandoned Club Lana'i. The status of the resort remains to be seen, although it could potentially provide a luxurious accommodation option for the island's eastern shoreline.

BED-AND-BREAKFASTS

The **Dreams Come True** (808/565-6961 www. dreamscometruelanai.com, $129) guesthouse has four rooms available for rent. While the house itself dates to 1925, it was largely renovated in 2000, with hardwood floors and Italian marble in the bathrooms. The local owners are a wealth of knowledge on all sort of island information. Breakfast is included, as is free Internet.

Hale Moe (502 Akolu St., 808/565-9520,

$85-95) is a modern, clean, and comfy island house on the south side of town that rents three rooms, each with a bathroom, or the entire house. Food for breakfast is available each morning, and guests can use the kitchen for other meals. Two rooms go for $85 and the third is $95; the whole house can be rented for $300.

VACATION RENTALS

To experience Lana'i from a more local perspective (i.e., not be spritzed by Evian bottles), consider one of the smaller, more affordable rental options scattered throughout Lana'i City.

Located in town is **Apo's House** (www.lanaicityrental.com, $195), a three-bedroom, two-bath house. The house is fully furnished, and there is a full kitchen. While it might be set in an older plantation home, you have the convenience of walking into Lana'i City and the feeling that you're part of the local community.

For those traveling in larger groups, the **Lana'i City Vacation Rental** (www.lanaiforvacation.com, $250), a three-bedroom house

WHERE TO STAY ON LANA'I

Name	Type	Price
Apo's House	vacation rental	$195
Dreams Come True	vacation rental	$129
(C Four Seasons Manele Bay	Resort	$450-1,500
Four Seasons Lodge at Koele	Resort	$350-1,200
Hale Moe	vacation rental	$85'95
(C Hotel Lana'i	hotel	$119-229
Hulopo'e Beach Park	camping	$30 + $15/person
Lana'i City Vacation Rental	vacation rental	$250

in the center of Lana'i City, rents for $250 per night with a three-night minimum. The plantation home is set in a tropical, relaxing surrounding, can accommodate groups of 9-11 people, and can arrange any holistic retreat options you're hoping to find on the island.

CAMPING

The only legal camping on the island of Lana'i is at **Hulopo'e Beach Park** a five-minute walk from the Manele Boat Harbor. Permits are available from the park ranger when you show up at the park. If you can't find him, don't worry, he's sure to find you. Only Lana'i residents are allowed to camp on the sand, so all visitors will need to camp in the grassy area on the far side of the parking lot. The campground has restrooms, beach showers, running water, and the convenience of waking up and being the first people on the beach. Other than the Four Seasons, however, there isn't any place for food, so pack some supplies with you or have a way of getting up into town. Fees are $30 for the campsite and $15 per person per night, with a maximum stay of three nights.

Other than Hulopo'e there is some "unofficial" camping that takes place on other island beaches, and while illegal, enforcement is rare.

Moloka'i

Moloka'i is gloriously free of resorts, and no buildings on the island are taller than a palm tree. Accommodation options on Moloka'i are restricted to condos, camping, and private vacation rentals, and all provide calming sanctuaries where you can relax and hear yourself think. Since most Moloka'i condos are managed through vacation rental agencies, contact **Moloka'i Vacation Properties** (808/553-8334, www.molokai-vacation-rental.net) or **Friendly** **Isle Realty** (808/553-3666, www.molokairealty.com) about their large selection of vacation rentals across the island.

WEST MOLOKA'I

While Kaluakoi was once the home of an oceanfront resort with an 18-hole golf course, the resort was shuttered with the closing of the Moloka'i Ranch. The benefits of staying in West Moloka'i are the comfortable, modern

Features	Why Go Here	Best Fit For
kitchen	affordable, location	couples, families
kitchen	affordable, location	couples, budget travelers
pool, golf, oceanfront	luxury, romantic	couples, honeymooners, luxury-lovers
croquet, gardens, golf	luxury, romantic	couples, honeymooners, luxury-lovers
kitchen, breakfast	affordable, quiet	budget travelers, couples
lanai, breakfast	romantic, location, historic	couples
restrooms, water, oceanfront	location, affordable	budget travelers, groups, families
kitchen, amenities	location, quiet	couples, groups, families

accommodations, the fact that you're within walking distance of the island's best beaches, and the fiery sunsets that take place each evening.

One of the largest complexes in West Moloka'i is the **Ke Nani Kai** (50 Kepuhi Pl., 800/490-9042, www.kenanikai.com, $100-200), an expansive complex that has a swimming pool, one- and two-bedroom units, and affordable rates.

Closer to the beach, the **Paniolo Hale** offers similar accommodation just steps from the shoreline. Units here rent for $110-225 per night with a two- to three-night minimum, although some units have longer minimum stays.

Some of the units at the old Kaluakoi Hotel complex, collectively called the **Kaluakoi Villas** (1121 Kaluakoi Rd., Maunaloa, HI 96770, 808/552-2721 or 800/367-5004, www.castleresorts.com, $150-190), are managed by Castle Resorts and Hotels. Each studio, suite, and cottage has been tastefully decorated and includes a color TV and a kitchen or kitchenette.

Camping

The only legal camping on this side of the island is at **Papohaku Beach Park,** which fronts the longest white sand beach on the island. The park area features restrooms, an outdoor showerhead, and potable water.

Permits for camping need to be obtained back in Kaunakakai through the County Parks Department (808/553-3204). Rates per night are $3/person for Hawai'i residents and $5/person for nonresidents Monday-Thursday, and $5/person and $8/person on Friday and the weekends. There is also plenty of unofficial camping that takes place at Hale O Lono and Kawakiu, and while camping on the beach is technically illegal, rarely is it enforced.

CENTRAL MOLOKA'I
Under $100

In the cool uplands of Kala'e, **Hale Manu Guesthouse** (808/567-9136, www.halemalu-molokai.com, $55-80) is a small, relaxed, one-bedroom accommodation with two guest rooms and a small cottage. Guest rooms share a bathroom, and all rooms have access to a full kitchen in the main house. Refreshingly basic and in a non-touristy part of the island, guest rooms are $55/night, with an $80 rate for the cottage. Discounts are available for longer stays, no credit cards accepted. The guesthouse is centrally located near the Kualapu'u Coffee Farms and Kalaupapa Peninsula.

Over $150

Kaunakakai has the island's widest

WHERE TO STAY

WHERE TO STAY ON MOLOKA'I

Name	Type	Price
◖ Aloha Beach House	vacation rental	$250
Dunbar Beachfront Cottages	vacation rental	$175
Halawa Valley	camping	free in summer, inquire ahead
Hale Manu Guesthouse	vacation rental	$55-80
◖ Hotel Moloka'i	hotel	$175-250
Ka Hale Mana	B&B	$80-
Kaluakoi Villas	condo	$150-190
Ke Nani Kai	condo	100-200
Moloka'i Beach House	vacation rental	$250
Moloka'i Shores	condo	$190-250
One Ali'i Beach Park	camping	$5
Pala'au State Park	camping	$18
Paniolo Hale	condo	110-225
Papohaku Beach Park	camping	$5
◖ Pu'u O Hoku Ranch	cottages	$200-300
Waikolu	camping	$18
Wavecrest Resort	condo	$100-200

accommodation options and offers the closest thing to an island "resort."

The ◖ **Hotel Moloka'i** (877/553-5347, www.hotelmolokai.com, $175-250) is set right on the water and offers A-frame accommodations in a resort-type setting. It offers a swimming pool and activities desk, free Wi-Fi, live entertainment on select evenings, and all rooms have a refrigerator and microwave. The rooms have been refurbished numerous times. Breakfast is complimentary. This is a convenient, comfortable, and relaxing option for those who are more comfortable in a semi-resort setting. Rates vary depending on room size and season.

The **Moloka'i Shores** is a condominium complex with a large number of individually owned units as well as others managed by **Castle Resorts** (808/553-5944). Set on a tiny sliver of a beach, the three-story complex has a large open courtyard area with barbecue facilities and a swimming pool. The trade winds here are pronounced in the afternoon, and the swimming out front is marginal at best, but this is another convenient and comfortable option for basing yourself toward the center of the island. Rates range from $190-250 for one- and two-bedroom units.

Camping

Along the shoreline, camping is available at **One Ali'i Beach Park** for a $3/person permit available from the Parks and Recreation office in Kaunakakai (808/553-3204). The beach here is too shallow for swimming, however, and I would only camp here if it were an emergency.

A better option for camping is at **Pala'au State Park** in the cool and forested uplands of Kala'e. From here you can walk to such sights as the Kalaupapa Overlook or the densely forested Phallic Rock, or even wake up early to make

Features	Why Go Here	Best Fit For
oceanfront, kitchen	location, romantic	couples, groups, families
oceanfront, kitchen	location, quiet	couples
toilets	oceanfront, affordable	budget travelers
kitchen	location, affordable	budget travelers, solo travelers, couples
kitchenette, pool, breakfast	modern, activities desk	couples, families
gardens, kitchen	quiet, affordable	budget travelers, couples, solo travelers
kitchen	close to beach, location	couples
pool, kitchen	close to beach, location	couples, families
oceanfront, kitchen	location, full amenities	couples, groups, families
pool, barbecue, kitchen, oceanfront	location	families, couples
restrooms, water, oceanfront	last resort	budget travelers
restrooms, pavilion	affordable, location	budget travelers
	oceanfront, kitchen	location, quiet
toilets, water	oceanfront, quiet	budget travelers
kitchen, views	quiet, retreat	couples, honeymooners, families
toilets, picnic tables	quiet, nearby hiking	budget travelers, adventure travelers
pool, tennis, amenities	oceanfront, modern	couples, families

the trek to the Kalaupapa Peninsula to meet up with a guided tour. Permits are available by either calling the State Parks office (808/984-8109) or by making a reservation online at www.camping.ehawaii.gov. You will need to create a free account, and rates are $18/night for nonresidents and $12/night for Hawai'i residents.

If you want to get off the grid and plan on doing some hiking in the Moloka'i Forest Reserve, the same State Park permits can also be obtained for **Waikolu** campground. A grassy area with a small pavilion, this is a cool and misty mountain retreat where you're nearly sure to have the place all to yourself. For reservations, visit www.camping.ehawaii.gov.

EAST MOLOKA'I

Along this eastern section of the island are the bulk of its vacation rentals, cottages, and B&Bs. Afternoons are punctuated by brisk trade winds and the setting is more tropical than arid West Moloka'i.

Bed-and-Breakfasts

Ka Hale Mala (808/553-9009, www.molokai-bnb.com, $80-90) is less than five miles east of Kaunakakai on Kamakana Place. This quiet vacation rental is the ground floor of a family house, set amid a tropical garden. Here you have a large living room, full kitchen and bath, separate bedroom, and a laundry room, plus use of snorkel gear. Rates are $80 without breakfast or $90 with. No credit cards. Good place, convenient location. For more information, contact hosts Cheryl or Chuck Corbiell.

Condominiums

The largest condo on the east end of the

island is the **Wavecrest Resort** (808/558-8101), at mile marker 13 and with individually owned units. While every unit is different, general amenities include a swimming pool, tennis court, laundry facilities, and a nicely manicured, five-acre setting. One- and two-bedroom units have full kitchens and look across the Pailolo Channel toward Maui, and rates vary between $100-200. There is a front desk that is open 7:30am-1:30pm Monday-Friday. Contact island rental agents for individual units.

Vacation Rentals

The 【 **Aloha Beach House** (808/828-1100 or 888/828-1008, www.molokaivacation.com) is a great little two-bedroom cottage right on the beach in Puko'o. This house is just down the road from a sundries store, so you can pick up supplies there. This beach house has a full kitchen and washer and dryer. With a view like the one looking across toward Maui, there's a good chance you'll never want to leave. Perhaps best of all, a swimmable beach is just out the front door. Rates are $250 a night with a three-night minimum, plus a $175 cleaning fee.

For two additional beachfront accommodations, the **Dunbar Beachfront Cottages** (808/558-8153, www.molokai-beachfront-cottages.com) are 2 two-bedroom cottages set right on a secluded section of beach. Neat and trim, each has a full kitchen, living room, laundry, and deck, and the beach is right in front of you. These are quiet places, perfect for a relaxing holiday, but you still have television and free Wi-Fi. Cottages can sleep up to four people comfortably, and rates run $175 a night, with a three-night minimum and $75 cleaning fee. No credit cards.

Some distance farther is the **Molokai Beach House** (808/599-3838, www.molokaibeachhouse.com), a three-bedroom, two-bath, oceanfront home with all the conveniences. A large yard with a picnic table spreads out before you on the ocean side, and inside this island-style house is a big living room, full kitchen, and laundry room. The house sleeps up to six and runs $250 per night or $1,600 per week, with a $125 cleaning fee and three-night minimum.

At the far eastern end of the island high on the eastern hillside sits 14,000-acre 【 **Pu'u O Hoku Ranch** (808/558-8109, www.puuohoku.com). The three cottages and one lodge are some of the best and most remote on the island. If you're looking for a place to get away from everything, this is it. This is a real, working ranch, and it's also minutes away from the shores of Halawa Bay. This is a great place to tap into Hawai'i's history and culture, but those who prefer large beach resorts should probably just stay away. Wi-Fi is available at a few spots, but most accommodations are "unplugged." Check in at the ranch office along the highway at mile marker 25, where there is a small sundries store that sells basic food and gift items.

The two-bedroom Sunrise Cottage is $225/night, has a full kitchen, covered lanai, and can accommodate up to four people. The larger, four-bedroom Grove Cottage is $300/night for four people and $30/night for each additional guest, and can comfortably accommodate up to eight people. From this cottage there are ocean views looking out toward Maui with amazing whale-watching in winter. Five miles closer to Kaunakakai along the main highway, the one-bedroom Sugar Mill cottage is $200/night, sleeps four people, has a full kitchen, and is walking distance from one of the island's nicest beaches. For groups of 14 or more, the all-inclusive lodge includes three meals a day and spacious accommodations for $165/person/night. All cottages have a minimum two-night stay and a $100 cleaning fee; the lodge has a four-night minimum.

Camping

Camping without permission in **Halawa**

Valley is a great way to get a tongue-lashing from protective valley locals. Recently, however, Pu'u O Hoku Ranch has installed temporary restroom facilities in the valley, and has begun issuing free permits to camp along the shoreline May-September. Inquire at the ranch office before you set up camp.

WHERE TO STAY

BACKGROUND

The Land

GEOGRAPHY

The island of Maui is 727 square miles, making it the 17th largest island in the United States and the second largest island in Hawai'i behind the massive, 4,029-square-mile Big Island of Hawai'i. There are 120 linear miles of coastline. At its widest point, the island is 26 miles from north to south and 48 miles from east to west.

Known as the "Valley Isle," Maui is the product of two volcanoes—Haleakala and the older Mauna Kahalawai—the output of which merged together into a central isthmus to form the island we know today. At 10,023 feet above sea level, Haleakala is estimated to be about 750,000 years old, making it half as old as Mauna Kahalawai (otherwise known as the West Maui Mountains), which has stood for 1.5 million years. In looking at the two mountains, it's evident that Mauna Kahalawai—with its deeply eroded valleys and dramatically carved peaks—has fought the forces of nature for longer than smooth Haleakala. However, Haleakala already shows signs of its age in the ravines of Kipahulu, the Kaupo Gap, and the cleft in the mountainside towering above Ke'anae.

Although the islands of Maui, Lana'i,

© KYLE ELLISON

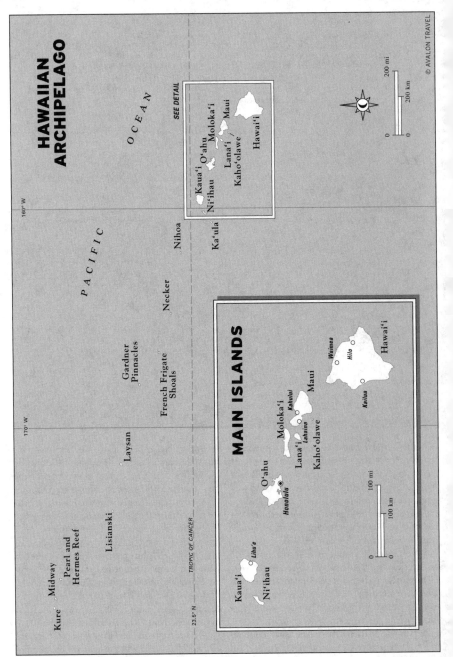

HAWAIIAN ARCHIPELAGO

PACIFIC   OCEAN

170° W

160° W

Kure

Midway

Pearl and
Hermes Reef

Lisianski

Laysan

Gardner
Pinnacles

French Frigate
Shoals

Necker

Nihoa

Ka'ula

TROPIC OF CANCER

23.5° N

SEE DETAIL

Kaua'i   O'ahu
Ni'ihau   Moloka'i
           Lana'i / Maui
           Kaho'olawe
           Hawai'i

© AVALON TRAVEL

0   200 mi
0   200 km

MAIN ISLANDS

Kaua'i
Lihu'e
Ni'ihau

O'ahu
Honolulu

Moloka'i
Lana'i   Kahului
Lahaina
Maui
Kaho'olawe

Waimea
Hilo
Kailua
Hawai'i

0   100 mi
0   100 km

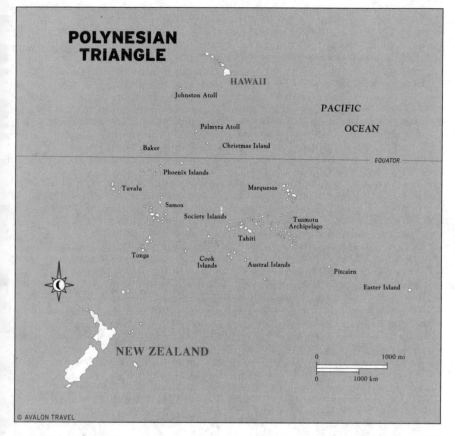

POLYNESIAN TRIANGLE

HAWAII

Johnston Atoll

PACIFIC

Palmyra Atoll

OCEAN

Baker   Christmas Island

EQUATOR

Phoenix Islands

Tuvalu   Marquesas

Samoa

Society Islands   Tuamotu
                                   Archipelago

Tahiti

Tonga   Cook
               Islands   Austral Islands

                                   Pitcairn

                                   Easter Island

NEW ZEALAND

0   1000 mi

0   1000 km

© AVALON TRAVEL

Moloka'i, and Kaho'olawe are four separate landmasses today, there was a time when all were connected in an island known as "Maui Nui," or "great Maui." This massive island was larger than the modern-day Big Island, and it's estimated that the islands were joined until as recently as 20,000 years ago when sea levels were lower as a result of an ice age.

If you look at a map of Hawai'i, you will notice that the islands drift to the northwest in a regular pattern. The Hawaiian Islands were formed by volcanoes which hover over a consistent hot spot in the core of the Earth while the tectonic plate containing the Hawaiian Islands drifts to the northwest at 3-5 inches per year, essentially creating an

"island conveyer belt." Over the course of millions of years islands will bubble up from the ocean floor, and as soon as they drift off the hot spot and their cores change into extinct volcanoes, they begin the torturous, northwestern drift of steady erosion until they become shorter, smaller, and more dramatically sculpted. This explains why the Big Island of Hawai'i (which has created 500 new acres of land in its most recent eruption) is the largest island with the tallest mountains, and why Maui—as the next island in the chain—is the second largest island with the second tallest mountain. Kaua'i is the oldest in the main Hawaiian chain at four million years old, and of the 132 islands which make up the state of

THE FORBIDDEN ISLAND

It's understandable that, after a five-hour plane ride where the view out the window is only of water, many visitors to Maui are geographically disoriented. It is more than just having their internal compass spun; having other islands looming on the horizon only makes it more geographically confusing. If you are in South Maui and you face the water, the island in the distance and to your right is Lana'i. Most island visitors know this much. Where many people stumble, however, is trying to determine what that *other* island is that sits silently to the left.

That mysterious island, as it turns out, has a fascinating history laced with crime, death, destruction, and rebirth. This is **Kaho'olawe** (Ka-HO-OH-LAW-vay), a place where there are no residents and no hotels, but more than a fair share of stories. It's a dry island reliant on rain from clouds extending out from Haleakala. Kaho'olawe was only sporadically settled during ancient times. During the mid-1800s, after the missionaries convinced Queen Ka'ahumanu to abolish capital punishment, the barren island was used as a penal colony. Life on the island was difficult and miserable. Many prisoners died of starvation. In 1841, a band of banished criminals swam from Kaho'olawe to Makena on the island of Maui, raided a settlement, loaded some canoes with food, and then paddled victoriously back to the emaciated prisoners. With food now in hand, the marooned prisoners focused solving their second problem: the lack of women. A team paddled across the channel to the island of Lana'i and returned with a boatful of volunteers from the women-only penal colony established there. Suddenly, all on Kaho'olawe was right again.

Once the penal colony was closed, there were a number of failed attempts at ranching on the island. After the Japanese invasion of Pearl Harbor in 1941, Kaho'olawe was placed under martial law. Over the next 50 years, the forbidden island served as a practice bombing range for the military. Longtime locals remember the island glowing orange in the evening due to the explosions.

Legions of native Hawaiian activists protested the bombing of a major Hawaiian island. The protests intensified in 1976 when a group of activists headed to Kaho'olawe itself. En route to the island, their boats were stopped by a U.S. Coast Guard helicopter. Nine landed and spend a few hours on the forbidden island before being detained. The island of Kaho'olawe became a catalyst for change—something that all native Hawaiian activists rallied around. The bombing finally ceased in 1990. Some island residents believe that the billions of dollars in real estate investments on the nearby Wailea shoreline made it stop. A political donation here, an old friend from college there, and *voila!*, no more bombing.

Today the island of Kaho'olawe is owned by the state of Hawai'i, although it exists under the stewardship of organizations such as the Kaho'olawe Island Reserve Commission and Protect Kaho'olawe Ohana. No commercial activities are permitted on the island, and long-term goals such as clearing the island of ordnance and replanting native foliage have already begun. The U.S. Navy spent $400 million dollars clearing the island of millions of pounds of military debris—the largest ordnance removal in the nation's history, Despite these efforts, vast, unknown quantities of debris remain. But there are also hundreds of recorded archaeological sites, ensuring that Kaho'olawe will forever be dedicated to Hawaiian culture.

Hawai'i, tiny Midway and Kure atolls form the northwestern reach.

A seamount known as Lo'ihi is already believed to be the next Hawaiian island in the long Pacific chain. Researchers estimate that the island of Lo'ihi will surface southeast of the Big Island in 10,000 years.

Rivers and Lakes

Maui has no navigable rivers, but there are hundreds of streams. Two of the largest are **Palikea Stream,** which runs through Kipahulu Valley forming 'Ohe'o Gulch, and **'Iao Stream,** which has sculpted the amazing monoliths in 'Iao Valley. A few reservoirs dot the island,

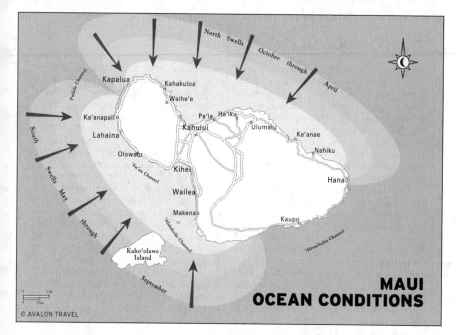

MAUI OCEAN CONDITIONS

© AVALON TRAVEL

but the two largest natural bodies of water are the 41-acre **Kanaha Pond** on the outskirts of Kahului and 500-acre **Kealia Pond** on the southern shore of the isthmus, both major bird and wildlife sanctuaries. Be aware of the countless streams and rivulets that can quickly turn from trickles to torrents, causing flash floods in valleys that were the height of hospitality only minutes before.

NATURAL DISASTERS

Although moderately free of most natural disasters, Maui has experienced a number of events which remain fresh in recent memory. Of all the disasters, the most dramatic was the 1946 **tsunami** that swept entire villages away along the flank of East Maui and flooded much of Halawa Valley on the eastern tip of Moloka'i. More recently, the same tsunami which struck Japan on March 11, 2011, also caused a big mess in Maui. While there was no loss of life, Lahaina Harbor completely drained on the outgoing pull, and the incoming water was strong enough to sink numerous

boats and destroy the docks at many of the harbors around the island. At Manele Harbor on Lana'i, the end of the ferry dock has yet to be fixed as of this writing.

Maui, thankfully, has always been spared the direct hit of any major hurricane. The last **hurricane** to affect Maui was Hurricane Iniki in 1992, and while Maui avoided the billions in damage which the storm leveraged on Kaua'i, waves destroyed the pier at Mala and sank numerous boats. Hurricane Iwa in 1982 crept close to the islands, although Maui is situated outside the hurricane belt.

Although **earthquakes** are rare, a large temblor on October 15, 2006, caused enough damage to close the "back road" to Hana for the better part of two years due to landslides and structural damage to bridges.

CLIMATE

Maui, Lana'i, and Moloka'i have weather similar to that of the rest of the Hawaiian Islands. The weather on Maui depends more on where you are than on the season, and the average daily temperature along the coast is about 78°F (25.5°C) in summer and about 72°F (22°C) in winter. On Haleakala summit, the average is 43-50°F (6-10°C), although snow can fall in rare winter storms. The lowest temperature ever recorded on Maui was atop Haleakala in 1961, when it dropped well below freezing to a low, low 11°F. In contrast, sunny Kihei has recorded a blistering 98°F.

Maui has wonderful weather, and because of near-constant breezes, the air is usually clear and clean. Traffic and weather conditions never create smog, but because of burning cane fields, Maui air will at times become smoky, a condition that usually rectifies itself in a day when the winds are blowing. On rarer occasions, a volcanic haze, known as VOG, will filter over the island from the Big Island. If it's hazy, doesn't smell of smoke, and nothing has been burning, it's probably VOG.

On Lana'i, the average summer temperature along the coast is about 80°F, while the average winter temperature is about 70°F. It can be as much as 10 degrees cooler in Lana'i City, which sits in the cooler uplands.

Precipitation

Rain on Maui is as much a factor as it is elsewhere in Hawai'i. On any day, somewhere on Maui it's raining, while other areas experience drought. A dramatic example of this phenomenon is a comparison of Lahaina with Pu'u Kukui, both in West Maui and separated by only seven miles. Lahaina, which translates as "Merciless Sun," is hot, arid, and gets only 15 inches of rainfall annually, while Pu'u Kukui can receive close to 400 inches (33 *feet!*) of precipitation. Other leeward towns get a comparable amount of rain to Lahaina, but as you move upcountry and around the north coast, the rains become more frequent. In Hana, rainfall is about five times as great as on the leeward side, averaging more than 80 inches per year.

The Trade Winds

Temperatures in the 50th state are both constant and moderate because of the trade winds, a breeze from the northeast that blows at about 10-25 miles per hour. These breezes are so prevalent that the northeast sides of the islands are always referred to as **windward,** regardless of where the wind happens to be blowing on any given day. You can count on the trades an average of 300 days per year, hardly missing a day during summer and occurring half the time in winter. Although usually calm in the morning, they pick up during the heat of the afternoon and weaken at night.

Kona Winds

Kona means "leeward" in Hawaiian, and when the trades stop blowing, these southerly winds often take over. To anyone from Hawai'i, "kona wind" is a euphemism for bad weather, for it brings in hot, sticky air. Luckily, kona winds are most common October-April, when they only appear roughly half the time. The temperatures drop slightly during the winter, so these hot winds are tolerable, and even useful for moderating the temperature.

A "kona storm" is another matter. These subtropical low-pressure storms develop west of the Hawaiian Islands, and as they move east, they draw winds up from the south. Usually occurring only in winter, they can cause heavy rainfall and considerable damage, often stretching for the better part of a week. For locals, this is "winter."

THE TSUNAMI SIREN

If you are visiting Maui on the first workday of the month, don't be alarmed when you hear a loud siren right around noon. This is the island's tsunami warning system. The sirens are systematically tested at the this time once a month. The loud wailing will last for about 30 seconds, after which the regularly scheduled peace and tranquility will resume. If, however, you hear the tsunami siren at any other time, ask your hotel about potential tsunami evacuations (which have occurred three times since 2011).

MICROCLIMATES

The weather in Maui can be confusing. Often it can be raining at your hotel but sunny two miles down the road, and the wind can be blowing 30 knots at one beach but completely still at another.

Why is that? While on the mainland frontal storm systems can stretch for thousands of miles, weather on Maui is regulated by microclimates. Since the trade winds blow from a northeasterly direction, towns on the northern or eastern coastlines lie on the windward side of the island and are prone to more wind and rain. Meanwhile, towns on the southern and western shorelines are tucked in the lee of the steep mountains and are consequently drier and calmer. This explains why parts of the island such as Kapalua, Napili, and Hana are wetter and drier than areas such as Lahaina or Kihei. Conversely, during the hot summer months when Lahaina can swelter in 90° heat, the northern areas of Napili and Kapalua can be 10 degrees cooler and blessed with a cooling breeze.

Many visitors only check the weather forecast for their upcoming vacation, on a site such as www.weather.com, which only displays the forecast for the Kahului Airport on the windier and wetter windward side of Maui. Consequently the forecast will almost always call for showers. Don't be discouraged! Chances are resort areas such as Wailea, Kihei, Lahaina, or Ka'anapali will be experiencing a completely different—often sunnier—forecast than what's being displayed. For a more accurate weather forecast, see local weather sites such as www.mauiweathertoday.com, which breaks down the island's forecasts by various regions.

Although microclimates control the majority of Maui's weather, they don't dictate the weather 100 percent of the time. October-April Maui can be affected by large cold fronts in the same way that areas on the mainland are. If a large cold front in the North Pacific (the same storm systems which will eventually drop snow and rain on the West Coast of the US) decides to swing south, this front can move across the chain and bring heavy rain to every part of the island. While these fronts often dissipate over Kaua'i and O'ahu before reaching Maui (and thereby make Kaua'i and O'ahu wetter than Maui), occasionally the front will envelop the entire state and bring up to a week of rain.

For locals, this is what's known as "winter." The island might not get snow (well, Haleakala might), but Maui is still prone to winter storms which can bring a lot of rain. No one wants to have a week of rain on their vacation. In the same way that a "normal" winter day in your hometown might include sun or it might include snow, a "normal" winter day in Hawaii can be 78° and sunny, or it can be also be 74° and rainy. But at least it's warm!

So what's the moral of the story? If you're staying in Kapalua, Napili, or Ka'anapali and it's windy and rainy at your hotel, don't just assume it's raining everywhere. If you are planning a vacation at any point in winter (particularly January or February), cross your fingers that you'll enjoy some midwinter sun!

Flora and Fauna

Anyone who loves a mystery will be intrigued by the speculation about how plants and animals first came to Hawai'i. The islands, more than 2,000 miles from any continental landfall, are isolated from the normal ecological spread of plants and animals. Even the most tenacious travelers of the flora and fauna kingdoms would be sorely tried in crossing the mighty Pacific. Those that made it by pure chance found a totally foreign ecosystem where they had to adapt or perish. The survivors evolved quickly, and many plants and birds became so specialized that they were limited not only to specific islands in the chain but to habitats that frequently consisted of a single isolated valley. It was as if after traveling so far, and finding a niche, they never budged again.

Before settlement, Hawai'i had no fruits, vegetables, coconut palms, edible land animals, conifers, mangroves, or banyans. The early Polynesians brought 27 varieties of plants they needed for food and other purposes. About 90 percent of plants on the Hawaiian Islands today were introduced after Captain Cook first set foot here. Tropical flowers, wild and vibrant as we know them today, were relatively few. In a land where thousands of orchids now brighten every corner, there were only four native varieties, the least in any of the 50 states. Today, the indigenous plants and animals have the highest rate of extinction anywhere on earth. By the beginning of the 21st century, native plants growing below 1,500 feet in elevation were almost completely extinct or totally replaced by introduced species, and the land and its living things have been greatly transformed by humans and their agriculture.

The silversword ('ahinahina) is endemic to Hawai'i.

FLORA
Introduced Plants

The majority of flora considered exotic by visitors was introduced either by the original Polynesians or by later settlers of European origin. The Polynesians who colonized Hawai'i brought foodstuffs, including coconuts, bananas, taro, breadfruit, sweet potatoes, yams, and sugarcane. Non-Hawaiian settlers have brought mangoes, papayas, passion fruit, pineapples, and the other tropical fruits and vegetables associated with the islands. Tthe flowers, including protea, plumeria, anthuriums, orchids, heliconia, ginger, and most hibiscus, have come from every continent on earth.

Native Trees

Koa and 'ohi'a are two indigenous trees still seen on Maui. Both have been greatly reduced by the foraging of introduced cattle and goats, and through logging and forest fires. The **koa,** a form of acacia, is Hawai'i's finest native tree. It can grow to more than 70 feet high and has a strong, straight trunk that can measure more than 10 feet in circumference. The Hawaiians used koa as the main log for their dugout canoes, and elaborate ceremonies were performed when a log was cut and dragged to a canoe shed. Koa wood was also preferred for paddles, spears, and surfboards, and today you will find fine Hawaiian galleries across the islands selling koa wood bowls and crafts.

The **'ohi'a** is a survivor and therefore the most abundant of all the native Hawaiian trees. The 'ohi'a produces a tuftlike flower—usually red, but occasionally orange, yellow, or white, the latter being rare and elusive—that resembles a natural pompon. The strong, hard wood was used to make canoes, poi bowls, and temple images. 'Ohi'a logs were also used as railroad ties and shipped to the mainland from Pahoa on the Big Island. It's believed that the "golden spike" finally linking the rail lines spanning the U.S. East and West Coasts in Ogden, Utah was driven into a Puna 'ohi'a log.

'Ahinahina (Silversword)

Found on the high alpine slopes of Haleakala

above the 6,000-foot level, the 'ahinahina plant is an iconic symbol for the beauty of Haleakala Crater. The plant may live for only a few years or for nearly a century, but each ends its life by sprouting a gorgeous stalk of hundreds of purplish-red flowers before withering from a majestic six-foot plant to a flat, gray skeleton. 'Ahinahina bloom mostly July-August, but they can bloom as early as May or as late as November. An endangered species, 'ahinahina are totally protected.

Protea

The slopes of leeward Haleakala between 2,000 and 4,000 feet are heaven to protea, as the growing conditions could not be more perfect. The days are warm, the nights are cool, and the well-drained volcanic soil has the exact combination of minerals on which protea thrive. Protea make excellent gifts that can be shipped anywhere, and although they are beautiful as fresh-cut flowers, they have the extra benefit of drying superbly. Just hang them in a dark, dry, well-ventilated area and they do the rest. You can see protea, along with other botanical specialties, at the gardens, flower farms, and gift shops in Kula.

FAUNA
Birds

One of the great tragedies of natural history is the continuing demise of Hawaiian bird life. Perhaps only 15 original species of birds remain of the more than 70 native families that thrived before the coming of humans, and since the arrival of Captain Cook in 1778, 23 species have become extinct, with 31 more in danger. Hawai'i's endangered birds account for 40 percent of the birds officially listed as endangered or threatened by the U.S. Fish and Wildlife Service. In the last 200 years, more than four times as many birds have become extinct in Hawai'i as in all of North America.

Despite the threats, however, a few cling to life in the remote reaches of the East Maui rainforest, with the **'akohekohe, 'i'iwi,** and **'amakihi** some of the notable varieties. While visitors aren't likely to encounter many of the island's forest birds, those who are interested in these fragile species should contact the **Maui Forest Bird Recovery Project** (www.mauiforestbird.org) for more information and ways in which you can volunteer.

Other than forest birds, two water birds found on Maui are the **Hawaiian stilt** *(ae'o)* and the **Hawaiian coot** *('alae ke'oke'o).* The stilt is about 16 inches tall and lives on Maui at Kanaha and Kealia Ponds, with a black body, white belly, and distinctively pink legs.

At Haleakala Crater, the dark-rumped petrel is found around the visitor's center at about one hour after dusk May-October, and the **nene goose**—the Hawaiian state bird—is a close cousin of the Canada goose and can be found in large numbers in the grass around Paliku Cabin.

Mammals

Hawai'i's only two indigenous land mammals are the Hawaiian monk seal and the hoary bat. All other mammals have been introduced. While **monk seals** are sometimes sighted along island shorelines and reefs, the most famous mammals are the whales and dolphins which ply the waters offshore. The channels between the islands of Maui County are home to the world's largest population of **humpback whales.** These acrobatic, aerial cetaceans are a delight for winter visitors, and there are few things like the thrill of a 45-ton animal erupting out of the water before your eyes. Humpbacks migrate to the islands from November-May to mate, birth, and care for their young, and during the course of their four-month stay, they won't eat anything at all. While whales are only observed during the winter, **dolphins** are year-round residents and a common sight around the islands. There are three distinct pods of Hawaiian spinner dolphins residing along West Maui, South Maui, and the southwestern coastline of Lana'i. The acrobatic spinners can complete up to seven full rotations in the air before splashing back down into the water. Larger bottlenose dolphins are also occasionally seen, while the pan-tropical spotted dolphins are confined to deeper waters.

© KYLE ELLISON

The *nene* goose is Hawai'i's state bird.

FLORA AND FAUNA OF LANA'I

Most of Lana'i's flora and fauna have been introduced. The **Cook pine** and the **mouflon sheep** were a human intervention attempting to improve the natural, often barren habitat. These species have adapted so well that they now symbolize Lana'i in the way that the pineapple once did. Besides the mouflon, Lana'i boasts **axis deer, Rio Grande turkeys,** and a number of **ring-necked pheasants.** Like the other islands of Hawai'i, Lana'i, unfortunately, is home to native birds that are headed for extinction, although the recent rediscovery of a colony of **'Ua'u shearwaters** on the summit of Lana'ihale has given hope that all is not yet lost. For more information on the native species of Lana'i, visit www.lanainativespeciesrecovery.org.

FLORA AND FAUNA OF MOLOKA'I

The *kukui,* or candlenut tree, is common to all of the Hawaiian Islands, and while it's the official tree for the state of Hawai'i, its tiny white blossom is Moloka'i's flower. The *kukui,* introduced centuries ago by the early Polynesians, grows on lower mountain slopes, is distinguished by its pale green leaves, and dominates the valleys of lush eastern Moloka'i.

Land animals on Moloka'i such as **pigs, goats,** and **axis deer** were introduced by humans. Moloka'i's feral pigs of the upper wetland forests of the northeast, indiscriminate in their relentless hunt for food, are ecological nightmares that virtually bulldoze the rainforest floor into fetid pools and gouged earth, where mosquitoes and other introduced species thrive while driving out the natives. Today, pigs are hunted, and fences keep them out of some fragile areas.

Offspring from a pair of goats left by Captain Cook on the island of Ni'ihau spread to all the islands, and they were well adapted to life on Moloka'i. Originally from the arid Mediterranean, goats could live well without any surface water, a condition quite prevalent over most of Moloka'i.

NO LAND PREDATORS!

Maui can be a hiker's dream—and not just because of the scenery. Unlike other parts of the world where hikers need to worry about grizzly bears, mountain lions, black bears, and snakes, Maui has no land predators to speak of whatsoever. Remote sections of the island are home to wild boars, axis deer, and mountain goats, although all of these flee at the sound of a footstep. There are technically centipedes and a small number of scorpions, although unless you're hiking through a compost pile you're not likely to encounter them. So when you set off hiking, there is nothing to worry about in the way of natural predators.

History

DISCOVERY OF THE ISLANDS

No one knows exactly when the first Polynesians arrived in Hawai'i, but the great deliberate migrations from the southern islands seem to have taken place AD 400–800, though anthropologists keep pushing the date back as new evidence becomes available. They arrived through an uncanny ability to sail and navigate without instruments, using the sun by day and the moon and rising stars by night. The first planned migrations were from the Marquesas, a group of 11 islands in eastern Polynesia, and for five centuries the Marquesans settled and lived peacefully on the new land.

Then, it appears that in the 12th century a deliberate exodus of warlike Tahitians arrived and subjugated the settled islanders. They came to conquer, and when a Tahitian priest named Pa'ao introduced the warlike god Ku and the rigid *kapu* system of laws, it forever altered the religious and social landscape. Voyages between Tahiti and Hawai'i continued for about 100 years, and Tahitian customs, legends, and language became the Hawaiian way of life. Then suddenly, for no recorded or apparent reason, the voyages discontinued, and Hawai'i returned to total isolation.

CAPTAIN COOK SIGHTS HAWAI'I

On January 18, 1778, Captain Cook's 100-foot flagship HMS *Resolution* and its 90-foot companion HMS *Discovery* first caught sight of the island of O'ahu. Two days later, Cook would venture ashore at the town of Waimea to reprovision his ships, and from this moment on, life would never be the same for Hawaiians. Though he didn't stay long in Waimea, Cook did note in his diary that the Hawaiians looked similar to other peoples of the Pacific he had encountered, specifically those of New Zealand.

Once the seafarers were onshore, brass medals were traded for a mackerel, and Cook noted that the Hawaiians were quite enamored with the ships. Sailors immediately took to mixing with the women, bringing the first venereal diseases to the island that would later ravage the native population. The highlights of the first meeting included mutual interest in each other, a few of the sailors' items being stolen, the trading of sex and venereal disease.

It wouldn't be until a year later that Cook returned, and his impact would become much more significant. Cook had named Hawai'i the Sandwich Islands in honor of one of his patrons, John Montague, the Earl of Sandwich. On his return voyage he spotted Maui on November 26, 1778. After eight weeks of seeking a suitable harbor the ships bypassed the island and finally found safe anchorage at Kealakekua Bay on the Kona coast of the Big Island. It is lucky for history that on board was Mr. Anderson, ship's chronicler, who left a handwritten record of the strange and tragic events that followed.

Coincidentally, when Cook landed on the Big Island, it was the time of the *makahiki,* a celebration dedicated to the beloved god Lono. For a few days, as Cook circled the island, the Hawaiians circled it too, parading a structure held overhead of a cross beam with two flowing white sheets of tapa which resembled a ship's mast. On January 16, 1779, as the Hawaiians reached Kealakekua Bay, Lono's sacred harbor, Cook's ship came into the port. Because of the timing with the *makahiki,* the Hawaiians believed Cook to be a god and welcomed him to shore with respect.

In the following weeks the Englishmen overstayed their welcome, but when they left, the *Resolution* broke down at sea. Cook returned to Kealakekua but was no longer well received. As the Hawaiians stole random items from the sailboat, the sailors became violent. Cook lost control after the Hawaiians stole a cutter which had been moored to a nearby buoy, and it would be a change in temper that would ultimately cost him his life. He went ashore with backup, intending to take Chief Kalaniopu'u hostage for ransom. When the violence escalated, Cook was killed. A bitter, protracted argument ensued over the return of Cook's bones (he was ceremoniously roasted to have the bones removed from the flesh), and upon finally receiving the bones of their leader, Cook's men sailed back to England.

At the time of Cook's visit, Hawai'i was in a state of political turmoil. In the 1780s the islands were divided into three kingdoms: Kalaniopu'u ruled the Big Island and the Hana district of Maui; Kahekili ruled the rest of Maui, Kaho'olawe, Lana'i, and eventually O'ahu; and Kaeo ruled Kaua'i. Soon after, the great warrior Kamehameha conquered all of the islands under one rule, and this dynasty would last for 100 years until the Hawaiian monarchy fell forever.

With regard to Western explorers, however, it became known that Hawai'i was a convenient stop on routes to the Pacific Northwest and China, leading to an influx of westerners and increased foreign trade. Hawai'i, it seemed, was no longer a secret.

THE OLOWALU MASSACRE

In 1790, as Western traders were still beginning their forays to the islands, the U.S. merchant ship *Eleanora,* commanded by Yankee captain Simon Metcalfe, was looking for a harbor after its long voyage from the Pacific Northwest. Following a day behind was the *Fair American,* a tiny ship sailed by Metcalfe's son, Thomas. While the elder Metcalfe's ship was anchored off the southern coastline of Maui, some natives slipped close in their canoes and stole a small boat, killing a sailor in the process. Upon learning that the perpetrators were from the village of Olowalu (about five miles south of Lahaina), Metcalfe decided to sail there and trick the Hawaiians by first negotiating a truce and then unleashing full fury upon them. Signaling he was willing to trade, he invited canoes of innocent natives to visit his ship. In the meantime, he ordered that all cannon and muskets be readied with scatter shot. When the canoes were within hailing distance, he ordered his crew to fire at will. More than 100 people were slain, and the Hawaiians remembered this killing as "the Day of Spilled Brains." Metcalfe then sailed away to Kealakekua Bay and, in an unrelated incident, succeeded in insulting a ruling chief named Kameiamoku who vowed to annihilate the next *haole* ship he saw.

Fate sent him the *Fair American* and young Thomas Metcalfe. The little ship was overrun by superior forces, and in the ensuing battle, the mate, Isaac Davis, so distinguished himself by open acts of bravery that his life alone was spared. Kameiamoku later turned over both Davis and the ship to Kamehameha. Meanwhile, while harbored at Kealakekua, the senior Metcalfe sent John Young to reconnoiter. Kamehameha, having learned of the capture of the *Fair American,* detained Young so he could not report, and Metcalfe, losing patience, marooned his own man and sailed off to Canton. Kamehameha quickly realized the significance of his two captives and the *Fair American* with its brace of small cannons. He appropriated the ship and made Davis and Young trusted advisers, eventually raising them to the rank of chief. They would all play a significant role in the unification of Hawai'i.

KAMEHAMEHA'S UNIFICATION OF THE ISLANDS

Kamehameha was born on the Big Island of Hawai'i, after a prophecy that he would become a "killer of chiefs." Because of this, other chiefs ordered the child to be killed, so his mother had to sneak off to the royal birthing stones near Mo'okini Heiau on the island's Kohala coast. After giving birth, she gave the child to a servant, who took him down the coast to raise him in solitude. As he grew and matured, Kamehameha proved himself a fierce and hardy warrior, and in due time became one of the strongest chiefs on the island of Hawai'i.

In 1790, Kamehameha invaded Maui with the assistance of cannons from the captured *Fair American*. In the Battle of Kepaniwai at 'Iao Valley, Kamehameha killed so many commoners it's said that he dammed the stream waters with their bloody bodies. After his decisive victory on Maui, Kamehameha was drawn back to the Big Island to quell uprisings on his home island. When the king of Maui—Kahekili—sailed to the Big Island to exact revenge for the slaughter at 'Iao, he was thoroughly beaten by Kamehameha's forces at the Battle of Waimanu Valley. Demoralized and defeated, Kahekili succumbed to the rule of Kamehameha, and the battle for Maui had been won.

By the time Kamehameha had won the Big Island and Maui, Hawai'i was becoming a regular stopover for ships seeking the lucrative sandalwood trade with China. In February 1791, Captain George Vancouver (who had originally sailed on Cook's ill-fated voyage), returned to Kealakekua and was greeted by a throng of 30,000. The captain at once recognized Kamehameha, who was wearing a Chinese dressing gown that he had received in tribute from another chief, who in turn had received it directly from the hands of Cook himself. Captain Vancouver became a trusted adviser of Kamehameha and told him about the westerners' form of worship, and the captain gave him gifts of beef cattle, fowl, and breeding stock of sheep and goats. The Hawaiians were cheerful and outgoing, and they showed remorse for the earlier incident when they indicated that the remainder of Cook's bones had been buried in a temple close to Kealakekua. Young, by this time firmly entrenched in Hawaiian society, made no request to sail away with Vancouver. During the next two decades of Kamehameha's rule, the French, Russians, English, and Americans discovered the great whaling waters off Hawai'i, and their increasing visits shook the ancient religion and social order of *kapu*.

Kamehameha's final victories over the other islands would come later, with a decisive conflict taking place in 1794 on the island of O'ahu. Kamehameha and 16,000 of his troops pushed Kalanikupule—the leader of O'ahu—back into the mountains of Nu'uanu to the edge of towering cliffs which form the backdrop of Honolulu. After fierce fighting, Kamehameha's men drove Kalanikupule's warriors over the cliffs, and with the dramatic victory, Kamehameha now took control of O'ahu. In 1796 Kamehameha put down a revolt on Hawai'i, and Kaumuali'i, the king of Kaua'i, recognizing his strength, gave up the island rather than suffer attack. For the first time in history, Kamehameha became the sole ruler of all of the islands in Hawai'i.

Under Kamehameha, social order was medieval, with *ali'i* (royalty) owing their military allegiance to the king and the serf-like *maka'ainana* paying tribute and working the lands.

The great king ruled until his death on May 8, 1819. Hawai'i knew a peaceful rule under Kamehameha. After years on Maui, he returned to his home in Kona on the Big Island where he eventually passed away. To this day, his burial place is unknown. His son, Liholiho, gained the kingdom (and would become Kamehameha II), although Kamehameha's wife Ka'ahumanu had a strong influence and power.

NO MORE *KAPU*

As Ka'ahumanu used her strength to counsel Kamehameha's son and successor Liholiho, she knew that the old ways would not carry Hawai'i into the future. In November 1819 she inspired Liholiho to eliminate the *kapu* system of laws which had so rigidly dominated Hawaiian society. Men eating with women was prohibited, as was women eating certain food, such as bananas and particular fish. To exhibit the end of the *kapu* system, Ka'ahumanu and Liholiho ate together in public, thereby shattering these important taboos and marking the demise of the old ways. As the first morsels passed Ka'ahumanu's lips, the ancient gods of Hawai'i tumbled. Throughout the land, revered *heiau* were burned and abandoned and idols knocked to the ground. Now the people had nothing but their weakened inner selves to rely on. Nothing and no one could answer their prayers; their spiritual lives were in shambles.

MISSIONARIES AND WHALERS

The year 1819 was of the utmost significance in Hawaiian history. It marked the death of Kamehameha, the overthrow of the ancient *kapu* system, the arrival of the first whaler in Lahaina, and the departure of Calvinist missionaries from New England, determined to convert the heathen islands. With the *kapu* system and all of the ancient gods abandoned (except for the fire goddess Pele of Kilauea), a great void existed in the souls of the Hawaiians.

Missionaries

Into this spiritual vortex sailed the brig *Thaddeus* on April 4, 1820. Coming ashore in Kailua-Kona, the Reverends Bingham and Thurston were granted a one-year trial missionary period by King Liholiho. They established themselves on the Big Island and O'ahu and from there began the transformation of Hawai'i. By 1824, the new faith had such a foothold that Chieftess Keopuolani, the first wife of Kamehameha and mother of Kamehameha II, climbed to the fire pit atop Kilauea and defied the volcano goddess Pele.

This was even more striking than the previous breaking of the food *kapu* because the strength of Pele could be seen. Keopuolani ate forbidden *'ohelo* berries and cried out, "Jehovah is my God."

The year 1824 also marked the death of Keopuolani, who was given a Christian burial. She had set the standard by accepting Christianity, and several of the *ali'i* had followed the queen's lead. Liholiho had sailed off to England, where he and his wife contracted measles and died. During these years, Ka'ahumanu allied herself with Reverend Richards, pastor of the first mission in the islands, and together they wrote Hawai'i's first code of laws based on the Ten Commandments. Foremost was the condemnation of murder, theft, brawling, and the desecration of the Sabbath by work or play. The early missionaries had the best of intentions, but they were blinded by the single-mindedness that was also their greatest ally. *Anything* native was felt to be inferior, and they set about wiping out all traces of the old ways. In their rampage they reduced the Hawaiian culture to ashes—more so than the diseases brought in by the whalers.

Whalers

A good share of the common sailors of the early 19th century came from the lowest levels of the Western world. Many a whoremongering drunkard had awoken from a stupor and found himself on the pitching deck of a ship, discovering to his dismay that he had been "pressed into naval service." These sailors were a filthy, uneducated, lawless rabble. Their present situation was dim, their future hopeless, and they would live to be 30 if they were lucky and didn't die from scurvy or a thousand other miserable fates. They snatched brief pleasure in every port and jumped ship at any opportunity, especially in an easy berth such as Lahaina. In exchange for *aloha* they gave drunkenness, sloth, and insidious death by disease. By the 1850s, the population of native Hawaiians had tumbled from the estimated 300,000 reported by Captain Cook in 1778 to barely 60,000. Common conditions such as colds, flu, venereal disease, and sometimes smallpox and cholera more than decimated the Hawaiians, who had no natural immunities to these foreign ailments.

Two Worlds Collide

The 1820s were a time of confusion for the Hawaiians. When Kamehameha II died, the kingdom passed to Kauikeaouli (Kamehameha III), who made his residence in Lahaina. The young king was only nine years old when the title passed to him. His childhood was spent during the cusp of the change from old ways to new, and he was often pulled in two directions by vastly differing beliefs. Since he was royally born, he was bound by age-old Hawaiian tradition to mate and produce an heir with the highest ranking *ali'i* in the kingdom. This mate happened to be his younger sister, Princess Nahi'ena'ena. To the old Hawaiian advisers, this arrangement was perfectly acceptable. To the influential missionaries, incest was an unimaginable abomination. The young king could not stand the mental pressure imposed by conflicting worlds, and he became a teenage alcoholic too royal to be restrained.

Meanwhile, Nahi'ena'ena was under even more pressure because she was a favorite of the missionaries, having been baptized into the church at age 12. At times she was a pious Christian, at others she drank all night. As the prince and princess grew into their late teens, they became even more attached to each other, and whenever possible, they lived together in a grass house built for the princess by her father. In 1832, the great Ka'ahumanu died, leaving the king on his own, and in 1833 Kamehameha III fell into total drunken confusion, one night attempting suicide. After this episode he seemed to straighten up a bit and mostly kept a low profile. In 1836, Princess Nahi'ena'ena was convinced by the missionaries to take a husband, and though she married Leleiohoku, a chief from the Big Island, she continued to sleep with her brother. It's uncertain who fathered the child, but Nahi'ena'ena gave birth to a baby boy in September 1836, though the young prince survived for only a few hours and Nahi'ena'ena never recovered. She died in December 1836 and was laid to rest in Lahaina. After the death of his sister, Kamehameha III became a sober and righteous ruler, and he governed longer than any other king until his death in 1854.

Missionaries Take Over

In 1823 the first mission was established in Lahaina, and within a few years many of the notable *ali'i* had been converted to Christianity. Construction began on Waine'e Church in 1828, while a struggle brewed between missionaries and whalers centering on public drunkenness and the servicing of sailors by native women. The missionaries placed a curfew on sailors and prohibited native women from boarding ships. As can be expected, the sailors were outraged. In 1825 the crew from the *Daniel* attacked the home of Reverend Richards, and in 1827, sailors from the whaler *John Palmer* fired their cannon at his house, prompting the construction of the Lahaina fort.

The Great Mahele

In 1840, Kamehameha III instituted a constitutional monarchy, bringing about the Hawaiian Bill of Rights. The most far-reaching change was the transition to private ownership of land, although the Hawaiians could not think in terms of "owning" land. No one could *possess* land, one could only *use* land, and its ownership was a strange foreign concept. As a result, naive Hawaiians gave up their lands for a song to unscrupulous traders, and land ownership issues remain a basic and unrectified problem even to this day. In 1847 Kamehameha III and his advisers separated the lands of Hawai'i into three groupings: crown land (belonging to the king), government land (belonging to the chiefs), and the people's land (the largest parcels). In 1848, 245 *ali'i* entered their land claims in the *Mahele Book*, assuring them ownership. In 1850 the commoners were given title in fee simple to the lands they cultivated and lived on as tenants, not including house lots in towns. Commoners without land could buy small *kuleana* (farms) from the government at $0.50 per acre. In

THE HAWAIIAN WRITTEN WORD

Prior to the arrival of the missionaries, the Hawaiian language—like all other Polynesian languages—had no written form. All information was passed along orally through song, chant, or dance. There wasn't even an alphabet upon which to base the language. The missionaries, however, found it difficult to convert Hawaiians to Christianity without the ability to read, write, or create a Hawaiian language Bible, so it was the missionaries themselves who took on the task of creating a Hawaiian alphabet and establishing a written form of the language. With a 12-letter alphabet in place (14 if the okina and kahako characters are included), the island's first printing press was shipped from Honolulu and housed here in Hale Pa'i in 1834. Not long after its arrival, the first printed newspaper west of the Rocky Mountains—a four-page publication called Ka Lama Hawai'i was printed on Valentine's Day of the same year. Along with the press came myriad other benefits of written language such as hymn books, written laws, and a Hawaiian Constitution. In the course of a single lifetime during the 1800s, the Native Hawaiians went from having no form of written communication to boasting one of the highest literacy rates in the world.

1850, foreigners were also allowed to buy land in fee simple, and the ownership of Hawai'i from that day forward slipped steadily from the hands of its indigenous people.

SUGAR

While the first successful sugar plantation was on Kaua'i, Maui wasn't far behind when it came to refining the sweet stuff. Many of the successful sugar barons were sons of New England missionaries, and by the mid-1800s sugar mills were springing up from Hana to Lahaina. Labor was the main issue, however. Upon realizing their contracts amounted to indentured servitude, many of the Hawaiians refused to work. Chinese laborers were brought in, but rather than slaving for three dollars a month, they often abandoned their contracts and went on to start other businesses. Japanese laborers were then tried, and they worked 10 hour days, 6 days a week, for $20 a month plus housing. Eventually sugar was doing so well the industry seemed promising to foreigners who needed work. Boatloads of immigrants from Japan, Portugal, Germany, and Russia came to the islands, and their religions, foods, customs, and cultures mixed together in the multiethnic plantation communities. As the sugar industry boomed, the plantation owners became the new "chiefs" of Hawai'i who would carve up the land and dispense favors. With the power of the sugar barons growing with each passing year, the writing was on the wall that the Hawaiian monarchy would soon be eliminated.

END OF THE MONARCHY

As with the Hawaiian people themselves, the Kamehameha dynasty was dying from within. King Kamehameha IV (Alexander Liholiho) ruled 1854-1863, and his only child died in 1862. He was succeeded by his older brother Kamehameha V (Lot Kamehameha), who ruled until 1872. With his passing, the Kamehameha line ended. William Lunalilo, elected king in 1873 by popular vote, was of royal, but not Kamehameha, lineage. He died after only a year in office and, being a bachelor, left no heirs. He was succeeded by David Kalakaua, known far and wide as the "Merrie Monarch," who made a world tour and was well received wherever he went. Kalakaua died in 1891 and was replaced by his sister, Lydia Lili'uokalani, last of the Hawaiian monarchs.

When Lili'uokalani took office in 1891, the native population was at a low of 40,000. When the McKinley Tariff of 1890 brought a decline in sugar profits, she made no attempt to improve the situation, and planters saw her as an

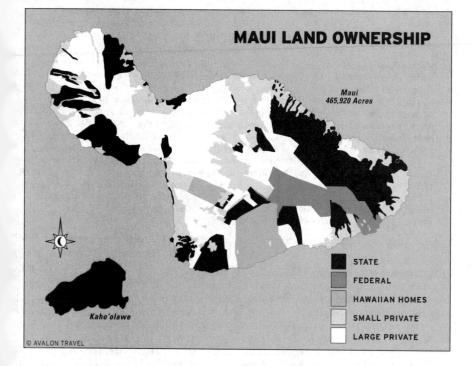

MAUI LAND OWNERSHIP

Maui
465,920 Acres

Kahoʻolawe

© AVALON TRAVEL

- STATE
- FEDERAL
- HAWAIIAN HOMES
- SMALL PRIVATE
- LARGE PRIVATE

obstacle to economic growth. Lorrin Thurston, a Honolulu publisher, gathered a group of 30 men and challenged the Hawaiian monarchy. Naturally, the conspirators could not have succeeded without some solid assurances from a secret contingent in the U.S. Congress as well as outgoing President Benjamin Harrison, who favored Hawaiʻi's annexation. Marines from the *Boston* went ashore to "protect American lives," and on January 17, 1893, the Hawaiian monarchy came to an end. As for Liliʻuokalani, she remained staunchly loyal to her people until her death in 1917, and her struggles are documented in *Hawaii's Story,* a powerful read detailing the history of the era.

ANNEXATION

In relinquishing the throne, Liliʻuokalani surrendered not to the conspirators, but to U.S. ambassador John Stevens. She believed that the U.S. government, which had assured her

of Hawaiian independence and had signed numerous friendly treaties, would be outraged by the overthrow. Indeed, incoming President Grover Cleveland was appalled at the events which had transpired in Hawaiʻi, and he sent a delegation to the islands to research their legality, with hopes of transferring lands back to the queen. Meanwhile, when the conspirators brought the movement for annexation to Congress, it failed to pass given the shaky ground on which it stood. Not to be deterred, they refused to reinstate Liliʻuokalani, and instead continued to operate as a republic with Sanford Dole at the helm.

An unsuccessful countercoup was staged in 1895. After a cache of weapons was found in the queen's garden, Liliʻuokalani was relegated to house arrest in a bedroom of ʻIolani Palace. Over the next couple of years, two more annexation movements would be offered to the U.S. Congress, although after witnessing the stiff resistance of the Hawaiian people to formal annexation (a petition of over 30,000 signatures known as the Ku'e Petition opposed joining the union), the movement failed in Congress three times.

Circumstances changed, however, when the United States was drawn into the Spanish-American War in 1898. Recognizing that Hawai'i was strategically situated for fighting the Spanish in the Philippines and that Pearl Harbor would make the perfect naval port, a joint resolution of Congress was signed which deemed it acceptable to annex Hawai'i as a circumstance of the impending war known as the Newlands Resolution.

There remains great debate today over the legality of the situation. In many ways it appears that since no formal annexation treaty was signed—particularly one pertaining to international lands which are extraterritorial of immediate borders—that Hawai'i technically may never have been annexed through proper and constitutional channels. Furthermore, whatever documents were in fact signed were done so as an agreement with the Republic of Hawai'i, and at no point was an agreement made with the original Hawaiian kingdom representing more than 90 percent of the population. Even now, over 120 years later, it remains a hotly contested issue (President Clinton signed an Apology Resolution in 1993 stating that the overthrow was illegal), and as time marches on, there is growing support for the kingdom which may have never ceased to exist.

Nevertheless, as Hawai'i entered the 20th century it became largely Americanized. Hawaiian language, religion, and culture were nearly gone. Everyone dressed like westerners and was Christian, and Asians made up 75 percent of plantation workers. By 1900 everyone was encouraged to attend school, and almost 90 percent of all Hawaiians were literate.

Interracial marriage was accepted, and Hawai'i became a true melting pot.

Pearl Harbor Attack

On December 7, 1941, the Japanese carrier *Akagi* received a broadcast over its PA system of island music from Honolulu station KGMB. Yet the crew were secretly listening for a different message of code coming from the Japanese mainland. When they heard the message "east wind rain," the attack on O'ahu was launched. At the end of the day, 2,325 U.S. military members and 57 civilians were dead, 188 planes were destroyed, 18 major warships were sunk or heavily damaged, and the United States was in World War II. It roared on for four years through the Nagasaki and Hiroshima bombings, and when it was over, in the hearts of a nation, Hawai'i was an integral part of the United States.

Statehood

During World War II, Hawai'i was placed under martial law, but no serious attempt to intern the Japanese population was made. Many Japanese-Americans went on to gain the respect of the American people through their outstanding fighting record during the war. Hawai'i's own 100th Battalion became the famous 442nd Regimental Combat Team, which would be *the* most decorated battalion in all of World War II. When these GIs returned home, *no one* was going to tell them that they were not loyal Americans. Many of these Americans of Japanese Ancestry (AJAs) took advantage of the GI Bill and received higher educations. They also rallied grassroots support for statehood. When the vote finally occurred, approximately 132,900 voted in favor of statehood with only 7,800 votes against. Congress passed the Hawai'i State Bill on March 12, 1959, and on August 21, 1959, President Eisenhower announced that Hawai'i was officially the 50th state.

THE "LAWFUL HAWAIIAN GOVERNMENT"

At Ho'okipa Lookout and Maliko Gulch you will notice signs proclaiming that the land is under the jurisdiction of the "Lawful Hawaiian Government." While the issue of Hawaiian sovereignty is lengthy and complex, here are the basics about the ongoing movement.

The kingdom of Hawai'i was formed in 1810 when King Kamehameha united all the islands under a single rule, and it lasted until 1893 when the monarchy was illegally overthrown in a bloodless coup by a group of Western businesspeople. While the kingdom existed under a monarchial system of rule 1810-1840, a notable change took place in 1840 when King Kamehameha III changed the system of governance to a constitutional monarchy similar to those found in modern-day Spain, Thailand, or Sweden. A congress was established, there were recognized officials, and a constitution was drafted which outlined the laws of the nation. Due to the efforts taken to create a legitimate form of government, the kingdom of Hawai'i was officially recognized by England and France in 1843, and the United States followed suit in 1846. Hawai'i had embassies in dozens of countries; there was a Hawaiian embassy in Washington D.C., as well as consulates in New York and San Francisco.

In 1893, however, western business interests overthrew Queen Lili'uokalani and formed the Republic of Hawai'i, which was governed by Sanford Dole. A motion was put forth to be annexed by the United States, but it failed when President Grover Cleveland ruled through an investigation of the takeover that it was not performed through legal means. Another annexation attempt would be put forth in 1897, but this too would be shot down due to a letter of protest from Queen Lili'uokalani (who remained under house arrest), along with tens of thousands of Hawaiian signatures. Finally, with the outbreak of the Spanish-American War in 1898, U.S. congressional legislation decided that Hawai'i would be occupied by U.S. military forces as a strategic military base in the Pacific. Once the war was over, the occupiers remained, and Hawai'i stayed a territory to the United States despite the end of the hostilities (it would later become a state in 1959). Since Hawai'i was never formally annexed by either treaty or war, however, the Hawaiian offices of government were consequently never abolished, and when Queen Lili'uokalani died in 1917, the offices sat vacant.

In 1993, President Bill Clinton signed the Apology Resolution which basically said that

History of Lana'i

There was once a time when the island of Lana'i was believed to have been dominated by spirits. Abandoned and considered as taboo, the island was open to settlement in the 1400s when a chief by the name of Kaka'alaneo banished his mischievous son Kaulula'au there, only to find that when Kaulula'au's campfire could be seen burning from Maui each night, it meant that the spirits had been driven out.

Lana'i passed through the next few hundred years as a satellite of Maui. Its population of 3,000 natives was ravaged in 1778 by Kalaniopu'u, aging king of the Big Island. The pillaging sent the population of the island into decline so that by the start of the 20th century only a handful of Hawaiians remained. The old order ended completely when one of the last traditional *kanaka,* a man named Ohua, hid the traditional fish-god Kunihi and died shortly thereafter in his grass hut in the year 1900.

No one knows his name, but all historians agree that a Chinese man tried his luck at raising sugarcane on Lana'i in 1802. He brought boiling pots and rollers to Naha on the east coast, but after a year of hard luck gave up and moved on. About 100 years later a large commercial sugar enterprise was attempted at the United States was sorry for overthrowing the Hawaiian monarchy, recognizing that it had officially done so. It was at this time that sovereignty leaders realized that even though the monarchy had ceased to exist with the death of Queen Lili'uokalani, the Hawaiian framework of government established had never actually disappeared. Since the framework was still in place, it simply needed to be reinstated with new officers, citizens, and elections.

Using the old electoral processes established in the 1864 constitution, elections began being held in 1999 to once again establish a congress for a kingdom which had never disappeared. Henry Noa was elected prime minister, there are now representatives to the congress from 24 districts across the state, and elections take place among the Hawaiian Kingdom citizens. In order to become a citizen of the Hawaiian Kingdom, you must swear an oath of allegiance to the kingdom and renounce your citizenship to the United States. As of July, 2011, there were 400 citizens in the Hawaiian Kingdom, with 7,000 citizenship applications also being processed. In addition to the elected offices, there are also a Department of Health and Department of Transportation. There is a slight chance you might see a vehicle displaying a Hawaiian Kingdom license plate on both the front and back of the car during your time on the island.

Citizens of the Hawaiian Kingdom are quick to point out, however, that they are not seceding from the United States, because the kingdom of Hawai'i was never formally ceded in the first place. At no point did the offices and system of government cease to exist, and after a 107-year vacancy the positions are being filled once again. This reinstated government has been officially recognized in numerous international proceedings, most recently at the International Criminal Court in 2012. No U.S. government grants are involved in the funding of the nation, and you will often see huli huli chicken stands (especially in the Wahikuli section of Lahaina) that help raise funds toward reinstating the lawful Hawaiian government.

Proponents of the Hawaiian Kingdom do not hope to seek "Nation within a Nation" status such as those granted to Native Americans because this would mean formally ceding the nation to the overall governance of the United States. Instead, they would prefer to continue with their sovereignty, which was never formally abolished.

Maunalei. Although this time the sugar company built a narrow-gauge railroad to carry the cane, again sugar cultivation was foiled. Scholars today suggest that since stones from native *heiau* were used to build the railroad, the desecration of a sacred place is what ultimately turned the water brackish and caused the plantation to fail.

Meanwhile, in 1854 a small band of Mormon elders tried to colonize Lana'i by starting a "City of Joseph" at Palawai Basin. Walter Murray Gibson came to Palawai to lead an idyllic settlement for the Latter-day Saints. While he set to work improving the land with funds from Utah, the only fly in Gibson's grand ointment occurred when the Mormon Church discovered that the acres of Palawai were not registered to the church at all, but to Gibson himself! He was excommunicated, and the bilked settlers relocated.

A few other business ventures proved uneconomical, and Lana'i languished. The last big attempt at cattle raising produced the Lana'i Ranch (1874-1951), part of whose lands make up the Cavendish Golf Course and the Lodge at Koele in Lana'i City. This enterprise did have one bright note in the New Zealander George Munro, who was hired as ranch manager. He imported all manner of seeds and cuttings in his attempt to foliate the island and create a watershed. Although the ranch eventually failed, Munro's legacy of Cook pines stands as a testament to this amateur horticulturist.

THE RISE AND FALL OF PINEAPPLES

In 1922 James D. Dole purchased much of Lana'i from the Baldwin family for $1.1 million dollars at just $12 per acre. Dole had experienced success with canning pineapple on other islands, and the expansive Palawai Basin seemed perfect for growing his business.

With pineapple well established on the world market, Lana'i finally had a firm economic base. From a few thousand fruits in the early days the flow at its peak reached a million fruits per day. They were shipped from the port at Kaumalapau, which was specially built in 1926 to accommodate Lana'i's "pines."

At the industry's height, Lana'i had 18,000 acres of pineapples under cultivation, making up the largest single pineapple plantation in the world. Virtually the entire island was operated by the Dole Co., whose name had become synonymous with pineapples. In one way or another, everyone on Lana'i owed his or her livelihood to pineapples, from the worker who twisted his ankle in a field to the technician at the community hospital who x-rayed it. As time wore on, however, the tiny island of Lana'i struggled to compete with foreign operation (particularly those in the Philippines), and due to continual economic hardship Dole Co. made the decision to cut its losses. In 1986 David Murdock—the CEO of Castle & Cooke—acquired all of Dole's holdings on the island and started the transition to luxury tourism.

THE CASTLE & COOKE ERA

While Murdock absorbed Dole's struggling pineapple operation on Lana'i, plans were put into place to create a more sustainable economy. By the time that the last pineapple was picked in 1992, the glitzy new Manele Bay Resort had been open for a year, with the equally luxurious Lodge at Koele having been built where the Lana'i Ranch headquarters once stood. Suddenly, with the introduction of the resorts and the addition of more than 1,000 resort employees and personnel the island's population nearly doubled from around 1,700 people to close to 3,000 residents. Today, with the resort having also developed some private homes on the point around Hulopo'e Bay, the island's population now rests around 3,300.

In addition to more jobs and a cleaned-up face, the resorts brought about a different way of life to once homey little Lana'i. The island during the plantation days offered a family-oriented, simple way of life. Many of the island's old-timers long for those times that now exist solely in memories. Despite the infusion of multisource capitalism, however, the community remains tight-knit and is the type of place where everyone knows each other's business and waves warmly as they pass in the streets. Lana'i City is still the island's only town, although the change is evident in refurbished homes and residential developments built to accommodate the swelling population.

THE LARRY ELLISON ERA

Just as soon as Lana'i residents had adjusted to life under Murdock, however, the Castle & Cooke CEO sold his stake in the island to Larry Ellison in June 2012 for upward of $500 million. Once again, the fate of the island hangs in the balance. Ellison received 98 percent of the island of Lana'i in the deal (the other 2 percent is comprised of federal and state property such as the boat harbors and personal plots of land owned by residents). At the time of publication rumors and speculation abound as to the future of the former pineapple plantation. While all official releases have pointed to Lana'i becoming a "model of sustainability," other rumblings have included a third hotel being built along the shoreline in Kahalepalaoa (of which construction is currently underway), the airport being expanded to accommodate direct flights from the mainland (Ellison also recently purchased Island Air, one of the lone carriers to fly to Lana'i), and there was once even talk of making the island a winter training ground for the Oracle fleet of racing sailboats. In the first phases of his ownership, Ellison has done much to spruce up the island including repaving the parking lot at Hulopo'e Beach Park, renovating the restrooms, reopening the public swimming pool in Lana'i City, and replacing all of the Asian decor in the resorts with more traditional Hawaiian handiwork. There is also talk that the resorts will soon only be able to accommodate ultra-elite A-listers due to their prices. Only time will tell.

History of Moloka'i

Ever since the days of ancient Hawai'i, Moloka'i has been steeped in mysticism and lore. It's believed to be home of Laka, goddess of the hula, and Halawa Valley is believed to be one of the oldest settlements in Hawai'i. Human sacrifices were performed at the 'Ili'ili'opae Heiau. Even today the power and *mana* of this little-known island is evident in everywhere you visit.

Captain James Cook first spotted Moloka'i on November 26, 1778, but because it looked bleak and uninhabited, he bypassed it. Eight years later Captain George Dixon sighted the island and decided to land although little about this first encounter was recorded in his ship's log. Moloka'i slipped from the attention of the Western world until Protestant missionaries arrived at Kalua'aha in 1832 and reported the native population at approximately 6,000.

CHANGING TIMES

From the time of missionary arrival until the 1850s, Moloka'i remained almost unchanged. The Great Mahele of 1848 provided for private ownership of land, and giant tracts were formed into the Moloka'i Ranch. About 1850, German immigrant Rudolph Meyer came to Moloka'i and married a high chieftess named Dorcas Kalama Waha. Together they had 11 children, with whose aid he turned the vast lands of the Moloka'i Ranch into productive pastureland. In 1875, Charles Bishop had bought half of the 70,000 acres of Moloka'i Ranch, and his wife, Bernice, a Kamehameha descendant, inherited the remainder. In 1898, the Moloka'i Ranch was sold to businesspeople in Honolulu for $251,000. This consortium formed the American Sugar Co. But after a few plantings, the available water on Moloka'i turned brackish, and once again Moloka'i Ranch was sold. Charles Cooke

bought controlling interest from the other businesspeople in 1908 and remained in control of the ranch until 1988.

In 1921, Congress passed the Hawaiian Homes Act, which set aside 43,000 acres on the island for people who had at least 50 percent Hawaiian blood. By this time, however, all agriculturally productive land in Hawai'i had already been claimed. The parcels given to the Hawaiians were poor and lacked adequate water. Also many Hawaiians had long since left the land and were raised in towns and cities. Now out of touch with the simple life of the taro patch, they found it difficult to readjust. However, to prevent the Hawaiians from selling their claims and losing the land forever, the Hawaiian Homes Act provided that the land be leased to them for 99 years. Making a go of these 40-acre (*kuleana*) parcels was so difficult that successful homesteaders were called "Moloka'i Miracles."

In 1923 Libby Corporation leased land from Moloka'i Ranch at Kaluakoi and went into pineapple production. Del Monte followed suit in 1927 at Kualapu'u. Both built company towns and imported Japanese and Filipino field laborers, swelling Moloka'i's population and stabilizing the economy. Many of the native Hawaiians subleased their *kuleana* tracts to the pineapple growers, and the Hawaiian Homes Act seemed to backfire. Instead of the homesteaders' working their own farms, they were given monthly checks and lured into a life of complacency. Those who grew little more than family plots became, in effect, permanent tenants on their own property. Much more important, they lost the psychological advantage of controlling their own future and regaining their pride, as envisioned in the Hawaiian Homes Act.

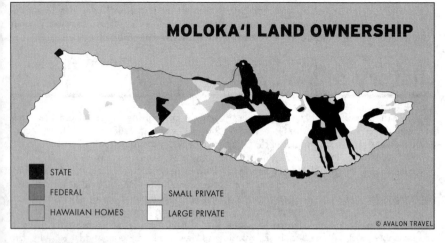

MOLOKA'I LAND OWNERSHIP

STATE

FEDERAL

HAWAIIAN HOMES

SMALL PRIVATE

LARGE PRIVATE

© AVALON TRAVEL

MODERN TIMES

For the next 50 years life was quiet. The pineapples grew, providing security. Another large ranch, **Pu'u O Hoku** (Hill of Stars) was formed on the eastern tip of the island. It was originally owned by Paul Fagan, the San Francisco entrepreneur who later developed the Hana Ranch on Maui. In 1955, Fagan sold Pu'u O Hoku to George Murphy, a Canadian industrialist, for a meager $300,000. The ranch, under Murphy, became famous for beautiful white Charolais cattle, a breed originating in France.

In the late 1960s, things started quietly happening on Moloka'i. The Moloka'i Ranch sold 6,700 oceanside acres to the Kaluakoi Corp., which it controlled along with the Louisiana Land and Exploration Company. In 1969 the long-awaited Moloka'i reservoir was completed at Kualapu'u; finally West Moloka'i had plenty of water. Shortly after Moloka'i's water problem appeared to be finally under control, Dole Co. bought out Libby in 1972, lost millions in the next few years, and shut down its pineapple production at Maunaloa in 1975. By 1977 the acreage sold to the Kaluakoi Corp. was starting to be developed. The Molokai Sheraton (later called the Kaluakoi Hotel, but now closed) opened along with low-rise condominiums and 270 fee-simple homesites ranging 5-43 acres. Plans then for this area included two

more resorts, additional condominiums, shopping facilities, bridle paths, and an airstrip (it's only 20 minutes to Honolulu). It seemed that sleepy old Moloka'i with the tiny Hawaiian Homes farms was now prime real estate and worth a fortune.

To complicate the picture even further, Del Monte shut down its operations in 1982, throwing more people out of work. In 1986 it did resume planting 250-acre tracts, but now all of the pineapple is gone. Recently, coffee has been put into production near the old pineapple town of Kualapu'u, some experimental plots of fruits and vegetables have been planted, and the Moloka'i Ranch has brought in sheep and cattle. After Brierly Investments (now known as GuocoLeisure) bought the Moloka'i Ranch in 1988, other changes started to take place, including a total face-lift for the town of Maunaloa and a greater emphasis on tourism. An 18-hole golf course was built, the town of Maunaloa surged, and luxury accommodations throughout West Moloka'i breathed life into the struggling economy.

All of that changed, however, in April 2008, when the ranch decided to cease all operations amid heavy opposition from locals critical of plans to develop La'au Point with over 200 luxury homes. Everything from the movie theater to the golf course to the hotels was closed, and over 120 employees lost their jobs. In 2013, the businesses still remain vacant. Though the ranch has claimed in recent years that the focus of growth will be on sustainable energy and agriculture, much of the island continues to struggle to find an economic foothold.

Government and Economy

GOVERNMENT

The government of Hawai'i is limited to two levels, the state and the county, of which the islands of Maui, Moloka'i, Lana'i, and Kaho'olawe comprise Maui County. Politics and government at one time were taken seriously in the Aloha State, which once consistently turned in the best national voting record per capita. For example, in the first state elections, 173,000 of 180,000 registered voters cast ballots—a whopping 94 percent of the electorate. These days, however, although there is still great voter turnout for state and local elections, Hawai'i boasts one of the worst voter turnouts for national presidential elections. In the 2012 election, Hawai'i had a measly 62 percent of registered voters cast ballots, which gave it the distinction of having the lowest turnout in the nation. Because of Hawai'i's location in the far west, when presidential elections are held, the results are often known before many in the state have time to cast their ballots. There is also a vocal minority that sees no point on voting in an election for a nation they would rather not be a part of.

Hawai'i is the only state to have just a single school district. A packed schoolroom in downtown Honolulu falls under the same set of guidelines as a one-room schoolhouse in West Moloka'i. Consequently, the idea of moving to a neighborhood where the schools are better isn't a part of Hawaiian life.

ECONOMY

Today, tourism and the military are the two prime sources of income for Hawai'i. Tourists come in anticipation of endless golden days on soothing beaches, while the military is provided with the strategic position of an unsinkable battleship. Each economic sector nets Hawai'i billions annually. Also contributing to the state revenue are, in descending proportions, manufacturing, construction, and agriculture.

Tourism

Maui is the second-most-frequently chosen Hawaiian destination after O'ahu and welcomes more than two million visitors annually. On any given day about 40,000 visitors are enjoying the island. Maui's most popular attractions are Haleakala National Park, Lahaina town, the Maui Ocean Center, the Whalers Village Museum, 'Iao Valley, and Hana.

Agriculture

Maui generates agricultural revenue through cattle, sugar, pineapples, and flowers, along with a substantial subculture for *pakalolo* (marijuana). Cattle grazing occurs on the western and southern slopes of Haleakala, where 30,000 acres are owned by the Haleakala Ranch and more than 18,000 acres by the Ulupalakua Ranch. The upper slopes of Haleakala around Kula are a gardener's dream, where delicious onions, potatoes, and all sorts of garden vegetables are grown.

Sugar is still important to Maui's economy, but without federal subsidies it probably wouldn't be a viable cash crop. The only acreage is in the central isthmus area, which is virtually all owned by the Alexander and Baldwin Company. Maui's one remaining operational mill is at Pu'unene. The Lahaina mill closed in 1996, and the cane fields on the Ka'anapali side have all been abandoned, the land given to pineapple or coffee production, developed into residential subdivisions, or left fallow.

Hali'imaile Pineapple Company grows

pineapples between Pa'ia and Makawao on the lower slope of Haleakala. Since Maui's last cannery closed down in 2007, the only way in which you can still buy pineapple is in the form of a whole fruit.

Meanwhile, renegade entrepreneurs grow patches of *pakalolo* wherever they can find a spot that has the right vibes and away from the prying eyes of authorities. Deep in the West Maui Mountains and along the Hana coast are favorite areas of island growers.

Military

The small military presence on Maui amounts to a tiny U.S. Army installation near Kahului, the U.S. Coast Guard facility at Ma'alaea, and an Air Force tracking station on top of Haleakala.

People and Culture

POPULATION

Hawai'i is a true ethnic melting pot where more than 50 diverse groups are represented. With 144,000 residents, Maui has the third-largest island population in Hawai'i, with about 7,000 residents on Moloka'i and 3,300 on Lana'i. Maui's population density is 176 people per square mile, with Moloka'i and Lana'i at 27 and 23 per square mile, respectively. The Kahului/Wailuku area has the island's greatest population with nearly 50,000 people, although the South Maui zip code is the islands largest with over 26,000 residents in Kihei and Wailea. The Upcountry population is just over 31,000 including Pa'ia and Ha'iku, and West Maui has 21,000. In East Maui about 5,000 live along the Hana Highway, although fewer than 2,000 reside in Hana itself. For Maui County, 78 percent are urban while 22 percent live rurally. The ethnic breakdown of Maui's 144,000 people is 36 percent Caucasian, 29 percent Asian, 23 percent mixed, 11 percent Hawaiian, and 1 percent other.

PEOPLE
Hawaiians

Any study of the native Hawaiians is ultimately a study in tragedy because it nearly ends in their demise as a viable people. When Captain Cook first sighted Hawai'i in 1778, there were an estimated 300,000 natives living in relative harmony with their ecological surroundings; within 100 years a scant 50,000 demoralized and dejected Hawaiians existed almost as wards of the state. Today, although more than 240,000 people claim varying degrees of Hawaiian blood, experts say that fewer than 1,000 are pure Hawaiian, and this might be stretching it.

It's easy to see why people of Hawaiian lineage could be bitter over what they have lost, being strangers in their own land, much like Native Americans. The overwhelming majority of Hawaiians are of mixed heritage, and the wisest take the best from all worlds. From the Hawaiian side comes simplicity, love of the land, and acceptance of people. It is the Hawaiian legacy of *aloha* that remains immortal and adds that special elusive quality that *is* Hawai'i.

POLYNESIAN ROOTS

The Polynesians' original stock is muddled and remains an anthropological mystery, but it's believed that they were nomadic wanderers who migrated from both the Indian subcontinent and Southeast Asia through Indonesia, where they learned to sail and navigate on protected waterways. As they migrated, they honed their sailing skills until they could take on the Pacific. As they moved, they absorbed people from other cultures and races until they had coalesced into Polynesians.

THE CASTE SYSTEM

Hawaiian society was divided into rankings by a strict caste system determined by birth and from which there was no chance of escaping.

The highest rank was the *ali'i*—the chiefs and royalty. Ranking passed from both father and mother, and custom dictated that the first mating of an *ali'i* be with a person of equal status.

A *kahuna* was a highly skilled person whose advice was sought before any major project was undertaken, such as building a house, hollowing a canoe log, or even offering a prayer.

Besides this priesthood of *kahuna,* there were other *kahuna* who were not *ali'i* but commoners. The two most important were the healers (*kahuna lapa'au*) and the black magicians (*kahuna 'ana'ana*). The *kahuna lapa'au* had a marvelous pharmacopoeia of herbs and spices that could cure more than 250 diseases common to the Hawaiians. The *kahuna 'ana'ana* could be hired to cast a love spell over a person or cause his or her untimely death.

The common people were called the *maka'ainana,* "the people of land"—the farmers, craftspeople, and fishers. The land that they lived on was controlled by the *ali'i,* but they were not bound to it. If the local *ali'i* was cruel or unfair, the *maka'ainana* had the right to leave and live on another's lands. The *maka'ainana* mostly loved their local *ali'i* much like a child loves a parent, and the feeling was reciprocal. All *maka'ainana* formed extended families called *ohana* who usually lived on the same section of land, called *ahupua'a.* Those farmers who lived inland would barter their produce with the fishers who lived on the shore, and thus all shared equally in the bounty of land and sea.

A special group called *kauwa* was an untouchable caste confined to reservations. Their origins were obviously Polynesian, but they appear to have been descendants of castaways who had survived and become perhaps the aboriginals of Hawai'i before the main migrations. It was *kapu* for anyone to go onto *kauwa* lands, and doing so meant instant death. If a human sacrifice was needed, the *kahuna* would summon a *kauwa,* who had no recourse but to mutely comply. To this day, to call someone *kauwa,* which now supposedly means only servant, is still considered a fight-provoking insult.

HAWAIIANS TODAY

Many of the Hawaiians who moved to the cities became more and more disenfranchised. Their folk society stressed openness and a giving nature but downplayed the individual and the ownership of private property. Ni'ihau, a privately owned island, is home to about 160 pure-blooded Hawaiians, representing the largest concentration of them, per capita, in the islands. The Robinson family, which owns the island, restricts visitors to invited guests only.

The second-largest concentration is on Moloka'i, where 2,700 Hawaiians, living mostly on 40-acre *kuleana* of Hawaiian Home Lands, make up 40 percent of that island's population. The majority of mixed-blood Hawaiians, 240,000 or so, live on O'ahu, where they are particularly strong in the hotel and entertainment fields.

Chinese

Next to Yankees from New England, the Chinese are the oldest migrant group in Hawai'i, and their influence has far outshone their meager numbers. They brought to Hawai'i, along with their individuality, Confucianism, Taoism, and Buddhism, although many have long since become Christians. The Chinese population at 56,000 makes up only 5 percent of the state's total, but the vast majority live on O'ahu. As a group they have done well and have succeeded in starting businesses lasting generations. The first Chinese were brought to Hawai'i in 1852 to work on sugar plantations. They were contracted to work for $3 a month plus room and board. After working 12-hour days six days a week, the Chinese nearly always moved on when their contracts were done and started their own businesses or shops.

Japanese

The first official Japanese to come to Hawai'i were ambassadors sent to Washington by the shogun who stopped in Honolulu on the way in 1860. A small group came eight years later to work on the plantations, and a large influx came in 1885. After an emigration of Japanese

LOCAL CUSTOM: NO SHOES IN THE HOUSE

One of the local customs visitors often find shocking is the removal of shoes before entering a house. Unless you're directly told otherwise, no shoes in the house is a definite rule. There are a few theories about where the custom came from. Some say it's common sense not to track added dirt and germs inside, while others say it's a Japanese custom relating to not following in other people's shoes (or paths, or footstep). Whatever the origins might be, follow it if you visit a local's home. It's even usually requested by the management of vacation rentals. This rule doesn't extend to hotels or businesses, but if you notice a pile of shoes at the door of a small business, it's probably a sign that the owner prefers the no-shoes rule. If you are a fan of the custom or already practice it at home, locally made Please Remove Shoes signs and tiles can be purchased around the island.

farmers who were sent over because of their famine, from 1897 to 1908 there was a steady influx. By 1900 there were more than 60,000 Japanese in the islands.

Caucasians

Next to Hawaiians themselves, Caucasians have the longest history in Hawai'i. They settled in earnest since the missionaries of the 1820s and were established long before any other migrant group. Caucasians have a distinction separating them from all other ethnic groups in Hawai'i in that they are lumped together as one. A person can be anything from a Protestant Norwegian dockworker to a Greek Orthodox shipping tycoon, but if his or her skin is light, in Hawai'i, he or she is a *haole*. What's more, a person could have arrived at Waikiki from Missoula, Montana, in the last 24 hours, or his or her *kama'aina* family can go back five generations, but again, if the person is Caucasian, he or she is a *haole*.

The word *haole* has a floating connotation that depends upon the spirit in which it's used. It can mean everything from a derisive "honky" or "cracker" to nothing more than "white person." The exact Hawaiian meaning is clouded, although it largely has to do with the fact that when white people first arrived, they lacked any true *ha*, which means "spirit," or "breath." Europeans did not "share breath" in the same way that many Polynesian cultures would (such as the traditional greeting of pressing noses

rather than hands), and this lack of "breath" lives on today in the semi-derogatory term.

Portuguese

Between 1878 and 1887, around 12,000 Portuguese came to Hawai'i. Later on, between 1906 and 1913, 6,000 more arrived. They were put to work on plantations and gained a reputation as good workers. Although they were European, for some reason they weren't *haole*, just somewhere in between. Nearly 27,000 Portuguese made up 11 percent of Hawai'i's population by 1920. They intermarried, and the Portuguese remain an ethnic group in Hawai'i today. One item they brought in that would influence local culture was the *cavaquinho*, a stringed instrument that would evolve into the ukulele.

Filipinos

The Filipinos who came to Hawai'i brought high hopes of amassing personal fortunes and returning home as rich heroes, but for most it was a dream that never came true. Filipinos had been U.S. nationals ever since the Spanish-American War of 1898 and as such weren't subject to immigration laws that curtailed the importation of other Asian workers. The first to arrive were 15 families in 1906, but a large number came in 1924 as strikebreakers. From the first, Filipinos were looked down upon by all the other immigrant groups and were considered particularly uncouth by the Japanese.

The value they placed on education was the lowest of any group, and even by 1930 only about half could speak rudimentary English, the majority remaining illiterate. They were billeted in the worst housing, performed the most menial jobs, and were the last hired and first fired.

One big difference between Filipinos and other groups was that the men brought no Filipino women to marry, so they clung to the idea of returning home. In 1930 there were 30,000 men and only 360 women. Many of these terribly lonely bachelors would feast and drink on weekends and engage in their gruesome but exciting pastime of cockfighting on Sundays. When some did manage to find wives, their mates were inevitably part Hawaiian. Filipino workers continued to be imported, although sporadically, until 1946, so even today there are a few old Filipino bachelors who never managed to get home.

Other Groups

About 10 percent of Hawai'i's population is a conglomerate of small ethnic groups. Of these, one of the largest and fastest growing is Korean, with 25,000 individuals. About 30,000 residents consider themselves Puerto Rican. 22,000 residents identify as black. Another fast-growing group is Samoans, with 16,000 currently settled in Hawai'i and with more on the way. Other lesser represented ethnic groups include 3,500 Native Americans, 4,000 Tongans, 7,000 other Pacific Islanders, and 8,000 Vietnamese.

FOOD

Although modern Hawaiian food is extremely meat based, traditionally Hawaiians were nearly vegetarian, reserving meat for celebrations rather than daily meals. Traditional Hawaiian food can still be found—your best bet would be at a *lu'au*—but a lot if it now is simply considered "local food" and blended with food from other cultures.

With ancient Hawaiians the ocean was a great source of food. Yet they still cultivated successful land crops such as taro, sweet potatoes, breadfruit, and sugarcane. They raised pigs and chickens for celebratory meals, although they wouldn't make use of the eggs.

The taro root was the staple crop, and it was the first thing they got going when settling the island. Taro would be mostly be pounded into poi, which is another meal staple often eaten with other foods. Taro is nutritious and starchy. Women avoided the starch while pregnant in hopes of avoiding growing a large baby.

Another treat is *haupia,* a custard-like substance made from coconut usually served as a dessert. *Lau lau* is a lu'au food that is served as a small package of meat, fish, or vegetables all wrapped in *ti* leaves and then baked or steamed. For fish, a local favorite is ahi *poke,* a dish which is served at many delis and supermarkets mixed with soy sauce, onions, seaweed, and other flavors and enjoyed as a snack or a meal.

THE ARTS

Since everything in old Hawai'i had to be fashioned by hand, almost every object was either a genuine work of art or the product of a highly refined craft. With the "civilizing" of the natives, most of the old ways disappeared, including the old arts and crafts. Most authentic Hawaiian art by master craftspeople exists only in museums. But with the resurgence of connecting to Hawaiian roots as part of the Hawaiian Renaissance, many old arts are being revitalized, and their legacy lives on in a number of proficient artists.

Hula

The hula is more than an ethnic dance; it's the soul of Hawai'i expressed in motion. It began as a form of worship during religious ceremonies and was danced only by highly trained men. As time went on, however, women were allowed to learn the hula, and today both sexes perform the dance equally.

During the 19th century, the hula almost vanished because the missionaries considered it vile and heathen. King Kalakaua is saved it during the late 1800s by forming his own troupe and encouraging the dancers to learn the old hula. Many of the original dances had been forgotten, but some were retained and are performed to this day.

Hula is art in swaying motion, and the true form is studied rigorously and taken seriously. Today, hula *halau* (schools) are active on every island, teaching hula and keeping the old ways and culture alive. (Ancient hula is called *hula kahiko,* and modern renditions are known as *hula auana.*) Performers still spend years perfecting their techniques. They show off their accomplishments during the fierce competition of the Merrie Monarch Festival in Hilo every April.

Canoes

The most respected artisans in old Hawai'i were the canoe makers. With little more than a stone adze and a pump drill, they built sleek and seaworthy canoes that could carry 200 people and last for generations. The main hull was usually a gigantic koa log, and the gunwale planks were minutely drilled and sewn to the sides with sennit rope. Apprenticeships lasted for years, and a young man knew that he had graduated when one day he was nonchalantly asked to sit down and eat with the master builders. Small family-size canoes with outriggers were used for fishing and perhaps carried a spear rack; large oceangoing double-hulled canoes were used for migration and warfare. On these, the giant logs had been adzed to about two inches thick. A mainsail woven from pandanus was mounted on a central platform, and the boat was steered by two long paddles. The hull was dyed with plant juices and charcoal. The entire village helped launch such a canoe.

Carving

Wood was one of the primary materials used by Hawaiian craftspeople. They almost exclusively relied on koa because of its density, strength, and natural luster. It was turned into canoes, woodware, calabashes, and furniture used by the *ali'i.* Temple idols were another major product of wood carving. A variety of stone artifacts were also turned out, including poi pounders, mirrors, fish sinkers, and small idols.

Weaving

Hawaiians became the best basket makers and mat weavers in all of Polynesia. *Ulana* (woven mats) were made from *lau hala* (pandanus) leaves. Once the leaf was split, the spine was removed and the fibers stored in large rolls. When needed these would be soaked, pounded, and then fashioned into various floor coverings and sleeping mats. Intricate geometrical patterns were woven in, and the edges were rolled and well fashioned. Coconut palms were not used to make mats in old Hawai'i, but a wide variety of basketry was fashioned from the aerial root *'ie'ie.* The shapes varied according to use. Some baskets were tall and narrow, some were cones, others were flat like trays, and many were woven around gourds and calabashes.

Featherwork

This highly refined art was practiced only on the islands of Tahiti, New Zealand, and Hawai'i, but the fashioning of feather helmets and idols was unique to Hawai'i. Favorite colors were red and yellow, which came only in a limited supply from a small number of birds such as the *'o'o, 'i'iwi, mamo,* and *'apapane.* Professional bird hunters in old Hawai'i paid their taxes to *ali'i* in prized feathers. The feathers were fastened to a woven net of *olona* cord and made into helmets, idols, and beautiful flowing capes and cloaks. These resplendent garments were made and worn only by men, especially during battle, when a fine cloak became a great trophy of war. Featherwork was also employed in the making of *kahili* and lei, which were highly prized by the *ali'i* women.

Lei Making

Any flower or blossom can be strung into a lei, but the most common are orchids or the lovely-smelling plumeria. Lei, like babies, are all beautiful, but special lei are highly prized by those who know what to look for. Of the different stringing styles, the most common is *kui*—stringing the flower through the middle or side. Most "airport-quality" lei are of this type. The *humuhumu* style, reserved for making flat lei, is made by sewing flowers and ferns to a *ti*, banana, or sometimes *hala* leaf. A *humuhumu* lei makes an excellent hatband. *Wili* is the winding together of greenery, ferns, and flowers into short, bouquet-type lengths. The most traditional form is *hili,* which requires no stringing at all but involves braiding fragrant ferns and leaves such as *maile.* If flowers are interwoven, the *hili* becomes the *haku* style, the most difficult and most beautiful type of lei.

Tapa Cloth

Tapa, cloth made from tree bark, was common throughout Polynesia and a woman's art. A few trees such as the *wauke* and *mamaki* produced the best cloth, but a variety of other types of bark could be used. First the raw bark was pounded into a feltlike pulp and beaten together to form strips (the beaters had distinctive patterns that helped make the cloth supple). The cloth was decorated by stamping (a form of block printing) and dyed with natural colors from plants and sea animals in shades of gray, purple, pink, and red. They were even painted with natural brushes made from pandanus fruit, with an overall gray color made from charcoal. The tapa cloth was sewn together to make bed coverings, and fragrant flowers and herbs were either sewn or pounded in to produce a permanent fragrance. Tapa cloth is still available today, but the Hawaiian methods have been lost, and most comes from other areas of Polynesia.

Festivals and Events

For such a small island, there is always something happening on Maui. From sporting events to film festivals and rodeos to wine festivals, Maui is a flurry of community fervor when it comes to annual events. Dates are rarely constant, however, so check local listings and websites for up-to-date information. While many events are annual affairs, the most consistent festive occasion is the **Friday Town Parties** (www.mauifridays.com), which take place every Friday night. Rotating between Wailuku, Lahaina, Makawao, and Kihei, these are great community events which are free to attend.

For other events of all sorts throughout the state, visit the calendar of events listing on the Hawai'i Visitors Bureau (HVB) website (www.calendar.gohawaii.com), or check out the weekly schedule of events on the *Maui Time* website (www.mauitime.com/calendar).

MAUI
January

The PGA golf tour kicks off each year with the **Hyundai Tournament of Champions** (www.kapalua.com/golf/hyundai-tournament-champions) held during the first week of January at the Kapalua Plantation Course.

February

Chinese New Year (www.visitlahaina.com) celebrations are held in the evening along Front Street in Lahaina and include a lion's dance, martial arts demonstrations, live music, food, and, of course, firecrackers.

For artists, the **Maui Open Studios** (www.mauiopenstudios.com) take place during each weekend in February, showcasing the talent of the island's local art community.

The **Maui Whale Festival** (www.mauiwhalefest.org) is sponsored by the Pacific Whale Foundation and features live music, festivals, fun runs, and community activities through the month of February. The annual **World Whale Day** takes place at Kihei's Kalama Park and is the largest event of the festival.

Seeing as February is the peak of whale season, it only makes sense that another event, **Whales Tales** (www.whaletrust.org), is held during the busy month. The event at the Maui Theatre supports local whale research teams such as the Whale Trust, Center for

THAR SHE BLOWS! WHALE SEASON

December-May the waters of Maui County house the largest population of humpback whales found anywhere in the world. If whale-watching is high on your list of iconic Maui experiences, it's important to time your visit during the peak of whale season and not show up in the summer.

Officially, whale season in Maui runs December 15-May 15, although the first sighting is usually mid-October and whales can linger through the end of May. For whale-watching, however, the peak season is the 10-week span of January 15-March 31. During the month of April, there are noticeably fewer whales by the day. Whale-watching tours will usually operate December 15-April 20, after which time there is no guarantee of seeing whales. (Boats will often advertise "whale searches" as opposed to a "whale watches" during the extreme beginning and end of the season, which is a casual way of saying you probably won't encounter whales, but your money will gladly be accepted.)

During the peak of the season, anyone setting out on a charter is 100 percent guaranteed to see whales. The question becomes a matter of not *if* you're going to see whales, but *which* whales you should look at since you'll end up being surrounded!

Whale Studies, and Hawai'i Whale Research Foundation.

March

The month usually kicks off with more whale-related events at the **Lahaina Whale and Ocean Arts Festival** (www.visitlahaina) held in downtown Lahaina.

March 26 is **Prince Kuhio Day,** a public state holiday observed in remembrance of Prince Kuhio, heir to the throne of the Hawaiian monarchy.

Toward the end of the month, the **Celebration of the Arts** (www.celebrationofthearts.org) at the Ritz-Carlton Hotel in Kapalua is a four-day event that spotlights various native art forms and cultural traditions. It's an absolute must-visit if you are in town.

April

Usually held on the first weekend in April at the Maui Tropical Plantation, the **Maui County Agricultural Festival** (www.mauicountyfarmbureau.org), aka the "Maui Ag Fest," celebrates the rich heritage of farming and agriculture on Maui.

The **East Maui Taro Festival** (www.tarofestival.org) is celebrated in Hana with traditional ceremonies, music, food markets, symposia, demonstrations, and exhibitions to honor one of the island's most basic food sources and the resurgence of Hawaiian cultural traditions.

In the world of art, the annual **Art Maui** is a juried art show of works by Maui County residents that's held for about one month in the Schaefer Gallery at the Maui Arts and Cultural Center.

In Lahaina, April 20-21 is the **Banyan Tree Birthday** (www.visitlahaina.com) celebration for the town's famous banyan tree.

April 22 is **Earth Day,** and there are numerous environmental cleanups and festivals across the island where visitors can get involved.

Upcountry, the **Haiku Ho'olaulea and Flower Fest** (www.haikuhoolaulea.org) is held at the Ha'iku Community Center with live music, auctions, "talk story" sessions, vendors, and a welcoming atmosphere that defines this rural town.

May

May 1 is **Lei Day** in Hawai'i. There are usually large lei day celebrations held in Wailea and various other places around the island.

At Whalers Village in Ka'anapali, the **Maui Onion Festival** (www.whalersvillage.com/onionfestival) celebrates everything about the Maui onion with food vendors, craft booths, recipe contests, chef demonstrations, and live entertainment.

Upcountry in Makawao, the **Seabury Hall Craft Fair** (www.seaburyhall.org) is held on the Saturday before Mother's Day and features Hawaiian craft vendors from across the state. With live music, food booths, and hundreds of artists, it's the perfect place for picking up a gift for mom.

At the Maui Arts and Cultural Center, the **Maui Brewers Festival** (www.mauiarts.org) celebrates the culture of craft brewing and the love of good beer.

June

The annual **Upcountry Fair** at the Eddie Tam Center, Makawao, is an old-fashioned farm fair right in the heart of Maui's *paniolo* country. Crafts, food, and competitions are all part of the fair, as are the county 4-H championship and auctions.

In Kapalua, foodies flock to the **Kapalua Wine and Food Festival** (www.kapaluawineandfoodfestival.com), a three-day event featuring some of the state's top sommeliers and chefs.

June 11 is **King Kamehameha Day** in Lahaina. Festivities include a parade through town, crafts, and lots of food and entertainment.

The annual **Slack Key Guitar Festival** (www.slackkeyfestival.com) at the Maui Arts and Cultural Center in Kahului features some of Hawai'i's best musicians.

The **Maui Film Festival** (www.mauifilmfestival.com) shows films at both the Maui Arts and Cultural Center as well as the Celestial Cinema on the golf course lawn in Wailea.

The **Da Kine Classic Windsurfing Event,** a professional windsailing competition for men and women, is held at Kanaha Beach, and is part of the summer long Maui Race Series.

July

Over the July 4 weekend, head for the coolness of Makawao for the annual **Makawao Rodeo.** *Paniolo* are an old and important tradition in Hawaiian life. Held at the Oskie Rice Arena, this old-time Upcountry rodeo can't be beat for fun and entertainment anywhere in the country. And it's always accompanied by the Paniolo Parade through town.

The **Fourth of July** brings the best fireworks display on Maui to the Lahaina Roadstead, and thousands congregate for the show.

July also has numerous Buddhist festivals taking place across the island, with one of the largest being the **Obon Festival** at the Mantokuji Soto Temple in Pa'ia.

August

Toward the end of August, the **Ka'anapali Fresh** (www.kaanapalifresh.com) food and wine festival features cuisine and demonstrations from some of the island's top chefs and sommeliers.

September

The Valley Island Road Runners (virr.com) sponsor the numerous races throughout September, including the **Hana Relay** (www.hanarelay.com) and **Maui Marathon** (www.mauimarathonhawaii.com). The Hana Relay sees over 1,200 runners run in costume from Kahului Airport to the downtown ballpark in Hana. The next week, the marathon takes runners from the Queen Ka'ahumanu Center in Kahului, down to Ma'alaea, and then along the ocean to Whalers Village in Ka'anapali. The weekend is also punctuated by the **Front Street Mile** event which has some of the world's top mileage runners tackle the flat course of Front Street.

October

The **Maui County Fair** at the Wailuku War Memorial Complex brings out the kid in everyone. An old-fashioned fair with western and homespun flavor, this popular event caters to more than 100,000 people every year and offers rides, booths, exhibits, and games, plus plenty of music and food.

In Lahaina, the **Lahaina Plantation Days** (www.lahainarestoration.org) is hosted by the Lahaina Restoration Foundation and features

The Hana Relay is a popular annual event.

live music, food booths, and movies held under the smokestack.

The **XTERRA World Championships** (www.xterraplanet.com/maui) are held in Kapalua. This is an off-road triathlon that combines a 1.5-mile ocean swim, 30-km mountain-bike ride, and an 11-km trail run.

At the end of the month, wild costumes and outlandish behavior set the mood for **Halloween** in Lahaina, the largest celebration of Halloween in Hawai'i, often called the "Mardi Gras of the Pacific."

November

The **Maui Invitational Basketball Tournament** (www.mauiinvitational.com) holds a preseason college team playoff at the Civic Center in Lahaina.

Each year the Ka'anapali Beach Hotel hosts **Hula O Na Keiki**, the state's only children's solo and partner hula contest. Two days of competition make this an entertaining event for everyone.

December

The **Holiday Lighting of the Banyan Tree** takes place in Lahaina, as well as decorating the Old Courthouse for Christmas.

MOLOKA'I

While there are numerous smaller festivals which take place on Moloka'i, the following are some of the larger annual events. For specific dates and more information, visit www.molokaievents.com.

January

The **Ka Moloka'i Makahiki Festival** is held for one day each January to celebrate the *makahiki*, a traditional time following the harvest when wars would cease in favor of arts, crafts, competition, and merriment. This tradition is carried on today at the Mitchell Pauole Center in Kaunakai.

May

The **Moloka'i Ka Hula Piko** festival is perhaps the largest annual event on the island

and celebrates the history of the hula at its legendary birthplace in West Moloka'i. For more information on this cultural event visit www.kahulapiko.com.

September

Moloka'i is well known for its outrigger canoe races, during which time the island buzzes with visitors from across the Pacific. The **Pailolo Challenge** (www.pailolo.com) features paddlers who race from Maui to Kauanakakai, and the **Na Wahine O Ke Kai** features all-girl paddle crews who race from Hale O Lono Harbor to the neighboring island of O'ahu.

October

More famous than the Pailolo is the **Moloka'i Hoe** (www.molokaihoe.com) outrigger canoe race in which paddlers race from West Moloka'i to O'ahu. More than 1,000 paddlers compete in the event. It's an exciting time to be visiting West Moloka'i.

The **Festivals of Aloha** is a community event which has been taking place for more than 50 years and is held in the city of Kaunakakai.

LANA'I

Despite only having a population of 3,300 people, Lana'i still has a full roster of events. The following are just a handful of occasions that pop up throughout the year.

March

The **Lana'i Jazz Festival** (www.lanaijazzfestival.com) features free events for jazz lovers with some of the state's top musicians.

June

The **Lana'i Ukulele Festival** (www.lanaiukulelefestival.com) features some of the state's top ukulele musicians all descending on the small island for a weekend of musical merriment.

July

Even though the last commercial pineapple was picked in 1992, the **Lana'i Pineapple Festival** (www.lanaipineapplefestival.com) features live entertainment, vendor booths, and a celebration of the island's pineapple heritage.

August

In keeping with the musical theme, the **Lana'i Slack Key Festival** brings some of the state's best *ki ho'alu* musicians to the people of Lana'i City.

November

While there are numerous races throughout the year, the largest event of the **TriLanai** (www.trilanai.com) race series is the off-road sprint triathlon that takes place in November.

ESSENTIALS

Getting There and Around

AIR

More likely than not you'll land at the **Kahului Airport** (1 Kahului Airport Rd., 808/872-3830, www.hawaii.gov/ogg), which is 30-45 minutes by car from the resort areas of Wailea and Kaʻanapali. Kahului has direct flights to a host of mainland cities and handful of international destinations, and it's serviced by most major carriers.

Other than Kahului there are two small airstrips in the areas of Kapalua and Hana. There are no direct flights to the mainland from here, although there are seven flights per day from the Kapalua Airport to the neighboring island of Oʻahu.

CAR
Car Rental

Although more expensive than the bus, rental cars are the easiest way for getting around and exploring the island. While there are a number of large corporate rental car companies which operate within the airport, there are also a number of locally-owned companies which can provide better rates and more "authentic" looking cars. A shiny new rental car is always nice to drive around in, but the downside is that rentals are usually the targets of car thieves. Having a car that looks like a local's can potentially save you the cost of a break-in.

© KYLE ELLISON

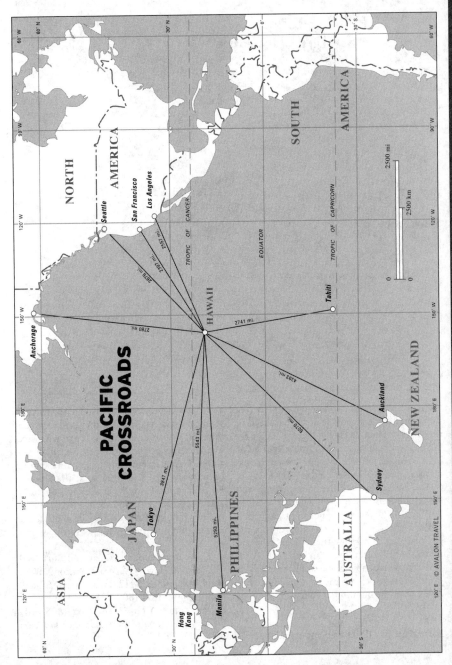

PACIFIC CROSSROADS

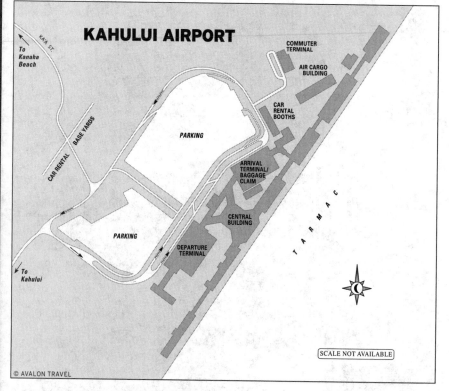

KAHULUI AIRPORT

© AVALON TRAVEL

SCALE NOT AVAILABLE

Most local rental car companies offer free transport to the airport if arranged ahead of time. Check **Maui Vans** (190 Papa Pl., 808/877-0090, www.mauivans.com), **Kimo's Rent a Car** (440 Alamaha St. 808/280-6327, www.kimos-rentacar.com), **Kihei Rent a Car** (96 Kio Loop, 808/879-7257, www.kiheirentacar.com), and **Manaloha Rent a Car** (375 West Kuiaha Rd., 808/283-8779, www.manaloharentacar.net).

Book ahead of time if traveling during the peak season, and know that drivers who are under 24 will often incur an extra fee. Also, in order to save some money, only rent a four-wheel-drive vehicle for the days you'll need it, rather than the duration of your trip.

Taxi

More than two dozen taxi companies operate an islandwide service on Maui, and besides providing normal taxi service they will also run tours all over the island. Taxis are expensive and metered by the distance traveled. From Kahului Airport, the fare to Lahaina should be roughly $65, $80 to Ka'anapali, $100 to Kapalua, and $55 to Wailea. Expect $5-10 in and around Kahului, and about $14 to the hostels in Wailuku. Any taxi may drop off at the airport, but only those with permits may pick up there.

Those in need of a taxi can call **Surf Taxi** (807/870-9974, www.surftaximaui.com), **West Maui Taxi** (808/661-1122, www.westmauitaxi.com), **Kihei Taxi** (808/298-1877, www.kiheitaxi.com), **Aloha Maui Taxi** (808/661-5432, www.alohamauitaxi.com), or **MJ Taxi** (808/283-9309).

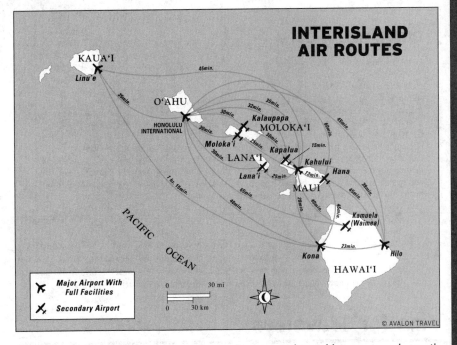

INTERISLAND AIR ROUTES

© AVALON TRAVEL

Shuttles

Robert's Hawaii (866/293-1782, www.robertshawaii.com/mauiexpress) connects the Kahului Airport to virtually anywhere on the island and operates daily during the hours that the planes fly.q1` With this door-to-door service, pickup can be either from the airport or from any hotel or condo if going to the airport. **Executive Airport Shuttle** (808/669-2300 or 800/833-2303) offers virtually the same service to and from the airport and to points around the island for marginally better rates, which will average around $50 per person from Kahului to Ka'anapali. Although these companies will service calls as soon as they can, they prefer several hours' or even 24 hours' notice if possible.

BUS

The **Maui Bus** (808/270-7511, www.co.maui.hi.us/bus) system has eight routes for an inexpensive way to get around to the major towns. Fares are $2 per boarding or $4 for a day pass, and monthly passes are also available. Although the bus does run to the airport, riders are not allowed to board with luggage which can't fit under their seat. For a full listing of island bus schedules refer to the timetables on the website.

BICYCLE

Maui is a great island for both serious road cyclers and those who prefer to just cruise around town. Towns such as Lahaina and Kihei are easily navigable by bicycle, although on many occasions cyclists will be forced to share the road with similarly slow-moving traffic. Rental shops can be found in Kahului, Pa'ia, Kihei, and Lahaina, and all will have island maps detailing the best rides.

SCOOTERS

Scooters are great for just running around town. Most rental operators will ask for a cash or credit card deposit. You must be at least 18 years old, have a valid driver's license, and often

DRIVE WITH ALOHA

Local customs come into play behind the wheel. You'll notice that even on highways drivers cruise along slowly. The maximum speed limit found anywhere on Maui is 55 mph, and in many places it's between 30 and 45. Off the main roads, it's essential to go slow in residential neighborhoods or on any side streets, especially when there are homes around. Going fast, even if it's not *really* speeding, can result in an angry fist shaken at your car or a call for you to slow down. Aside from speed issues, car horns are *only* to be used in an emergency (or when your friend walks by!), aggressive driving is severely frowned upon, and it's common courtesy—if not expected—to stop and allow waiting cars into traffic. Drivers are known to wave or throw *shakas* at each other, and there's a good chance you'll encounter at least one "Slow Down! This ain't the Mainland!" bumper sticker during your drive around the island.

Remember, you're here on an island to slow down and relax. So instead of racing to get somewhere, leave earlier and take time to enjoy the ride.

stay within a certain area from your rental office. Legally, mopeds can have only one rider.

On the west side of the island you can get scooters from **Motoroshi** (129 Lahainaluna Rd., 808/661-0006), and on the south side you will find **Aloha Motorsports** (2463 S. Kihei Rd., 808/667-7000, www.alohamotorpsports.com) in addition to other providers.

Tips for Travelers

TRAVELING WITH CHILDREN

Traveling with children on Maui can be a memorable experience—for better or for worse. Consider the kind of trip you want and book activities accordingly.

One of the best sites on the island for kids (other than the beach) is the **Maui Ocean Center,** which is full of hands-on activities and educational experiences. On the other hand, if you want to bring the little ones on vacation, but want to sneak away for a romantic dinner, the best service on the island for a short-term sitter is **The Nanny Connection** (808/875-4777, www.thenannyconnection.com), where professional sitting staff will meet you at your hotel and take care of your loved one in your absence.

TRAVELERS WITH DISABILITIES

A person with a disability can have a wonderful time in Hawai'i; all that's needed is a little planning. The key for a smooth trip is to make as many arrangements ahead of time as possible. Tell the transportation companies and hotels you'll be dealing with the nature of your disability in advance so they can make arrangements to accommodate you. Bring your medical records and notify medical establishments of your arrival if you'll be needing their services. Travel with a friend or make arrangements for an aide on arrival. Bring your own wheelchair if possible and let airlines know if it is battery-powered. Boarding interisland carriers sometimes requires steps. They'll board wheelchairs early on special lifts, but they must know that you're coming. Most hotels and restaurants accommodate people with disabilities, but always call ahead just to make sure.

Information

The state Commission on Persons with Disabilities was designed to aid disabled people. It is an invaluable source of information and

MAUI FOR FREE

Maui can be expensive, but it doesn't have to be. A number of Maui activities don't cost a thing:

- A morning stroll on the Kapalua Coastal Trail or Baldwin Beach
- Bodysurfing at D.T. Fleming Beach Park
- Watching the sunset at Haleakala and staying to watch the stars come out
- Free hula performances at the Lahaina Cannery Mall
- Hiking in Polipoli, Makena, or Hana
- Watching fishers sell their catch at Lahaina Harbor
- Swimming beneath a waterfall on the Road to Hana

- People-watching beneath the banyan tree
- A morning swim off Ka'anapali Beach
- Free evening entertainment at Whalers Village
- Volunteering with a local environmental organization
- Watching the surfers at Lahaina or Honolua Bay
- Watching the windsurfers at Kanaha Beach Park or Ho'kipa
- "Talking story" with a local
- Window-shopping in Makawao, Pa'ia, or Front Street
- Whale-watching from the Pali Lookout between Ma'alaea and Lahaina

distributes self-help booklets, published jointly by the Disability and Communication Access Board and the Hawai'i Centers for Independent Living. Any person with disabilities heading to Hawai'i should write first or visit the office of the **Hawai'i Centers for Independent Living** (414 Kuwili St., #102, Honolulu, HI 96817, 808/522-5400). On Maui, contact the **Maui Center for Independent Living** (220 Imi Kala St., Ste. 103, Wailuku, HI 96793, 808/242-4966). Additional information is available on the **Disability and Communication Access Board website** (www.hawaii.gov/health/dcab/home).

LGBT TRAVELERS

Gay and lesbian travelers are welcome throughout Hawai'i. While acceptance is part of the general state of mind, Maui has a smaller gay and lesbian community in the way of nighclubs, bars, or other gathering places for members of the LGBT community than O'ahu does, for example. In 2011, Hawai'i became the seventh state to legalize civil unions for same-sex couples.

For an accommodation option specifically geared toward LGBT travelers, check out the **Maui Sunseeker** in North Kihei (551 S. Kihei Rd., 808/879-1261 or 800/532-6284, www. mauisunseeker.com).

For all information LGBT-related on Maui, the website www.mauigayinfo.com has a listing of upcoming events, and www.gogayhawaii. com has detailed listings of dining, nightlife, and accommodation options which are specific to the LGBT community. Another source to consult is the **International Gay and Lesbian Travel Association** (954/630-1637, www.iglta. org), which can connect you with gay-friendly organizations and tour help.

Health and Safety

Every year Hawai'i consistently ranks among one of the healthiest states in America. Citizens here live longer than those anywhere else in the country, with an average life span of about 80 years. Lifestyle, heredity, and diet help with these figures, but Hawai'i is still an oasis in the middle of the ocean, and germs just have a tougher time getting here. There are no cases of malaria, cholera, or yellow fever, and because of a strict quarantine law, rabies is nonexistent.

Due to the perfect weather, soothing negative ionization from the sea, and carefree lifestyle, everyone seems to feel better in the islands. Hawai'i is just what the doctor ordered: a beautiful, natural health spa. That's one of its main drawing cards. The food and water are perfectly safe, and the air quality is the best in the country.

On the other hand, tooth decay, perhaps because of the wide use of sugar and the enzymes present in certain tropical fruits, is 30 percent above the national average. Obesity and related heart problems, as well as hard-drug use—especially crystal meth, or "ice"—are prevalent among native Hawaiians.

WATER SAFETY

Hawai'i has a sad claim to fame: More people drown here than anywhere else in the world. Moreover, there are dozens of victims of scuba, snorkeling, and boogie boarding accidents yearly with broken necks and backs or other injuries. These statistics shouldn't keep you out of the water, however, since the majority of visitors go home unscathed. The best remedy is to avoid situations you can't handle, and ask lifeguards or beach attendants about conditions and follow their advice. If local people refuse to go in, there's a good reason. Even experts can get in trouble in Hawaiian waters, and while some beaches are as gentle as a lamb, others can be frothing giants.

While beachcombing, or especially when walking out on rocks, never turn your back to the ocean. Always be aware of what is going on with the water. Undertows (the water drawing back into the sea) can knock you off your feet and pull you into the shorebreak. Observe the water well before you go in. Study it for rocks, breakers, and reefs. Look for ocean currents, especially those within reefs that can cause riptides when the water washes out a channel. Note where others are swimming or snorkeling and go there. Don't swim alone if possible, and obey all warning signs. When snorkeling, come ashore *before* you get tired.

When the wind comes up, get out. Stay out of water during periods of high surf. High surf often creates riptides, powerful currents that can drag you out to sea. Mostly they peter out not too far from shore, and you can often see their choppy waters on the surface. If you get caught in a "rip," don't fight by swimming directly against it. You'll only exhaust yourself. Swim diagonally across it, while letting it carry you, and try to stay parallel to the shore until you are out of the strong pull.

When bodysurfing, never ride straight in with your hands out in front you. This is the number one cause of broken necks in Hawai'i. Instead, ride the wave at a 45-degree angle, and try to kick out the back of the wave instead of letting it slam you into the sand. Remember, waves come in sets, and little ones can be followed by giants, so watch the action awhile instead of plunging right in. Standard procedure is to duck under a breaking wave. You can survive even thunderous oceans using this technique. Don't try to swim through a heavy froth and never turn your back and let it smash you.

Sharks and Marine Life

Some visitors fear that the moment their feet can no longer touch the sand they will be immediately attacked by **sharks.** Sharks live in all the oceans of the world and are largely harmless. More people die every year from falling coconuts and vending machines than from shark attacks. The chances of even seeing a large shark are remarkably slim. Hawaiian sharks are well fed—on fish—and don't usually bother with unsavory humans. To avoid sharks, avoid rivermouths, murky water, and especially murky water around dusk and dawn when there isn't as much natural light.

Portuguese man-of-wars and other jellyfish put out long, floating tentacles that sting if they touch you. It seems that many floating jellyfish are blown into shore by winds on the eighth, ninth, and 10th days after the full moon. Don't wash a sting off with freshwater because this will only aggravate it. Hot saltwater will take away the sting, as will alcohol (the drinking or the rubbing kind), aftershave lotion, or meat tenderizer. After rinsing, soak with a wet towel. Antihistamines may also bring relief. Expect to start to feel better in about a half hour.

Coral can give you a nasty cut and is known for causing infections because it's a living organism. Wash the cut immediately and apply an antiseptic. Keep it clean and covered, and watch for infection. With coral cuts, it's best to have a professional look at it.

Poisonous **sea urchins** found in tidepools and shallow reefs can be beautiful creatures, but if you step on them, their spines will enter your foot, break off, and burn like blazes. This is known to locals as *wana* (pronounced: Vah-na). Soaking a couple of times in vinegar for a half hour or so should stop the burning, or if that's not available, the Hawaiian solution is urine. It might seem gross, but it should put the fire out. Don't worry, the spines will wear off in a few days, and there are generally no long-term effects.

Hawaiian reefs also have their share of **moray eels.** These creatures are ferocious in appearance but will never initiate an attack. You'll have to poke around in their holes while snorkeling or scuba diving to provoke them. Sometimes this is inadvertent on the diver's part, so be careful where you stick your hand while underwater.

Present in streams, ponds, and muddy soil, leptospirosis is a freshwater-borne bacteria, deposited by the urine of infected animals. Two to 20 days after the bacteria enter the body, there will be a *sudden* onset of fever accompanied by chills, sweats, headache, and sometimes vomiting and diarrhea. Preventive measures include staying out of freshwater sources and mud where cattle and other animals wade and drink, not swimming in freshwater if you have an open cut, and not drinking stream water. Leptospirosis may be fatal in some cases if left untreated.

SAFETY IN THE OUTDOORS
Hiking

Other than bodysurfing and swimming, the most common way that visitors end up hurt or in trouble is taking unnecessary risks while hiking. Remember that wet rocks are slippery, and that stream crossings can be dangerous since flash floods can occur without warning. Stay away from the tops of waterfalls (where something as unpredictable as a gust of wind can send you one step farther than you had originally planned). If you are doing any cliff jumping, be sure you've scouted the landing zone for rocks and that it's been verified as safe by someone in the know. When hiking along the sea, remember that large surf can unpredictably crash onto the shoreline, so keep a safe distance from turbid seas and slippery rocks. While ACE bandages and disinfectants are great for curing cuts and scrapes, the most important thing to pack with you before heading out on an adventure is a healthy dose of common sense; don't go out in conditions with which you're unfamiliar, and never push yourself outside of your comfort zone when wandering off your own. As the motto says, "If in doubt, don't go out." Remember that the moment you set foot on a trail—whether in the mountains, the rainforest, or along the shoreline—every action is a direct result of choices you made. It isn't the fault of the landowner that wet rocks on his property are slippery, so be prepared to accept the personal responsibility for keeping yourself safe while exploring.

Sun

Many can't wait to strip down and lie on the sand like beached whales. But the tropical sun will burn you to a cinder if you aren't diligent about sunscreen. Burning rays come through more easily in Hawai'i because of the sun's angle and you don't feel them as much because there's always a cool breeze. The worst part of the day is 11am–3pm. Even though Maui lies about 21° north latitude and is not even close to the equator, it's still more than 1,000 miles south of sunny Southern California beaches. While spray-on sunscreens might be convenient, they stain the decks of boats, end up in your neighbor's mouth, and can ignite your skin if you stand next to an open flame (yikes!). The best—albeit most expensive—option is a sunscreen which isn't petroleum-based so that the chemicals don't slough off in the water and damage the coral. The best local sunscreen is **Doc Martin's**, which was developed by a local dermatologist and surfer himself to be highly water-resistant and great for covering your face.

Whether you are on the beach, in the mountains, or just strolling around town, beware of dehydration. The sun and wind sap your energy and your store of liquid. Bottled water in various sizes is readily available in all parts of Hawai'i. Carry some with you or stop at a store or restaurant for a fill'er-up.

MOSQUITOES, ROACHES, AND CENTIPEDES

Everyone seems to have some sort of aversion to bugs, and while Hawai'i isn't infested with a wide variety, it does have its share. Mosquitoes were unknown in the islands until their larvae stowed away in the water barrels of the *Wellington* in 1826 and were introduced at Lahaina. They bred easily in the tropical climate and rapidly spread to all the islands. They are a particular nuisance in the rainforests. Be prepared, and bring a natural repellent such as citronella oil, available in most health food stores on the islands or a commercial product available in grocery and drugstores. Campers will be happy to have mosquito coils to burn at night.

Cockroaches are a common sight in Hawai'i and offer nothing to worry about. They love the climate like everyone else, and it's a real problem keeping them under control.

Perhaps the most dangerous of all the island critters are the fearsome-looking centipedes which will wiggle their way into dark places of the home—particularly after the grass is mowed or the neighboring field harvested. Centipedes can deliver a nasty bite—with the babies packing more venom than the adults—and the best way for dealing with them is to give them the old rubbah slippah!

While you aren't likely to encounter too many spiders while on vacation, brown, spindly cane spiders can grow to be about the size of your hand, although there isn't too much to worry about in terms of getting a bite.

HAOLE ROT

A peculiar skin condition caused by the sun and damp towels is referred to locally as *haole* rot because it supposedly affects only people of European descent, but you'll notice some dark-skinned folks with the same condition. Basically, the skin becomes mottled with white spots that refuse to tan. You get a blotchy effect, mostly on the shoulders and back. Dermatologists have a fancy name for it, and they'll give you a fancy prescription with a fancy price tag to cure it. It's common knowledge throughout the islands, however, that Selsun Blue shampoo has an ingredient that stops the white mottling effect. Just wash your hair with it and then make sure to rub the lather over the affected areas, and it should clear up.

MEDICAL SERVICES
Hospital

Between downtown Kahului and downtown Wailuku, **Maui Memorial Medical Center** (221 Mahalani St., 808/244-9056) is the only full-service hospital on the island.

Medical Clinics

Several clinics are dotted around the island, including the following in Kihei: **Urgent Care**

Maui/Kihei Physicians (1325 S. Kihei Rd., Ste. 103, 808/879-7781), **Kihei-Wailea Medical Center** (808/874-8100) in the Piʻilani Village Shopping Center, and **Kihei Clinic** (2349 S. Kihei Rd., 808/879-1440). **Kaiser Permanente** has clinics in Lahaina (910 Waineʻe, 808/662-6800), Wailuku (80 Mahalani St., 808/243-6800), and Kihei (1279 S. Kihei Rd., 808/891-6800). In West Maui, the **West Maui Healthcare Center** (808/667-9721) maintains an office at the Whalers Village shopping mall, and in Hana, the **Hana Community Health Center** (808/248-8294) is along the highway just as you enter town.

Information and Services

TOURIST INFORMATION
Free Travel Literature

Free tourist literature is well done and loaded with tips, discounts, maps, happenings, and so forth. Found at the airport arrival lounge and on some street stands, they include the narrow-format *This Week Maui, Maui Gold, Maui Magazine, Maui Beach and Activity Guide, Maui Activities and Attractions,* and the magazine-style *Maui Drive Guide,* with excellent maps and tips, given out free by many car rental agencies. *101 Things to Do in Maui* is a great resource for activities and also has money-saving coupons. Aside from these, you'll find other magazines for Maui shops, art and culture, and golf.

Visitors Bureaus

The **Hawaiʻi Visitors Bureau or HVB** (www.gohawaii.com) is a top-notch organization providing help and information to all of Hawaiʻi's visitors. Anyone contemplating a trip to Hawaiʻi should visit a nearby office or check out its website for any specific information that might be required. The HVB's advice and excellent brochures on virtually every facet of living in, visiting, or enjoying Hawaiʻi are free.

The best information on Maui is dispensed by the **Maui Visitors Bureau** (1727 Wili Pa Loop, Wailuku, HI 96793, 808/244-3530 or 800/525-6284, www.visitmaui.com). Two other helpful organizations are the **Molokaʻi Visitors Association** (P.O. Box 960, Kaunakakai, HI 96748, 800/553-0404 interisland, 808/553-3876 or 800/800-6367 mainland and Canada, www.molokai-hawaii.com) and **Destination Lanaʻi** (P.O. Box 700, Lanaʻi City, HI 96763, 808/565-7600 or 800/947-4774, fax 808/565-9316, www.visitlanai.net). Additional online information pertaining to Maui County can be found at the official **County of Maui website** (www.co.maui.hi.us).

Weather Reports and Surfing Conditions

Remember that Maui has microclimates with weather unlike that on the mainland. To check what the weather is going to be in a certain part of the island, refrain from using large, national websites such as www.weather.com, and instead opt for a local site which is much more in tune with the island nuances. For weather, the absolute best site around is www.mauiweathertoday.com by Glenn James, which offers both weather and surf conditions (surf heights in Hawaiian scale). For surf forecasting, the best local resource is www.omaui.com (surf heights in face size), and there is also a detailed weather forecast at the bottom of the page.

Consumer Protection

If you encounter problems with accommodations, bad service, or downright rip-offs, try the following: **Maui Chamber of Commerce** (313 Ano St., Kahului, 96732, 808/871-7711, www.mauichamber.com), the state **Office of Consumer Protection** (808/984-8244 or 808/587-3222, www.hawaii.gov/dcca/ocp), or the **Better Business Bureau** (Oʻahu, 877/222-6551).

MONEY
Currency

U.S. currency is among the drabbest in the world. It's all the same size, with little variation in color; those unfamiliar with it should spend some time getting acquainted to avoid making costly mistakes. Coinage in use is one cent (penny), five cents (nickel), 10 cents (dime), 25 cents (quarter), 50 cents (half dollar), and $1; paper currency is $1, $2 (uncommon), $5, $10, $20, $50, $100. Bills larger than $100 are not in common use. Since 1996, new designs have been issued for the $100, $50, $20, $10, and $5 bills, although both the old and new bills are accepted as valid currency.

Travelers Checks

Travelers checks are accepted throughout Hawai'i at hotels, restaurants, car rental agencies, and in most stores and shops. However, to be readily acceptable, they should be in U.S. currency. Some larger hotels that frequently have Japanese and Canadian guests will accept those currencies. Banks accept foreign-currency travelers checks, but it'll mean an extra trip and inconvenience. It's best to get most of your travelers checks in $20 or $50 denominations; anything larger may be hard to cash in shops and boutiques, although not in hotels.

Credit Cards

Credit cards are the accepted method for virtually all business transactions in Maui. Almost every form of accommodation, shop, restaurant, and amusement takes them, although a handful of local mom-and-pop shops still only accept cash.

COMMUNICATIONS AND MEDIA
Telephone

The telephone system on the main islands is modern and comparable to any system on the mainland. For land lines, any phone call to a number on that island is a local call; it's long-distance when dialing to another island or beyond the state.

Cell (mobile) phone reception is good throughout the state of Hawai'i. However, as anywhere, you will find pockets where reception is not good or nonexistent.

For directory assistance, dial 1-411 (local), 1-555-1212 (interisland), 1-area code/555-1212 (mainland), 1-800/555-1212 (toll-free).

The area code for all the islands of Hawai'i is 808.

Newspapers

The major local newspaper available on Maui is the daily *Maui News* (www.mauinews.com), which has decent coverage and a good listing of local events. The *Lahaina News* (www.lahainanews.com) is a weekly community paper with news, feature stories, and entertainment listings. Free local weekly and biweekly newspapers include the *Maui Time* (www.mauitime.com) and *Maui Weekly* (www.mauiweekly.com), with the former focusing heavily on island entertainment options and political commentary.

WEIGHTS AND MEASURES

Hawai'i, like the rest of the United States, employs the imperial system of measurements for weights and distances. Basically, dry weights are in ounces and pounds; liquid measures are in ounces, quarts, and gallons; and distances are measured in inches, feet, yards, and miles. The metric system is known but not in general use.

Electricity

The same electrical current is in use in Hawai'i as on the U.S. mainland. The system functions on 110 volts, 60 cycles of alternating current (AC); type A (two-pin) and type B (three-pin) plugs are used. Appliances from Japan will work, but there is some danger that they will burn out, while those requiring the normal European voltage of 220, with other types of plugs, will not work.

Time Zones

There is no daylight saving time in Hawai'i. When daylight saving time is not observed on the mainland, Hawai'i is two hours behind the West Coast, four hours behind the Midwest, five hours behind the East Coast, and 11 hours behind Germany. During the other half of the year when the mainland is observing daylight savings time, Hawai'i is consequently three hours behind the West Coast and six hours behind the East Coast. Hawai'i, being just east of the International Date Line, is almost a full day behind most Asian and Oceanian cities. Hours behind these countries and cities are: Japan, 19 hours; Singapore, 18 hours; Sydney, 20 hours; New Zealand, 22 hours; Fiji, 22 hours.

RESOURCES

Glossary

HAWAIIAN

There was once a point in time when it was illegal to speak Hawaiian. The language was reserved to the home, children were punished for speaking it in school, and a census performed in 1983 determined there were only 50 island youths who could speak their native tongue. It wasn't until 1978 that the language began a monumental comeback as part of a greater movement known as the Hawaiian Renaissance, and today, Hawaiian is fluently spoken by approximately 8,000 people, not counting the tens of thousands of locals who pepper their daily speech with intermittent Hawaiian words.

While English is the official language of tourism and daily life, the following list provides a basic vocabulary of words you are likely to hear. You might even discover some Hawaiian words that are so perfectly expressive they'll become regular parts of your vocabulary.

'a'a: rough clinker lava; 'A'a has become the correct geological term to describe this type of lava found anywhere in the world.

'ae: yes

ahupua'a: pie-shaped land divisions running from mountain to sea that were governed by *konohiki*, local *ali'i* who owed their allegiance to a reigning chief

aikane: friend; pal; buddy

'aina: land; the binding spirit to all Hawaiians. Love of the land is paramount in traditional Hawaiian beliefs.

akamai: smart; clever; wise

akua: a god, or divine

ali'i: a Hawaiian chief or noble

aloha: the most common greeting in the islands; can mean both hello and good-bye, welcome and farewell. It can also mean romantic love, affection, or best wishes.

anuenue: rainbow

'a'ole: no

'aumakua: a personal or family god, often an ancestral spirit

auwe: alas; ouch! When a great chief or loved one died, it was a traditional wail of mourning.

halakahiki: pineapple

halau: school, as in hula school

hale: house or building; often combined with other words to name a specific place, such as Haleakala (House of the Sun).

hana: work; combined with *pau* means end of work or quitting time

hanai: literally "to feed." Part of the true aloha spirit. A *hanai* is a permanent guest, or an adopted family member, usually an old person or a child. This is an enduring cultural phenomenon in Hawai'i, in which a child from one family (perhaps that of a brother or sister, and quite often one's grandchild) is raised as one's own without formal adoption.

haole: a word that at one time meant foreigner, but which now means a white person or Caucasian

hapa: half, as in a mixed-blooded person being referred to as *hapa haole*

hapai: pregnant; used by all ethnic groups when a *keiki* is on the way

haupia: a coconut custard dessert often served at a lu'au

HAWAIIAN LANGUAGE PRONUNCIATION GUIDE

Many visitors are baffled by the Hawaiian language. Seemingly chaotic, endless chains of vowels blend to create ridiculously long words. Confronted with the task of pronouncing words like *Honoapiʻilani* (aka "Highway 30") or *Kealaikahiki,* many give up.

The Hawaiian language is actually straightforward once you understand it. The first step is proper pronunciation. Follow these guidelines, and all those long stretches of vowels will suddenly start to make sense.

Vowels are pronounced differently in Hawaiian than they are in English. Rather than the standard "a, e, i, o, u" that all English-speakers find familiar, there are "aw, eh, ee, oh, ooh," much the same as in Spanish. Take the word *la* (which means "sun"), and you will find that it's pronounced phonetically as "law," as opposed to "lah." The word *ala* (which means "road" or "path") is pronounced as "aw-law" as opposed to "aah-laah," as it would be in English. Got it?

The next step in pronouncing Hawaiian is the ability to say those *really* long words. They look daunting, but it's easier to understand if you know that long Hawaiian words—much like German words—are actually many smaller words scrunched together. Take, for example, *Haleakala,* Maui's famous mountain, and try to pronounce it right now. How did that go? Is it any easier when you break it into smaller words such as *Hale-a-ka-la.* Say those four words right now, remembering the vowel pronunciation (phonetically: Haw-lay-aw-kaw-LAW). Any better? When broken into four smaller words, it's not only easier to pronounce, but the name

makes sense. *Hale* means "house," *a* means "of," *ka* means "the," and *la* means "sun," so a full translation is "house of the sun." Easy, right?

Let's try it again with the big, scary words from the beginning of this section, *Honoapiʻilani,* and *Kealaikahiki.* The first word, *Honoapiʻilani,* can be broken down as *Hono-a-Piʻilani,* which translates as *Hono* (bay) *a* (of) *Piʻilani* (an ancient king of Maui), or completely, "the bays of Piʻilani." This is a fitting name for highway, seeing as Piʻilani was the great king of Maui who once created a footpath around much of the island as a way of connecting all the areas in his domain.

For a final example, look at *Kealaikahiki,* which can be broken down as *Ke-ala-i-kahiki.* The translations are *Ke* (the) *ala* (road) *i* (to) *kahiki* (Tahiti), or completely, "The road to Tahiti." (For "kahiki," the "k" and the "t" are interchangeable in many Polynesian languages, and lacking a "t" in modern Hawaiian, the "k" is substituted). Seeing as this name refers to the channel between the islands of Lanaʻi and Kahoʻolawe—which points south—it would only make sense that "the road to Tahiti" would signify the direction that voyaging canoes would head when journeying back to their ancestral homeland.

Whew! You got all that? It's a lot to take in. But it's worth the effort. By pronouncing the vowels correctly, and by breaking longer words into the shorter words contained within, the scary Hawaiian language suddenly becomes much more manageable.

---

heʻenalu: surfing

heiau: A platform made of skillfully fitted rocks, upon which temporary structures were built as temples and offerings made to the gods.

hono: bay, as in Honolulu (Sheltered Bay)

honu: green sea turtle; endangered

hoʻolauleʻa: any happy event, but especially a family outing or picnic

huhu: angry; irritated

hui: a group; meeting; society. Often used to refer to Chinese businesspeople or family

members who pool their money to get businesses started.

hukilau: traditional shoreline fish-gathering in which everyone lends a hand to *huki* (pull) the huge net.

hula: a native Hawaiian dance in which the rhythm of the islands is captured by swaying hips and stories told by lyrically moving hands. A *halau* is a group or school of hula.

huli huli: barbecue, as in *huli huli* chicken

imu: underground oven filled with hot rocks and

used for baking. The main cooking method featured at a lu'au, used to steam-bake pork and other succulent dishes. The tending of the *imu* was traditionally for men only.

ipo: sweetheart; lover; girlfriend or boyfriend

kahuna: priest; sorcerer; doctor; skillful person. In old Hawai'i *kahuna* had tremendous power, which they used for both good and evil. The *kahuna ana'ana* was a feared individual who practiced black magic and could pray a person to death, while the *kahuna lapa'au* was a medical practitioner bringing aid and comfort to the people.

kai: the sea. Many businesses and hotels employ *kai* as part of their name.

kalua: means roasted underground in an *imu*. A favorite island food is *kalua* pork.

kama'aina: a child of the land; an old-timer; a longtime island resident of any ethnic background; a resident of Hawai'i or native son or daughter. Hotels and airlines often offer discounts called "*kama'aina* rates" to anyone who can prove island residency.

kanaka: man or commoner; later used to distinguish a Hawaiian from other races.

kane: means man, but is actually used to signify a relationship such as husband or boyfriend. Written on a lavatory door it means "men's room."

kapu: forbidden; taboo; keep out; do not touch

kaukau: slang word meaning food or chow; grub. Some of the best food in Hawai'i comes from the *kaukau* wagons, trucks that sell plate lunches and other morsels.

keiki: child or children; used by all ethnic groups. "Have you hugged your *keiki* today?"

kiawe: an algaroba tree from South America commonly found in Hawai'i along the shore. It grows a nasty long thorn that can easily puncture a tire. Legend has it that the trees were introduced to the islands by a misguided missionary who hoped the thorns would coerce natives into wearing shoes. Actually, they are good for fuel, as fodder for hogs and cattle, and for reforestation, none of which you'll appreciate if you step on one of the thorns or flatten a tire on your rental car!

kokua: help. As in "Your *kokua* is needed to keep Hawai'i free from litter."

kolohe: rascal

kona wind: a muggy subtropical wind that blows from the south and hits the leeward side of the islands. It usually brings sticky hot weather and one of the few times when air-conditioning will be appreciated.

ko'olau: windward side of the island

kukui: a candlenut tree whose pods are polished and then strung together to make a beautiful lei. Traditionally the oil-rich nuts were strung on the rib of a coconut leaf and used as a candle.

kuleana: home site; the old homestead; small farms. Especially used to describe the small spreads on Hawaiian Home Lands on Moloka'i.

Kumulipo: ancient Hawaiian genealogical chant that records the pantheon of gods, creation, and the beginning of humankind

kupuna: a grandparent or old-timer; usually means someone who has gained wisdom. The statewide school system now invites *kupuna* to talk to the children about the old ways and methods.

la: the sun. Often combined with other words to be more descriptive, such as Lahaina (Merciless Sun) or Haleakala (House of the Sun).

lanai: veranda or porch. You'll pay more for a hotel room if it has a lanai with an ocean view.

lani: sky or the heavens

lau hala: traditional Hawaiian weaving of mats, hats, etc., from the prepared fronds of the pandanus (screw pine)

lei: a traditional garland of flowers or vines. One of Hawai'i's most beautiful customs. Given at any auspicious occasion, but especially when arriving or leaving Hawai'i.

lele: the stone altar at a *heiau*

limu: edible seaweed of various types. Gathered from the shoreline, it makes an excellent salad. It's used to garnish many island dishes and is a favorite at lu'au.

lolo: crazy, as in *lolo buggah* (stupid or crazy guy)

lomi lomi: traditional Hawaiian massage; also, raw salmon made into a vinegared salad with chopped onion and spices

lua: the toilet; the head; the bathroom

UNDERSTANDING THE OKINA

You will often notice what appears to be a backward apostrophe inserted in the middle of Hawaiian words such as Lanaʻi and Kaʻanapali. This marking is known as the *okina*, and rather than letting it confuse you even further, use the *okina* to help in determining the proper pronunciation.

To a professional linguist the *okina* denotes a glottal stop, which in layman's terms essentially means that you pronounce both of the vowels it's sandwiched between. To use the above examples, when pronouncing the name of island of Lanaʻi you would verbalize both the "a" as well as the "i," for a phonetic pronunciation of "Lah-NA-ee." The *incorrect* pronunciation is to blend the final two words together and say "Lah-Nai," which in the Hawaiian language means "a porch," and is spelled *lanai*.

Similarly, the major resort area of Kaʻanapali is correctly pronounced by verbalizing both the first as well as the second "a," which phonetically looks like "Kah-ah-naw-PAW-lee." The *incorrect* way to pronounce the word is to slur the two vowels together by saying "KAW-nah-paw-lee," or even worse, the dreaded "Ka-NAH-poli."

The *okina* serves as an instructional guide as to which vowels to pronounce individually and which to blend together. The town of Lahaina—which you notice does not have an *okina*—is correctly pronounced as "Law-HIGH-nah," whereas if it were to be spelled with an *okina* such as Lahaʻina, it would then be pronounced as "Law-HUH-ee-na."

Make sense?

luakini: a human-sacrifice temple. Introduced to Hawaiʻi in the 13th century at Wahaʻula Heiau on the Big Island.

luʻau: a Hawaiian feast featuring poi, *imu-* baked pork, and other traditional foods. Good ones provide some of the best gastronomic delights in the world.

luna: foreman or overseer in the plantation fields. They were often mounted on horseback and were renowned for either their fairness or their cruelty. Representing the middle class, they served as a buffer between plantation workers and white plantation owners.

mahalo: thank you. *Mahalo nui* means "big thanks" or "thank you very much."

mahele: division. The Great Mahele of 1848 changed Hawaiʻi forever when the traditional common lands were broken up into privately owned plots.

mahimahi: a favorite eating fish. Often called a dolphin, but a mahimahi is a true fish, not a cetacean.

mahu: a homosexual; often used derisively

maile: a fragrant vine used in traditional lei. It looks ordinary but smells delightful.

makaʻainana: a commoner; a person "belonging" to the *ʻaina* (land), who supported the *aliʻi*

by fishing and farming and as a warrior

makai: toward the sea; used by most islanders when giving directions

make: dead; deceased

malihini: what you are if you have just arrived: a newcomer; a tenderfoot; a recent arrival

malo: the native Hawaiian loincloth. Never worn anymore except at festivals or pageants.

mana: power from the spirit world; innate energy of all things animate or inanimate; the grace of god. Mana could be passed on from one person to another, or even stolen. Great care was taken to protect the *aliʻi* from having their *mana* defiled. Commoners were required to lie flat on the ground and cover their faces whenever a great *aliʻi* approached. *Kahuna* were often employed in the regaining or transference of *mana*.

manini: small; stingy; tight

mauka: toward the mountains; used by most islanders when giving directions

mauna: mountain. Often combined with other words to be more descriptive, such as Mauna Kea (White Mountain)

mele: a song or chant in the Hawaiian oral tradition that records the history and genealogies of the *aliʻi*

Menehune: the legendary "little people" of Hawai'i. Like leprechauns, they are said to shun humans and possess magical powers.

moa: chicken; fowl

moana: the ocean; the sea.

moe: sleep

mo'olelo: ancient tales kept alive by the oral tradition and recited only by day

nani: beautiful

nui: big; great; large; as in *mahalo nui* (thank you very much)

'ohana: a family; the fundamental social division; extended family. Now often used to denote a social organization with grassroots overtones.

oli: chant not done to a musical accompaniment

'ono: delicious; delightful; the best.

'opihi: a shellfish or limpet that clings to rocks and is gathered as one of the islands' favorite *pupu*. Custom dictates that you never remove all of the *'opihi* from a rock; some are always left to grow for future generations.

'opu: belly; stomach

pahoehoe: smooth, ropy lava that looks like burnt pancake batter. It is now the correct geological term used to describe this type of lava found anywhere in the world.

pakalolo: "crazy smoke"; grass; smoke; dope; marijuana

pake: a Chinese person. Can be derisive, depending on the tone in which it is used. It is a bastardization of the Chinese word meaning "uncle."

pali: a cliff; precipice. Hawai'i's geology makes them quite common. The most famous are the *pali* of O'ahu where a major battle was fought.

paniolo: a Hawaiian cowboy. Derived from the Spanish *español*. The first cowboys brought to Hawai'i during the early 19th century were Mexicans from California.

pau: finished; done; completed. Often combined into *pau hana*, which means end of work or quitting time.

pilau: stink; bad smell; stench

pilikia: trouble of any kind, big or small; bad times

poi: a glutinous paste made from the pounded corm of taro, which ferments slightly and has a light sour taste. Purplish in color, it's a staple at lu'au, where it is called "one-, two-, or three-finger" poi, depending upon its thickness.

pono: righteous or excellent

pua: flower

puka: a hole of any size. *Puka* is used by all island residents, whether talking about a pinhole in a rubber boat or a tunnel through a mountain.

pupu: an appetizer; a snack; hors d'oeuvres; can be anything from cheese and crackers to sushi. Often, bars or nightclubs offer them free.

pupule: crazy; nuts; out of your mind

pu'u: hill, as in Pu'u 'Ula'ula (Red Hill)

tapa: a traditional paper cloth made from beaten bark. Intricate designs were stamped in using beaters, and natural dyes added color. The tradition was lost for many years but is now making a comeback, and provides some of the most beautiful folk art in the islands. Also called Kapa.

taro: the staple of old Hawai'i. A plant with a distinctive broad leaf that produces a starchy root. It was brought by the first Polynesians and was grown on magnificently irrigated plantations. According to the oral tradition, the life-giving properties of taro hold mystical significance for Hawaiians, since it was created by the gods at about the same time as humans.

ti: a broad-leafed plant that was used for many purposes, from plates to hula skirts. Especially used to wrap religious offerings presented at the *heiau.*

tutu: grandmother; granny; older woman. Used by all as a term of respect and endearment.

ukulele: *uku* means "flea" and *lele* means "jumping," so "jumping flea." The way the Hawaiians perceived the quick finger movements used on the banjo-like Portuguese folk instrument called a *cavaquinho.*

wahine: young woman; female; girl; wife. Used by all ethnic groups. When written on a lavatory door it means "women's room."

wai: freshwater; drinking water

wela: hot.

wiki: quickly; fast; in a hurry. Often seen as *wiki wiki* (very fast), as in "Wiki Wiki Messenger Service."

Useful Phrases

Aloha ahiahi Good afternoon
Aloha au ia 'oe I love you
Aloha kakahiaka Good morning
Aloha nui loa Much love
E komo mai Welcome
Ha'uoli la hanau Happy Birthday
Ha'uoli makahiki hou Happy New Year
Mahalo nui loa Thank you very much
Mele Kalikimaka Merry Christmas

PIDGIN

More so than Hawaiian, pidgin is the language of choice that you will notice being spoken around the islands. A creole which borrows words from English, Hawaiian, and a host of other languages, it has a lilt, cadence, and grammar entirely unto itself. Born out of the sugar plantation camps, pidgin was developed as a melding of languages of workers in the field.

Today, pidgin is likely to be heard spoken among most island locals, and even those *kama'aina* who can speak perfect English can turn their pidgin on and off just like flipping a switch. To most visitors, however, pidgin can be completely undecipherable, mainly because of the sentence structure and introduction of foreign words. For example, the past tense in pidgin is created by placing the word "wen" (as in "went") in front of the present tense of a verb. Examples would be "wen go" (went), "wen eat" (ate), "wen drive" (drove), etc.

A full example of a pidgin sentence might go something like: "Braddah wen drive da odda side and was shaking his *okole* the whole time cuz he needed fo' use da lua," which translates as "Braddah (general subject) drove to the other side (of the island) and was shaking his butt (*okole*) the whole time because he needed to use the bathroom (*lua*)."

In other instances, grammar instructors would be astonished at the blatant disregard for the tenses of the English language, as seen in the common phrase "Try wait brah, I stay coming" ("Hold on, I'm on my way"), or the assertion that "he get choke mangoes already that guy" ("his mango tree is already full").

For those who were raised without the language it can take years to fully understand pidgin, although for the *keiki* who were raised here it comes as naturally as a native tongue. While you probably won't become fluent any time soon, here are some basic phrases for helping you get by.

an' den and then? big deal; so what's next?
auntie respected elderly woman
bumbye Later; after a while.
blalah brother, but actually only refers to a large, heavy-set, good-natured Hawaiian man
brah all the bros in Hawaii are brahs; brother; pal. Used to call someone's attention. One of the most common words even among people who are not acquainted. After a fill-up at a gas station, a person would say "Tanks, brah."
chicken skin goose bumps
choke lots of something
cockaroach steal; rip off.
da kine a catchall word of many meanings that epitomizes the essence of pidgin. Da kine is a euphemism for pidgin and is substituted whenever the speaker is at a loss for a word or just wants to generalize.
geev um give it to them; give them hell; go for it. Can be used as an encouragement. If a surfer is riding a great wave, the people on the beach might yell, "Geev um, brah!"
grinds food
hana hou again. Especially after a concert the audience shouts "hana hou" (one more!).
hele on let's get going
howzit? as in "howzit, brah?" What's happening? How's it going? The most common greeting, used in place of the more formal "How do you do?"
lesgo let's go! do it!
li'dis an' li'dat like this or that
lolo stupid, crazy
mo' bettah A better way of doing something.
pakalolo "crazy smoke"; marijuana; grass; reefer
pau a Hawaiian word meaning finished; done; over and done with. Pau hana means end of work or quitting time. Once used by plantation workers, now used by everyone.

seestah sister, female

shaka hand wave where only the thumb and baby finger stick out, meaning "thank you, all right!"

shoots Whatever, sure, in agreement. Example: "What, you like go Makena today?" "Shoots!"

rubbah sleepah rubber slippers, sandals, flip-flops. Referring to slippers as sandals is only something that "mainlanders" would do.

stink eye Basically frowning at someone; using facial expression to show displeasure. Hard looks. What you'll get if you give local people a hard time.

talk story spinning yarns; shooting the breeze; throwing the bull; a rap session. If you're lucky enough to be around to hear *kupuna* (elders) "talk story," you can hear some fantastic tales in the tradition of old Hawai'i.

tanks, brah thanks, thank you

to da max all the way

wea stay? literally, "where stay?," as in to ask a location. Examples are "wea the car stay?," "wea you stay?," or the gloriously grammatical "wea you stay going" (where are you going).

We go Let's go! Usually used in conjunction with "shoots," as in "shoots we go!"

Suggested Reading

Many publishers print books on Hawai'i. Following are a few that focus on Hawaiian topics: **University of Hawai'i Press** (www.uhpress.hawaii.edu) has the best overall general list of titles on Hawai'i. The **Bishop Museum Press** (www.bishopmuseum.org/press) puts out many scholarly works on Hawaiiana, as does **Kamehameha Schools Press** (http://kspress.ksbe.edu). Also good, with a more general-interest list, are **Bess Press** (www.besspress.com), **Mutual Publishing** (www.mutualpublishing.com), and **Petroglyph Press** (www.basicallybooks.com). In addition, a website specifically oriented toward books on Hawai'i, Hawaiian music, and other things Hawaiian is **Hawaii Books** (www.hawaiibooks.com).

ASTRONOMY

Rhoads, Samuel. *The Sky Tonight—A Guided Tour of the Stars over Hawaii.* Honolulu: Bishop Museum, 1993. Four pages per month of star charts—one each for the horizon in every cardinal direction. Exceptional!

COOKING

Choy, Sam. *Cooking from the Heart with Sam Choy.* Honolulu: Mutual Publishing, 1995. This beautiful, hand-bound cookbook contains many color photos by Douglas Peebles.

Wong, Alan. *New Wave Luau.* Berkeley: Ten Speed Press, 1999. With his book, Hawai'i's prized chef shares wonderful recipes across the board of Hawaiian and local food.

CULTURE

Hartwell, Jay. *Na Mamo: Hawaiian People Today.* Honolulu: 'Ai Pohaku Press, 1996. Profiles 12 people practicing Hawaiian traditions in the modern world.

Kamehameha Schools Press. *Life in Early Hawai'i: The Ahupua'a.* 3rd ed. Honolulu: Kamehameha Schools Press, 1994. Written for schoolchildren to better understand the basic organization of old Hawaiian land use and its function, this slim volume is a good primer for people of any age who wish to understand this fundamental societal fixture.

Kirch, Patrick V. *Feathered Gods and Fishhooks: An Introduction to Hawaiian Archaeology and Prehistory.* Honolulu: University of Hawai'i Press, 1997. This scholarly, lavishly illustrated, yet readable book gives new insight into the development of precontact Hawaiian civilization. It focuses on the sites and major settlements of old Hawai'i and chronicles the main cultural developments while weaving in the social climate that contributed to change.

McBride, Likeke. *Petroglyphs of Hawaii*. Hilo, HI: Petroglyph Press, 1997. A revised and updated guide to petroglyphs found in the Hawaiian Islands. A basic introduction to these old Hawaiian picture stories.

McBride, L. R. *Practical Folk Medicine of Hawaii*. Hilo, HI: Petroglyph Press, 1975. An illustrated guide to Hawai'i's medicinal plants as used by the *kahuna lapa'au* (medical healers). Includes a thorough section on ailments, diagnosis, and the proper folk remedy. Illustrated by the author, a renowned botanical researcher and former ranger at Hawai'i Volcanoes National Park.

FAUNA

Fielding, Ann, and Ed Robinson. *An Underwater Guide to Hawai'i*. Honolulu: University of Hawai'i Press, 1987. If you've ever had a desire to snorkel/scuba the living reef waters of Hawai'i and to be familiar with what you're seeing, get this small but fact-packed book. The amazing array of marine life found throughout the archipelago is captured in glossy photos with accompanying informative text. Both the scientific and common names of specimens are given. This book will enrich your underwater experience and serve as an easily understood reference guide for years.

Hoover, John P. *Hawaii's Fishes: A Guide for Snorkelers and Divers*. Honolulu: Mutual Publishing, 2007. The definitive resource for identifying the fish of Hawai'i.

Kay, Alison, and Olive Schoenberg-Dole. *Shells of Hawai'i*. Honolulu: University of Hawai'i Press, 1991. Color photos and tips on where to look.

Van Riper, Charles, and Sandra van Riper. *A Field Guide to the Mammals of Hawaii*. Honolulu: Oriental Publishing. A guide to the surprising number of mammals introduced into Hawai'i. Full-color pages document description, uses, tendencies, and habitat. Small and thin, this book makes a worthwhile addition to any serious hiker's backpack.

FLORA

Kepler, Angela. *Hawaiian Heritage Plants*. Honolulu: University of Hawai'i Press, 1998. A treatise on 32 utilitarian plants used by the early Hawaiians.

Kepler, Angela. *Hawai'i's Floral Splendor*. Honolulu: Mutual Publishing, 1997. A general reference to flowers of Hawai'i.

Miyano, Leland. *A Pocket Guide to Hawai'i's Flowers*. Honolulu: Mutual Publishing, 2001. A small guide to readily seen flowers in the state. Good for the backpack or back pocket.

Teho, Fortunato. *Plants of Hawaii—How to Grow Them*. Hilo, HI: Petroglyph Press, 1992. A small but useful book for those who want their backyards to bloom into tropical paradises.

Valier, Kathy. *Ferns of Hawaii*. Honolulu: University of Hawai'i Press, 1995. One of the few books that treat the state's ferns as a single subject.

HISTORY

Ashdown, Inez MacPhee. *Recollections of Kaho'olawe*. Honolulu: Topgallant Publishing, 1979. The tortured story of the lonely island of Kaho'olawe by a member of the family who owned the island until it was turned into a military bombing target during World War II. This is a first-person account of life on the island and is rife with myths, legends, and historical facts about Kaho'olawe.

Barnes, Phil. *A Concise History of the Hawaiian Islands*. Hilo, HI: Petroglyph Press, 1999. An examination of the main currents of Hawaiian history and its major players, focusing on the important factors in shaping the social, economic, and political trends of the islands. An easy read.

Cordy, Ross. *Exalted Sits the Chief.* Honolulu, Mutual Publishing, 2000. An in-depth examination from archaeological and cultural records of the ancient Hawaiian civilization up until the coming of the Western explorers.

Davenport, Kiana. *Shark Dialogues.* New York: Penguin Books, 1995. A fictional account of Hawai'i's history based upon historical events. Captivating read which is given from the perspective of Hawaiians.

Daws, Gavan. *Shoal of Time, A History of the Hawaiian Islands.* Honolulu: University of Hawai'i Press, 1974. A highly readable history of Hawai'i dating from its "discovery" by the Western world down to its acceptance as the 50th state. Good insight into the psychological makeup of influential characters who helped form Hawai'i's past.

Ellis, William. *A Narrative of an 1823 Tour Through Hawai'i.* Reprint. Honolulu: Mutual Publishing, 2004. Reprint of the 1825 journal by an early missionary of a journey around the island of Hawai'i and impressions of the land and its people. One of the first descriptions of Hawai'i for the West.

Fornander, Abraham. *An Account of the Polynesian Race; Its Origins and Migrations, and the Ancient History of the Hawaiian People to the Times of Kamehameha I.* Rutland, VT: C.E. Tuttle Co., 1969. This is a reprint of a three-volume opus originally published 1878-1885. It is still one of the best sources of information on Hawaiian myth and legend.

Ii, John Papa. *Fragments of Hawaiian History.* Honolulu: Bishop Museum, 1959. Hawai'i's history under Kamehameha I as told by a Hawaiian who actually experienced it.

Joesting, Edward. *Hawaii: An Uncommon History.* New York: W.W. Norton Co., 1978. A truly uncommon history told in a series of vignettes relating to the lives and personalities of the first Caucasians in Hawai'i, Hawaiian nobility, sea captains, writers, and adventurers. Brings history to life.

Kamakau, S. M. *Ruling Chiefs of Hawaii,* revised edition. Honolulu: Kamehameha Schools Press, 1992. A history of Hawai'i from the legendary leader 'Umi to the mid-Kamehameha dynasty, from oral tales and a Hawaiian perspective.

Lili'uokalani. *Hawaii's Story by Hawaii's Queen.* Reprint, Honolulu: Mutual Publishing, 1990. Originally written in 1898, this moving personal account recounts Hawai'i's inevitable move from monarchy to U.S. Territory by its last queen, Lili'uokalani. The facts can be found in other histories, but none provides the emotion or point of view expressed by Hawai'i's deposed monarch. This is a must-read to get the whole picture.

Nickerson, Roy. *Lahaina, Royal Capital of Hawaii.* Honolulu: Hawaiian Service, 1978. The story of Lahaina from whaling days to present, spiced with ample photographs.

Tabrah, Ruth M. *Ni'ihau: The Last Hawaiian Island.* Kailua, Hawai'i: Press Pacifica, 1987. Sympathetic history of the privately owned island of Ni'ihau.

Takaki, Ronald. *Pau Hana: Plantation Life and Labor in Hawaii.* Honolulu: University of Hawai'i Press, 1983. The story of immigrant labor and the sugar industry in Hawai'i until the 1920s from the workers' perspective.

LANGUAGE

Elbert, Samuel, and Mary Pukui. *Hawaiian Dictionary.* Honolulu: University of Hawai'i Press, 1986. The best dictionary available on the Hawaiian language. The *Pocket Hawaiian Dictionary* is a less expensive, condensed version of this dictionary and adequate for most travelers with a general interest in the language.

Pukui, Mary Kawena, Samuel Elbert, and Esther T. Mookini. *Place Names of Hawaii.* Honolulu: University of Hawai'i Press, 1974. The most current and comprehensive listing of Hawaiian and foreign place names in the state, giving pronunciation, spelling, meaning, and location.

MYTHOLOGY, LEGEND, AND LITERATURE

Beckwith, Martha. *Hawaiian Mythology.* Reprint. Honolulu: University of Hawai'i Press, 1976. Originally printed in 1940, this work remains the definitive text on Hawaiian mythology. Beckwith compiled this book from many sources, giving exhaustive cross-references to genealogies and legends expressed in the oral tradition. If you are only going to read one book on Hawai'i's folklore, this should be it.

Beckwith, Martha. *The Kumulipo.* Reprint. Honolulu: University of Hawai'i Press, 1972.

Translation of the Hawaiian creation chant, originally published in 1951.

Kalakaua, His Hawaiian Majesty, King David. *The Legends and Myths of Hawaii.* Edited by R. M. Daggett, with a foreword by Glen Grant. Honolulu: Mutual Publishing, 1990. In this book originally published in 1888, Hawai'i's own King Kalakaua draws upon his scholarly and formidable knowledge of the classic oral tradition to bring alive ancient tales from precontact Hawai'i. A powerful yet Victorian voice from Hawai'i's past speaks clearly and boldly, especially about the intimate role of pre-Christian religion in the lives of the Hawaiian people.

Pukui, Mary Kawena, and Caroline Curtis. *Hawaii Island Legends.* Honolulu: The Kamehameha Schools Press, 1996. Hawaiian tales and legends for preteens.

Pukui, Mary Kawena, and Caroline Curtis. *Tales of the Menehune.* Honolulu: The Kamehameha Schools Press, 1960. Compilation of legends relating to Hawai'i's "little people."

Internet Resources

www.co.maui.hi.us
The official website of Maui County. Includes, among other items, information on city government, the county-sponsored bus system, disability access, and a calendar of events.

www.gohawaii.com
This official site of the Hawai'i Visitors and Convention Bureau, the state-run tourism organization, has information about all of the major Hawaiian Islands: transportation, accommodations, eating, activities, shopping, Hawaiian products, an events calendar, a travel planner and resource guide for a host of topics, as well as information about meetings, conventions, and the organization itself.

www.visitmaui.com
The official site of the Maui Visitors Bureau, a branch of the Hawai'i Visitors and Convention Bureau, has much the same information as the previous website but specific to the island of Maui. Tourist information specific to Moloka'i and Lana'i, can be found at **www.molokai-hawaii.com** and **www.visitlanai.net.**

www.mauiinformationguide.com
A large, informative, and modern website that offers insights into everything from activities and trip planning to helpful tips and safety guidelines.

www.bestplaceshawaii.com
Produced and maintained by H&S Publishing,

this first-rate commercial site has general and specific information about all major Hawaiian Islands, a vacation planner, and suggestions for things to do and places to see. For a nongovernment site, this is a great place to start a search for tourist information about the state or any of its major islands. One of dozens of sites on the Internet with a focus on Hawai'i tourism-related information.

www.alternative-hawaii.com
Alternative source for ecofriendly general information and links to specific businesses, with some cultural, historical, and events information.

www.hawaiiecotourism.org
Official Hawaii Ecotourism Association website. Lists goals, members, and activities, and provides links to member organizations and related ecotourism groups.

http://calendar.gohawaii.com
For events of all sorts happening throughout the state, visit the calendar of events listing on the Hawai'i Visitors Bureau website. Information can be accessed by island, date, or type.

www.state.hi.us/sfca
This site of the State Foundation of Culture and the Arts features a calendar of arts and cultural events, activities, and programs held throughout the state.

www.mele.com
Check out the Hawaiian music scene at Hawaiian Music Island, one of the largest music websites that focuses on Hawaiian music, books, and videos related to Hawaiian music and culture, concert schedules, Hawaiian music awards, and links to music companies and musicians. Others with broad listings and general interest information are **www.nahenahe.net** and **www.hawaii-music.com**.

www.uhpress.hawaii.edu
This University of Hawai'i Press website has the best overall list of titles for books published on Hawaiian themes and topics. Other publishers to check for substantial lists of books on Hawaiiana are the Bishop Museum Press, **www.bishopmuseum. org;** Kamehameha Schools Press, **http:// kspress.ksbe.edu;** Bess Press, **www. besspress.com;** Mutual Publishing, **www. mutualpublishing.com;** and Petroglyph Press, **www.basicallybooks.com.**

www.hawaiimuseums.org
This site is dedicated to the promotion of museums and cultural attractions in the state of Hawai'i with links to member sites on each of the islands. A member organization.

www.mauinews.com
Website of Maui's largest newspaper, *Maui News*. It has a concentration of news coverage about Maui, but also covers major news from the neighboring islands.

www.oha.org
Official site for the state-mandated organization that deals with native Hawai'i-related affairs.

www.reinstated.org
Site of Reinstated Hawaiian Government, one of the organizations of native Hawaiians advocating for sovereignty and independence. Other native Hawaiian rights organizations include Kingdom of Hawai'i (**www. freehawaii.org**) and **www.pixi.com/~kingdom**) Hawaiian Independence (**www.hawaii-nation. org**) and the Hawaiian Kingdom, (**www. hawaiiankingdom.org**).

Index

List of Maps

Acknowledgments

The first edition of *Moon Maui* was published in 1986. Its original author was J.D. Bisignani (1947-1997), whose *Japan Handbook* (1983) was one of Moon's founding publications. The next seven editions of *Moon Maui* were revised by Joe and by Robert Nilsen (also the author of *Moon South Korea*), who took over as sole author after Joe's death in 1997. Joe and Bob brought the same spirit of adventure to their Hawai'i coverage as they did to Moon's pioneering coverage of Asia. We wish them both aloha.

www.moon.com

DESTINATIONS | ACTIVITIES | BLOGS | MAPS | BOOKS

MOON.COM is ready to help plan your next trip! Filled with fresh trip ideas and strategies, author interviews, informative travel blogs, a detailed map library, and descriptions of all the Moon guidebooks, Moon.com is all you need to get out and explore the world—or even places in your own backyard. While at Moon.com, sign up for our monthly e-newsletter for updates on new releases, travel tips, and expert advice from our on-the-go Moon authors. As always, when you travel with Moon, expect an experience that is uncommon and truly unique.

KEEP UP WITH MOON ON FACEBOOK AND TWITTER
JOIN THE MOON PHOTO GROUP ON FLICKR

MAP SYMBOLS

▦▦▦	Expressway	◖	Highlight	✗	Airfield	♨	Golf Course
	Primary Road	○	City/Town	✈	Airport	ⓟ	Parking Area
	Secondary Road	◉	State Capital	▲	Mountain	⬭	Archaeological Site
- - - -	Unpaved Road	⊛	National Capital	✛	Unique Natural Feature	⬘	Church
- - -	Trail	★	Point of Interest			⬚	Gas Station
··········	Ferry	•	Accommodation	≋	Waterfall	◌	Glacier
⊷⊷⊷	Railroad	▾	Restaurant/Bar	▲	Park	◰	Mangrove
▥▥▥	Pedestrian Walkway	▪	Other Location	❶	Trailhead	◱	Reef
▦▦▦	Stairs	⋀	Campground	✗	Skiing Area	◲	Swamp

CONVERSION TABLES

$°C = (°F - 32) / 1.8$
$°F = (°C \times 1.8) + 32$
1 inch = 2.54 centimeters (cm)
1 foot = 0.304 meters (m)
1 yard = 0.914 meters
1 mile = 1.6093 kilometers (km)
1 km = 0.6214 miles
1 fathom = 1.8288 m
1 chain = 20.1168 m
1 furlong = 201.168 m
1 acre = 0.4047 hectares
1 sq km = 100 hectares
1 sq mile = 2.59 square km
1 ounce = 28.35 grams
1 pound = 0.4536 kilograms
1 short ton = 0.90718 metric ton
1 short ton = 2,000 pounds
1 long ton = 1.016 metric tons
1 long ton = 2,240 pounds
1 metric ton = 1,000 kilograms
1 quart = 0.94635 liters
1 US gallon = 3.7854 liters
1 Imperial gallon = 4.5459 liters
1 nautical mile = 1.852 km

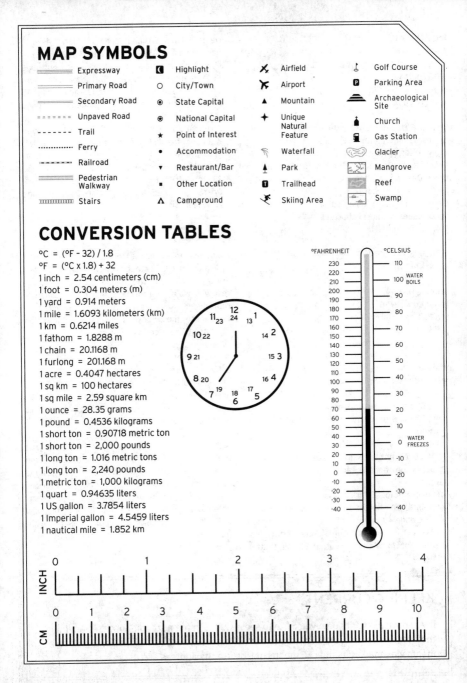

MOON MAUI

Avalon Travel
a member of the Perseus Books Group
1700 Fourth Street
Berkeley, CA 94710, USA
www.moon.com

Editors: Elizabeth Hansen, Kevin McLain
Series Manager: Kathryn Ettinger
Copy Editor: Ashley Benning
Graphics and Production Coordinator: Darren Alessi
Cover Designer: Darren Alessi
Map Editor: Mike Morgenfeld
Cartographer: Stephanie Poulain
Proofreader: Megan Mulholland
Indexer: Rachel Kuhn

ISBN: 978-1-61238-110-7
ISSN: 1099-8772

Printing History
1st Edition – 1986
9th Edition – March 2014
5 4 3 2 1

Front cover photo: Maui, Makena Beach, Wave breaking on shore © Pacific Stock - Design Pics / SuperStock
Title page photo: © Mark Driessen
Color interior photos: all photos © Kyle Ellison, except page 4 © Heather Ellison; page 6 (top left) © Mark Driessen, (top right) © Jenna Strubhar; page 7 (bottom left) © Heather Ellison, (bottom right) © Jenna Strubhar; page 8 © Mark Driessen; page 9 (top) © Heather Ellison, (bottom left) © Mark Driessen; page 10 © Mark Driessen; page 12 © Heather Ellison; page 13 (top right) © Mark Driessen; page 14 © Tom Tietz/123rf.com; page 15 © Jenna Strubhar; page 16 © Heather Ellison; page 17 (top left) © Mark Driessen, (bottom left) © Jenna Strubhar, (bottom right) © Heather Ellison; page 19 (all photos) © Mark Driessen; page 21 (top left and bottom left) © Mark Driessen, (bottom right) © Heather Ellison; page 22 © Mark Driessen; page 23 (top left) © Heather Ellison; page 24 © Mark Driessen; page 25 (top left) © Mark Driessen; page 28 © Mark Driessen

Printed in Canada by Friesens

KEEPING CURRENT

If you have a favorite gem you'd like to see included in the next edition, or see anything that needs updating, clarification, or correction, please drop us a line. Send your comments via email to feedback@moon.com, or use the address above.